Controversies in
CONSTITUTIONAL LAW

COLLECTIONS OF DOCUMENTS AND ARTICLES
ON MAJOR QUESTIONS OF AMERICAN LAW

PAUL FINKELMAN
GENERAL EDITOR
Virginia Polytechnic Institute and State University

A Garland Series

≡ Contents ≡
of the Series

THE CONSTITUTION AND THE FLAG

PRAYER IN PUBLIC SCHOOLS
AND THE CONSTITUTION, 1961-1992

GUN CONTROL AND THE CONSTITUTION
Sources and Explorations
on the Second Amendment

PRAYER IN PUBLIC SCHOOLS AND  THE CONSTITUTION 1961–1992

Volume 1

Government-Sponsored Religious Activities in Public Schools and the Constitution

Edited with an Introduction by

Robert Sikorski

DUKE UNIVERSITY
CENTER FOR INTERNATIONAL STUDIES

Garland Publishing, Inc.
New York & London
1993

Library of Congress Cataloging-in-Publication Data

Prayer in the public schools and the constitution, 1961–1992 :
    government-sponsored religious activities in public schools and the
    constitution / edited by Robert Sikorski.
        p.   cm. — (Controversies in constitutional law)
    ISBN 0–8153–1272–5 (alk. paper)
        1. Prayer in the public schools—Law and legislation—United States.
I. Sikorski, Robert, 1949–   . II. Series.
KF4162.P73   1993
344.73'0796—dc20
[347.304796]   92–42959
                                                                           CIP

Printed on acid-free, 250-year-life paper
Manufactured in the United States of America

To Hannah and Merc,
for the years of traveling around together

CONTENTS

GENERAL INTRODUCTION

This series provides teachers, scholars, and students with convenient access to the law, debates, and scholarly literature surrounding major questions of constitutional law. Each set of books—from two to four volumes—consists of four elements: an extended introduction to the problem by the editor; reprints of a few of the significant cases and briefs on the subject; Congressional testimony, and other primary documents on the problem; and the best scholarly articles on the subject. By conveniently gathering all this material in one place, each set of volumes allows users to quickly become familiar with the arguments and issues surrounding a particular constitutional controversy.

Scholars and students interested in constitutional law and public policy are often overwhelmed by the sheer amount of material published on controversial subjects. The topics in *Controversies in Constitutional Law* are timely, controversial, politically significant, and intellectually compelling. They are the issues that bring the legal academy, courts, politicians, and general public together, although not always in harmony.

Many scholars are barely able to keep up with the scholarship in their own fields. Yet, we need to learn about issues beyond our own specialties. A new course may require a quick introduction to a problem; our own research may lead us to a new issue. *Controversies in Constitutional Law* is designed to meet these needs. It will enable scholars and teachers to quickly come up to speed on the topics of each volume.

This series will also serve students at all levels of higher education. Students often encounter controversial topics without a background in how the problem developed. These volumes provide such a background. The important cases are reprinted in full; the introductions provide students with a map to the issues; the briefs, congressional testimony, and scholarly articles give convenient access to the arguments and debates.

The volumes bring together in one place a wide variety of sources and materials that are unlikely to be found in any one library. The primary documents include reported cases, briefs, testimony from legislative committee hearings, and, on occasion, executive branch publications. Few law libraries, university libraries, or public libraries will have all these materials. The secondary literature comes from the scholarly literature of law, history, political science, economics, criminology, and other relevant fields. Some of the articles are also from serious non-academic journals. All the articles and primary sources in these volumes sample a wide range of sources.

The related government publications, briefs and congressional testimony, are particularly important. Too often scholars overlook them. We tend to focus on court opinions—what the Court said. This is obviously important for understanding doctrine, but, briefs, especially amicus briefs, are also an important source of information about the larger constitutional controversy the case represents. The politics of a case is often more apparent in them than in either the oral arguments or the courts opinion. Similarly, Congressional hearings illustrate the social, philosophical, and political dimensions of these questions. These sources are an important supplement to the scholarly literature.

Our goal of limiting each collection to two to four focused volumes and our inability to secure copyright permission for some important articles forced us to make hard and judicious choices. Important articles that we could not reprint are listed in the further reading sections at the end of the author's introduction.

Controversies in Constitutional Law provides in one single place a comprehensive introduction to a topic that will satisfy most lawyers, scholars, and students. By combining cases, briefs, legislative debates and testimony from committee hearings with secondary articles, we hope to facilitate access to the problem set out in each set of volumes.

INTRODUCTION

Thirty years of United States Supreme Court litigation over schoolhouse religion have not lessened our interest and concern in testing new purposes, places, and limits for religious practices in public schools. The first decisions— *Engel v. Vitale* and *Abington v. Schempp*—brought forth a wealth of legal writings and political science research. The earliest legal writings reflected a search in the Court's opinions for a constitutional standard whereby to measure future conflicts. Some, like Jesse Choper in this volume, attempted to establish their own constitutional standard as a guide to the courts. Political scientists were more intrigued with the impact of the decisions on states and local communities.

More recent legal writings have moved away from the search for neutral principles of constitutional evaluation. Major pieces—with notable exceptions such as Douglas Laycock in this collection—are likely to be partisan and advocate extrajudicial positions.[1] Political scientists have shifted their interests away from impact studies to studies of interest-group activity and the legislative process in which schoolhouse religion provides a case study. These trends are represented in the readings.

This introductory essay provides a possible frame of reference for thinking about schoolhouse religion, judicial opinions, and the secondary literature. In this essay I step back from the debate's immediacy to suggest that the debate—and not simply one side of it—can be understood through appreciating the fundamental tension contained within our political and constitutional system. This tension, as examined here, is in how the United States responds to the intertwined issues of individual rights, community values and community rights, and state actions and institutions.

To begin, I suggest that we can note, over the last thirty years, two highly consistent features. First, Supreme Court decisions have been nearly uniform in excluding institutionalized religious practices from the public schools. Second, despite such consistency in decisions, cases which raise only marginally different issues keep returning to the Court—and it keeps accepting them.

The recurrence of schoolhouse-religion cases reflects our continuing national uncertainty about the places of religion and of public schools in public life, as opposed to their places in our personal (and economic lives). The section of the First Amendment of the U.S. Constitution to which the cases and this essay are addressed—"Congress shall make no law respecting an establishment of religion, or prohibit the free exercise thereof"—is subject to multiple readings deriving not just from uncertainty of meaning, but also from uncertainty of values to which people adhere, antecedent to entering into constitutional debate.

Unlike many sets of decisions by the Supreme Court, those dealing with conflicts over schoolhouse religion are not particularly arcane or opaque. Since *Engel v. Vitale*[2] in 1962, the Supreme Court has managed a straightforward line of constitutional jurisprudence which, in theory, should have left little room for public discussion of what future acts were constitutional. In fact, I would suggest that with very few exceptions—most notably some recent and passionate dissents—the Court has been not only highly consistent, but also predictable.

Yet we continue to witness a regular flow of schoolhouse-religion cases to the Court, cases which are only variations on the theme of *Engel v. Vitale*. But when such cases do enter the Court, they do not partake of the circus-like atmosphere surrounding conflicts over other such issues as reproductive choice, racial segregation and discrimination, and freedom of expression. This is true despite the emotionally charged nature of conflicts over the place and purpose of religion in public schools. Public concern appears very broad, but not very deep.[3]

The seeming paradox of Court consistency, continuing and highly emotional conflicts, and less than overwhelming popular passion is what makes the subject of constitutional litigation over schoolhouse religion so intriguing. The purpose of this introductory essay is, then, to suggest a possible framework within which to read the following materials and to think about the continuing salience of the issue in U.S. popular political culture. The essay is not intended as a contribution to the constitutional debate, but rather as a schema that allows the reader of these and related materials to have one way of understanding the broad issue of schoolhouse religion in the courts and in the community.

For purposes of this essay, *popular political culture* encompasses those ideas, images, customs, and actions around and through which people define and identify their political and moral positions within an open forum. This excludes both unarticulated, privately held beliefs and unexpressed motivations, and concentrates on those words and deeds addressed to a nonexclusive public audience.

United States Supreme Court decisions are ingredients of our public culture; however the conferences within which the justices hammer out decisions are not. Similarly, while advocates' public beliefs are part of political culture, their truth-value may not be.

We can identify two significant themes in our popular political culture which, taken together, illuminate both the Supreme Court decisions, including their simplicity, and the continuing presence of schoolhouse religion as a constitutional problem. The first theme is the tension between liberal and communitarian values, which often find direct and clear expression in the Court's opinions (holdings, concurrences, and dissents). The second is the place we have ascribed to our public schools: sites of knowledge acquisition and of citizenship training. I utilize these two themes as a framework for discussing the cases presented in these volumes.

ENGEL VERSUS VITALE AND AFTER

In 1951, the New York State Board of Regents prepared a short prayer which it then recommended for adoption by the state's school systems. "Almighty God, we acknowledge our dependence upon Thee, and we beg Thy blessings upon us, our parents, our teachers and our Country."[4] In 1958, the New Hyde Park Board of Education implemented the Regents' prayer as part of school-day activities, upon which action parents lodged complaints with the local school board. *Engel v. Vitale* was the culmination of those events.

The Court's holding in the case was direct and unambiguous: "We think that by using its public school system to encourage recitation of the Regents' prayer, the State of New York has adopted a practice *wholly* inconsistent with the Establishment Clause."[5] The Court continued in strong and straightforward language to find that the prayer violated a fundamental principle of U.S. constitutional life in that it was "no part of the business of government to compose official prayers for any group of the American people to recite as part of a religious program carried on by the government."[6]

Following this general statement of principle, the decision provided, as have most subsequent schoolhouse-religion decisions, the historical background underpinning its decision. Clearly, the Court felt the need to look behind the words of the First Amendment in order to articulate the culture in which the amendment was born and fostered. The essential feature of this historical interlude in the Court's decision was the majority's reflection on religious beliefs as personal.

The historical reconstruction of the Founders' views on government and religion are a formulaic feature of the Court's opinions on schoolhouse religion. The Court's historical reconstructions little resemble works of historical scholarship, if for no other reason than their decidedly teleological nature. Furthermore, the Justices' various reconstructions are best read in terms of achieving one's goals and should be read in terms of an ongoing debate between liberal and communitarian members of the Court, legal profession, and public.

While underlining that the establishment clause, unlike the free exercise clause, did not require the demonstration of government coercion, the Court stated that "religion is too *personal*, too sacred, too holy, to permit its 'unhallowed perversion' by a civil magistrate."[7] The Court was focusing on the issue that there need be no obvious coercion to create a defensible right under the establishment clause; thus the families did not have to demonstrate that their children were injured. I wish, however, to take a second reading of this passage to demonstrate one of the reasons for the consistency of subsequent decisions and one of the reasons why the decision has often been a nullity in local communities.

In the introduction I referred to the theme of liberal versus communitarian beliefs. *Engel* opens this theme both in the court's decision and in how U.S. communities responded to that decision. The theme looks at civil society, the locus for expression of political views and social living. A liberal understanding of civil society focuses on the rights guaranteed to individual members, secured from the tyranny of the majority and from the state. A communitarian understanding of civil society stresses a sense of personhood and bondedness among persons, which is to be strengthened through shared values and their public expression. A society is weakened when individual members advocate for personal rights too strenuously over community rights.[8]

The decision in *Engel* constitutes a liberal interpretation of civil society. Many protesting the decision expressed or acted upon a communitarian stance. In several studies that examined the impact of *Engel* and subsequent decisions upon public school policy making at the community level, we find interesting results.

William Muir's[9] study of one community's response to the schoolhouse-religion issue found the relative ease with which the community decided to conform to the decisions, once they felt that the Court had left no "loophole" (this meant, however, not excluding religious practices entirely but allowing for moments of silence). An essential fact of Muir's story is the role taken by a local lawyer and member of the school board to convince others that recitations of prayers and Bible verses as part of the formal school day were unconstitutional. The lawyer was Jewish and a close and supportive student of the Supreme Court. He articulated a liberal understanding of civil society and the place of religious practice.

In contrast to Muir's findings for "Midland," Kenneth Dolbeare and Phillip Hammond[10] found in their study of the state of "Midway" little change in school board policies. Significantly, the authors noted the presence of a relatively homogeneous society. The consequence was that while administrators would state that they were abiding by the Court's decisions, they also admitted to little or no change in school practices. What the authors found is consistent with a communitarian understanding of civil society: schools and teachers continued prayers and Bible-readings as a means of drawing their students together and underlining the importance of shared values. Teachers recognized the possibility of dissent, but felt that dissenters should not interfere with their fellow students' opportunity to share publicly certain central religious values. The dissenters should sit by quietly while the other students participate. The religious practices in the schoolhouse were expressions of community, not of the state.

Other research confirms that "traditional" communities ignored the decision or implemented only cosmetic changes. H. Frank Way's "Survey Research on Judicial Decisions," Kirk W. Elifson's and C. Kirk Hadaway's "Prayer in Public Schools," and John C. Green's and James L. Guth's "The Missing Link" each demonstrate that southern and New England states, evangelical groups, and other new right groups were more likely than Jewish groups, old line conservatives, midwestern states, and national mainline-Protestant organizations to endorse the continued presence of prayer and Bible reading in the public schools. Many of these regions and groups who affirmed the role of religious practices in the schools also stressed strongly negative views of the Supreme Court and on decisions that would expand individual civil rights.[11]

What many local school systems expressed by their continuing practice was also expressed in Justice Potter Stewart's dissent in *Engel*: "I think that to deny the wish of these school children to join in reciting this prayer is to deny them the opportunity of sharing in the spiritual heritage of our Nation."[12] Stewart's communitarian dissent is the first in a series that continues through today with the dissents is *Lee v. Weisman* (1992).

Although it was *Engel* which opened judicial and popular discussion on school prayer, *Abington v. Schempp*[13] established the contours of school prayer jurisprudence and firmly situated the Court in a liberal tradition.

The case grew from a parent's challenge to a 1948 Pennsylvania law requiring—without exception—reading of Bible passages at the opening of each school day. Once a three-judge court had ruled the law unconstitutional, the Pennsylvania legislature amended the law to include an excusal policy, thus making hearing of the morning readings voluntary. The parent, Edward Schempp, maintained his challenge, viewing the amended statute as also violative of the establishment clause.

It was the challenge to the amended law that was argued before the Court. Joined to *Schempp* was a similar case, arising in the City of Baltimore, *Murray v. Curlett*.[14] In an eight-one decision, the Court held both the Pennsylvania law and the Baltimore School Board rule to be unconstitutional.

Justice Clark, writing for the Court, established in *Schempp* the first two prongs of what has become the standard establishment clause test (the *Lemon* test): "the test may be stated as follows: what are the purpose and the primary effect of the enactment."[15] Justice Brennan's concurrence offered a variant, examining whether the governmental institutions "(a) serve the essentially religious activities of religious institutions; (b) employ the organ of government for essentially religious purposes; or (c) use essentially religious means to serve governmental ends where secular means would suffice."[16]

A decade later, Chief Justice Berger enunciated a third prong to Clark's first two, when in *Lemon v. Kurtzman*[17] he included the question of "excessive entanglement" of the state with a religious institution. A violation of any single prong was sufficient to find a violation of the establishment clause.

Justice Clark, in outlining his tests, distinguishes between this test for violations of the establishment clause and one that might be articulated under the free exercise clause: "The distinction between the two clauses is apparent—a violation of the Free Exercise Clause is predicated on coercion while the establishment clause violation need not be so attended."[18] Although the establishment/free exercise contrast was easily established in *Engel*, *Schempp* begins a line of discussion in which the justices attempt to identify the relationship between the two clauses, worried that the sweep of one will overburden the constraining influence of the other.

The attempt in *Schempp* to construct a constitutional jurisprudence for both clauses occasioned the espousal of an essential liberal view of schoolhouse-religion conflicts. Clark writes, "While the Free Exercise Clause clearly prohibits the use of state action to deny the rights of free exercise to *anyone*, it has never meant that a majority could use the machinery of the State to practice its beliefs."[19] Earlier Clark writes that the purpose of the free exercise clause "is to secure religious liberty in the *individual* by prohibiting any invasion thereof by civil authority."[20]

Despite any number of statements as to the difficult, subtle terrain that is schoolhouse religion, Justice Clark's opinion can be understood and applied easily if one steps back to view the cases in broader political and sociological perspectives. Since the Founding Era, two conceptions of political life have dominated debate over the construction, purpose, and boundary of U.S. public life. Those studying eighteenth-century Anglo-American politics contrast *civic republicanism* with *liberalism*.[21] Civic republicanism is one example of communitarianism, which had other manifestations even in the eighteenth century (for example, the Society of Friends or the Moravians). The basic points of contrast between the various forms of communitarianism, on the one side, and liberalism, on the other, is the individual's relationship to the state and the meaning of government. For communitarianism, government should be a manifestation of community, through which common choices are made and common values adhered to. Individuals should respect and submit to government for the good of the common community. Communitarianism is concerned with the advancement of individual rights to the extent that such rights become a threat to the logic and life of the common community. The view is not a disguising of majoritarianism, but emphasizes the process through which members collectively define and maintain an identity and system of values and it accepts the validity of other potential communities with differing collective values. The danger of communitarianism is the extent to which it can lead to an absolute tyranny of collective interests over individual rights. It can, obviously, drift or plummet into a majoritarianism or totalitarianism of either a left or right variety.

For liberalism, constitutional government is a mediating structure to assure individual protection against the force of another individual or group which might come to dominate the political process. Government should guarantee the rights of an individual to manifest a unique identity without fear of that identity being repressed. Ultimately, government is about maintaining a mechanism securing fairness toward each individual while providing for the security of the whole. Liberalism understands that this guardian role of government can become custodial, ultimately transforming itself into a totalitarian regime in which individual identity is subjugated not to the community but to the state.

With this distinction before us, Justice Clark's opinion can be described as a clear articulation of liberalism and shows that concerns about potential conflicts between the establishment clause and free exercise clause are needless. Both clauses are intended to preserve the rights of the individual: that of the establishment clause from the community using the state to suppress an individual's autonomy of religious belief and that of the free exercise clause from the state itself repressing individual religious belief or attempting to force beliefs and actions contrary to an individual's religious convictions (for example, studying sex education or saying the Pledge of Allegiance).

The establishment and free exercise clauses, following this line, are clearly situated in the mainstream of liberal thought. They were created and have persisted as protectors of an individual's religious rights against all comers.

The rub to the liberal interpretation is that not all accept that the constitutional guarantees are there to protect the individual exclusively, and that even a liberal jurisprudence becomes confused when it focuses on the place of public schools in U.S. society. Normally, the court addresses constitutional issues and tries to avoid political questions. The place and purpose of public schools is such a question. Yet addressing the role of public schools is extremely pertinent to the issue of a student's religious rights in that school.

While Clark and others in the *Schempp* majority are clearly decided on a liberal stance in explicating the clauses, such is not the case when defining the place of public schools. And it is because of the drifting, shadowy understanding of the public schools that so much uncertainty has emerged in the schoolhouse-religion cases. It is not the Constitution that is being read variously, but the place of the schools.[22]

The Court generally supports prohibition of coercion by school authorities when First Amendment interests are at stake. Yet frequently, school officials can cite an excusal policy which the Court will find adequate to guarantee the student's free exercise rights. What happens, of course, is that the student must elect to remove himself or herself from the community of classmates and teachers and to announce by removal a rejection of that portion of the shared bond of identity.[23] Thus a liberal jurisprudence finds itself addressing an institution that people—including the justices—variously perceive as liberal or communitarian. And such views have generally remained in the unarticulated background of most decisions.

Brennan's overlong concurrence begins with the place of public schools: "Americans regard the public schools as a most vital civic institution for the preservation of a democratic system of government. It is therefore understandable that the constitutional prohibitions encounter their severest test when they are sought to be applied in the school classroom."[24] And later he continues: "It is implicit in the history and character of American public education that the public schools serve a uniquely *public* function: the training of American citizens in an atmosphere free of parochial, divisive, or separatist influences of any sort— an atmosphere in which children may assimilate a heritage common to all American groups and religions . . . this is a heritage . . . simply civic and patriotic."[25]

Here we read of a melding of liberal and communitarian concerns, which may be appropriate but nonetheless plays havoc with liberal constitutional jurisprudence. We see this most particularly in comments which seem to lay out a future place for religion and religious practices until the question is litigated and held unconstitutional. The classic case is Justice O'Connor's concurrence in *Wallace v. Jaffree.*

The Court accepts only a limited notion of the public schools as community in practice, though it is very willing to articulate elegant nonbinding professions of the school as community. It sees that the public school community is for instilling the political values of citizenship and patriotism, but even these must be tempered with provisos that permit the individual student to opt out[26] nor is the public school is not a place in which the individual student leaves his or her liberal constitutional guarantees at the front door.[27] It is under these conditions that the Equal Access Act—an act which has the potential to affect school life radically—passed constitutional muster, and yet a short, innocuous baccalaureate benediction in a voluntary graduation exercise is held to violate the establishment clause. The Court offers a rhetoric in which public schools are a reflection of the community and a reality of decisions in which the community is an intrusive feature (and sometimes a not to be trusted one, at that). The line of decisions from *Engel* may be consistent, but it is not consistent with a communitarian concept of public schools (the holding of constitutionality of the Equal Access Act may, in the long run, establish an even more complicated relationship between strict liberal constitutionalism and a more mixed understanding of the public schools).

One communitarian view of public schools that would also develop a qualified communitarian constitutional jurisprudence begins with Stewart's dissents in *Engel* and *Schempp*. Stewart articulates a view of public schools as places of community, not simply as state institutions. He carries this perspective forward to his understanding of the establishment clause. As quoted above, Stewart writes in *Engel* about wishing not to deny students the right to join in prayers.[28] And in *Schempp*, he finds, "In these cases . . . what is involved is not state action based on impermissible categories, but rather an attempt by the State to accommodate these differences which the existence in our society of a variety of religious beliefs makes inevitable."[29] Stewart's view should be contrasted with that of Brennan. Both assert that the public school is a place for education in community values. The contrast is that Brennan contends that the public school can assert only the broadest, most encompassing community—that of the nation and its values of citizenship and patriotism. Stewart, in contrast, takes a less grand view of community and believes that public schools should be able to accommodate a plurality of communities (cautioning that this should not be confused with a plurality of individual private beliefs which is a mainstay of liberal constitutionalism).

ATTEMPTING TO RECONFIGURE SCHOOLHOUSE RELIGION

If the Court had an easy time with the constitutional dimension and a difficult, if not so clearly recognized, time with the political question of the role of schools, how did local communities respond?

Following the decisions in *Engel* and *Schempp*, we find states reassessing their role in fostering religiosity (even the Pennsylvania law that was the basis for the *Schempp* decision is an early example of such attempts as reconfiguring). Most reassessments came only gradually. The initial response of many school systems was to ignore the decision, to make cosmetic changes, or to delegate choice in the matter to classroom teachers.

Birby found that Tennessee schools by early 1965 had yet to undertake changes modifying policy on religious activities in the public schools. And as Way indicates, this was true throughout the South; greater changes or professed changes were noted in other regions with New England most like the South and the remainder of the country inaugurating major changes or continuing with changes that preceded the Court decisions.[30]

One might advance the hypothesis that where there is a common community identity coterminous with the boundaries of the school system (or school), local leaders will be inclined to ignore the Court's decisions. Anecdotal evidence suggests that this was and remains the case. Where, however, a school system encompasses many communities and the children of these communities are mixed in school, we shall discover a greater adherence to the decisions (either voluntarily or through the complaints of parents). The research by Muir, and by Dolbeare and Hammond, as noted earlier, bear this out.

What is fascinating to follow is not the refusal to change, but the charges brought against those school officials who do enforce the changes. For some advocates of schoolhouse religion, the problem has been "not so much Supreme Court decisions as it is the ignorance of school officials, acting out of fear that any religious activity, however voluntary or student initiated, could be challenged in the courts, necessitating payment of costly legal fees."[31] Such reactions by school officials appear most commonly in larger urban areas that display greater religious diversity. They also emerge, one might consider, from a growing shift of the concept of public schools from community institution to state institution. Official reaction against religious activity may well be a spinoff, a dependent condition, from other forces acting upon the school system, especially the increasing bureaucratization and formalization of schooling. The more a school is responsible to agencies outside the community, the less impact the community will have within the school, including various aspects of socialization.

Moreover, school officials may think that failure to act to exclude religion is tantamount to endorsing its presence. The issue of religion in the school without official endorsement entered a first round of judicial jousting in the "silent prayer" cases.

JUSTICE O'CONNOR AND *WALLACE* *VERSUS JAFFREE*

The litigation in *Jaffree* arose from three related Alabama statutes: the first, passed in 1978, authorized a moment of silence for meditation; the second, from 1981, authorized a period of silence "for meditation or voluntary prayer"; while the third, passed in 1982, authorized teachers to lead willing students in a prescribed prayer.[32]

The district court found the second and third statutes to encourage religion in the schools, but held that they were constitutional, because "Alabama had the power to establish a state religion." The Eleventh Circuit agreed with the lower court that the second and third statutes established religion, but rightly found that they were unconstitutional. The Supreme Court agreed that the third statute—on teachers leading willing students in prayer—violated the establishment clause. Futhermore, all parties agreed not to litigate the constitutionality of the first statute (this action and nonbinding comments in the opinions in the decision were almost the same as saying that the first would pass constitutional muster, absent a "smoking gun").

What remained for the Court to decide was whether the 1981 statute breached the establishment clause boundary. In a five-three decision the Court affirmed, with Justice Stevens writing for four justices and Justice O'Connor concurring in the judgment. Berger, White, and Rehnquist dissented.

Although Stevens wrote the opinion of the Court, what are important here are O'Connor's concurrence and Rehnquist's dissent. Stevens applies a straightforward *Lemon* test, focussing on the legislative record which indisputably demonstrated that the sponsor of the act was hoping to return vocal prayer to the classroom.[33]

O'Connor clearly believes that moments of silence can be constitutional and that students, if they so chose, could use the moments for silent prayer: "Nothing in the United States Constitution as interpreted by this Court or in the laws of the State of Alabama prohibits public school students from voluntarily praying at any time before, during, or after the school day."[34] One should add that this applies to silent prayers and to unintrusive prayers and rituals; I would suggest that this is an example of thinking which construes religious activity as personal and private, and not a feature of public communal life.

What O'Connor finds objectionable is "that the purpose and likely effect of this . . . enactment is to endorse and sponsor voluntary prayer in public schools."[35] Legislative intent is here at issue and not how the school officials implemented the act.

The importance of O'Connor's opinion is its role as a rebuttal to the logic, law, and implications of Rehnquist's dissent, which is the first clear and lengthy expression of communitarian constitutional jurisprudence by a justice. O'Connor begins with a basic premise that "In this country, church and state must operate within the same community. Because of this coexistence, it is inevitable that the secular interests of government and the religious interests of various sects and their adherents will frequently intersect, conflict, and combine."[36]

She identifies the ambiguous terrain that the Court must map in defining a boundary between state and church. Yet, for her, it is mandatory that such a boundary be established. As with real territory, a legal conflict can appear different depending upon where one is standing. O'Connor builds her argument around the supposition that there can exist an objective observer, who understands constitutional standards and who can act appropriately in determining resolutions of real-life situations. Deviation from this vantage point endangers constitutional principles.[37]

O'Connor must confront the point raised by Rehnquist and the United States in its *amicus* brief that at issue here is not a question only of violating the establishment clause, but also of accommodating to the free exercise clause. Thus in O'Connor's and Rehnquist's opinions we observe the merging of a new dominating approach to the religion clauses—that of accommodation.[38] Central to her pursuit of a reasonable accommodation is the belief that either clause "if expanded to a logical extreme would tend to clash with the other."[39] Such limits on government support of religion, or action to exclude it are necessary, but these limits should be determined by an objective observer as to whether the state action removes a burden placed on the free exercise of religion, or whether it attempts to "remove burdens imposed by the Constitution itself."[40] The state, thus, should act in such a manner as to keep from burdening an individual's free exercise rights; thus she is able to remind us that nothing in Court decisions has outlawed an individual's right to pray in school. The state also should not act in such a way as to foster a religious activity, institution, theology, or environment. O'Connor sees that the Alabama statue does nothing to relieve a burden placed on an individual, but does attempt to remove a burden placed on the state by the Constitution.

In her opinion, then, O'Connor is focused on two perspectives: that of the individual and that of the state. The perspective of the community hardly comes into play, other than as being illegitimately intruded into an individual's life by action of the state. The feeling of her language, with its stress on the objective observer, highlights the opinion's strong liberal constitutionalism, with a concentration on the protection of individual rights against the state. She allows no place for the funneling of religious beliefs and institutions through a state institution into the life of a student.

Rehnquist founds his alternative reading of the clauses in an historical reconstruction of the drafting and ratifying of the religion clauses.[41] The first goal of Rehnquist's attack through history is the breaching of the "wall of separation," but such an attack is ill-directed since the *Lemon* test effectively ended any absolutist approach to the two clauses. Yet he insists that *Lemon* is heir to the same historical misconstructions: "The three-part test represents a determined effort to craft a workable rule from an historically faulty doctrine;

but the rule can only be as sound as the doctrine it attempts to serve."[42] He finds, finally that, "Nothing in the Establishment Clause of the First Amendment, properly understood, prohibits any such generalized 'endorsement' of prayer."[43]

In his dissent, Rehnquist addresses the negative and positive roles of states in promoting religious traditions. The two roles relate to two different aspects of religion. The negative role of government is nonpreferential treatment of churches and sects. The positive role is for government to support, if it chooses—and he seems to feel that it should—a general religious environment. Combined, the two articulate a communitarian interpretation of the religion clauses. The government can establish a general climate that promotes the growth of churches, of communities, of religious values, but it should do so even-handedly.

Although he does not deal directly with the problem that such a state position can foster separatism and lead to religious conflict, he does seem to believe that religious diversity is to be fostered by the state. He does not address the specific place of public schools in the arrangement of state, community, and citizen, and we are left to wonder, here, whether Rehnquist views schools as state institutions, communities, or some hybrid. What we know is that it is proper for schools and other state institutions to foster a general religious environment—which could relate either to the individual or the corporate/community group.

STARTING FRESH: FREE EXERCISE AND THE PUBLIC SCHOOLS

After the *Engel* decision, interest groups appealed to Congress to support a constitutional amendment authorizing school prayer. Such amendments have come before the Congress on a regular basis, and just as regularly been rejected despite overwhelming public support for school prayer. As long as the interest groups focused on challenging the Court's understanding of the establishment clause, their efforts failed. But in the early 1980s, an alternative emerged, one which achieved a broad consensus and was able to secure passage and withstand constitutional challenges. The alternative is the Equal Access Act of 1984, signed into law in the summer of that year.

The Act began life as the Religious Speech Protection Act,[44] pressed forward by the Christian Legal Society. In this early incarnation it could not gather adequate support for passage. But continued pressure and renegotiations produced a new coalition in support. The support came from fundamentalists, mainline-Protestant and Catholic organizations, and First Amendment advocates.[45] Such was made possible by the broadening of the proposed Act's language which made it unlawful for any school "which has a limited open forum to deny equal access or a fair opportunity to, or discriminate against, any students who wish to conduct a meeting within that limited open forum on the basis of the religious, political, philosophical, or other content of the speech at such meetings."[46]

The Act thus transformed one approach to schoolhouse religion into a question of free speech, and thereby shifted the focus from what burdens a school could or could not impose, to what burdens it should and must lift. The issue of concern here is where the Equal Access Act fits within the traditions of liberalism and communitarianism. The answer seems that, for now at least, it is a satisfactory piece of legislation from either perspective.

In its constitutional test case, *Westside Community Schools v. Mergens,* Stevens was the lone dissenter, while O'Connor wrote for the Court.

The case involved Bridget Mergens and several friends who proposed organizing a Christian club at their school, only to have their request denied. The school argued that it was not "a limited public forum" and thus did not fall within the purview of the Equal Access Act.[47] O'Connor found to the contrary. The school also argued that even if it was a limited public forum, authorizing the Christian club would have violated the establishment clause. Again, O'Connor disagreed.[48] And it is this point of disagreement that concerns me now.

The issue is whether allowing the Christian club to hold meetings on school grounds and, generally, within the school day would be consistent with an impermissible endorsement of religion and constitute an entanglement of state and religion, violating a prong of the *Lemon* test. O'Connor argues that permission for the club to operate would be a "message of neutrality rather than endorsement; if a State refused to let religious groups use facilities open to others, then it would demonstrate not neutrality but hostility toward religion."[49] And the purpose of the Equal Access Act was "to prevent discrimination against religious and other types of speech," a clearly secular intent.[50]

O'Connor underlines what is, for her, "a crucial difference between *government* speech endorsing religion, which the establishment clause forbids, and *private* speech endorsing religion, which the Free Speech and Free Exercise Clauses protect."[51] The contrast, which the justice articulates, is that between the state and what it cannot do and the individual and what she/he is secured in doing. In opening the public school to various groups, the Congress and the Court agree that they are utilizing a *forum.* This is quite different from the state being employed to support the advancement of corporate religious values and institutions.

Kennedy, in concurring, suggests that the standard of "endorsement" may be too vague. School approval may constitute endorsement in a common-sense use and that neutrality in principle can mask hostility in practice. He argues for a focus on whether the school's role in any way indicates coercion of a student to participate in an organization. But he stresses that recognition (or endorsement) of itself does not have to give way to coercion. In laying out this variation, Kennedy, like O'Connor, is focused on the state and the individual: "But no constitutional violation occurs if the school's action is based upon a recognition of the fact that membership in a religious club is one of many permissible ways for a student to further his or her *own personal enrichment*."[52]

What are we to make of this opinion's place in the contrast of liberal and communitarian jurisprudence?

Perhaps one way to understand *Mergens* is to begin with a personal anecdote: While lecturing on schoolhouse religion to school teachers, I would naturally talk about the relationship between state action and the establishment clause. I found early on that most teachers needed to be reminded that they were state agents and that their work constituted state action. Especially with growing moves toward parental involvement and community intervention in the schools, teachers and their administrators feel themselves more a part of their community than an instrument of the state. Similarly some members of the Court view the Equal Access Act as expanding the role of the school in strengthening the community through support of student associations. Other members of the Court see equal access as personally enriching and that the state has an important role in insuring that individual students have the experience of their rights within a supportive environment.

The members of the Court are thus able to join temporarily a liberal and a communitarian interpretation of the clauses as they relate directly to the school's attempt to continue a ban on student prayer groups. For the liberal interpretation, the decision removes a state-imposed burden on the constitutional freedom of the individual student. For the communitarian interpretation, the decision underlines the role of the school and the state in promoting collective religious values.

How long this concurrence of opinions will last is a fascinating question. To pose a hypothetical one: A school has a limited open forum and abiding by the Equal Access Act permits students to join in prayer groups. The prayer groups become active centers of cultural and religious identify, fostering a climate of separatism within the school and among the students. Would, at this point, the two interpretations continue to agree on outcome, if not the reasons behind such?

SCHOOL PRAYER REDUX

The decision in *Mergens* and the perceived direction of the Court toward a more communitarian direction led many observers to believe that prayers/benedictions given outside the regular schoolroom instructional period would find support in the Supreme Court. The decision in *Lee v. Weisman* came, then, as a rude shock (or unanticipated blessing) to many.

The case arose over a benediction said at a middle school graduation ceremony in Rhode Island during 1989. Rabbi Leslie Gutterman from a local temple was asked by the school principal to deliver the benediction. The principal provided Rabbi Gutterman with a pamphlet entitled *Guidelines for Civic Occasion*, which suggested prayers that were nonsectarian and prepared with sensitivity toward inclusiveness and diversity. Daniel Weisman, a parent and Jewish, protested to the school principal prior to the ceremony and when rebuffed sought a temporary restraining order. The request was denied for lack of adequate time to review the case. The child and her parents attended the graduation ceremony and afterwards the father filed an amended complaint seeking a permanent injunction barring the saying of invocations and benedictions at graduation exercises.[53]

Writing for a five-judge majority, Justice Kennedy found that the invocation and benediction violated the establishment clause. The arguments by the members of the Court continued the issue of accommodation developed in *Wallace v. Jaffree* and the "balancing" of the two religion clauses. Kennedy writes: "The principle that government may accommodate the free exercise of religion does not supersede the fundamental limitations imposed by the Establishment Clause."[54] And he continues, "The question is not the good faith of the school [or the school as a social institution of the community as such a notion of good faith implies] in attempting to make the prayer acceptable to most persons, but the legitimacy of its undertaking the enterprise at all."[55]

Kennedy follows this with an exploration of the place of schools in society in which he makes clear what is inchoate in many liberal interpretations: "To endure the speech of false ideas or offensive content and then to counter it is part of learning how to live in a pluralistic society, a society which insists upon open discourse towards the end of a tolerant citizenry. And tolerance presupposes some mutuality of obligation."[56] One can almost hear the echo of Justice Holmes' "marketplace of ideas," a quintessential liberal concept. The state performs the task of education, part of which is to teach students how to challenge ideas with which they do not agree. But important here is that the challenge must remain within the limits of a tolerant and diverse society, where differences of ideas and interests can be freely expressed. The individual is pre-eminent here. Society rests on the ability of individuals to remain open to debate and difference.

Kennedy finds that *Engel* and *Schempp* are determinative to the point that the public school context requires special reflection. Students are learning to act within society and their mini-society should not impose burdens upon them which the student could easily avoid in the broader world and which might place pressure on the student to conform and repress the opportunity to articulate difference.[57]

Public schools are meeting-groups for diversity and training-grounds for young citizens. Support of one religious sect or several over nonreligion defies the idea of tolerance and denies the practice in the use of individual rights.

Scalia penned the four-justice dissent and continued the pressing forward of a communitarian jurisprudence. Just as in Kennedy's opinion one finds strong echoes of liberalism, one finds in Scalia's marked attraction to the language of communitarianism: "I may add . . . that maintaining respect for the religious observances of others is a fundamental civic virtue that government (including the public schools) can and should cultivate—so that even if it were the case that the displaying of such respect might be mistaken for taking part in the prayer, I would deny that the dissenter's interest in avoiding *even the appearance of participation* constitutionally trumps the government's interest in fostering respect for religion generally."[58]

We could not ask for a clearer articulation of the differences between the liberal and the communitarian, and the view each has of the school's place. For the liberal, toleration is the principle and that means a willingness to permit the articulation of alternative viewpoints to one's own, and also an ability to challenge those alternatives. Schools are to teach tolerance and the skills required to explore differences. For the communitarian, civic virtue—giving of oneself to the community—and respect are core. Respect here implies a recognition of difference but a separatism as well (I agree to respect the boundary between your world and beliefs and my own). Respect acted upon leads one into the world of civic virtue: I will act to maintain the sanctity of my community through respecting the sanctity of other people's communities. Scalia takes this one step forward by moving from a skeleton of civic virtue to suggesting one important element—religion.

Scalia spends considerable space in tracing the historical tradition of American public culture in order to demonstrate that state support for religion generally is a fundamental principle of American society. Without such support we break with our past and its traditions. Religion is a core element in the making of American society, one that helps to distinguish us from other societies/nations. While liberalism would suggest that our political system and culture could take root anywhere, communitarianism argues for exceptionalism. Any variation on the scheme would produce a different society.

Scalia underlines this exceptionalism and the importance of community in an extremely revealing passage near the close of his dissent: "Church and state would not be such a difficult subject if religion were, as the Court apparently thinks it to be, some purely personal avocation that can be indulged entirely in secret, like pornography, in the privacy of one's room. For most believers it is *not* that and has never been."[59] Scalia is biting in establishing the contrast. And for all the harshness of tone, he accurately states the communitarian understanding of the establishment clause—that it is fundamental about the relationship between state and church (i.e. communities of members) and not about the relationship between the state and the individual.

CONCLUSION

Kennedy and Scalia articulate two categorically different points of views. Each is persuaded that his is correct. One is true, while the other is false. Looking through the thirty-year record of schoolhouse religion, one should be struck to the extent that the opinions of the Court have consistently opposed these two views. Over time, I think, the justices have become more articulate concerning the meaning and impact of each view. Both, though, were there in *Engel* and continue their presence. Whether liberal or communitarian jurisprudence is correct is beside the point of this essay. What is essential is to establish that there is a continuing frame of reference that helps one to understand the consistency of the Court's opinions, the continuing presence of schoolhouse-religion cases, and why the Court's opinions are not accepted by everyone.

To summarize the liberal constitutional view of the two clauses: the establishment clause prevents any community/collectivity from employing the state to impose religious beliefs—general or specific—and the free exercise clause prevents an autonomously acting state from interfering with an individual's religious beliefs. In this view, one must accept that it is inconceivable that the state acting for itself—rather than for the electorate and its representatives—would attempt to impose religious beliefs. We must also accept that we as a people are tolerant of other individual beliefs, to the extent that others display a similar tolerance, or do not act in such a manner as to threaten the state of tolerance. The liberal view focuses on the holding of views, and on the ability of people to engage in debate over their views.

To summarize the communitarian view of the two clauses: the establishment clause is to insure that no church receive preferential treatment over another church or sect. It does not forbid the state from supporting a general religious atmosphere. In fact, such an atmosphere is essential air to American political culture. The free exercise clause insures that the state respects the autonomy of specific religious groups and that the role of the state would be to remove burdens placed on the free exercise of religious beliefs. The communitarian interpretation of the free exercise clause encompasses protection of action by individuals and groups from state interference. Communitarians have a separatist notion of community. Respect, according to this view, is what holds the different communities together and prevents them from mutual attacks.

The continuing tension of these two views appears built into the fabric of American political culture, the Constitution, and the decisions of the Court. But only very rarely—as in Scalia's dissent in *Lee v. Weisman*—does one find an unmixed articulation of one view as opposed to the other. This is especially the case with schoolhouse religion, where the conflict arises as much over the role of public schools as over the place of religion in those schools.

NOTES

1. Law review notes continue a genre of typology-making with an emphasis on close readings of the judicial texts. The best of these law-student pieces provide insights into the nuanced differences among justices' conceptualizations of the Establishment and Free Exercise clauses.

2. *Engel v. Vitale*, 370 U.S. 421 (1962).

3. The role of fundamentalist and evangelical religious movements and school prayer amendment movements is herein discussed. Even where personal passions and interest-group articulation occurs, they have not combined to forge a substantial popular movement. We continue to see effective interest-group actions and uncoordinated popular actions (such as congressional letter writing campaigns). These do not constitute a political or social movement in the same way as the fight over reproductive rights.

4. *Engel v. Vitale* at 422.

5. Id.

6. Id. at 425.

7. Id. at 432.

8. The debates over liberalism and communitarianism are becoming more and more extensive, finding expressions across the political spectrum. For illustrations of the two views, see Michael Walzer, "The Communitarian Critique of Liberalism," *Political Theory* 18, 1 (1990) 6-23, and Will Kymlicka, *Liberalism and Community* (Oxford, 1991).

9. William K. Muir, Jr., *Prayer in the Public Schools: Law and Attitude Change* (Chicago: University of Chicago Press, 1967), see especially 17-20.

10. Kenneth M. Dolbeare and Phillip E. Hammond, *The School Prayer Decisions: From Court Policy to Local Practice* (Chicago: University of Chicago Press, 1971).

11. John L. Green and James L. Guth, "The Missing Link: Political Activists and Support for School Prayer," *Public Opinion Quarterly*, 53 (1989) 45-50.

12. *Engel v. Vitale* at 445.

13. *Abington v. Schempp,* 374 U.S. 203 (1963).

14. The plaintiff in this case, Madeleine Murray, received a disproportionate amount of publicity. Her stance was the one most directly antagonistic to communitarian values.

15. *Abington v. Schempp* at 222.

16. Id. at 231.

17. *Lemon v. Kultzman,* 403 U.S. 602 (1974).

18. *Abington v. Schempp* at 223; see also *Engel v. Vitale* at 430.

19. Id. at 226; emphasis in the original.

20. Id. at 223; emphasis added.

21. cites to Wood, Bailyn, Pocock, Banning, Appleby.

22. Of course, various minority opinions in these cases stress an alternative reading of the establishment clause. I would contend, however, that an alternative reading is a dependent variable with the definition of public school's place as the independent variable. If one adheres to a communitarian understanding of the public schools, one is forced toward a "reconstructed" history of the meaning of the establishment clause.

    An interesting example of the conflict between communitarian view of the school and adherence to a liberal rendering of the constitutional protection is Justice O'Connor and her establishment clause decisions.

23. In this regard, schoolhouse-religion cases concerning an individual's free exercise rights are of a different impact than those which have developed around employment issues and more like those that have developed around the military. Contrast the highly liberal view of the state's role in the market with the extremely communitarian view of individual versus collective identity in the Army. See *Sherbert v. Verner,* 374 U.S. 398 and *Goldman v. Weinberger,* 475 U.S. 503 (1986). Further twists in the relationship between accepted alternative communities (voluntary or imposed) can be read in *Wisconsin v. Yoder,* 406 U.S. 205 (1972) and a Third Circuit opinion in *Africa v. Pennsylvania* 662 F.2d 1025 (3rd Cir., 1981).

24. *Abington v. Schempp* at 230.

25. Id. at 241–242; emphasis in the original.

26. *West Virginia v. Barnette,* 319 U.S. 624 (1943).

27. *Tinker v. Des Moines, 393 U.S. 503 (1969) and* Hazelwood School Dist. v. Kuhlmeier, *484 U.S. 260 (1988).*

28. *Engel v. Vitale* at 445.

29. *Abington v. Schempp* at 317.

30. See both Birby and Way in these volumes.

31. Allen D. Hertzke, *Representing God in Washington*, (Knoxville: University of Tennessee Press, 1988), 163.

32. *Wallace v. Jaffree*, 471 U.S. 38, 40 (1985). For a discussion of the plaintiff, Ishmal Jaffree, see Peter Irons, *The Courage of Their Convictions* (New York, 1988).

33. *Wallace v. Jaffree* at 59-61.

34. Id. at 67.

35. Id. at 67.

36. Id. at 69.

37. Id. at 76, 83.

38. Id. at 79-82; see M. McConnell, "Accommodation of Religion," 1985 *Supreme Court Review* 1-59, especially for a discussion of "individual accommodation" and "institutional accommodation."

39. Id. at 87, quoting *Walz* 397 U.S. 668-669.

40. Id. at 84.

41. One need not undertake a detailed critical study of Rehnquist's history to have grave doubts about its seriousness. The references to the colonies debating the Constitution is enough to make one hesitate at the door. *Wallace v. Jaffree* at 92-93. See above, page xi–xii, and Charles Miller, *The Supreme Court and the Uses of History* (Cambridge, 1969).

42. *Wallace v. Jaffree* at 113.

43. Id. at 113-114.

44. See Teitel, at footnote 7, in this collection.

45. Hertzke, *Representing God*, p. 162 and Laycock below.

46. *Equal Access Act* 20 *U.S.C.* §4071(a); without going into a detailed discussion of the meaning of "limited open forum" suffice it to say that most public schools would fall within the term's coverage.

47. *Westside Community Schools v. Mergens*, 58 U.S.L.W. 1720 (1990), at 1721–22.

48. *Mergens* at 1725-1726.

49. Id. at 1726.

50. Id. at 1726.

51. Id. at 1726.

52. Id. at 1729 (emphasis added). Of interest is the fact that Scalia joined Kennedy in this concurring opinion. One can only imagine, as seen later, that this was a

temporary convergence of two lines of constitutional interpretation and that Scalia could read into the opinions a place for community, which O'Connor and Kennedy were leaving out.

53. *Lee v. Weisman*, 60 *U.S.L.W.* 4723 (1992) at 4724–25.

54. Id. at 4725.

55. Id. at 4725.

56. Id. at 4726.

57. Id. at 4728.

58. Id. at 4739.

59. Id. at 4740.

ENGEL ET AL. *v.* VITALE ET AL.

CERTIORARI TO THE COURT OF APPEALS OF NEW YORK.

No. 468.   Argued April 3, 1962.—Decided June 25, 1962.

Because of the prohibition of the First Amendment against the enactment of any law "respecting an establishment of religion," which is made applicable to the States by the Fourteenth Amendment, state officials may not compose an official state prayer and require that it be recited in the public schools of the State at the beginning of each school day—even if the prayer is denominationally neutral and pupils who wish to do so may remain silent or be excused from the room while the prayer is being recited.   Pp. 422–436.

10 N. Y. 2d 174, 176 N. E. 2d 579, reversed.

William J. Butler argued the cause for petitioners. With him on the briefs was *Stanley Geller.*

Bertram B. Daiker argued the cause for respondents. With him on the briefs was *Wilford E. Neier.*

Porter R. Chandler argued the cause for intervenors-respondents.   With him on the briefs were *Thomas J. Ford* and *Richard E. Nolan.*

Charles A. Brind filed a brief for the Board of Regents of the University of the State of New York, as *amicus curiae,* in opposition to the petition for certiorari.

Briefs of *amici curiae,* urging reversal, were filed by *Herbert A. Wolff, Leo Rosen* and *Nancy Wechsler* for the American Ethical Union; *Louis Caplan, Edwin J. Lukas, Paul Hartman, Theodore Leskes* and *Sol Rabkin* for the American Jewish Committee et al.; and *Leo Pfeffer, Lewis H. Weinstein, Albert Wald, Shad Polier* and *Samuel Lawrence Brennglass* for the Synagogue Council of America et al.

A brief of *amici curiae,* urging affirmance, was filed by *Roger D. Foley,* Attorney General of Nevada, *Robert*

Pickrell, Attorney General of Arizona, *Frank Holt,* Attorney General of Arkansas, *Albert L. Coles,* Attorney General of Connecticut, *Richard W. Ervin,* Attorney General of Florida, *Eugene Cook,* Attorney General of Georgia, *Frank Benson,* Attorney General of Idaho, *Edwin K. Steers,* Attorney General of Indiana, *William M. Ferguson,* Attorney General of Kansas, *Jack P. F. Gremillion,* Attorney General of Louisiana, *Thomas B. Finan,* Attorney General of Maryland, *Joe T. Patterson,* Attorney General of Mississippi, *William Maynard,* Attorney General of New Hampshire, *Arthur J. Sills,* Attorney General of New Jersey, *Earl E. Hartley,* Attorney General of New Mexico, *Leslie R. Burgum,* Attorney General of North Dakota, *David Stahl,* Attorney General of Pennsylvania, *J. Joseph Nugent,* Attorney General of Rhode Island, *Daniel R. McLeod,* Attorney General of South Carolina, *A. C. Miller,* Attorney General of South Dakota, *Will Wilson,* Attorney General of Texas, and *C. Donald Robertson,* Attorney General of West Virginia.

MR. JUSTICE BLACK delivered the opinion of the Court.

The respondent Board of Education of Union Free School District No. 9, New Hyde Park, New York, acting in its official capacity under state law, directed the School District's principal to cause the following prayer to be said aloud by each class in the presence of a teacher at the beginning of each school day:

> "Almighty God, we acknowledge our dependence upon Thee, and we beg Thy blessings upon us, our parents, our teachers and our Country."

This daily procedure was adopted on the recommendation of the State Board of Regents, a governmental agency created by the State Constitution to which the New York Legislature has granted broad supervisory, executive, and

legislative powers over the State's public school system.[1]
These state officials composed the prayer which they
recommended and published as a part of their "Statement on Moral and Spiritual Training in the Schools,"
saying: "We believe that this Statement will be subscribed to by all men and women of good will, and we call
upon all of them to aid in giving life to our program."

Shortly after the practice of reciting the Regents'
prayer was adopted by the School District, the parents of
ten pupils brought this action in a New York State Court
insisting that use of this official prayer in the public
schools was contrary to the beliefs, religions, or religious
practices of both themselves and their children. Among
other things, these parents challenged the constitutionality of both the state law authorizing the School District
to direct the use of prayer in public schools and the School
District's regulation ordering the recitation of this particular prayer on the ground that these actions of official
governmental agencies violate that part of the First
Amendment of the Federal Constitution which commands
that "Congress shall make no law respecting an establishment of religion"—a command which was "made
applicable to the State of New York by the Fourteenth
Amendment of the said Constitution." The New York
Court of Appeals, over the dissents of Judges Dye and
Fuld, sustained an order of the lower state courts which
had upheld the power of New York to use the Regents'
prayer as a part of the daily procedures of its public
schools so long as the schools did not compel any pupil
to join in the prayer over his or his parents' objection.[2]

---

[1] See New York Constitution, Art. V, § 4; New York Education
Law, §§ 101, 120 *et seq.*, 202, 214–219, 224, 245 *et seq.*, 704, and
801 *et seq.*

[2] 10 N. Y. 2d 174, 176 N. E. 2d 579. The trial court's opinion,
which is reported at 18 Misc. 2d 659, 191 N. Y. S. 2d 453, had
made it clear that the Board of Education must set up some sort

3

We granted certiorari to review this important decision involving rights protected by the First and Fourteenth Amendments.[3]

We think that by using its public school system to encourage recitation of the Regents' prayer, the State of New York has adopted a practice wholly inconsistent with the Establishment Clause. There can, of course, be no doubt that New York's program of daily classroom invocation of God's blessings as prescribed in the Regents' prayer is a religious activity. It is a solemn avowal of divine faith and supplication for the blessings of the Almighty. The nature of such a prayer has always been

---

of procedures to protect those who objected to reciting the prayer: "This is not to say that the rights accorded petitioners and their children under the 'free exercise' clause do not mandate safeguards against such embarrassments and pressures. It is enough on this score, however, that regulations, such as were adopted by New York City's Board of Education in connection with its released time program, be adopted, making clear that neither teachers nor any other school authority may comment on participation or nonparticipation in the exercise nor suggest or require that any posture or language be used or dress be worn or be not used or not worn. Nonparticipation may take the form either of remaining silent during the exercise, or if the parent or child so desires, of being excused entirely from the exercise. Such regulations must also make provision for those nonparticipants who are to be excused from the prayer exercise. The exact provision to be made is a matter for decision by the board, rather than the court, within the framework of constitutional requirements. Within that framework would fall a provision that prayer participants proceed to a common assembly while nonparticipants attend other rooms, or that nonparticipants be permitted to arrive at school a few minutes late or to attend separate opening exercises, or any other method which treats with equality both participants and nonparticipants." 18 Misc. 2d, at 696, 191 N. Y. S. 2d, at 492–493. See also the opinion of the Appellate Division affirming that of the trial court, reported at 11 App. Div. 2d 340, 206 N. Y. S. 2d 183.

[3] 368 U. S. 924.

religious, none of the respondents has denied this and the trial court expressly so found:

> "The religious nature of prayer was recognized by Jefferson and has been concurred in by theological writers, the United States Supreme Court and State courts and administrative officials, including New York's Commissioner of Education. A committee of the New York Legislature has agreed.
>
> "The Board of Regents as *amicus curiae,* the respondents and intervenors all concede the religious nature of prayer, but seek to distinguish this prayer because it is based on our spiritual heritage. . . ." [4]

The petitioners contend among other things that the state laws requiring or permitting use of the Regents' prayer must be struck down as a violation of the Establishment Clause because that prayer was composed by governmental officials as a part of a governmental program to further religious beliefs. For this reason, petitioners argue, the State's use of the Regents' prayer in its public school system breaches the constitutional wall of separation between Church and State. We agree with that contention since we think that the constitutional prohibition against laws respecting an establishment of religion must at least mean that in this country it is no part of the business of government to compose official prayers for any group of the American people to recite as a part of a religious program carried on by government.

It is a matter of history that this very practice of establishing governmentally composed prayers for religious services was one of the reasons which caused many of our early colonists to leave England and seek religious freedom in America. The Book of Common Prayer,

---

[4] 18 Misc. 2d, at 671–672, 191 N. Y. S. 2d, at 468–469.

which was created under governmental direction and
which was approved by Acts of Parliament in 1548 and
1549,[5] set out in minute detail the accepted form and
content of prayer and other religious ceremonies to be
used in the established, tax-supported Church of England.[6] The controversies over the Book and what should
be its content repeatedly threatened to disrupt the peace
of that country as the accepted forms of prayer in the
established church changed with the views of the particular ruler that happened to be in control at the time.[7]
Powerful groups representing some of the varying religious views of the people struggled among themselves to
impress their particular views upon the Government and

---

[5] 2 & 3 Edward VI, c. 1, entitled "An Act for Uniformity of Service
and Administration of the Sacraments throughout the Realm"; 3 & 4
Edward VI, c. 10, entitled "An Act for the abolishing and putting
away of divers Books and Images."

[6] The provisions of the various versions of the Book of Common
Prayer are set out in broad outline in the Encyclopaedia Britannica,
Vol. 18 (1957 ed.), pp. 420–423. For a more complete description,
see Pullan, The History of the Book of Common Prayer (1900).

[7] The first major revision of the Book of Common Prayer was
made in 1552 during the reign of Edward VI. 5 & 6 Edward VI, c. 1.
In 1553, Edward VI died and was succeeded by Mary who abolished
the Book of Common Prayer entirely. 1 Mary, c. 2. But upon the
accession of Elizabeth in 1558, the Book was restored with important
alterations from the form it had been given by Edward VI. 1 Elizabeth, c. 2. The resentment to this amended form of the Book was
kept firmly under control during the reign of Elizabeth but, upon her
death in 1603, a petition signed by more than 1,000 Puritan ministers
was presented to King James I asking for further alterations in the
Book. Some alterations were made and the Book retained substantially this form until it was completely suppressed again in 1645 as a
result of the successful Puritan Revolution. Shortly after the restora-
tion in 1660 of Charles II, the Book was again reintroduced, 13 & 14
Charles II, c. 4, and again with alterations. Rather than accept this
form of the Book some 2,000 Puritan ministers vacated their benefices.
See generally Pullan, The History of the Book of Common Prayer
(1900), pp. vii–xvi; Encyclopaedia Britannica (1957 ed.), Vol. 18,
pp. 421–422.

obtain amendments of the Book more suitable to their
respective notions of how religious services should be conducted in order that the official religious establishment
would advance their particular religious beliefs.[8] Other
groups, lacking the necessary political power to influence
the Government on the matter, decided to leave England
and its established church and seek freedom in America
from England's governmentally ordained and supported
religion.

It is an unfortunate fact of history that when some of
the very groups which had most strenuously opposed the
established Church of England found themselves sufficiently in control of colonial governments in this country
to write their own prayers into law, they passed laws making their own religion the official religion of their respective colonies.[9] Indeed, as late as the time of the Revolu-

---

[8] For example, the Puritans twice attempted to modify the Book of
Common Prayer and once attempted to destroy it. The story of
their struggle to modify the Book in the reign of Charles I is vividly
summarized in Pullan, History of the Book of Common Prayer, at
p. xiii: "The King actively supported those members of the Church
of England who were anxious to vindicate its Catholic character and
maintain the ceremonial which Elizabeth had approved. Laud,
Archbishop of Canterbury, was the leader of this school. Equally
resolute in his opposition to the distinctive tenets of Rome and of
Geneva, he enjoyed the hatred of both Jesuit and Calvinist. He
helped the Scottish bishops, who had made large concessions to the
uncouth habits of Presbyterian worship, to draw up a Book of Common Prayer for Scotland. It contained a Communion Office resem-
bling that of the book of 1549. It came into use in 1637, and met
with a bitter and barbarous opposition. The vigour of the Scottish
Protestants strengthened the hands of their English sympathisers.
Laud and Charles were executed, Episcopacy was abolished, the use
of the Book of Common Prayer was prohibited."

[9] For a description of some of the laws enacted by early theocratic
governments in New England, see Parrington, Main Currents in
American Thought (1930), Vol. 1, pp. 5–50; Whipple, Our Ancient
Liberties (1927), pp. 63–78; Wertenbaker, The Puritan Oligarchy
(1947).

7

tionary War, there were established churches in at least
eight of the thirteen former colonies and established religions in at least four of the other five.[10] But the successful Revolution against English political domination was
shortly followed by intense opposition to the practice of
establishing religion by law. This opposition crystallized
rapidly into an effective political force in Virginia where
the minority religious groups such as Presbyterians, Lutherans, Quakers and Baptists had gained such strength
that the adherents to the established Episcopal Church
were actually a minority themselves. In 1785–1786,
those opposed to the established Church, led by James
Madison and Thomas Jefferson, who, though themselves
not members of any of these dissenting religious groups,
opposed all religious establishments by law on grounds
of principle, obtained the enactment of the famous
"Virginia Bill for Religious Liberty" by which all religious
groups were placed on an equal footing so far as the
State was concerned.[11] Similar though less far-reaching

---

[10] The Church of England was the established church of at least
five colonies: Maryland, Virginia, North Carolina, South Carolina
and Georgia. There seems to be some controversy as to whether that
church was officially established in New York and New Jersey but
there is no doubt that it received substantial support from those
States. See Cobb, The Rise of Religious Liberty in America (1902),
pp. 338, 408. In Massachusetts, New Hampshire and Connecticut,
the Congregationalist Church was officially established. In Pennsylvania and Delaware, all Christian sects were treated equally in most
situations but Catholics were discriminated against in some respects.
See generally Cobb, The Rise of Religious Liberty in America (1902).
In Rhode Island all Protestants enjoyed equal privileges but it is not
clear whether Catholics were allowed to vote. Compare Fiske, The
Critical Period in American History (1899), p. 76 with Cobb, The
Rise of Religious Liberty in America (1902), pp. 437–438.

[11] 12 Hening, Statutes of Virginia (1823), 84, entitled "An act for
establishing religious freedom." The story of the events surrounding
the enactment of this law was reviewed in *Everson* v. *Board of
Education*, 330 U. S. 1, both by the Court, at pp. 11–13, and in the

legislation was being considered and passed in other States.[12]

By the time of the adoption of the Constitution, our history shows that there was a widespread awareness among many Americans of the dangers of a union of Church and State. These people knew, some of them from bitter personal experience, that one of the greatest dangers to the freedom of the individual to worship in his own way lay in the Government's placing its official stamp of approval upon one particular kind of prayer or one particular form of religious services. They knew the anguish, hardship and bitter strife that could come when zealous religious groups struggled with one another to obtain the Government's stamp of approval from each King, Queen, or Protector that came to temporary power. The Constitution was intended to avert a part of this danger by leaving the government of this country in the hands of the people rather than in the hands of any monarch. But this safeguard was not enough. Our Founders were no more willing to let the content of their prayers and their privilege of praying whenever they pleased be influenced by the ballot box than they were to let these vital matters of personal conscience depend upon the succession of monarchs. The First Amendment was added to the Constitution to stand as a guarantee that neither the power nor the prestige of the Federal Government would be used to control, support or influence the kinds of prayer the American people can say—

---

dissenting opinion of Mr. Justice Rutledge, at pp. 33–42. See also Fiske, The Critical Period in American History (1899), pp. 78–82; James, The Struggle for Religious Liberty in Virginia (1900); Thom, The Struggle for Religious Freedom in Virginia: The Baptists (1900); Cobb, The Rise of Religious Liberty in America (1902), pp. 74–115, 482–499.

[12] See Cobb, The Rise of Religious Liberty in America (1902), pp. 482–509.

that the people's religions must not be subjected to the pressures of government for change each time a new political administration is elected to office. Under that Amendment's prohibition against governmental establishment of religion, as reinforced by the provisions of the Fourteenth Amendment, government in this country, be it state or federal, is without power to prescribe by law any particular form of prayer which is to be used as an official prayer in carrying on any program of governmentally sponsored religious activity.

There can be no doubt that New York's state prayer program officially establishes the religious beliefs embodied in the Regents' prayer. The respondents' argument to the contrary, which is largely based upon the contention that the Regents' prayer is "non-denominational" and the fact that the program, as modified and approved by state courts, does not require all pupils to recite the prayer but permits those who wish to do so to remain silent or be excused from the room, ignores the essential nature of the program's constitutional defects. Neither the fact that the prayer may be denominationally neutral nor the fact that its observance on the part of the students is voluntary can serve to free it from the limitations of the Establishment Clause, as it might from the Free Exercise Clause, of the First Amendment, both of which are operative against the States by virtue of the Fourteenth Amendment. Although these two clauses may in certain instances overlap, they forbid two quite different kinds of governmental encroachment upon religious freedom. The Establishment Clause, unlike the Free Exercise Clause, does not depend upon any showing of direct governmental compulsion and is violated by the enactment of laws which establish an official religion whether those laws operate directly to coerce nonobserving individuals or not. This is not to say, of course, that laws officially prescribing a particular form of religious worship do not involve coercion of such individuals. When the power, prestige and financial support of government is placed behind a particular religious belief, the indirect coercive pressure upon religious minorities to conform to the prevailing officially approved religion is plain. But the purposes underlying the Establishment Clause go much further than that. Its first and most immediate purpose rested on the belief that a union of government and religion tends to destroy government and to degrade religion. The history of governmentally established religion, both in England and in this country, showed that whenever government had allied itself with one particular form of religion, the inevitable result had been that it had incurred the hatred, disrespect and even contempt of those who held contrary beliefs.[13] That same history showed that many people had lost their respect for any religion that had relied upon the support of government to spread its faith.[14] The Establishment Clause

---

[13] "[A]ttempts to enforce by legal sanctions, acts obnoxious to so great a proportion of Citizens, tend to enervate the laws in general, and to slacken the bands of Society. If it be difficult to execute any law which is not generally deemed necessary or salutary, what must be the case where it is deemed invalid and dangerous? and what may be the effect of so striking an example of impotency in the Government, on its general authority." Memorial and Remonstrance against Religious Assessments, II Writings of Madison 183, 190.

[14] "It is moreover to weaken in those who profess this Religion a pious confidence in its innate excellence, and the patronage of its Author; and to foster in those who still reject it, a suspicion that its friends are too conscious of its fallacies, to trust it to its own merits. . . . [E]xperience witnesseth that ecclesiastical establishments, instead of maintaining the purity and efficacy of Religion, have had a contrary operation. During almost fifteen centuries, has the legal establishment of Christianity been on trial. What have been its fruits? More or less in all places, pride and indolence in the Clergy; ignorance and servility in the laity; in both, superstition,

11

thus stands as an expression of principle on the part of the Founders of our Constitution that religion is too personal, too sacred, too holy, to permit its "unhallowed perversion" by a civil magistrate.[15] Another purpose of the Establishment Clause rested upon an awareness of the historical fact that governmentally established religions and religious persecutions go hand in hand.[16] The Founders knew that only a few years after the Book of Common Prayer became the only accepted form of religious services in the established Church of England, an Act of Uniformity was passed to compel all Englishmen to attend those services and to make it a criminal offense to conduct or attend religious gatherings of any other kind [17]—a law

bigotry and persecution. Enquire of the Teachers of Christianity for the ages in which it appeared in its greatest lustre; those of every sect, point to the ages prior to its incorporation with Civil policy." *Id.*, at 187.

[15] Memorial and Remonstrance against Religious Assessments, II Writings of Madison, at 187.

[16] "[T]he proposed establishment is a departure from that generous policy, which, offering an asylum to the persecuted and oppressed of every Nation and Religion, promised a lustre to our country, and an accession to the number of its citizens. What a melancholy mark is the Bill of sudden degeneracy? Instead of holding forth an asylum to the persecuted, it is itself a signal of persecution. . . . Distant as it may be, in its present form, from the Inquisition it differs from it only in degree. The one is the first step, the other the last in the career of intolerance. The magnanimous sufferer under this cruel scourge in foreign Regions, must view the Bill as a Beacon on our Coast, warning him to seek some other haven, where liberty and philanthropy in their due extent may offer a more certain repose from his troubles." *Id.*, at 188.

[17] 5 & 6 Edward VI, c. 1, entitled "An Act for the Uniformity of Service and Administration of Sacraments throughout the Realm." This Act was repealed during the reign of Mary but revived upon the accession of Elizabeth. See note 7, *supra.* The reasons which led to the enactment of this statute were set out in its preamble: "Where there hath been a very godly Order set forth by the Authority of Parliament, for Common Prayer and Administration of the Sacra-

which was consistently flouted by dissenting religious groups in England and which contributed to widespread persecutions of people like John Bunyan who persisted in holding "unlawful [religious] meetings . . . to the great disturbance and distraction of the good subjects of this kingdom . . . ." [18] And they knew that similar persecutions had received the sanction of law in several of the colonies in this country soon after the establishment of official religions in those colonies.[19] It was in large part to get completely away from this sort of systematic religious persecution that the Founders brought into being our Nation, our Constitution, and our Bill of Rights with its prohibition against any governmental establishment of religion. The New York laws officially prescribing the Regents' prayer are inconsistent both with the purposes of the Establishment Clause and with the Establishment Clause itself.

It has been argued that to apply the Constitution in such a way as to prohibit state laws respecting an

---

ments to be used in the Mother Tongue within the Church of *England,* agreeable to the Word of God and the Primitive Church, very comfortable to all good People desiring to live in Christian Conversation, and most profitable to the Estate of this Realm, upon the which the Mercy, Favour and Blessing of Almighty God is in no wise so readily and plenteously poured as by Common Prayers, due using of the Sacraments, and often preaching of the Gospel, with the Devotion of the Hearers: (1) And yet this notwithstanding, a great Number of People in divers Parts of this Realm, following their own Sensuality, and living either without Knowledge or due Fear of God, do wilfully and damnably before Almighty God abstain and refuse to come to their Parish Churches and other Places where Common Prayer, Administration of the Sacraments, and Preaching of the Word of God, is used upon *Sundays* and other Days ordained to be Holydays."

[18] Bunyan's own account of his trial is set forth in A Relation of the Imprisonment of Mr. John Bunyan, reprinted in Grace Abounding and The Pilgrim's Progress (Brown ed. 1907), at 103–132.

[19] For a vivid account of some of these persecutions, see Wertenbaker, The Puritan Oligarchy (1947).

establishment of religious services in public schools is to indicate a hostility toward religion or toward prayer. Nothing, of course, could be more wrong. The history of man is inseparable from the history of religion. And perhaps it is not too much to say that since the beginning of that history many people have devoutly believed that "More things are wrought by prayer than this world dreams of." It was doubtless largely due to men who believed this that there grew up a sentiment that caused men to leave the cross-currents of officially established state religions and religious persecution in Europe and come to this country filled with the hope that they could find a place in which they could pray when they pleased to the God of their faith in the language they chose.[20] And there were men of this same faith in the

---

[20] Perhaps the best example of the sort of men who came to this country for precisely that reason is Roger Williams, the founder of Rhode Island, who has been described as "the truest Christian amongst many who sincerely desired to be Christian." Parrington, Main Currents in American Thought (1930), Vol. 1, at p. 74. Williams, who was one of the earliest exponents of the doctrine of separation of church and state, believed that separation was necessary in order to protect the church from the danger of destruction which he thought inevitably flowed from control by even the best-intentioned civil authorities: "The unknowing zeale of *Constantine* and other Emperours, did more hurt to *Christ Jesus* his Crowne and Kingdome, then the raging fury of the most bloody *Neroes*. In the *persecutions* of the later, *Christians* were sweet and fragrant, like spice pounded and beaten in morters: But those *good* Emperours, persecuting some erroneous persons, *Arrius, &c.* and advancing the professours of some Truths of Christ (for there was no small number of *Truths* lost in those times) and maintaining their *Religion* by the materiall Sword, I say by this meanes *Christianity* was *ecclipsed,* and the Professors of it fell asleep . . . ." Williams, The Bloudy Tenent, of Persecution, for cause of Conscience, discussed in A Conference betweene Truth and Peace (London, 1644), reprinted in Narragansett Club Publications, Vol. III, p. 184. To Williams, it was no part of the business or competence of a civil magistrate to interfere in religious matters: "[W]hat imprudence and *indiscretion* is it in the most common

power of prayer who led the fight for adoption of our Constitution and also for our Bill of Rights with the very guarantees of religious freedom that forbid the sort of governmental activity which New York has attempted here. These men knew that the First Amendment, which tried to put an end to governmental control of religion and of prayer, was not written to destroy either. They knew rather that it was written to quiet well-justified fears which nearly all of them felt arising out of an awareness that governments of the past had shackled men's tongues to make them speak only the religious thoughts that government wanted them to speak and to pray only to the God that government wanted them to pray to. It is neither sacrilegious nor antireligious to say that each separate government in this country should stay out of the business of writing or sanctioning official prayers and leave that purely religious function to the people themselves and to those the people choose to look to for religious guidance.[21]

---

affaires of Life, to conceive that *Emperours, Kings* and *Rulers* of the earth must not only be qualified with *politicall* and *state abilities* to *make* and *execute* such *Civill Lawes* which may concerne the common *rights, peace* and *safety* (which is worke and businesse, load and burthen enough for the ablest shoulders in the Commonweal) but also furnished with such *Spirituall* and heavenly *abilities* to governe the *Spirituall* and *Christian Commonweale* . . . ." *Id.,* at 366. See also *id.,* at 136–137.

[21] There is of course nothing in the decision reached here that is inconsistent with the fact that school children and others are officially encouraged to express love for our country by reciting historical documents such as the Declaration of Independence which contain references to the Deity or by singing officially espoused anthems which include the composer's professions of faith in a Supreme Being, or with the fact that there are many manifestations in our public life of belief in God. Such patriotic or ceremonial occasions bear no true resemblance to the unquestioned religious exercise that the State of New York has sponsored in this instance.

15

It is true that New York's establishment of its Regents' prayer as an officially approved religious doctrine of that State does not amount to a total establishment of one particular religious sect to the exclusion of all others— that, indeed, the governmental endorsement of that prayer seems relatively insignificant when compared to the governmental encroachments upon religion which were commonplace 200 years ago. To those who may subscribe to the view that because the Regents' official prayer is so brief and general there can be no danger to religious freedom in its governmental establishment, however, it may be appropriate to say in the words of James Madison, the author of the First Amendment:

> "[I]t is proper to take alarm at the first experiment on our liberties. . . . Who does not see that the same authority which can establish Christianity, in exclusion of all other Religions, may establish with the same ease any particular sect of Christians, in exclusion of all other Sects? That the same authority which can force a citizen to contribute three pence only of his property for the support of any one establishment, may force him to conform to any other establishment in all cases whatsoever?" [22]

The judgment of the Court of Appeals of New York is reversed and the cause remanded for further proceedings not inconsistent with this opinion.

Reversed and remanded.

Mr. Justice Frankfurter took no part in the decision of this case.

Mr. Justice White took no part in the consideration or decision of this case.

---

[22] Memorial and Remonstrance against Religious Assessments, II Writings of Madison 183, at 185–186.

MR. JUSTICE DOUGLAS, concurring.

It is customary in deciding a constitutional question to treat it in its narrowest form. Yet at times the setting of the question gives it a form and content which no abstract treatment could give. The point for decision is whether the Government can constitutionally finance a religious exercise. Our system at the federal and state levels is presently honeycombed with such financing.[1] Nevertheless, I think it is an unconstitutional undertaking whatever form it takes.

First, a word as to what this case does not involve.

---

[1] "There are many 'aids' to religion in this country at all levels of government. To mention but a few at the federal level, one might begin by observing that the very First Congress which wrote the First Amendment provided for chaplains in both Houses and in the armed services. There is compulsory chapel at the service academies, and religious services are held in federal hospitals and prisons. The President issues religious proclamations. The Bible is used for the administration of oaths. N. Y. A. and W. P. A. funds were available to parochial schools during the depression. Veterans receiving money under the 'G. I.' Bill of 1944 could attend denominational schools, to which payments were made directly by the government. During World War II, federal money was contributed to denominational schools for the training of nurses. The benefits of the National School Lunch Act are available to students in private as well as public schools. The Hospital Survey and Construction Act of 1946 specifically made money available to non-public hospitals. The slogan 'In God We Trust' is used by the Treasury Department, and Congress recently added God to the pledge of allegiance. There is Bible-reading in the schools of the District of Columbia, and religious instruction is given in the District's National Training School for Boys. Religious organizations are exempt from the federal income tax and are granted postal privileges. Up to defined limits—15 per cent of the adjusted gross income of individuals and 5 per cent of the net income of corporations—contributions to religious organizations are deductible for federal income tax purposes. There are no limits to the deductibility of gifts and bequests to religious institutions made under the federal gift and estate tax laws. This list of federal 'aids' could easily be expanded, and of course there is a long list in each state." Fellman, The Limits of Freedom (1959), pp. 40–41.

17

Plainly, our Bill of Rights would not permit a State or the Federal Government to adopt an official prayer and penalize anyone who would not utter it. This, however, is not that case, for there is no element of compulsion or coercion in New York's regulation requiring that public schools be opened each day with the following prayer:

> "Almighty God, we acknowledge our dependence upon Thee, and we beg Thy blessings upon us, our parents, our teachers and our Country."

The prayer is said upon the commencement of the school day, immediately following the pledge of allegiance to the flag. The prayer is said aloud in the presence of a teacher, who either leads the recitation or selects a student to do so. No student, however, is compelled to take part. The respondents have adopted a regulation which provides that "Neither teachers nor any school authority shall comment on participation or non-participation . . . nor suggest or request that any posture or language be used or dress be worn or be not used or not worn." Provision is also made for excusing children, upon written request of a parent or guardian, from the saying of the prayer or from the room in which the prayer is said. A letter implementing and explaining this regulation has been sent to each taxpayer and parent in the school district. As I read this regulation, a child is free to stand or not stand, to recite or not recite, without fear of reprisal or even comment by the teacher or any other school official.

In short, the only one who need utter the prayer is the teacher; and no teacher is complaining of it. Students can stand mute or even leave the classroom, if they desire.[2]

---

[2] West Point Cadets are required to attend chapel each Sunday. Reg., c. 21, § 2101. The same requirement obtains at the Naval Academy (Reg., c. 9, § 0901, (1)(a)), and at the Air Force Academy except First Classmen. Catalogue, 1962–1963, p. 110. And see Honey-

McCollum v. *Board of Education,* 333 U. S. 203, does not decide this case. It involved the use of public school facilities for religious education of students. Students either had to attend religious instruction or "go to some other place in the school building for pursuit of their secular studies. . . . Reports of their presence or absence were to be made to their secular teachers." *Id.,* at 209. The influence of the teaching staff was therefore brought to bear on the student body, to support the instilling of religious principles. In the present case, school facilities are used to say the prayer and the teaching staff is employed to lead the pupils in it. There is, however, no effort at indoctrination and no attempt at exposition. Prayers of course may be so long and of such a character as to amount to an attempt at the religious instruction that was denied the public schools by the *McCollum* case. But New York's prayer is of a character that does not involve any element of proselytizing as in the *McCollum* case.

The question presented by this case is therefore an extremely narrow one. It is whether New York oversteps the bounds when it finances a religious exercise.

What New York does on the opening of its public schools is what we do when we open court. Our Crier has from the beginning announced the convening of the Court and then added "God save the United States and this Honorable Court." That utterance is a supplication, a prayer in which we, the judges, are free to join, but which we need not recite any more than the students need recite the New York prayer.

What New York does on the opening of its public schools is what each House of Congress[3] does at the open-

---

well, Chaplains of the United States Army (1958); Jorgensen, The Service of Chaplains to Army Air Units, 1917–1946, Vol. I (1961).

[3] The New York Legislature follows the same procedure. See, *e. g.,* Vol. 1, N. Y. Assembly Jour., 184th Sess., 1961, p. 8; Vol. 1, N. Y. Senate Jour., 184th Sess., 1961, p. 5.

19

ing of each day's business.[4] Reverend Frederick B. Harris is Chaplain of the Senate; Reverend Bernard Braskamp is Chaplain of the House. Guest chaplains of various denominations also officiate.[5]

---

[4] Rules of the Senate provide that each calendar day's session shall open with prayer. See Rule III, Senate Manual, S. Doc. No. 2, 87th Cong., 1st Sess. The same is true of the Rules of the House. See Rule VII, Rules of the House of Representatives, H. R. Doc. No. 459, 86th Cong., 2d Sess. The Chaplains of the Senate and of the House receive $8,810 annually. See 75 Stat. 320, 324.

[5] It would, I assume, make no difference in the present case if a different prayer were said every day or if the ministers of the community rotated, each giving his own prayer. For some of the petitioners in the present case profess no religion.

The Pledge of Allegiance, like the prayer, recognizes the existence of a Supreme Being. Since 1954 it has contained the words "one Nation *under God,* indivisible, with liberty and justice for all." 36 U. S. C. § 172. The House Report recommending the addition of the words "under God" stated that those words in no way run contrary to the First Amendment but recognize "only the guidance of God in our national affairs." H. R. Rep. No. 1693, 83d Cong., 2d Sess., p. 3. And see S. Rep. No. 1287, 83d Cong., 2d Sess. Senator Ferguson, who sponsored the measure in the Senate, pointed out that the words "In God We Trust" are over the entrance to the Senate Chamber. 100 Cong. Rec. 6348. He added:

"I have felt that the Pledge of Allegiance to the Flag which stands for the United States of America should recognize the Creator who we really believe is in control of the destinies of this great Republic.

"It is true that under the Constitution no power is lodged anywhere to establish a religion. This is not an attempt to establish a religion; it has nothing to do with anything of that kind. It relates to belief in God, in whom we sincerely repose our trust. We know that America cannot be defended by guns, planes, and ships alone. Appropriations and expenditures for defense will be of value only if the God under whom we live believes that we are in the right. We should at all times recognize God's province over the lives of our people and over this great Nation." *Ibid.* And see 100 Cong. Rec. 7757 *et seq.* for the debates in the House.

The Act of March 3, 1865, 13 Stat. 517, 518, authorized the phrase "In God We Trust" to be placed on coins. And see 17 Stat. 427. The first mandatory requirement for the use of that motto on coins

In New York the teacher who leads in prayer is on the
public payroll; and the time she takes seems minuscule as
compared with the salaries appropriated by state legislatures and Congress for chaplains to conduct prayers in the
legislative halls. Only a bare fraction of the teacher's
time is given to reciting this short 22-word prayer,
about the same amount of time that our Crier spends
announcing the opening of our sessions and offering a
prayer for this Court. Yet for me the principle is the
same, no matter how briefly the prayer is said, for in
each of the instances given the person praying is a public
official on the public payroll, performing a religious exercise in a governmental institution.[6] It is said that the

---

was made by the Act of May 18, 1908, 35 Stat. 164. See H. R. Rep.
No. 1106, 60th Cong., 1st Sess.; 42 Cong. Rec. 3384 *et seq.* The use
of the motto on all currency and coins was directed by the Act of July
11, 1955, 69 Stat. 290. See H. R. Rep. No. 662, 84th Cong., 1st Sess.;
S. Rep. No. 637, 84th Cong., 1st Sess. Moreover, by the Joint Reso-
lution of July 30, 1956, our national motto was declared to be "In God
We Trust." 70 Stat. 732. In reporting the Joint Resolution, the
Senate Judiciary Committee stated:

"Further official recognition of this motto was given by the adoption
of the Star-Spangled Banner as our national anthem. One stanza
of our national anthem is as follows:

" 'O, thus be it ever when freemen shall stand
    Between their lov'd home and the war's desolation!
    Blest with vict'ry and peace may the heav'n rescued land
    Praise the power that hath made and preserved us a nation!
    Then conquer we must when our cause it is just,
    And this be our motto—"In God is our trust."
    And the Star-Spangled Banner in triumph shall wave
    O'er the land of the free and the home of the brave.'

"In view of these words in our national anthem, it is clear that 'In
God we trust' has a strong claim as our national motto." S. Rep.
No. 2703, 84th Cong., 2d Sess., p. 2.

[6] The fact that taxpayers do not have standing in the federal courts
to raise the issue (*Frothingham* v. *Mellon*, 262 U. S. 447) is of course
no justification for drawing a line between what is done in New
York on the one hand and on the other what we do and what Congress
does in this matter of prayer.

element of coercion is inherent in the giving of this prayer. If that is true here, it is also true of the prayer with which this Court is convened, and of those that open the Congress. Few adults, let alone children, would leave our courtroom or the Senate or the House while those prayers are being given. Every such audience is in a sense a "captive" audience.

At the same time I cannot say that to authorize this prayer is to establish a religion in the strictly historic meaning of those words.[7] A religion is not established in the usual sense merely by letting those who choose to do so say the prayer that the public school teacher leads. Yet once government finances a religious exercise it inserts a divisive influence into our communities.[8] The New York Court said that the prayer given does not conform to all of the tenets of the Jewish, Unitarian, and Ethical Culture groups. One of the petitioners is an agnostic.

"We are a religious people whose institutions presuppose a Supreme Being." *Zorach* v. *Clauson*, 343 U. S. 306, 313. Under our Bill of Rights free play is given for

---

[7] The Court analogizes the present case to those involving the traditional Established Church. We once had an Established Church, the Anglican. All baptisms and marriages had to take place there. That church was supported by taxation. In these and other ways the Anglican Church was favored over the others. The First Amendment put an end to placing any one church in a preferred position. It ended support of any church or all churches by taxation. It went further and prevented secular sanction to any religious ceremony, dogma, or rite. Thus, it prevents civil penalties from being applied against recalcitrants or nonconformists.

[8] Some communities have a Christmas tree purchased with the taxpayers' money. The tree is sometimes decorated with the words "Peace on earth, goodwill to men." At other times the authorities draw from a different version of the Bible which says "Peace on earth to men of goodwill." Christmas, I suppose, is still a religious celebration, not merely a day put on the calendar for the benefit of merchants.

22

making religion an active force in our lives.[9] But "if a religious leaven is to be worked into the affairs of our people, it is to be done by individuals and groups, not by the Government." *McGowan* v. *Maryland,* 366 U. S. 420, 563 (dissenting opinion). By reason of the First Amendment government is commanded "to have no interest in theology or ritual" (*id.,* at 564), for on those matters "government must be neutral." *Ibid.* The First Amendment leaves the Government in a position not of hostility to religion but of neutrality. The philosophy is that the atheist or agnostic—the nonbeliever—is entitled to go his own way. The philosophy is that if government interferes in matters spiritual, it will be a divisive force. The First Amendment teaches that a government neutral in the field of religion better serves all religious interests.

My problem today would be uncomplicated but for *Everson* v. *Board of Education,* 330 U. S. 1, 17, which allowed taxpayers' money to be used to pay "the bus fares of parochial school pupils as a part of a general program under which" the fares of pupils attending public and other schools were also paid. The *Everson* case seems in retrospect to be out of line with the First Amendment. Its result is appealing, as it allows aid to be given to needy children. Yet by the same token, public funds could be used to satisfy other needs of children in parochial schools—lunches, books, and tuition being obvious examples. Mr. Justice Rutledge stated in dissent what I think is durable First Amendment philosophy:

"The reasons underlying the Amendment's policy have not vanished with time or diminished in force.

---

[9] Religion was once deemed to be a function of the public school system. The Northwest Ordinance, which antedated the First Amendment, provided in Article III that "Religion, morality, and knowledge being necessary to good government and the happiness of mankind, schools and the means of education shall forever be encouraged."

Now as when it was adopted the price of religious freedom is double. It is that the church and religion shall live both within and upon that freedom. There cannot be freedom of religion, safeguarded by the state, and intervention by the church or its agencies in the state's domain or dependency on its largesse. Madison's Remonstrance, Par. 6, 8. The great condition of religious liberty is that it be maintained free from sustenance, as also from other interferences, by the state. For when it comes to rest upon that secular foundation it vanishes with the resting. *Id.,* Par. 7, 8. Public money devoted to payment of religious costs, educational or other, brings the quest for more. It brings too the struggle of sect against sect for the larger share or for any. Here one by numbers alone will benefit most, there another. That is precisely the history of societies which have had an established religion and dissident groups. *Id.,* Par. 8, 11. It is the very thing Jefferson and Madison experienced and sought to guard against, whether in its blunt or in its more screened forms. *Ibid.* The end of such strife cannot be other than to destroy the cherished liberty. The dominating group will achieve the dominant benefit; or all will embroil the state in their dissensions. *Id.,* Par. 11." *Id.,* pp. 53–54.

What New York does with this prayer is a break with that tradition. I therefore join the Court in reversing the judgment below.

Mr. Justice Stewart, dissenting.

A local school board in New York has provided that those pupils who wish to do so may join in a brief prayer at the beginning of each school day, acknowledging their dependence upon God and asking His blessing upon them and upon their parents, their teachers, and their country. The Court today decides that in permitting this brief non-denominational prayer the school board has violated the Constitution of the United States. I think this decision is wrong.

The Court does not hold, nor could it, that New York has interfered with the free exercise of anybody's religion. For the state courts have made clear that those who object to reciting the prayer must be entirely free of any compulsion to do so, including any "embarrassments and pressures." Cf. *West Virginia State Board of Education* v. *Barnette,* 319 U. S. 624. But the Court says that in permitting school children to say this simple prayer, the New York authorities have established "an official religion."

With all respect, I think the Court has misapplied a great constitutional principle. I cannot see how an "official religion" is established by letting those who want to say a prayer say it. On the contrary, I think that to deny the wish of these school children to join in reciting this prayer is to deny them the opportunity of sharing in the spiritual heritage of our Nation.

The Court's historical review of the quarrels over the Book of Common Prayer in England throws no light for me on the issue before us in this case. England had then and has now an established church. Equally unenlightening, I think, is the history of the early establishment and later rejection of an official church in our own States. For we deal here not with the establishment of a state church, which would, of course, be constitutionally impermissible, but with whether school children who want to begin their day by joining in prayer must be prohibited from doing so. Moreover, I think that the Court's task, in this as in all areas of constitutional adjudication, is not responsibly aided by the uncritical invocation of metaphors like the "wall of separation," a phrase nowhere to be found in the Constitution. What is relevant to the issue here is not the history of an established church in sixteenth century England or in eighteenth century America, but the history of the religious traditions of our people, reflected in countless practices of the institutions and officials of our government.

At the opening of each day's Session of this Court we stand, while one of our officials invokes the protection of God. Since the days of John Marshall our Crier has said, "God save the United States and this Honorable Court." [1] Both the Senate and the House of Representatives open their daily Sessions with prayer.[2] Each of our Presidents, from George Washington to John F. Kennedy, has upon assuming his Office asked the protection and help of God.[3]

---

[1] See Warren, The Supreme Court in United States History, Vol. 1, p. 469.

[2] See Rule III, Senate Manual, S. Doc. No. 2, 87th Cong., 1st Sess. See Rule VII, Rules of the House of Representatives, H. R. Doc. No. 459, 86th Cong., 2d Sess.

[3] For example:

On April 30, 1789, President George Washington said:

"... it would be peculiarly improper to omit in this first official act my fervent supplications to that Almighty Being who rules over the universe, who presides in the councils of nations, and whose providential aids can supply every human defect, that His benediction may consecrate to the liberties and happiness of the people of the United States a Government instituted by themselves for these essential purposes, and may enable every instrument employed in its administration to execute with success the functions allotted to his charge. In tendering this homage to the Great Author of every public and private good, I assure myself that it expresses your sentiments not less than my own, nor those of my fellow-citizens at large less than either. No people can be bound to acknowledge and adore the Invisible Hand which conducts the affairs of men more than those of the United States. . . .

. . . . .

"Having thus imparted to you my sentiments as they have been awakened by the occasion which brings us together, I shall

Footnote 3—Continued.

take my present leave; but not without resorting once more to
the benign Parent of the Human Race in humble supplication
that, since He has been pleased to favor the American people
with opportunities for deliberating in perfect tranquillity, and
dispositions for deciding with unparalleled unanimity on a form
of government for the security of their union and the advancement of their happiness, so His divine blessing may be equally
conspicuous in the enlarged views, the temperate consultations,
and the wise measures on which the success of this Government
must depend."

On March 4, 1797, President John Adams said:

"And may that Being who is supreme over all, the Patron of
Order, the Fountain of Justice, and the Protector in all ages
of the world of virtuous liberty, continue His blessing upon this
nation and its Government and give it all possible success and
duration consistent with the ends of His providence."

On March 4, 1805, President Thomas Jefferson said:

". . . I shall need, too, the favor of that Being in whose hands
we are, who led our fathers, as Israel of old, from their native
land and planted them in a country flowing with all the neces-
saries and comforts of life; who has covered our infancy with His
providence and our riper years with His wisdom and power, and
to whose goodness I ask you to join in supplications with me
that He will so enlighten the minds of your servants, guide their
councils, and prosper their measures that whatsoever they do
shall result in your good, and shall secure to you the peace,
friendship, and approbation of all nations."

On March 4, 1809, President James Madison said:

"But the source to which I look . . . is in . . . my fellow-
citizens, and in the counsels of those representing them in the
other departments associated in the care of the national interests.
In these my confidence will under every difficulty be best placed,
next to that which we have all been encouraged to feel in the
guardianship and guidance of that Almighty Being whose power
regulates the destiny of nations, whose blessings have been so
conspicuously dispensed to this rising Republic, and to whom
we are bound to address our devout gratitude for the past, as
well as our fervent supplications and best hopes for the future."

[*Footnote 3 continued on p. 448*]

Footnote 3—Continued.

On March 4, 1865, President Abraham Lincoln said:

". . . Fondly do we hope, fervently do we pray, that this mighty scourge of war may speedily pass away. Yet, if God wills that it continue until all the wealth piled by the bondsman's two hundred and fifty years of unrequited toil shall be sunk, and until every drop of blood drawn with the lash shall be paid by another drawn with the sword, as was said three thousand years ago, so still it must be said 'the judgments of the Lord are true and righteous altogether.'

"With malice toward none, with charity for all, with firmness in the right as God gives us to see the right, let us strive on to finish the work we are in, to bind up the nation's wounds, to care for him who shall have borne the battle and for his widow and his orphan, to do all which may achieve and cherish a just and lasting peace among ourselves and with all nations."

On March 4, 1885, President Grover Cleveland said:

". . . And let us not trust to human effort alone, but humbly acknowledging the power and goodness of Almighty God, who presides over the destiny of nations, and who has at all times been revealed in our country's history, let us invoke His aid and His blessing upon our labors."

On March 5, 1917, President Woodrow Wilson said:

". . . I pray God I may be given the wisdom and the prudence to do my duty in the true spirit of this great people."

On March 4, 1933, President Franklin D. Roosevelt said:

"In this dedication of a Nation we humbly ask the blessing of God. May He protect each and every one of us. May He guide me in the days to come."

On January 21, 1957, President Dwight D. Eisenhower said:

"Before all else, we seek, upon our common labor as a nation, the blessings of Almighty God. And the hopes in our hearts fashion the deepest prayers of our whole people."

On January 20, 1961, President John F. Kennedy said:

"The world is very different now. . . . And yet the same revolutionary beliefs for which our forebears fought are still at issue around the globe—the belief that the rights of man come

The Court today says that the state and federal governments are without constitutional power to prescribe any particular form of words to be recited by any group of the American people on any subject touching religion.[4] One of the stanzas of "The Star-Spangled Banner," made our National Anthem by Act of Congress in 1931,[5] contains these verses:

> "Blest with victory and peace, may the heav'n
>   rescued land
>   Praise the Pow'r that hath made and preserved
>   us a nation!
> Then conquer we must, when our cause it is just,
>   And this be our motto 'In God is our Trust.' "

In 1954 Congress added a phrase to the Pledge of Allegiance to the Flag so that it now contains the words "one Nation *under God,* indivisible, with liberty and justice for all."[6] In 1952 Congress enacted legislation calling upon the President each year to proclaim a National Day of Prayer.[7] Since 1865 the words "IN GOD WE TRUST" have been impressed on our coins.[8]

---

not from the generosity of the state but from the hand of God.

.   .   .   .   .

"With a good conscience our only sure reward, with history the final judge of our deeds, let us go forth to lead the land we love, asking His blessing and His help, but knowing that here on earth God's work must truly be our own."

[4] My brother DOUGLAS says that the only question before us is whether government "can constitutionally finance a religious exercise." The official chaplains of Congress are paid with public money. So are military chaplains. So are state and federal prison chaplains.

[5] 36 U. S. C. § 170.

[6] 36 U. S. C. § 172.

[7] 36 U. S. C. § 185.

[8] 13 Stat. 517, 518; 17 Stat. 427; 35 Stat. 164; 69 Stat. 290. The current provisions are embodied in 31 U. S. C. §§ 324, 324a.

Countless similar examples could be listed, but there is no need to belabor the obvious.[9] It was all summed up by this Court just ten years ago in a single sentence: "We are a religious people whose institutions presuppose a Supreme Being." *Zorach* v. *Clauson,* 343 U. S. 306, 313.

I do not believe that this Court, or the Congress, or the President has by the actions and practices I have mentioned established an "official religion" in violation of the Constitution. And I do not believe the State of New York has done so in this case. What each has done has been to recognize and to follow the deeply entrenched and highly cherished spiritual traditions of our Nation— traditions which come down to us from those who almost two hundred years ago avowed their "firm Reliance on the Protection of divine Providence" when they proclaimed the freedom and independence of this brave new world.[10]

I dissent.

---

[9] I am at a loss to understand the Court's unsupported *ipse dixit* that these official expressions of religious faith in and reliance upon a Supreme Being "bear no true resemblance to the unquestioned religious exercise that the State of New York has sponsored in this instance." See *ante,* p. 435, n. 21. I can hardly think that the Court means to say that the First Amendment imposes a lesser restriction upon the Federal Government than does the Fourteenth Amendment upon the States. Or is the Court suggesting that the Constitution permits judges and Congressmen and Presidents to join in prayer, but prohibits school children from doing so?

[10] The Declaration of Independence ends with this sentence: "And for the support of this Declaration, with a firm reliance on the protection of divine Providence, we mutually pledge to each other our Lives, our Fortunes and our sacred Honor."

SCHOOL DISTRICT OF ABINGTON TOWNSHIP, PENNSYLVANIA, ET AL. *v.* SCHEMPP ET AL.

APPEAL FROM THE UNITED STATES DISTRICT COURT FOR THE EASTERN DISTRICT OF PENNSYLVANIA.

No. 142. Argued February 27–28, 1963.—Decided June 17, 1963.*

Because of the prohibition of the First Amendment against the enactment by Congress of any law "respecting an establishment of religion," which is made applicable to the States by the Fourteenth Amendment, no state law or school board may require that passages from the Bible be read or that the Lord's Prayer be recited in the public schools of a State at the beginning of each school day— even if individual students may be excused from attending or participating in such exercises upon written request of their parents. Pp. 205–227.

201 F. Supp. 815, affirmed.

228 Md. 239, 179 A. 2d 698, reversed.

John D. Killian III, Deputy Attorney General of Pennsylvania, and *Philip H. Ward III* argued the cause for appellants in No. 142. With them on the brief were *David Stahl,* Attorney General of Pennsylvania, *Percival R. Rieder* and *C. Brewster Rhoads.*

Henry W. Sawyer III argued the cause for appellees in No. 142. With him on the brief was *Wayland H. Elsbree.*

Leonard J. Kerpelman argued the cause and filed a brief for petitioners in No. 119.

Francis B. Burch and *George W. Baker, Jr.* argued the cause for respondents in No. 119. With them on the brief were *Nelson B. Seidman* and *Philip Z. Altfeld.*

---

*Together with No. 119, *Murray et al.* v. *Curlett et al.,* Constituting the Board of School Commissioners of Baltimore City,* on certiorari to the Court of Appeals of Maryland, argued February 27, 1963.

Thomas B. Finan, Attorney General of Maryland, argued the cause for the State of Maryland, as *amicus curiae,* urging affirmance in No. 119. With him on the brief were *James P. Garland* and *Robert F. Sweeney,* Assistant Attorneys General of Maryland. *Richmond M. Flowers,* Attorney General of Alabama, *Robert Pickrell,* Attorney General of Arizona, *Bruce Bennett,* Attorney General of Arkansas, *Richard W. Ervin,* Attorney General of Florida, *Eugene Cook,* Attorney General of Georgia, *Allan G. Shepard,* Attorney General of Idaho, *William M. Ferguson,* Attorney General of Kansas, *Jack P. F. Gremillion,* Attorney General of Louisiana, *Frank E. Hancock,* Attorney General of Maine, *Joe T. Patterson,* Attorney General of Mississippi, *William Maynard,* Attorney General of New Hampshire, *Arthur J. Sills,* Attorney General of New Jersey, *Earl E. Hartley,* Attorney General of New Mexico, *Thomas Wade Bruton,* Attorney General of North Carolina, *J. Joseph Nugent,* Attorney General of Rhode Island, *Daniel R. McLeod,* Attorney General of South Carolina, *Frank R. Farrar,* Attorney General of South Dakota, and *George F. McCanless,* Attorney General of Tennessee, joined in the brief on behalf of their respective States, as *amici curiae.*

Briefs of *amici curiae,* urging affirmance in No. 142 and reversal in No. 119, were filed by *Morris B. Abram, Edwin J. Lukas, Burnett Roth, Arnold Forster, Paul Hartman, Theodore Leskes* and *Sol Rabkin* for the American Jewish Committee et al.; by *Leo Pfeffer, Lewis H. Weinstein, Albert Wald, Shad Polier, Samuel Lawrence Brennglass* and *Theodore R. Mann* for the Synagogue Council of America et al.; and by *Herbert A. Wolff, Leo Rosen, Morris L. Ernst* and *Nancy F. Wechsler* for the American Ethical Union.

MR. JUSTICE CLARK delivered the opinion of the Court.

Once again we are called upon to consider the scope of the provision of the First Amendment to the United States Constitution which declares that "Congress shall make no law respecting an establishment of religion, or prohibiting the free exercise thereof . . . ." These companion cases present the issues in the context of state action requiring that schools begin each day with readings from the Bible. While raising the basic questions under slightly different factual situations, the cases permit of joint treatment. In light of the history of the First Amendment and of our cases interpreting and applying its requirements, we hold that the practices at issue and the laws requiring them are unconstitutional under the Establishment Clause, as applied to the States through the Fourteenth Amendment.

I.

The Facts in Each Case: No. 142. The Commonwealth of Pennsylvania by law, 24 Pa. Stat. § 15–1516, as amended, Pub. Law 1928 (Supp. 1960) Dec. 17, 1959, requires that "At least ten verses from the Holy Bible shall be read, without comment, at the opening of each public school on each school day. Any child shall be excused from such Bible reading, or attending such Bible reading, upon the written request of his parent or guardian." The Schempp family, husband and wife and two of their three children, brought suit to enjoin enforcement of the statute, contending that their rights under the Fourteenth Amendment to the Constitution of the United States are, have been, and will continue to be violated unless this statute be declared unconstitutional as violative of these provisions of the First Amendment. They sought to enjoin the appellant school district, wherein the Schempp children attend school, and its officers and the

Superintendent of Public Instruction of the Commonwealth from continuing to conduct such readings and recitation of the Lord's Prayer in the public schools of the district pursuant to the statute. A three-judge statutory
District Court for the Eastern District of Pennsylvania
held that the statute is violative of the Establishment
Clause of the First Amendment as applied to the States
by the Due Process Clause of the Fourteenth Amendment
and directed that appropriate injunctive relief issue. 201
F. Supp. 815.[1] On appeal by the District, its officials and
the Superintendent, under 28 U. S. C. § 1253, we noted
probable jurisdiction. 371 U. S. 807.

The appellees Edward Lewis Schempp, his wife Sidney, and their children, Roger and Donna, are of the
Unitarian faith and are members of the Unitarian Church
in Germantown, Philadelphia, Pennsylvania, where they,
as well as another son, Ellory, regularly attend religious
services. The latter was originally a party but having
graduated from the school system *pendente lite* was voluntarily dismissed from the action. The other children
attend the Abington Senior High School, which is a public
school operated by appellant district.

On each school day at the Abington Senior High School
between 8:15 and 8:30 a. m., while the pupils are attending their home rooms or advisory sections, opening exer-

---

[1] The action was brought in 1958, prior to the 1959 amendment
of § 15–1516 authorizing a child's nonattendance at the exercises
upon parental request. The three-judge court held the statute and
the practices complained of unconstitutional under both the Establishment Clause and the Free Exercise Clause. 177 F. Supp. 398.
Pending appeal to this Court by the school district, the statute was
so amended, and we vacated the judgment and remanded for further
proceedings. 364 U. S. 298. The same three-judge court granted
appellees' motion to amend the pleadings, 195 F. Supp. 518, held a
hearing on the amended pleadings and rendered the judgment, 201
F. Supp. 815, from which appeal is now taken.

cises are conducted pursuant to the statute.   The exercises are broadcast into each room in the school building through an intercommunications system and are conducted under the supervision of a teacher by students attending the school's radio and television workshop. Selected students from this course gather each morning in the school's workshop studio for the exercises, which include readings by one of the students of 10 verses of the Holy Bible, broadcast to each room in the building.   This is followed by the recitation of the Lord's Prayer, likewise over the intercommunications system, but also by the students in the various classrooms, who are asked to stand and join in repeating the prayer in unison.   The exercises are closed with the flag salute and such pertinent announcements as are of interest to the students.   Participation in the opening exercises, as directed by the statute, is voluntary.   The student reading the verses from the Bible may select the passages and read from any version he chooses, although the only copies furnished by the school are the King James version, copies of which were circulated to each teacher by the school district. During the period in which the exercises have been conducted the King James, the Douay and the Revised Standard versions of the Bible have been used, as well as the Jewish Holy Scriptures.   There are no prefatory statements, no questions asked or solicited, no comments or explanations made and no interpretations given at or during the exercises.   The students and parents are advised that the student may absent himself from the classroom or, should he elect to remain, not participate in the exercises.

It appears from the record that in schools not having an intercommunications system the Bible reading and the recitation of the Lord's Prayer were conducted by the

699–272 O–63—17

home-room teacher,[2] who chose the text of the verses and read them herself or had students read them in rotation or by volunteers. This was followed by a standing recitation of the Lord's Prayer, together with the Pledge of Allegiance to the Flag by the class in unison and a closing announcement of routine school items of interest.

At the first trial Edward Schempp and the children testified as to specific religious doctrines purveyed by a literal reading of the Bible "which were contrary to the religious beliefs which they held and to their familial teaching." 177 F. Supp. 398, 400. The children testified that all of the doctrines to which they referred were read to them at various times as part of the exercises. Edward Schempp testified at the second trial that he had considered having Roger and Donna excused from attendance at the exercises but decided against it for several reasons, including his belief that the children's relationships with their teachers and classmates would be adversely affected.[3]

---

[2] The statute as amended imposes no penalty upon a teacher refusing to obey its mandate. However, it remains to be seen whether one refusing could have his contract of employment terminated for "wilful violation of the school laws." 24 Pa. Stat. (Supp. 1960) § 11–1122.

[3] The trial court summarized his testimony as follows:

"Edward Schempp, the children's father, testified that after careful consideration he had decided that he should not have Roger or Donna excused from attendance at these morning ceremonies. Among his reasons were the following. He said that he thought his children would be 'labeled as "odd balls"' before their teachers and classmates every school day; that children, like Roger's and Donna's classmates, were liable 'to lump all particular religious difference[s] or religious objections [together] as "atheism"' and that today the word 'atheism' is often connected with 'atheistic communism,' and has 'very bad' connotations, such as 'un-American' or 'anti-Red,' with overtones of possible immorality. Mr. Schempp pointed out that due to the events of the morning exercises following in rapid succession, the Bible reading, the Lord's Prayer, the Flag Salute, and

---

36

Expert testimony was introduced by both appellants and appellees at the first trial, which testimony was summarized by the trial court as follows:

"Dr. Solomon Grayzel testified that there were marked differences between the Jewish Holy Scriptures and the Christian Holy Bible, the most obvious of which was the absence of the New Testament in the Jewish Holy Scriptures. Dr. Grayzel testified that portions of the New Testament were offensive to Jewish tradition and that, from the standpoint of Jewish faith, the concept of Jesus Christ as the Son of God was 'practically blasphemous.' He cited instances in the New Testament which, assertedly, were not only sectarian in nature but tended to bring the Jews into ridicule or scorn. Dr. Grayzel gave as his expert opinion that such material from the New Testament could be explained to Jewish children in such a way as to do no harm to them. But if portions of the New Testament were read without explanation, they could be, and in his specific experience with children Dr. Grayzel observed, had been, psychologically harmful to the child and had caused a divisive force within the social media of the school.

"Dr. Grayzel also testified that there was significant difference in attitude with regard to the respective Books of the Jewish and Christian Religions in that Judaism attaches no special significance to the reading of the Bible *per se* and that the Jewish Holy Scriptures are source materials to be studied. But Dr. Grayzel did state that many portions of the New,

---

the announcements, excusing his children from the Bible reading would mean that probably they would miss hearing the announcements so important to children. He testified also that if Roger and Donna were excused from Bible reading they would have to stand in the hall outside their 'homeroom' and that this carried with it the imputation of punishment for bad conduct." 201 F. Supp., at 818.

as well as of the Old, Testament contained passages of great literary and moral value.

"Dr. Luther A. Weigle, an expert witness for the defense, testified in some detail as to the reasons for and the methods employed in developing the King James and the Revised Standard Versions of the Bible. On direct examination, Dr. Weigle stated that the Bible was non-sectarian. He later stated that the phrase 'non-sectarian' meant to him non-sectarian within the Christian faiths. Dr. Weigle stated that his definition of the Holy Bible would include the Jewish Holy Scriptures, but also stated that the 'Holy Bible' would not be complete without the New Testament. He stated that the New Testament 'conveyed the message of Christians.' In his opinion, reading of the Holy Scriptures to the exclusion of the New Testament would be a sectarian practice. Dr. Weigle stated that the Bible was of great moral, historical and literary value. This is conceded by all the parties and is also the view of the court." 177 F. Supp. 398, 401–402.

The trial court, in striking down the practices and the statute requiring them, made specific findings of fact that the children's attendance at Abington Senior High School is compulsory and that the practice of reading 10 verses from the Bible is also compelled by law. It also found that:

"The reading of the verses, even without comment, possesses a devotional and religious character and constitutes in effect a religious observance. The devotional and religious nature of the morning exercises is made all the more apparent by the fact that the Bible reading is followed immediately by a recital in unison by the pupils of the Lord's Prayer. The fact that some pupils, or theoretically all pupils, might be excused from attendance at the exercises does not mitigate the obligatory nature of the ceremony for . . . Section 1516 . . . unequivocally requires the exercises to be held every school day in every school in the Commonwealth. The exercises are held in the school buildings and perforce are conducted by and under the authority of the local school authorities and during school sessions. Since the statute requires the reading of the 'Holy Bible,' a Christian document, the practice . . . prefers the Christian religion. The record demonstrates that it was the intention of . . . the Commonwealth . . . to introduce a religious ceremony into the public schools of the Commonwealth." 201 F. Supp., at 819.

No. 119. In 1905 the Board of School Commissioners of Baltimore City adopted a rule pursuant to Art. 77, § 202 of the Annotated Code of Maryland. The rule provided for the holding of opening exercises in the schools of the city, consisting primarily of the "reading, without comment, of a chapter in the Holy Bible and/or the use of the Lord's Prayer." The petitioners, Mrs. Madalyn Murray and her son, William J. Murray III, are both professed atheists. Following unsuccessful attempts to have the respondent school board rescind the rule, this suit was filed for mandamus to compel its rescission and cancellation. It was alleged that William was a student in a public school of the city and Mrs. Murray, his mother, was a taxpayer therein; that it was the practice under the rule to have a reading on each school morning from the King James version of the Bible; that at petitioners' insistence the rule was amended [4] to permit children to

---

[4] The rule as amended provides as follows:

"Opening Exercises. Each school, either collectively or in classes, shall be opened by the reading, without comment, of a chapter in the Holy Bible and/or the use of the Lord's Prayer. The Douay version may be used by those pupils who prefer it. Appropriate

be excused from the exercise on request of the parent and that William had been excused pursuant thereto; that nevertheless the rule as amended was in violation of the petitioners' rights "to freedom of religion under the First and Fourteenth Amendments" and in violation of "the principle of separation between church and state, contained therein. . . ." The petition particularized the petitioners' atheistic beliefs and stated that the rule, as practiced, violated their rights

> "in that it threatens their religious liberty by placing a premium on belief as against non-belief and subjects their freedom of conscience to the rule of the majority; it pronounces belief in God as the source of all moral and spiritual values, equating these values with religious values, and thereby renders sinister, alien and suspect the beliefs and ideals of your Petitioners, promoting doubt and question of their morality, good citizenship and good faith."

The respondents demurred and the trial court, recognizing that the demurrer admitted all facts well pleaded, sustained it without leave to amend. The Maryland Court of Appeals affirmed, the majority of four justices holding the exercise not in violation of the First and Fourteenth Amendments, with three justices dissenting. 228 Md. 239, 179 A. 2d 698. We granted certiorari. 371 U. S. 809.

II.

It is true that religion has been closely identified with our history and government. As we said in *Engel* v. *Vitale*, 370 U. S. 421, 434 (1962), "The history of man is inseparable from the history of religion. And . . . since

---

patriotic exercises should be held as a part of the general opening exercise of the school or class. Any child shall be excused from participating in the opening exercises or from attending the opening exercises upon the written request of his parent or guardian."

the beginning of that history many people have devoutly believed that 'More things are wrought by prayer than this world dreams of.'" In *Zorach* v. *Clauson,* 343 U. S. 306, 313 (1952), we gave specific recognition to the proposition that "[w]e are a religious people whose institutions presuppose a Supreme Being." The fact that the Founding Fathers believed devotedly that there was a God and that the unalienable rights of man were rooted in Him is clearly evidenced in their writings, from the Mayflower Compact to the Constitution itself. This background is evidenced today in our public life through the continuance in our oaths of office from the Presidency to the Alderman of the final supplication, "So help me God." Likewise each House of the Congress provides through its Chaplain an opening prayer, and the sessions of this Court are declared open by the crier in a short ceremony, the final phrase of which invokes the grace of God. Again, there are such manifestations in our military forces, where those of our citizens who are under the restrictions of military service wish to engage in voluntary worship. Indeed, only last year an official survey of the country indicated that 64% of our people have church membership, Bureau of the Census, U. S. Department of Commerce, Statistical Abstract of the United States (83d ed. 1962), 48, while less than 3% profess no religion whatever. *Id.,* at p. 46. It can be truly said, therefore, that today, as in the beginning, our national life reflects a religious people who, in the words of Madison, are "earnestly praying, as . . . in duty bound, that the Supreme Lawgiver of the Universe . . . guide them into every measure which may be worthy of his [blessing . . . .]" Memorial and Remonstrance Against Religious Assessments, quoted in *Everson* v. *Board of Education,* 330 U..S. 1, 71–72 (1947) (Appendix to dissenting opinion of Rutledge, J.).

This is not to say, however, that religion has been so identified with our history and government that religious freedom is not likewise as strongly imbedded in our public and private life. Nothing but the most telling of personal experiences in religious persecution suffered by our forebears, see *Everson* v. *Board of Education, supra,* at 8–11, could have planted our belief in liberty of religious opinion any more deeply in our heritage. It is true that this liberty frequently was not realized by the colonists, but this is readily accountable by their close ties to the Mother Country.[5] However, the views of Madison and Jefferson, preceded by Roger Williams,[6] came to be incorporated not only in the Federal Constitution but likewise in those of most of our States. This freedom to worship was indispensable in a country whose people came from the four quarters of the earth and brought with them a diversity of religious opinion. Today authorities list 83 separate religious bodies, each with membership exceeding 50,000, existing among our people, as well as innumerable smaller groups. Bureau of the Census, *op. cit., supra,* at 46–47.

III.

Almost a hundred years ago in *Minor* v. *Board of Education of Cincinnati,*[7] Judge Alphonso Taft, father

---

[5] There were established churches in at least eight of the original colonies, and various degrees of religious support in others as late as the Revolutionary War. See *Engel* v. *Vitale, supra,* at 428, n. 10.

[6] "There goes many a ship to sea, with many hundred souls in one ship, whose weal and woe is common, and is a true picture of a commonwealth, or human combination, or society. It hath fallen out sometimes, that both Papists and Protestants, Jews and Turks, may be embarked in one ship; upon which supposal, I affirm that all the liberty of conscience I ever pleaded for, turns upon these two hinges, that none of the Papists, Protestants, Jews, or Turks be forced to come to the ship's prayers or worship, nor compelled from their own particular prayers or worship, if they practice any."

[7] Superior Court of Cincinnati, February 1870. The opinion is not reported but is published under the title, The Bible in the Com-

of the revered Chief Justice, in an unpublished opinion stated the ideal of our people as to religious freedom as one of

> "absolute equality before the law, of all religious opinions and sects . . . .
>
> .   .   .   .   .
>
> "The government is neutral, and, while protecting all, it prefers none, and it *disparages* none."

Before examining this "neutral" position in which the Establishment and Free Exercise Clauses of the First Amendment place our Government it is well that we discuss the reach of the Amendment under the cases of this Court.

First, this Court has decisively settled that the First Amendment's mandate that "Congress shall make no law respecting an establishment of religion, or prohibiting the free exercise thereof" has been made wholly applicable to the States by the Fourteenth Amendment. Twenty-three years ago in *Cantwell* v. *Connecticut,* 310 U. S. 296, 303 (1940), this Court, through Mr. Justice Roberts, said:

> "The fundamental concept of liberty embodied in that [Fourteenth] Amendment embraces the liberties guaranteed by the First Amendment. The First Amendment declares that Congress shall make no law respecting an establishment of religion or prohibiting the free exercise thereof. The Fourteenth Amend-

---

mon Schools (Cincinnati: Robert Clarke & Co. 1870). Judge Taft's views, expressed in dissent, prevailed on appeal. See *Board of Education of Cincinnati* v. *Minor,* 23 Ohio St. 211, 253 (1872), in which the Ohio Supreme Court held that:

"The great bulk of human affairs and human interests is left by any free government to individual enterprise and individual action. Religion is eminently one of these interests, lying outside the true and legitimate province of government."

ment has rendered the legislatures of the states as incompetent as Congress to enact such laws. . . ." [8]

In a series of cases since *Cantwell* the Court has repeatedly reaffirmed that doctrine, and we do so now. *Murdock* v. *Pennsylvania,* 319 U. S. 105, 108 (1943); *Everson* v. *Board of Education, supra; Illinois ex rel. McCollum* v. *Board of Education,* 333 U. S. 203, 210–211 (1948); *Zorach* v. *Clauson, supra; McGowan* v. *Maryland,* 366 U. S. 420 (1961); *Torcaso* v. *Watkins,* 367 U. S. 488 (1961); and *Engel* v. *Vitale, supra.*

Second, this Court has rejected unequivocally the contention that the Establishment Clause forbids only governmental preference of one religion over another. Almost 20 years ago in *Everson, supra,* at 15, the Court said that "[n]either a state nor the Federal Government can set up a church. Neither can pass laws which aid one religion, aid all religions, or prefer one religion over another." And Mr. Justice Jackson, dissenting, agreed:

> "There is no answer to the proposition . . . that the effect of the religious freedom Amendment to our Constitution was to take every form of propagation of religion out of the realm of things which could directly or indirectly be made public business and thereby be supported in whole or in part at taxpayers' expense. . . . This freedom was first in the Bill of Rights because it was first in the forefathers' minds; it was set forth in absolute terms, and its strength is its rigidity." *Id.,* at 26.

---

[8] Application to the States of other clauses of the First Amendment obtained even before *Cantwell.* Almost 40 years ago in the opinion of the Court in *Gitlow* v. *New York,* 268 U. S. 652, 666 (1925), Mr. Justice Sanford said: "For present purposes we may and do assume that freedom of speech and of the press—which are protected by the First Amendment from abridgment by Congress—are among the fundamental personal rights and 'liberties' protected by the due process clause of the Fourteenth Amendment from impairment by the States."

Further, Mr. Justice Rutledge, joined by Justices Frankfurter, Jackson and Burton, declared:

> "The [First] Amendment's purpose was not to strike merely at the official establishment of a single sect, creed or religion, outlawing only a formal relation such as had prevailed in England and some of the colonies. Necessarily it was to uproot all such relationships. But the object was broader than separating church and state in this narrow sense. It was to create a complete and permanent separation of the spheres of religious activity and civil authority by comprehensively forbidding every form of public aid or support for religion." *Id.,* at 31–32.

The same conclusion has been firmly maintained ever since that time, see *Illinois ex rel. McCollum, supra,* at pp. 210–211; *McGowan* v. *Maryland, supra,* at 442–443; *Torcaso* v. *Watkins, supra,* at 492–493, 495, and we reaffirm it now.

While none of the parties to either of these cases has questioned these basic conclusions of the Court, both of which have been long established, recognized and consistently reaffirmed, others continue to question their history, logic and efficacy. Such contentions, in the light of the consistent interpretation in cases of this Court, seem entirely untenable and of value only as academic exercises.

IV.

The interrelationship of the Establishment and the Free Exercise Clauses was first touched upon by Mr. Justice Roberts for the Court in *Cantwell* v. *Connecticut, supra,* at 303–304, where it was said that their "inhibition of legislation" had

> "a double aspect. On the one hand, it forestalls compulsion by law of the acceptance of any creed or the practice of any form of worship. Freedom of

conscience and freedom to adhere to such religious organization or form of worship as the individual may choose cannot be restricted by law. On the other hand, it safeguards the free exercise of the chosen form of religion. Thus the Amendment embraces two concepts,—freedom to believe and freedom to act. The first is absolute but, in the nature of things, the second cannot be."

A half dozen years later in *Everson* v. *Board of Education, supra,* at 14–15, this Court, through MR. JUSTICE BLACK, stated that the "scope of the First Amendment . . . was designed forever to suppress" the establishment of religion or the prohibition of the free exercise thereof. In short, the Court held that the Amendment

"requires the state to be a neutral in its relations with groups of religious believers and non-believers; it does not require the state to be their adversary. State power is no more to be used so as to handicap religions than it is to favor them." *Id.,* at 18.

And Mr. Justice Jackson, in dissent, declared that public schools are organized

"on the premise that secular education can be isolated from all religious teaching so that the school can inculcate all needed temporal knowledge and also maintain a strict and lofty neutrality as to religion. The assumption is that after the individual has been instructed in worldly wisdom he will be better fitted to choose his religion." *Id.,* at 23–24.

Moreover, all of the four dissenters, speaking through Mr. Justice Rutledge, agreed that

"Our constitutional policy . . . does not deny the value or the necessity for religious training, teaching or observance. Rather it secures their free exercise. But to that end it does deny that the state can undertake or sustain them in any form or degree. For this reason the sphere of religious activity, as distinguished from the secular intellectual liberties, has been given the twofold protection and, as the state cannot forbid, neither can it perform or aid in performing the religious function. The dual prohibition makes that function altogether private." *Id.*, at 52.

Only one year later the Court was asked to reconsider and repudiate the doctrine of these cases in *McCollum* v. *Board of Education.* It was argued that "historically the First Amendment was intended to forbid only government preference of one religion over another . . . . In addition they ask that we distinguish or overrule our holding in the *Everson* case that the Fourteenth Amendment made the 'establishment of religion' clause of the First Amendment applicable as a prohibition against the States." 333 U. S., at 211. The Court, with Mr. Justice Reed alone dissenting, was unable to "accept either of these contentions." *Ibid.* Mr. Justice Frankfurter, joined by Justices Jackson, Rutledge and Burton, wrote a very comprehensive and scholarly concurrence in which he said that "[s]eparation is a requirement to abstain from fusing functions of Government and of religious sects, not merely to treat them all equally." *Id.*, at 227. Continuing, he stated that:

"the Constitution . . . prohibited the Government common to all from becoming embroiled, however innocently, in the destructive religious conflicts of which the history of even this country records some dark pages." *Id.*, at 228.

In 1952 in *Zorach* v. *Clauson, supra,* Mr. Justice Douglas for the Court reiterated:

"There cannot be the slightest doubt that the First Amendment reflects the philosophy that Church and State should be separated. And so far as interference with the 'free exercise' of religion and an 'establishment' of religion are concerned, the separation must be complete and unequivocal. The First Amendment within the scope of its coverage permits no exception; the prohibition is absolute. The First Amendment, however, does not say that in every and all respects there shall be a separation of Church and State. Rather, it studiously defines the manner, the specific ways, in which there shall be no concert or union or dependency one on the other. That is the common sense of the matter." 343 U. S., at 312.

And then in 1961 in *McGowan* v. *Maryland* and in *Torcaso* v. *Watkins* each of these cases was discussed and approved. CHIEF JUSTICE WARREN in *McGowan*, for a unanimous Court on this point, said:

"But, the First Amendment, in its final form, did not simply bar a congressional enactment *establishing a church;* it forbade all laws *respecting an establishment of religion.* Thus, this Court has given the Amendment a 'broad interpretation . . . in the light of its history and the evils it was designed forever to suppress. . . .'" 366 U. S., at 441–442.

And MR. JUSTICE BLACK for the Court in *Torcaso*, without dissent but with Justices Frankfurter and HARLAN concurring in the result, used this language:

"We repeat and again reaffirm that neither a State nor the Federal Government can constitutionally force a person 'to profess a belief or disbelief in any religion.' Neither can constitutionally pass laws or impose requirements which aid all religions as against non-believers, and neither can aid those religions based on a belief in the existence of God as against those religions founded on different beliefs." 367 U. S., at 495.

Finally, in *Engel* v. *Vitale,* only last year, these principles were so universally recognized that the Court, without the citation of a single case and over the sole dissent of MR. JUSTICE STEWART, reaffirmed them. The Court found the 22-word prayer used in "New York's program of daily classroom invocation of God's blessings as prescribed in the Regents' prayer . . . [to be] a religious activity." 370 U. S., at 424. It held that "it is no part of the business of government to compose official prayers for any group of the American people to recite as a part of a religious program carried on by government." *Id.*, at 425. In discussing the reach of the Establishment and Free Exercise Clauses of the First Amendment the Court said:

> "Although these two clauses may in certain instances overlap, they forbid two quite different kinds of governmental encroachment upon religious freedom. The Establishment Clause, unlike the Free Exercise Clause, does not depend upon any showing of direct governmental compulsion and is violated by the enactment of laws which establish an official religion whether those laws operate directly to coerce non-observing individuals or not. This is not to say, of course, that laws officially prescribing a particular form of religious worship do not involve coercion of such individuals. When the power, prestige and financial support of government is placed behind a particular religious belief, the indirect coercive pressure upon religious minorities to conform to the prevailing officially approved religion is plain." *Id.*, at 430–431.

And in further elaboration the Court found that the "first and most immediate purpose [of the Establishment Clause] rested on the belief that a union of government and religion tends to destroy government and to degrade religion." *Id.*, at 431. When government, the Court said, allies itself with one particular form of religion, the

49

inevitable result is that it incurs "the hatred, disrespect and even contempt of those who held contrary beliefs." *Ibid.*

V.

The wholesome "neutrality" of which this Court's cases speak thus stems from a recognition of the teachings of history that powerful sects or groups might bring about a fusion of governmental and religious functions or a concert or dependency of one upon the other to the end that official support of the State or Federal Government would be placed behind the tenets of one or of all orthodoxies. This the Establishment Clause prohibits. And a further reason for neutrality is found in the Free Exercise Clause, which recognizes the value of religious training, teaching and observance and, more particularly, the right of every person to freely choose his own course with reference thereto, free of any compulsion from the state. This the Free Exercise Clause guarantees. Thus, as we have seen, the two clauses may overlap. As we have indicated, the Establishment Clause has been directly considered by this Court eight times in the past score of years and, with only one Justice dissenting on the point, it has consistently held that the clause withdrew all legislative power respecting religious belief or the expression thereof. The test may be stated as follows: what are the purpose and the primary effect of the enactment? If either is the advancement or inhibition of religion then the enactment exceeds the scope of legislative power as circumscribed by the Constitution. That is to say that to withstand the strictures of the Establishment Clause there must be a secular legislative purpose and a primary effect that neither advances nor inhibits religion. *Everson* v. *Board of Education, supra; McGowan* v. *Maryland, supra,* at 442. The Free Exercise Clause, likewise considered many times here, withdraws from legislative power, state and federal, the exertion of any restraint on the free exercise of religion.   Its purpose is to secure religious liberty in the individual by prohibiting any invasions thereof by civil authority.   Hence it is necessary in a free exercise case for one to show the coercive effect of the enactment as it operates against him in the practice of his religion.   The distinction between the two clauses is apparent—a violation of the Free Exercise Clause is predicated on coercion while the Establishment Clause violation need not be so attended.

Applying the Establishment Clause principles to the cases at bar we find that the States are requiring the selection and reading at the opening of the school day of verses from the Holy Bible and the recitation of the Lord's Prayer by the students in unison.   These exercises are prescribed as part of the curricular activities of students who are required by law to attend school.   They are held in the school buildings under the supervision and with the participation of teachers employed in those schools.   None of these factors, other than compulsory school attendance, was present in the program upheld in *Zorach* v. *Clauson*.   The trial court in No. 142 has found that such an opening exercise is a religious ceremony and was intended by the State to be so.   We agree with the trial court's finding as to the religious character of the exercises.   Given that finding, the exercises and the law requiring them are in violation of the Establishment Clause.

There is no such specific finding as to the religious character of the exercises in No. 119, and the State contends (as does the State in No. 142) that the program is an effort to extend its benefits to all public school children without regard to their religious belief.   Included within its secular purposes, it says, are the promotion of moral values, the contradiction to the materialistic trends of our times, the perpetuation of our institutions and the teaching of literature.   The case came up

699-272 O-63-18

on demurrer, of course, to a petition which alleged that the uniform practice under the rule had been to read from the King James version of the Bible and that the exercise was sectarian. The short answer, therefore, is that the religious character of the exercise was admitted by the State. But even if its purpose is not strictly religious, it is sought to be accomplished through readings, without comment, from the Bible. Surely the place of the Bible as an instrument of religion cannot be gainsaid, and the State's recognition of the pervading religious character of the ceremony is evident from the rule's specific permission of the alternative use of the Catholic Douay version as well as the recent amendment permitting nonattendance at the exercises. None of these factors is consistent with the contention that the Bible is here used either as an instrument for nonreligious moral inspiration or as a reference for the teaching of secular subjects.

The conclusion follows that in both cases the laws require religious exercises and such exercises are being conducted in direct violation of the rights of the appellees and petitioners.[9] Nor are these required exercises mitigated by the fact that individual students may absent

---

[9] It goes without saying that the laws and practices involved here can be challenged only by persons having standing to complain. But the requirements for standing to challenge state action under the Establishment Clause, unlike those relating to the Free Exercise Clause, do not include proof that particular religious freedoms are infringed. *McGowan* v. *Maryland, supra,* at 429–430. The parties here are school children and their parents, who are directly affected by the laws and practices against which their complaints are directed. These interests surely suffice to give the parties standing to complain. See *Engel* v. *Vitale, supra.* Cf. *McCollum* v. *Board of Education, supra; Everson* v. *Board of Education, supra.* Compare *Doremus* v. *Board of Education,* 342 U. S. 429 (1952), which involved the same substantive issues presented here. The appeal was there dismissed upon the graduation of the school child involved and because of the appellants' failure to establish standing as taxpayers.

themselves upon parental request, for that fact furnishes
no defense to a claim of unconstitutionality under the
Establishment Clause. See *Engel* v. *Vitale, supra,* at 430.
Further, it is no defense to urge that the religious practices here may be relatively minor encroachments on the
First Amendment. The breach of neutrality that is today
a trickling stream may all too soon become a raging torrent
and, in the words of Madison, "it is proper to take alarm
at the first experiment on our liberties." Memorial and
Remonstrance Against Religious Assessments, quoted in
Everson, supra, at 65.

It is insisted that unless these religious exercises are
permitted a "religion of secularism" is established in the
schools. We agree of course that the State may not
establish a "religion of secularism" in the sense of affirma-
tively opposing or showing hostility to religion, thus "preferring those who believe in no religion over those who do
believe." *Zorach* v. *Clauson, supra,* at 314. We do not
agree, however, that this decision in any sense has that
effect. In addition, it might well be said that one's education is not complete without a study of comparative
religion or the history of religion and its relationship to
the advancement of civilization. It certainly may be said
that the Bible is worthy of study for its literary and historic qualities. Nothing we have said here indicates that
such study of the Bible or of religion, when presented objectively as part of a secular program of education, may
not be effected consistently with the First Amendment.
But the exercises here do not fall into those categories.
They are religious exercises, required by the States in
violation of the command of the First Amendment that
the Government maintain strict neutrality, neither aiding
nor opposing religion.

Finally, we cannot accept that the concept of neutrality,
which does not permit a State to require a religious exercise even with the consent of the majority of those

affected, collides with the majority's right to free exercise of religion.[10] While the Free Exercise Clause clearly prohibits the use of state action to deny the rights of free exercise to *anyone,* it has never meant that a majority could use the machinery of the State to practice its beliefs. Such a contention was effectively answered by Mr. Justice Jackson for the Court in *West Virginia Board of Education* v. *Barnette,* 319 U. S. 624, 638 (1943):

> "The very purpose of a Bill of Rights was to withdraw certain subjects from the vicissitudes of political controversy, to place them beyond the reach of majorities and officials and to establish them as legal principles to be applied by the courts. One's right to . . . freedom of worship . . . and other fundamental rights may not be submitted to vote; they depend on the outcome of no elections."

The place of religion in our society is an exalted one, achieved through a long tradition of reliance on the home, the church and the inviolable citadel of the individual heart and mind. We have come to recognize through bitter experience that it is not within the power of government to invade that citadel, whether its purpose or effect be to aid or oppose, to advance or retard. In the relationship between man and religion, the State is firmly committed to a position of neutrality. Though the application of that rule requires interpretation of a delicate sort, the rule itself is clearly and concisely stated in the words of the First Amendment. Applying that rule to the facts of these cases, we affirm the judgment in No. 142.

---

[10] We are not of course presented with and therefore do not pass upon a situation such as military service, where the Government regulates the temporal and geographic environment of individuals to a point that, unless it permits voluntary religious services to be conducted with the use of government facilities, military personnel would be unable to engage in the practice of their faiths.

In No. 119, the judgment is reversed and the cause remanded to the Maryland Court of Appeals for further proceedings consistent with this opinion.

It is so ordered.

Mr. Justice Douglas, concurring.

I join the opinion of the Court and add a few words in explanation.

While the Free Exercise Clause of the First Amendment is written in terms of what the State may not require of the individual, the Establishment Clause, serving the same goal of individual religious freedom, is written in different terms.

Establishment of a religion can be achieved in several ways. The church and state can be one; the church may control the state or the state may control the church; or the relationship may take one of several possible forms of a working arrangement between the two bodies.[1] Under all of these arrangements the church typically has a place in the state's budget, and church law usually governs such matters as baptism, marriage, divorce and separation, at least for its members and sometimes for the entire body politic.[2] Education, too, is usually high on the priority

---

[1] See Bates, Religious Liberty: An Inquiry (1945), 9–14, 239–252; Cobb, Religious Liberty in America (1902), 1–2, cc. IV, V; Gledhill, Pakistan, The Development of its Laws and Constitution (8 British Commonwealth, 1957), 11–15; Keller, Church and State on the European Continent (1936), c. 2; Pfeffer, Church, State, and Freedom (1953), c. 2; I Stokes, Church and State in the United States (1950), 151–169.

[2] See III Stokes, *op. cit., supra,* n. 1, 42–67; Bates, *op. cit., supra,* n. 1, 9–11, 58–59, 98, 245; Gledhill, *op. cit., supra,* n. 1, 128, 192, 205, 208; Rackman, Israel's Emerging Constitution (1955), 120–134; Drinan, Religious Freedom in Israel, America (Apr. 6, 1963), 456–457.

list of church interests.[3]   In the past schools were often made the exclusive responsibility of the church.   Today in some state-church countries the state runs the public schools, but compulsory religious exercises are often required of some or all students.   Thus, under the agreement Franco made with the Holy See when he came to power in Spain, "The Church regained its place in the national budget.   It insists on baptizing all children and has made the catechism obligatory in state schools." [4]

The vice of all such arrangements under the Establishment Clause is that the state is lending its assistance to a church's efforts to gain and keep adherents.   Under the First Amendment it is strictly a matter for the individual and his church as to what church he will belong to and how much support, in the way of belief, time, activity or money, he will give to it.   "This pure Religious Liberty" "declared . . . [all forms of church-state relationships] and their fundamental idea to be oppressions of conscience and abridgments of that liberty which God and nature had conferred on every living soul." [5]

In these cases we have no coercive religious exercise aimed at making the students conform.   The prayers announced are not compulsory, though some may think they have that indirect effect because the nonconformist student may be induced to participate for fear of being called an "oddball."   But that coercion, if it be present,

---

[3] See II Stokes, *op. cit., supra,* n. 1, 488–548; Boles, The Bible, Religion, and the Public Schools (2d ed. 1963), 4–10; Rackman, *op. cit., supra,* n. 2, at 136–141; O'Brien, The *Engel* Case From A Swiss Perspective, 61 Mich. L. Rev. 1069; Freund, Muslim Education in West Pakistan, 56 Religious Education 31.

[4] Bates, *op. cit., supra,* n. 1, at 18; Pfeffer, *op. cit., supra,* n. 1, at 28–31; Thomas, The Balance of Forces in Spain, 41 Foreign Affairs 208, 210.

[5] Cobb, *op. cit., supra,* n. 1, at 2.

has not been shown; so the vices of the present regimes are different.

These regimes violate the Establishment Clause in two different ways. In each case the State is conducting a religious exercise; and, as the Court holds, that cannot be done without violating the "neutrality" required of the State by the balance of power between individual, church and state that has been struck by the First Amendment. But the Establishment Clause is not limited to precluding the State itself from conducting religious exercises. It also forbids the State to employ its facilities or funds in a way that gives any church, or all churches, greater strength in our society than it would have by relying on its members alone. Thus, the present regimes must fall under that clause for the additional reason that public funds, though small in amount, are being used to promote a religious exercise. Through the mechanism of the State, all of the people are being required to finance a religious exercise that only some of the people want and that violates the sensibilities of others.

The most effective way to establish any institution is to finance it; and this truth is reflected in the appeals by church groups for public funds to finance their religious schools.[6] Financing a church either in its strictly religious activities or in its other activities is equally unconstitutional, as I understand the Establishment Clause. Budgets for one activity may be technically separable from budgets for others.[7] But the institution is an inseparable whole, a living organism, which is strengthened in proselytizing when it is strengthened in any department by contributions from other than its own members.

---

[6] See II Stokes, *op. cit., supra,* n. 1, at 681–695.

[7] See Accountants' Handbook (4th ed. 1956) 4.8–4.15.

Such contributions may not be made by the State even in a minor degree without violating the Establishment Clause. It is not the amount of public funds expended; as this case illustrates, it is the use to which public funds are put that is controlling. For the First Amendment does not say that some forms of establishment are allowed; it says that "no law respecting an establishment of religion" shall be made. What may not be done directly may not be done indirectly lest the Establishment Clause become a mockery.

No. 90–1014

ROBERT E. LEE, INDIVIDUALLY AND AS PRINCIPAL OF NATHAN BISHOP MIDDLE SCHOOL, ET AL., PETITIONERS *v.* DANIEL WEISMAN ETC.

ON WRIT OF CERTIORARI TO THE UNITED STATES COURT OF APPEALS FOR THE FIRST CIRCUIT

Syllabus

No. 90–1014. Argued November 6, 1991—Decided June 24, 1992

Principals of public middle and high schools in Providence, Rhode Island, are permitted to invite members of the clergy to give invocations and benedictions at their schools' graduation ceremonies. Petitioner Lee, a middle school principal, invited a rabbi to offer such prayers at the graduation ceremony for Deborah Weisman's class, gave the Rabbi a pamphlet containing guidelines for the composition of public prayers at civic ceremonies, and advised him that the prayers should be nonsectarian. Shortly before the ceremony, the District Court denied the motion of respondent Weisman, Deborah's father, for a temporary restraining order to prohibit school officials from including the prayers in the ceremony. Deborah and her family attended the ceremony, and the prayers were recited. Subsequently, Weisman sought a permanent injunction barring Lee and other petitioners, various Providence public school officials, from inviting clergy to deliver invocations and benedictions at future graduations. It appears likely that such prayers will be conducted at Deborah's high school graduation. The District Court enjoined petitioners from continuing the practice at issue on the ground that it violated the Establishment Clause of the First Amendment. The Court of Appeals affirmed.

Held: Including clergy who offer prayers as part of an official public school graduation ceremony is forbidden by the Establishment Clause.

(a) This Court need not revisit the questions of the definition and scope of the principles governing the extent of permitted accommodation by the State for its citizens' religious beliefs and practices, for the controlling precedents as they relate to prayer and religious exercise in primary and secondary public schools compel the holding here. Thus, the Court will not reconsider its decision in *Lemon* v. *Kurtzman*, 403 U. S. 602. The principle that government may accommodate the free exercise of religion does not supersede the fundamental limitations imposed by the Establishment Clause, which guarantees at a minimum that a government may not coerce anyone to support or participate in religion or its exercise, or otherwise act in a way that "establishes a [state] religion or religious faith, or tends to do so." *Lynch* v. *Donnelly*, 465 U. S. 668, 678.

(b) State officials here direct the performance of a formal religious exercise at secondary schools' promotional and graduation ceremonies. Lee's decision that prayers should be given and his selection of the religious participant are choices attributable to the State. Moreover, through the pamphlet and his advice that the prayers be nonsectarian, he directed and controlled the prayers' content. That the directions may have been given in a good faith attempt to make the prayers acceptable to most persons does not resolve the dilemma caused by the school's involvement, since the government may not establish an official or civic religion as a means of avoiding the establishment of a religion with more specific creeds.

(c) The Establishment Clause was inspired by the lesson that in the hands of government what might begin as a tolerant expression of religious views may end in a policy to indoctrinate and coerce. Prayer exercises in elementary and secondary schools carry a particular risk of indirect coercion. *Engel* v. *Vitale*, 370 U. S. 421; *Abington School District* v. *Schempp*, 374 U. S. 203. The school district's supervision and control of a high school graduation ceremony places subtle and indirect public and peer pressure on attending students to stand as a group or maintain respectful silence during the invocation and benediction. A reasonable dissenter of high school age could believe that standing or remaining silent signified her own participation in, or approval of, the group exercise, rather than her respect for it. And the State may not place the student dissenter in the dilemma of participating or protesting. Since adolescents are often susceptible to peer pressure, especially in matters of social convention, the State may no more use social pressure to enforce orthodoxy than it may use direct means. The embarrassment and intrusion of the religious exercise cannot be refuted by arguing that the prayers are those for whom the prayers have meaning, and since any intrusion was both real and a violation of the objectors' rights.

(d) Petitioners' argument that the option of not attending the ceremony excuses any inducement or coercion in the ceremony itself is rejected. In this society, high school graduation is one of life's most significant occasions, and a student is not free to absent herself from the exercise in any real sense of the term "voluntary." Also not dispositive is the contention that prayers are an essential part of these ceremonies because for many persons the occasion would lack meaning without the recognition that human achievements cannot be understood apart from their spiritual essence. This position fails to acknowledge that what for many was a spiritual imperative was for the Weismans religious conformance compelled by the State. It also gives insufficient recognition to the real conflict of conscience faced by a student who would have to choose whether to miss graduation or conform to the state-sponsored practice, in an environment where the risk of compulsion is especially high.

(e) Inherent differences between the public school system and a session of a state legislature distinguish this case from *Marsh* v. *Chambers*, 463 U. S. 783, which condoned a prayer exercise. The atmosphere at a state legislature's opening, where adults are free to enter and leave with little comment and for any number of reasons, cannot compare with the constraining potential of the one school event most important for the student to attend.

908 F. 2d 1090, affirmed.

KENNEDY, J., delivered the opinion of the Court, in which BLACKMUN, STEVENS, O'CONNOR, and SOUTER, JJ., joined. BLACKMUN, J., and SOUTER, J., filed concurring opinions, in which STEVENS and O'CONNOR, JJ., joined. SCALIA, J., filed a dissenting opinion, in which REHNQUIST, C. J., and WHITE and THOMAS, JJ., joined.

JUSTICE KENNEDY delivered the opinion of the Court.

School principals in the public school system of the city of Providence, Rhode Island, are permitted to invite members of the clergy to offer invocation and benediction prayers as part of the formal graduation ceremonies for middle schools and for high schools. The question before us is whether including clerical members who offer prayers as part of the official school graduation ceremony is consistent with the Religion Clauses of the First Amendment, provisions the Fourteenth Amendment makes applicable with full force to the States and their school districts.

I

A

Deborah Weisman graduated from Nathan Bishop Middle School, a public school in Providence, at a formal ceremony in June 1989. She was about 14 years old. For many years it has been the policy of the Providence School Committee and the Superintendent of Schools to permit principals to invite members of the clergy to give invocations and benedictions at middle school and high school graduations. Many, but not all, of the principals elected to include prayers as part of the graduation ceremonies. Acting for himself and his daughter, Deborah's father, Daniel Weisman, objected to any prayers at Deborah's middle school graduation, but to no avail. The school principal, petitioner Robert E. Lee, invited a rabbi to deliver prayers at the graduation exercises for Deborah's class. Rabbi Leslie Gutterman, of the Temple Beth El in Providence, accepted.

It has been the custom of Providence school officials to provide invited clergy with a pamphlet entitled "Guidelines for Civic Occasions," prepared by the National Conference of Christians and Jews. The Guidelines recommend that public prayers at nonsectarian civic ceremonies be composed with "inclusiveness and sensitivity," though they acknowledge that "[p]rayer of any kind may be inappropriate on some civic occasions." App. 20–21. The principal gave Rabbi Gutterman the pamphlet before the graduation and advised him the invocation and benediction should be nonsectarian. Agreed Statement of Facts ¶17, *id.*, at 13.

"INVOCATION

"God of the Free, Hope of the Brave:

"For the legacy of America where diversity is celebrated and the rights of minorities are protected, we thank You. May these young men and women grow up to enrich it.

"For the liberty of America, we thank You. May these new graduates grow up to guard it.

"For the political process of America in which all its citizens may participate, for its court system where all may seek justice we thank You. May those we honor this morning always turn to it in trust.

"For the destiny of America we thank You. May the graduates of Nathan Bishop Middle School so live that they might help to share it.

"May our aspirations for our country and for these young people, who are our hope for the future, be richly fulfilled.

AMEN"

"BENEDICTION

"O God, we are grateful to You for having endowed us with the capacity for learning which we have celebrated on this joyous commencement.

"Happy families give thanks for seeing their children achieve an important milestone. Send Your blessings upon the teachers and administrators who helped prepare them.

"The graduates now need strength and guidance for the future, help them to understand that we are not complete with academic knowledge alone. We must each strive to fulfill what You require of us all: To do justly, to love mercy, to walk humbly.

"We give thanks to You, Lord, for keeping us alive, sustaining us and allowing us to reach this special, happy occasion.

AMEN"

Id., at 22–23.

The record in this case is sparse in many respects, and we are unfamiliar with any fixed custom or practice at middle school graduations, referred to by the school district as "promotional exercises." We are not so constrained with reference to high schools, however. High school graduations are such an integral part of American cultural life that we can with confidence describe their customary features, confirmed by aspects of the record and by the parties' representations at oral argument. In the Providence school system, most high school graduation ceremonies are conducted away from the school, while most middle school ceremonies are held on school premises. Classical High School, which Deborah now attends, has conducted its graduation ceremonies on school premises. Agreed Statement of Facts ¶37, *id.,* at 17. The parties stipulate that attendance at graduation ceremonies is voluntary. Agreed Statement of Facts ¶41, *id.,* at 18. The graduating students enter as a group in a processional, subject to the direction of teachers and school officials, and sit together, apart from their families. We assume the clergy's participation in any high school graduation exercise would be about what it was at Deborah's middle school ceremony. There the students stood for the Pledge of Allegiance and remained standing during the Rabbi's prayers. Tr. of Oral Arg. 38. Even on the assumption that there was a respectful moment of silence both before and after the prayers, the Rabbi's two presentations must not have extended much beyond a minute each, if that. We do not know whether he remained on stage during the whole ceremony, or whether the students received individual diplomas on stage, or if he

helped to congratulate them.

The school board (and the United States, which supports it as *amicus curiae*) argued that these short prayers and others like them at graduation exercises are of profound meaning to many students and parents throughout this country who consider that due respect and acknowledgement for divine guidance and for the deepest spiritual aspirations of our people ought to be expressed at an event as important in life as a graduation. We assume this to be so in addressing the difficult case now before us, for the significance of the prayers lies also at the heart of Daniel and Deborah Weisman's case.

B

Deborah's graduation was held on the premises of Nathan Bishop Middle School on June 29, 1989. Four days before the ceremony, Daniel Weisman, in his individual capacity as a Providence taxpayer and as next friend of Deborah, sought a temporary restraining order in the United States District Court for the District of Rhode Island to prohibit school officials from including an invocation or benediction in the graduation ceremony. The court denied the motion for lack of adequate time to consider it. Deborah and her family attended the graduation, where the prayers were recited. In July 1989, Daniel Weisman filed an amended complaint seeking a permanent injunction barring petitioners, various officials of the Providence public schools, from inviting the clergy to deliver invocations and benedictions at future graduations. We find it unnecessary to address Daniel Weisman's taxpayer standing, for a live and justiciable controversy is before us. Deborah Weisman is enrolled as a student at Classical High School in Providence and from the record it appears likely, if not certain, that an invocation and benediction will be conducted at her high school graduation. Agreed Statement of Facts ¶38, *id.,* at 17.

The case was submitted on stipulated facts. The District Court held that petitioners' practice of including invocations and benedictions in public school graduations violated the Establishment Clause of the First Amendment, and it enjoined petitioners from continuing the practice. 728 F. Supp. 68 (RI 1990). The court applied the three-part Establishment Clause test set forth in *Lemon* v. *Kurtzman,* 403 U. S. 602 (1971). Under that test as described in our past cases, to satisfy the Establishment Clause a governmental practice must (1) reflect a clearly secular purpose; (2) have a primary effect that neither advances nor inhibits religion; and (3) avoid excessive government entanglement with religion. *Committee for Public Education & Religious Liberty* v. *Nyquist,* 413 U. S. 756, 773 (1973). The District Court held that petitioners' actions violated the second part of the test, and so did not address either the first or the third. The court decided, based on its reading of our precedents, that the effects test of *Lemon* is violated whenever government action "creates an identification of the state with a religion, or with religion in general," 728 F. Supp., at 71, or when "the effect of the governmental action is to endorse one religion over another, or to endorse religion in general." *Id.,* at 72. The court determined that the practice of including invocations and benedictions, even so-called nonsectarian ones, in public school graduations creates an identification of governmental power with religious practice, endorses religion, and violates the Establishment Clause. In so holding the court expressed the determination not to follow *Stein* v. *Plainwell Community Schools,* 822 F.2d 1406 (1987), in which the Court of Appeals for the Sixth Circuit, relying on our decision in *Marsh* v. *Chambers,* 463 U. S. 783 (1983), held that benedictions and invocations at public school graduations are not always unconstitutional. In *Marsh* we upheld the constitutionality of the Nebraska State Legislature's practice of opening each of its sessions with a prayer offered by a chaplain paid out of public funds. The District Court in this case disagreed with the Sixth Circuit's reasoning because it believed that *Marsh* was a narrow decision, "limited to the unique situation of legislative prayer," and did not have any relevance to school prayer cases. 728 F. Supp., at 74.

On appeal, the United States Court of Appeals for the First Circuit affirmed. The majority opinion by Judge Torruella adopted the opinion of the District Court. 908 F.2d 1090 (1990). Judge Bownes joined the majority, but wrote a separate concurring opinion in which he decided that the practices challenged here violated all three parts of the *Lemon* test. Judge Bownes went on to agree with the District Court that *Marsh* had no application to school prayer cases and that the *Stein* decision was flawed. He concluded by suggesting that under Establishment Clause rules no prayer, even one excluding any mention of the Deity, could be offered at a public school graduation ceremony. 908 F.2d, at 1090–1097. Judge Campbell dissented, on the basis of *Marsh* and *Stein*. He reasoned that if the prayers delivered were nonsectarian, and if school officials ensured that persons representing a variety of beliefs and ethical systems were invited to present invocations and benedictions, there was no violation of the Establishment Clause. 908 F.2d, at 1099. We granted certiorari, 499 U. S. ___ (1991), and now affirm.

II

These dominant facts mark and control the confines of our decision: State officials direct the performance of a formal religious exercise at promotional and graduation ceremonies for secondary schools. Even for those students who object to the religious exercise, their attendance and participation in the state-sponsored religious activity are in a fair and real sense obligatory, though the school district does not require attendance as a condition for receipt of the diploma.

This case does not require us to revisit the difficult questions dividing us in recent cases, questions of the definition and full scope of the principles governing the extent of permitted accommodation by the State for the religious beliefs and practices of many of its citizens. See *Allegheny County* v. *Greater Pittsburgh ACLU*, 492 U. S. 573 (1989); *Wallace* v. *Jaffree*, 472 U. S. 38 (1985); *Lynch* v. *Donnelly*, 465 U. S. 668 (1984). For without reference to those principles in other contexts, the controlling precedents as they relate to prayer and religious exercise in primary and secondary public schools compel the holding here that the policy of the city of Providence is an unconstitutional one. We can decide the case without reconsidering the general constitutional framework by which public schools' efforts to accommodate religion are measured. Thus we do not accept the invitation of petitioners and *amicus* the United States to reconsider our decision in *Lemon* v. *Kurtzman, supra*. The government involvement with religious activity in this case is pervasive, to the point of creating a state-sponsored and state-directed religious exercise in a public school. Conducting this formal religious observance conflicts with settled rules pertaining to prayer exercises for students, and that suffices to determine the question before us.

The principle that government may accommodate the free exercise of religion does not supersede the fundamental limitations imposed by the Establishment Clause. It is beyond dispute that, at a minimum, the Constitution guarantees that government may not coerce anyone to support or participate in religion or its exercise, or other-

wise act in a way which "establishes a [state] religion or religious faith, or tends to do so." *Lynch, supra*, at 678; see also *Allegheny County, supra*, at 591 quoting *Everson* v. *Board of Education of Ewing*, 330 U. S. 1, 15–16 (1947). The State's involvement in the school prayers challenged today violates these central principles.

That involvement is as troubling as it is undenied. A school official, the principal, decided that an invocation and a benediction should be given; this is a choice attributable to the State, and from a constitutional perspective it is as if a state statute decreed that the prayers must occur. The principal chose the religious participant, here a rabbi, and that choice is also attributable to the State. The reason for the choice of a rabbi is not disclosed by the record, but the potential for divisiveness over the choice of a particular member of the clergy to conduct the ceremony is apparent.

Divisiveness, of course, can attend any state decision respecting religions, and neither its existence nor its potential necessarily invalidates the State's attempts to accommodate religion in all cases. The potential for divisiveness is of particular relevance here though, because it centers around an overt religious exercise in a secondary school environment where, as we discuss below, see *infra*, at __, subtle coercive pressures exist and where the student had no real alternative which would have allowed her to avoid the fact or appearance of participation.

The State's role did not end with the decision to include a prayer and with the choice of clergyman. Principal Lee provided Rabbi Gutterman with a copy of the "Guidelines for Civic Occasions," and advised him that his prayers should be nonsectarian. Through these means the principal directed and controlled the content of the prayer. Even if the only sanction for ignoring the instructions were that the rabbi would not be invited back, we think no religious representative who valued his or her continued reputation and effectiveness in the community would incur the State's *displeasure in this regard. It is a cornerstone principle of our Establishment Clause jurisprudence that "it is no part of the business of government to compose official prayers for any group of the American people to recite as a part of a religious program carried on by government," *Engel* v. *Vitale*, 370 U. S. 421, 425 (1962), and that is what the school officials attempted to do.

Petitioners argue, and we find nothing in the case to refute it, that the directions for the content of the prayers were a good-faith attempt by the school to ensure that the sectarianism which is so often the flashpoint for religious animosity be removed from the graduation ceremony. The concern is understandable, as a prayer which uses ideas or images identified with a particular religion may foster a different sort of sectarian rivalry than an invocation or benediction in terms more neutral. The school's explanation, however, does not resolve the dilemma caused by its participation. The question is not the good faith of the school in attempting to make the prayer acceptable to most persons, but the legitimacy of its undertaking that enterprise at all when the object is to produce a prayer to be used in a formal religious exercise which students, for all practical purposes, are obliged to attend.

We are asked to recognize the existence of a practice of nonsectarian prayer, prayer within the embrace of what is known as the Judeo-Christian tradition, prayer which is more acceptable than one which, for example, makes explicit references to the God of Israel, or to Jesus Christ, or to a patron saint. There may be some support, as an empirical observation, to the statement of the Court of Appeals for the Sixth Circuit, picked up by Judge Campbell's dissent in the Court of Appeals in this case, that there has emerged in this country a civic religion, one which is tolerated when sectarian exercises are not. *Stein*, 822 F. 2d, at 1409; 908 F. 2d 1090, 1098–1099 (CA1 1990) (Campbell, J., dissenting) (case below); see also Note, Civil Religion and the Establishment Clause, 95 Yale L.J. 1237 (1986). If common ground can be defined which permits once conflicting faiths to express the shared conviction that there is an ethic and a morality which transcend human invention, the sense of community and purpose sought by all decent societies might be advanced. But though the First Amendment does not allow the government to stifle prayers which aspire to these ends, neither does it permit the government to undertake that task for itself.

The First Amendment's Religion Clauses mean that religious beliefs and religious expression are too precious to be either proscribed or prescribed by the State. The design of the Constitution is that preservation and transmission of religious beliefs and worship is a responsibility and a choice committed to the private sphere, which itself is promised freedom to pursue that mission. It must not be forgotten then, that while concern must be given to define the protection granted to an objector or a dissenting nonbeliever, these same Clauses exist to protect religion from government interference. James Madison, the principal author of the Bill of Rights, did not rest his opposition to a religious establishment on the sole ground of its effect on the minority. A principal ground for his view was: "[E]xperience witnesseth that ecclesiastical establishments, instead of maintaining the purity and efficacy of Religion, have had a contrary operation." Memorial and Remonstrance Against Religious Assessments (1785), in 8 Papers of James Madison 301 (W. Rachal, R. Rutland, B. Ripel, & F. Teute eds. 1973).

These concerns have particular application in the case of school officials, whose effort to monitor prayer will be perceived by the students as inducing a participation they might otherwise reject. Though the efforts of the school officials in this case to find common ground appear to have been a good-faith attempt to recognize the common aspects of religions and not the divisive ones, our precedents do not permit school officials to assist in composing prayers as an incident to a formal exercise for their students. *Engel* v. *Vitale, supra*, at 425. And these same precedents caution us to measure the idea of a civic religion against the central meaning of the Religion Clauses of the First Amendment, which is that all creeds must be tolerated and none favored. The suggestion that government may establish an official or civic religion as a means of avoiding the establishment of a religion with more specific creeds strikes us as a contradiction that cannot be accepted.

The degree of school involvement here made it clear that the graduation prayers bore the imprint of the State and thus put school-age children who objected in an untenable position. We turn our attention now to consider the position of the students, both those who desired the prayer and she who did not.

To endure the speech of false ideas or offensive content and then to counter it is part of learning how to live in a pluralistic society, a society which insists upon open discourse towards the end of a tolerant citizenry. And tolerance presupposes some mutuality of obligation. It is argued that our constitutional vision of a free society requires confidence in our own ability to accept or reject ideas of which we do not approve, and that prayer at a high school graduation does nothing more than offer a choice. By the time they are seniors, high school students no doubt have been required to attend classes and assemblies and to complete assignments exposing them to ideas they find distasteful or immoral or absurd or all of these. Against this background, students may consider it an odd measure

of justice to be subjected during the course of their education to ideas deemed offensive and irreligious, but to be denied a brief, formal prayer ceremony that the school offers in return. This argument cannot prevail, however. It overlooks a fundamental dynamic of the Constitution.

The First Amendment protects speech and religion by quite different mechanisms. Speech is protected by insuring its full expression even when the government participates, for the very object of some of our most important speech is to persuade the government to adopt an idea as its own. *Meese* v. *Keene*, 481 U. S. 465, 480–481 (1987); see also *Keller* v. *State Bar of California*, 496 U. S. 1, 10–11 (1990); *Abood* v. *Detroit Board of Education*, 431 U. S. 209 (1977). The method for protecting freedom of worship and freedom of conscience in religious matters is quite the reverse. In religious debate or expression the government is not a prime participant, for the Framers deemed religious establishment antithetical to the freedom of all. The Free Exercise Clause embraces a freedom of conscience and worship that has close parallels in the speech provisions of the First Amendment, but the Establishment Clause is a specific prohibition on forms of state intervention in religious affairs with no precise counterpart in the speech provisions. *Buckley* v. *Valeo*, 424 U. S. 1, 92–93, and n. 127 (1976) *(per curiam)*. The explanation lies in the lesson of history that was and is the inspiration for the Establishment Clause, the lesson that in the hands of government what might begin as a tolerant expression of religious views may end in a policy to indoctrinate and coerce. A state-created orthodoxy puts at grave risk that freedom of belief and conscience which are the sole assurance that religious faith is real, not imposed.

The lessons of the First Amendment are as urgent in the modern world as in the 18th Century when it was written. One timeless lesson is that if citizens are subjected to state-sponsored religious exercises, the State disavows its own duty to guard and respect that sphere of inviolable conscience and belief which is the mark of a free people. To compromise that principle today would be to deny our own tradition and forfeit our standing to urge others to secure the protections of that tradition for themselves.

As we have observed before, there are heightened concerns with protecting freedom of conscience from subtle coercive pressure in the elementary and secondary public schools. See, *e.g.*, *Abington School District* v. *Schempp*, 374 U. S. 203, 307 (1963) (Goldberg, J., concurring); *Edwards* v. *Aguillard*, 482 U. S. 578, 584 (1987); *Westside Community Bd. of Ed.* v. *Mergens*, 496 U. S. 226, 261–262 (1990) (KENNEDY, J., concurring). Our decisions in *Engel* v. *Vitale*, 370 U. S. 421 (1962), and *Abington School District, supra*, recognize, among other things, that prayer exercises in public schools carry a particular risk of indirect coercion. The concern may not be limited to the context of schools, but it is most pronounced there. See *Allegheny County v. Greater Pittsburgh ACLU*, 492 U. S., at 661 (KENNEDY, J., concurring in judgment in part and dissenting in part). What to most believers may seem nothing more than a reasonable request that the nonbeliever respect their religious practices, in a school context may appear to the nonbeliever or dissenter to be an attempt to employ the machinery of the State to enforce a religious orthodoxy.

We need not look beyond the circumstances of this case to see the phenomenon at work. The undeniable fact is that the school district's supervision and control of a high school graduation ceremony places public pressure, as well as peer pressure, on attending students to stand as a group or, at least, maintain respectful silence during the Invocation and Benediction. This pressure, though subtle and indirect, can be as real as any overt compulsion. Of course, in our culture standing or remaining silent can signify adherence to a view or simple respect for the views of others. And no doubt some persons who have no desire to join a prayer have little objection to standing as a sign of respect for those who do. But for the dissenter of high school age, who has a reasonable perception that she is being forced by the State to pray in a manner her conscience will not allow, the injury is no less real. There can be no doubt that for many, if not most, of the students at the graduation, the act of standing or remaining silent was an expression of participation in the Rabbi's prayer. That was the very point of the religious exercise. It is of little comfort to a dissenter, then, to be told that for her the act of standing or remaining in silence signifies mere respect, rather than participation. What matters is that, given our social conventions, a reasonable dissenter in this milieu could believe that the group exercise signified her own participation or approval of it.

Finding no violation under these circumstances would place objectors in the dilemma of participating, with all that implies, or protesting. We do not address whether that choice is acceptable if the affected citizens are mature adults, but we think the State may not, consistent with the Establishment Clause, place primary and secondary school children in this position. Research in psychology supports the common assumption that adolescents are often susceptible to pressure from their peers towards conformity, and that the influence is strongest in matters of social convention. Brittain, Adolescent Choices and Parent-Peer Cross-Pressures, 28 Am. Sociological Rev. 385 (June 1963); Clasen & Brown, The Multidimensionality of Peer Pressure in Adolescence, 14 J. of Youth and Adolescence 451 (Dec. 1985); Brown, Clasen, & Eicher, Perceptions of Peer Pressure, Peer Conformity Dispositions, and Self-Reported Behavior Among Adolescents, 22 Developmental Psychology 521 (July 1986). To recognize that the choice imposed by the State constitutes an unacceptable constraint only acknowledges that the government may no more use social pressure to enforce orthodoxy than it may use more direct means.

The injury caused by the government's action, and the reason why Daniel and Deborah Weisman object to it, is that the State, in a school setting, in effect required participation in a religious exercise. It is, we concede, a brief exercise during which the individual can concentrate on joining its message, meditate on her own religion, or let her mind wander. But the embarrassment and the intrusion of the religious exercise cannot be refuted by arguing that these prayers, and similar ones to be said in the future, are of a *de minimis* character. To do so would be an affront to the Rabbi who offered them and to all those for whom the prayers were an essential and profound recognition of divine authority. And for the same reason, we think that the intrusion is greater than the two minutes or so of time consumed for prayers like these. Assuming, as we must, that the prayers were offensive to the student and the parent who now object, the intrusion was both real and, in the context of a secondary school, a violation of the objectors' rights. That the intrusion was in the course of promulgating religion that sought to be civic or nonsectarian rather than pertaining to one sect does not lessen the offense or isolation to the objectors. At best it narrows their number, at worst increases their sense of isolation and affront. See *supra*, at __.

There was a stipulation in the District Court that attendance at graduation and promotional ceremonies is voluntary. Statement of Agreed Facts ¶41, App. 18. Petitioners and the United States, as *amicus*, made this a center point of the case, arguing that the option of not attending the graduation excuses any inducement or coercion in the ceremony itself. The argument lacks all persuasion. Law reaches past formalism. And to say a teenage student has a real choice not to attend her high school graduation is formalistic in the extreme. True, Deborah could elect not to attend commencement without renouncing her diploma; but we shall not allow the case to turn on this point. Everyone knows that in our society and in our culture high school graduation is one of life's most significant occasions. A school rule which excuses attendance is beside the point. Attendance may not be required by official decree, yet it is apparent that a student is not free to absent herself from the graduation exercise in any real sense of the term "voluntary," for absence would require forfeiture of those intangible benefits which have motivated the student through youth and all her high school years. Graduation is a time for family and those closest to the student to celebrate success and express mutual wishes of gratitude and respect, all to the end of impressing upon the young person the role that it is his or her right and duty to assume in the community and all of its diverse parts.

The importance of the event is the point the school district and the United States rely upon to argue that a formal prayer ought to be permitted, but it becomes one of the principal reasons why their argument must fail. Their contention, one of considerable force were it not for the constitutional constraints applied to state action, is that the prayers are an essential part of these ceremonies because for many persons an occasion of this significance lacks meaning if there is no recognition, however brief, that human achievements cannot be understood apart from their spiritual essence. We think the Government's position that this interest suffices to force students to choose between compliance or forfeiture demonstrates fundamental inconsistency in its argumentation. It fails to acknowledge that what for many of Deborah's classmates and their parents was a spiritual imperative was for Daniel and Deborah Weisman religious conformance compelled by the State. While in some societies the wishes of the majority might prevail, the Establishment Clause of the First Amendment is addressed to this contingency and rejects the balance urged upon us. The Constitution forbids the State to exact religious conformity from a student as the price of attending her own high school graduation. This is the calculus the Constitution commands.

The Government's argument gives insufficient recognition to the real conflict of conscience faced by the young student. The essence of the Government's position is that with regard to a civic, social occasion of this importance it is the objector, not the majority, who must take unilateral and private action to avoid compromising religious scruples, here by electing to miss the graduation exercise. This turns conventional First Amendment analysis on its head. It is a tenet of the First Amendment that the State cannot require one of its citizens to forfeit his or her rights and benefits as the price of resisting conformance to state-sponsored religious practice. To say that a student must remain apart from the ceremony at the opening invocation and closing benediction is to risk compelling conformity in an environment analogous to the classroom setting, where we have said the risk of compulsion is especially high. See *supra*, at __. Just as in *Engel* v. *Vitale*, 370 U. S., at 430, and *Abington School District* v. *Schempp*, 374 U. S., at 224-225, we found that provisions within the challenged legislation permitting a student to be voluntarily excused from attendance or participation in the daily prayers did not shield those practices from invalidation, the fact that attendance at the graduation ceremonies is voluntary in a legal sense does not save the religious exercise.

Inherent differences between the public school system and a session of a State Legislature distinguish this case from *Marsh* v. *Chambers*, 463 U. S. 783 (1983). The considerations we have raised in objection to the invocation and benediction are in many respects similar to the arguments we considered in *Marsh*. But there are also obvious differences. The atmosphere at the opening of a session of a state legislature where adults are free to enter and leave with little comment and for any number of reasons cannot compare with the constraining potential of the one school event most important for the student to attend. The influence and force of a formal exercise in a school graduation are far greater than the prayer exercise we condoned in *Marsh*. The *Marsh* majority in fact gave specific recognition to this distinction and placed particular reliance on it in upholding the prayers at issue there. 463 U. S., at 792. Today's case is different. At a high school graduation, teachers and principals must and do retain a high degree of control over the precise contents of the program, the speeches, the timing, the movements, the dress, and the decorum of the students. *Bethel School Dist. No. 403* v. *Fraser*, 478 U. S. 675 (1986). In this atmosphere the state-imposed character of an invocation and benediction by clergy selected by the school combine to make the prayer a state-sanctioned religious exercise in which the student was left with no alternative but to submit. This is different from *Marsh* and suffices to make the religious exercise a First Amendment violation. Our Establishment Clause jurisprudence remains a delicate and fact-sensitive one, and we cannot accept the parallel relied upon by petitioners and the United States between the facts of *Marsh* and the case now before us. Our decisions in *Engel* v. *Vitale, supra,* and *Abington School District* v. *Schempp, supra,* require us to distinguish the public school context.

We do not hold that every state action implicating religion is invalid if one or a few citizens find it offensive. People may take offense at all manner of religious as well as nonreligious messages, but offense alone does not in every case show a violation. We know too that sometimes to endure social isolation or even anger may be the price of conscience or nonconformity. But, by any reading of our cases, the conformity required of the student in this case was too high an exaction to withstand the test of the Establishment Clause. The prayer exercises in this case are especially improper because the State has in every practical sense compelled attendance and participation in an explicit religious exercise at an event of singular importance to every student, one the objecting student had no real alternative to avoid.

Our jurisprudence in this area is of necessity one of line-drawing, of determining at what point a dissenter's rights of religious freedom are infringed by the State.

> "The First Amendment does not prohibit practices which by any realistic measure create none of the dangers which it is designed to prevent and which do not so directly or substantially involve the state in religious exercises or in the favoring of religion as to have meaningful and practical impact. It is of course true that great consequences can grow from small beginnings, but the measure of constitutional adjudication is the ability and willingness to distinguish between real threat and mere shadow." *Abington School District* v. *Schempp, supra,* at 308 (Goldberg, J., concurring).

Our society would be less than true to its heritage if it lacked abiding concern for the values of its young people, and we acknowledge the profound belief of adherents to many faiths that there must be a place in the student's life

for precepts of a morality higher even than the law we today enforce. We express no hostility to those aspirations, nor would our oath permit us to do so. A relentless and all-pervasive attempt to exclude religion from every aspect of public life could itself become inconsistent with the Constitution. See *Abington School District, supra,* at 306 (Goldberg, J., concurring). We recognize that, at graduation time and throughout the course of the educational process, there will be instances when religious values, religious practices, and religious persons will have some interaction with the public schools and their students. See *Westside Community Bd. of Ed.* v. *Mergens*, 496 U. S. 226 (1990). But these matters, often questions of accommodation of religion, are not before us. The sole question presented is whether a religious exercise may be conducted at a graduation ceremony in circumstances where, as we have found, young graduates who object are induced to conform. No holding by this Court suggests that a school can persuade or compel a student to participate in a religious exercise. That is being done here, and it is forbidden by the Establishment Clause of the First Amendment.

For the reasons we have stated, the judgment of the Court of Appeals is

Affirmed.

JUSTICE BLACKMUN, with whom JUSTICE STEVENS and JUSTICE O'CONNOR join, concurring.

Nearly half a century of review and refinement of Establishment Clause jurisprudence has distilled one clear understanding: Government may neither promote nor affiliate itself with any religious doctrine or organization, nor may it obtrude itself in the internal affairs of any religious institution. The application of these principles to the present case mandates the decision reached today by the Court.

I

This Court first reviewed a challenge to state law under the Establishment Clause in *Everson* v. *Board of Education*, 330 U. S. 1 (1947).[1] Relying on the history of the Clause, and the Court's prior analysis, Justice Black outlined the considerations that have become the touchstone of Establishment Clause jurisprudence: Neither a State nor the Federal Government can pass laws which aid one religion, aid all religions, or prefer one religion over another. Neither a State nor the Federal Government, openly or secretly, can participate in the affairs of any religious

---

[1]A few earlier cases involving federal laws touched on interpretation of the Establishment Clause. In *Reynolds* v. *United States*, 98 U. S. 145 (1879), and *Davis* v. *Beason*, 133 U. S. 333 (1890), the Court considered the Clause in the context of federal laws prohibiting bigamy. The Court in *Reynolds* accepted Thomas Jefferson's letter to the Danbury Baptist Association "almost as an authoritative declaration of the scope and effect" of the First Amendment. 98 U. S., at 164. In that letter Jefferson penned his famous lines that the Establishment Clause built "a wall of separation between church and State." *Ibid. Davis* considered that "[t]he first amendment to the Constitution . . . was intended . . . to prohibit legislation for the support of any religious tenets, or the modes of worship of any sect." 133 U. S., at 342. In another case, *Bradfield* v. *Roberts*, 175 U. S. 291 (1899), the Court held that it did not violate the Establishment Clause for Congress to construct a hospital building for caring for poor patients, although the hospital was managed by sisters of the Roman Catholic Church. The Court reasoned: "That the influence of any particular church may be powerful over the members of a non-sectarian and secular corporation, incorporated for a certain defined purpose and with clearly stated powers, is surely not sufficient to convert such a corporation into a religious or sectarian body." *Id.*, at 298. Finally, in 1908 the Court held that "the spirit of the Constitution" did not prohibit the Indians from using their money, held by the United States Government, for religious education. See *Quick Bear* v. *Leupp*, 210 U. S. 50, 81.

organization and vice versa.[2] "In the words of Jefferson, the clause against establishment of religion by law was intended to erect 'a wall of separation between church and State.'" *Everson*, 330 U. S., at 16, quoting *Reynolds* v. *United States*, 98 U. S. 145, 164 (1879). The dissenters agreed: "The Amendment's purpose . . . was to create a complete and permanent separation of the spheres of religious activity and civil authority by comprehensively forbidding every form of public aid or support for religion." 330 U.S., at 31–32 (Rutledge, J., dissenting, joined by Frankfurter, Jackson, and Burton, JJ.).

In *Engel* v. *Vitale*, 370 U. S. 421 (1962), the Court considered for the first time the constitutionality of prayer in a public school. Students said aloud a short prayer selected by the State Board of Regents: "Almighty God, we acknowledge our dependence upon Thee, and we beg Thy blessings upon us, our parents, our teachers and our Country." *Id.*, at 422. Justice Black, writing for the Court, again made clear that the First Amendment forbids the use of the power or prestige of the government to control, support, or influence the religious beliefs and practices of the American people. Although the prayer was "denominationally neutral" and "its observance on the part of the students [was] voluntary," *id.*, at 430, the Court found that it violated this essential precept of the Establishment Clause.

A year later, the Court again invalidated government-sponsored prayer in public schools in *Abington School District* v. *Schempp*, 374 U. S. 203 (1963). In *Schempp*, the school day for Baltimore, Maryland, and Abington Township, Pennsylvania, students began with a reading from the Bible, or a recitation of the Lord's Prayer, or both. After a thorough review of the Court's prior Establishment Clause cases, the Court concluded:

"[T]he Establishment Clause has been directly considered by this Court eight times in the past score of years and, with only one Justice dissenting on the point, it has consistently held that the clause withdrew all legislative power respecting religious belief or the expression thereof. The test may be stated as follows: what are the purpose and the primary effect of the enactment? If either is the advancement or inhibition of religion, then the enactment exceeds the scope of legislative power as circumscribed by the Constitution." *Id.*, at 222.

Because the schools' opening exercises were government-sponsored religious ceremonies, the Court found that the primary effect was the advancement of religion and held, therefore, that the activity violated the Establishment Clause. *Id.*, at 223–224.

Five years later, the next time the Court considered whether religious activity in public schools violated the Establishment Clause, it reiterated the principle that government "may not aid, foster, or promote one religion or religious theory against another or even against the militant opposite." *Epperson* v. *Arkansas*, 393 U. S. 97, 104 (1968). "'If [the purpose or primary effect] is the advancement or inhibition of religion then the enactment exceeds the scope of legislative power as circumscribed by the Constitution.'" *Id.*, at 107 (quoting *Schempp*, 374 U. S., at 222). Finding that the Arkansas law aided religion by preventing the teaching of evolution, the Court invalidated it.

In 1971, Chief Justice Burger reviewed the Court's past decisions and found: "Three . . . tests may be gleaned from our cases." *Lemon* v. *Kurtzman*, 403 U. S. 602, 612. In order for a statute to survive an Establishment Clause challenge, "[f]irst, the statute must have a secular legislative purpose; second, its principal or primary effect must be one that neither advances nor inhibits religion; finally, the statute must not foster an excessive government entanglement with religion." *Id.*, at 612–613 (internal quotation marks and citations omitted).[3] After *Lemon*, the Court continued to rely on these basic principles in resolving Establishment Clause disputes.[4]

Application of these principles to the facts of this case is straightforward. There can be "no doubt" that the "invocation of God's blessings" delivered at Nathan Bishop Middle School "is a religious activity." *Engel*, 370 U. S., at 424. In the words of *Engel*, the Rabbi's prayer "is a solemn avowal of divine faith and supplication for the blessings of the Almighty. The nature of such a prayer has always been religious." *Ibid.* The question then is whether the government has "plac[ed] its official stamp of approval" on the prayer. *Id.*, at 429. As the Court ably demonstrates, when the government "compose[s] official prayers," *id.*, at 425, selects the member of the clergy to deliver the prayer, has the prayer delivered at a public school event that is planned, supervised and given by school officials, and pressures students to attend and participate in the prayer, there can be no doubt that the government is advancing and promoting religion.[5] As our prior decisions teach us, it is this that the Constitution prohibits.

II

I join the Court's opinion today because I find nothing in it inconsistent with the essential precepts of the Establishment Clause developed in our precedents. The Court holds that the graduation prayer is unconstitutional because the State "in effect required participation in a religious exercise." *Ante*, at 14. Although our precedents make clear that proof of government coercion is not necessary to prove

---

[2]The Court articulated six examples of paradigmatic practices that the Establishment Clause prohibits: "The 'establishment of religion' clause of the First Amendment means at least this: Neither a state nor the Federal Government can set up a church. Neither can pass laws which aid one religion, aid all religions, or prefer one religion over another. Neither can force or influence a person to go to or to remain away from church against his will or force him to profess a belief or disbelief in any religion. No person can be punished for entertaining or professing religious beliefs or disbeliefs, for church attendance or non-attendance. No tax in any amount, large or small, can be levied to support any religious activities or institutions, whatever they may be called, or whatever form they may adopt to teach or practice religion. Neither a state nor the Federal Government can, openly or secretly, participate in the affairs of any religious organizations or groups and *vice versa*." *Everson* v. *Bd. of Ed.*, 330 U. S. 1, 15 (1947).

[3]The final prong, excessive entanglement, was a focus of *Walz* v. *Tax Comm'n*, 397 U. S. 664, 674 (1970), but harkens back to the final example in *Everson*: "Neither a state nor the Federal Government can, openly or secretly, participate in the affairs of any religion organizations or groups and *vice versa*." *Everson*, 330 U. S., at 16. The discussion in *Everson* reflected the Madisonian concern that secular and religious authorities must not interfere with each other's respective spheres of choice and influence. See generally, The Complete Madison 298–312 (S. Padover ed. 1953).

[4]Since 1971, the Court has decided 31 Establishment Clause cases. In only one instance, the decision of *Marsh* v. *Chambers*, 463 U. S. 783 (1983), has the Court not rested its decision on the basic principles described in *Lemon*. For example, in the most recent Establishment Clause case, *Westside Community Bd. of Ed.* v. *Mergens*, 496 U. S. 226 (1990), the Court applied the three-part *Lemon* analysis to the Equal Access Act, which made it unlawful for public secondary schools to deny equal access to any student wishing to hold religious meetings. *Id.*, at 248–253 (plurality opinion); *id.*, at 262 (Marshall, J., concurring). In no case involving religious activities in public schools has the Court failed to apply vigorously the *Lemon* factors.

[5]In this case, the religious message it promotes is specifically Judeo-Christian. The phrase in the benediction: "We must each strive to fulfill what you require of us all, to do justly, to love mercy, to walk humbly" obviously was taken from the Book of the Prophet Micah, ch. 6, v. 8.

an Establishment Clause violation, it is sufficient. Government pressure to participate in a religious activity is an obvious indication that the government is endorsing or promoting religion.

But it is not enough that the government restrain from compelling religious practices: it must not engage in them either. See *Schempp*, 374 U. S., at 305 (Goldberg, J., concurring). The Court repeatedly has recognized that a violation of the Establishment Clause is not predicated on coercion. See, *e. g., id.*, at 223; *id.*, at 229 (Douglas, J., concurring); *Wallace* v. *Jaffree*, 472 U. S. 38, 72 (1985) (O'CONNOR, J., concurring in judgment) ("The decisions [in *Engel* and *Schempp*] acknowledged the coercion implicit under the statutory schemes, but they expressly turned only on the fact that the government was sponsoring a manifestly religious exercise" (citation omitted)); *Comm. for Public Ed.* v. *Nyquist*, 413 U. S. 756, 786 (1973) ("[P]roof of coercion . . . [is] not a necessary element of any claim under the Establishment Clause"). The Establishment Clause proscribes public schools from "conveying or attempting to convey a message that religion or a particular religious belief is *favored* or *preferred*," *County of Allegheny* v. *ACLU*, 492 U. S. 573, 593 (1989) (internal quotations omitted) (emphasis in original), even if the schools do not actually "impos[e] pressure upon a student to participate in a religious activity."[6] *Westside Community Bd. of Ed.* v. *Mergens*, 496 U. S. 226, 261 (1990) (KENNEDY, J., concurring).

The scope of the Establishment Clause's prohibitions developed in our case law derives from the Clause's purposes. The First Amendment encompasses two distinct guarantees—the government shall make no law respecting an establishment of religion or prohibiting the free exercise thereof—both with the common purpose of securing religious liberty.[7] Through vigorous enforcement of both clauses, we "promote and assure the fullest possible scope of religious liberty and tolerance for all and . . . nurture the conditions which secure the best hope of attainment of that end." *Schempp*, 374 U. S., at 305 (Goldberg, J., concurring).

There is no doubt that attempts to aid religion through government coercion jeopardize freedom of conscience. Even subtle pressure diminishes the right of each individual to choose voluntarily what to believe. Representative Carroll explained during congressional debate over the Establishment Clause: "[T]he rights of conscience are, in their nature, of peculiar delicacy, and will little bear the gentlest touch of governmental hand." I Annals of Cong. 757 (August 15, 1789).

Our decisions have gone beyond prohibiting coercion, however, because the Court has recognized that "the fullest possible scope of religious liberty," *Schempp*, 374 U. S., at 305 (Goldberg, J., concurring), entails more than freedom from coercion. The Establishment Clause protects religious liberty on a grand scale; it is a social compact that guarantees for generations a democracy and a strong religious community—both essential to safeguarding religious liberty. "Our fathers seem to have been perfectly sincere in their belief that the members of the Church would be more

patriotic, and the citizens of the State more religious, by keeping their respective functions entirely separate." Religious Liberty, in Essays and Speeches of Jeremiah S. Black 53 (C. Black ed. 1885) (Chief Justice of the Commonwealth of Pennsylvania).[8]

The mixing of government and religion can be a threat to free government, even if no one is forced to participate. When the government puts its imprimatur on a particular religion, it conveys a message of exclusion to all those who do not adhere to the favored beliefs.[9] A government cannot be premised on the belief that all persons are created equal when it asserts that God prefers some. Only "[a]nguish, hardship and bitter strife" result "when zealous religious groups struggl[e] with one another to obtain the Government's stamp of approval." *Engel*, 370 U. S., at 429; see also *Lemon*, 403 U. S., at 622–623; *Aguilar* v. *Felton*, 473 U. S. 402, 416 (1985) (Powell, J., concurring).[10] Such a struggle can "strain a political system to the breaking point." *Walz* v. *Tax Commission*, 397 U. S. 664, 694 (1970) (opinion of Harlan, J.).

When the government arrogates to itself a role in religious affairs, it abandons its obligation as guarantor of democracy. Democracy requires the nourishment of dialogue and dissent, while religious faith puts its trust in an ultimate divine authority above all human deliberation. When the government appropriates religious truth, it "transforms rational debate into theological decree." Nuechterlein, Note, The Free Exercise Boundaries of Permissible Accommodation Under the Establishment Clause, 99 Yale L.J. 1127, 1131 (1990). Those who disagree no longer are questioning the policy judgment of the elected but the rules of a higher authority who is beyond reproach.

Madison warned that government officials who would use religious authority to pursue secular ends "exceed the commission from which they derive their authority and are Tyrants. The People who submit to it are governed by laws made neither by themselves, nor by an authority derived from them, and are slaves." Memorial and Remonstrance against Religious Assessments (1785) in The Complete Madison 300 (S. Padover, ed. 1953). Democratic govern-

---

[6]As a practical matter, of course, anytime the government endorses a religious belief there will almost always be some pressure to conform. "When the power, prestige and financial support of government is placed behind a particular religious belief, the indirect coercive pressure upon religious minorities to conform to the prevailing officially approved religion is plain." *Engel* v. *Vitale*, 370 U. S. 421, 431 (1962).

[7]See, *e. g., Everson*, 330 U. S., at 40 (Rutledge, J., dissenting) (" 'Establishment' and 'free exercise' were correlative and coextensive ideas, representing only different facets of the single great and fundamental freedom"); *Abington School Dist.* v. *Schempp*, 374 U. S. 203, 227 (1963) (Douglas, J., concurring); *id.*, at 305 (Goldberg, J., concurring); *Wallace* v. *Jaffree*, 472 U. S. 38, 50 (1985).

[8]See also *Engel*, 370 U. S., at 431 (The Clause's "first and most immediate purpose rested on the belief that a union of government and religion tends to destroy government and to degrade religion"); *McCollum* v. *Board of Education*, 333 U. S. 203, 212 (1948) ("[T]he First Amendment rests upon the premise that both religion and government can best work to achieve their lofty aims if each is left free from the other within its respective sphere").

[9]"[T]he Establishment Clause is infringed when the government makes adherence to religion relevant to a person's standing in the political community. Direct government action endorsing religion or a particular religious practice is invalid under this approach because it sends a message to nonadherents that they are outsiders, not full members of the political community, and an accompanying message to adherents that they are insiders, favored members of the political community." *Wallace* v. *Jaffree*, 472 U. S., at 69 (O'CONNOR, J., concurring) (internal quotations omitted).

[10]Sigmund Freud expressed it this way: "a religion, even if it calls itself the religion of love, must be hard and unloving to those who do not belong to it." S. Freud, Group Psychology and the Analysis of the Ego 51 (1922). James Madison stated the theory even more strongly in his "Memorial and Remonstrance" against a bill providing tax funds to religious teachers: "It degrades from the equal rank of Citizens all those whose opinions in Religion do not bend to those of the Legislative authority. Distant as it may be, in its present form, from the Inquisition it differs from it only in degree. The one is the first step, the other the last in the career of intolerance." The Complete Madison, at 303. Religion has not lost its power to engender divisiveness. "Of all the issues the ACLU takes on—reproductive rights, discrimination, jail and prison conditions, abuse of kids in the public schools, police brutality, to name a few—by far the most volatile issue is that of school prayer. Aside from our efforts to abolish the death penalty, it is the only issue that elicits death threats." Parish, Graduation Prayer Violates the Bill of Rights, 4 Utah Bar J. 19 (June/July 1991).

ment will not last long when proclamation replaces persuasion as the medium of political exchange.

Likewise, we have recognized that "[r]eligion flourishes in greater purity, without than with the aid of Gov[ern-ment]."[11] *Id.*, at 309. To "make room for as wide a variety of beliefs and creeds as the spiritual needs of man deem necessary," *Zorach* v. *Clauson*, 343 U. S. 306, 313 (1952), the government must not align itself with any one of them. When the government favors a particular religion or sect, the disadvantage to all others is obvious, but even the favored religion may fear being "taint[ed] . . . with a corrosive secularism." *Grand Rapids School Dist.* v. *Ball*, 473 U. S. 373, 385 (1985). The favored religion may be compromised as political figures reshape the religion's beliefs for their own purposes; it may be reformed as government largesse brings government regulation.[12] Keeping religion in the hands of private groups minimizes state intrusion on religious choice and best enables each religion to "flourish according to the zeal of its adherents and the appeal of its dogma." *Zorach*, 343 U. S., at 313.

It is these understandings and fears that underlie our Establishment Clause jurisprudence. We have believed that religious freedom cannot exist in the absence of a free democratic government, and that such a government cannot endure when there is fusion between religion and the political regime. We have believed that religious freedom cannot thrive in the absence of a vibrant religious community and that such a community cannot prosper when it is bound to the secular. And we have believed that these were the animating principles behind the adoption of the Establishment Clause. To that end, our cases have prohibited government endorsement of religion, its sponsorship, and active involvement in religion, whether or not citizens were coerced to conform.

I remain convinced that our jurisprudence is not misguided, and that it requires the decision reached by the Court today. Accordingly, I join the Court in affirming the judgment of the Court of Appeals.

JUSTICE SOUTER, with whom JUSTICE STEVENS and JUSTICE O'CONNOR join, concurring.

I join the whole of the Court's opinion, and fully agree that prayers at public school graduation ceremonies indirectly coerce religious observance. I write separately nonetheless on two issues of Establishment Clause analysis that underlie my independent resolution of this case: whether the Clause applies to governmental practices that do not favor one religion or denomination over others, and whether state coercion of religious conformity, over and above state endorsement of religious exercise or belief, is a necessary element of an Establishment Clause violation.

I

Forty-five years ago, this Court announced a basic principle of constitutional law from which it has not strayed: the Establishment Clause forbids not only state practices that "aid one religion . . . or prefer one religion

over another," but also those that "aid all religions." *Everson* v. *Board of Education of Ewing*, 330 U. S. 1, 15 (1947). Today we reaffirm that principle, holding that the Establishment Clause forbids state-sponsored prayers in public school settings no matter how nondenominational the prayers may be. In barring the State from sponsoring generically Theistic prayers where it could not sponsor sectarian ones, we hold true to a line of precedent from which there is no adequate historical case to depart.

A

Since *Everson*, we have consistently held the Clause applicable no less to governmental acts favoring religion generally than to acts favoring one religion over others.[1] Thus, in *Engel* v. *Vitale*, 370 U. S. 421 (1962), we held that the public schools may not subject their students to readings of any prayer, however "denominationally neutral." *Id.*, at 430. More recently, in *Wallace* v. *Jaffree*, 472 U. S. 38 (1985), we held that an Alabama moment-of-silence statute passed for the sole purpose of "returning voluntary prayer to public schools," *id.*, at 57, violated the Establishment Clause even though it did not encourage students to pray to any particular deity. We said that "when the underlying principle has been examined in the crucible of litigation, the Court has unambiguously concluded that the individual freedom of conscience protected by the First Amendment embraces the right to select any religious faith or none at all." *Id.*, at 52–53. This conclusion, we held,

> "derives support not only from the interest in respecting the individual's freedom of conscience, but also from the conviction that religious beliefs worthy of respect are the product of free and voluntary choice by the faithful, and from recognition of the fact that the political interest in forestalling intolerance extends beyond intolerance among Christian sects—or even intolerance among 'religions'—to encompass intolerance of the disbeliever and the uncertain." *Id.*, at 53–54 (footnotes omitted).

Likewise, in *Texas Monthly, Inc.* v. *Bullock*, 489 U. S. 1 (1989), we struck down a state tax exemption benefiting only religious periodicals; even though the statute in question worked no discrimination among sects, a majority of the Court found that its preference for religious publications over all other kinds "effectively endorses religious belief." *Id.*, at 17 (plurality opinion); see *id.*, at 28 (BLACKMUN, J., concurring in judgment) ("A statutory preference for the dissemination of religious ideas offends our most basic understanding of what the Establishment Clause is all about and hence is constitutionally intolerable"). And in *Torcaso* v. *Watkins*, 367 U. S. 488 (1961), we struck down a provision of the Maryland Constitution requiring public officials to declare a "'belief in the existence of God,'" *id.*, at 489, reasoning that, under the Religion Clauses of the First Amendment, "neither a State nor the Federal Government . . . can constitutionally pass laws or impose requirements which aid all religions as against non-believers . . . ," *id.*, at 495. See also *Epperson* v. *Arkansas*, 393 U. S. 97, 104 (1968) ("The First Amendment mandates governmental neutrality between religion and religion, and between religion and nonreligion"); *School Dist. of Abington* v. *Schempp*, 374 U. S. 203, 216 (1963) ("this Court has rejected unequivocally the contention that the Establishment Clause forbids only governmental preference of one religion over another"); *id.*, at 319–320 (Stewart, J., dissenting) (the Clause applies "to each of us,

---

[11] The view that the Establishment Clause was primarily a vehicle for protecting churches was expounded initially by Roger Williams. "[W]ordly corruptions . . . might consume the churches if sturdy fences against the wilderness were not maintained." M. Howe, The Garden and the Wilderness 6 (1965).

[12] "[B]ut when a religion contracts an alliance of this nature, I do not hesitate to affirm that it commits the same error as a man who should sacrifice his future to his present welfare; and in obtaining a power to which it has no claim, it risks that authority which is rightfully its own." A. de Tocqueville, Democracy in America 315 (H. Reeve transl. 1900).

[1] Cf. *Larson* v. *Valente*, 456 U. S. 228 (1982) (subjecting discrimination against certain religious organizations to test of strict scrutiny).

be he Jew or Agnostic, Christian or Atheist, Buddhist or Freethinker").

Such is the settled law. Here, as elsewhere, we should stick to it absent some compelling reason to discard it. See *Arizona* v. *Rumsey,* 467 U. S. 203, 212 (1984); *Payne* v. *Tennessee,* 501 U. S. ——, —— (1991) (slip op., at 8) (SOUTER, J., concurring).

B

Some have challenged this precedent by reading the Establishment Clause to permit "nonpreferential" state promotion of religion. The challengers argue that, as originally understood by the Framers, "[t]he Establishment Clause did not require government neutrality between religion and irreligion nor did it prohibit the Federal Government from providing nondiscriminatory aid to religion." *Wallace, supra,* at 106 (REHNQUIST, J., dissenting); see also R. Cord, Separation of Church and State: Historical Fact and Current Fiction (1988). While a case has been made for this position, it is not so convincing as to warrant reconsideration of our settled law; indeed, I find in the history of the Clause's textual development a more powerful argument supporting the Court's jurisprudence following *Everson.*

When James Madison arrived at the First Congress with a series of proposals to amend the National Constitution, one of the provisions read that "[t]he civil rights of none shall be abridged on account of religious belief or worship, nor shall any national religion be established, nor shall the full and equal rights of conscience be in any manner, or on any pretext, infringed." 1 Annals of Cong. 434 (1789). Madison's language did not last long. It was sent to a Select Committee of the House, which, without explanation, changed it to read that "no religion shall be established by law, nor shall the equal rights of conscience be infringed." *Id.,* at 729. Thence the proposal went to the Committee of the Whole, which was in turn dissatisfied with the Select Committee's language and adopted an alternative proposed by Samuel Livermore of New Hampshire: "Congress shall make no laws touching religion, or infringing the rights of conscience." See *id.,* at 731. Livermore's proposal would have forbidden laws having anything to do with religion and was thus not only far broader than Madison's version, but broader even than the scope of the Establishment Clause as we now understand it. See, *e. g., Corporation of Presiding Bishop of Church of Jesus Christ of Latter-Day Saints* v. *Amos,* 483 U. S. 327 (1987) (upholding legislative exemption of religious groups from certain obligations under civil rights laws).

The House rewrote the amendment once more before sending it to the Senate, this time adopting, without recorded debate, language derived from a proposal by Fisher Ames of Massachusetts: "Congress shall make no law establishing Religion, or prohibiting the free exercise thereof, nor shall the rights of conscience be infringed." 1 Documentary History of the First Federal Congress of the United States of America 136 (Senate Journal) (L. de Pauw ed. 1972); see 1 Annals of Cong. 765 (1789). Perhaps, on further reflection, the Representatives had thought Livermore's proposal too expansive, or perhaps, as one historian has suggested, they had simply worried that his language would not "satisfy the demands of those who wanted something said specifically against establishments of religion." L. Levy, The Establishment Clause 81 (1986) (hereinafter Levy). We do not know; what we do know is that the House rejected the Select Committee's version, which arguably ensured only that "no religion" enjoyed an official preference over others, and deliberately chose instead a prohibition extending to laws establishing "religion" in general.

The sequence of the Senate's treatment of this House proposal, and the House's response to the Senate, confirm that the Framers meant the Establishment Clause's prohibition to encompass nonpreferential aid to religion. In September 1789, the Senate considered a number of provisions that would have permitted such aid, and ultimately it adopted one of them. First, it briefly entertained this language: "Congress shall make no law establishing One Religious Sect or Society in preference to others, nor shall the rights of conscience be infringed." 1 Documentary History, *supra,* at 151 (Senate Journal). After rejecting two minor amendments to that proposal, see *ibid.,* the Senate dropped it altogether and chose a provision identical to the House's proposal, but without the clause protecting the "rights of conscience," *ibid.* With no record of the Senate debates, we cannot know what prompted these changes, but the record does tell us that, six days later, the Senate went half circle and adopted its narrowest language yet: "Congress shall make no law establishing articles of faith or a mode of worship, or prohibiting the free exercise of religion." *Id.,* at 166. The Senate sent this proposal to the House along with its versions of the other constitutional amendments proposed.

Though it accepted much of the Senate's work on the Bill of Rights, the House rejected the Senate's version of the Establishment Clause and called for a joint conference committee, to which the Senate agreed. The House conferees ultimately won out, persuading the Senate to accept this as the final text of the Religion Clauses: "Congress shall make no law respecting an establishment of religion, or prohibiting the free exercise thereof." What is remarkable is that, unlike the earliest House drafts or the final Senate proposal, the prevailing language is not limited to laws respecting an establishment of "a religion," "a national religion," "one religious sect," or specific "articles of faith."[2] The Framers repeatedly considered and deliberately rejected such narrow language and instead extended their prohibition to state support for "religion" in general.

Implicit in their choice is the distinction between preferential and nonpreferential establishments, which the weight of evidence suggests the Framers appreciated. See, *e. g.,* Laycock, "Nonpreferential" Aid 902–906; Levy 91–119. But cf. T. Curry, The First Freedoms 208–222 (1986). Of particular note, the Framers were vividly familiar with efforts in the colonies and, later, the States to impose general, nondenominational assessments and other incidents of ostensibly ecumenical establishments. See generally Levy 1–62. The Virginia Statute for Religious Freedom, written by Jefferson and sponsored by Madison, captured the separationist response to such measures. Condemning all establishments, however nonpreferentialist, the Statute broadly guaranteed that "no man shall be compelled to frequent or support any religious worship, place, or ministry whatsoever," including his own. Act for Establishing Religious Freedom (1785), in 5 The Founders' Constitution 84, 85 (P. Kurland & R. Lerner eds. 1987). Forcing a citizen to support even his own church would, among other things, deny "the ministry those temporary

---

[2] Some commentators have suggested that by targeting laws respecting "an" establishment of religion, the Framers adopted the very nonpreferentialist position whose much clearer articulation they repeatedly rejected. See, *e. g.,* R. Cord, Separation of Church and State: Historical Fact and Current Fiction 11–12 (1988). Yet the indefinite article before the word "establishment" is better seen as evidence that the Clause forbids any kind of establishment, including a nonpreferential one. If the Framers had wished, for some reason, to use the indefinite term to achieve a narrow meaning for the Clause, they could far more aptly have placed it before the word "religion." See Laycock, "Nonpreferential" Aid to Religion: A False Claim About Original Intent, 27 Wm. & Mary L. Rev. 875, 884–885 (1986) (hereinafter Laycock, "Nonpreferential" Aid).

rewards, which proceeding from an approbation of their personal conduct, are an additional incitement to earnest and unremitting labours for the instruction of mankind." *Id*, at 84. In general, Madison later added, "religion & Govt. will both exist in greater purity, the less they are mixed together." Letter from J. Madison to E. Livingston, 10 July 1822, in 5 The Founders' Constitution, at 105, 106.

What we thus know of the Framers' experience underscores the observation of one prominent commentator, that confining the Establishment Clause to a prohibition on preferential aid "requires a premise that the Framers were extraordinarily bad drafters—that they believed one thing but adopted language that said something substantially different, and that they did so after repeatedly attending to the choice of language." Laycock, "Nonpreferential" Aid 882–883; see also *Allegheny County* v. *American Civil Liberties Union, Greater Pittsburgh Chapter*, 492 U. S. 573, 647–648 (1989) (opinion of STEVENS, J.). We must presume, since there is no conclusive evidence to the contrary, that the Framers embraced the significance of their textual judgment.[3] Thus, on balance, history neither contradicts nor warrants reconsideration of the settled principle that the Establishment Clause forbids support for religion in general no less than support for one religion or some.

C

While these considerations are, for me, sufficient to reject the nonpreferentialist position, one further concern animates my judgment. In many contexts, including this one, nonpreferentialism requires some distinction between "sectarian" religious practices and those that would be, by some measure, ecumenical enough to pass Establishment Clause muster. Simply by requiring the enquiry, nonpreferentialists invite the courts to engage in comparative theology. I can hardly imagine a subject less amenable to the competence of the federal judiciary, or more deliberately to be avoided where possible.

This case is nicely in point. Since the nonpreferentiality of a prayer must be judged by its text, JUSTICE BLACKMUN pertinently observes, *ante*, at 6, n. 5, that Rabbi Gutterman drew his exhortation "[t]o do justly, to love mercy, to walk humbly" straight from the King James version of Micah, ch. 6, v. 8. At some undefinable point, the similarities between a state-sponsored prayer and the sacred text of a specific religion would so closely identify the former with the latter that even a nonpreferentialist would have to concede a breach of the Establishment Clause. And even if Micah's thought is sufficiently generic for most believers, it still embodies a straightforwardly Theistic premise, and so does the Rabbi's prayer. Many Americans who consider themselves religious are not Theistic; some, like several of the Framers, are Deists who would question Rabbi Gutterman's plea for divine advancement of the country's political and moral good. Thus, a nonpreferentialist who would condemn subjecting public school graduates to, say, the Anglican

liturgy would still need to explain why the government's preference for Theistic over non-Theistic religion is constitutional.

Nor does it solve the problem to say that the State should promote a "diversity" of religious views; that position would necessarily compel the government and, inevitably, the courts to make wholly inappropriate judgments about the number of religions the State should sponsor and the relative frequency with which it should sponsor each. In fact, the prospect would be even worse than that. As Madison observed in criticizing religious presidential proclamations, the practice of sponsoring religious messages tends, over time, "to narrow the recommendation to the standard of the predominant sect." Madison's "Detached Memoranda," 3 Wm. & Mary Q. 534, 561 (E. Fleet ed. 1946) (hereinafter Madison's "Detached Memoranda"). We have not changed much since the days of Madison, and the judiciary should not willingly enter the political arena to battle the centripetal force leading from religious pluralism to official preference for the faith with the most votes.

II

Petitioners rest most of their argument on a theory that, whether or not the Establishment Clause permits extensive nonsectarian support for religion, it does not forbid the state to sponsor affirmations of religious belief that coerce neither support for religion nor participation in religious observance. I appreciate the force of some of the arguments supporting a "coercion" analysis of the Clause. See generally *Allegheny County, supra*, at 655–679 (opinion of KENNEDY, J.); McConnell, Coercion: The Lost Element of Establishment, 27 Wm. & Mary L. Rev. 933 (1986). But we could not adopt that reading without abandoning our settled law, a course that, in my view, the text of the ⸱Clause would not readily permit. Nor does the extratextual evidence of original meaning stand so unequivocally at odds with the textual premise inherent in existing precedent that we should fundamentally reconsider our course.

A

Over the years, this Court has declared the invalidity of many noncoercive state laws and practices conveying a message of religious endorsement. For example, in *Allegheny County, supra*, we forbade the prominent display of a nativity scene on public property; without contesting the dissent's observation that the crèche coerced no one into accepting or supporting whatever message it proclaimed, five Members of the Court found its display unconstitutional as a state endorsement of Christianity. *Id.*, at 589–594, 598–602. Likewise, in *Wallace* v. *Jaffree*, 472 U. S. 38 (1985), we struck down a state law requiring a moment of silence in public classrooms not because the statute coerced students to participate in prayer (for it did not), but because the manner of its enactment "convey[ed] a message of state approval of prayer activities in the public schools." *Id.*, at 61; see also *id.*, at 67–84 (O'CONNOR, J., concurring in judgment). Cf. *Engel* v. *Vitale*, 370 U. S., at 431 ("When the power, prestige and financial support of government is placed behind a particular religious belief, the indirect coercive pressure upon religious minorities to conform to the prevailing officially approved religion is plain. But the purposes underlying the Establishment Clause go much further than that").

In *Epperson* v. *Arkansas*, 393 U. S. 97 (1968), we invalidated a state law that barred the teaching of Darwin's theory of evolution because, even though the statute obviously did not coerce anyone to support religion or participate in any religious practice, it was enacted for a singularly religious purpose. See also *Edwards* v. *Aguillard*, 482 U. S. 578, 593 (1987) (statute requiring instruction in "creation science" "endorses religion in

---

[3]In his dissent in *Wallace* v. *Jaffree*, 472 U. S. 38 (1985), THE CHIEF JUSTICE rested his nonpreferentialist interpretation partly on the postratification actions of the early national government. Aside from the willingness of some (but not all) early Presidents to issue ceremonial religious proclamations, which were at worst trivial breaches of the Establishment Clause, see *infra*, at 22–23, he cited such seemingly preferential aid as a treaty provision, signed by Jefferson, authorizing federal subsidization of a Roman Catholic priest and church for the Kaskaskia Indians. 472 U. S., at 103. But this proves too much, for if the Establishment Clause permits a special appropriation of tax money for the religious activities of a particular sect, it forbids virtually nothing. See Laycock, "Nonpreferential" Aid 915. Although evidence of historical practice can indeed furnish valuable aid in the interpretation of contemporary language, acts like the one in question prove only that public officials, no matter when they serve, can turn a blind eye to constitutional principle. See *infra*, at 18.

violation of the First Amendment"). And in *School Dist. of Grand Rapids* v. *Ball*, 473 U. S. 373 (1985), we invalidated a program whereby the State sent public school teachers to parochial schools to instruct students on ostensibly nonreligious matters; while the scheme clearly did not coerce anyone to receive or subsidize religious instruction, we held it invalid because, among other things, "[t]he symbolic union of church and state inherent in the [program] threatens to convey a message of state support for religion to students and to the general public." *Id.*, at 397; see also *Texas Monthly, Inc.* v. *Bullock*, 489 U. S., at 17 (plurality opinion) (tax exemption benefiting only religious publications "effectively endorses religious belief"); *id.*, at 28 (BLACKMUN, J., concurring in judgment) (exemption unconstitutional because State "engaged in preferential support for the communication of religious messages").

Our precedents may not always have drawn perfectly straight lines. They simply cannot, however, support the position that a showing of coercion is necessary to a successful Establishment Clause claim.

B

Like the provisions about "due" process and "unreasonable" searches and seizures, the constitutional language forbidding laws "respecting an establishment of religion" is not pellucid. But virtually everyone acknowledges that the Clause bans more than formal establishments of religion in the traditional sense, that is, massive state support for religion through, among other means, comprehensive schemes of taxation. See generally Levy 1–62 (discussing such establishments in the colonies and early States). This much follows from the Framers' explicit rejection of simpler provisions prohibiting either the establishment of a religion or laws "establishing religion" in favor of the broader ban on laws "respecting an establishment of religion." See *supra*, at 4–6.

While some argue that the Framers added the word "respecting" simply to foreclose federal interference with State establishments of religion, see, *e. g.*, Amar, The Bill of Rights as a Constitution, 100 Yale L. J. 1131, 1157 (1991), the language sweeps more broadly than that. In Madison's words, the Clause in its final form forbids "everything like" a national religious establishment, see Madison's "Detached Memoranda" 558, and, after incorporation, it forbids "everything like" a State religious establishment.[4] Cf. *Allegheny County*, 492 U. S., at 649 (opinion of STEVENS, J.). The sweep is broad enough that Madison himself characterized congressional provisions for legislative and military chaplains as unconstitutional "establishments." Madison's "Detached Memoranda" 558–559; see *infra*, at 16–17, and n. 6.

While petitioners insist that the prohibition extends only to the "coercive" features and incidents of establishment, they cannot easily square that claim with the constitutional text. The First Amendment forbids not just laws "respecting an establishment of religion," but also those "prohibiting the free exercise thereof." Yet laws that coerce nonadherents to "support or participate in any religion or its exercise," *Allegheny County*, *supra*, at 659–660 (opinion of KENNEDY, J.), would virtually by definition violate their right to religious free exercise. See *Employment Div., Dept. of Human Resources of Ore.* v. *Smith*, 494 U. S. 872, 877 (1990) (under Free Exercise Clause, "government may not compel affirmation of religious belief"), citing *Torcaso* v.

---

[4]In *Everson* v. *Board of Education of Ewing*, 330 U. S. 1 (1947), we unanimously incorporated the Establishment Clause into the Due Process Clause of the Fourteenth Amendment and, by so doing, extended its reach to the actions of States. *Id.*, at 14–15; see also *Cantwell* v. *Connecticut*, 310 U. S. 296, 303 (1940) (dictum). Since then, not one Member of this Court has proposed disincorporating the Clause.

Watkins, 367 U. S. 488 (1961); see also J. Madison, Memorial and Remonstrance Against Religious Assessments (1785) (compelling support for religious establishments violates "free exercise of Religion"), quoted in 5 The Founders' Constitution, at 82, 84. Thus, a literal application of the coercion test would render the Establishment Clause a virtual nullity, as petitioners' counsel essentially conceded at oral argument. Tr. of Oral Arg. 18.

Our cases presuppose as much; as we said in *School Dist. of Abington*, *supra*, "[t]he distinction between the two clauses is apparent—a violation of the Free Exercise Clause is predicated on coercion while the Establishment Clause violation need not be so attended." 374 U. S., at 223; see also Laycock, "Nonpreferential" Aid 922 ("If coercion is . . . an element of the establishment clause, establishment adds nothing to free exercise"). While one may argue that the Framers meant the Establishment Clause simply to ornament the First Amendment, cf. T. Curry, The First Freedoms 216–217 (1986), that must be a reading of last resort. Without compelling evidence to the contrary, we should presume that the Framers meant the Clause to stand for something more than petitioners attribute to it.

Petitioners argue from the political setting in which the Establishment Clause was framed, and from the Framers' own political practices following ratification, that government may constitutionally endorse religion so long as it does not coerce religious conformity. The setting and the practices warrant canvassing, but while they yield some evidence for petitioners' argument, they do not reveal the degree of consensus in early constitutional thought that would raise a threat to *stare decisis* by challenging the presumption that the Establishment Clause adds something to the Free Exercise Clause that follows it.

The Framers adopted the Religion Clauses in response to a long tradition of coercive state support for religion, particularly in the form of tax assessments, but their special antipathy to religious coercion did not exhaust their hostility to the features and incidents of establishment. Indeed, Jefferson and Madison opposed any political appropriation of religion, see *infra*, at 15–18 and, even when challenging the hated assessments, they did not always temper their rhetoric with distinctions between coercive and noncoercive state action. When, for example, Madison criticized Virginia's general assessment bill, he invoked principles antithetical to all state efforts to promote religion. An assessment, he wrote, is improper not simply because it forces people to donate "three pence" to religion, but, more broadly, because "it is itself a signal of persecution. It degrades from the equal rank of Citizens all those whose opinions in Religion do not bend to those of the Legislative authority." J. Madison, Memorial and Remonstrance Against Religious Assessments (1785), in 5 The Founders' Constitution, at 83. Madison saw that, even without the tax collector's participation, an official endorsement of religion can impair religious liberty.

Petitioners contend that because the early Presidents included religious messages in their inaugural and Thanksgiving Day addresses, the Framers could not have meant the Establishment Clause to forbid noncoercive state endorsement of religion. The argument ignores the fact, however, that Americans today find such proclamations less controversial than did the founding generation, whose published thoughts on the matter belie petitioners' claim. President Jefferson, for example, steadfastly refused to issue Thanksgiving proclamations of any kind, in part because he thought they violated the Religion Clauses. Letter from Thomas Jefferson to Rev. S. Miller (Jan. 23, 1808), in 5 The Founders' Constitution, at 98. In explaining his views to the Reverend Samuel Miller, Jefferson effectively anticipated, and rejected, petitioners' position:

> "[I]t is only proposed that I should *recommend*, not prescribe a day of fasting & prayer. That is, that I should *indirectly* assume to the U. S. an authority over religious exercises which the Constitution has directly precluded from them. It must be meant too that this recommendation is to carry some authority, and to be sanctioned by some penalty on those who disregard it; not indeed of fine and imprisonment, but of some degree of proscription perhaps in public opinion." *Id.*, at 98–99 (emphasis in original).

By condemning such noncoercive state practices that, in "recommending" the majority faith, demean religious dissenters "in public opinion," Jefferson necessarily condemned what, in modern terms, we call official endorsement of religion. He accordingly construed the Establishment Clause to forbid not simply state coercion, but also state endorsement of religious belief and observance.[5] And if he opposed impersonal presidential addresses for inflicting "proscription in public opinion," all the more would he have condemned less diffuse expressions of official endorsement.

During his first three years in office, James Madison also refused to call for days of thanksgiving and prayer, though later, amid the political turmoil of the War of 1812, he did so on four separate occasions. See Madison's "Detached Memoranda," 562, and n. 54. Upon retirement, in an essay condemning as an unconstitutional "establishment" the use of public money to support congressional and military chaplains, *id.*, at 558–560,[6] he concluded that "[r]eligious proclamations by the Executive recommending thanksgivings & fasts are shoots from the same root with the

---

[5] Petitioners claim that the quoted passage shows that Jefferson regarded Thanksgiving proclamations as "coercive": "Thus, while one may disagree with Jefferson's view that a recommendatory Thanksgiving proclamation would nonetheless be coercive . . . one cannot disagree that Jefferson believed coercion to be a necessary element of a First Amendment violation." Brief for Petitioners 34. But this is wordplay. The "proscription" to which Jefferson referred was, of course, by the public and not the government, whose only action was a noncoercive recommendation. And one can call any act of endorsement a form of coercion, but only if one is willing to dilute the meaning of "coercion" until there is no meaning left. Jefferson's position straightforwardly contradicts the claim that a showing of "coercion," under any normal definition, is prerequisite to a successful Establishment Clause claim. At the same time, Jefferson's practice, like Madison's, see *infra*, at 16–17, sometimes diverged from principle, for he did include religious references in his inaugural speeches. See Inaugural Addresses of the Presidents of the United States 17, 22–23 (1989); see also *supra* note 3. Homer nodded.

Petitioners also seek comfort in a different passage of the same letter. Jefferson argued that presidential religious proclamations violate not just the Establishment Clause, but also the Tenth Amendment, for "what might be a right in a state government, was a violation of that right when assumed by another." Letter from Thomas Jefferson to Rev. S. Miller (Jan. 23, 1808), in 5 The Founders' Constitution 99 (P. Kurland & R. Lerner eds. 1987). Jefferson did not, however, restrict himself to the Tenth Amendment in condemning such proclamations by a national officer. I do not, in any event, understand petitioners to be arguing that the Establishment Clause is exclusively a structural provision mediating the respective powers of the State and National Governments. Such a position would entail the argument, which petitioners do not make, and which we would almost certainly reject, that incorporation of the Establishment Clause under the Fourteenth Amendment was erroneous.

[6] Madison found this practice "a palpable violation of . . . Constitutional principles." Madison's "Detached Memoranda" 558. Although he sat on the committee recommending the congressional chaplainship, see R. Cord, Separation of Church and State: Historical Fact and Current Fiction 23 (1988), he later insisted that "it was not with my approbation, that the deviation from [the immunity of Religion from civil jurisdiction] took place in Congs., when they appointed Chaplains, to be paid from the Natl. Treasury." Letter from J. Madison to E. Livingston (July 10, 1822), in 5 The Founders' Constitution, at 105.

legislative acts reviewed. Altho' recommendations only, they imply a religious agency, making no part of the trust delegated to political rulers." *Id.*, at 560. Explaining that "[t]he members of a Govt . . . can in no sense, be regarded as possessing an advisory trust from their Constituents in their religious capacities," *ibid.*, he further observed that the state necessarily freights all of its religious messages with political ones: "the idea of policy [is] associated with religion, whatever be the mode or the occasion, when a function of the latter is assumed by those in power." *Id.*, at 562 (footnote omitted).

Madison's failure to keep pace with his principles in the face of congressional pressure cannot erase the principles. He admitted to backsliding, and explained that he had made the content of his wartime proclamations inconsequential enough to mitigate much of their impropriety. See *ibid* ; see also Letter from J. Madison to E. Livingston (July 10, 1822), in 5 The Founders' Constitution, at 105. While his writings suggest mild variations in his interpretation of the Establishment Clause, Madison was no different in that respect from the rest of his political generation. That he expressed so much doubt about the constitutionality of religious proclamations, however, suggests a brand of separationism stronger even than that embodied in our traditional jurisprudence. So too does his characterization of public subsidies for legislative and military chaplains as unconstitutional "establishments," see *supra*, at 16–17, and n. 6, for the federal courts, however expansive their general view of the Establishment Clause, have upheld both practices. See *Marsh* v. *Chambers*, 463 U. S. 783 (1983) (legislative chaplains); *Katcoff* v. *Marsh*, 755 F. 2d 223 (CA2 1985) (military chaplains).

To be sure, the leaders of the young Republic engaged in some of the practices that separationists like Jefferson and Madison criticized. The First Congress did hire institutional chaplains, see *Marsh* v. *Chambers, supra*, at 788, and Presidents Washington and Adams unapologetically marked days of "public thanksgiving and prayer," see R. Cord, Separation of Church and State 53 (1988). Yet in the face of the separationist dissent, those practices prove, at best, that the Framers simply did not share a common understanding of the Establishment Clause, and, at worst, that they, like other politicians, could raise constitutional ideals one day and turn their backs on them the next. "Indeed, by 1787 the provisions of the state bills of rights had become what Madison called mere 'paper parchments'—expressions of the most laudable sentiments, observed as much in the breach as in practice." Kurland, The Origins of the Religion Clauses of the Constitution, 27 Wm. & Mary L. Rev. 839, 852 (1986) (footnote omitted). Sometimes the National Constitution fared no better. Ten years after proposing the First Amendment, Congress passed the Alien and Sedition Acts, measures patently unconstitutional by modern standards. If the early Congress's political actions were determinative, and not merely relevant, evidence of constitutional meaning, we would have to gut our current First Amendment doctrine to make room for political censorship.

While we may be unable to know for certain what the Framers meant by the Clause, we do know that, around the time of its ratification, a respectable body of opinion supported a considerably broader reading than petitioners urge upon us. This consistency with the textual considerations is enough to preclude fundamentally reexamining our settled law, and I am accordingly left with the task of considering whether the state practice at issue here violates our traditional understanding of the Clause's proscriptions.

III

While the Establishment Clause's concept of neutrality is not self-revealing, our recent cases have invested it with specific content: the state may not favor or endorse either religion generally over nonreligion or one religion over others. See, *e. g.*, *Allegheny County*, 492 U. S., at 589–594, 598–602; *Texas Monthly*, 489 U. S., at 17 (plurality opinion); *id.*, at 28 (BLACKMUN, J., concurring in judgment); *Edwards* v. *Aguillard*, 482 U. S., at 593; *School Dist. of Grand Rapids*, 473 U. S., at 389–392; *Wallace* v. *Jaffree*, 472 U. S., at 61; see also Laycock, Formal, Substantive, and Disaggregated Neutrality Toward Religion, 39 De Paul L. Rev. 993 (1990); *cf. Lemon* v. *Kurtzman*, 403 U. S. 602, 612–613 (1971). This principle against favoritism and endorsement has become the foundation of Establishment Clause jurisprudence, ensuring that religious belief is irrelevant to every citizen's standing in the political community, see *Allegheny County*, *supra*, at 594; J. Madison, Memorial and Remonstrance Against Religious Assessments (1785), in 5 The Founders' Constitution, at 82–83, and protecting religion from the demeaning effects of any governmental embrace, see *id.*, at 83. Now, as in the early Republic, "religion & Govt. will both exist in greater purity, the less they are mixed together." Letter from J. Madison to E. Livingston (10 July 1822), in 5 The Founders' Constitution, at 106. Our aspiration to religious liberty, embodied in the First Amendment, permits no other standard.

A

That government must remain neutral in matters of religion does not foreclose it from ever taking religion into account. The State may "accommodate" the free exercise of religion by relieving people from generally applicable rules that interfere with their religious callings. See, *e. g.*, *Corporation of Presiding Bishop of Church of Jesus Christ of Latter-Day Saints* v. *Amos*, 483 U. S. 327 (1987); see also *Sherbert* v. *Verner*, 374 U. S. 398 (1963). Contrary to the views of some,[7] such accommodation does not necessarily signify an official endorsement of religious observance over disbelief.

In everyday life, we routinely accommodate religious beliefs that we do not share. A Christian inviting an Orthodox Jew to lunch might take pains to choose a kosher restaurant; an atheist in a hurry might yield the right of way to an Amish man steering a horse-drawn carriage. In so acting, we express respect for, but not endorsement of, the fundamental values of others. We act without expressing a position on the theological merit of those values or of religious belief in general, and no one perceives us to have taken such a position.

The government may act likewise. Most religions encourage devotional practices that are at once crucial to the lives of believers and idiosyncratic in the eyes of nonadherents. By definition, secular rules of general application are drawn from the nonadherent's vantage and, consequently, fail to take such practices into account. Yet when enforcement of such rules cuts across religious sensibilities, as it often does, it puts those affected to the choice of taking sides between God and government. In such circumstances, accommodating religion reveals nothing beyond a recognition that general rules can unnecessarily offend the religious conscience when they offend the conscience of secular society not at all. Cf. *Welsh* v. *United States*, 398 U. S. 333, 340 (1970) (plurality opinion). Thus, in freeing the Native American Church from federal laws forbidding peyote use, see Drug Enforcement Administra-

tion Miscellaneous Exemptions, 21 C. F. R. § 1307.31 (1991), the government conveys no endorsement of peyote rituals, the Church, or religion as such; it simply respects the centrality of peyote to the lives of certain Americans. See Note, The Free Exercise Boundaries of Permissible Accommodation Under the Establishment Clause, 99 Yale L. J. 1127, 1135–1136 (1990).

B

Whatever else may define the scope of accommodation permissible under the Establishment Clause, one requirement is clear: accommodation must lift a discernible burden on the free exercise of religion. See *Allegheny County*, *supra*, at 601, n. 51; *id.*, at 631–632 (opinion of O'CONNOR, J.); *Corporation of Presiding Bishop*, *supra*, at 348 (O'CONNOR, J., concurring in judgment); see also *Texas Monthly*, *supra*, at 18, 18–19, n. 8 (plurality opinion); *Wallace* v. *Jaffree*, 472 U. S., at 57–58, n. 45. But see *Allegheny County*, *supra*, at 663, n. 2 (opinion of KENNEDY, J.). Concern for the position of religious individuals in the modern regulatory state cannot justify official solicitude for a religious practice unburdened by general rules; such gratuitous largesse would effectively favor religion over disbelief. By these lights one easily sees that, in sponsoring the graduation prayers at issue here, the State has crossed the line from permissible accommodation to unconstitutional establishment.

Religious students cannot complain that omitting prayers from their graduation ceremony would, in any realistic sense, "burden" their spiritual callings. To be sure, many of them invest this rite of passage with spiritual significance, but they may express their religious feelings about it before and after the ceremony. They may even organize a privately sponsored baccalaureate if they desire the company of likeminded students. Because they accordingly have no need for the machinery of the State to affirm their beliefs, the government's sponsorship of prayer at the graduation ceremony is most reasonably understood as an official endorsement of religion and, in this instance, of Theistic religion. One may fairly say, as one commentator has suggested, that the government brought prayer into the ceremony "precisely because some people want a symbolic affirmation that government approves and endorses their religion, and because many of the people who want this affirmation place little or no value on the costs to religious minorities." Laycock, Summary and Synthesis: The Crisis in Religious Liberty, 60 Geo. Wash. L. Rev. 841, 844 (1992).[8]

Petitioners would deflect this conclusion by arguing that graduation prayers are no different from presidential religious proclamations and similar official "acknowledgments" of religion in public life. But religious invocations in Thanksgiving Day addresses and the like, rarely noticed, ignored without effort, conveyed over an impersonal

---

[7]See, *e. g.*, *Thomas* v. *Review Bd. of Indiana Employment Security Div.*, 450 U. S. 707, 726 (1981) (REHNQUIST, J., dissenting); Choper, The Religion Clauses of the First Amendment: Reconciling the Conflict, 41 U. Pitt. L. Rev. 673, 685–686 (1980); see also *Walz* v. *Tax Comm'n of New York City*, 397 U. S. 664, 668–669 (1970); *Sherbert* v. *Verner*, 374 U. S. 398, 414, 416 (1963) (Stewart, J., concurring in result); *cf. Wallace* v. *Jaffree*, 472 U. S., at 83 (O'CONNOR, J., concurring in judgment).

[8]If the State had chosen its graduation day speakers according to wholly secular criteria, and if one of those speakers (not a state actor) had individually chosen to deliver a religious message, it would have been harder to attribute an endorsement of religion to the State. Cf. *Witters* v. *Washington Dept. of Services for Blind*, 474 U. S. 481 (1986). But that is not our case. Nor is this a case where the State has, without singling out religious groups or individuals, extended benefits to them as members of a broad class of beneficiaries defined by clearly secular criteria. See *Widmar* v. *Vincent*, 454 U. S. 263, 274–275 (1981); *Walz*, *supra*, at 696 (opinion of Harlan, J.) ("In any particular case the critical question is whether the circumference of legislation encircles a class so broad that it can be fairly concluded that religious institutions could be thought to fall within the natural perimeter"). Finally, this is not a case like *Marsh* v. *Chambers*, 463 U. S. 783 (1983), in which government officials invoke spiritual inspiration entirely for their own benefit without directing any religious message at the citizens they lead.

medium, and directed at no one in particular, inhabit a pallid zone worlds apart from official prayers delivered to a captive audience of public school students and their families. Madison himself respected the difference between the trivial and the serious in constitutional practice. Realizing that his contemporaries were unlikely to take the Establishment Clause seriously enough to forgo a legislative chaplainship, he suggested that "[r]ather than let this step beyond the landmarks of power have the effect of a legitimate precedent, it will be better to apply to it the legal aphorism de minimis non curat lex . . . ." Madison's "Detached Memoranda" 559; see also Letter from J. Madison to E. Livingston, 10 July 1822, in 5 The Founders' Constitution, at 105. But that logic permits no winking at the practice in question here. When public school officials, armed with the State's authority, convey an endorsement of religion to their students, they strike near the core of the Establishment Clause. However "ceremonial" their messages may be, they are flatly unconstitutional.

JUSTICE SCALIA, with whom THE CHIEF JUSTICE, JUSTICE WHITE, and JUSTICE THOMAS join, dissenting.

Three Terms ago, I joined an opinion recognizing that the Establishment Clause must be construed in light of the "[g]overnment policies of accommodation, acknowledgment, and support for religion [that] are an accepted part of our political and cultural heritage." That opinion affirmed that "the meaning of the Clause is to be determined by reference to historical practices and understandings." It said that "[a] test for implementing the protections of the Establishment Clause that, if applied with consistency, would invalidate longstanding traditions cannot be a proper reading of the Clause." *Allegheny County* v. *Greater Pittsburgh ACLU*, 492 U. S. 573, 657, 670 (1989) (KENNEDY, J., concurring in judgment in part and dissenting in part).

These views of course prevent me from joining today's opinion, which is conspicuously bereft of any reference to history. In holding that the Establishment Clause prohibits invocations and benedictions at public-school graduation ceremonies, the Court—with nary a mention that it is doing so—lays waste a tradition that is as old as public-school graduation ceremonies themselves, and that is a component of an even more longstanding American tradition of nonsectarian prayer to God at public celebrations generally. As its instrument of destruction, the bulldozer of its social engineering, the Court invents a boundless, and boundlessly manipulable, test of psychological coercion, which promises to do for the Establishment Clause what the *Durham* rule did for the insanity defense. See *Durham* v. *United States*, 94 U. S. App. D. C. 228, 214 F. 2d 862 (1954). Today's opinion shows more forcefully than volumes of argumentation why our Nation's protection, that fortress which is our Constitution, cannot possibly rest upon the changeable philosophical predilections of the Justices of this Court, but must have deep foundations in the historic practices of our people.

I

Justice Holmes' aphorism that "a page of history is worth a volume of logic," *New York Trust Co.* v. *Eisner*, 256 U. S. 345, 349 (1921), applies with particular force to our Establishment Clause jurisprudence. As we have recognized, our interpretation of the Establishment Clause should "compor[t] with what history reveals was the contemporaneous understanding of its guarantees." *Lynch* v. *Donnelly*, 465 U. S. 668, 673 (1984). "[T]he line we must draw between the permissible and the impermissible is one which accords with history and faithfully reflects the understanding of the Founding Fathers." *Abington School District* v. *Schempp*,

374 U. S. 203, 294 (1963) (Brennan, J., concurring). "[H]istorical evidence sheds light not only on what the draftsmen intended the Establishment Clause to mean, but also on how they thought that Clause applied" to contemporaneous practices. *Marsh* v. *Chambers*, 463 U. S. 783, 790 (1983). Thus, "[t]he existence from the beginning of the Nation's life of a practice, [while] not conclusive of its constitutionality . . . , is a fact of considerable import in the interpretation" of the Establishment Clause. *Walz* v. *Tax Comm'n of New York City*, 397 U. S. 664, 681 (1970) (Brennan, J., concurring).

The history and tradition of our Nation are replete with public ceremonies featuring prayers of thanksgiving and petition. Illustrations of this point have been amply provided in our prior opinions, see, *e.g.*, *Lynch*, *supra*, at 674–678; *Marsh*, *supra*, at 786–788; see also *Wallace* v. *Jaffree*, 472 U. S. 38, 100–103 (1985) (REHNQUIST, J., dissenting); *Engel* v. *Vitale*, 370 U. S. 421, 446–450, and n. 3 (1962) (Stewart, J., dissenting), but since the Court is so oblivious to our history as to suggest that the Constitution restricts "preservation and transmission of religious beliefs . . . to the private sphere," *ante*, at 10, it appears necessary to provide another brief account.

From our Nation's origin, prayer has been a prominent part of governmental ceremonies and proclamations. The Declaration of Independence, the document marking our birth as a separate people, "appeal[ed] to the Supreme Judge of the world for the rectitude of our intentions" and avowed "a firm reliance on the protection of divine Providence." In his first inaugural address, after swearing his oath of office on a Bible, George Washington deliberately made a prayer a part of his first official act as President:

> "it would be peculiarly improper to omit in this first official act my fervent supplications to that Almighty Being who rules over the universe, who presides in the councils of nations, and whose providential aids can supply every human defect, that His benediction may consecrate to the liberties and happiness of the people of the United States a Government instituted by themselves for these essential purposes." Inaugural Addresses of the Presidents of the United States 2 (1989).

Such supplications have been a characteristic feature of inaugural addresses ever since. Thomas Jefferson, for example, prayed in his first inaugural address: "may that Infinite Power which rules the destinies of the universe lead our councils to what is best, and give them a favorable issue for your peace and prosperity." *Id.*, at 17. In his second inaugural address, Jefferson acknowledged his need for divine guidance and invited his audience to join his prayer:

> "I shall need, too, the favor of that Being in whose hands we are, who led our fathers, as Israel of old, from their native land and planted them in a country flowing with all the necessaries and comforts of life; who has covered our infancy with His providence and our riper years with His wisdom and power, and to whose goodness I ask you to join in supplications with me that He will so enlighten the minds of your servants, guide their councils, and prosper their measures that whatsoever they do shall result in your good, and shall secure to you the peace, friendship, and approbation of all nations." *Id.*, at 22–23.

Similarly, James Madison, in his first inaugural address, placed his confidence

> "in the guardianship and guidance of that Almighty Being whose power regulates the destiny of nations,

whose blessings have been so conspicuously dispensed to this rising Republic, and to whom we are bound to address our devout gratitude for the past, as well as our fervent supplications and best hopes for the future." *Id.*, at 28.

Most recently, President Bush, continuing the tradition established by President Washington, asked those attending his inauguration to bow their heads, and made a prayer his first official act as President. *Id.*, at 346.

Our national celebration of Thanksgiving likewise dates back to President Washington. As we recounted in *Lynch*,

"The day after the First Amendment was proposed, Congress urged President Washington to proclaim 'a day of public thanksgiving and prayer, to be observed by acknowledging with grateful hearts the many and signal favours of Almighty God.' President Washington proclaimed November 26, 1789, a day of thanksgiving to 'offe[r] our prayers and supplications to the Great Lord and Ruler of Nations, and beseech him to pardon our national and other transgressions . . . .'" 465 U. S., at 675, n. 2 (citations omitted).

This tradition of Thanksgiving Proclamations—with their religious theme of prayerful gratitude to God—has been adhered to by almost every President. *Id.*, at 675, and nn. 2 and 3; *Wallace* v. *Jaffree, supra*, at 100–103 (REHNQUIST, J., dissenting).

The other two branches of the Federal Government also have a long-established practice of prayer at public events. As we detailed in *Marsh*, Congressional sessions have opened with a chaplain's prayer ever since the First Congress. 463 U. S., at 787–788. And this Court's own sessions have opened with the invocation "God save the United States and this Honorable Court" since the days of Chief Justice Marshall. 1 C. Warren, The Supreme Court in United States History 469 (1922).

In addition to this general tradition of prayer at public ceremonies, there exists a more specific tradition of invocations and benedictions at public-school graduation exercises. By one account, the first public-high-school graduation ceremony took place in Connecticut in July 1868—the very month, as it happens, that the Fourteenth Amendment (the vehicle by which the Establishment Clause has been applied against the States) was ratified—when "15 seniors from the Norwich Free Academy marched in their best Sunday suits and dresses into a church hall and waited through majestic music and long prayers." Brodinsky, Commencement Rites Obsolete? Not At All, A 10–Week Study Shows, Updating School Board Policies, Vol. 10, p. 3 (Apr. 1979). As the Court obliquely acknowledges in describing the "customary features" of high school graduations, *ante*, at 3–4, and as respondents do not contest, the invocation and benediction have long been recognized to be "as traditional as any other parts of the [school] graduation program and are widely established." H. McKown, Commencement Activities 56 (1931); see also Brodinsky, *supra*, at 5.

II

The Court presumably would separate graduation invocations and benedictions from other instances of public "preservation and transmission of religious beliefs" on the ground that they involve "psychological coercion." I find it a sufficient embarrassment that our Establishment Clause jurisprudence regarding holiday displays, see *Allegheny County* v. *Greater Pittsburgh ACLU*, 492 U. S. 573 (1989), has come to "requir[e] scrutiny more commonly associated with interior decorators than with the judiciary." *American Jewish Congress* v. *Chicago*, 827 F. 2d 120, 129 (Easterbrook, J., dissenting). But interior decorating is a rock-hard science compared to psychology practiced by amateurs. A few citations of "[r]esearch in psychology" that have no particular bearing upon the precise issue here, *ante*, at 14, cannot disguise the fact that the Court has gone beyond the realm where judges know what they are doing. The Court's argument that state officials have "coerced" students to take part in the invocation and benediction at graduation ceremonies is, not to put too fine a point on it, incoherent.

The Court identifies two "dominant facts" that it says dictate its ruling that invocations and benedictions at public-school graduation ceremonies violate the Establishment Clause. *Ante*, at 7. Neither of them is in any relevant sense true.

A

The Court declares that students' "attendance and participation in the [invocation and benediction] are in a fair and real sense obligatory." *Ibid.* But what exactly is this "fair and real sense"? According to the Court, students at graduation who want "to avoid the fact or appearance of participation," *ante*, at 8, in the invocation and benediction are *psychologically* obligated by "public pressure, as well as peer pressure, . . . to stand as a group or, at least, maintain respectful silence" during those prayers. *Ante*, at 13. This assertion—*the very linchpin of the Court's opinion*—is almost as intriguing for what it does not say as for what it says. It does not say, for example, that students are psychologically coerced to bow their heads, place their hands in a Dürer-like prayer position, pay attention to the prayers, utter "Amen," or in fact pray. (Perhaps further intensive psychological research remains to be done on these matters.) It claims only that students are psychologically coerced "to stand . . . or, at least, maintain respectful silence." *Ibid.* (emphasis added). Both halves of this disjunctive (*both* of which must amount to the fact or appearance of participation in prayer if the Court's analysis is to survive on its own terms) merit particular attention.

To begin with the latter: The Court's notion that a student who simply *sits* in "respectful silence" during the invocation and benediction (when all others are standing) has somehow joined—or would somehow be perceived as having joined—in the prayers is nothing short of ludicrous. We indeed live in a vulgar age. But surely "our social conventions," *ibid.*, have not coarsened to the point that anyone who does not stand on his chair and shout obscenities can reasonably be deemed to have assented to everything said in his presence. Since the Court does not dispute that students exposed to prayer at graduation ceremonies retain (despite "subtle coercive pressures," *ante*, at 8) the free will to sit, cf. *ante*, at 14, there is absolutely no basis for the Court's decision. It is fanciful enough to say that "a reasonable dissenter," standing head erect in a class of bowed heads, "could believe that the group exercise signified her own participation or approval of it," *ibid.* It is beyond the absurd to say that she could entertain such a belief while pointedly declining to rise.

But let us assume the very worst, that the nonparticipating graduate is "subtly coerced" . . . to stand! Even that half of the disjunctive does not remotely establish a "participation" (or an "appearance of participation") in a religious exercise. The Court acknowledges that "in our culture standing . . . can signify adherence to a view or simple respect for the views of others." *Ante*, at 13. (Much more often the latter than the former, I think, except perhaps in the proverbial town meeting, where one votes by standing.) But if it is a permissible inference that one who is standing is doing so simply out of respect for the prayers of others that are in progress, then how can it possibly be said that a "reasonable dissenter . . . could believe that the group exercise signified her own participation or approval"?

Quite obviously, it cannot. I may add, moreover, that maintaining respect for the religious observances of others is a fundamental civic virtue that government (including the public schools) can and should cultivate—so that even if it were the case that the displaying of such respect might be mistaken for taking part in the prayer, I would deny that the dissenter's interest in avoiding *even the false appearance of participation* constitutionally trumps the government's interest in fostering respect for religion generally.

The opinion manifests that the Court itself has not given careful consideration to its test of psychological coercion. For if it had, how could it observe, with no hint of concern or disapproval, that students stood for the Pledge of Allegiance, which immediately preceded Rabbi Gutterman's invocation? *Ante*, at 4. The government can, of course, no more coerce political orthodoxy than religious orthodoxy. *West Virginia Board of Education* v. *Barnette*, 319 U. S. 624, 642 (1943). Moreover, since the Pledge of Allegiance has been revised since *Barnette* to include the phrase "under God," recital of the Pledge would appear to raise the same Establishment Clause issue as the invocation and benediction. If students were psychologically coerced to remain standing during the invocation, they must also have been psychologically coerced, moments before, to stand for (and thereby, in the Court's view, take part in or appear to take part in) the Pledge. Must the Pledge therefore be barred from the public schools (both from graduation ceremonies and from the classroom)? In *Barnette* we held that a public-school student could not be compelled to *recite* the Pledge; we did not even hint that she could not be compelled to observe respectful silence—indeed, even to *stand* in respectful silence—when those who wished to recite it did so. Logically, that ought to be the next project for the Court's bulldozer.

I also find it odd that the Court concludes that high school graduates may not be subjected to this supposed psychological coercion, yet refrains from addressing whether "mature adults" may. *Ante*, at 14. I had thought that the reason graduation from high school is regarded as so significant an event is that it is generally associated with transition from adolescence to young adulthood. Many graduating seniors, of course, are old enough to vote. Why, then, does the Court treat them as though they were first-graders? Will we soon have a jurisprudence that distinguishes between mature and immature adults?

B

The other "dominant fac[t]" identified by the Court is that "[s]tate officials direct the performance of a formal religious exercise" at school graduation ceremonies. *Ante*, at 7. "Direct[ing] the performance of a formal religious exercise" has a sound of liturgy to it, summoning up images of the principal directing acolytes where to carry the cross, or showing the rabbi where to unroll the Torah. A Court professing to be engaged in a "delicate and fact-sensitive" line-drawing, *ante*, at 18, would better describe what it means as "prescribing the content of an invocation and benediction." But even that would be false. All the record shows is that principals of the Providence public schools, acting within their delegated authority, have invited clergy to deliver invocations and benedictions at graduations; and that Principal Lee invited Rabbi Gutterman, provided him a two-page flyer, prepared by the National Conference of Christians and Jews, giving general advice on inclusive prayer for civic occasions, and advised him that his prayers at graduation should be nonsectarian. How these facts can fairly be transformed into the charges that Principal Lee "directed and controlled the content of [Rabbi Gutterman's] prayer," *ante*, at 9, that school officials "monitor prayer,"

ante, at 10, and attempted to "'compose official prayers,'" *ante*, at 9, and that the "government involvement with religious activity in this case is pervasive," *ante*, at 7, is difficult to fathom. The Court identifies nothing in the record remotely suggesting that school officials have ever drafted, edited, screened or censored graduation prayers, or that Rabbi Gutterman was a mouthpiece of the school officials.

These distortions of the record are, of course, not harmless error: without them the Court's solemn assertion that the school officials could reasonably be perceived to be "enforc[ing] a religious orthodoxy," *ante*, at 13, would ring as hollow as it ought.

III

The deeper flaw in the Court's opinion does not lie in its wrong answer to the question whether there was state-induced "peer-pressure" coercion; it lies, rather, in the Court's making violation of the Establishment Clause hinge on such a precious question. The coercion that was a hallmark of historical establishments of religion was coercion of religious orthodoxy and of financial support *by force of law and threat of penalty.* Typically, attendance at the state church was required; only clergy of the official church could lawfully perform sacraments; and dissenters, if tolerated, faced an array of civil disabilities. L. Levy, The Establishment Clause 4 (1986). Thus, for example, in the colony of Virginia, where the Church of England had been established, ministers were required by law to conform to the doctrine and rites of the Church of England; and all persons were required to attend church and observe the Sabbath, were tithed for the public support of Anglican ministers, and were taxed for the costs of building and repairing churches. *Id.*, at 3–4.

The Establishment Clause was adopted to prohibit such an establishment of religion at the federal level (and to protect state establishments of religion from federal interference). I will further acknowledge for the sake of argument that, as some scholars have argued, by 1790 the term "establishment" had acquired an additional meaning—"financial support of religion generally, by public taxation"—that reflected the development of "general or multiple" establishments, not limited to a single church. *Id.*, at 8–9. But that would still be an establishment coerced *by force of law.* And I will further concede that our constitutional tradition, from the Declaration of Independence and the first inaugural address of Washington, quoted earlier, down to the present day, has, with a few aberrations, see *Holy Trinity Church* v. *United States*, 143 U. S. 457 (1892), ruled out of order government-sponsored endorsement of religion—even when no legal coercion is present, and indeed even when no ersatz, "peer-pressure" psycho-coercion is present—where the endorsement is sectarian, in the sense of specifying details upon which men and women who believe in a benevolent, omnipotent Creator and Ruler of the world, are known to differ (for example, the divinity of Christ). But there is simply no support for the proposition that the officially sponsored nondenominational invocation and benediction read by Rabbi Gutterman—with no one legally coerced to recite them—violated the Constitution of the United States. To the contrary, they are so characteristically American they could have come from the pen of George Washington or Abraham Lincoln himself.

Thus, while I have no quarrel with the Court's general proposition that the Establishment Clause "guarantees that government may not coerce anyone to support or participate in religion or its exercise," *ante*, at 8, I see no warrant for expanding the concept of coercion beyond acts backed by threat of penalty—a brand of coercion that, happily, is readily discernible to those of us who have made a career of reading the disciples of Blackstone rather than of Freud. The Framers were indeed opposed to coercion of religious worship by the National Government; but, as their own sponsorship of nonsectarian prayer in public events demonstrates, they understood that "[s]peech is not coercive; the listener may do as he likes." *American Jewish Congress* v. *Chicago*, 827 F. 2d, at 132 (Easterbrook, J., dissenting).

This historical discussion places in revealing perspective the Court's extravagant claim that the State has "for all practical purposes," *ante*, at 9, and "in every practical sense," *ante*, at 18, compelled students to participate in prayers at graduation. Beyond the fact, stipulated to by the parties, that attendance at graduation is voluntary, there is nothing in the record to indicate that failure of attending students to take part in the invocation or benediction was subject to any penalty or discipline. Contrast this with, for example, the facts of *Barnette*: Schoolchildren were required by law to recite the Pledge of Allegiance; failure to do so resulted in expulsion, threatened the expelled child with the prospect of being sent to a reformatory for criminally inclined juveniles, and subjected his parents to prosecution (and incarceration) for causing delinquency. 319 U. S., at 629-630. To characterize the "subtle coercive pressures," *ante*, at 8, allegedly present here as the "practical" equivalent of the legal sanctions in *Barnette* is . . . well, let me just say it is not a "delicate and fact-sensitive" analysis.

The Court relies on our "school prayer" cases, *Engel* v. *Vitale*, 370 U. S. 421 (1962), and *Abington School District* v. *Schempp*, 374 U. S. 203 (1963). *Ante*, at 13. But whatever the merit of those cases, they do not support, much less compel, the Court's psycho-journey. In the first place, *Engel* and *Schempp* do not constitute an exception to the rule, distilled from historical practice, that public ceremonies may include prayer, see *supra*, at 3–6; rather, they simply do not fall within the scope of the rule (for the obvious reason that school instruction is not a public ceremony). Second, we have made clear our understanding that school prayer occurs within a framework in which legal coercion to attend school (*i. e.*, coercion under threat of penalty) provides the ultimate backdrop. In *Schempp*, for example, we emphasized that the prayers were "prescribed as part of the curricular activities of students who are *required by law* to attend school." 374 U. S., at 223 (emphasis added). *Engel's* suggestion that the school-prayer program at issue there—which permitted students "to remain silent or be excused from the room," 370 U. S., at 430—involved "indirect coercive pressure," *id.*, at 431, should be understood against this backdrop of legal coercion. The question whether the opt-out procedure in *Engel* sufficed to dispel the coercion resulting from the mandatory attendance requirement is quite different from the question whether forbidden coercion exists in an environment *utterly devoid of legal compulsion*. And finally, our school-prayer cases turn in part on the fact that the classroom is inherently an instructional setting, and daily prayer there—where parents are not present to counter "the students' emulation of teachers as role models and the children's susceptibility to peer pressure," *Edwards* v. *Aguillard*, 482 U. S. 578, 584 (1987)—might be thought to raise special concerns regarding state interference with the liberty of parents to direct the religious upbringing of their children: "Families entrust public schools with the education of their children, but condition their trust on the understanding that the classroom will not purposely be used to advance religious views that may conflict with the private beliefs of the student and his or her family." *Ibid.*; see *Pierce* v. *Society of Sisters*, 268 U. S. 510, 534–535 (1925). Voluntary prayer at graduation—a one-time

ceremony at which parents, friends and relatives are present—can hardly be thought to raise the same concerns.

IV

Our religion-clause jurisprudence has become bedeviled (so to speak) by reliance on formulaic abstractions that are not derived from, but positively conflict with, our long-accepted constitutional traditions. Foremost among these has been the so-called *Lemon* test, see *Lemon* v. *Kurtzman*, 403 U. S. 602, 612–613 (1971), which has received well-earned criticism from many members of this Court. See, *e.g.*, *Allegheny County*, 492 U. S., at 655–656 (opinion of KENNEDY, J.); *Edwards* v. *Aguillard*, *supra*, at 636–640 (1987) (SCALIA, J., dissenting); *Wallace* v. *Jaffree*, 472 U. S. at 108–112 (REHNQUIST, J., dissenting); *Aguilar* v. *Felton*, 473 U. S. 402, 426–430 (1985) (O'CONNOR, J., dissenting); *Roemer* v. *Maryland Bd. of Public Works*, 426 U. S. 736, 768–769 (1976) (WHITE, J., concurring in judgment). The Court today demonstrates the irrelevance of *Lemon* by essentially ignoring it, see *ante*, at 7, and the interment of that case may be the one happy byproduct of the Court's otherwise lamentable decision. Unfortunately, however, the Court has replaced *Lemon* with its psycho-coercion test, which suffers the double disability of having no roots whatever in our people's historic practice, and being as infinitely expandable as the reasons for psychotherapy itself.

Another happy aspect of the case is that it is only a jurisprudential disaster and not a practical one. Given the odd basis for the Court's decision, invocations and benedictions will be able to be given at public-school graduations next June, as they have for the past century and a half, so long as school authorities make clear that anyone who abstains from screaming in protest does not necessarily participate in the prayers. All that is seemingly needed is an announcement, or perhaps a written insertion at the beginning of the graduation Program, to the effect that, while all are asked to rise for the invocation and benediction, none is compelled to join in them, nor will be assumed, by rising, to have done so. That obvious fact recited, the graduates and their parents may proceed to thank God, as Americans have always done, for the blessings He has generously bestowed on them and on their country.

               * * *

The reader has been told much in this case about the personal interest of Mr. Weisman and his daughter, and very little about the personal interests on the other side. They are not inconsequential. Church and state would not be such a difficult subject if religion were, as the Court apparently thinks it to be, some purely personal avocation that can be indulged entirely in secret, like pornography, in the privacy of one's room. For most believers it is *not* that, and has never been. Religious men and women of almost all denominations have felt it necessary to acknowledge and beseech the blessing of God as a people, and not just as individuals, because they believe in the "protection of divine Providence," as the Declaration of Independence put it, not just for individuals but for societies; because they believe God to be, as Washington's first Thanksgiving Proclamation put it, the "Great Lord and Ruler of Nations." One can believe in the effectiveness of such public worship, or one can deprecate and deride it. But the longstanding American tradition of prayer at official ceremonies displays with unmistakable clarity that the Establishment Clause does not forbid the government to accommodate it.

The narrow context of the present case involves a community's celebration of one of the milestones in its young citizens' lives, and it is a bold step for this Court to seek to banish from that occasion, and from thousands of similar celebrations throughout this land, the expression of gratitude to God that a majority of the community wishes to make. The issue before us today is not the abstract philosophical question whether the alternative of frustrating this desire of a religious majority is to be preferred over the alternative of imposing "psychological coercion," or a feeling of exclusion, upon nonbelievers. Rather, the question is *whether a mandatory choice in favor of the former has been imposed by the United States Constitution.* As the age-old practices of our people show, the answer to that question is not at all in doubt.

I must add one final observation: The founders of our Republic knew the fearsome potential of sectarian religious belief to generate civil dissension and civil strife. And they also knew that nothing, absolutely nothing, is so inclined to foster among religious believers of various faiths a toleration—no, an affection—for one another than voluntarily joining in prayer together, to the God whom they all worship and seek. Needless to say, no one should be compelled to do that, but it is a shame to deprive our public culture of the opportunity, and indeed the encouragement, for people to do it voluntarily. The Baptist or Catholic who heard and joined in the simple and inspiring prayers of Rabbi Gutterman on this official and patriotic occasion was inoculated from religious bigotry and prejudice in a manner that can not be replicated. To deprive our society of that important unifying mechanism, in order to spare the nonbeliever what seems to me the minimal inconvenience of standing or even sitting in respectful nonparticipation, is as senseless in policy as it is unsupported in law.

For the foregoing reasons, I dissent.

CHARLES J. COOPER, Washington, D.C. (MICHAEL A. CARVIN, PETER J. FERRARA, ROBERT J. CYNKAR, SHAW, PITTMAN, POTTS & TROWBRIDGE, JOSEPH A. ROTELLA, and JAY ALAN SEKULOW, on the briefs) for petitioner; KENNETH W. STARR, Solicitor General (STUART M. GERSON, Asst. Atty. Gen., JOHN G. ROBERTS JR., Dpty. Sol. Gen., JOHN O. McGINNIS, Dpty. Asst. Atty. Gen., RICHARD H. SEAMON, Asst. to Sol. Gen., on the briefs) for U.S. as amicus curiae; SANDRA A. BLANDING, Warwick, R.I. (REVENS, BLANDING, REVENS & ST. PIERRE, STEVEN R. SHAPIRO, and JOHN A. POWELL, on the briefs) for respondent.

Supreme Court of the United States

October Term, 1961

No. 468

————o————

In the Matter of the Application

of

STEVEN I. ENGEL, DANIEL LICHTENSTEIN, MONROE LERNER, LENORE LYONS, and LAWRENCE ROTH,

Petitioners,

against

WILLIAM J. VITALE, JR., PHILIP J. FREED, MARY HARTE, ANNE BIRCH and RICHARD SAUNDERS, constituting the Board of Education of Union Free School District Number Nine, New Hyde Park, New York,

Respondents,

directing them to discontinue a certain school practice

and

HENRY HOLLENBERG, ROSE LEVINE, MARTIN ABRAMS, HELEN SWANSON, WALTER F. GIBB, JANE EHLEN, RALPH B. WEBB, VIRGINIA ZIMMERMAN, VIRGINIA DAVIS, VIOLET S. COX, EVELYN KOSTER, IRENE O'ROURKE, ROSEMARIE PETELENZ, DANIEL J. REEHIL, THOMAS DELANEY and EDWARD L. MACFARLANE,

Intervenors-Respondents.

————o————

BRIEF FOR PETITIONERS

Opinions Below

The opinion of the Special Term of the Supreme Court of the State of New York, Nassau County (R. 50-116), is reported at 18 Misc. 2d 659, 191 N. Y. S. 2d 453. The majority and concurring opinions of the Appellate Division of the Supreme Court of the State of New York, Second

Department (R. 123-40), are reported at 11 App. Div. 2d 340, 206 N. Y. S. 2d 183. The majority, concurring and dissenting opinions of the Court of Appeals of the State of New York (R. 142-55) are reported at 10 N. Y. 2d 174, 184 N. Y. S. 2d 659, 176 N. E. 2d 579.

Jurisdiction of This Court

The jurisdiction of this Court is invoked under 28 U. S. C. § 1257(3).

The judgment of the Court of Appeals was announced on July 7, 1961 (R. 156-7), and entered on October 23, 1961 (R. 158-9). The petition for a writ of certiorari was filed on October 4, 1961, and granted on December 3, 1961 (R. 160).

Constitutional and Statutory Provisions Involved

The constitutional provisions involved in this case are the First and Fourteenth Amendments.

The pertinent part of the First Amendment reads as follows:

> "Congress shall make no law respecting an establishment of religion, or prohibiting the free exercise thereof; * * *."

Section 1 of the Fourteenth Amendment reads as follows:

> "All persons born or naturalized in the United States, and subject to the jurisdiction thereof, are citizens of the United States and of the State wherein they reside. No State shall make or enforce any law which shall abridge the privileges or immunities of citizens of the United States; nor shall any State deprive any person of life, liberty, or property, without due process of law; nor deny to any person within its jurisdiction the equal protection of the laws."

Strictly speaking, there are no statutory provisions involved in this case. A critical part of the State action under consideration, however, is a resolution of respondents, as the Board of Education of Union Free School District Number 9, New Hyde Park, New York, which was adopted at an official meeting on July 8, 1958, and is recorded in the minutes of the meeting as follows (R. 40):

> "Mrs. Harte moved, seconded by Mr. Saunders, that the regents prayer be said daily in our schools. Motion carried by majority vote, Mr. Fried voted 'nay.'
> The Board of Education gave direction to the District Principal that this be instituted as a daily procedure to follow the Salute to the flag."

Question Presented

Does not State action requiring that a prayer to God, composed by State officials, acting in their official capacity, be said as a daily procedure, following the Pledge of Allegiance to the Flag, in all the public schools of a local school district, violate the guarantee of separation of church and state in the Establishment Clause of the First Amendment to the United States Constitution, made applicable to the States by the Fourteenth Amendment?

Statement of the Case

1. The Facts

Petitioners, five citizens of the State of New York and taxpayers residing in Union Free School District Number 9, New Hyde Park, New York, where their children attend the local public schools, seek to compel respondents, the five members of the local board of education, to discontinue the saying of a prayer now required to be said in those schools (R. 11-13). They are opposed by sixteen intervenors, as well as by respondents (R. 43-7).

Two of the petitioners are of the Jewish faith. One belongs to the Society for Ethical Culture. One is a member of the Unitarian Church. And one is a non-believer (R. 11-12). All are subject to the Education Law of New York, which requires parents to cause their children between the ages of seven and sixteen years to attend a course of full-time day instruction, under penalty of punishment by fine or imprisonment for failure to comply (R. 13, 61).

The prayer under consideration is required to be said pursuant to a resolution adopted by respondents at an official meeting on July 8, 1958 (R. 13). The minutes of the meeting show that, by a vote of 4-1, respondents resolved "that the regents prayer be said daily in our schools," and "gave direction to the District Principal that this be instituted as a daily procedure to follow the Salute to the flag" (R. 40).

The name of the prayer derives from the fact that it was composed by the Board of Regents, the governing body of the Department of Education of the State of New York, and recommended in a statement of belief entitled "The Regents Statement on Moral and Spiritual Training in the Schools," which was unanimously adopted at the Regents' regular meeting on November 30, 1951 (R. 13-14, 28-9, 390), The words of the prayer are as follows (R. 14):

> "Almighty God, we acknowledge our dependence upon Thee, and we beg Thy blessings upon us, our parents, our teachers and our country."

Pursuant to respondents' resolution of July 8, 1958, the prayer is said aloud, daily, at the commencement of the school day, in each class of each public school within the local school district (R. 14, 66). It is said in the presence of the teacher, and is either led by the teacher or by a student selected by the teacher (R. 14, 24-7, 66). Though respondents' resolution does not so provide, respondents claim that they have always directed principals and teachers not to force or to encourage any child to join in the prayer (R. 27, 66).

Prior to this case, respondents claim to have received only one request that a child be excused from saying the prayer, and they claim to have respected that request (R. 26-7, 66), but Special Term, the only court below which considered the question, has found, as a matter of fact, that the saying of the prayer and the manner and setting in which it is said are contrary to the religions and religious practices of those petitioners who have a religion and contrary to the beliefs held by the petitioner who professes none (R. 15, 66-7).

2. The Proceedings Below

This case began in January, 1959, when petitioners instituted a proceeding at Special Term, under Article 78 of the Civil Practice Act of New York, in which they requested an order in the nature of mandamus directing respondents to discontinue the saying of the prayer (R. 9-10, 54). Such a proceeding, under New York law, is summary and may be decided on papers, and this one was. The "facts" in this case, as stated above, have been taken from those allegations in the petition which have not been explicitly denied in the answer of respondents or the accompanying affidavit of respondent Vitale, a procedure followed by Special Term in arriving at its decision (R. 65-7).

The relief requested by petitioners was denied by Special Term, but the case was remanded to respondents, as the local board of education, for further proceedings in accordance with the opinion expressed by the court that certain features of the procedure connected with the prayer were objectionable because "compulsory" (R. 6-8, 105-9). From this interlocutory order, an appeal was taken by petitioners to the Appellate Division, where the order was unanimously affirmed (R. 123-40).

The case proceeded no further until the proceedings provided for in the interlocutory order were taken by respondents. These consisted of adopting a set of regulations at an official meeting on September 3, 1959, transmitting them to the principals and teachers in the local school district, and sending a letter to each parent and taxpayer in the district (R. 170-3).

The regulations were as follows (R. 171-2):

> "1. Neither teachers nor any school authority shall comment on participation or non-participation in the exercise nor suggest or request that any posture or language be used or dress be worn or be not used or not worn.
>
> 2. Provision is to be made for those children who are to be excused from participating or from the room during the prayer exercise.
>
> 3. Any child may be excused on written request of the parent or legal guardian and all parents will be so advised that the request should be so made, addressed to the principal of the school which the child attends."

The critical part of the letter was intended to supplement regulation number "3" (R. 172-3):

> "Any parent or guardian who does not wish his child to say the prayer is requested to write a letter to the principal of the school his child attends, indicating whether he wants his child excused from the room or to remain silent in the room while the prayer is being said."

Thereafter, a motion was made by respondents at Special Term for a final order dismissing the petition on the basis of the proceedings taken pursuant to the interlocutory order (R. 169). In an affidavit in support of this motion, respondent Freed stated that, although respondents had received requests that children be excused from saying the prayer, they had received none requesting that children be excused from the classroom, and they had decided "to defer any decision with respect to the exact provision to be made for any such children until such request is made * * * " (R. 173).

The final order was granted, and an appeal taken therefrom directly to the Court of Appeals (R. 164-8). That appeal brought into question the validity of the interlocutory order and its affirmance by the Appellate Division. The interlocutory order was sustained and the final order affirmed by a vote of 5-2 (R. 142-57).

Summary of Argument

1. The State action under consideration violates the Establishment Clause of the First Amendment.

(a) The Establishment Clause has been made applicable by the Fourteenth Amendment to acts of State and local officials, and it prohibits any such acts respecting an establishment of religion, and not merely an establishment of a church or sect. "Religion" within the meaning of the Establishment Clause may be nothing more nor less than a single religious belief, such as belief in the existence of God.

(b) The Regents' Prayer is sectarian and denominational, since it includes a declaration of belief in the existence of God, which is a belief not shared by several faiths in this country, including the Society for Ethical Culture, to which one petitioner belongs. It also involves belief in a set form of worship and belief in the practice of asking God's blessings on behalf of the worshipper. Moreover, Special Term found, as a fact, that the prayer is contrary to the religions of petitioners who have a religion and to the beliefs of petitioner who professes none.

(c) The Regents' Prayer is not part of any national "tradition" or "heritage," although prayer in general may be, since the Regents' Prayer was composed by laymen who are State officials, in their official capacity, in the hope of finding a form of worship acceptable to all. Such a prayer has no tradition behind it in this country, and is not believed to be in use in the public schools of any State outside the State of New York.

(d) The significance of the Regents' Prayer should not be judged by its brevity or simplicity, but by the importance of the beliefs involved in it and the significance of a determination that prayers may be composed by State officials and recited under their direct supervision in public schools. The prayer involved in this case should be judged by the fact that it is part of a recognized drive in this country to introduce religious education and observances in public schools.

(e) The essential and primary purpose and effect of the State action under consideration is to aid religion. The form of the State action, and, specifically, the fact that it may not be "instruction", is immaterial. The statement of belief of the Board of Regents makes it clear that the purpose and intended effect of the Regents in recommending the prayer, and of respondents in instituting it as a daily procedure in the public schools of the local school district, is to promote belief in God. The means or form of achieving that purpose, if not "instruction", is a higher or more extreme form of religious activity.

(f) The factual situation in this case is basically the same as that in *McCollum*. The State action under consideration permits, even requires, religious activity in public school buildings during school hours; it requires pupils not participating in the religious activity to remain in school; and it involves the use of tax-supported buildings to aid religion.

(g) The only factual difference between the present case and *McCollum* makes this case a stronger one for application of the doctrine of separation. Whereas in *McCollum* State officials merely cooperated with religious ministers, here they perform the functions of religious ministers. This violates the most fundamental concept in the doctrine of separation, as developed in this country, which is that civil magistrates have no competence in, or jurisdiction over, religious matters.

(h) The element of coercion in this case is stronger than in *McCollum*. The impact of the compulsory school system is, if anything, stronger here because pupils are not merely compelled to attend school; they are compelled to say the Regents' Prayer unless excused. Morever, as the record shows, because of the brevity of the prayer and its recitation in conjunction with the Pledge of Allegiance, even those pupils who are excused do not leave the classroom. Most important of all, the influence on the minds of pupils necessarily exerted by the fact that education officials, including their teachers, advocate certain religious beliefs cannot be avoided by permitting the pupils to leave their classroom, or even the school building.

(i) The State action under consideration rejects the belief on which the "Founding Fathers" built our national government, belief in the necessity for absolute separation of church and state. It threatens not merely to breach the "wall of separation", but to undermine it completely.

Argument

1. **The State action in this case violates the guarantee of separation of church and state in the Establishment Clause of the First Amendment, made applicable to the States by the Fourteenth Amendment.**

(a) Certain propositions are beyond the area of legitimate dispute.

Petitioners assume that certain propositions are now beyond the area of legitimate dispute in this Court.

(1) We assume that the Establishment Clause of the First Amendment, though in terms applicable only to laws enacted by Congress, has been made applicable by the Fourteenth Amendment to the laws of a State government and to the acts of State and local officials which have the force of such laws (*Cantwell* v. *State of Connecticut,* 310 U. S. 296, 303; *Everson* v. *Board of Education,* 330 U. S. 1, 5; *People of State of Illinois* ex rel. *McCollum* v. *Board of Education,* 333 U. S. 203, 210; *McGowan* v. *State of Maryland,* 366 U. S. 420, 429; *Torcaso* v. *Watkins,* 367 U. S. 488, 492).

(2) We assume that the Establishment Clause prohibits more than laws establishing a church or sect; it bars any law *respecting an establishment of religion* (*People of State of Illinois* ex rel. *McCollum* v. *Board of Education, supra; Torcaso* v. *Watkins, supra; Everson* v. *Board of Education, supra,* 330 U. S. at pages 14-15; *McGowan* v. *State of Maryland, supra,* 366 U. S. at pages 441-2).

This second proposition does not appear to have been accepted by the majority in the Court of Appeals. In the opinion of the court written by Chief Judge Desmond, the word "law" and the word "respecting", which appear in the Establishment Clause, are treated as if they were not part of the clause at all (R. 143):

"Saving this simple prayer may be, according to the broadest possible dictionary definition, an act of 'religion', *but when the Founding Fathers prohibited an 'establishment of religion' they were referring to official adoption of, or favor to, one or more sects.*" (Emphasis added.)

(3) Lastly, petitioners assume that the word "religion", as used in the First Amendment may mean nothing more nor less than a single religious belief, such as belief in the existence of God (*Torcaso* v. *Watkins, supra*).

This, too, does not seem to have been accepted by the majority below. Running through both the opinion of Chief Judge Desmond and the concurring opinion of Judge Froessel is the notion that belief in the existence of God is so elementary or "essential" that it is outside the scope of religion, at least as that word is used in the First Amendment. The notion is stated in the opinion of Judge Froessel as follows (R. 145):

"History and common experience teach us that the perception of a Supreme Being, commonly called God, is experienced in the lives of most human beings. Some, it is true, escape it, or think they do for a time. In any event, that perception is manifest, independent of any particular religion or church, and has become the foundation of virtually every recognized religious faith—indeed, the common denominator. *One may earnestly believe in God, without being attached to any particular religion or church. Hence a rule permitting public school children, willing to do so, to acknowledge their dependence upon Him, and to invoke His blessings, can hardly be called a 'law respecting an establishment of religion'* or 'prohibiting the free exercise thereof' in transgression of the First Amendment, which in nowise prohibits the recognition of God, or laws respecting such recognition." (Emphasis added.)

Any such notion, however, would seem to have been rejected by this Court in the recent *Torcaso* case, *supra,* where the only "religion" under consideration was belief in the existence of God. In *Torcaso,* Maryland's refusal to issue to an individual, otherwise qualified, a commission to serve as a notary public because he would not declare his belief in God was held by this Court to be a violation of the First Amendment. The State action was characterized in the opinion of the Court written by Mr. Justice Black as follows (367 U. S. at page 490):

> "The power and authority of the State of Maryland thus is put on the side of one particular sort of believers—those who are willing to say they believe in 'the existence of God'."

The State action under consideration in *Torcaso* may not be comparable to that in the present case in all respects. If, however, a declaration of belief in the existence of God was a matter of religion in *Torcaso,* petitioners respectfully submit that a prayer including precisely the same declaration must be so here.

(b) The Regents' Prayer is sectarian and denominational.

The corollary assumption in the opinions of Chief Judge Desmond and Judge Froessel that the Regents' Prayer is non-sectarian and non-denominational would seem to be contrary to a fact judicially noted by this Court in the *Torcaso* case and to one of the few findings of fact made by the court of first instance in this case.

In the opinion of this Court in *Torcaso,* the observation was made that belief in the existence of God is not among the tenets of several faiths practiced in this country. Mr. Justice Black specifically noted that one such faith was "Ethical Culture," the faith of one of the petitioners in the present case (367 U. S. at page 495, note 11).

Moreover, the opinion of Special Term, the only court below which considered the question, contains the express finding of fact that the saying of the Regents' Prayer and the manner and setting in which it is said are contrary to the religions and religious practices of all the petitioners who have a religion, as well as to the beliefs of the petitioner who professes none (R. 66-7). Special Term held that such a finding necessarily resulted from respondents' failure to challenge the good faith of petitioners' claim that the prayer was contrary to their beliefs (R. 66-7).

Despite this finding, it is true, Special Term subsequently concluded that the prayer was non-sectarian (R. 113):

> "The fact that the prayer and the manner of its saying may not conform to all of the tenets of the Jewish, Unitarian and Ethical Culture groups, or of any other group, does not mean that the prayer is sectarian."

Petitioners respectfully submit, however, that Special Term's conclusion is both unwarranted and self-contradictory. We submit that, by definition, a prayer which conforms to *all* of the tenets of one or more faiths and only to *some,* but not all, of the tenets of others, is sectarian and denominational, particularly if the tenets to which it does not conform are important. We would assume that even respondents and intervenors would agree that belief in the existence of God is important. The Regents' Prayer also involves belief in a set form of worship and belief in the practice of asking God's blessings on behalf of the worshipper.

(c) The Regents' Prayer is not part of any national "tradition" or "heritage."

The majority and concurring opinions of the Court of Appeals, the concurring opinion of the Appellate Division and the opinion of Special Term refer to the Regents' Prayer as part of a national "tradition" or "heritage"

(R. 70, 132, 144). Petitioners respectfully submit that, although *prayer in general* may be an integral part of our national tradition and heritage, a prayer such as that involved in this case, which has been composed by laymen who are State officials, acting in their official capacity, in the hope of finding a form of worship acceptable to all, is most certainly not part of any national tradition or heritage.

In this respect it is significant that, although the well-documented opinion of Special Term begins by stating that ''the attempt to find a commonly acceptable prayer is not new'' (R. 51), the opinion cites only two instances in which the attempt was made, one, by Benjamin Franklin, being merely an attempt to modify the Lord's Prayer.

The other attempt noted in the opinion of Special Term was recorded by James Madison in a letter to Edward Everett on March 19, 1823, and it was made by William Livingston, before he became Governor of New Jersey, at a time when he was merely a member of the Committee of Trustees for the Lottery Fund for King's College (now Columbia University). In 1753, Livingston composed a prayer which he thought might be said by all of the Protestant students at King's College, when that institution should be built. The prayer was never put in use, and it was roundly criticized in the newspaper in which it was originally published.*

This is what Madison had to say about Livingston's prayer:

> ''I recollect to have seen many years ago, a project of a prayer by Governor Livingston, father of the present judge, intended to comprehend and conciliate college students of every Christian denomination, by a form composed wholly of texts and phrases of Scripture. If a trial of the expedient was

---

* MAHONEY, THE RELATION OF THE STATE TO RELIGIOUS EDUCATION IN EARLY NEW YORK, 1633-1825 (1941), pp. 74-6.

ever made, it must have failed, notwithstanding its winning aspect, from the single cause that many sects reject all set forms of worship." *

In 1823, it appears, Madison had to think back over a span of almost three-quarters of a century even to recall a significant attempt at composition of a commonly accepted prayer. As far as he was concerned, that isolated attempt was doomed to failure. And, in any event, it was not made by government officials acting in their official capacity.

Today, the statistics would appear to be much the same. Petitioners do not believe that there is any prayer in use in the public schools of any State in this country which, like the prayer involved in this case, has been composed by State officials for use in such schools. In 1955, a prayer virtually identical with the Regents' Prayer was presented to the Honorable Edmund G. Brown, now the Governor but then the Attorney General of California. In the only official opinion on the specific question presented in this case, other than those of the courts below, Governor Brown ruled that the prayer presented to him was a violation of the Establishment Clause of the First Amendment, citing the *Everson, McCollum* and *Zorach* decisions of this Court (25 Cal. Ops. Atty. Gen. 316, 1955). This is the "tradition" and "heritage" behind the Regents' Prayer.

(d) The true significance of the Regents' Prayer is not to be judged by its brevity or simplicity.

The opinions of the courts below sustaining the Regents' Prayer emphasize its brevity and simplicity, as if to indicate that the measure of its significance should be its size and form (R. 105, 126, 143, 145). Of course, this emphasis is more than inconsistent with the importance which the same opinions attach to the main belief expressed in the

---

* BLAKELY, AMERICAN STATE PAPERS ON FREEDOM AND RELIGION (1943), p. 592.

prayer, and, as petitioners will point out below, the only real effect of the brevity of the prayer is to strengthen the element of coercion already present in the State action under consideration in this case. These "physical" characteristics of the prayer, however, have much the same type of distorting effect as an optical illusion, and, petitioners respectfully submit, they require the same degree of concentration to overcome.

If State educational officials are now held legally competent to compose and conduct the recitation of a 22-word prayer at the beginning of the school day, on the theory that the beliefs expressed in that prayer are acceptable to the vast majority of citizens, it is difficult to see why they will not be held equally competent to compose and conduct the recitation of a 220-word prayer, or a *second* brief prayer at the *end* of the school day. Moreover, if such other prayer involves beliefs other than belief in God, belief in a set form of worship, and belief in the practice of asking God's blessing on the worshipper, who will judge whether those other beliefs are acceptable to the vast majority?

Madison was faced with a similar problem in 1784 when he opposed "A Bill Establishing a Provision for Teachers of the Christian Faith," in the Virginia Assembly. After the long dark years of religious persecution in England and the Colonies, a bill levying a tax to provide support for religious teachers of their own choosing must have appeared to be a rather modest and even liberal proposal to many of the God-fearing citizens of Virginia. In his famous "Memorial and Remonstrance against Religious Assessments," however, Madison opposed the bill, among other reasons—

> "3. Because it is proper to take alarm at the first experiment on our liberties * * * Who does not see that the same authority which can establish Christianity, in exclusion of all other Religions, may estab-

lish with the same ease any particular sect of Christianity in exclusion of all other Sects? * * * '' *

The Regents' Prayer may not be a ''first experiment,'' but the State action connected with it is part of one of two great and powerful drives recognized in the minority opinion of this Court written by Mr. Justice Rutledge in the *Everson* case, *supra* (330 U. S. at page 63), and more recently recognized in the majority opinion of the Court in the *McGowan* case (366 U. S. at page 444). Those drives are described and commented upon in the opinion of Mr. Justice Rutledge as follows (330 U. S. at page 63):

> ''Two great drives are constantly in motion to abridge, in the name of education, the complete division of religion and civil authority which our forefathers made. *One is to introduce religious education and observances into the public schools.* The other, to obtain public funds for the aid and support of various private religious schools * * * In my opinion both avenues were closed by the Constitution. Neither should be opened by this Court.''

Petitioners respectfully submit that, although the Regents' Prayer is brief and simple, the State action under consideration in this case constitutes a gross violation of the guarantee of church and state in the Establishment Clause of the First Amendment.

(e) The essential or primary, if not the only, purpose and effect of the State action under consideration in this case is to aid religion.

Petitioners assume that the classic expression of the latitude of the Establishment Clause is to be found in the majority opinion of this Court in the *Everson* case, *supra,* 330 U. S. at pages 15-16:

---

* Both the bill referred to and Madison's ''Memorial and Remonstrance'' are set forth in appendices to the dissenting opinion of Mr. Justice Rutledge in the *Everson* case, *supra,* 330 U. S. at pages 63-74.

"The 'establishment of religion' clause of the First Amendment means at least this: Neither a state nor the Federal Government can set up a church. Neither can pass laws which aid one religion, aid all religions, or prefer one religion over another. Neither can force nor influence a person to go to or to remain away from church against his will or force him to profess a belief or disbelief in any religion. No person can be punished for entertaining or professing religious beliefs or disbeliefs, for church attendance or nonattendance. No tax in any amount, large or small, can be levied to support any religious activities or institutions, whatever they may be called, or whatever form they may adopt to teach or practice religion. Neither a state nor the Federal Government can, openly or secretly, participate in the affairs of any religious organization or groups and *vice versa*. In the words of Jefferson, the clause against establishment of religion by law was intended to erect 'a wall of separation between Church and State'."

In the *Everson* case, the State action consisted of the repayment of money to parents of school children for bus fares which the children had paid to attend parochial schools. Although such State action provided some indirect aid to religion, this Court held, by a vote of 5-4, that the action did not violate the Establishment Clause because it was in the nature of "public welfare legislation," and its essential purpose and effect was to aid public education (330 U. S. at page 17).

In the *McCollum* case, *supra*, which followed *Everson*, there was no real issue as to the nature of the State action. There, a local board of education permitted religious instruction during school hours in public school buildings, and required those children who chose not to attend to remain in their classrooms. Such instruction, this Court held, was "beyond all question a utilization of the tax-established public school system to aid religious groups to spread their faith. And it falls squarely under the ban of the First Amendment * * *." (330 U. S. at page 210.)

The present case, petitioners respectfully submit, falls into precisely the same category. Although it may be true that the State action under consideration in this case is not, in form, "instruction," that aspect of the case would seem to be immaterial, and the confusion which it created in the courts below would seem to have been entirely unnecessary.*

Petitioners share part of the responsibility for this confusion. Because the decision in the *McCollum* case was favorable to our position in this case, and because the religious activity involved in the prior case was in the form of instruction, we characterized the religious activity in this case as "instruction". For the same reasons, respondents and intervenors argued to the contrary. The dispute, however, was a battle over words which raised form over substance.

The interpretation of the Establishment Clause in the *Everson* case, quoted above, includes the following warning (330 U. S. at page 16):

> "No tax in any amount, large or small, can be levied to support *any religious activities or institutions, whatever they may be called, or whatever form they may adopt to teach or practice religion.*"

Moreover, the recent decisions of this Court in the *Sunday Closing Law Cases* (366 U. S. 420 et seq.), particularly in the *McGowan* case, *supra,* point out that the real question in a case of this type relates not to the *form* of the State action, but rather to its substance or essential *pur-*

---

* The concurring opinion of Mr. Justice Beldock in the Appellate Division gives as his "sole" reason for affirming the interlocutory order of Special Term his belief that "the prayer here involved *does not constitute religious teaching * * *.* It gives no training or instruction of a religious nature whatever" (R. 129; emphasis in original). The majority opinion of the Court of Appeals also denies that the prayer is "religious education" (R. 143).

pose and effect. Thus, the Sunday Closing Laws of Maryland and other States were sustained because their essential purpose and effect was to provide the general public with a "uniform day of rest," rather than to encourage the observance of Sunday as a religious holiday (366 U. S. at page 445).

Two Justices of this Court concurred in the decisions in the *Sunday Closing Law* cases, but expressed the opinion that State action should not be held invalid under the Establishment Clause so long as it appeared to serve any legitimate and substantial secular end. Although this concurring opinion is perhaps more favorable than the majority opinion to State action which is being examined in the light of the Establishment Clause, it contains a caveat (366 U. S. at page 466):

> " * * * If the primary end achieved by a form of regulation is the affirmation or promotion of religious doctrine—primary, in the sense that all secular ends which it purportedly serves are derivative from, not wholly independent of, the advancement of religion—the regulation is beyond the power of the state. This was the case in *McCollum.*"

This, petitioners respectfully submit, is also the case now before this Court. Whether or not the State action under consideration here is deemed to be "instruction," "teaching" or "education," the conclusion seems inescapable that its essential or primary, if not its only, purpose and effect is to promote belief in the existence of God.

The Board of Regents have admitted as much in the statement of belief in which they first recommended the prayer that now bears their name. That statement begins as follows (R. 28):

> "BELIEF IN and dependence upon Almighty God was the very cornerstone upon which our Founding Fathers builded."

After thus stating their thesis, the Regents proceed to unfold their purpose (R. 28):

> " * * * In our opinion, the securing of the peace and safety of our country and our State against such dangers points to *the essentiality of teaching our children, as set forth in the Declaration of Independence, that almighty God is their Creator,* and that by Him they have been endowed with their inalienable rights of life, liberty and the pursuit of happiness." (Emphasis added.)

Not petitioners, but the Regents themselves, it will be noted, first used the word "teaching" in connection with the saying of the Regents' Prayer. Moreover, although the Regents mention a secular goal, "the securing of the peace and safety of our country," they indicate quite clearly that it is secondary and derivative in that it is intended to follow and result from teaching children to believe in God.

Immediately after the foregoing quotation, the Regents recommend the saying of the prayer, together with "the act of allegiance to the Flag." Then they repeat and emphasize their initially stated purpose (R. 29):

> "We believe that thus *the school will fulfill its high function of supplementing the training of the home, ever intensifying in the child that love for God,* for parents and for home which is the mark of true character training and the sure guarantee of a country's welfare." (Emphasis added.)

By "school," of course, the Regents mean the compulsory public school system of New York. They apparently consider "intensifying" in pupils a "love for God" to be not only a function, but a "high function," of that system.

Petitioners respectfully submit that the Regents' purpose in recommending the prayer, and respondents' purpose in instituting it as a daily procedure in the public schools of their district, is to promote belief in God by daily prayer. Moreover, if the means or form of accomplish-

ing that purpose is not accurately described as "instruction," "teaching" or "education," it is nonetheless a
religious activity; and, since prayer is merely putting into
practice the beliefs in which the practitioner has previously
been instructed, it is, if anything, a higher or more extreme
form of religious activity.

(f) The factual situation in this case is basically the same as that in *McCollum*.

The opinion of this Court in the *McGowan* case, *supra,*
lists the fatal defects in the State action under consideration
in *McCollum* as follows (366 U. S. at page 452):

> " * * * In McCollum, state action permitted re-
> ligious instruction in public school buildings during
> school hours and required students not attending the
> religious instruction to remain in their classrooms
> during that time. The Court found that this system
> had the effect of coercing the children to attend re-
> ligious classes; * * * In McCollum, the only alterna-
> tive available to the nonattending students was to
> remain in their classrooms; * * * In McCollum, there
> was direct cooperation between state officials and
> religious ministers; * * * In McCollum, tax supported
> buildings were used to aid religion; * * *."

(1) In the present case, the State action also "permits"
religious activity in public school buildings during school
hours, and requires students who do not choose to participate to remain in their classrooms.

The State action under consideration in *McCollum,* was,
if anything, more truly permissive than that under consideration here. Under the program involved in *McCollum;*
there was provision for religious instruction only to the
extent that particular religious sects requested the privilege
of giving instruction in their respective faiths, and the
majority opinion in *McCollum* noted that instruction in
the Jewish faith had been discontinued because there was
no request for it (333 U. S. at pages 208-9). Under the

procedure involved in this case, there is provision for the saying of the Regents' Prayer, as a daily procedure in all the schools of the district, *regardless of whether a single parent requests the prayer to be said.* The resolution adopted by respondents on July 8, 1958, *requires,* rather than permits, 'that the Regents' Prayer be said daily in our schools' '' (R. 40).

Moreover, under the program involved in *McCollum,* there was an element of choice; the pupils participating in that program could select the particular faith in which they desired instruction (333 U. S. at pages 208-9). Here, there is no such choice: the pupils who wish to join in prayer with their classmates may only join in the Regents' Prayer, no other.

(2) In the present case, as in *McCollum,* the only alternative available to pupils not choosing to participate is to remain ''in their classrooms.''

On this point, some clarification is necessary. This Court's opinion in the *McGowan* case uses the phrase ''in their classrooms'' (366 U. S. at page 452), but petitioners assume that the phrase is intended to convey no more than the Court's understanding that the pupils not choosing to participate in the program involved in *McCollum* were required to remain *in school.* The Court's opinion in the *McCollum* case states the actual fact as follows (333 U. S. at page 209):

> ''Students who did not choose to take the religious instruction were not released from public school duties; *they were required to leave their classrooms and go to some other place in the school building for the pursuit of their secular studies.''* (Emphasis added.)

In the present case, as the affidavit of respondent Freed in support of respondents' motion for a final order shows (R. 173), the pupils not choosing to participate in the saying of the prayer actually remain in their classrooms, in the sense that they do not leave the classrooms in which the prayer is said and go to some other place in the school building. According to respondent Freed, this situation results from the fact that no parents have requested that their child be excused from the classroom in which the prayer is being said. There is nothing in the record, however, to indicate that if parents did request that their child be excused from the classroom, the child would be free to leave the school building, or free from school discipline. On the contrary, although the prayer is required to be said at the commencement of the school day, it is definitely required to be said *after* that day has begun, and at a time when attendance at school is compulsory.

(3) Here, as in *McCollum,* tax-supported buildings are used to aid religion.

This final similarity between the factual situation in *McCollum* and the présent case requires only the briefest comment. The fact is admitted that, pursuant to the resolution adopted by respondents on July 8, 1958, the Regents' Prayer is being said daily in all the schools of the local school district (R. 20).

> **(g) The only difference in the factual situation in *McCollum* and that in the present case makes the present case a stronger one for the application of the guarantee of separation in the Establishment Clause.**

The only difference between the factual situation in the *McCollum* case and that in the present case lies in the fact that ''[i]n McCollum, there was direct cooperation between state offiicals and religious ministers'' (366 U. S. at page 452). In the present case, no such cooperation appears to exist, but this one difference, petitioners respectfully submit, makes this case a stronger one for the application of the guarantee of separation incorporated in the Establishment Clause of the First Amendment.

In this case, instead of merely cooperating with religious ministers, the State officials have performed the functions of ministers. Acting in their capacity as State officials, they have inquired into religious matters and expressed their beliefs on those matters; they have composed a prayer which incorporates their beliefs; they have instituted that prayer as a daily procedure in the public schools of a local school district; and they are now supervising and conducting the saying of the prayer in those schools. It is certainly the fact that a teacher is present whenever the prayer is said, thus not only making certain that it is said, but also that it is said in an orderly and proper way (R. 66). It also appears to be undisputed that if the teacher does not actually lead the saying of the prayer, he or she selects the student who does (R. 14, 24-7, 66).

Undoubtedly, to a limited extent, cooperation between State officials and religious ministers is necessary and proper (*Zorach* v. *Clauson,* 343 U. S. 306). Petitioners respectfully submit, however, that the State action under consideration in this case violates the most fundamental concept in the entire philosophy of separation of church and state, as that philosophy has been developed in this country and incorporated in the Constitution.

If there was any one belief that was shared by all of the Founding Fathers, it was the belief that the civil magistrate had no competence in, or jurisdiction over, religious matters. First expressed by the English philosopher John Locke, this belief was adopted and adapted to the American scene by Thomas Jefferson and James Madison, and it was even shared by "moderates" such as George Washington.

This Court has described "A Bill for Establishing Religious Freedom," which Jefferson wrote, Madison sponsored, and Virginia enacted into law in 1785, "as best reflecting the long and intensive struggle for religious freedom in America, as particularly relevant in the search for the First Amendment's meaning" (*McGowan* v. *State of Maryland, supra,* 366 U. S. at page 437). In that document, Jefferson stated:

> " * * * that the opinions of men are not the object of civil government, nor under its jurisdiction; that to suffer the civil magistrate to extend his powers into the field of opinion and to restrain a profession or propagation of principles on supposition of their ill tendency is a dangerous fallacy, which at once destroys all religious liberty, because he being of course judge of that tendency will make his opinions the rule of judgment and approve or condemn the sentiments of others only as they shall square with or suffer from his own; that it is time enough for the rightful purposes of civil government for its officers to interfere when principles break out into overt acts against peace and good order; * * *." *

This Court has also acknowledged the "Memorial and Remonstrance Against Religious Assessments," written by Madison, as an important original source for determining the meaning of the First Amendment (*Reynolds* v. *United States,* 98 U. S. 145; see also Mr. Justice Rutledge's dissenting opinion in *Everson* v. *Board of Education, supra,* 330 U. S. at page 68). Among other reasons, Madison opposed religious assessments—

> "2. Because if religion be exempt from the authority of Society at large, still less can it be subject to that of the Legislative Body. * * *
>
> *   *   *
>
> 5. Because the bill implies that the Civil Magistrate is a competent Judge of Religious truths or that he may employ Religion as an engine of Civil policy. The first is an arrogant pretention, falsified by the contradictory opinions of rulers in all ages and throughout the world; the second, an unhallowed perversion of the means of salvation.

---

* Quoted in PADOVER, THE COMPLETE JEFFERSON, p. 947.

6. Because the establishment proposed by the Bill is not requisite for the support of the Christian Religion. To say that it is, is a contradiction to the Christian Religion itself, for every page of it disavows a dependence on the powers of this world; it is a contradiction to fact; for it is known that this Religion both existed and flourished, not only without the support of human laws, but in spite of every opposition from them; * * *

* * *

8. Because the establishment in question is not necessary for the support of Civil Government. If it be urged as necessary for the support of Civil Government only as it is a means of supporting religion, and it be not necessary for the latter purpose, it cannot be necessary for the former. If Religion be not within [the] cognizance of Civil Government, how can its legal establishment be said to be necessary to civil Government * * * Rulers who wished to subvert the public liberty, may have found an established clergy convenient auxiliaries. A just government, instituted to secure and perpetuate it needs them not. Such a government will best be supported by protecting every citizen in the enjoyment of his Religion with the same equal hand which protects his person and his property; by neither invading the equal rights of any Sect, nor suffering any Sect to invade those of another." *

As pointed out above, even Washington, who was more moderate than Jefferson and Madison in his views on separation, shared the latter's belief concerning the civil magistrate's incompetence in, and lack of jurisdiction over, religious matters. In a letter written at the end of 1789 to Presbyterians of Massachusetts and New Hampshire who had expressed dismay over the omission in the new Constitution of any reference to the Christian religion, he said the following:

---

* The "Remonstrance" is set forth in full in an appendix to Mr. Justice Rutledge's dissenting opinion in the *Everson* case, *supra*, 330 U. S. beginning at page 63.

"And here, I am persuaded, you will permit me to observe, that *the path of true piety is so plain, as to require but little* POLITICAL *direction.*

To this consideration we ought to ascribe the absence of any regulation respecting religion from the Magna Charta of our country. To the guidance of the Ministers of the Gospel, this important object is, perhaps, more properly committed. It will be your [the Presbyterians'] care to instruct the ignorant and to reclaim the devious; And in the progress of morality and science, to which our Government will give every furtherance, we may confidently expect the advancement of true religion, and the completion of our happiness." * (Emphasis in original.)

There is one more document, written by Jefferson, which is particularly applicable to the State action under consideration in this case. It is a letter to Reverend Samuel Miller in 1808 on the subject of Presidential proclamations of days of thanksgiving, and it contains the following general comment:

"Certainly, no power to prescribe any religious exercise, or to assume authority in religious discipline, has been delegated to the General Government * * * I do not believe it is for the interest of religion to invite the civil magistrate to direct its exercises, its disciplines or its doctrines; nor of the religious societies, that the General Government should be invested with the power of effecting any uniformity of time or matter among them. Fasting and praying are religious exercises; the enjoining them an act of discipline. Every religious society has a right to determine for itself the time for these exercises, and the subjects proper for them, according to their own particular tenets; * * * " **

---

* Quoted in I STOKES, CHURCH AND STATE IN THE UNITED STATES, p. 537.

** I STOKES, *ibid.,* pp. 490-1.

In the present case, the New York officials would seem to have committed every single act condemned by the Founding Fathers in the statements quoted above. They have advocated belief in the existence of God, belief in a set form of worship and belief in the practice of asking God's blessings on behalf of the worshipper. They have composed and are now supervising and conducting, on a daily basis, a prayer incorporating those religious beliefs. They have attempted to justify their acts by stating that the promotion of those religious beliefs is in the interests of securing the peace and safety of our country, but in so doing they have merely compounded their original error by employing religion "as an engine of civil policy."

All of this, of course, is in addition to the fact that these same State officials, have, by making the saying of the Regents' Prayer a daily procedure in the schools of a local school district, utilized the compulsory school system and school buildings, facilities, supplies and personnel in the promotion of religious beliefs and the conduct of religious activities.

(h) The element of coercion present in this case is also stronger than that in *McCollum*.

The opinions of this Court in the *McCollum* case indicate that the only element of "coercion," "compulsion" or "pressure" present in that case lay in the impact of the "compulsory" public school system upon the program of religious instruction under consideration. The majority opinion, delivered by Mr. Justice Black, describes this element as follows (333 U. S. at pages 209-10):

> "The operation of the state's compulsory education system thus assists and is integrated with the program of religious instruction carried on by separate religious sects. Pupils compelled by law to go to school for secular education are released in part from their legal duty upon the condition that they attend the religious classes."

The concurring opinion of Mr. Justice Frankfurter, in which four Justices of the Court joined, is to the same effect (333 U. S. at page 227):

> "Religious education so conducted on school time and property is patently woven into the working scheme of the school. The Champaign arrangement thus presents powerful elements of inherent pressure by the school system in the interest of religious sects."

In this concurring opinion, there is also mention of another form of pressure, but it, too, is generated by the compulsory public school system (333 U. S. at page 227):

> "That a child is offered an alternative may reduce the constraint; it does not eliminate the operation of influence by the school in matters sacred to conscience and outside the school's domain. The law of imitation operates, and non-conformity is not an outstanding characteristic of children. The result is an obvious pressure upon children to attend."

In his separate concurring opinion, Mr. Justice Jackson took exception to the above-quoted comment. He saw no "legal compulsion" of any kind in the State action under consideration (333 U. S. at pages 232-3). *Yet, he, also, believed that such action was prohibited by the Establishment Clause.*

Needless to say, Mr. Justice Reed, who dissented, saw no element of coercion, compulsion or pressure (333 U. S. at pages 238-56).

The situation in the present case, petitioners respectfully submit, is little different from that in *McCollum*. If anything, the impact of the compulsory school system is stronger here, in at least three ways.

(1) In *McCollum*, the only "coercion" lay in the fact the pupils were compelled to attend school to obtain a secular education. They were not thereafter compelled to

participate in the program of religious instruction unless their parents requested that they do so. When they participated in the program of religious instruction, they were deemed to have been "released," and it was for that reason that the program was called a "released time" program (333 U. S. at page 222). In the present case, not only are the pupils compelled to attend school to obtain a secular education, but also, when they attend, they are compelled to participate in the saying of the Regents' Prayer, *unless their parents request that they be excused.* Here, the burden of taking action is on the parents of the pupils. If no action is taken, the pupils participate in the religious activity.

(2) In *McCollum*, the program of religious instruction was one of several classes which occurred during the school day, and it lasted for about 30-45 minutes (333 U. S. at pages 207-8). Those pupils who did not wish to participate in the program pursued their regular secular studies during that period (*ibid.* at page 209). In the present case, the Regents' Prayer is said in conjunction with the Pledge of Allegiance to the Flag. This is required by the resolution adopted by respondents on July 8, 1958 (R. 40), and it is recommended in the statement of belief adopted by the Regents on November 30, 1951 (R. 28). Moreover, the prayer contains only 22 words and takes less than one minute to say. Any pupil, therefore, who wishes to participate in the Pledge of Allegiance, but who does not choose to be present at the recitation of the prayer, must dash out of the classroom immediately after the Pledge of Allegiance and return in a matter of seconds. Under these circumstances, it is hardly surprising that although respondents have received requests that children be excused from saying the prayer, they have received none requesting that any child be excused from the classroom.

Both the timing and the brevity of the prayer, therefore, have the effect of encouraging some form of participation in its recitation even by those children who have been excused from saying it. They see and hear their teacher and classmates say the prayer. They have been excused from saying it, at the request of their parents, but nothing in the record indicates that they will be prohibited from saying it if they choose to do so. Petitioners respectfully submit that the "law of imitation" cited in the concurring opinion of Mr. Justice Frankfurter in the *McCollum* case (333 U. S. at page 227) is in full force and effect here.

(3) Most important of all, even more than the State action considered in *McCollum*, the State action being considered in this case necessarily exerts an influence on the minds of the children involved which cannot be avoided by any system of alternatives. Here, State educational officials charged with the duty of imparting knowledge to minor children have, in their official capacity, advocated religious beliefs. The same officials who teach children, and demand that the latter learn, that two plus two equals four and that "c-a-t" spells "cat", now say that there is a God, to Whom children should say a specified daily prayer, and from Whom children may ask, and expect to receive, blessings for themselves as well as others. Under these circumstances, petitioners respectfully submit, the effect on the children involved will be much the same whether they say the Regents' Prayer, or remain silent while it is said, or even if they leave the classroom or the school building during its recitation.

(i) The State action under consideration in this case rejects the belief concerning religion on which the "Founding Fathers" built.

The Board of Regents of the State of New York have stated that "[b]elief in and dependence upon Almighty God was the very cornerstone upon which our Founding Fathers builded" (R. 28). Petitioners disagree.

We are aware, of course, that belief in God exerted a strong influence on the thoughts and actions of many of the "Founding Fathers" in their personal lives, but we respectfully submit that another belief concerning religion dominated their thinking and conduct in the sphere of politics and government. We submit that the true corner-stone, or rather the "wall", on which they based their hope of creating a national government under which religion would flourish was "the wall of separation of Church and State."

That wall, we submit, the State action under consideration in this case threatens not merely to breach, but to undermine completely.

Conclusion

It is respectfully submitted that the decision of the Court of Appeals of the State of New York should be reversed and this case remanded to that Court with a direction to grant the relief requested in the original petition presented to the Special Term of the Supreme Court of the State of New York, Nassau County, together with such other and further relief as may be appropriate.

Respectfully submitted,

WILLIAM J. BUTLER and
STANLEY GELLER,
Attorneys for Petitioners.

BUTLER, JABLOW & GELLER,
of Counsel.

Supreme Court of the United States

OCTOBER TERM, 1961

No. 468

In the Matter of the Application

of

STEVEN I. ENGEL, DANIEL LICHTENSTEIN, MONROE LERNER,
LENORE LYONS and LAWRENCE ROTH,

Petitioners,

against

WILLIAM J. VITALE, JR., PHILIP J. FREED, MARY HARTE,
ANNE BIRCH and RICHARD SAUNDERS, constituting the
Board of Education of Union Free School District Number Nine, New Hyde Park, New York,

Respondents,

directing them to discontinue a certain school practice

and

HENRY HOLLENBERG, ROSE LEVINE, MARTIN ABRAMS, HELEN
SWANSON, WALTER F. GIBB, JANE EHLEN, RALPH B.
WEBB, VIRGINIA ZIMMERMAN, VIRGINIA DAVIS, VIOLET S.
COX, EVELYN KOSTER, IRENE O'ROURKE, ROSEMARIE PETE-
LENZ, DANIEL J. REEHIL, THOMAS DELANEY and EDWARD
L. MACFARLANE,

Intervenors-Respondents.

BRIEF OF RESPONDENTS

Opinions Below

The opinion of the Special Term of the Supreme Court
of the State of New York, Nassau County (R. 50-116), is
reported at 18 Misc. 2d 659, 191 N. Y. S. 2d 453. The

majority and concurring opinions of the Appellate Division
of the Supreme Court of the State of New York, Second
Department (R. 123-40), are reported at 11 App. Div. 2d
340, 206 N. Y. S. 2d 183. The majority, concurring and dissenting opinions of the Court of Appeals of the State of
New York (R. 142-55) are reported at 10 N. Y. 2d 174, 184
N. Y. S. 2d 659, 176 N. E. 2d 579.

Constitutional and Statutory Provisions Involved

While petitioners in their brief (pp. 2-3) have set forth
the First and Fourteenth Amendments to the Federal
Constitution, as well as the resolution of the respondent
Board of Education of July 8, 1958 (R. 40), pursuant to
which the saying of the Regents' Prayer was instituted as
a daily procedure in the schools of the District, there
should also be included at this point the regulation adopted
by respondents on September 3, 1959, which read (R.
171-2):

> "1. Neither teachers nor any school authority
> shall comment on participation or non-participation
> in the exercise nor suggest or request that any posture
> or language be used or dress be worn or be not used
> or not worn.
>
> 2. Provision is to be made for those children who
> are to be excused from participating or from the room
> during the prayer exercise.
>
> 3. Any child may be excused on written request
> of the parent or legal guardian and all parents will
> be so advised that the request should be so made,
> addressed to the principal of the school which the
> child attends."

Each parent and taxpayer received a letter (R. 172-3)
which advised that opening exercises at school included

the Regents' Prayer, set forth at length, after which, the letter read:

"Any parent or guardian who does not wish his child to say the prayer is requested to write a letter to the principal of the school his child attends, indicating whether he wants his child excused from the room or to remain silent in the room while the prayer is being said."

Question Presented

Do the First and Fourteenth Amendments compel the total abolition of a brief non-denominational prayer composed by the Board of Regents of the University of the State of New York in language taken from the preambles of various State Constitutions, in accordance with an historic tradition of public prayer and recommended by the Regents for voluntary recital by public school pupils in conjunction with the pledge of allegiance to the flag in an attempt to provide in the public schools of New York a simple recognition of this country's moral and spiritual heritage, where there is no showing of any compulsion upon any pupil to participate, and when any pupil whose parents object is excused from participation?

Statement of the Case

A. The Background of the Litigation.

The petitioners in a special proceeding under Article 78 of the New York Civil Practice Act (R. 9-18) sought an order directing the respondents, the Board of Education of Union Free School District Number Nine, New Hyde Park, New York (hereinafter sometimes referred to as the "Board"), to require them to discontinue or cause to be discontinued in the schools of said school district the saying of the prayer (sometimes referred to herein as the

"Regents' Prayer") daily in said schools following the Salute to the Flag pursuant to a resolution passed by respondents (R. 40).

The New York Supreme Court, Special Term (Meyer, J.), in a lengthy and careful opinion (R. 50-116; 18 Misc. 2d 659), held that the Regents' Prayer did not violate either the Federal or the State Constitutions. It ruled that the "establishment" clause of the First Amendment did not prohibit the non-compulsory saying in the public schools of that Prayer but that the "free exercise" provision of the First Amendment required that parents be advised of the adoption of the School Board's resolution so requiring, of the wording of the Prayer and of the procedure to be followed in its recital, so that a conscious choice could be made whether a child should or should not participate.

In arriving at these conclusions, the Court below reasoned:

> The question involved is one of constitutional power, not of policy.
> There is in our constitutional history, however, and in the history of public education a long tradition of prayer.
> Nothing in the history of the First or Fourteenth Amendments or in the personal views of Franklin, Madison or Jefferson suggests any intention to exclude non-compulsory prayer from the schools.
> Freedom of religion includes the right publicly to express religious beliefs.
> The "establishment" clause prohibits direct compulsion on individuals in matters of religion, but prohibits indirect compulsion (through tax payments, for example) only when the state and religion are too closely connected. "The democratic nature of our government precludes the imposition of sanctions in the field of religion; the religious nature of the governed sanctions

the inclusion of religion in the processes of democratic life; the dividing line between permitted accommodation and proscribed compulsion is a matter of degree, to be determined anew in each new fact situation." (R. 96)

The religion clauses protect non-believers as well as believers; every individual has a constitutional right personally to be free from religion, but he may not compel others to adopt the same attitude.

The Regents' Prayer is not religious instruction. Recital of it is not within prohibited degree as an indirect compulsion.

Religious tensions and division over the saying of the prayer is not a constitutional reason for not permitting it to be said. "The genius of the American experiment has been not a lack of difference in point of view, but absolute equality in matters of thought and belief despite all differences." (R. 112)

The Regents' Prayer is not sectarian merely because it does not fully accord with the tenets of all of petitioners' or any group's beliefs. So long as "each is free to follow his own predilection with respect to prayer, to participate in a prayer exercise or to refuse to do so, the exercise cannot be deemed preferential." (R. 113)

The order entered upon this determination in Supreme Court, Nassau County (to the extent relevant to appellate proceedings) denied the petition (and accordingly refused to order the discontinuance of the Regents' Prayer), denied petitioners' demand for a jury trial, and directed that the matter be remanded to the respondent Board of Education for proceedings not inconsistent with the Court's opinion (R. 6-8). That opinion in substance directed the Board to adopt certain specific safeguards, confirming its existing practice, to ensure that the recital of the Regents' Prayer was a voluntary matter, to be observed or not at the election of the child or his parents (R. 8, 105-09).

On appeal to the Appellate Division, Second Department, this order was affirmed *per curiam,* one Justice concurring in part and dissenting in part (R. 124-25; 11 App. Div. 2d 340). A final order was then entered in Supreme Court, Nassau County, dismissing the proceeding on the merits on the ground that respondent School Board, by taking the steps recited at page 2 above, had complied with the directions of Special Term, as affirmed (R. 148-49).

The Court of Appeals, by a 5 to 2 vote, affirmed the decisions below (10 N. Y. 2d 174). That Court first held that there were:

> "* * * adequate provisions to ensure that no pupil need take part in or be present during the act of reverence so any question of 'compulsion' or 'free exercise' is out of the case (see Zorach v. Clauson, 343 U. S. 306)."

The Court went on to hold that the vountary recital of the Prayer was not an "establishment of religion," saying:

> "The 'Regents prayer' is an acknowledgment of our dependence upon Almighty God and a petition for the bestowal of His blessings. It includes an acknowledgment of the existence of a Supreme Being just as does the Declaration of Independence and the Constitutions of each of the 50 States of the Union, including our own. In construing even a Constitution some attention must be paid to the obvious intent of those who drafted it and adopted it (*Matter of Carey* v. *Morton,* 297 N. Y. 361). That the First Amendment was ever intended to forbid as an 'establishment of religion' a simple declaration of belief in God is so contrary to history as to be impossible of acceptance.

Judge Froessel, in his concurring opinion, said:

> "The narrow question presented is: Do the Federal and State Constitutions prohibit the recitation by chil

dren in our public schools of the 22 words acknowledging dependence upon Almighty God, and invoking His
blessing upon them, their parents and teachers, and
upon our country? To say that they do seems to me to
stretch the so-called separation of church and State
doctrine beyond reason.

* * * * *

One may earnestly believe in God, without being attached to any particular religion or church. Hence a
rule permitting public school children, willing to do so,
to acknowledge their dependence upon Him, and to invoke His blessings, can hardly be called a 'law respecting an establishment of religion' or 'prohibiting the
free exercise thereof'' in transgression of the First
Amendment which in nowise prohibits the recognition
of God, or laws respecting such recognition.

The challenged recitation follows the pledge of allegiance, which itself refers to God. School children
are permitted to sing 'America', the fourth stanza of
which is indeed a prayer, invoking the protection of
'God', 'Author of Liberty'. The preamble to our State
Constitution, which is taught in our public schools, provides: 'We the People of the State of New York, grateful to Almighty God for our Freedom'. Virtually every
State Constitution in the United States, as well as the
Declaration of Independence, contains similar references. To say that such references, and others of like
nature employed in the executive, legislative and judicial branches of our Government (see *Zorach* v. *Clauson*, 343 U. S. 306, at pp. 312-313), unrelated to any
particular religion or church, may be sanctioned by
public officials everywhere but in the public school
room defies understanding.

* * * * *

Here no partiality is shown, nor are classrooms
being turned over to religious instructors as in

McCollum v. *Board of Educ.* (333 U. S. 203). Any effort of a particular group to promote its own beliefs, doctrines, tenets and dogma must be carried on outside the public school, and any law to the contrary would violate the First Amendment. (*McCollum* v. *Board of Educ., supra.*)

As we see it, then, the challenged recitation was rightly upheld. It is not compulsory, is clearly nonsectarian in language, and neither directly nor indirectly even suggests belief in any form of organized or established religion. It permits each child to express gratitude to God and to invoke His blessing, to be steadfast in the faith of his acceptance if he has one; it compels no one, directly or indirectly, to do anything, if that be his or his parents' wish. All remain free, and thus we do not show preference as between 'those who believe in no religion' and 'those who do believe' (*Zorach* v. *Clauson, supra,* p. 314).''

B. The Regents' Prayer.

The Regents' Prayer, the voluntary recital of which petitioners now seek to prohibit in all the public schools of the State, say simply this:

> "Almighty God, we acknowledge our dependence upon Thee, and we beg Thy blessings upon us, our parents, our teachers and our Country."

This prayer was adopted by the respondent Board in accordance with the Statement of Belief adopted by the New York State Board of Regents on November 13, 1951 (R. 28-29) and the Supplemental Statement of 1955 setting forth the Regents Recommendation for School Programs on America's Moral and Spiritual Heritage (R. 30-39). Its language was borrowed from provisions appearing in the Constitutions of nearly all of the states of the Union. (*Cf.* Appendix A to this Brief.)

The Prayer was recommended by the Regents as a means of:

"* * * stressing the moral and spiritual heritage which is America's, the trust which our pioneering ancestors placed in Almighty God, their gratitude to Him from Whom they freely and frequently acknowledged came their blessings and their freedom and their abiding belief in the free way of life and in the universal brotherhood of man based upon their acknowledgment of the fatherhood of their Creator, Almighty God, Whom they loved and reverenced in diverse ways." (Regents' Statement on Moral and Spiritual Training in the Schools) (R. 28-29)

In this Statement the Regents declared:

"Belief in and dependence upon Almighty God was the very cornerstone upon which our Founding Fathers builded.

Our State Constitution opens with these solemn words: 'We, the People of the State of New York, grateful to Almighty God for our Freedom, in order to secure its blessings, do establish this Constitution.'

We are convinced that this fundamental belief and dependence of the American—always a religious—people is the best security against the dangers of these difficult days. In our opinion, the securing of the peace and safety of our country and our State against such dangers points to the essentiality of teaching our children, as set forth in the Declaration of Independence, that Almighty God is their Creator, and that by Him they have been endowed with their inalienable rights of life, liberty, and the pursuit of happiness" (R. 28).

The same principles were repeated by the Regents four years later in their unanimous "Recommendation

for School Programs on America's Moral and Spiritual
Heritage'' (R. 30-39).

" 'All men are created equal' is the basic principle
of the Brotherhood of Man, and 'endowed by their
Creator with life, liberty and the pursuit of happiness'
is the recognition of the Fatherhood of God, and that
these most precious rights come from the Creator and
not from the kings, princes or other men. The proposition that 'government derives its just powers from
the consent of the governed' is a recognition of the
dignity, worth and sovereignty of each individual
under God and of the concept of the individual as a
sovereign citizen who, with his fellow citizens, is
master of the state they have created and not its
servant.

The American people have always been a religious
people, believing in God each in accordance with his
own conscience. As our Supreme Court well stated,
'We are a religious people whose institutions presuppose a Supreme Being' '' (R. 33-34).

* * * * *

''The same will give to the student an understanding
and appreciation of his role as an individual endowed
by his Creator with inalienable rights and as a member of a group similarly endowed; of respect for
others, particularly parents and teachers, of devotion
to freedom and of reverence for Almighty God'' (R.
38).

In recommending this program, which is nothing more
than a reaffirmation of our long historical traditions, the
Regents specifically warned:

''In putting such recommendations into effect
teachers will be mindful always of the fundamental
American doctrine of the separation of church and
state, and careful at all times to avoid any and all

sectarianism or religious instruction which advocates, teaches or prefers any religious creed. Formal religion is not to be injected into the public school. It is a matter for the church and the home, for the religious leaders and the parents of each child'' (R. 32).

There is no evidence in this case that any pupil in the schools operated by respondent School Board has been subjected in the schools to any sectarian or other formal religious teaching. Undisguised, petitioners' attack is against any voluntary public recognition of belief and trust in God in an effort to obliterate from our public schools any recognition—even on a voluntary basis—of the existence of a Divine Being. In their briefs and arguments below and in their Petition to this Court they attack not merely the Regents' Prayer but any form of prayer whatsoever. They deny to every public school the right to suggest to any child that God is our Creator and the Author of our liberties or to encourage any public expression of gratitude to Him for those liberties, regardless of the wishes of the child or his parents and regardless of the historical and constitutional tradition of this nation.

Summary of Argument

1. The establishment clause of the First Amendment does not prohibit a recognition of Almighty God in public prayer, but on the contrary the history and growth of the United States as evidenced in documents from the earliest days of our nation to the present time would indicate such recognition as a part of our national heritage.

2. The establishment clause of the First Amendment was intended to prohibit a State religion but not to prevent the growth of a religious State. Non-compulsory recitation of the Regents' Prayer does not breach the principle of separation of church and State.

3. The saying of a prayer in public assemblies is traditional in this nation and in the State of New York where it has existed for over a century.

4. The authorities support the position that the noncompulsory recitation of the Regents' Prayer causes no pocket book injury; that voluntary expressions of belief in God should not be abolished because they are allegedly in conflict with the beliefs of some; that, as in the case of the Pledge to the Flag, those who object because of an alleged conflict with their belief should be permitted to refrain from participating, as in the case before the Court, but there should not be an abolition of such voluntary recital.

ARGUMENT

POINT I

Recognition of Almighty God in public prayer is an integral part of our national heritage.

Referring to the First Amendment to the Constitution of the United States, the New York Special Term has said that it agrees that:

"* * * the 'establishment' clause cannot have been intended to outlaw the practice in schools any more than from the rest of public life; that is, that prayer in the schools is permissible not as a means of teaching 'spiritual values' but because traditionally, and particularly at the time of the adoption of the First and Fourteenth Amendments, this was the accepted practice." (R. 70-71)

Every adult will recall that he came to know, in his earliest days in school through courses variously designated as History or Citizenship Education, or perhaps even earlier at his father's knee through learning about the Fourth of July celebration, the significance of the Declaration of Independence. That historic document refers to Almighty God in no less than four instances:

(a) "* * * laws of nature and of nature's God entitled them * * *"

(b) "* * * All men are endowed by their Creator with certain inalienable rights * * *."

(c) "* * * the Supreme Judge of the world * * *."

(d) "* * * with a firm reliance on the protection of Divine Providence * * *."

These references were not accidental but on the contrary were in accord with the basic traditions of both those who originally settled our land and those who came later. The feeling was not restricted to those relatively few men who had a part in establishing this country as a nation but also was a recognition observed by those in whose hands was placed the destiny of the various States which made up the Union. In this connection there have been collected in Appendix A hereto extracts from the Preambles or Constitutions of 49 of the 50 States making similar references.

The Congress of the United States which was responsible in the first instance for adopting the First and Fourteenth Amendments has throughout its history opened the sessions of both houses each day with a prayer seeking Divine guidance and acknowledging the existence of Almighty God.

It is, of course, a matter of common knowledge that both the New York State Senate and Assembly commence their legislative sessions with prayer.

Further recognition of the official observance of prayer is contained in Section 24 of the New York State General Construction Law where in defining the term holiday is included "* * * each day appointed by the president of the United States or by the governor of this state as a day of general thanksgiving, general fasting and prayer, or other religious observances * * *.''

Nor was the subject of our national heritage overlooked when our Legislature established the New York State Education Law for, we find the Regents being directed (Sec. 801) to prescribe courses of instruction " in the history, meaning, significance and effect of the provisions of the constitution of the United States, the amendments thereto, the declaration of independence, the constitution of the state of New York and the amendments thereto * * *.'' Special Term, in a slightly different vein in its opinion below, has traced "the history of the constitutional provisions and of public education'' (R. 71-82) on which respondents will rely, without unnecessary repetition in this brief.

POINT II

The Constitution of the United States is incapable of being so interpreted as to require that the wall of separation of church and State become an iron curtain.

"God who gave us life, gave us liberty. Can the liberties of a nation be secure when we have removed the conviction that these liberties are the gift of God?'' These are the words of Thomas Jefferson (referred to in Appendix C, hereto) who, it has been recorded, is the author of some of our fundamental historic documents and the famous phrase "wall of separation of church and State.''

Zorach v. *Clauson,* 303 N. Y. 161 (1951), 343 U. S. 306, is one of the most recent and most famous cases involving the separation of church and State in either this State or in the history of the United States Supreme Court. There was there involved the released time program which had been authorized by the State Legislature in 1940, resulting in the promulgation of regulations relating thereto by the Commissioner of Education of the State of New York and, in that particular case, additional rules established by the New York City Board of Education.

There, as in the instant case, the choice of whether to join in the program or not was that of the parents and the children and there, too, many if not all of the charges contained in the petitioners' pleading herein were voiced (as a matter of fact the language of the pleading in that case and in this case are almost identical). After the courts of New York had consistently upheld "released time" against constitutional attack, this Court affirmed their rulings, holding that government and religion need not be implacably hostile but could, to a reasonable extent, accommodate each other's legitimate interests.

The intent of the First Amendment has more recently been the subject of a judicial decision in New York State as it appears in the opinion of Mr. Justice Bookstein in *Lewis* v. *Allen,* 5 Misc. 2d 68, 159 N.Y.S. 2d 897, in the following language:

"If I properly apprehend the intent, design and purposes of the First Amendment, it was conceived to prevent and prohibit the establishment of a *State Religion;* it was not intended to prevent or prohibit the growth and development of a *Religious State.*

This concept finds judicial support in Holy Trinity Church v. United States, 1892, 143 U. S. 457, at page 470, 12 S. Ct. 511, at page 516, 36 L. Ed. 226, where the Court says 'this is a religious nation'.

In 1951, that Court said in Zorach v. Clauson, 343 U. S. 306, at page 313, 72 S. Ct. 679, at page 684, 96 L. Ed. 954, 'We are a religious people whose institutions presuppose a Supreme Being'.

The Declaration of Independence refers to 'the Supreme Judge of the world', and 'the protection of Divine Providence'. Lincoln, at Gettysburg, spoke of 'this nation, under God'. Even the preamble to the New York Constitution expresses gratitude 'to Almighty God for our Freedom'. Indeed, the presidential oath of office concludes, 'So Help Me, God'. By Act of Congress, our coins are inscribed, 'In God we trust'.

If petitioners' contention be sound, it may be wondered whether the public school curriculum might properly include the Declaration of Independence and the Gettysburg address. Could 'America' ('* * * Protect us by thy might, Great God, our King!') be sung in a public school without offending the First Amendment? And might not the presidential oath of office have questionable constitutional status?'' (p. 812; Italics by the Court)

Nor were the rhetorical questions left unanswered by the Court for the Justice found support once more in authoritative judicial and legislative interpretation as follows:

"These questions find their answer in House Report No. 1693,* note 2, supra. There the Committee on Judiciary notes:

"The Supreme Court has clearly indicated that the references to the Almighty which run through our laws, our public rituals and our ceremonies in no way flout the provisions of the first amendment (Zorach v. Clauson, 343 N. S. 306, 312-313 '72 S. Ct. 679, 96 L. Ed. 954'). In so construing the first amendment, the Court pointed out that if this recognition of the Almighty was not so, then even a fastidious atheist or agnostic could object to the way in which the Court itself opens each of its sessions, namely, 'God save the United States and the Honorable Court' (Id., [343 U. S.] 313 [72 S. Ct. 683])". (pp. 812-813)

---

* This Report is set forth in Appendix B hereto.

The facts in the foregoing case, *Lewis* v. *Allen,* 5 Misc.
2d 68, 159 N.Y.S. 2d 807, show that the proceeding was
brought on by petition under Article 78 to compel the Commissioner of Education to perform a duty which allegedly
he had failed to perform with respect to a regulation calling for the use of the phrase "Under God" in the Pledge
of Allegiance to the Flag of America. Petitioners there
contended that, as in the instant case, there was some
nebulous "non-discretionary duty" on the part of the Commissioner of Education to rescind his regulations regarding
the new Pledge, as it had been enacted by Congress in 1954.
There, too, as here, the petitioners claimed there was some
compulsory aspect about even a voluntary reference to God
by others, and that such compulsion violates the same portions of the Federal and State Constitutions as petitioners
have referred to in the instant case. The Court there
noted (as we would respectfully urge the Court here to
note) that there was "no compulsory aspect. No penalties
attached to a failure or refusal to recite the Pledge. The
Pledge is made voluntarily and no penalties are imposed
for non-compliance" (p. 811).

POINT III

**Judicial, legislative, administrative and text writers
have agreed that what the framers of the First Amendment had in mind did not project the idea of wall of
separation of church and State into a "governmental
hostility to religion" which would be "at war with our
national tradition."**

For a century and a half, the First Amendment has been
a guide to the religious freedom of this country and, while
it has existed, public recognition of God, of religion and of
prayer has continued and flourished. Throughout the field
of text writing, judicial pronouncements, legislative enactments and administrative implementation for all of this
period we find a pattern which recognizes the intent and

meaning of the framers of the First Amendment which is confirmatory of their own public pronouncements.

As stated by Judge Desmond in his concurring opinion in *Zorach* v. *Clauson*, 303 N. Y. 161, 175, if the idea that any governmental recognition of God's existence is unconstitutional,

> "then every President has offended by invoking the Deity in his oath of office, by issuing Thanksgiving proclamations and calling on our people to pray for victory in war, or for peace, or for our soldiers' safety. If petitioners are right, then there is a violation every time a chaplain opens a Congressional session with prayer, or an army bugler sounds 'Church call'. If petitioners are right, then the Pilgrims were wrong as was every President who officially urged our people to train themselves in, and practice, religion. Our own State Constitution, on petitioners' theory offends against American Constitutionalism at the point in its preamble where it expresses gratitude 'to Almighty God' for our freedom. Petitioners would have this court now deny the declarations of the Supreme Court in the *Church of Holy Trinity* v. *United States* case, 143 U. S. 457, 12 S. Ct. 511, 36 L. Ed. 226 and of Chief Justice Kent in the *People* v. *Ruggles* case, 8 Johns. 290, in 1811, that ours is a religious nation. I stand on Chief Justice Kent's declaration, long ago in the *Ruggles* case, 8 Johns. at page 296, that the Constitution 'never meant to withdraw religion in general, and with it the best sanctions of moral and social obligation, from all consideration and notice of the law'."

Nor did Judge Froessel, also writing in *Zorach* v. *Clauson*, 303 N. Y. 169, at page 170, overlook the thought that the constitutional provisions regarding the relationship of religion and the State were two-fold, in that while on the one hand they prohibited the establishment of a State church, on the other hand they also prohibited any law interfering with the "free exercise" of religious profession. Thus, in quoting from a previous Court of Appeals case (*Lewis* v. *Graves,* 245 N. Y. 198), he calls attention to the language:

"Neither the Constitution nor the law discriminate against religion. Denominational religion is merely put in its proper place outside of public aid or support."

Again, in his opinion Judge Froessel points to the fallacy of eliminating every "friendly gesture" between church and State on the theory of "separation" when he says (at p. 172):

"It is thus clear beyond cavil that the Constitution does not demand that every friendly gesture between church and State shall be discountenanced. The so-called 'wall of separation' may be built so high and so broad as to impair both State and church, as we have come to know them. Indeed, we should convert this 'wall', which in our 'religious nation', *Church of Holy Trinity* v. *United States,* 143 U. S. 457, 470, 12 S. Ct. 511, 36 L. Ed. 226, is designed as a reasonable line of demarcation between friends, into an 'iron curtain' as between foes, were we to strike down this sincere and most scrupulous effort of our State legislators, the elected representatives of the People, to find an accommodation between constitutional prohibitions and the right of parental control over children. In so doing we should manifest 'a governmental hostility to religion' which would be 'at war with our national tradition', *People of State of Illinois ex rel. McCollum* v. *Board of Education of School Dist. No. 71 supra,* 333 U. S. at page 211, 68 S. Ct. at page 465, and would disregard the basic tenet of constitutional law that 'the public interests imperatively demand—that legislative enactments should be recognized and enforced by the courts as embodying the will of the people, unless they are plainly and palpably, beyond all question, in violation of the fundamental law of the Constitution', *Atkin* v. *State of Kansas,* 191 U. S. 207, 223, 24 S. Ct. 124, 128, 48 L. Ed. 148.

"While extreme care must, of course, be exercised to protect the constitutional rights of these appellants, it must also be remembered that the First Amendment not only forbids laws 'respecting an establishment of religion' but also laws 'prohibiting the free exercise thereof'. We must not destroy one in an effort to preserve the other."

Further in establishing the intent of Congress, Cooley's Principles of Constitutional Law, 224-225, 3rd ed. (1898) read as follows:

"By establishment of religion is meant the setting up or recognition of a state church, or at least the conferring upon one church of special favors and advantages which are denied to others (citing 1 Tuck, Bl. Com. App. 296; 2 id., App., Note G). It was never intended by the Constitution that the government should be prohibited from recognizing religion, * * * where it might be done without drawing any invidious distinctions between different religious beliefs, organizations, or sects."

The emphasis, indeed, reemphasis of America's moral and spiritual heritage, as promulgated by the New York State Board of Regents, the Commissioner of Education and the respondent School Board through the daily voluntary use of the Regents' prayer draws no "invidious distinctions between different religious beliefs, organizations, or sects" as referred to in the preceding quotation.

As said by Mr. Justice Douglas, speaking for the majority of this Court in *Zorach* v. *Clauson,* 343 U. S. 306 (1952):

"The First Amendment, however, does not say that in every and all respects there shall be a separation of church and State * * * otherwise, the State and religion would be aliens to each other—hostile, suspicious and even unfriendly * * *. A fastidious atheist or agnostic could even object to the supplication with which the Court opens each session: 'God save the United States and this Honorable Court.' * * *. We are a religious people whose institutions presuppose a Supreme Being. We guarantee the freedom to worship as one chooses. We make room for as wide a variety of beliefs and creeds as the spiritual needs of man deem necessary. We sponsor an attitude on the part of government that shows no partiality to any one group and that lets each flourish according to the zeal of its adherents and the appeal of its dogma. When the state encourages religious instruction or cooperates with religious authorities by adjusting the schedule of public events to sectarian needs, it follows the best of our traditions. For it then respects the religious nature of our people and accommodates the public service to their spiritual needs. To hold that it may not would be to find in the Constitution a requirement that the government show a callous indifference to religious groups. That would be preferring those who believe in no religion over those who do believe. Government may not finance religious groups nor undertake religious instruction nor blend secular and sectarian education nor use secular institutions to force one or some religion on any person. But we find no constitutional requirement which makes it necessary for government to be hostile to religion and to throw its weight against efforts to widen the effective scope of religious influence. The government must be neutral when it comes to competition between sects. It may not thrust any sect on any person. It may not make a religious observance compulsory. It may not coerce anyone to attend church, to observe a religious holiday, or to take religious instruction. But it can close its doors or suspend its operations as to those who want to repair to their religious sanctuary for worship or instruction. No more than that is undertaken here.''

As the facts indicate, there is no compulsory aspect attached to the saying of the Regents' prayer in the School District in question, nor is there any effort to foster sectarian religion in the schools any more so than when, as Mr. Justice Douglas pointed out above, the Court itself commences its day with a prayer.

One might wonder if the Supreme Court prayer were slightly reworded so as to read ''God save the United States and this School District'' whether our opponents might then say that this is ''an establishment of religion.'' Could petitioners then say that such a prayer is forcing ''some religion on any person'' or that this is thrusting ''any sect on any person'' or that it makes ''a religious observance compulsory'' or amounts to ''religious instruction''?

Does the prayer used by this Court amount to ''an establishment of religion''? Is this sectarian? Would this infringe the rights of either the judiciary or the attorneys appearing on behalf of litigants? Rather would it not be in keeping with our American tradition of voluntary public prayer and our moral and spiritual heritage? We submit that it is the latter.

Attention should also be drawn to House Report No. 1693 set forth in toto in Appendix B to Respondents' brief, where Representative Rabaut who introduced the resolution which led to the insertion of the words "under God" in the Pledge of Allegiance, stated:

> "Children and Americans of all ages must know that this is one Nation which 'under God' means liberty and justice for all"

and again he said:

> "By the addition of the phrase 'under God' to the pledge, the consciousness of the American people will be more alerted to the true meaning of our country and its form of government. In this full awareness we will, I believe, be strengthened for the conflict now facing us and more determined to preserve our precious heritage.
>
> "More importantly, the children of our land, in the daily recitation of the pledge in school, will be daily impressed with a true understanding of our way of life and its origins. As they grow and advance in this understanding, they will assume the responsibilities of self-government equipped to carry on the traditions that have been given to us. Fortify our youth in their allegiance to the flag by their dedication to 'one Nation, under God'."

The report itself did not overlook the First Amendment and the establishment clause for, after tracing many of the public pronouncements in which God had been clearly recognized, the report says:

> "It should be pointed out that the adoption of this legislation in no way runs contrary to the provisions of the first amendment to the Constitution. This is not an act establishing a religion or one interfering with the 'free exercise' of religion. A distinction must be made between the existence of a religion as an institution and a belief in the sovereignty of God."

Finally, we come to the well known rule of law that administrative interpretation of a statute is to be given great weight in determining its intent, meaning and purpose. While by no means contending that such an interpretation is infallible, a long continued practical and contemporaneous construction is entitled to great significance. See *Dole* v. *City of New York,* 44 N.Y.S. 2d 250 (1943), where the Court said:

> "Considerable force must be attached to the practical construction of the statute by 'public officers whose duty is to enforce it, acquiesced in by all for a long period of time'." (Citing cases) (pp. 252-253)

At the very outset of the Special Term's opinion below, the learned Justice refers to and quotes a policy statement adopted by the Superintendent of the New York public schools in 1837 (154-159). It is apparent from a reading thereof that over 120 years ago the trustees of a school system were given the approval of the Superintendent "to commence the business of the day by public prayer" (R. 53). The opinion of the Superintendent not only has been on record for many years but (as the Special Term pointed out) the ruling originally promulgated in 1837 was repeatedly reaffirmed by successive superintendents right down to 1909. We, therefore, have difficulty in reconciling a statement heretofore made by petitioners that respondents "seek to end the constitutionally-sanctioned and time honored trend of separation of church and state, by the introduction of a new-fangled Prayer into the schools of a District in which prayers were not heretofore said."

The Regents of the State of New York, by way of administrative interpretation, in 1951 first promulgated the prayer which is the subject of this litigation and recommended it for use in the school districts under their jurisdiction, suggesting that "at the commencement of each school day the act of allegiance to the Flag might well be joined with this act of reverence to God" (R. 53-54) and pursuant to such recommendations, it has become a matter of public knowledge many of the school districts here on Long Island have adopted the recommended procedure of having the prayer said daily in the class rooms as part of the opening exercises (See Exhibit "A" of Affidavit of William J. Vitale, Jr. attached to respondents' answer for 1951 promulgation by Regents (R. 28-29)). In 1955 the Board of Regents saw fit to supplement the 1951 statement (Id. Exhibit "B" (R. 30-39)).

POINT IV

A few seconds of voluntary prayer in the schools, acknowledging dependence on Almighty God, is consistent with our heritage of "securing" the blessings of freedom which are recognized in both the Federal and State Constitutions as having emanated from Almighty God.

Focus upon the petitioners' claim in paragraph 10 of the petition (R. 14) at this point is deemed necessary in view of the dependence of succeeding paragraphs of the petition on such paragraph, as well as the arguments in their brief which rely on this claim. There, where the pleader purports to state carefully how the prayer is led and said, there is studiously avoided any assertion that "the manner" of saying the prayer is pursuant to the *direction* or lack of direction that the teachers in the Herricks School District may be responsible for. Petitioners must be aware that no child is *required* to join in the prayer and that it is conceivable through the training of any particular child that he or she *may* hold their hands in a particular manner and that likewise there may be hundreds of children who hold their hands entirely differently or who do not in any way take a physical posture which reflects a prayerful attitude.

Similar comment can be made regarding the assertion that during the saying of the prayer no student is permitted to leave the class room. This is simply not true. On request any student may be excused in accordance with established procedure.

The petitioners, however, again and again (R. 15-17) refer to the "saying of the prayer and the manner in which it is said", seeking to pull themselves up by their own bootstraps, as it were, having first made a faulty statement of facts and then relying continuously on such faulty statement. For this reason and since these identical charges have been raised again and again and again through the cases involving comparable questions, respondents feel it incumbent to take the petition, paragraph by paragraph starting at paragraph 11 (R. 15) and set forth what the authorities have had to say on each of these subjects.

(a) The use of the public school system and the time and efforts of the teachers and staff of the schools.

Paragraph 11 (R. 15) of the petition contains merely an assertion, unsupported, that the saying of the prayer entails the use of the school system and the time and efforts of teachers and staff. The petition fails to allege anything regarding a separate tax having been levied for this purpose, any specific public monies being used for this purpose, or any damage of any kind to the petitioners. Nor is any invasion of any right of petitioners alleged.

Anticipating petitioners' claim that the ideas expressed in the foregoing paragraph are to be *inferred* from paragraph 11, it must still be concluded, based upon the judicial decisions in which this problem has been before the Court, that they have not suffered any "pocket book injury" as it is sometimes called.

This was the conclusion in *Doremus* v. *Board of Education*, 5 N. J. 435, 75 A. 2d 880 (1950), app. dis. 342 U. S. 429 (1952), where the Supreme Court of the State of New Jersey had upheld the constitutionality of a New Jersey

Statute which provided for the reading, without comment, of five verses of the Old Testament at the opening of each public school day. In this Court, Mr. Justice Jackson, writing for the majority, said:

"Appellants, apparently seeking to bring themselves within Illinois ex rel. McCollum v. Board of Education, 333 U. S. 203, 92 L. ed. 648, 68 S. Ct. 461, 2 A.L.R. 2d 1338, assert a challenge to the Act in two capacities— one as parent of a child subject to it, and both as tax-payers burdened because of its requirements. * * *

"Klein is set out as a citizen and taxpayer of the Borough of Hawthorne in the State of New Jersey, and it is alleged that Hawthorne has a high school supported by public funds. In this school the Bible is read, according to statute. There is no allegation that this activity is supported by any separate tax or paid for from any particular appropriation or that it adds any sum whatever to the cost of conducting the school. No information is given as to what kind of taxes are paid by appellants and there is no averment that the Bible reading increases any tax they do pay or that as taxpayers they are, will, or possibly can be out of pocket because of it. * * *

"Without disparaging the availability of the remedy by taxpayer's action to restrain unconstitutional acts which result in direct pecuniary injury, we reiterate what the Court said of a federal statute as equally true when a state Act is assailed: 'The party who invokes the power must be able to show not only that the statute is valid but that he has sustained or is immediately in danger of sustaining some direct injury as a result of its enforcement, and not merely that he suffers in some indefinite way in common with people generally.' Massachusetts v. Mellon, supra (262 U. S. at 488, 67 L. Ed. 1085, 43 S. Ct. 597)."

New York State's highest Court has long reiterated this necessity of damage. The Court of Appeals held in *Adler* v. *Metropolitan Elevated Ry. Co.,* 138 N. Y. 173, 180:

"* * * nor will the Court exert its equitable power of injunction in a case of a violation of a mere abstract right, unaccompanied with any substantial injury."

Mr. Justice Sutherland, speaking for this Court on the sufficiency of a plaintiff's interest in a constitutional issue raised by him, said:

"That question may be considered only when the justification for some direct injury suffered or threatened, presenting a justiciable issue, is made to rest upon such an act. * * * The party who invokes the power (of judicial review) must be able to show not only that the statute is invalid but that he has sustained or is immediately in danger of sustaining some direct injury as the result of its enforcement, and not merely that he suffers in some indefinite way in common with people generally." *Frothingham* v. *Mellon,* 262 U. S. 447, 488.

(b) The saying of the Regents' prayer as the teaching of religion and religious practices, contrary to the beliefs of the petitioners "who are believers" and their children and contrary to the beliefs of the petitioner and his children "who are non-believers" and therefore, allegedly offensive to such petitioners and their children.

This topical heading is the substance of the allegations in paragraphs 12 and 13 (R. 15) of the petition.

"The term 'religion' has reference to one's views of his relations to His Creator and to the obligations they impose of reverence for His being and character and of obedience to His will. It is often confounded with the cultus or form of worship of a particular sect, but is distinguishable from the latter." Thus said the New York Appellate Division, Third Department in *Drozda* v. *Bassos,* 260 App. Div. 408, 23 N.Y.S. 2d 544 (1940), quoting with approval from *Davis* v. *Beason,* 133 U. S. 333.

In Appendix C to this brief, there have been set forth the innumerable instances in which reference to Almighty God has been made in our currency, in public pronouncements, in Statutes,—indeed in almost every mode of activity of our Government. Surely, petitioners cannot seriously argue that each such instance represents a "religion" or a "religious practice" and that they find these things offensive to themselves and to their children.

As a matter of fact the petitioners must find themselves in a strangely anomalous position for on the one hand they purport to object to these references as constituting "religion" and "religious practices" and yet they rely on these very documents to support their position in this petition. Their position must be likened to that of the petitioner Joseph Lewis, who in an action against the Board of Education of the City of New York in 1953 (157 Misc. 520, 285 N. Y. Supp. 164) sought among other things to forbid the "use" of school buildings for the reading of the Bible in the public school assemblies. Of the many arguments advanced by the plaintiff there, comparable to those advanced here, the Court said:

> "Undisguised, the plaintiffs attack is on a belief and trust in God and in any system or policy or teaching which enhances or fosters or countenances or even recognizes that belief and trust. Such belief and trust, however, regardless of one's own belief, has received recognition in state and judicial documents from the earliest days of our republic." (p. 167)

The Court there focused the question as being one of "power" not policy, pointing out that the policy had already been decided and the question of power was an issue in the sense that the determination sought was whether a constitutional guarantee or any other provision or concept of law had been violated. The statement of the Court is as follows:

> "Let it be emphasized that the concern here is with power not policy. Within the boundaries of law what shall and shall not be done in the public schools is an educational function to be determined by those intrusted with the conduct and administration of the public schools. Lewis v. Board of Education of the City of New York, 258 N. Y. 117, 122, 179 N. E. 315, 317." (p. 167)

After quoting the Declaration of Independence, the motto "In God We Trust" and the opening lines of our State Constitution, the opinion continues:

> "Nor have the courts ignored the existence of this declared policy. In People ex rel. Lewis v. Graves, 219 App. Div. 233, 238, 219 N.Y.S. 189, 195, it was said: 'A belief in religion is not foreign to our system of government.'
>
> Our highest court, in Holy Trinity Church v. United States, 143 U. S. 457, 465, 12 S. Ct. 511, 514, 36 L. Ed. 226, said: 'This is a religious people. This is historically true. From the discovery of this continent to the present hour, there is a single voice making this affirmation.'
>
> These quotations are not intended to convey the thought that state and church should be brought into closer harmony. Their separation is a fundamental of immutable virility. Nor do the excerpts indicate the approval or proposal of a policy that religion be taught in the public schools. The principle that religion has no place in public temporal education is so inexorable that a reaffirmation of it would be supererogatory.

These concepts are not repugnant to the constitutional guaranty which safeguards freedom of conscience and of worship and the free entertainment and pursuit of religious beliefs. They are not hostile to section 3 of article 1 of the State Constitution, which declares that: 'The free exercise and enjoyment of religious profession and worship, without discrimination or preference, shall forever be allowed in this State to all mankind'." (p. 168)

* * * * *

"The sanctified principle of freedom of religious belief does not distinguish between believers and non-believers. It embraces both, and accords one as much protection and freedom as the other. A sect or tenet which is intolerant of those of a different sect or tenet is the precise antithesis of religious liberty. Freedom is negated if it does not comprehend freedom for those who believe as well as those who disbelieve. The law is astute and zealous in seeing to it that all religious beliefs or disbeliefs be given unfettered expression. Authentic free thinking involves the indubitable right to believe in God, as well as the unfettered license not to believe or to disbelieve in a Deity.

To examine into the sectarianism of those seeking access to public school buildings would make a travesty of our glorified liberty of conscience. Liberty for non-believers in God, but denial to believers in a Deity, would be a mock liberty." (pp. 169-170)

Although frequently referred to in petitioners' brief, the decision of this Court in *McGowan* v. *Maryland*, 366 U. S. 420, reviewing Sunday Closing statutes adds little support to petitioners' position. In upholding such laws, it was apparent that the Court recognized the public purpose involved and that any incidental benefit to religion did not warrant removing from the body of our laws those which recognized an integral part of our national heritage and tradition.

(c) The saying of the prayer as allegedly resulting in the exercise of coercion.

The admitted fact is that the prayer is said daily in the public schools of Union Free School District Number 9. Likewise the admitted fact must be that "we are essentially a religious people" and likewise the admitted fact must be that no child can grow up in this country of ours without hearing a constant reference to Almighty God, this being the very nature of our heritage and institutions.

The rule of the respondent Board of Education is that no child is to be required or encouraged to join in the saying of the Regents' Prayer (and if it were otherwise it is a certainty that petitioners would have emphatically so alleged in their petition). There is thus a clear distinction between the instant situation and *West Virginia Board of Education* v. *Barnette,* 319 U. S. 625 (1943), where this Court held unconstitutional the regulation of West Virginia State Board of Education requiring children in the public schools to salute the American flag and pledge allegiance to it under penalty of expulsion. The injunction was issued there, not because those whose religious beliefs were infringed upon were required to *listen* to the salute but because they were required to *join* in the Salute to the flag. It is noteworthy, however, that in recognizing the rights of those whose religion (Jehovah's Witnesses) assertedly prevented them from participating in the Salute and Pledge, the Court did not *abolish* the practice for all others. The observation of Mr. Justice Murphy in his concurring opinion in that case is worthy of note:

> "But there is before us the right of freedom to believe, freedom to worship one's Maker according to the dictates of one's conscience, a right which the Constitution specifically shelters. Reflection has convinced me that as a Judge I have no loftier duty or responsibility than to uphold that spiritual freedom to its farthest reaches." (p. 645)

Mr. Justice Douglas, speaking for the Court in *Zorach* v. *Clauson,* 343 U. S. 306, upholding the New York City release time program again indicated the unwillingness of that Court to strike from our public practices and procedures any reference to God, although it is evident from his language that he was aware that there were those who believed in no religion and who might therefore in some way claim that they were "offended." The Court's statement on the point is as follows:

"There is much talk of the separation of Church and State in the history of the Bill of Rights and in the decisions clustering around the First Amendment. See Everson v. Board of Education, 330 U. S. 1; McCollum v. Board of Education, supra. There cannot be the slightest doubt that the First Amendment reflects the philosophy that Church and State should be separated. And so far as interference with the 'free exercise' of religion as an 'establishment' of religion are concerned, the separation must be complete and unequivocal. The First Amendment within the scope of its coverage permits no exception; the prohibition is absolute. The First Amendment, however, does not say that in every and all respects there shall be a separation of Church and State."

"We would have to press the concept of separation of Church and State to these extremes to condemn the present law on constitutional grounds."

The recent case before this Court of *Torcaso* v. *Watkins,* 367 U. S. 203, is readily distinguishable from the principles laid down in *Zorach.* There, as a condition to becoming a notary public, deemed to be a public office, the applicant was required to profess a belief in God. This was concluded to be a "religious test oath" violative of our Constitution since it *obligated* a person "to profess a belief or disbelief" in religion (363 U. S. at p. 987). Certainly, there can be no parallel between such compulsion and the voluntary Regents' Prayer in accordance with our fundamental national tradition.

(d) **The saying of the prayer as a sectarian or denominational practice allegedly favoring one or more religions or religious practices over others and favoring religion over non-belief.**

We have already seen above that the saying of a prayer as such cannot constitute religion, *per se*. Paragraphs 15 and 16 (R. 16) of the petition, summarized as in the topical heading above, can only be thought to mean, therefore, that there is some ''practice'' which is sectarian and denominational and favors belief in religion over non-belief. Somehow petitioners overlooked completely the inconsistency of their position in asserting their right not to believe, which no one disputes, and at the same time asserting their right to impose on all others who do believe in a Supreme Being and Almighty God, their claimed right to eliminate reference thereto.

This apparently was the claim of the plaintiffs in *Doremus* v. *Board of Education,* 5 N. J. 435, 75 A. 2d 880 (1950), app. dis. 342 U. S. 429 (1952), in New Jersey which, when it was before the Supreme Court of that State, was answered by the Court's reference to *Cooley* (Constitutional Limitations, Eighth Edition, Volume 2, p. 974) where the author says:

> ''While thus careful to establish, protect, and defend religious freedom and equality, the American constitutions contain no provision which prohibit the authorities from such solemn recognition of a superintending Providence in public transactions and exercises as the general religious sentiment of mankind inspires, and as seems meet and proper infinite and dependent beings. Whatever may be the shades of religious belief, all must acknowledge the fitness of recognizing in important human affairs the superintending care and control of the Great governor of the

Universe, and of acknowledging with thanksgiving His boundless favors, of bowing in contrition when visited with the penalties of His broken laws.''

Reduced to the barest simplicity, what petitioners are seeking to argue in paragraphs 15 and 16 (R. 16) of their petition is that the alleged holding of children's hands in a manner specified in paragraph 10 (R. 14) coupled with the saying of the prayer constitutes a sectarian or denominational practice favoring one or more religions and religious practices over others and favoring religion over non-belief in religion. This then means that they are disregarding, for the moment at least, whether or not the *adoption* of the procedure of saying a prayer is constitutional or not and are now saying, in effect, that even if it were constitutional, the *method* allegedly used makes the law unconstitutional. This, we submit, cannot be so. It would appear to require no citation of authority to establish in the Court's mind that no law or regulation, otherwise constitutional, can be held by a Court to be unconstitutional because of the *manner* in which some participants carry it out, namely, the practice of some children holding their hands in a certain way because of their own beliefs. This has no more foundation than would the argument that a law or regulation otherwise unconstitutional, if followed by a certain practice, could by the fact be made constitutional.

The foregoing is very similar to what the complaining parties in *Zorach* v. *Clauson,* 303 N. Y. 161, aff. 343 U. S. 306, alleged, namely, that some teacher in the New York City school system so interpreted the release time program as to adopt a practice which the petitioners felt was unconstitutional. No more credence was given by either the Court of Appeals or the United States Supreme Court in that case than should be given by this Court in the instant proceeding.

This proposition is nicely summed up by Mr. Justice Bookstein in *Lewis* v. *Allen,* 5 Misc. 2d 68, 159 N.Y.S. 2d

897, the case involving the revised rendition of the Pledge of Allegiance in the State of New York, where he said:

> "To grant this application 'would be preferring those who believe in no religion over those who do believe.' Zorach v. Clauson, supra, 343 U. S. at page 314, 72 S. Ct. at page 684. The First Amendment does not require this.
>
> Petitioners' right to disbelieve is guaranteed by the First Amendment, and neither they nor their children can be compelled to recite the word 'under God' in the pledge of allegiance. But the First Amendment affords them no preference over those who do believe in God and who, pledging their allegiance, choose to express that belief". (159 N.Y.S. 2d 813)

(e) The saying of the prayer as resulting in "divisiveness".

There are at least five school districts within a few miles of the school district represented by the respondent Board of Education which have adopted the identical prayer on the recommendation of the New York State Board of Regents. In each case this procedure has been in effect for several years and in some, five or six years, yet the students at these schools seem to be normal, well adjusted, healthy American children, not at all warped in their thinking as a result of this daily reference to Almighty God. The respondents meet weekly as a Board of Education and since the prayer was instituted there was noted no "divisiveness" among parents or children and certainly none was brought in writing to the Board of Education until petitioners served their demand, heretofore referred to. Any parent may disagree with the "advisability" of some "policy" undertaken by a Board of Education but this disagreement does not warrant a striking down of such policy as being unconstitutional.

We have already seen that in *Zorach v. Clauson*, 303 N. Y. 161, aff. 343 U. S. 306, released time has been held constitutional in the State of New York yet some of the children avail themselves of one hour weekly pursuant to the release time program for religious training and others do not. Our State Courts and the United States Supreme Court, however, did not hold that the "divisiveness" thereby created, if any, would warrant striking down the release time program.

There are many occasions during a school year when children are excused for absence for the purpose of observance of religious holidays. When this occurs some children stay away from school while others attend. On still other holidays some children stay away to attend worship. Is this what petitioners call 'divisive"? Would the petitioners have this Court hold that such holiday observances should be banned because they identify one or more children with one religion or another? Certainly to do so would strike down one of our basic constitutional guarantees, i.e, religious liberty.

Complete secularism to the entire exclusion of religion or even recognition of Almighty God would be the watchword of petitioners. They would rewrite the books in which it has been held that "this is a religious people" or, as stated by the United States Supreme Court before the turn of the century, in *Holy Trinity Church* v. *United States*, 143 U. S. 457 (1892):

> "But beyond all these matters no purpose of action against religion can be imputed to any legislation, state or national, because this is a religious people. This is historically true. From the discovery of this continent to the present hour, there is single voice making this affirmation." (p. 465)

In claiming "divisiveness", again we have reliance by petitioners on the *People of the State of Illinois ex rel. McCollum* v. *Board of Education of School District No. 71, Champaign County, Illinois, et al.*, 333 U. S. 203 (1949), but we find an apt answer in the opinion of Mr. Justice Jackson when he observed, 333 U. S. at pages 232-233, 68 S. Ct. at page 476:

> "The complaint is that when others join and he does not, it sets him apart as a dissenter, which is humiliating. Even admitting this to be true, it may be doubted whether the Constitution which, of course, protects the right to dissent, can be construed also to protect one from the embarrassment that always attends non-conformity, whether in religion, politics, behavior or dress. Since no legal compulsion is applied to complainant's son himself and no penalty is imposed or threatened from which we may relieve him, we can hardly base jurisdiction on this ground."

(f) The saying of the Regents' Prayer as affected by (1) the prohibition against laws respecting an establishment of religion, or (2) prohibiting the free exercise thereof, or (3) the free exercise and enjoyment of religious profession and worship, without discrimination or preference.

This topical heading summarizes the allegations of paragraphs 18, 19 and 20 (R. 16-17) of the petition which, in toto, sumarize the language of the First Amendment to the United States Constitution and Article 1, Section 3 of the New York State Constitution.

As to the charge, here repeated, that the saying of the prayer constitutes an "establishment" of religion, we are content to rely on the points heretofore made that this is neither a logical nor legal conclusion which can be drawn.

As to there being a prohibition against laws which prohibit the free exercise of religion respondents can readily admit that the Constitution so provides. In the instant case, however, there is no "law" to which the petitioners can point as having "established" a religion.

We have here, not "acts which aid in the establishment of a religion, but acts whose purpose is to prevent the restriction of freedom to worship" (*64th St. Residences* v. *City of New York,* 173 N.Y.S. 2d 700, affd. 4 N. Y. 2d 268 (1958)).

Again as stated by the New York Court of Appeals in *Zorach* v. *Clauson* (303 N. Y. at p. 172):

> "* * * it must * * * be remembered that the First Amendment not only forbids laws 'respecting an establishment of religion' but also laws 'prohibiting the free exercise thereof'. We must not destroy one in an effort to preserve the other."

Again, in that same case, Judge Froessel said that instances abound which prove that not "every friendly gesture between church and State shall be discountenanced" (303 N. Y. at pp. 171-172).

(g) The saying of the Regents' Prayer as being in excess of respondents' statutory authority and in violation of their statutory duties.

In paragraphs 21 through 24 (R. 17) of the petition the petitioners have alleged, respectively, that respondents have exceeded their authority under Section 1709 of the Education Law; that if respondents relied on the Board of Regents' "Statement of Belief" then the Statement of Belief violates State and Federal Constitutions; that respondents' failure to discontinue the procedure regarding the saying of the prayer is illegal and constitutes a dereliction of duty; and that the discontinuance of the prayer is a non-discretionary duty imposed upon residents by the State and Federal Constitutions.

For the convenience of the Court we should first examine Section 1709 of the New York State Education Law. This Section is entitled: "Powers and Duties of Boards of Education" and applies particularly to Union Free School Districts.

By subparagraph 2 of Section 1709 of the Education Law a Board of Educators is given power "and it shall be its duty" to establish rules and regulations "concerning the order and discipline of the school * * * as they may deem necessary to secure the best educational results."

Should there have been anything missing from the above, there is an omnibus subparagraph 33 reading:

> "33. To have in all respects the superintendence, management and control of the educational affairs of the district, and, therefore, shall have all the powers reasonably necessary to exercise powers granted expressly or by implication and to discharge duties imposed expressly or by implication by this chapter or other statutes."

We come now to the the charge contained in paragraph 23 (R. 17) of the petition which asserts that respondents' refusal to discontinue the saying of the prayer upon demand of petitioners "is illegal and constitutes a dereliction of duty"; or, conversely, that the petitioners having made their claim, there is now a "non-discretionary duty" on the part of the respondents imposed by the Federal and State Constitutions (Petition, paragraph 24 (R. (17)).

We must now go back once more to the Declaration of Independence in its assertion of "self-evident truths" that "all men are endowed by their Creator with certain inalienable Rights." This was followed with the assertion that "to *secure* these Rights, Governments are instituted among Men." Resorting once more to the United States Supreme Court for emphasis with respect to the "securing" of these inalienable rights, we find this language in the concurring opinion by Mr. Justice Field in *Butcher's Union, etc., Co.* v. *Crescent City, etc., Co.,* 111 U. S. 746 (at p. 756):

> "As in our intercourse with our fellowmen certain principles of morality are assumed to exist, without

which society would be impossible, so certain inherent
rights, lie at the foundation of all action, and upon a
recognition of them alone can free institutions be
maintained. These inherent rights have never been
more happily expressed than in the Declaration of
Independence, that new evangel of liberty to the people: 'We hold these truths to be self-evident,' that is,
so plain that their truth is recognized upon their mere
statement, 'that all men are endowed', not by edicts of
Employers or decrees of Parliament or acts of Congress, but 'by their Creator, with certain inalienable
rights', that is, rights which cannot be bartered away
or given away or taken away except in punishment of
crime, 'and that among these are life, liberty and the
pursuit of happiness, and to secure these' not grant
them but secure them, 'governments are instituted
among men, deriving their just powers from the consent of the governed'.''

Apparently the "same duty" was referred to and relied
upon by the petitioners in the proceeding before Justice
Bookstein in *Lewis* v. *Allen,* 5 Misc. 2d 68, 159 N.Y.S. 2d
897, involving the Flag Salute where we find the terse
comment:

"No statutory duty has been shown which requires
respondent to rescind or revoke the regulation. So it
cannot be said that respondent has failed to perform
a duty imposed upon him by Statute."

But there, as here, the petitioners contended that the
duty was imposed on the respondents by the First and
Fourteenth Amendments to the United States Constitution
and by Article 1, Section 3, among others, of the New
York State Constitution. After reviewing the Education
Law provisions (as well as the Federal Code, applicable in that case) the Court concluded that in making a

regulation regarding the Flag Salute the "respondent was performing his duties." The Court went on to say:

> "Respondent has made a regulation pursuant to express direction of a Statute of this State and in conformance with a law of the United States. How then can he be charged with failing to perform his duty?" (p. 809)

In that case the Commissioner of Education made a specific regulation regarding the Flag Salute. In the instant case, his superiors, the Board of Regents, made a recommendation which has been urged by him as a proper subject of adoption by school districts such as that in which respondents constitute the Board of Education. Here too it might be asked: "How then can he be charged with failing to perform his duty?"

By analysis to Mr. Justice Bookstein's opinion, the petitioners' contention is reduced to a claim that the respondents should not perform the duties or abide by the recommendations of either the Board of Regents or the State Commissioner of Education since to do so violates the State and Federal Constitutions. On this subject, the opinion reads (5 Misc. 2d 68, 159 N.Y.S. 2d 897):

> "To sustain that contention implies respondent has not only the right, but the duty, to determine the constitutionality of an Act of the State Legislature or of the Congress and to refuse to perform, where in his judgment, such act is unconstitutional.
> "Clearly, this is the exclusive domain of the judiciary. It is not a function of administrative officials."

We believe, that Mr. Justice Bookstein had a complete and final answer to allegations of this type and apparently both the New York Court of Appeals and the United States Supreme Court felt similarly in *Zorach* v. *Clauson*,

303 N. Y. 161, 343 U. S. 306, where, the record on appeal in that case shows (p. 22 of that record) that these identical charges were contained in the petition and were apparently considered to be without merit in view of the failure of either Court to agree with petitioners.

Conclusion

The noncompulsory saying of the "Regents' Prayer" does not violate any Statute giving rise to either a clear legal duty on the part of respondents to discontinue such practice, nor has there been any violation by the saying of such prayer, consistent with the basic national traditions of a religious country, as our highest Courts have said we are, which would authorize the issuance of an injunction as sought by petitioners to abolish the Prayer.

The order appealed from should be affirmed.

Respectfully submitted,

BERTRAM B. DAIKER,
Attorney for Respondents.

WILFORD E. NEIER,
Of Counsel.

APPENDIX A

The State Constitutions or Preambles thereto of 49 States of the United States acknowledge that the rights and liberties of the people issue from God and express gratefulness therefor.

Alabama (Adopted in 1901)

We, the people of the State of Alabama, in order to establish justice, insure domestic tranquility and secure the blessings of liberty to ourselves and our posterity, invoking the favor and guidance of Almighty God, do ordain and establish the following Constitution and form of government for the State of Alabama.

Alaska (Adopted April 24, 1956)

We the people of Alaska, grateful to God and to those who founded our nation and pioneered this great land, in order to secure and transmit to succeeding generations our heritage of political, civil, and religious liberty within the Union of States, do ordain and establish this Constitution for the State of Alaska.

Arizona (Adopted in 1912)

We, the people of the State of Arizona, grateful to Almighty God for our liberties, do ordain this Constitution.

Arkansas (Adopted in 1874)

We, the people of the State of Arkansas, grateful to Almighty God for the privilege of choosing our own form of government, for our civil and religious liberty, and desiring to perpetuate its blessings and secure the same to ourselves and posterity, do ordain and establish this Constitution.

Appendix A

California (Adopted in 1879)

We, the people of the State of California, grateful to Almighty God for our freedom, in order to secure and perpetuate its blessings, do establish this Constitution.

Colorado (Adopted in 1876)

We, the people of Colorado, with profound reverence for the Supreme Ruler of the Universe, in order to form a more independent and perfect government; establish justice; insure tranquillity; provide for the common defense; promote the general welfare and secure the blessings of liberty to ourselves and our posterity; do ordain and establish this Constitution for the "State of Colorado".

Connecticut (Adopted in 1818)

The people of Connecticut acknowledging with gratitude, the good providence of God, in having permitted them to enjoy a free government, do, in order more effectually to define, secure, and perpetuate the liberties, rights and privileges which they have derived from their ancestors, hereby, after a careful consideration and revision, ordain and establish the following Constitution and form of civil government.

Delaware (Adopted in 1897)

Through Divine goodness, all men have by nature the rights of worshiping and serving their Creator according to the dictates of their consciences, of enjoying and defending life and liberty, of acquiring and protecting reputation and property and in general of obtaining objects suitable to their condition, without injury by one to another; and as these rights are essential to their welfare, for the due exercise thereof, power is inherent in them; and therefore all just authority in the institutions of political society is derived from the people, and established with their con-

Appendix A

sent, to advance their happiness; and they may for this end, as circumstances require, from time to time alter their Constitution of government.

Florida (Adopted in 1887)

We, the people of the State of Florida, grateful to Almighty God for our constitutional liberty, in order to secure its blessings and to form a more perfect government, insuring domestic tranquillity, maintaining public order, and guaranteeing equal civil and political rights to all, do ordain and establish this Constitution.

Georgia (Adopted in 1887)

To perpetuate the principles of free government, insure justice to all, preserve peace, promote the interest and happiness of the citizen, and transmit to posterity the enjoyment of liberty, we, the people of Georgia, relying upon the protection and guidance of Almighty God, do ordain and establish this Constitution.

Hawaii (1959)

We the people of the State of Hawaii, grateful for Divine Guidance, and mindful of our Hawaiian heritage, reaffirm our belief in a government of the people, by the people and for the people, and with an understanding heart toward all the peoples of the earth, do hereby ordain and establish this Constitution for the State of Hawaii.

Idaho (Adopted in 1890)

We, the people of the State of Idaho, grateful to Almighty God, for our freedom, to secure its blessings and promote our common welfare, do establish this Constitution.

Appendix A

Illinois (Adopted in 1870)

We, the people of the State of Illinois grateful to Almighty God for the civil, political and religious liberty which He hath so long permitted us to enjoy, and looking to Him for a blessing upon our endeavors to secure and transmit the same unimpaired to succeeding generations—in order to form a more perfect government, establish justice, insure domestic tranquillity, provide for the common defense, promote the general welfare, and secure the blessing of liberty to ourselves and our posterity, do ordain and establish this Constitution for the State of Illinois.

Indiana (Adopted in 1851)

To the end that justice be established, public order maintained, and liberty perpetuated: We, the people of the State of Indiana, grateful to Almighty God for the free exercise of the right to choose our own form of government, do ordain this Constitution.

Iowa (Adopted in 1857)

We, the people of the State of Iowa, grateful to the Supreme Being for the blessings hitherto enjoyed, and feeling our dependence on Him for a continuation of those blessings, do ordain and establish a free and independent government, by the name of the State of Iowa, the boundaries whereof shall be as follows. . . .

Kansas (Adopted in 1863)

We, the people of Kansas, grateful to Almighty God for our civil and religious privileges, in order to insure the full enjoyment of our rights as American citizens, do ordain and establish this Constitution of the State of Kansas, with the following boundaries. . . .

Appendix A

Kentucky (Adopted in 1891)

We, the people of the Commonwealth of Kentucky, grateful to Almighty God for the civil, political and religious liberties we enjoy, and invoking the continuance of these blessings, do ordain and establish this Constitution.

Louisiana (Adopted in 1921)

We, the people of the State of Louisiana, grateful to Almighty God for the civil, political and religious liberties we enjoy and desiring to secure the continuance of these blessings, do ordain and establish this Constitution.

Maine (Adopted in 1820 and 1876)

We, the people of Maine, in order to establish justice, insure tranquillity, provide for our mutual defense, promote our common welfare, and secure to ourselves and our posterity the blessings of liberty, acknowledging with grateful hearts the goodness of the Sovereign Ruler of the Universe in affording us an opportunity, so favorable to the design; and, imploring His aid and direction in its accomplishment, do agree to form ourselves into a free and independent State, by the style and title of the State of Maine, and do ordain and establish the following Constitution for the government of the same.

Maryland (Adopted in 1867)

We, the people of the State of Maryland, grateful to Almighty God for our civil and religious liberty, and taking into our serious consideration for best means of establishing a good Constitution in this State for the sure foundation and more permanent security thereof, declare. . . .

Massachusetts (Adopted in 1790)

We, therefore, the people of Massachusetts, acknowledging, with grateful hearts, the goodness of the great Legislator of the universe, in affording us, in the course of His

Appendix A

providence, an opportunity, deliberately and peaceably, without fraud, violence, or surprise, of entering into an original, explicit, and solemn compact with each other; and for forming a new Constitution of civil government, for ourselves and posterity; and devoutly imploring His direction in so interesting a design, do agree upon, ordain, and establish the following Declaration of Rights, and Frame of Government, as the Constitution of the Commonwealth of Massachusetts.

Michigan (Adopted in 1909)

We, the people of the State of Michigan, grateful to Almighty God for the blessings of freedom, and earnestly desiring to secure these blessings undiminished to ourselves and our posterity, do ordain and establish the Constitution.

Minnesota (Adopted in 1857)

We, the people of the State of Minnesota, grateful to God for our civil and religious liberty and desiring to perpetuate its blessings and secure the same to ourselves and our posterity, do ordain and establish this Constitution.

Mississippi (Adopted in 1890)

We, the people of Mississippi in convention assembled, grateful to Almighty God, and invoking His Blessing on our work, do ordain and establish this Constitution.

Missouri (Adopted in 1945)

We, the people of Missouri, with profound reverence for the Supreme Ruler of the Universe, and grateful for His goodness, do establish this Constitution for the better government of the State.

Appendix A

Montana (Adopted in 1889)

We, the people of Montana, grateful to Almighty God for the blessings of liberty, in order to secure the advantages of a State government, do in accordance with the provisions of the enabling act of Congress, approve the twenty-second of February A. D. 1889, ordain and establish this Constitution.

Nebraska (Adopted in 1875)

We, the people, grateful to Almighty God for our freedom, do ordain and establish the following declaration of rights and frame of government, as the Constitution of the State of Nebraska.

Nevada (Adopted in 1864)

We, the people of the State of Nevada, grateful to Almighty God for our freedom, in order to secure its blessings, insure domestic tranquillity, and form a more perfect government, do establish this Constitution.

New Hampshire (Adopted in 1784)

Every individual has a natural and unalienable right to worship God according to the dictates of his own conscience, and reason . . . morality and piety, rightly grounded on evangelical principles, will give the best and greatest security to government, and will lay, in the hearts of men, the strongest obligations to due subjection; and the knowledge of these is most likely to be propogated through society by the institution of the public worship of the Deity.

New Jersey (Adopted in 1844)

We, the people of the State of New Jersey, grateful to Almighty God for the civil and religious liberty which He has so long permitted us to enjoy, and looking to Him for

Appendix A

a blessing upon our endeavors to secure and transmit the same unimpaired to succeeding generations, do ordain and establish this Constitution.

New Mexico (Adopted in 1912)

We, the people of New Mexico, grateful to Almighty God for the blessings of liberty, in order to secure the advantages of a State government, do ordain and establish this Constitution.

New York (Adopted in 1895)

We, the people of the State of New York, grateful to Almighty God for our freedom, in order to secure its blessings, do establish this Constitution.

North Carolina (Adopted in 1876)

We, the people of the State of North Carolina, grateful to Almighty God, and the Sovereign Ruler of Nations, for the preservation of the American Union and the existence of our civil, political and religious liberties, and acknowledging our dependence upon Him for the continuance of these blessings to us and our posterity, do, for the more certain security thereof and for the better government of this State, ordain and establish this Constitution.

North Dakota (Adopted in 1889)

We, the people of North Dakota, grateful to Almighty God for the blessings of civil and religious liberty, do ordain and establish this Constitution.

Ohio (Adopted in 1851)

We, the people of the State of Ohio, grateful to Almighty God for our freedom, to secure its blessings and promote our common welfare, do establish this Constitution.

Appendix A

Oklahoma (Adopted in 1907)

Invoking the guidance of Almighty God in order to secure and perpetuate the blessings of liberty; to secure just and rightful government; to promote our mutual welfare and happiness, we the people of the State of Oklahoma, do ordain and establish this Constitution.

Oregon (Adopted in 1859)

All men shall be secured in the natural right to worship Almighty God according to the dictates of their own consciences.

Pennsylvania (Adopted in 1874)

We, the people of the Commonwealth of Pennsylvania, grateful to Almighty God for the blessings of civil and religious liberty, and humbly invoking His guidance, do ordain and establish this Constitution.

Rhode Island (Adopted in 1843)

We, the people of the State of Rhode Island and Providence Plantations, grateful to Almighty God for the civil and religious liberty which He hath so long permitted us to enjoy, and looking to Him for a blessing upon our endeavors to secure and to transmit the same unimpaired to succeeding generations do ordain and establish this Constitution of Government.

South Carolina (Adopted in 1895)

We, the people of the State of South Carolina, in convention assembled, grateful to God for our liberties, do ordain and establish this Constitution for the preservation and perpetuation of the same.

South Dakota (Adopted in 1889)

We, the people of South Dakota, grateful to Almighty God for our civil and religious liberties, in order to form a more perfect and independent government, establish jus-

Appendix A

tice, insure tranquillity, provide for the common defense, promote the generel welfare and preserve to ourselves and to our posterity the blessings of liberty, do ordain and establish this Constitution for the State of South Dakota.

Tennessee (Adopted in 1870)

That all men have a natural and indefeasible right to worship Almighty God according to the dictates of their conscience; that no man can of right, be compelled to attend, erect or support any place of worship, or to maintain any minister against his consent; that no human authority can, in any case whatever, control or interefere with the rights of conscience; and that no preference shall ever be given, by law, to any religious establishment or mode of worship.

Texas (Adopted in 1876)

Humbly invoking the blessings of Almighty God, the people of the State of Texas, do ordain and establish this Constitution.

Utah (Adopted in 1895)

Grateful to Almighty God for life and liberty, we, the people of Utah, in order to secure and perpetuate the principles of free government, do ordain and establish this Constitution.

Vermont (Adopted in 1793)

That all men have a natural and unalienable right, to worship Almighty God, according to the dictates of their own consciences and understandings, as in their opinion shall be regulated by the word of God; and that no man ought to or of right can be compelled to attend any religious worship, or erect or support any place of worship, or maintain any minister, contrary to the dictates of his conscience, nor can any man be justly deprived or abridged of

Appendix A

any civil right as a citizen, on account of his religious sentiments, or peculiar mode of religious worship; and that no
authority can, or ought to be vested in, or assumed by,
any power whatever, that shall in any case interefere with,
or in any manner control the rights of conscience, in the
free exercise of religious worship. Nevertheless, every sect
or denomination of Christians ought to observe the Sabbath or Lord's day, and keep up some sort of religious worship, which to them shall seem most agreeable to the revealed will of God.

Virginia (Adopted in 1902)

That religion or the duty which we owe to our Creator,
and the manner of discharging it, can be directed only by
reason and conviction, not by force or violence; and, therefore, all men are equally entitled to the free exercise of
religion, according to the dictates of conscience; and that
it is the mutual duty of all to practice Christian forbear-
ance, love and charity towards each other.

Washington (Adopted in 1889)

We, the people of the State of Washington, grateful to
the Supreme Ruler of the Universe for our liberties, do
ordain this Constitution.

Wisconsin (Adopted in 1848)

We, the people of Wisconsin, grateful to Almighty God
for our freedom, in order to secure its blessings, form a
more perfect government, insure domestic tranquillity and
promote the general welfare, do establish this Constitution.

Wyoming (Adopted in 1889)

We, the people of the State of Wyoming, grateful to God
for our civil, political and religious liberties, and desiring
to secure them to ourselves and perpetuate them to our
posterity, do ordain and establish this Constitution.

APPENDIX B

HOUSE OF REPRESENTATIVES

| 83D CONGRESS | REPORT |
| 2d *Session* | No. 1693 |

AMENDING THE PLEDGE OF ALLEGIANCE TO THE FLAG
OF THE UNITED STATES

MAY 28, 1954.—Referred to the House Calendar
and ordered to be printed

Mr. JONAS of Illinois, from the Committee on the
Judiciary, submitted the following

REPORT

[To accompany H. J. Res. 243]

The Committee on the Judiciary, to whom was referred
the joint resolution (H. J. Res. 243) to amend the pledge
of allegiance to the flag of the United States of America,
having considered the same, report favorably thereon with
an amendment and recommend that the joint resolution, as
amended, do pass.

The Amendment is as follows:

Page 2, line 1, strike out the comma after the words
"one Nation".

Appendix B

Purpose

The act of June 22, 1942 (ch. 435, 56 Stat. 1074), as amended, relates to rules and customs pertaining to the display and use of the flag of the United States of America. Section 7 of that act contains the pledge of allegiance to the flag; and it is the purpose of this proposed legislation to amend that pledge by adding the words "under God" so as to make it read, in appropriate part, "one Nation under God, indivisible,".

Statement

Since the introduction of this legislation the committee and a great number of the individual Members of Congress have received communications from all over the United States urging the enactment of this measure.

At this moment of our history the principles underlying our American Government and the American way of life are under attack by a system whose philosophy is at direct odds with our own. Our American Government is founded on the concept of the individuality and the dignity of the human being. Underlying this concept is the belief that the human person is important because he was created by God and endowed by Him with certain inalienable rights which no civil authority may usurp. The inclusion of God in our pledge therefore would further acknowledge the dependence of our people and our Government upon the moral directions of the Creator. At the same time it would serve to deny the atheistic and materialistic concepts of communism with its attendant subservience of the individual.

The Supreme Court ruled in 1892 that "this is a religious nation."[1] It reiterated this holding, more recently (1951), when it stated:

---

[1] *Church of the Holy Trinity v. U. S.* (1892) (143 U. S. 457, 470).

Appendix B

We are a religious people whose institutions presuppose a supreme being.[2]

Those words by our Supreme Court are true in a very fundamental and realistic sense. From the time of our earliest history our peoples and our institutions have reflected the traditional concept that our Nation was founded on a fundamental belief in God. For example our colonial forebears recognized the inherent truth that any government must look to God to survive and prosper. In the year 1620, the Mayflower compact, a document which contained the first constitution in America for complete self-government, declared in the opening sentence "In the name of God. Amen." This was an open recognition, by our forebears, of the need for the official conjunction of the laws of God and with the laws of the land.

It was William Penn who said: "Those people who are not governed by God will be ruled by tyrants."

Four years before the Declaration of Independence, we find George Mason arguing to the General Court of Virginia that—

> All acts of legislature apparently contrary to the natural right and justice are, in our laws, and must be in the nature of things considered as void. The laws of nature are the laws of God, whose authority can be superseded by no power on earth.

On July 4, 1776, our Founding Fathers proclaimed our Declaration of Independence which no less than four times refers to the existence of the Creator. It states in part:

> When in the Course of human events, it becomes necessary for one people to dissolve the political bands which have connected them with another and to assume among the powers of the earth, the separate and equal

---

[2] *Zorach* v. *Clauson* (1951) (343 U. S. 306, 313).

Appendix B

station to which the Laws of Nature and of Nature's God entitle them, a decent respect to the opinions of mankind requires that they should declare the causes which impel them to the separation.

We hold these truths to be self-evident, that all men are created equal, that they are endowed by their Creator with certain unalienable Rights, that among these are Life, Liberty, and the pursuit of Happiness.

This same document appeals to ''The Supreme Judge of the world that this Nation be free, and pledges our Nation to support the Declaration ''with a firm reliance on the protection of divine Providence.''

During the Presidency of Abraham Lincoln, the Congress passed the act of April 22, 1864, directing that the inscription ''In God we trust'' be placed on our coins. This avowal of faith has been imprinted on billions and billions of coins during the last 90 years.

Later at Gettysburg on November 19, 1863, Lincoln said:

That we here highly resolve that these dead shall not have died in vain; that this Nation, under God, shall have a new birth of freedom, and that government of the people, by the people, for the people shall not perish from the earth:

Recently President Eisenhower joined with Bishop Fulton J. Sheen, Dr. Norman Vincent Peale, Rabbi Norman Salit, and the American Legion Commander, Arthur J. Connell, in the American Legion's Back to God appeal in connection with its Four Chaplains' Day, Commemorating the four military chaplains who heroically gave their lives when the troopship *Dorchester* was sunk in 1943. The President declared that ''all the history of America'' bears witness to the truth that ''in time of test or trial we instinctively turn to God.'' ''Today, as then (Gettysburg), there is need for positive acts of renewed recognition that faith is our surest * * * strength, our greatest resource.''

Appendix B

Representative Louis C. Rabaut who testified at the hearing before the subcommittee aptly stated the need for this legislation in the following words:

> By the addition of the phrase "under God" to the pledge, the consciousness of the American people will be more altered to the true meaning of our country and its form of government. In this full awareness we will, I believe, be strengthened for the conflict now facing us and more determined to preserve our precious heritage.
>
> More importantly, the children of our land, in the daily recitation of the pledge in school, will be daily impressed with a true understanding of our way of life and its origins. As they grow and advance in this understanding, they will assume the responsibilities of self-government equipped to carry on the traditions that have been given to us. Fortify our youth in their allegiance to the flag by their dedication to "one Nation, under God."

Since our flag is symbolic of our Nation, its constitutional government and the morality of our people, the committee believes it most appropriate that the concept of God be included in the recitations of the pledge of allegience to the flag. It should be pointed out that the adoption of this legislation in no way runs contrary to the provisions of the first amendment to the Constitution. This is not an act establishing a religion or one interfering with the "free exercise" of religion. A distinction must be made between the existence of a religion as an institution and a belief in the sovereignty of God. The phrase "under God" recognizes only the guidance of God in our national affairs. The Supreme Court has clearly indicated that the references to the Almighty which run thorugh our laws, our public rituals, and our ceremonies in no way flout the provisions of the first amendment (*Zorach* v. *Clauson* (343 U. S. 306,

Appendix B

312-313)). In so construing the first amendment, the Court pointed out that, if this recognition of the Almighty was not so, then even a fastidious atheist or agnostic could object to the way in which the Court itself opens each of its sessions, namely, "God save the United States and this Honorable Court" (id., 313).

Included as a part of this report is an opinion from the Legislative Reference Service of the Library of Congress, concerning the proper placement of the words "Under God" in the pledge of allegiance.

MAY 11, 1954.

To: Mr. Cyril F. Brickfield [Assistant Counsel], House Committee on the Judiciary.

Subject: Placing of the words "under God" in the pledge of allegiance.

The pledge of allegiance to the flag was recognized and codified by Congress in the Flag Code of 1942 (act of June 22, 1942, amended December 22, 1942, U. S. C. 36:172). The pledge law now reads: "I pledge allegiance to the flag of the United States of America and to the Republic for which it stands, one Nation indivisible, with liberty and justice for all."

Currently, several proposals are pending, to insert in this pledge the word "under God." These present several alternatives as to placement and punctuation:

(1) * * * Republic for which it stands, one Nation, under God, indivisible, with liberty * * *

(2) * * * Republic for which it stands, one Nation under God, indivisible, with liberty * * *

(3) * * * Republic for which it stands, one Nation indivisible under God, with liberty * * *

You have asked for a brief memorandum on the question of placement and punctuation, and whether the rules of grammar point to one form rather than

Appendix B

another. The present statement is limited to this narrow point. Of course, before any judgment can be expressed, the fundamental question must be met— what is the exact meaning intended by the proposed insertion? On this point, we have some remarks in the Congressional Record as a guide.

Representative Rabaut, who introduced Joint Resolution 243, explained his measure in the Congressional Record of February 12, 1954, page A-1115. "Unless we are willing to affirm our belief in the existence of God and His creator-creature relationship to man, we drop man himself to the significance of a grain of sand. * * * Children and Americans of all ages must know that this is one Nation which "under God" means "liberty and justice for all."

Senator Ferguson, who introduced Senate Joint Resolution 126, commented that "Our Nation was founded on a fundamental belief in God * * * communism, on the contrary, rejects the very existence of God." (See Congressional Record, April 1, 1954, p. A-2527.)

It seems unlikely, then, that the insertion is intended as a general affirmance of the proposition that the United States of America, is "founded on a fundamental belief in God." The new language should therefore be inserted, and punctuated, so as most clearly to indicate this general thought. Under the generally accepted rules of grammar, a modifier should normally be placed as close as possible to the word it modifies. In the present instance, this would indicate that the phrase "under God," being intended as a fundamental and basic characterization of our Nation, might well be put immediately following the word "Nation." Further, since the basic idea is a Nation founded on a belief in God, there would seem to be no reason for a comma after Nation; "one Nation under

Appendix B

God" thus becomes a single phrase, emphasizing precisely the idea desired by the authors noted above.

This reading, will be noted, substitutes the basic concept of "one Nation under God" for the phrase now in law, "one Nation indivisible"; and "indivisible" becomes a separate prime modifier.

In the alternative reading, "one Nation indivisible under God," the phrase "under God" would be the normal rules of grammar be read as modify "indivisible," rather than "Nation." By the same reasoning, in the reading "one Nation under God indivisible," indivisible would naturally be construed as modifying the word "God."

It may be noted in passing that as the expression is used in Lincoln's Gettysburg Address [that this Nation, under God, shall have a new birth of freedom * * *] the phrase "under God" seems to mean "with the help of God." Lincoln was solemnly asking his people to resolve that the Nation, with God's help, should have a new birth of freedom. The difference in context seems adequate reason for the punctuation as given.

W. C. GILBERT, *Assistant Director.*

CHANGES IN EXISTING LAW

In compliance with clause 3 of rule XIII of the House of Representatives there is printed below in roman type without brackets existing law in which no change is proposed by enactment of this bill: New provisions proposed to be inserted are shown in italic.

Appendix B

Title 28, United States Code

§ 172. Pledge of Allegiance to the Flag; Manner of Delivery

The following is designated as the pledge of allegiance to the flag: "I pledge allegiance to the flag of the United States of America and to the Republic for which it stands, one Nation *under God,* indivisible, with liberty and justice for all." Such pledge should be rendered by standing with the right hand over the heart. However, civilians will always show full respect to the flag when the pledge is given by merely standing at attention, men removing the headdress. Persons in uniform shall render the military salute.

APPENDIX C

1. THE MAYFLOWER COMPACT—41 pilgrims on the deck of the Mayflower in 1620 prepared the first written constitution of our land. It opened with these words: "In the name of God, Amen," and stated that the long and difficult voyage to the new world had been "undertaken for the glory of God." They signed it "solemnly and mutually in the presence of God."

2. THE LIBERTY BELL—When the bell was cast in 1751, these words of Moses were inscribed on it: "Proclaim liberty throughout the land unto all the inhabitants thereof." (Lev. 25:10)

3. DECLARATION OF INDEPENDENCE ON GOD—On June 12, 1775, a year before the signing of the Declaration of Independence, the Continental Congress officially called on all citizens to observe "the twentieth day of July next" to be set aside as a day of public humiliation, fasting and prayer; that we may, with united hearts and voices, unfeignedly confess and deplore our many sins, and offer up our joint supplications to the all-wise, omnipotent and merciful Disposer of all events . . . "

4. THE AMERICAN SEAL—On every dollar bill the seal is pictured with the "Eye of God" directly above the pyramid. The words "Annuit Coeptis" signify: "He (God) has favored our undertakings." Congress approved this design on June 20, 1782.

5. OATH OF OFFICE—The oath taken by government employees, witnesses in court and those seeking passports concludes with the prayerful petition: "So help me God." This practice was originated by George Washington when he took his first oath of office as President of the United States, April 30, 1789.

Appendix C

6. NORTHWEST ORDINANCE—This document played an important part in United States history. Congress passed it on July 13, 1787, and thereby established federal control of the territory west of the Allegheny Mountains and north of the Ohio River. It included this stipulation:

"Religion, morality, and knowledge, being necessary to good government and the happiness of mankind, schools and the means of education shall forever be encouraged."

7. THANKSGIVING DAY—From its very start, our nation has set aside one day to render thanks to Almighty God. The Chief Executive officially asks each citizen to express gratitude to a bountiful Creator. In his proclamation for a national Thanksgiving Day, George Washington, shortly after his inauguration, said: "Whereas it is the duty of all nations to acknowledge the Providence of Almighty God, to obey His will, to be grateful for His benefits, and humbly to implore His protection and favor. I do recognize and assign Thursday, the 26th day of November next, to be devoted by the people of these states to the service of that great and glorious Being who is the beneficent Author of all the good that was, that is, or will be."

8. WASHINGTON'S ORDER REGARDING CHAPLAINS—On July 9, 1776, less than a week after the signing of the Declaration of Independence, General George Washington issued the following order:

"The honorable Continental Congress having been pleased to allow a chaplain to each regiment, the colonels or commanding officers of each regiment are directed to procure chaplains accordingly, persons of good character and exemplary lives, and to see that all inferior officers and soldiers pay them a suitable respect. The blessings and protection of Heaven are at

Appendix C

all times necessary, but especially so in times of public distress and danger.''

All branches of the U. S. Armed Services are now officially staffed by thousands of chaplains.

9. NATIONAL ANTHEM—Francis Scott Key composed the ''Star Spangled Banner'' during the bombardment of Fort McHenry on the night of September 13, 1814. He scribbled it on an old envelope. For 117 years, this song was popular as a patriotic hymn. On March 3, 1931 Congress adopted the ''Star Spangled Banner'' as our national anthem . . . It closes with this reverent praise of God:

''Praise the Power that hath made and preserved us a nation.

Then conquer we must, when our cause it is just
And this is our motto—'In God is our Trust'.''

10. MOTTO ON COINS—During the Civil War, a Protestant minister, Rev. M. R. Watkinson of Ridleyville, Pa., wrote the Secretary of the Treasury, Salmon P. Chase, on Nov. 13, 1861, requesting ''the recognition of the Almighty God on our coins.'' He concluded his letter to Mr. Chase with this petition: ''This would put us openly under the Divine protection we have personally claimed. From my heart I have felt our national shame in disowning God as not the least of our present national disasters.''

On Dec. 9, 1863, after several wordings and designs had been submitted, Mr. Chase instructed Mr. James Pollock, director of the U. S. Mint in Philadelphia, to start inscribing the words ''In God We Trust'' on all coins.

11. EVERY PRESIDENT PAID TRIBUTE TO GOD—All Presidents without exception, from George Washington

Appendix C

to Dwight D. Eisenhower, have publicly recognized the dependence of this nation on Almighty God. These excerpts are from some of their Inaugural Addresses:

WASHINGTON—" . . . in this first official act my fervent supplications to that Almighty Being Who rules over the universe . . ."

THOMAS JEFFERSON—". . . acknowledging and adoring an overruling Providence . . . May that Infinite Power, . . . lead our councils to what is best . . ."

JAMES MADISON—". . . in the guardianship and guidance of that Almighty Being Whose power regulates the destiny of nations . . ."

ANDREW JACKSON—". . . a firm reliance on the goodness of that Power Whose Providence protected our national infancy and has since upheld our liberties in various vicissitudes . . ."

ABRAHAM LINCOLN—". . . with firmness in the right as God gives us to see the light, let us strive on to finish the work we are in . . ."

WILLIAM HOWARD TAFT—". . . I invoke . . . the aid of the Almighty God in the discharge of my responsible duties."

WOODROW WILSON—" . . . God helping me, I will not fail them . . ."

HERBERT HOOVER—". . . I ask the help of Almighty God in this service to my country . . ."

FRANKLIN D. ROOSEVELT—" . . . We humbly ask the blessing of God . . . May He guide me in the days to come . . ."

Appendix C

HARRY S. TRUMAN—". . . We believe that all men are created equal because they are created in the image of God . . ."

DWIGHT D. EISENHHOWER—". . . In our quest of understanding, we beseech God's guidance . . ."

12. NATIONAL MOTTO—A Joint Resolution was also adopted by Congress on July 20, 1956, establishing "In God we trust" as the national motto of the United States. Here are the words of the official resolution:

"Resolved by the Senate and House of Representatives of the United States of America in Congress assembled, that the national motto of the United States is hereby declared to be 'In God we trust'."

13. TOMB OF UNKNOWN SOLDIER—In the National Cemetery at Arlington, Va., the official inscription on the tomb of the unknown soldier reads:

"Here lies in honored glory, an American soldier, known but to God."

14. NATIONAL MONUMENTS—They bear further tribute to the dependence of our country upon Almighty God.

WASHINGTON MONUMENT—The numerous spiritual inscriptions on its walls include these words of the Divine Master:

"Suffer the little children to come unto me and forbid them not, for of such is the kingdom of heaven." (Luke 18:16)

LINCOLN MEMORIAL—Near the massive statute of Abraham Lincoln, his words are chiseled into the granite wall:

Appendix C

". . . that this nation under God shall have a new birth of freedom, and that government of the people, by the people, for the people, shall not perish from the earth."

JEFFERSON MEMORIAL—The forceful words of Thomas Jefferson inscribed in the monument remind all who behold them of the dire results that may follow if we forget God is the Source of our Liberty:

"God who gave us life gave us liberty. Can the liberties of a nation be secure when we have removed the conviction that these liberties are the gift of God?"

IN THE

SUPREME COURT OF THE UNITED STATES

October Term, 1962

No. 142

School District of Abington Township, Pennsylvania, James F. Koehler, O. H. English, Eugene Stull, M. Edward Northam, and Charles H. Boehm, Superintendent of Public Instruction, Commonwealth of Pennsylvania,

Appellants

v.

Edward Lewis Schempp, Sidney Gerber Schempp, Individually and as Parents and Natural Guardians of Roger Wade Schempp and Donna Kay Schempp,

Appellees

On Appeal From a District Court of Three Judges for the Eastern District of Pennsylvania.

BRIEF FOR APPELLANTS

OPINIONS BELOW

———

The opinion with findings of fact and conclusions of law of the three-judge District Court for the Eastern District of Pennsylvania declaring the former Bible reading statute unconstitutional is reported in 177 F. Supp. 398 (R. 177). The opinion of such court permitting appellees to file their supplemental pleading is reported in 195 F. Supp. 518 (R. 201). The subsequent opinion of such court, with findings of fact and conclusions of law, declaring the amended Bible reading statute unconstitutional, is reported in 201 F. Supp. 815 (R. 228).

JURISDICTION

The final decree of the three-judge District Court for the Eastern District of Pennsylvania was entered on February 1, 1962 (R. 236). Notice of appeal was filed in that court on March 28, 1962 (R. 237). The jurisdictional statement was filed May 24, 1962 and probable jurisdiction was noted October 8, 1962 (R. 241).

The jurisdiction of the Supreme Court to review this decision by direct appeal is conferred by Title 28, United States Code, Section 1253.

STATUTES INVOLVED

The statute of Pennsylvania previously declared unconstitutional by the three-judge court, as it read at the time appellees' original complaint was filed and the final decree of September 7, 1959 issued, was as follows:

"Section 1516. Bible To Be Read in Public Schools.—At least ten verses from the Holy Bible shall be read, or caused to be read, without comment, at the opening of each public school on each school day, by the teacher in charge: Provided, That where any teacher has other teachers under and subject to direction, then the teacher exercising such authority shall read the Holy Bible, or cause it to be read, as herein directed.

If any school teacher, whose duty it shall be to read the Holy Bible, or cause it to be read, shall fail or omit so to do, said school teacher shall, upon charges preferred for such failure or omission, and proof of the same, before the board of school directors of the school district, be discharged.''

Section 1516 of the Public School Code of 1949, the Act of March 10, 1949, P.L. 30, as amended May 9, 1949, P.L. 939, 24 Purdon's Pa. Stats. Ann. Section 15-1516.

The amended statute of Pennsylvania that was declared unconstitutional by the three-judge court in its opinion and decree dated February 1, 1962, is as follows:

"Section 1516.   Bible Reading in Public Schools.—
At least ten verses from the Holy Bible shall be read,
without comment, at the opening of each public school
on each school day.   Any child shall be excused from
such Bible reading, or attending such Bible reading,
upon the written request of his parent or guardian."

> Section 1516 of the Public School Code of 1949,
> the Act of March 10, 1949, P.L. 30, as amended
> December 17, 1959, P.L. 1928, 24 Purdon's Pa.
> Stats. Ann. Section 15-1516.

The First Amendment of the Constitution of the
United States, provides as follows:

"Congress shall make no law respecting an establishment of religion, or prohibiting the free exercise
thereof; or abridging the freedom of speech, or of
the press; or the right of the people peaceably to as-
semble, and to petition the Government for a redress
of grievances."

The Fourteenth Amendment, Section 1, provides as
follows:

"Section 1.   All persons born or naturalized in the
United States, and subject to the jurisdiction thereof,
are citizens of the United States and of the State
wherein they reside.   No State shall make or enforce
any law which shall abridge the privileges or immunities of citizens of the United States; nor shall
any State deprive any person of life, liberty, or property, without due process of law; nor deny to any
person within its jurisdiction the equal protection of
the laws."

QUESTIONS PRESENTED

1. Is Pennsylvania's Bible reading statute, Section 1516 of the Public School Code of 1949, the Act of March 10, 1949, P.L. 30, as amended by the Act of December 17, 1959, P.L. 1928, a law respecting an establishment of religion or prohibiting the free exercise thereof within the prohibition of the First Amendment to the United States Constitution as applied to the States by the Fourteenth Amendment, by providing for the reading without comment at the opening of each public school on each school day, of at least ten verses from the Holy Bible, subject to the excuse of any child from attending such Bible reading upon the written request of his parent or guardian?

2. Have appellees been deprived of any constitutionally protected right when, in the absence of compulsion on them to believe, disbelieve, participate in or attend a Bible reading exercise in violation of their religious consciences, they have not sought to be excused under a statute which provides the right of excuse, and no measurable tax burden upon them resulting from the Bible reading exercise has been shown?

STATEMENT OF THE CASE

On February 14, 1958, appellees, students in the public schools of Abington Township, Pennsylvania, and their parents, filed their complaint (R. 1) alleging that appellant School District of Abington Township and certain employees thereof were violating the religious consciences and liberties of appellees by causing the Bible to be read in the classrooms of the Abington Township School District pursuant to the then existing Section 1516 of the Public School Code of 1949, the Act of March 10, 1949, P.L. 30, as amended May 9, 1949, P.L. 939, which read as follows.:

"Section 1516. Bible To Be Read in Public Schools.—At least ten verses from the Holy Bible shall be read, or caused to be read, without comment, at the opening of each public school on each school day, by the teacher in charge: Provided, That where any teacher has other teachers under and subject to direction, then the teacher exercising such authority shall read the Holy Bible, or cause it to be read, as herein directed.

If any school teacher, whose duty it shall be to read the Holy Bible, or cause it to be read, shall fail or omit so to do, said school teacher shall, upon charges preferred for such failure or omission, and proof of the same, before the board of school directors of the school district, be discharged."

As the complaint prayed that appellants be enjoined from enforcing this statute, jurisdiction was assumed by

a three-judge court, pursuant to 28 U.S.C. Sections 2281
and 2284, as an action seeking a permanent injunction
restraining the enforcement, operation and execution of a
State statute.

After trial, the three-judge court, on September 16,
1959, issued its opinion declaring unconstitutional such
Bible reading statute and the practice thereunder, on the
grounds that it provided for an establishment of religion
and interfered with appellees' free exercise of religion (R.
177). The conclusion of the court below was predicated on
its factual finding that attendance by all pupils and participation by the teachers were compulsory. In its Eighth
Finding of Fact (R. 194), the three-judge court stated:

> "(8) The attendance of all students in both of
> the aforesaid schools at the ceremony of the Bible
> reading and recitation of the Lord's Prayer is com-
> pulsory."

On the same day, the three-judge court issued its final
decree which perpetually enjoined appellants from causing
to be read to the students in the public schools of Abington
Township the Holy Bible as directed by the Pennsylvania
Public School Code, or as part of any ceremony, observance, exercise or school routine (R. 196).

On September 21, 1959, the three-judge court issued its
order staying the operation and enforcement of the final
decree until final determination of an appeal, and on
November 12, 1959, notice of appeal to the Supreme Court
of the United States was filed by appellants.

On December 17, 1959 the Legislature of Pennsylvania,
to eliminate the compulsory features of the then existing
statute amended Section 1516 of the Public School Code to
read as follows:

"Section 1516.—Bible Reading in Public Schools.—
At least ten verses from the Holy Bible shall be read,
without comment, at the opening of each public school
on each school day.

Any child shall be excused from such Bible reading, or attending such Bible reading, upon the written
request of his parent or guardian."

This amended statute differs from the old statute in
that the amendment deletes any provision requiring teachers, on pain of discharge, to cause the Bible to be read,
and contains the entirely new provision for excusing any
child from Bible reading or from attendance at the Bible
reading on the written request of his parent or guardian.
Following the passage of this amendment, the Abington
Township School District altered its practice and now will
excuse any child from attendance at Bible reading upon
the written request of his parent or guardian (R. 205, par.
10).

On December 23, 1959, appellants filed with the three-
judge court their Motion for Relief from Judgment and
Final Decree under Rule 60(b) of the Federal Rules of
Civil Procedure. Such motion prayed that the final decree
be vacated on the grounds, *inter alia,* that the passage of
the amendment and the changes it brought about in the
Bible reading practice in the Abington Township School
District had eliminated any controversy between the parties and had rendered the issues moot.

On June 9, 1960, the three-judge court denied appellants' Motion for Relief from Judgment and Final Decree
on the ground that it lacked jurisdiction either to entertain
or adjudicate the motion and held that jurisdiction had

passed to and was lodged exclusively with the Supreme Court of the United States.

On August 5, 1960, appellants filed their Jurisdictional Statement and on October 24, 1960, this Court issued its *per curiam* order, which read as follows:

"The judgment is vacated and the case is remanded to the District Court for such further proceedings as may be appropriate in light of Act No. 700 of the Laws of the General Assembly of the Commonwealth of Pennsylvania, passed at the Session of 1959 and approved by the Governor of the Commonwealth on December 17, 1959." (364 U.S. 298.)

On January 5, 1961, because of the deep concern of the Commonwealth of Pennsylvania in its amended Bible reading statute, the Superintendent of Public Instruction petitioned the three-judge court and subsequently was permitted to intervene in this case as a party defendant (R. 200).

On January 4, 1961, appellees filed their motion for leave to file a supplemental pleading (R. 199), and, after filing of briefs and oral argument, the three-judge court, on June 22, 1961, filed its Opinion and Order granting leave to appellees to file such supplemental pleading (R. 201). Appellants filed their Answer to this supplemental pleading on July 10, 1961 (R. 204), and on October 17, 1961, trial was held before the three-judge court.

At this second trial appellees called Edward Schempp and his son, Roger, and rested their case on the brief testimony given by these two (R. 211-221) and on the evidence that had been previously introduced at the former trial under the old non-excusatory Act (R. 221-225).

On February 1, 1962, the three-judge court issued its opinion declaring the amended statute unconstitutional on the ground that it violates the "establishment of religion" clause of the First Amendment made applicable to the Commonwealth of Pennsylvania by the Fourteenth Amendment (R. 228). The court held that the reading without comment of ten verses of the Holy Bible each morning, at an exercise from which any or all students could be excused, constituted an obligatory religious observance (R. 232).

On the same day, the three-judge court issued its final decree which perpetually enjoined appellants from reading and causing to be read or permitting anyone subject to their control and direction to read to students in the Abington Township Senior High School, any work or book known as the Holy Bible as directed by Section 1516 of the Public School Code of 1949, the Act of March 10, 1949, P.L. 30, as amended December 17, 1959, P.L. 1928, in conjunction with, or not in conjunction with, the saying, the reciting, or the reading of the Lord's Prayer (R. 236). Thereafter, on February 5, 1962, the three-judge court issued its Order staying the operation and enforcement of the final decree until final disposition of the case by this Court.

SUMMARY OF ARGUMENT

The activity found by the court below to have violated the First Amendment to the Constitution of the United States was the practice of reading without comment ten verses of the Holy Bible at the opening exercises of the Abington Township High School pursuant to the Public School Code of Pennsylvania. It did not involve coercion of the pupils, any of whom were privileged to be excused upon the written request of their parents. It did not affect the appellees as taxpayers, or in any manner impair their right to exercise freely their religious beliefs.

The holding of the court below that this practice of Bible reading in Pennsylvania's public schools constitutes an unconstitutional "establishment of religion" in violation of the First Amendment is erroneous as a matter of law. The statutory Bible reading practice is not a religious practice. It requires only that those who wish to do so may listen to daily readings without discussion or comment from a great work that possesses many values, including religious, moral, literary and historical. Unlike the program of religious education struck down in *McCollum v. Board of Education,* 333 U.S. 203 (1948), the Pennsylvania practice does not involve proselytizing, persuasion, or religious indoctrination. It involves no avowal of faith, acceptance of doctrine, or statement of belief. Listening to the Bible being read, unlike the religious oath of office in *Torcaso v. Watkins,* 367 U.S. 488 (1961), and the solemn avowal of prayer in *Engel v. Vitale,* 370 U.S. 421 (1962), is not a religious act.

This Court has affirmed that we are a religious people, and that many of our customs compel the conclusion that our public life contains a religious leaven (*Zorach v. Clauson,* 343 U.S. 306 (1952)). Nothing in the Constitution requires that the courts or the government should be hostile to religion. In *Zorach* and *Engel* this Court has stated that the First Amendment requires only that the government be neutral, not friendly or hostile, to religion. The maintenance of such neutrality in the matter of religion in a nation that has this traditional religious leaven in its public life requires that the government neither add to nor subtract from such leaven. The appellants here contend that this Court is not required, under the First Amendment, to eradicate from this nation's public life all voluntary customs and established traditions which some might consider to have religious connotations. It is contended that the Legislature of Pennsylvania cannot be forced by a few persons to abandon a voluntarily attended Bible reading practice which has been traditional in Pennsylvania for generations, on the ground that such reading provides for "an establishment of religion," as held by the court below.

A decision by this Court that the Pennsylvania Bible reading practice is unconstitutional would provide a precedent whereby there could be eliminated from the public life of this nation all those customs and traditions that evidence the religious nature and origin of our country and are now and have long been cherished and accepted by a vast majority of the people. A decision by this Court upholding the constitutionality of the Pennsylvania Bible reading practice would be consistent with its prior holdings. It would reaffirm the constitutional requirement of neutrality to religion, for just as this Court refused to allow the introduction of religious instruction into the public schools in the *McCollum* case or the creation of an official prayer for public school children in the *Engel* case, so did it permit to continue in public life the voluntary religious oath of office in the *Torcaso* case.

There is a complete absence of proof that the Pennsylvania Bible reading practice affects the appellees as taxpayers or interferes with their right to exercise freely their religion or their religious beliefs. Under the doctrine of *Doremus v. Board of Education,* 342 U.S. 429 (1952), such a failure of proof would have compelled the conclusion that appellees had no standing to maintain this action. Although it is recognized that the decision in *Engel v. Vitale,* 370 U.S. 421 (1962), indicates that this Court may have revised its previous holdings concerning the doctrine of "standing in court," it is contended that by reason of the total failure of appellees to establish any compulsion against them or pecuniary loss, this Court should conclude that appellees have not established standing sufficient to invoke the jurisdiction of this Court.

ARGUMENT

POINT I

APPELLEES HAVE BEEN UNABLE TO SHOW THAT THE BIBLE READING PRACTICE INTERFERES WITH THE FREE EXERCISE OF THEIR RELIGIOUS BELIEFS

A. The Traditional Practice of Bible Reading in Pennsylvania

The practice of reading the Bible at the opening of each school day is a traditional custom that has existed in Pennsylvania since the early times and has been codified since 1913.[1] The practice has always been conducted in a secular manner, devoid of any attempt at proselytizing or the inculcation of religious belief.

The exact origin of Bible reading in Pennsylvania cannot be determined precisely because the custom originated before the practice of maintaining school records developed. That the Bible reading custom existed in the earliest schools may today only be demonstrated inferentially. The various reports of County Superintendents of

---

[1] The Act of May 20, 1913, P.L. 226. The preamble to this Act stated in part that "it is in the interest of good moral training, of a life of honorable thought and of good citizenship, that the public school children should have lessons of morality brought to their attention during their school days."

Schools contained in *Report of the Superintendent of Common Schools of the Commonwealth of Pennsylvania for the year ending June 4, 1866* (Harrisburg 1867), indicate that the custom had been a long established one as early as 1866. That the Bible reading custom was shared by other states is evidenced by the *Annual Report to the Massachusetts Board of Education* submitted by Horace Mann in 1847, in which he stated:

> "The use of the Bible in the schools is not expressly enjoined by law, but both its letter and its spirit are consonant with that use, and, as a matter of fact, *I suppose there is not, at the present time, a single town in the commonwealth in whose schools it is not read.*" (Emphasis supplied)[2]

Further light on the history of this practice in Pennsylvania is furnished by the opinion of Judge Edwards of the Court of Common Pleas of Lackawanna County in *Stevenson v. Hanyon,* 7 Pa. Dist. Rep. 585 (1898), at page 588:

> ". . . It is worthy of comment and reflects creditably upon the good sense of the people of Pennsylvania, that, although our common school system has been in existence for many years, and that, as a general rule, in a large number of school districts throughout the State, portions of the holy scriptures have been read as a part of the daily opening exercises, nobody up to this time has taken such interest in the question as to secure a decision upon it from our court of last resort . . ."

Although the Supreme Court of Pennsylvania has never had before it a case involving the practice of reading

---

[2] FULLER, HORACE MANN ANNUAL REPORTS, 595 (1868).

selections from the Bible in the public schools, such practice was held constitutional in several decisions of the Courts of Common Pleas:

> *Hart v. School District,* 2 Chester County Reports 521 (1895);
>
> *Curran v. White,* 22 Pa. County Reports 201 (1898);
>
> *Stevenson v. Hanyon,* supra.

While the question of Bible reading was being settled by the courts of Pennsylvania, the then Superintendent of Public Instruction, Dr. Nathan C. Schaeffer, edited a book of Bible readings for schools and stated in the Preface as follows:

> "* * * Bible readings cannot be omitted from the exercises of the school without the gravest loss and the most serious consequences.
>
> It is, of course, not the mission of the public school to teach the creed or the doctrines of any religious denomination. That is the province of the home, the church, and the Sabbath School. In making this collection of Bible readings, the aim has been to bring together selections that appeal strongly to the moral nature of the child. In modern education it has become proverbial to say that the perpetuity and prosperity of the state depend upon the intelligence and virtue of the people. . . ."[3]

The first statutory enactment covering Bible reading in Pennsylvania was the Act of May 20, 1913, P.L. 226. The intent of the Act was stated in its preamble which read as follows:

---

[3] AMERICAN BOOK COMPANY, BIBLE READINGS FOR SCHOOLS (1897).

"Whereas, The rules and regulations governing the reading of the Holy Bible in the public schools of this Commonwealth are not uniform; and

"Whereas, It is in the interest of good moral training, of a life of honorable thought and of good citizenship, that the public school children should have lessons of morality brought to their attention during their school-days . . ."

The practice of Bible reading developed as an aid to moral training, and not for the purpose of introducing religion or sectarian instruction into public education. The people of Pennsylvania, speaking through their Constitution and Legislature, have long followed the policy of avoiding religion or sectarianism in their public schools.[4]

---

[4] Article I, Section 3 of the Pennsylvania Constitution of 1874 provides:

"All men have a natural and indefeasible right to worship Almighty God according to the dictates of their own consciences; no man can of right be compelled to attend, erect or support any place of worship, or to maintain any ministry against his consent; no human authority can, in any case whatever, control or interfere with the rights of conscience and no preference shall ever be given by law to any religious establishments or modes of worship."

Article X, Section 2 of the same Constitution, provides:

"No money raised for the support of the public schools of the Commonwealth shall be appropriated to or used for the support of any sectarian school."

Section 108 of the Public School Code of 1949, the Act of March 10, 1949, P.L. 30, 24 Purdon's Penna. Stat. Ann., Section 1-108, provides:

"No religious or political test or qualification shall be required of any director, visitor, superintendent, teacher, or other officer, appointee, or employe in the public schools of this Commonwealth."

This same provision was included as Section 2801 of the Pennsylvania School Code of May 18, 1911, P.L. 309.

B. The Bible Reading Practice in Abington Township School District

Since the passage of the 1913 Act the Bible reading practice has been continuously prescribed by statute in the Commonwealth of Pennsylvania. The present Superintendent of Public Instruction of Pennsylvania, Dr. Charles H. Boehm, considers that the practice has both educational and moral value for the students (R. 89-90).

At the Abington Senior High School the practice is conducted as follows: Between 8:15 and 8:30 of each school morning, while the students are in their Home Rooms or Advisory Sections, there is heard over the public address system a morning program which includes the reading of ten verses of the Bible without comment, the saying of the Lord's Prayer, the flag salute, and the school announcements for that particular day (R. 102-103, 108-109). The persons who conduct this opening exercise over the public address system are students of the radio and television course, which is part of the teaching program of the school (R. 109). Participation in this course is voluntary with

---

Section 1112(a) of the Public School Code of 1949, the Act of March 10, 1949, P.L. 30, 24 Purdon's Penna. Stat. Ann. Section 11-1112(a), further provides:

"That no teacher in any public school shall wear in said school or while engaged in the performance of his duty as such teacher any dress, mark, emblem, or insignia indicating the fact that such teacher is a member or adherent of any religious order, sect or denomination."

This provision, in substantially the same language had appeared as Section 1 in the Act of June 27, 1895, P.L. 395. This Section 1 was preceded by the following preamble:

"Whereas, It is important that all appearances of sectarianism should be avoided in the administration of the public schools of this Commonwealth."

the student (R. 131). The student who reads the verses from the Bible may use any version of the Bible. The King James version, the Catholic Douay version, the Jewish Holy Scriptures and the Revised Standard version have been so used (R. 109-112). The particular verses to be read are selected by the student who does the reading (R. 103-104, 113).

With regard to the actual reading of the Bible, there are no prefatory statements made, no questions are solicited, no comments or explanations are made before, during or after its reading. No instruction is contemplated; no interpretation is given. As the statute specifically provides that the reading be "without comment" the ten verses are simply read to those students who have elected to participate. They may listen, they may accept, reject, believe or disbelieve any part or all of what they hear. No participatory act is required and what significance the student draws from this practice is completely a matter of his own choice, as there is and can be no promotion, dissuasion or persuasion, and in addition, the student knows that neither he nor any of his classmates need be present during the Bible reading.

Although the practice of Bible reading has been followed for many years in the Commonwealth, there is no evidence that, with the exception of the present appellees, there ever has been a complaint concerning such practice lodged by any student or parent, and the Superintendent of Public Instruction of Pennsylvania, the Superintendent of Schools of Abington Township, and the Principal of the Abington Senior High School have testified that in all their long experience they have received no such complaint (R. 89, 125, 104). Nor has any evidence been introduced that would indicate that the superintendent, administrators, teachers, students, parents, or anyone else, coerced, or attempted to coerce, any child to attend or not attend the Bible reading period or that any stigma is attached to a student who is excused from attending.

C. The Evidence Offered by Appellees

The appellees contend that the continuance of this traditional Bible reading custom violates their constitutional rights and in support of their contention offered the following evidence at the second trial when testimony was taken concerning the operation of the presently existing Bible reading statute which provides for the excuse of those students who do not wish to attend.

Edward Lewis Schempp, the father, testified that under the prior Act, which made no provision for excuse, he had objected to his children being exposed to the reading of the King James Bible because it was against his family's religious beliefs. He stated that "theoretically" he would have liked to have had his children excused from the earlier Bible reading practice (R. 214). He testified that he was familiar with the excuse provision of the new Act (R. 211), but that he had not elected to have his children excused because by so doing he believed that his children would be considered "odd balls", atheists, un-American, "immoral and other things" (R. 214). He stated that under the "mechanics", as he described them, of the Bible reading practice at Abington High School (R. 215-218) it would be difficult for the school to arrange to excuse a child (R. 216, 218) and that being made to stand outside the classroom in the hall was a form of punishment at the school (R. 218). On cross-examination, Mr. Schempp admitted that his only knowledge of the Bible reading practice conducted at Abington High School was what his children had told him (R. 219), that he had never heard of a child at the Abington High School being made to stand outside a classroom for not attending Bible reading (R. 219), and that he had never discussed the problem of Bible reading or being excused therefrom with the Superintendent or any administrative officer in the Abington Township School District (R. 219).

Roger Schempp, the son, testified that he was a student at Abington High School, that he had been present at the morning "routine" at that school and that his father had correctly described such routine in his testimony (R. 221).

The foregoing represents all of the evidence produced by appellees in support of their contention that the amended Bible reading act of the Commonwealth of Pennsylvania which is before this Court violates their constitutional rights and should be struck down.

Counsel for appellees argues that appellees' case also rests upon the testimony offered at the first trial under the old Bible reading statute (R. 221). Such testimony, we submit, has no probative value now since it concerned only the former practice which required that all students attend, and that teachers must conduct the Bible reading on pain of dismissal.

Ellory Schempp's testimony at the first trial that he was compelled to attend Bible reading is now totally irrelevant not only because he has been graduated from the Abington High School but also because, under the new Act, he admittedly could have been excused.

All of the testimony of Donna and Roger Schempp concerning the Bible reading practice at the Huntingdon Junior High School is now equally irrelevant since neither is now a student at the Huntingdon Junior High School. Nor can the testimony of appellees' expert, Dr. Grayzel, as to the effect on a Jewish student of listening to New Testament reading, be of any probative value now since, under the present law, no student need be present when the Bible, Old Testament or New, is being read. In short, every word of appellees' testimony, offered at the first trial, was concerned with a practice in which all the children, including these minor appellees, were compelled to attend. Such practice no longer exists.

The weakness of appellees' case is most clearly understood when it is realized that none of them testified that the present excusatory Bible reading practice, which is the subject of this suit, deprives them of their religious freedoms or interferes with the free exercise of their religious beliefs. Donna (R. 81-82), Roger (R. 77-79) and Ellory (R. 13-14) testified in the first trial that under the old compulsory Act the Bible reading practice confused and aggrieved them; yet not one of them has come forward to say that the practice under the new Act also confuses and aggrieves them. Since Ellory has been graduated the case as to him is moot, but Donna did not testify at the hearing held following the passage of the new Act, and Roger, who did testify, said only that his father had correctly described the new practice. Roger did not complain of the new practice as he had complained at the first trial of the old non-excusatory practice.

D. There Is No Interference With Appellees' Free Exercise of Religion

---

A most thorough and sympathetic scrutiny of appellees' evidence indicates that it shows not that their right to exercise freely their religious consciences or beliefs are affected, but only that Mr. Schempp himself believes that his son would be considered an "odd ball" if he were to be excused from the Bible reading practice, a belief which, surprisingly enough, his son Roger did not support by his own testimony.   This is rather slender support for a charge of unconstitutionality.   Such evidence does not show that Roger was considered by his classmates to be an "odd ball" nor that his father believed his classmates considered him an "odd ball".   All it showed was the father's belief that if Roger were excused from the practice Roger's classmates would consider him an "odd ball".   The applicability of the Constitution to the contentions here asserted was well stated by the late Mr. Justice Jackson in his concurring opinion in *McCollum v. Board of Education,* 333 U.S. 203 (1948), at pp. 232-33:

> "But here, complainant's son may join religious classes if he chooses and if his parents so request, or he may stay out of them.   The complaint is that when others join and he does not, it sets him apart as a dissenter, which is humiliating.   Even admitting this to be true, it may be doubted whether the Constitution which, of course, protects the right to dissent, can be construed also to protect one from the embarrassment that always attends nonconformity, whether in religion, politics, behavior or dress. *Since no legal compulsion is applied to complainant's son*

*himself and no penalty is imposed or threatened from
which we may relieve him, we can hardly base jurisdiction on this ground.''*

In the final opinion of the court below, Judge Biggs
stated (R. 233):

"We hold the statute as amended unconstitutional
on the ground that it violates the 'Establishment of
Religion' clause of the First Amendment made applicable to the Commonwealth of Pennsylvania by the
Fourteenth Amendment. We find it unnecessary to
pass upon any other contention made by the plaintiffs
in respect to the unconstitutionality of the statute or
of the practices thereunder."

Although this would appear to rule out of the case the
question of "free exercise", prudent advocacy demands
exposition of this point.

The Bible reading practice in question does not entail
worship by those attending; it does not require any profession of faith or expression of belief.[5] To the extent
that attendance alone may be regarded as a violation of
conscience (as in *Barnette*), the excuse provision in the
1959 Act precludes this from being a violation of conscience.

Appellees argue that the excuse provision is not
enough. They contend that the need for requesting excuse
is a governmental forcing of a profession of belief or dis-

---

[5] In this sense, the Bible reading practice is clearly less "religious" than the flag salute exercise in *West Virginia State Board
of Education v. Barnette*, 319 U.S. 624 (1943), where Mr. Justice
Jackson, in the opinion of the Court, found: "Here, however, we
are dealing with a compulsion of students to declare a belief."
(319 U.S. 624, at 631.)

belief, and results in social disapproval of those excused. This contention is totally unsupported by logic or by the facts. No profession of belief or belief itself is required of those attending, and choosing to exercise the excuse provision merely reflects some unidentifiable ground for non-attendance.

While there is no evidence of social disapproval in the record, if it is assumed that social disapproval would result, this does not render the prescribed practice unconstitutional. The "free exercise" clause should and does protect and encourage individual freedom of conscience, but it does not and should not compel the cessation of practices, otherwise legitimate, merely to protect individual "dissenters" thereto from possible unpopularity or embarrassment. This much is clear from *Barnette*[6] and from Justice Jackson's concurring opinion in *McCollum, supra*.

---

[6] This clear meaning of the "free exercise" clause was also delineated by Mr. Justice Frankfurter in his dissent in *Barnette*, 319 U.S. at 662:

"That which to the majority may seem essential for the welfare of the state may offend the consciences of a minority. But, so long as no inroads are made upon the actual exercise of religion by the minority, to deny the political power of the majority to enact laws concerned with civil matters, simply because they may offend the consciences of a minority, really means that the consciences of a minority are more sacred and more enshrined in the Constitution than the consciences of a majority."

POINT II

THE COURT BELOW ERRED WHEN IT HELD THIS CASE WAS GOVERNED BY McCOLLUM V. BOARD OF EDUCATION FOR THE BIBLE READING PRACTICE IS FUNDAMENTALLY DIFFERENT FROM THE PROGRAM OF RELIGIOUS INSTRUCTION IN McCOLLUM AND FROM ALL OTHER RELIGIOUS PRACTICES HERETOFORE CONSIDERED BY THIS COURT. APPELLEES' ATTACK UPON THE BIBLE READING PRACTICE RAISES A CONSTITUTIONAL ISSUE NEVER BEFORE DETERMINED BY THIS COURT

The First Amendment to the Constitution reads in part as follows:

"Congress shall make no law respecting an establishment of religion or prohibiting the free exercise thereof . . ."

In light of the decision of the court below, this Court must determine whether the Pennsylvania Bible reading practice prescribed by Section 1516 of the Public School Code of 1949, as amended December 17, 1959, constitutes an "establishment of religion" within the meaning of the First Amendment.

A. The Pennsylvania Bible Reading Practice Does Not Involve Proselytizing, Religious Indoctrination or Instruction

In the final opinion of the court below (201 F. Supp. 815) Judge Biggs stated (R. 233):

"The case at bar is governed by *McCollum v.
Board of Education,* 333 U.S. 203 (1948). Its essen-
tial facts and those of *McCollum* are quite similar.
They need not be compared here. . . ."

We respectfully submit that the court below erred in holding that this case is governed by *McCollum.*

In *McCollum,* this Court held unconstitutional a program of "released time" religious education operated in
the classrooms of the public schools of Champaign, Illinois.
The declared and the only purpose of the Champaign
program was to provide formal religious instruction for
students grouped according to their sectarian preferences.
In the words of Mr. Justice Frankfurter, at 333 U.S. 226,
the "candid purpose" of the Champaign program was
"sectarian teaching". This is not true of the Bible reading
practice at the Abington High School. The record here is
devoid of evidence to show that the "essential facts" in
the instant case are "quite similar" to those in *McCollum*
as stated by Judge Biggs. Unlike *McCollum* there is not
at Abington nor can there be any instruction, teaching,
proselytizing or indoctrination in connection with Bible
reading because the statute itself provides that no comment can be made. The voluntary listening to ten verses
of the Bible, selected and read without comment by one of
the students of the radio and television course is not
even remotely similar to the program for religious instruction struck down in the *McCollum* case. That the element
of proselytizing and religious instruction must be present
to warrant the application of the *McCollum* doctrine was
recently expressed by Mr. Justice Douglas in his concurring
opinion in *Engel v. Vitale,* 370 U.S. 421 (1962), at p. 439:

"McCollum v. Board of Education, 333 U.S. 203,
does not decide this case. It involved the use of pub-

lic school facilities for religious education of students. . . In the present case, school facilities are used to say the prayer and the teaching staff is employed to lead the pupils in it. There is, however, no effort at indoctrination and no attempt at exposition. Prayers, of course, may be so long and of such a character as to amount to an attempt at the religious instruction that was denied the public schools by the McCollum case. But New York's prayer is of a character that does not involve any element of proselytizing as in the McCollum case.''

B. The Pennsylvania Bible Reading Practice Does Not Require or Contemplate the Performance of a Religious Act

---

In *Torcaso v. Watkins,* 367 U.S. 488 (1961), this Court held unconstitutional a Maryland statute that required an individual to profess a belief in a Supreme Being as a condition to holding public office. In *Engel v. Vitale,* 370 U.S. 421 (1962), this Court held unconstitutional both the action of the State Board of Regents of New York in composing an official prayer and suggesting its daily recitation in the public schools and the school district's resolution ordering such recitation. Saying such prayer, this Court held, would be "a solemn avowal of divine faith and supplication for the blessings of the Almighty.''

In both of these cases the statute or regulation held unconstitutional either required or suggested the performance of an affirmative act which would evidence the religious belief of the actor. This is not true of the Bible reading practice for the suggested passive act of listening can in no way evidence the religious beliefs or disbeliefs of the listener. It contemplates merely the exposure to a book which is undoubtedly one of the greatest written sources of the ethical structure of our society. No affirmative act of accepting, professing or believing in what is being listened to is either required by the Bible reading practice or necessary to give meaning and purpose to the practice. This follows because readings from the Bible, wholly apart from whatever religious significance they may have, also may contain literary beauty, historical significance and moral values. Thus, any student, regardless of his religious beliefs or disbeliefs can gain much of secular value from listening to the Bible being read. This is not so with the Maryland oath of office or the Regents' prayer, for an oath professing belief in a Supreme Being or a prayer asking His mercy is and can be nothing other than a purely religious act.

Appellees claim that the student's act of choosing whether he will be present during the Bible reading is an act that professes his belief or disbelief. This cannot be true, for if the student elects to listen no one can tell whether he believes or disbelieves what he hears, whether he listens just because his classmates do, whether he finds beauty in the language, or whether he remains in his seat for any of a countless number of other reasons. If he elects to absent himself, it could mean that he disbelieves so strongly that he cannot bear to even listen, that he believes so strongly that he will listen only when it is read liturgically, that he holds a shade of belief or disbelief between these two extremes, or that he has a reason for absenting himself wholly unrelated to matters of religion, conscience or belief.

In *West Virginia State Board of Education v. Barnette,* 319 U.S. 624 (1942), this Court struck down a regulation of the State Board of Education which required all teachers and students to make a daily pledge of allegiance to the flag for it was shown that performing such pledge was considered an anti-religious act by Jehovah's Witnesses. The pledge of allegiance, unlike the Maryland oath or the Regents' prayer, is not a purely religious act, in fact only a few consider it so. However, as to those few, this Court held that they need not comply since otherwise they would be forced to perform what they considered to be an affirmative anti-religious act. In the Bible reading practice no affirmative act, religious or otherwise, is required of anyone whether he chooses to listen to the Bible or not.

It is therefore respectfully submitted that it is totally unrealistic to argue that listening to the reading of ten verses of the Bible daily at the opening of Pennsylvania's public schools is an "establishment of religion" within the meaning of the First Amendment in the absence of any compulsion to perform an act of faith, to assert a belief or disbelief of any kind, or to participate in any program designed to indoctrinate or proselytize.

C. Appellees' Objection to the Pennsylvania Bible Reading Practice Is Based on the Novel Contention That a Practice Which Evidences the Religious Origins and Traditions of the Nation Constitutes an "Establishment of Religion" in Violation of the First Amendment

---

Since the Bible reading program is completely voluntary for all students, since it is not designed to provide religious indoctrination for even those students who wish to participate, and since it does not require or even sug-

gest the performance of a religious act, the only basis for
appellees' contention that the practice be forbidden to all
must be their belief that since the Bible itself, as a document, does possess religious significance, that any use of
it authorized by the state must, of necessity, violate the
First Amendment to the Constitution. Because the vast
majority of the people of Pennsylvania may believe that
the Bible possesses religious significance, that it is in many
ways a symbol of the religious origins and traditions not
only of Pennsylvania but this nation, it does not follow
that daily reading of the Bible at the opening of public
schools constitutes a religious ceremony or is an unconstitutional "establishment of religion". By their long-stand-
ing acceptance and support of this program, culminating
in the amendment to the statute here under consideration,
the people of Pennsylvania have long demonstrated that
the reading of the Bible is a good custom in their schools
for they believe that much of secular value can be gained
by the listener regardless of what, if any, religious significance he attributes to the text being read.

Consequently, the fundamental issue in this case is
what does the First Amendment to the Constitution require us to do with one of the old established customs of
our country [7]—a custom that, although voluntary and with

---

[7] Annexed to this brief as an Appendix is a compilation of
statutory, decisional and administrative references showing that
twenty-four other states and the District of Columbia require or
expressly permit the reading of the Bible in public schools. In
1961 there were 23,146,376 pupils enrolled in full-time public
elementary and secondary day schools in these Bible reading juris-
dictions according to the United States Department of Health,
Education and Welfare, Office of Education, Publication OE-
20007-61, Circular No. 676 (1962) entitled "Fall 1961 Enrollment-
Teachers and School Housing", page 10.

secular values, also in some way reflects the religious origin and tradition of this nation. It is respectfully submitted that this question is novel with this Court and that the cases heretofore decided did not concern this precise issue with which the Court is now confronted.

POINT III

THE NEUTRALITY TO RELIGION REQUIRED BY THE FIRST AMENDMENT MEANS THAT THE GOVERNMENT CANNOT BE FORCED BY THE RELIGIOUS OR BY THE NONRELIGIOUS TO ADD TO OR SUBTRACT FROM THE TRADITIONAL AND VOLUNTARY RELIGIOUS LEAVEN THAT HAS ALWAYS EXISTED IN OUR PUBLIC LIFE

A. This Nation Is and Always Has Been a Religious People as Is Evidenced by Many of the Customs and Traditions in Our Public Life

---

An analysis of the cases dealing with the application of the First Amendment reveals a consistently reiterated judicial concept concerning the status of religion in this nation in relation to the religious freedoms protected by the Constitution. The inevitable conclusion from the decided cases is that we are today and always have been a religious people. We believe this conclusion would be accepted by even a casual student of this nation's history or routine observer of this nation's present public life. We need not here set forth the religious convictions of the Founding Fathers, the invocations of the Almighty in our cherished national documents, the prayers in our legislative halls, the military chaplains, the use of religious inscriptions on our coinage, the tax exemptions for church property and the myriad other manifestations of the religious leaven in our public life.[8] They are well known to this Court and their significance has often been affirmed by it.

> "There is no dissonance in these declarations. There is a universal language pervading them all, having one meaning; they affirm and reaffirm that this is a religious nation. These are not individual sayings, declarations of private persons: they are organic utterances; they speak the voice of the entire people."
>
> *Holy Trinity Church v. United States,* 143 U.S. 457, 470 (1892).

*   *   *   *   *   *   *   *

> "We are a religious people whose institutions presuppose a Supreme Being."
>
> *Zorach v. Clauson,* 343 U.S. 306, 313 (1952).

A further conclusion to be found in the cases is that the First Amendment does not require that the government be hostile or unfriendly to religion. Rather, it presupposes and requires an attitude of neutrality on the part of the government.

> "The First Amendment, however, does not say that in every and all respects there shall be a separation of Church and State . . . That is the common sense of the matter. Otherwise the state and religion would be aliens to each other—hostile, suspicious, and even unfriendly. Churches could not be required to pay even property taxes. Municipalities would not be

---

[8] For an excellent summation of such manifestations, reference may be made to Appendices to Brief of Respondents filed in *Engel v. Vitale,* at No. 468 October Term, 1961, in the Supreme Court of the United States.

permitted to render police or fire protection to religious groups. Policemen who helped parishioners into their places of worship would violate the Constitution. Prayers in our legislative halls; the appeals to the Almighty in the messages of the Chief Executive; the proclamations making Thanksgiving Day a holiday; 'so help me God' in our courtroom oaths—these and all other references to the Almighty that run through our laws, our public rituals, our ceremonies would be flouting the First Amendment. A fastidious atheist or agnostic could even object to the supplication with which the Court opens each session: 'God save the United States and this Honorable Court' ".

Zorach v. Clauson, 343 U.S. at 312-13.

* * * * * * * *

". . . The First Amendment leaves the Government in a position not of hostility to religion but of neutrality. The philosophy is that the atheist or agnostic—the nonbeliever—is entitled to go his own way. The philosophy is that if government interferes in matters spiritual, it will be a divisive force. The First Amendment teaches that a government neutral in the field of religion better serves all religious interests."

Engel v. Vitale, 370 U.S. 421, 443 (concurring opinion, 1962).

That the Constitution permits the government to cooperate with religious authorities was indicated by Mr. Justice Douglas in the *Zorach* case, *supra,* when he said at page 314:

". . . To hold that it may not would be to find in the Constitution a requirement that the government show a callous indifference to religious groups. That would be preferring those who believe in no religion over those who do believe . . ."

To strike down as a violation of the First Amendment Pennsylvania's amended Bible reading statute would constitute a departure from the traditional relationship between government and religion and would in fact be hostile to those who wish to preserve in our public schools a practice reflecting and consistent with the legal concept that this nation is indeed a religious people.

B. Neutrality Means That the Government Shall Neither Add to Nor Subtract From the Religious Leaven of This Nation

---

Our nation admittedly has a leaven of religious content in its public life. The Constitution requires our government to be neutral toward religion. The legal problem is how should this Court combine these two concepts in determining the constitutionality of Pennsylvania's traditional Bible reading practice? We here suggest that the solution is that government should neither help nor harm either the religious or the nonreligious; that it should not allow the religious to add to the religious leaven nor permit the nonreligious to subtract from it? In Mr. Justice Douglas' concurring opinion in *Engel v. Vitale,* 370 U.S. 421, 443, he said:

> "But 'if a religious leaven is to be worked into the affairs of our people, it is to be done by individuals and groups, not by the Government'. McGowan v. Maryland."

If the government must be neutral rather than hostile to religion, would not the above quotation be equally valid if it read:

> ". . . if a religious leaven is to be worked *out* of the affairs of our people, it is to be done by individuals and groups, not by the Government."

The Bible reading practice in our public schools, like the prayers in our legislative halls, the chaplains in our military forces, "So help me God" in our courtroom oaths and the numerous similar traditions and customs that exist in our public affairs, is all a part of a way of life that has been accepted and cherished by generations of Americans. They make up the religious leaven of our culture and evidence the religious origin and nature of our people. Would it be neutral for the government now to rip out all such customs from our public life? Certainly this Court, in its most recent decision concerning the First Amendment, did not indicate that such customs, even though translated into statutes by the states, must be removed. In *Engel v. Vitale*, 370 U.S. 421, at footnote 21, page 435, the Court said:

> "There is of course nothing in the decision reached here that is inconsistent with the fact that school children and others are officially encouraged to express love for our country by reciting historical documents such as the Declaration of Independence which contain references to the Deity or by singing officially espoused anthems which include the composer's professions of faith in a Supreme Being, or with the fact that there are many manifestations in our public life of belief in God. Such patriotic or ceremonial occasions bear no true resemblance to the

unquestioned religious exercise that the State of New York has sponsored in this instance.''

Is it neutral for the government to aid the nonreligious in their attempt to establish nonreligion as the ruling concept?[9] Does not the religious neutrality required by the First Amendment mean that neither the religious nor the nonreligious may use the government to improve their respective positions? The only alternative to such neutrality would be a policy that required the government to remove from public life all of the admittedly existing religious leaven and in its place establish an absolute nonreligious state. Such a policy could not be considered by reasonable men to be anything other than one of hostility toward religion as a matter of law.

---

[9] Dean Emeritus Luther A. Weigle of the Yale Divinity School in his introduction to the book GOD IN OUR PUBLIC SCHOOLS, by W. S. Fleming, at page 26, said the following in this connection:

''A system of education which gives no place to religion is not in reality neutral but exerts an influence, unintentional though it be, against religion . . . The omission of religion from the public schools conveys a condemnatory suggestion to the children.''

William Clayton Bower, a former professor in the University of Chicago, in his book, THE CHURCH AND STATE IN EDUCATION (University of Chicago Press), page 33, has this to say:

''In the church and in the religious home the growing person is led to believe that religion is the most important concern of life, while in the school religion is relegated to a position of unimportance by being treated with silence and neglect. The result is more serious than appears on the surface. Without intending it, the school is placed in the position of exerting a negative influence regarding religion, since what appears to be neutrality turns out practically to be a discrediting of religion.''

C. The Policy of Neutrality Is Consistent With
the Prior Decisions of This Court

———

We submit that the neutrality to religion required by
the First Amendment impels the conclusion that the court
below erred in holding Pennsylvania's Bible reading practice unconstitutional as an "establishment of religion".
To reverse the court below would be consistent with the
prior decisions of this Court wherein the Court disallowed
attempts to *add* to the religious leaven of the nation when
it struck down a plan to introduce admittedly religious instruction in the public schools (*McCollum v. Board of Education,* 333 U.S. 203 (1948)) and when it prevented public officials from writing a *new* prayer to be said in the
public schools (*Engel v. Vitale,* 370 U.S. 421 (1962)).
Neither religious instruction in the public schools nor the
composing of school prayers by public officials was part
of the religious tradition of this country.   That there is a
valid distinction between the newly composed and the traditional was noted by Professor Arthur E. Sutherland, Jr.
in his recent article, *Establishment According to Engel,*
76 Harv. L. Rev. 25 (1962), where he says, at p. 38:

> ". . . And a constitutional flaw of the Regents'
> Prayer may be its comparative novelty. *America* is
> an old song.   There is common sense in the distinc-
> tion between the long-established and the novel.   A
> man can reasonably say that what has become tradi-
> tional is less constitutionally objectionable than an
> innovation.[36]   At the margins of the minimally toler-
> able, such fine differences are not ridiculous."

> " [36] The degree of obscenity which is legally tol-
> erated seems to bear a relation to the age of the lit-

erature. In modern dress the Miller's Tale and the Reeve's Tale would raise interesting questions under Roth v. United States, 354 U.S. 476 (1957). And in measuring procedural due process, what men are used to is relevant. See, e.g., the opinion in Den *ex dem.* Murray v. Hoboken Land & Improvement Co., 59 U.S. (18 How.) 272 (1856)."

In the same pattern of neutrality this Court did not subtract from the religious leaven of the country when it held a religious oath of office need not be observed by a nonbeliever for it did not hold that the oath could not be made by a believer (*Torcaso v. Watkins,* 367 U.S. 488 (1961)). In the *Barnette* case (319 U.S. 624 (1942)) this Court likewise did not hold that the custom of pledging allegiance must be denied to all school children. Again in the Sunday Blue Laws case, this Court held that although the traditional observance of Sunday as a day of rest may be amply justified under the police powers of the state, such customary observance need not be struck down merely because it happened to be part of the religious leaven of our country (*McGowan v. Maryland,* 366 U.S. 420 (1961)).

D. A Decision by This Court To Strike Down the Bible Reading Practice Would Provide the Means Whereby Every Vestige of the Religious Traditions of This Nation Could Be Removed From Public Life

---

If this Court were to strike down Pennsylvania's Bible reading practice it would open a Pandora's box of litigation which could serve to remove from American public life every vestige of our religious heritage. Since the

Bible reading practice is voluntary and has secular values, its prohibition by this Court would logically impel the conclusion that the other traditions must fall. Certainly "God save this Honorable Court", "So help me God" and "In God We Trust" would fall, for such expressions have no secular meaning, there is nothing voluntary about a court of law and no one has a choice as to which currency he will use. The chaplains of our legislative bodies and our military forces could not be allowed to continue to conduct, at the nonreligious taxpayers' expense, their religious functions. Tax exemptions for church property would also fall, as well as statutory draft exemptions for conscientious objectors. With regard to the public schools, perhaps established school holidays could continue if they were renamed, but even this might be construed as only colorable compliance with the requirements of the Constitution. It would seem that any official use of the Christian calendar with its B.C. and A.D. must be discontinued and the seven day week, being of Biblical origin, should become either a six or an eight day period. The traditional day of rest, rather than falling on the Christian Sunday, or the Jewish Sabbath, should fall on a nonreligious Wednesday or Thursday, although the latter, being a corruption of Thor's day, may be objectionable because of its Germanic religious connotations.

The task facing this Court, if it undertook to remove from the public schools all practices that some might claim contain religious connotations, is well set forth in the following statements by Mr. Justice Jackson and Mr. Justice Frankfurter:

"To me, the sweep and detail of these complaints is a danger signal which warns of the kind of local

controversy we will be required to arbitrate if we
do not place appropriate limitation on our decision
and exact strict compliance with jurisdictional requirements. * * * If we are to eliminate everything
that is objectionable to any of these warring sects or
inconsistent with any of their doctrines, we will leave
public education in shreds. Nothing but educational
confusion and a discrediting of the public school
system can result from subjecting it to constant law
suits.

*   *   *   *   *   *   *   *

"I think it remains to be demonstrated whether
it is possible, even if desirable, to comply with such
demands as plaintiff's completely to isolate and cast
out of secular education all that some people may
reasonably regard as religious instruction. . .

*   *   *   *   *   *   *   *

"We must leave some flexibility to meet local conditions, some chance to progress by trial and error.
* * * The task of separating the secular from the
religious in education is one of magnitude, intricacy
and delicacy. * * * If with no surer legal guidance
we are to take up and decide every variation of this
controversy, raised by persons not subject to penalty
or tax but who are dissatisfied with the way schools
are dealing with the problem, we are likely to have
much business of the sort." (Jackson, J., concurring
in *McCollum,* 333 U.S. at 235, 237-38.)

". . . The requirement of Bible-reading has been
justified by various state courts as an appropriate
means of inculcating ethical precepts and familiarizing pupils with the most lasting expression of great

English literature. Is this Court to overthrow such
variant state educational policies by denying states
the right to entertain such convictions in regard to
their school systems, because of a belief that the King
James version is in fact a sectarian text to which
parents of the Catholic and Jewish faiths and of some
Protestant persuasions may rightly object to having
their children exposed? On the other hand the religious consciences of some parents may rebel at the
absence of any Bible-reading in the schools. See
Washington ex rel. Clithero v. Showalter, 284 U.S.
573. Or is this Court to enter the old controversy
between science and religion by unduly defining the
limits within which a state may experiment with its
school curricula? The religious consciences of some
parents may be offended by subjecting their children
to the Biblical account of creation, while another state
may offend parents by prohibiting a teaching of biol-
ogy that contradicts such Biblical account. Compare
Scopes v. State, 154 Tenn. 105, 289 S.W. 363. What of
conscientious objections to what is devoutly felt by
parents to be the poisoning of impressionable minds
of children by chauvinistic teaching of history? This
is very far from a fanciful suggestion for in the belief
of many thoughtful people nationalism is the seed-bed
of war.

*   *   *   *   *   *   *   *

"That which to the majority may seem essential
for the welfare of the state may offend the consciences
of a minority. But, so long as no inroads are made
upon the actual exercise of religion by the minority,
to deny the political power of the majority to enact
laws concerned with civil matters, simply because they

may offend the consciences of a minority, really means that the consciences of a minority are more sacred and more enshrined in the Constitution than the consciences of a majority." (Frankfurter, J., dissenting in *Barnette,* 319 U.S. at 659, 660 and 662.)

While we do not suggest that these other traditions would immediately fall upon the invalidation of our Bible reading statute, it is not far-fetched to believe that many of these customs could eventually meet the same fate.

POINT IV

APPELLEES DO NOT HAVE STANDING TO IN-VOKE THE JURISDICTION OF THIS COURT

Appellees have contended that even if the provision for excuse from attending Bible reading disposes of their argument that the Bible reading statute prohibited the free exercise of religion, it does not affect their argument that the statute is an establishment of religion. Such contention ignores the fundamental principle that if the appellees are not deprived of any constitutionally protected freedom, they have no standing to invoke the Constitution, and the Court has no jurisdiction to pass upon the constitutionality of the Act in question.

The First Amendment becomes binding upon the states only by virtue of the due process clause of the Fourteenth Amendment. In order to have the Court pass on their contention that an Act of the General Assembly of the Commonwealth of Pennsylvania constitutes an unconstitutional establishment of religion, the appellees must show that they are persons who, as a result of the enforcement of the Act, are deprived of life, liberty or property without due process of law.

Even more fundamental than the requirement that the plaintiff show a deprivation of liberty or property under the Fourteenth Amendment is the limitation on the power of this or any Federal court to declare a legislative act unconstitutional. Under Article III, Section 1 of the Constitution, the only power exercised by the Supreme

Court and any Federal court is *judicial* power. Under Article III, Section 2, this power extends only to "cases or controversies" within its meaning. It has therefore become well settled that the Court has no jurisdiction to render an advisory opinion as to the constitutionality of any legislative act of either Congress or a State Legislature. This fundamental limitation on the judicial power under the Constitution remains today, as stated by Chief Justice Marshall in *Cohens v. Virginia,* 6 Wheat. 264, 405 (1821):

> ". . . The article does not extend the judicial power to every violation of the constitution which may possibly take place, but to 'a case in law or equity,' in which a right, under such law, is asserted in a court of justice. If the question cannot be brought into a court, then there is no case in law or equity, and no jurisdiction is given by the words of the article. But if, in any controversy depending in a court, the cause should depend on the validity of such a law, that would be a case arising under the constitution, to which the judicial power of the United States would extend."

A "case or controversy" within the judicial power of the United States courts exists only when there is a litigation affecting the rights of the parties as to their persons or property. It is essential to the existence of jurisdiction that the plaintiff show a legally protected interest, personal to him, which is invaded or threatened by the actions of the defendant. In *Frothingham v. Mellon,* 262 U.S. 447, 488 (1922), the Court, speaking through Mr. Justice Sutherland, said:

> " * * * We have no power *per se* to review and annul acts of Congress on the ground that they are

unconstitutional. That question may be considered only when the justification for some direct injury suffered or threatened, presenting a justiciable issue, is made to rest upon such an act. Then the power exercised is that of ascertaining and declaring the law applicable to the controversy. It amounts to little more than the negative power to disregard an unconstitutional enactment, which otherwise would stand in the way of the enforcement of a legal right. The party who invokes the power must be able to show not only that the statute is invalid but that he has sustained or is immediately in danger of sustaining some direct injury as the result of its enforcement, and not merely that he suffers in some indefinite way in common with people generally. If a case for preventive relief be presented the court enjoins, in effect, not the execution of the statute, but the acts of the official, the statute notwithstanding."

This Court, in *Poe v. Ullman,* 367 U.S. 497 (1961), declined to pass on the constitutionality of the Connecticut statute prohibiting the use of contraceptive devices and the giving of medical advice on the use of such devices, on the ground that there was not a sufficient showing on the record that the plaintiffs were threatened with imminent prosecution.

The Opinion of the Court by Mr. Justice Frankfurter heavily underscores the limitations upon the power of the Supreme Court and Federal Courts to adjudicate constitutional issues. The necessity of a "case or controversy" is only one of the limitations on that power, which is further circumscribed by the principle that the Court will not entertain constitutional questions except in cases

where the constitutional determination is strictly necessary in order for it to decide a real case. The Court said
(367 U.S. 503-505):

" 'The best teaching of this Court's experience ad-
monishes us not to entertain constitutional questions
in advance of the strictest necessity.' Parker v. County of Los Angeles, 338 U.S. 327, 333. See also Liver-
pool, N. Y. & P.S.S. Co. v. Commissioners, 113 U.S. 33,
39. The various doctrines of 'standing,'[5] 'ripeness,'[6]
and 'mootness,'[7] which this Court has evolved with
particular, though not exclusive, reference to such
cases are but several manifestations—each having its
own 'varied application'[8]—of the primary conception
that federal judicial power is to be exercised to strike
down legislation, whether state or federal, only at the
instance of one who is himself immediately harmed,
or immediately threatened with harm, by the challenged action . . . Sterns v. Wood, 236 U.S. 75;
Texas v. Interstate Commerce Comm'n, 258 U.S. 158;
United Public Workers v. Mitchell, 330 U.S. 75, 89-90.
'This court can have no right to pronounce an abstract
opinion upon the constitutionality of a State law.
Such law must be brought into actual, or threatened
operation upon rights properly falling under judicial
cognizance, or a remedy is not to be had here.' Georgia v. Stanton, 6 Wall. 50, 75, approvingly quoting
Mr. Justice Thompson, dissenting, in Cherokee Nation v. Georgia, 5 Pet. 1, 75; also quoted in New Jersey
v. Sargent, 269 U.S. 328, 331. 'The party who invokes the power [to annul legislation on grounds of its
unconstitutionality] must be able to show not only that
the statute is invalid but that he has sustained or is
immediately in danger of sustaining some direct in-

jury as the result of its enforcement. . .' Massachusetts v. Mellon, 262 U.S. 447, 488.[9] "

Thus, in *Doremus v. Board of Education,* 342 U.S. 429 (1952), in which the plaintiffs contended that a New Jersey statute providing for reading the Bible in public schools was unconstitutional, the Supreme Court dismissed the appeal as moot because the child of the plaintiff-parent had graduated from school and the rights of such child were therefore moot. Despite plaintiffs' contention that they were still entitled to maintain the appeal as citizens and taxpayers, the Supreme Court held that the suit could not be maintained as a taxpayer's action because the plaintiffs had not shown that as taxpayers they had any financial interest in the case, or were in any immediate danger of sustaining direct injury in measurable amount, or that the practice of reading the Bible in the school added any sum to .the cost of conducting the school. The appeal was dismissed for lack of a justiciable controversy.

The present action cannot be maintained as a taxpayer's suit, nor has it ever been seriously argued that it could be. The appellees do not even allege that they pay any taxes to the Abington Township School District. They have not alleged that the practice of Bible reading adds any measurable amount to the cost of conducting the schools. In any event, it is clear under the decision of the Supreme Court in the *Doremus* case that such a minimal expenditure as might be involved in the purchase of Bibles is not a measurable appropriation of public funds of which a taxpayer is entitled to complain.

The appellees attempt to bring themselves within the decision of the Supreme Court in *McCollum v. Board of Education,* 333 U.S. 203 (1948), wherein the plaintiff was permitted to maintain an action in the dual capacity as taxpayer and parent of a child in school. However, that case involved the use of classrooms for programs of admittedly protracted religious instruction by priests, rabbis, and ministers. Subsequent decisions of the Court in the *Doremus* case and in *Zorach v. Clauson,* 343 U.S. 306 (1952), demonstrate that the Court will not invalidate a practice alleged to be an unconstitutional establishment of religion unless the plaintiffs show that they have sustained injury either as taxpayers or as parents of pupils compelled to participate in a religious ceremony in violation of their constitutional freedom of worship. In *Zorach* the Court sustained the constitutionality of the New York released time program on the ground that participation in the program of religious instruction was entirely voluntary, and because there was no use of the tax-supported school property for religious purposes. The Court distinguished *McCollum* on the ground that all of the costs of the New York program were paid by the religious organizations and not by the public school district.

The position of the Supreme Court in *Doremus* was foreshadowed in the concurring opinion of Mr. Justice Jackson in the *McCollum* case itself. He there pointed out that a Federal court may not interfere with local school authorities unless they are invading either a property right or a personal liberty protected by the Federal Constitution. Such a challenge to a local statute or practice should come before the Court in either of two ways: (1) when a person is required to submit to some religious rite or instruction as in *West Virginia State Board of Education v. Barnette,* 319 U.S. 624 (1943); or (2) when a taxpayer charges that there is a measurable burden on taxpayers for funds expended for unconstitutional purposes, as in *Everson v. Board of Education,* 330 U.S. 1 (1947).

Applying these principles to the facts of the instant case, it is apparent that as to one of the original plaintiffs, the son Ellory Schempp, the situation is now the same as in *Doremus.* Ellory has been graduated from the Abington Township High School and no injunction which this Court might otherwise grant can protect or affect his rights. But the other Schempp children are still in the Abington Township High School, and the case is not moot as to them in the sense that it is moot as to Ellory. Nevertheless, their action under the amended Act of 1959 cannot be maintained on their behalf by themselves or their parents since there has been no evidence presented to show that they have been compelled to relinquish any constitutional liberty. No such showing could be made since the statute and practice presently before this Court make attendance at Bible reading exercises purely voluntary.

Although it is recognized that the decision in *Engel v. Vitale,* 370 U.S. 421 (1962), indicates that this Court may have revised its previous holdings concerning the doctrine of "standing in court",[10] appellants contend that since appellees have no legally protected interest which is

---

[10] Sutherland, Arthur E., Jr., *Establishment According to Engel,* 76 Harv. L. Rev. at 26-27, 35 (1962):

". . . But in the *Prayer Case* the Court finds no actionable coercion of children to demonstrate dissent;[3] the majority opinion adopts, instead, a quite different formula—that a classroom exercise, if once found to be an 'establishment of religion,' becomes enjoinable under the fourteenth amendment, even if no schoolchild is subject to 'coercion,' and even if no plaintiff demonstrates any unconstitutional expenditure of taxpayers' money. One finds asserted in *Engel* no requirement that a litigant, if he would invoke judicial power to

injured or threatened by the Bible reading statute, they have no standing to maintain the action and the Court has no jurisdiction to determine in the abstract whether the statute would otherwise be unconstitutional.

---

forbid governmental action, must show that by it he 'has sustained or is immediately in danger of sustaining some direct injury as the result of its enforcement, and not merely that he suffers in some indefinite way in common with people generally.'[4] *Engel* thus suggests that the Supreme Court has somewhat revised its previous ideas concerning 'standing in court,' concerning, that is, the type of grievance a litigant must experience before the federal judiciary will intervene to forbid state governmental activity. The opinions seem to take as premise a judicial function rather more expanded than most lawyers had come to find usual. Here, rather than in the specific issue decided, may turn out to be the ultimate importance of the case."

* * * * * * * *

"In the *Prayer Case,* the Supreme Court, finding insufficient jurisdictional hardship imposed on the plaintiffs' children, would conventionally have denied certiorari. Absence of proof that the prayer added to school costs had eliminated the only other possible standing, unless *Doremus* was to be disregarded. But the *School Prayer* opinion did not expressly overrule *Doremus;* one wonders if it was overruled in silence. Is there in *Engel* a new doctrine concerning the wrongs against which the fourteenth amendment, judicially enforced, will protect all persons? Where a state does something amounting to 'establishment,' will the Supreme Court enjoin it on the suit of any member of society who dislikes the policy? And is this new doctrine likely to spread beyond religious establishment to other policy judgments?"

CONCLUSION

We accordingly respectfully submit that:

1.   The Pennsylvania Bible reading practice does not interfere with appellees' free exercise of religion.

2.   Since the Bible reading practice does not involve religious instruction or proselytizing nor require or suggest the performance of a religious act, it is not an establishment of religion within the meaning of the First Amendment to the Constitution.

3.   The neutrality to religion required of the government by the First Amendment to the Constitution means that the government cannot be forced by appellees to strike down a traditional and voluntary Bible reading practice simply because it may have, in addition to its secular values, certain religious connotations.

4.   Appellees do not have standing to invoke the jurisdiction of this Court.

We therefore respectfully submit that the judgment of the court below be reversed, the final decree below be vacated and the case be remanded to the District Court with a direction to enter judgment for appellants.

Dated: January 4, 1963.

Respectfully submitted,
PERCIVAL R. RIEDER,
1067 Old York Road,
Abington, Pennsylvania,

C. BREWSTER RHOADS,

PHILIP H. WARD, III,

1421 Chestnut Street,

Philadelphia 2, Pennsylvania,

Attorneys for Appellants, School District of Abington Township, Pennsylvania, James F. Koehler, O. H. English, Eugene Stull and M. Edward Northam,

JOHN D. KILLIAN III,

Deputy Attorney General,

DAVID STAHL,

Attorney General,

State Capitol,

Harrisburg, Pennsylvania,

Attorneys for Charles H. Boehm, Superintendent of Public Instruction, Commonwealth of Pennsylvania.

MONTGOMERY, MCCRACKEN, WALKER & RHOADS,

Of Counsel.

APPENDIX

The following is a summary of state constitutional, legislative, judicial and administrative provisions or rulings requiring or permitting Bible reading in the public schools.

ALABAMA

Bible reading is required daily in all public schools. Ala. Code, tit. 52, §542 (Recomp. 1958).

ARKANSAS

Bible reading is required daily in all public schools. Pupils may be excused upon request. Ark. Stat. Ann. §§80-1606, 80-1607 (1947).

COLORADO

Bible reading without comment is permitted on a voluntary basis under *People ex rel. Vollmar v. Stanley,* 81 Colo. 276, 255 Pac. 610 (1927).

DISTRICT OF COLUMBIA

Bible reading is required daily in all public schools. Pupils may be excused upon request. Board of Educ., By-Laws, c. 6, §4.

DELAWARE

Bible reading is required in all public schools. 14 Del. Code Ann. §§4102, 4103 (1953).

FLORIDA

Bible reading "without sectarian comment" is required daily in all public schools, pursuant to 1 Fla. Stat.

§231.09 (2) (1959). This practice was upheld on a voluntary basis in 1961 in *Chamberlin v. Dade County Board of Public Instruction* (Circuit Ct., Dade Co., case nos. 59-C-4928 and 59-C-8873) (30 U.S.L. Week 2623, Fla. Sup. Ct., June 6, 1962).

GEORGIA

One chapter from the Bible is required daily reading in the public schools and provision is made for the excuse of any pupils who do not wish to participate. Ga. Code Ann. §§32-705, 32-9903 (1952). See: *Wilkerson v. City of Rome,* 152 Ga. 762, 110 S.E. 895 (1922).

IDAHO

From 12 to 20 verses must be read without comment from the Bible each day in all public schools. Idaho Code §§33-2705-07 (1947).

INDIANA

Daily Bible reading is permitted in the public schools. Ind. Stat. Ann. §28-5105 (Burns 1948).

IOWA

Daily Bible reading in the public schools is permitted and students not wishing to participate may be excused. 1 Iowa Code §280.9 (1958). See: *Knowlton v. Baumhover,* 182 Iowa 691, 166 N.W. 202 (1918); *Moore v. Monroe,* 64 Iowa 367, 20 N.W. 475 (1884).

KANSAS

Daily Bible reading in the public schools is permitted. Kans. Gen. Stat. Ann. §72-1628 (Supp. 1961). See: *Billiard v. Board of Education,* 69 Kans. 53, 76 Pac. 422 (1904).

KENTUCKY

Daily Bible reading in the public schools is required and students not wishing to participate may be excused. Ky. Rev. Stat. §158.170 (Baldwin 1955). This practice was upheld against attack on constitutional grounds in *Hackett v. Brooksville Graded School Dist.*, 120 Ky. 608, 87 S.W. 792 (1905).

MAINE

"[R]eadings from the scriptures with special emphasis upon the Ten Commandments, the Psalms of David, the Proverbs of Solomon, the Sermon on the Mount and the Lord's Prayer" are required daily in the public schools. "[E]ach student shall give respectful attention but shall be free in his own forms of worship." 2 Me. Rev. Stat. §145 (1954). See: *Donahoe v. Richards*, 38 Me. 379 (1854).

MARYLAND

Bible reading in public schools on a voluntary basis, pursuant to a rule of the Board of School Commissioners of Baltimore City, has been sustained in *Murray v. Curlett*, 228 Md. 239, 179 A. 2d 698 (1962), *cert. granted*, 31 U.S.L. Week 3116 (U.S. Oct. 8, 1962) No. 119, 1962 Term.

MASSACHUSETTS

Bible reading is required daily in the public schools. Pupils not wishing to participate may be excused. Mass. Ann. Laws, c. 71, §71-31 (1958). See: *Spiller v. Inhabitants of Woburn*, 94 Mass. (12 Allen) 127 (1866).

MICHIGAN

Bible reading upheld by court without benefit of statute: *Pfeiffer v. Board of Education*, 118 Mich. 560, 77 N.W. 250 (1898).

MINNESOTA

Bible reading in the public schools on a voluntary basis is permitted under *Kaplan v. Independent School Dist.*, 171 Minn. 142, 214 N.W. 18 (1927).

MISSISSIPPI

Bible reading in the public schools is permitted on a voluntary basis. Const. Art. III, §18, contained in 1 Miss. Code Ann. (1942).

NEW JERSEY

At least 5 verses of the Old Testament are required to be read without comment each day in each public school classroom. N. J. S. A. §§18:14-77, 18:14-78 (1940). See *Doremus v. Board of Education*, 5 N.J. 435, 75 A. 2d 880 (1950), *appeal dismissed*, 342 U.S. 429 (1952).

NEW YORK

Bible reading in the public schools on a voluntary basis is permitted. See *Lewis v. Board of Education*, 157 Misc. 520, 285 N.Y.S. 164 (Sup. Ct., N. Y. Co. 1935), *modified* and *affirmed* 247 App. Div. 106, 286 N.Y.S. 174 (1st Dept. 1936), *appeal dismissed*, 246 N.Y. 490, 12 N.E. 2d 172 (1937).

NORTH DAKOTA

Bible reading in the public schools is permitted and provision is made for pupils not wishing to participate. 3 N. D. Cent. Code §15:38-12 (1960).

OHIO

Bible reading in the public schools is permitted. *Nessle v. Hum*, 2 O.D. 60, 1 Ohio N.P. 140 (1894). Cf., *Board of Educ. v. Paul*, 10 O.D. 17, 7 Ohio N.P. 58 (1900).

OKLAHOMA

Bible reading in the public schools is permitted. Okla. Stat., tit. 70, §11-1 (1941).

TENNESSEE

Bible reading in the public schools is required daily, Tenn. Code Ann., §49-1307(4) (1955). See *Carden v. Bland,* 199 Tenn. 665, 288 S.W. 2d 718 (1956).

TEXAS

Bible reading is permitted on a voluntary basis in the public schools. *Church v. Bullock,* 104 Tex. 1, 109 S.W. 115 (1908).

Supreme Court of the United States.

October Term, 1962.

No. 142.

SCHOOL DISTRICT OF ABINGTON TOWNSHIP, PENNSYLVANIA, JAMES F. KOEHLER, O. H. ENGLISH, EUGENE STULL, M. EDWARD NORTHAM, and CHARLES H. BOEHM, Superintendent of Public Instruction, Commonwealth of Pennsylvania,

Appellants,

v.

EDWARD LEWIS SCHEMPP, SIDNEY GERBER SCHEMPP, Individually and as Parents and Natural Guardians of ROGER WADE SCHEMPP and DONNA KAY SCHEMPP,

Appellees.

On Appeal From a District Court of Three Judges for the Eastern District of Pennsylvania.

BRIEF FOR APPELLEES.

STATEMENT OF THE CASE.

(a) Jurisdictional Statement.

Appellees are the Schempp family—husband and wife and two minor children. By their complaint they sought a preliminary injunction, and a permanent injunction after trial, enjoining the ceremonial reading of the King James Version of The Bible and recitation, in ceremonial unison, of the Lord's Prayer in the Schools of Abington Township,

Montgomery County, Pennsylvania, presently attended by the appellees Roger and Donna Schempp.

This action is brought under Title 28 § 1343 of the U. S. Code (28 U. S. C. A. § 1343) and was heard by a three-judge court pursuant to Title 28 § 2284 of the U. S. Code (28 U. S. C. A. § 2284).

The parent appellees complained on behalf of themselves as parents and as the natural guardians of Roger and Donna, their minor children. At the time of the filing of the action the older son, Ellory, formerly a plaintiff, was a student at the Abington Senior High School but graduated therefrom prior to trial. It is agreed that the application for an injunction is moot as to him.

The practice of reading The Bible in the public schools of Pennsylvania was, at the time suit was filed, made compulsory by section 1516 of the Public School Code of March 10, 1949, P. L. 30, as amended (24 PS § 15-1516) which read in full as follows:

> "At least ten verses from the Holy Bible shall be read, or caused to be read, without comment, at the opening of each public school on each school day, by the teacher in charge: Provided, That where any teacher has other teachers under and subject to direction, then the teacher exercising such authority shall read the Holy Bible, or cause it to be read, as herein directed.
>
> "If any school teacher, whose duty it shall be to read the Holy Bible, or cause it to be read, shall fail or omit so to do, said school teacher shall, upon charges preferred for such failure or omission, and proof of the same, before the board of school directors of the school district, be discharged."

After trial and decree as reported in 177 F. Supp. 398 [R. 177], and pending perfection of appellants' appeal from that decision, the statute was amended (December 17, 1959, P. L. 1928) to read in full as follows:

"At least ten verses from the Holy Bible shall be read, without comment, at the opening of each public school on each school day. Any child shall be excused from such Bible reading, or attending such Bible reading, upon the written request of his parent or guardian."

On October 24, 1960, this Court vacated the judgment of the District Court and remanded the case to the District Court for further proceedings in the light of the amendment to the original Bible reading statute.

On June 22, 1961, appellees obtained leave to file a supplemental complaint under Rule 15(d). The supplemental complaint consisted solely of the substitution in the complaint of the new citation and text of the amended statute in place of the former citation and text, and the elimination of paragraphs in the complaint relating to Ellory Schempp.

Appellant school district and intervenor appellant, the Superintendent of Public Instruction of the Commonwealth of Pennsylvania, thereafter filed an answer to the supplemental complaint.

After taking further testimony the District Court, on February 1, 1962, declared the amended statute unconstitutional, 201 F. Supp. 815 [R. 228] and issued a final decree enjoining appellants from carrying out the provisions of the statute. That decree has been stayed pending disposition by this Court.

Appellees contend that their rights under the Fourteenth Amendment are and have been violated and will continue to be violated unless this Court declares this statute unconstitutional and enjoins the appellant school district and appellant officers thereof from continuing to conduct the practices of which complaint is made.

(b) Statement of Facts.

The appellees Edward Lewis Schempp and Sidney Gerber Schempp are of the Unitarian faith and are members of the Unitarian Church in Germantown, Philadelphia, Pennsylvania, which they regularly attend together with their three children, Ellory, Roger and Donna.

Ellory was 18 at the time of the original trial and had attended Roslyn Elementary School, Abington Township, the Abington Junior High School and the Abington Senior High School from which he had graduated in June of 1958.

Roger, who was 15 at the time of the trial, was an eighth-grade student in the Huntingdon Junior High School in Abington Township during the academic year previous to the trial, which was held during the summer recess.

Donna Schempp was 12 years old at the time of the trial and also a student at the Abington Junior High School and in the academic year preceding the trial had been in the seventh grade.

At the time of their second appearance at the hearing on the Amended Complaint both children were students at Abington High School.

All of the three children testified at the trial and their evidence discloses that it is the practice in the various schools of the Township which they had attended to observe the opening period of school on each day by a brief ceremony consisting of the reading of ten verses of the King James Version of the Bible, followed by a standing recitation in unison of that portion of the New Testament known in the Christian faith as "The Lord's Prayer",[1] and that generally the ceremony was followed by the familiar Pledge of Allegiance to the Flag, followed by routine school announcements.

Beyond this, however, the three children described a substantial number of variations in the manner and technique employed in the execution of this ceremony. In all of the schools which any of the three children had attended, except one, the Bible reading and the recitation of the prayer was conducted by the individual home room teacher, who either chose a text and read the ten verses herself or

1. Matthew 6:9.

delegated both choice of text and reading to the students, either in rotation or to volunteers [R. 10, 76, 79]. The only exception to these practices was recounted by Ellory Schempp, who stated that after the Senior High School had moved to a new building equipped with a public address system, the Bible was read over the loud speaker in each classroom following which the voice on the loud speaker directed the children to rise and repeat The Lord's Prayer [R. 11].

Ellory and Donna Schempp testified that during the reading of the Bible, a particularly high standard of physical deportment and attention was exacted and Donna testified that this deportment was not always required when other works were being read [R. 12, 81].

The three Schempp children and their father also testified as to the points of religious doctrine purveyed by the King James Version of the Bible which were contrary to the religious belief which they held and which the father and mother were teaching to their children, specifically, the divinity of Christ, the Immaculate Conception, an anthropomorphic God and the concept of the Trinity.

The father, Edward L. Schempp, pointed out that the manner of presentation, ten verses without comment, was that of a religious ceremony, the material being given a degree of authority and religious significance above normal school authority [R. 31]. In content, the father objected to material in the Old Testament regarding blood sacrifices, uncleanness, and leprosy, together with the whole concept of the Old Testament God which was contrary to the concept of deity which he endeavored to instill in his children. He testified that he did not want his children to acquire an image of Jehovah, the God of vengeance. He pointed out that in the very midst of the Ten Commandments was a verse asserting that God would visit the sins of the father upon the fourth generation—a particular verse he testified had been read in the Abington High School—and the witness went on to assert that this concept of God was in sharp contrast with the God of his own church and as taught in the Schempp family [R. 30-32].

Mr. Schempp also testified that there were innumerable bits of anecdotal material which were quite foreign to his concept of what is good, religious and moral, such as the injunction that one should not eat meat that dies of itself but that it may be fed to "the stranger within thy gates" [R. 32]. (Dr. Solomon Grayzel, who subsequently testified for the plaintiffs as an expert, pointed this out as an example of the unfortunate errors attendant upon ceremonial reading of The Bible without explanation, and stated that this passage meant only that it might be fed to those not governed by religious dietary laws) [R. 50].

Roger Schempp, the younger son, testified that he also attended a Unitarian Sunday school and sometimes church services with his family and that he believed that Christ was a great man but did not believe other things that the King James Version of The Bible asserted concerning Christ and the events of his life and did not believe in the divinity of Christ [R. 75-78].

Donna Schempp, a student in the seventh grade in Huntingdon Junior High School, likewise testified that she attended the Unitarian Sunday school and cited several points of religious belief contrary to that asserted by what she had heard read to her from the King James Version of the Bible in school. She also recounted the reaction of a Jewish friend and fellow student who objected to a reading of the portion of the New Testament. Donna said that she had never made any complaint about the reading of the Bible [R. 79-85].

There is evidence in the record that the combined ceremony of Bible reading and the saying of the prayer was, on frequent occasions, although not uniformly, referred to by both students and teachers as the "morning devotions" [R. 22, 80].

Roger Schempp referred to the ceremony as "morning exercises"; counsel for the School District referred to the ceremony as "devotional services" or "devotional exercises" [R. 23-24, 76].

On behalf of the appellees, Dr. Solomon Grayzel, editor of the Jewish Publication Society, also testified. Dr. Grayzel, after graduation from the City College of New York and Columbia University, attended a Jewish theological seminary, was ordained a Rabbi and received a doctorate of Philosophy from the Dropsie College of Philadelphia, an institution of rabbinical, Semitic and Hebrew studies. The Jewish Publication Society, of which Dr. Grayzel is the editor, was the publisher of the "Holy Scriptures According to the Masoretic Text" and is presently engaged in a retranslation into English from the Hebrew. As part of the translation committee, Dr. Grayzel testified that he was familiar with the King James Version, the Revised Standard Version and both the Douay and the Knox Catholic Versions. Dr. Grayzel testified that there were marked differences between the Jewish Holy Scriptures and the Christian Holy Bible, the most obvious of which was the absence of the New Testament in the Jewish Holy Scriptures [R. 35-43].

Dr. Grayzel testified that from the standpoint of the Jewish faith, the entire New Testament and the concept of Jesus Christ as the Son of God was "practically blasphemous" [R. 44]. He cited at random incidents in the New Testament which were not only sectarian in nature but which tended to ridicule or scorn the Jews or, more particularly, the Jewish religious hierarchy, such as the address of Jesus in Matthew 23, in which the scribes and Pharisees are described as hypocrites [R. 52].

The witness also cited the famous scene portrayed in Matthew 27, in which the trial of Jesus before Pilate is described and in which, as related by the Christian New Testament, the Jews are portrayed as refusing to exchange Barabbas for the release of Jesus but insisting upon crucifixion in spite of the attempts of Pilate to placate the mob, the washing of the hands by Pilate, and then the verse 25; "Then answered all the people, and said, 'His blood be on us, and on our children' ", concerning which the witness stated that that single verse had been the cause of more anti-Jewish riots throughout the ages than anything else in history [R. 52-53].

On the basis of his experience as a teacher of Jewish children in religious subjects, both in New York and in Gratz College, Philadelphia, Dr. Grayzel gave the opinion that such material from the New Testament, particularly that having to do with the trial and the crucifixion of Jesus, was capable of being explained to Jewish children in such a way as to do no harm but if merely read without explanation, it would be, and in his specific experience with children had been, psychologically harmful to the child and a divisive force within the social media of the school [R. 59].

Dr. Grayzel also acknowledged that there were excerpts from the New Testament which were not objectionable but when counsel for the School District suggested the story of the Good Samaritan,[2] as an example, the witness emphatically stated that the story was deliberately tampered with when inserted in the New Testament and that the Samaritan had been substituted for an Israelite as "a slap at the Jews of that day who refused to join the Christian church", since it was obvious that the characters of the original story would have been representatives of the divisions of the Jewish society of the time, namely, Priests, Levites and Israelites, and so told it would have had a certain moral teaching upon which Dr. Grayzel elucidated. As presented in the New Testament, Dr. Grayzel pointed out that the Christian child could well reproach the Jewish child with the cruelty of the people from whom the Jewish child was descended; that, therefore, such a story should not be read in public schools [R. 67-68].

In addition, there were specific instances in which the King James Old Testament had, in the view of the Jewish religion, been imbued with a Christological significance [R. 48].

---

2. Luke 10:30.

Dr. Grayzel also explained that there was a significant difference in attitude with regard to the respective holy books of the Jewish and Christian religions in that Judaism attaches no special virtue to the reading of the Bible per se, that the Jewish Holy Scriptures are source materials to be studied, and the witness gave examples of confusion which had arisen in children's minds where passages of the Bible were read without benefit of explanation or comment [R. 49].

For the appellants, Orlando English, Superintendent of Schools of Abington Township, testified that a King James Version of the Bible was purchased by the School District and one copy issued to every teacher in the district. No other versions of the Bible or other religious work or text were ever purchased [R. 127].

All of the witnesses connected with the School District agreed that the method of selection of the verses for daily reading varied. In all of the schools, including Abington Senior High School, prior to the availability of the public address system, discretion as to selection and method of selection was left to the individual teacher, some of whom delegated this function to the students [R. 97].

According to the testimony of William Young, an English teacher at Abington Senior High School in charge of something known as the "radio and television workshop", a particular practice was followed in that school, under which the approximately 30 students of the radio and television workshop did the actual reading of the Bible and the leading of the school in the saying of The Lord's Prayer. Inasmuch as Mr. Young desired the students in this class to practice in advance the reading of whatever material was to be read by them over the microphone, he himself adopted a practice of sometimes having the students practice at home with their own Bibles, out of which they were to select a section, and consequently there had been occasions when the Jewish and the Catholic students had read from their Bibles which they had brought to school for the

purpose. Only the King James Version, however, was supplied by the school. Mr. Young did not say what the Jewish
students did about The Lord's Prayer, it not being included in the Jewish Holy Scriptures [R. 108-122].

The principal of the Abington Senior High School, Dr.
Eugene Stull, testified that there was in use in the school,
supplied by the township school authorities, a roll book for
the teachers' use in keeping attendance and marking the
students and in the front of this book there were suggested texts for Bible reading. Whether or not these suggestions were followed was apparently up to the teacher.
The book was not an official publication of the school district or of the state but was procured from a private publisher and neither Dr. Stull nor Dr. English knew how
these verses were selected by the publisher or what verses
they were [R. 105-106, 129-130].

The appellants likewise presented an expert witness,
Dr. Luther A. Weigle, an ordained Lutheran minister, then
holding a Congregational ministry in his capacity as Dean
Emeritus of the Yale Divinity School.

Dr. Weigle testified at some length as to his experience
and background in matters concerning theology, all of which
was within the discipline of the Protestant sects. On the
basis of this experience he testified that, although one of
the outstanding issues of the Protestant Reformation was
the feeling of Luther, Calvin and others that there must be
a return to the original Hebrew text for a new translation
of the Bible, the King James Version was not a sectarian
work [R. 147]. It developed, however, under questioning
by the Court that in Dr. Weigle's opinion, it would be a
sectarian practice if the Hebrew Scriptures, in English,
were read to the exclusion of other works; and it was the
witness's opinion that this might not satisfy the requirement that "The Holy Bible" be read [R. 152-153]. Subsequently on cross-examination, the witness defined his statement that the Bible was "non-sectarian" as meaning non-

sectarian among the various Christian bodies with a caveat as to the Catholic Church [R. 161.]

Of the various Christian denominations, the witness disclaimed any particular knowledge of the Catholic viewpoint but pointed out that unlike the King James Version the Catholic church put in notes to any translations made and approved by them setting forth "what the authorized theology of the Church is with respect to that particular point" [R. 161].

On direct examination Dr. Weigle had testified at considerable length on the New Revised Standard Version of the Protestant Bible and his part in the work of translating and editing this book. He acknowledged that as late as 1952, shortly after its publication, there were organizations within the Protestant church who bitterly opposed the New Revised Standard Version and that there were public burnings of books of this version [R. 156-157].

Dr. Weigle stated that he thought there was educational value in reading the King James Version, both because of the moral teachings contained therein and the high literary value, but he acknowledged on cross-examination that such aspects were incidental when he endorsed the following statement from the book of which he was the author:

"The message of the Bible is the central thing, its style is but an instrument for conveying the message. The Bible is not a mere historical document to be preserved. And it is more than a classic of English literature to be cherished and admired. The Bible contains the Word of God to man. And men need the Word of God in our time and hereafter as never before." [R. 164]

And he further stated that the reason that the Bible had moral, literary and historical values was "because people have believed it, because they believe that there is something revelatory in it of what true morals are. It is

253

not simply a literary exercise but its literature has arisen out of that faith'' [R. 166].

At the hearing on the amended complaint Mr. Schempp testified they had decided not to request that their children be excused from the morning devotions because, although they still felt that ''the reading of the King James Version of the Bible . . . was against our particular family religious beliefs'', the price which would be exacted was that of having the children labeled as ''odd balls'' day after day for every day of the year [R. 214]. Mr. Schempp stated that he was concerned that classmates of Roger and Donna would so react and would tend to equate the religious difference or religious objection with atheism, which, in turn, has a number of unpopular connotations in the milieu of the Abington community. Mr. Schempp felt that it is even likely to be equated with un-Americanism and immorality. He pointed out that the pledge of allegiance to the flag follows directly upon the recitation of the Lord's Prayer [R. 214, 216].

Mr. Schempp, in giving his reason for deciding not to request an excuse for his children, also pointed out that excuse from the morning devotions would also mean missing the daily announcements which, as he said, "are very important to a child" [R. 216].

He also testified that in Abington High School a common form of punishment is exclusion from the classroom and standing in the hall, and that excuse from the Bible reading would be undistinguishable in practice from such punishment and would carry the same stigma [R. 218]. Finally, Mr. Schempp testified that he felt these necessarily distinguishing actions would set apart his children from their classmates and "would be very detrimental to the psychological well-being of our children" [R. 217].

SUMMARY OF ARGUMENT.

As children and parents of children in the public schools of Pennsylvania the appellees have standing to challenge the constitutionality of the Pennsylvania statute requiring the reading of ten verses of the Holy Bible each day. The evidence is, as the District Court found, that this practice is a religious ceremony and, as such, violates the establishment portion of the religious clause of the First Amendment. In order to further the design of the Pennsylvania legislature, (as set forth in the Preamble of the Bible statute) to foster "a life of honorable thought" by teaching "lessons of morality" the state has employed religion as an engine of civil policy and has aided religion. The provision of the statute permitting children to be excused from the Morning Devotions is irrelevant to the transgression upon the establishment clause.

In addition, the evidence produced by both appellants and appellees establishes, as found by the District Court, that the only Holy Bible purchased and supplied by the state to all teachers, the King James Version, is a sectarian sacred work of certain sects of Protestantism. It is also not contested that the requirement of the language of the statute, which calls for the "Holy Bible" to be read, could only be satisfied by the sacred sectarian work of some particular religious sect. Thus the statute requires, and the practice as actually carried out in the schools constitutes, an aid to one religion over all others and a preference by the state in violation of both the establishment and free exercise clauses of the First Amendment.

Irrespective of the sectarian nature of the Holy Bible, the statute aids all religions. The First Amendment is not an "equal protection" clause among religions. The statute violates the establishment clause regardless of its excuse provision.

The appellees' constitutionally guaranteed rights to the free exercise of religion includes complete freedom to shape and mold the religious orientation of their minor children. It is of record that much that is promulgated by the King James Version is contrary to the religious beliefs and teaching of the plaintiffs and some is personally offensive to them. In order to be free of interference by the state in the religious training of their children plaintiff parents are required, by the written excuse provision, to profess publicly a belief or disbelief and to label publicly and identify their children on each day of the school year as dissenters.

The statute interferes with the free exercise of religion. The excuse provision does not eliminate the operation of influence by the State because the statute requires that appellees take public action in order to exercise their right not to attend a religious ceremony. The effect of the statute is to compel a "profession of disbelief" by a parent who requests an excuse for his children. At the same time the statute exerts pressure upon children to attend the religious ceremony. The statute injects a religious prejudice into the school by singling out those who attend and those who dissent from attending the Bible reading ceremony.

The statute is therefore unconstitutional and the decree of the District Court should be affirmed.

ARGUMENT.

Point I.

The Practice Required by the Pennsylvania Statute Constitutes a Religious Ceremony or Observance.

The statute here involved necessarily provides for a reading of the Bible as a devotional or religious act; the ritual must be done each day and only at the prescribed time. Comment is expressly barred. The terms are mandatory.

Any contention that the Bible reading in question is required merely or even primarily for its literary, historic or moral value is belied by the terms of the statute itself and the practice under it. The statute requires the reading specifically of the "Holy" Bible, and enjoins any comment upon what is read. No other book or writing, of whatever historical or literary merit, has been so singled out and made a compulsory subject of reading by teachers in the schools of Pennsylvania. No other work is presented without comment; there is no provision for excusing a child from any pedagogical exercise.

Moreover, the reading is not confined to passages of recognized literary grace, nor is any effort required or made to select passages of particular historical or moral value, even assuming agreement could be reached on the identity of such passages. The fact that the reading must be without comment necessarily means that the pedagogical benefits, if there can be any when comment and discussion are forbidden, are relegated to an inconsequential role in comparison with the religious significance of the reading.

The record establishes that the form and atmosphere of the daily reading is not that of instruction or teaching of educational material. Rather, the proceedings are formal and ceremonial, with the children instructed to be especially attentive and respectful [R. 80-81]. The reading is part of what are commonly called "Morning Devotions," and even counsel for the School District referred to it as "devotional services" [R. 23].

The School District's expert, Dr. Weigle, testified that the literary and historical aspects of the Bible are secondary to its inherently religious significance [R. 164]. The fact cannot be escaped that the Bible is essentially a religious work, and that its reading under these ritualistic circumstances is undeniably a religious exercise.

Appellees do not and need not contend that any version of the Bible or of any other major religious work is *incapable* of being used as pedagogical source material or is disqualified from any possible use in schools.[3] The contention is that it is not so used in the schools of Abington Township and was not intended by the legislature to be so used. This is plainly demonstrated by the fact that the Lord's Prayer, which clearly has no significance other than the religious one, is recited immediately after the Bible reading. Not only is the practice of mass compulsory recitation of the prayer unconstitutional in itself,[4] but the juxtaposition of this incantation following the Bible reading removes all doubts, if any there be, as to the religious character of the Bible reading.

The legislature has required, under criminal penalty, that all children in the Commonwealth attend school. It has provided that there must be each day a religious observance by teachers who face dismissal for failure to do so.[5] The law under attack, therefore, is one which estab-

---

3. The decree submitted by plaintiffs and adopted by the District Court expressly provides, "that nothing herein shall be construed as interfering with or prohibiting the use of any books or works as educational, source, or reference material; . . ." [R. 236].

4. There is no need for a separate provision in the decree with respect to the saying of The Lord's Prayer since it is a part of the Holy Bible and therefore within the terms of the Decree.

5. While the statute now provides no specific penalty in its own terms upon the teacher who refuses to observe its mandate, such a teacher can be dismissed for "wilful violation of the school laws." Public School Code of 1949, 24 PS § 11-1122.

lishes a mandatory religious ceremony with penalties for non-compliance.

Appellants argue that the Bible reading practice required by the statute does not require the performance of a religious act, and that listening to the reading does not constitute an "establishment of religion" within the meaning of the First Amendment (Appellants' brief, 29-31). Appellants attempt to distinguish listening to the reading of the Bible from the saying of an official prayer, held unconstitutional in *Engel v. Vitale,* 370 U. S. 421 (1962).

The attempted distinction is spurious. Whether the practice of Bible reading constitutes an "establishment of religion" certainly does not depend upon the listener's verbal participation in the practice. Certainly the official prayer in *Engel v. Vitale* would have been an "establishment of religion" had the prayers been required to be made by a teacher without any pupil participation. The listening pupil remains passive whether the teacher reads the Bible as here, or recites a prayer, or delivers a sermon. The listener's passivity in either case has not the slightest bearing on the nature of the ceremony.

Point II.

The Practice Required by the Statute Constitutes an Establishment of Religion in Violation of the Establishment Clause of the First Amendment.

The clause of the First Amendment dealing with religion is of dual thrust,—forbidding an establishment of religion and guaranteeing the free exercise of religion. Thus it is both a limitation upon the state and an affirmation of inviolate personal right.

Herein we treat of the establishment clause, bearing in mind that the written excuse provision of the Pennsylvania statute is irrelevant to this aspect of that statute's unconstitutionality.

The establishment clause of the First Amendment forbids not merely an established *church;* it forbids any law "respecting an establishment of *religion.*" Whether its meaning and scope be fathomed by analysis of the literal words used, the stirring historical background of its adoption or review of the judicial precedents interpreting it, one must conclude that it forbids any interference, whether positive or negative, by the state in things religious. The state may neither hinder nor aid religion,—either any religion or all religions. For what the state may aid, it may hinder; what it may foster, however slightly or indirectly, it may impede grossly and directly. In short, the Amendment has been accepted as creating a wall of separation between church and state.

Appellees submit that *Engel v. Vitale,* 370 U. S. 421 (1962) controls this case. There this Court held that the action of state officials in requiring a prayer composed by them to be recited in the public schools at the beginning of each school day violated the prohibition of the First Amendment even though the prayer was denominationally neutral, and pupils who wished to do so were excused from the room while the prayer was being recited. In the language of Mr. Justice Black for the Court: "We think that the Constitutional prohibition against laws respecting an establishment of religion must at least mean that in this country it is no part of the business of government to compose official prayers for any group of the American people to recite as a part of a religious program carried on by the government" (370 U. S. at 425).

Is it any more the business of government to require the reading of a prescribed number of verses from the sacred work of any religious sect as part of a ceremony opening each day's program in the public schools?

As in *Engel v. Vitale* the classrooms are used for conducting of this observance, the aegis and discipline of the state schools are employed to promulgate it, the children having been assembled to listen by the compulsion of the state's school attendance law and, finally, the state's employees, the teachers, supervise the proceedings.

There runs through appellants' argument the idea that a little ceremonial Bible reading is de minimus as an establishment. The Regents' Prayer in *Engel v. Vitale,* with its twenty-two words, was surely even lesser in magnitude, if such things can be measured. But this court said:

"It is true that New York's establishment of its Regents' Prayer as an officially approved religious doctrine of that State does not amount to a total establishment of one particular religious sect to the exclusion of all others—that, indeed, the governmental endorsement of that prayer seems relatively insignificant when compared to the governmental encroachments upon religion which were commonplace 200 years ago. To those who may subscribe to the view that because the Regents' official prayer is so brief and general there can be no danger to religious freedom in its governmental establishment, however, it may be appropriate to say in the words of James Madison, the author of the First Amendment:

" '(I)t is proper to take alarm at the first experiment on our liberties. . . . Who does not see that the same authority which can establish Christianity, in exclusion of all other Religions, may establish with the same ease any particular sect of Christians, in exclusion of all other Sects? That the same authority which can force a citizen to contribute three pence only of his property for the support of any one establishment, may force him to conform to any other establishment in all cases whatsoever?' " (370 U. S. at 436)

The application of the religious guaranty provision of the First Amendment in *Engel v. Vitale* required no extension of the "wall of separation" nor any departure from constitutional lines previously drawn by this court in a number of cases involving the public schools. Even without the guidance of *Engel v. Vitale* the District Court in the instant case found *McCollum v. Board of Education* controlling (333 U. S. 203 (1948)).

In the *McCollum* case, a parent and taxpayer objected to a released time program in which religious instruction was given to public school children during school hours and on school premises; private teachers (required to be approved by the school authorities) presented this instruction in various classes arranged according to religious faith. Classes consisted of pupils whose parents signed cards requesting that their children be permitted to attend. The Court held the program unconstitutional as a violation of the principle of separation of church and state, repeating the classic summation of the "establishment" clause which it had laid down in *Everson v. Board of Education,* 330 U. S. 1 (1947):

> "Neither a state nor the Federal Government can set up a church. Neither can pass laws which aid one religion, aid all religions, or prefer one religion over another. Neither can force nor influence a person to go to or remain away from church against his will or force him to profess a belief or disbelief in any religion. No person can be punished for entertaining or professing religious beliefs or disbeliefs, for church attendance or non-attendance. No tax in any amount, large or small, can be levied to support any religious activities or institutions, whatever they may be called, or whatever form they may adopt to teach or practice religion. Neither a state nor the Federal Government can, openly or secretly, participate in the affairs of any religious organizations or groups and *vice versa.* In the words of Jefferson, the clause against establishment of religion by law was intended to erect 'a wall of separation between church and State.' " (330 U. S. at 15-16; 333 U. S. at 210-11)

In *Zorach v. Clauson,* 343 U. S. 306 (1952), a different type of released time program was upheld by the Court (three Justices dissenting). There, the religious instruction was not given on public school premises, and it was presented by private teachers selected by the parents or churches of the children concerned; parents desiring to participate in the program merely notified the school authorities, and their children were released at designated times. The Court based its ruling on the differences between that program and the program in the *McCollum* case:

> "In the McCollum case the classrooms were used for religious instruction and the force of the public school was used to promote that instruction. Here, as we have said, the public schools do no more than accommodate their schedules to a program of outside religious instruction. We follow the McCollum case." (343 U. S. at 315)

Appellants urge that the program in *McCollum* unlike the case here was invalid because the classrooms there were used to provide formal religious instruction involving indoctrination (Appellants' brief, 28). Irrespective however of the fact that the Bible reading is without comment, it is undeniably indoctrination in the religious ideas contained in the Bible. At least it is so intended, in order, as the preamble of the act states, to foster "good moral training" and "a life of honorable thought".[6] As in *McCollum*, classrooms are used for the instruction, the force of the public school is used to promote it, and in addition public school teachers, the State's representatives, directly supervise it using Bibles supplied by the school district from public funds, a circumstance not present in *McCollum*. We do not think that the sweep of the *McCollum* case was limited to the circumstance that sectarian teaching was undertaken. In any event, *Engel v. Vitale* makes it clear beyond question that the element of proselytizing is not a factor in determining whether violation of the "establishment" clause exists.

---

6. Act of May 20, 1913, P. L. 226.

Appellants have invented and press an argument that what is required by the First Amendment is neutrality by "the government", which, in turn, means that the traditional religious leaven should remain undisturbed. The fact that it is the legislature of Pennsylvania which has not been neutral is apparently tacitly conceded, but the rejoinder is made that this non-neutrality is traditional. So was the segregation of students on the basis of race.

This is a curious and ingenious argument. Its initial fallacy is the equation of this Court with "the government." It blithely ignores the obvious fact that what these plaintiffs are complaining about is that "the government" in the person of the legislature of Pennsylvania has not observed the "neutrality towards religion" which appellants so rightly commend. In such a situation to urge this Court to be "neutral" by not interfering is to be oblivious to the very function of the judiciary and, because one branch of the government is induced to remain supine, the non-neutrality of the other is allowed to continue. This is neutrality with a vengeance!

In sum, appellants' argument here comes down to this: Bible reading in the schools has been a traditional religious practice over a long period of years. By not disturbing this practice the government's policy of neutrality toward religion will be preserved.

This is a plea for maintaining the status quo. It apparently assumes that governmental support of Bible reading in public schools would be objectionable were it not for the fact that such support has existed for a long time. Under this view, any long established practice in our public schools violative of church-state separation ought to be sanctioned if the effect of its removal would be a disturbance of the "religious leaven."

We find no support for abdication of judicial review of laws or customs having the sanction of law but honored by age alone. On the contrary, this court has not hesitated to review and declare invalid such laws where violative of rights protected by the Fourteenth Amendment. The "separate but equal" doctrine adopted in *Plessy v. Ferguson,* 163 U. S. 537 (1896) was acknowledged as law in the field of public education from 1896 until 1954. In finding the doctrine invalid this court felt it necessary to "consider public education in the light of its full development and its present place in American life throughout the Nation": *Brown v. Board of Education,* 347 U. S. 483, 492-93.

In this same context appellants argue that if this statute is struck down a chain of public catastrophies will inevitably ensue such as discontinuance of chaplains for the armed forces, the elimination of the rubric on our coins, courtroom oaths and the official use of the Christian calendar.

The law knows well how to deal with such a relentless pursuit of logic. Some of these matters are de minimus and courts will have no hesitancy in saying so. As to most of them, it is difficult to see how any plaintiff would have legal standing to object.

Others, like chaplains in the armed forces, are subject to countervailing rights. In that case the right of one who by compulsion of the state is separated physically from access to his church to be provided with a substitute. If chaplains were not provided, the state, through its military service laws, would be preventing the free exercise of religion.

A. THE STATUTE AIDS AND PREFERS ONE RELIGION TO ALL OTHERS.

Christianity is the religion favored by this act to the exclusion of all other religions. More than this, a particular sect of Christians is preferred over other sects, for while the statute does not specify which version of the Bible shall be read, manifestly any book which can qualify as a "Holy Bible" is by definition a religious book of a particular Christian faith, creed or sect. And as the record in this case eloquently shows, invariably the version of the Bible used, if not entirely clear from the statute, will be the one favored by the dominant sect in the community, or at least that favored by the predominant sect among the personnel of the school administration.[7]

In *Tudor v. Board of Education of Rutherford,* 14 N. J. 31, 100 A. 2d 857 (1953), cert. den., 348 U. S. 816 (1954), the Supreme Court of New Jersey condemned as violative of the Fourteenth Amendment a school board resolution permitting the distribution of Gideon Bibles of the King James Version. Chief Justice Vanderbilt for the court stated:

> "To permit the distribution of the King James version of the Bible in the public schools of this State would be to cast aside all the progress made in the United States and throughout New Jersey in the field of religious toleration and freedom." (14 N. J. at 52).[8]

---

7. The superintendent of schools of Montgomery County, in which Abington Township is located, Dr. Allen C. Harman, also teaches at the Willow Grove Methodist Church. The four superintendents of schools in Philadelphia and adjacent suburban counties are all past or present Protestant church school teachers. *The Evening Bulletin,* col. 1, p. 52, October 9, 1962.

8. A number of other state courts have considered Bible reading in the public schools where the issue was usually confined to the question whether the use of the Bible was "sectarian" within the meaning of a provision in the State Constitution prohibiting sectarian teaching or giving preference to any religious sect:

a. Upheld where participation not directly compelled by law:

Nessle v. Hum, 1 Ohio, N. P. 140, 2 Ohio Dec. 60 (1894); *Stevenson v. Hanyon,* 7 Pa. Dist. 585 (1898); *Lewis v. Board of Education,* 157 Misc. 520, 285 N. Y. Supp. 164 (1935), modified and affirmed, 247 App. Div. 106, 286 N. Y. Supp. 174 (1936), appeal dismissed, 246 N. Y. 490, 12 N. E. 2d 172 (1937); *Pfeiffer v. Board of Education,* 118 Mich. 560, 77 N. W. 250 (1898); *People ex rel. Vollmar v. Stanley,* 81 Colo. 276, 255 Pac. 610 (1927); in this case the court relied on the Fourteenth Amendment in holding children could not be required to attend reading against parents' wishes; *Kaplan v. Independent School Dist.,* 171 Minn. 142, 214 N. W. 18 (1927);

The practice struck down in the *Tudor* case was far less objectionable. There was no reading of the Bible in the school, the distribution was carried out privately, upon individual request of parents, and without cost to the school system. Although care was taken to insure that the children were under no pressure to apply for a Bible, yet the court concluded there was coercion in fact.

The particular Holy Bible read in the schools of Abington Township and throughout the state of Pennsylvania and the only Bible purchased by the state and supplied to all teachers is the King James Version [9] which is the official

---

Wilkerson v. Rome, 152 Ga. 762, 110 S. E. 895 (1922) ; *Moore v. Monroe,* 64 Iowa 367, 20 N. W. 475 (1884) ; *Hackett v. Brooksville Graded School Dist.,* 120 Ky. 608, 87 S. W. 792 (1905) ; *State ex rel. Finger v. Weedman,* 55 S. D. 343, 226 N. W. 348 (1929), reading permitted but Catholic children allowed to absent themselves.

    b. Upheld where legal compulsion present :

Church v. Bullock, 104 Tex. 1, 109 S. W. 115 (1908); *Spiller v. Inhabitants of Woburn,* 94 Mass. (12 Allen) 127 (1866) ; *Doremus v. Board of Education,* 5 N. J. 435, 75 A. 2d 880 (1950), app. dism'd, 342 U. S. 429 (1952) ; *Carden v. Bland,* 199 Tenn. 665, 288 S. W. 2d 718 (1956). In the latter case plaintiffs also urged invalidity under the First and Fourteenth Amendments. *Billard v. Board of Education,* 69 Kan. 53, 76 Pac. 422 (1904) ; *Donahoe v. Richards,* 38 Me. 379 (1854).

    c. Held unconstitutional where compulsory :

People ex rel. Ring v. Board of Education, 245 Ill. 334, 92 N. E. 251 (1910) ; *State ex rel. Freeman v. Scheve,* 65 Neb. 853, 91 N. W. 846 (1902) ; *State ex rel. Weiss v. District Board,* 76 Wis. 177, 44 N. W. 967 (1890) ; *Herold v. Parish Board,* 136 La. 1034, 68 So. 116 (1915); Cf. *State ex rel. Dearle v. Frazier,* 102 Wash. 369, 173 Pac. 35 (1918). Compulsory attendance at reading but not the Bible reading itself was held void in *People ex rel. Vollmar v. Stanley,* 81 Colo. 276, 255 Pac. 610 (1927).

    d. Held unconstitutional where not compulsory :

People ex rel. Ring v. Board of Education, supra, note; *State ex rel. Weiss v. District Board, supra,* note; *Herold v. Parish Board, supra,* note.

    9. [R. 127]. The fact that under an innovation of one teacher some students may occasionally use other versions does not, of course,

Bible of certain of the Protestant sects of the Christian
religion. It is a sectarian religious work, both in purpose
and content. Its dedication is anti-Catholic [10] [R. 162]; it
has been called by the Catholic Church the "chief arm of
the Protestant revolt".[11] The New Testament, known to
Protestants as the Gospel, was written as, and for 1900
years has been, the principal vehicle for the promulgation
of the Christian religion and it is, therefore, as sectarian
vis-a-vis Judaism as it is possible for a religious work to
be. Mere changes in language in the Revised Standard
Version have within the decade led to public burnings of
the new translation [R. 157].

The record contains considerable material excerpted
from Encyclicals of the Popes and the Canons of the Roman
Catholic church. Pope Leo XII labeled the Protestant
version as a perversion and warned that the very practice
followed in Abington (and according to the testimony of
State Superintendent Boehm, throughout the Commonwealth), that of *"indiscriminate"* Bible reading may do
"more harm than good". Pius IX asserted that the Protestant vernacular translations were filled with error and
false explanations and degraded the Sacred Book "by
using it as an instrument of proselytism". Naturally no
more fertile field for proselytism could be found than the
public schools. Whether, in fact, the Protestant Bible was
selected for such purposes is immaterial if, in fact, the
Catholics so believe. It was just such occasions for divi-

---

make the practice any less sectarian, for the listening children of other
faiths must then be attentive to the reader's particular version [R.
109-112].

10. The translators' dedicatory preface states that the purpose
of the translation was to give "such a blow unto that Man of Sin
[the Pope] as will not be healed" and "to make God's holy truth
to be yet more and more known to the people, whom they ['Papist
persons at home or abroad'] desire still to be kept in ignorance and
darkness."

11. *A Catholic Commentary on Holy Scripture* (imprimatur and
nihil obstat), London, 1953, p. 11.

sive recrimination that the First Amendment was designed to avoid. The very practice of reading the Bible "without comment" has been vigorously condemned by Catholic authority which has decreed, "Believing herself to be the divinely appointed custodian and interpreter of Holy Writ, she cannot without turning traitor to herself approve the distribution of Scripture 'without note or comment' ". The same authority has asserted that the "impelling motive" of those who distribute such Bibles is their knowlege that "Private interpretation of the Scriptures" is a "fundamental fallacy".[12] The most disgraceful and violent episode in Philadelphia's religious history arose over what version of the Bible was to be read in the public schools.[13]

The record contains considerable material delineating the difference in content and concept of the King James Version as compared to the Douay (Catholic) version and the Jewish Holy Scriptures.[14] Furthermore, the leading faiths differ not only in their translation and interpretation of particular Biblical passages, and as to the books which together constitute their "Bible", they also differ in their

---

12. *The Catholic Encyclopedia,* Robert Appleton Company, New York 1907, vol. 2, p. 545.

13. In 1844 took place the infamous Nativist Riots in Philadelphia. Within the shadow of the site where stands the courthouse in which the instant case was heard, Catholic churches were burned and at least ten persons killed. The trigger of this episode was a controversy over the reading of the King James Version of The Bible to Catholic children in the public schools. Bishop Kenrick had protested and asked for equal treatment. The Native American Party, forerunner of the Know-Nothings, seized upon this protest as evidence of a Popish Plot to oust the King James Bible from the schools. Hailing The Bible as the source of all morality, "Friends of The Bible" committees were set up to oppose "naturalized and unnaturalized foreigners" who wanted to "eject it therefrom." The bloodshed followed. *Irish Emigrant and American Nativism,* Berger, Pennsylvania Magazine (1946); O'Gorman, *History of the Roman Catholic Church in the United States,* New York (1895).

14. See particularly the testimony of Dr. Solomon Grayzel, Editor of the Jewish Publication Society, and of Dr. Luther A. Weigle, Dean Emeritus of the Yale Divinity School [R. 41-74, R. 142-169].

views as to the Bible's essential character. For the Jews
the Bible (i.e., the Old Testament) is a record of a covenant
between God and Abraham and the latter's descendants,
the children of Israel: to them the New Testament is not
"sacred" literature [R. 43], in fact the concept of the
divinity of Christ is blasphemous [R. 44]. For Catholics
the Bible is a church document whose meaning the Church
reserves the exclusive right to interpret.[15] For Protestants,
while the essence of the Bible is the New Testament, each
denomination reserves the right to interpret it to fit its own
particular beliefs and practices,[16] and this reservation has
led to exceedingly bitter controversy in this century.

The concept of an anthropomorphic God, the concept
of a God of vengeance, the doctrine of the Trinity, the doctrines of the Virgin Birth, the divinity of Christ, the trans-
figuration, the miracles,—all these *religious* beliefs are contrary to the religious beliefs of the appellees, both parents
and children. In a religiously free society, the Schempp
parents should not be put to contradicting in the home
what their children are subjected to in the school.

---

15. Catholics hold that: "The Bible, as the inspired record of
revelation, contains the word of God; that is, it contains those revealed truths which the Holy Ghost wishes to be transmitted in
writing." and further, that "though the inspiration of any writer and
the sacred character of his work be antecedent to its recognition by
the Church yet we are dependent upon the Church for our knowledge
of the existence of this inspiration. She is the appointed witness and
guardian of revelation. From her alone we know what books belong
to the Bible." *The Catholic Encyclopedia,* Robert Appleton Company, New York 1907, vol. 2, p. 543.

16. Many Protestant denominations appeal to the Bible to justify their own sectarian beliefs. Examples of this are too numerous
to recite here but the point is illustrated by the following: The Latter
Day Saints, according to an authoritative pronouncement, believe in
universal "salvation". See Richard L. Evans, "What is a Mormon?",
in *A Guide to the Religions of America,* ed. Leo Rosten, New York
1955, p. 95. On the other hand, the Jehovah's Witnesses say that
"The reward of Spiritual life with Christ Jesus in heaven for men
on earth is limited to those who inherit the Kingdom of God. In
Revelation 7:4, the number of these is given as exactly 144,000."
See Milton G. Henschel, "Who Are Jehovah's Witnesses?", in *A
Guide to the Religions of America, Ibid.,* at p. 61.

The Schempps ask no more than that which one would suppose they were entitled to as citizens of the United States: the right to form and mold and guide the spiritual life of their own children themselves without interference or "help" from the State, however well-intentioned.

To brush aside these differences in belief as mere quibbles is, to say the least, an extraordinary rewriting of the records of centuries of religious conflict and bloodshed. To treat them this lightly is to denigrate the value of specific religious belief. The result is to foster a kind of colorless national, or public school creed, a religiosity without religion, a sanctimonious eclecticism cut adrift from theology.[17]

The characterization of the Holy Bible of any religion as "non-sectarian" is, of course, almost inevitable on the part of the hierarchy of that particular church or religion. All religions claim universality; all believe, and must believe, that their truth is truth and that the "truth" of other religions is, at best, error. Likewise, the writings or sacred texts upon which the religion founds its particular beliefs, if admitted by the adherents of the religion to be "sectarian" are thus conceded to be less than fundamental and universal in origin and application, or at least, sug-

---

17. "There is an inclination in educational circles particularly to develop a kind of common, national, public-school creed which rigidly excludes any theological concern as divisive and dangerous to 'democratic unity'. Such a point of view is naturally offensive to the believer, for it misunderstands the necessarily transcendent and all-encompassing relevance of his beliefs.

* * *

When men feel compelled to subscibe to religious affirmations they do not truly accept, the civil liberties problem is plain enough. Failure on the religious side is important too. The kind of religion that results from this common civic faith is a religion-in-general, superficial and syncretistic, destructive of the profounder elements of faith. Part of what drops away is the note of judgment and, more broadly, the whole transcendent dimension of religious truth." William Lee Miller, *Religion in the American Way of Life,* Fund for the Republic (1958), pp. 13, 14.

gest that the faith in question is but one of many competing and co-equal religions.[18]

---

18. No better summation of the case against the claimed non-
sectarianism of The Bible can be stated than the one contained in
People ex rel. Ring v. Board of Education, 245 Ill. 334, 92 N. E. 251
(1910). In that case Catholic parents complained that their children were compelled to attend public school where the King James
Version of The Bible was read. The court in holding the practice invalid as sectarian instruction within the meaning of the Illinois Constitution said:

"Christianity is a religion. The Catholic church and the
various Protestant churches are sects of that religion. These two
versions of the Scriptures are the bases of the religion of the
respective sects. Protestants will not accept the Douay Bible as
representing the inspired word of God. As to them it is a sectarian book containing errors, and matter which is not entitled
to their respect as a part of the Scriptures. It is consistent with
the Catholic faith but not the Protestant. Conversely, Catholics
will not accept King James' version. As to them it is a sectarian
book inconsistent in many particulars with their faith, teaching
what they do not believe. The differences may seem to many
so slight as to be immaterial, yet Protestants are not found to
be more willing to have the Douay Bible read as a regular exercise in the schools to which they are required to send their children, than are Catholics to have the King James' version read
in schools which their children must attend. (pp. 344-345)

* * *

"The reading of the Bible in school is instruction. Religious
instruction is the object of such reading, but whether it is so or
not, religious instruction is accomplished by it. The Bible has
its place in the school, if it is read there at all, as the living word
of God, entitled to honor and reverence. Its words are entitled
to be received as authoritative and final. The reading or hearing
of such words cannot fail to impress deeply the pupil's minds.
It is intended and ought to so impress them. They cannot hear
the Scriptures read without being instructed as to the divinity
of Jesus Christ, the Trinity, the resurrection, baptism, predes-
tination, a future state of punishments and rewards, the authority
of the priesthood, the obligation and effect of the sacraments, and
many other doctrines about which the various sects do not agree.
Granting that instruction on these subjects is desirable, yet the
sects do not agree on what instruction shall be given. Any instruction on any one of the subjects is necessarily sectarian, because, while it may be consistent with the doctrines of one or
many of the sects, it will be inconsistent with the doctrine of one
or more of them. The petitioners are Catholics. They are com-

The testimony of Dr. Weigle, although he was called as a witness for the defendant School District, well illustrates this point. As an ordained Lutheran minister, it is not surprising that he felt that the King James Version was non-sectarian (which he later amended to non-sectarian within the Christian religion and further qualified this by saying that he was not a Catholic and could not speak for the Catholic Church), but asserted that the reading of the Jewish Holy Scriptures would be "a sectarian practice" [R. 150, 153, 161].

A practice of having a religious ceremony which consists solely of the reading of a Bible and/or the mass recitation of the Lord's Prayer is sectarian in a further sense.

---

pelled by law to contribute to the maintenance of this school and are compelled to send their children to it, or, besides contributing to its maintenance, to pay the additional expense of sending their children to another school. What right have the teachers of the school to teach those children religious doctrine different from that which they are taught by their parents? Why should the state compel them to unlearn the Lord's Prayer as taught in their homes and by their Church and use the Lord's Prayer as taught by another sect? If Catholic children may be compelled to read the King James' version of the Bible in schools taught by Protestant teachers, the same law will authorize Catholic teachers to compel Protestant children to read the Catholic version. The same law which subjects Catholic children to Protestant domination in school districts which are controlled by Protestant influences will subject the children of Protestants to Catholic control where the Catholics predominate. In one part of the state the King James' version of the Bible may be read in the public schools, in another the Douay Bible, while in school districts where the sects are somewhat evenly divided, a religious contest may be expected at each election of school director to determine which sect shall prevail in the school. Our Constitution has wisely provided against any such contest by excluding sectarian instruction altogether from the school. (pp. 346-347)

* * *

". . . The Bible is not read in the public schools as mere literature or mere history. It cannot be separated from its character as an inspired book of religion. It is not adapted for use as a text book for the teaching, alone, of reading, of history, or of literature, without regard to its religious character." (p. 348)

Regardless of the content of the particular Bible which might be read, the practice is a reflection of a concept of bibliolatry (sometimes called monobiblicism) characteristic of the fundamentalist Protestant faiths. Neither the Jewish nor the Catholic faiths, nor the Unitarians or Society of Friends [19] or other such Protestant dissenters, emphasize Bible reading per se without study, comment, discussion or elucidation. In fact, distinguished Catholic authority specifically charges the concept of monobiblicism to Calvin and ascribes to this practice great significance in the strategy of the Reformation.[20] And the saying of a prayer, with or without Bible reading, is sectarian regardless of content, at least under the method of mass recitation employed in the schools, since it embodies both a belief in the significance and exercise of petitional prayer, and the concept of direct access of the individual to an imminent God, neither of which are by any means universally accepted by all religions or individuals.

If this statute can be upheld it would be as justifiable and consistent, for example, for the Mormons (Latter Day Saints), in areas where they predominate, to insist that the Book of Mormon, which they regard as inspired by God, be read in public schools; or for Christian Scientists to insist that Mary Baker Eddy's "Science and Health with Key to the Scriptures", which they regard as inspired, to be read; or for Swedenborgians (New Church) to insist upon the reading of writings of Emanuel Swedenborg, such as "Arcana Celestia" or "Heaven and Hell"; or for fol-

19. "Nevertheless because they are only a declaration of the fountain, and not the fountain itself, therefore they are not to be esteemed the principal ground of all truth and knowledge, nor yet the adequate primary rule of faith and manners." Robert Barclay, The Confession of the Society of Friends, Commonly called Quakers, A. D. 1675 (*Barclay's Apology*), Third Proposition: Concerning the Scriptures.

20. Dom Bernard Orchard, Rev. Edmund Sutcliffe, Rev. Reginald C. Fuller, Dom Ralph Russell, editorial committee, A Catholic Commentary on Holy Scripture, p. 11 (with imprimatur and nihil obstat), London, 1953.

lowers of Eastern Religions, of which there are many in this country (and who constitute a majority in Hawaii), to insist upon the reading of the holy books of the East such as the Confucian classics, the Buddha Scriptures and the Koran.[21] Today in this country there are at least 254 religious sects or denominations, including many non-Christian groups.[22] Under the U. S. Constitution there is or should be no difference in the principles applicable to a small minority religious group and to a large dominant religious group. The First Amendment does not select any group or type of religion for preferred treatment: *United States v. Ballard,* 322 U. S. 78, 87 (1944).

The appellants seek to meet the inherently preferential aspect of the practice under the statute by insisting upon the absence of proselytizing or indoctrination which they say follows from the "without comment" proviso. This is wrong in theory and in fact,—in theory because proselytizing is not an essential ingredient of constitutional infirmity; in fact because, as their own expert testified, the Bible is the message of God to man and the New Testament the message of Christianity. No book in all history has demonstrated a more powerful ability to indoctrinate.

B. The Statute Aids All Religions.

We have stated at considerable length our reasons for contending this statute bad as giving a clear preference to

---

21. The I AM cult (which has a temple in Philadelphia and members throughout the area), the conviction of whose leaders for mail fraud was reversed in *United States v. Ballard,* 322 U. S. 78, 87 (1944), would insist upon the reading of the literature written by Guy and Edna Ballard which they regard as inspired by certain celestial "ascendant masters" and delivered to the Ballards by the divine messenger, St. Germain. Although characterized as "humbug" by this Court, this cult was accorded the protection of a religion under the First Amendment.

22. According to the Yearbook of the American Churches in 1961 (National Council of Churches, 297 4th Avenue, New York), there is a total church membership of 112,226,905 persons in the United States divided into 254 bodies, including Buddhist, Eastern churches, Jewish, Roman Catholic and Protestant.

one religion. We do not however mean to suggest that
its ailment would be remedied in the least degree if the
words "Holy Bible" were interpreted to include only the
books thereof acceptable to the Jews or if the various
versions currently used by Protestants and Catholics were
in some fashion made available for use in public schools
without discrimination, nor indeed would it vary the case
one bit if this statute were widened to include the "holy"
books of every religious group that claims adherents in the
United States today; this Court has made clear beyond
quibble that the state may not "aid all religions" any
more than it may prefer one over another.

This Court's classic declaration in the *Everson* case
was the fruit of long and careful historical research into
the evolution and meaning of the religion clause of the
Amendment and its announcement has since become the
most authoritative exposition of that meaning. Within a
year after the *Everson* decision was handed down, the
Court was called upon in the *McCollum* case to repudiate
this interpretation of the First Amendment, and this the
Court refused to do. On the contrary, it went out of its
way to repeat in full the detailed meaning of the Amendment set forth in the *Everson* case. It reaffirmed that interpretation and held the Illinois released time program
unconstitutional, expressly stating that it made no difference that the aid was non-preferential and non-discriminatory. Again in *Zorach v. Clauson, supra,* this Court reaffirmed its adherence to this view, unambiguously stating that "government cannot finance religious groups"
whether preferentially or otherwise. Finally, there is recent reaffirmance in *Engel v. Vitale.*

The First Amendment is thus not an "equal protection" clause among religions; it was framed to meet the
demands of the states for an express and absolute prohibition against government power to deal with religion
in any form or manner. To uphold such a statute as the
present one would be to run directly in the face of the

constitutional prohibition, and to ignore the clear, un-equivocal expressions of the Supreme Court in *Everson, McCollum,* and *Engel.*

Perhaps none of the provisions of the Bill of Rights are so illuminated by study of the immediate history behind their adoption as the clause which is involved in this case. We refer to the fight against the Assessment Bill in the legislature of Virginia during 1784 and 1785. This bill was designed to support religion in general; each taxpayer having the privilege of selecting the church which should receive his share of the tax *or,* if he preferred, his share could be designated by him for education. Thus there was neither overt preference for one sect over another nor enforced contribution to some church since the tax could be used for secular purposes.

However, Madison and Jefferson fought the Assessment Bill, were ultimately successful and, in the succeeding legislature, there was passed Jefferson's Bill for Establishing Religious Freedom. As part of the fight against the Assessment Bill, Madison published one of the great landmarks in the history of human freedom,—the famous *Memorial and Remonstrance.*

A complete and definitive discussion of the history of the religious clause of the First Amendment and the role of Madison and Jefferson is set forth in Justice Rutledge's fifty-seven page dissent in the *Everson* case. It is pointless here to reproduce the material contained there and summary fails to do justice to it. The full text of the Remonstrance, together with the text of the Assessment Bill itself, is printed as an appendix to that opinion. In view of Madison's subsequent draftsmanship of the religious clause of the First Amendment, the Remonstrance is more than an historical curiosity; it declares the very basis of policy upon which, a few years later, the First Amendment clause was founded.

Madison's position was that religion is wholly exempt from the cognizance of civil society and hence beyond the power of the legislature to treat in any way—by aid or hindrance, large or small. The fact that the Bill was non-discriminatory and non-sectarian, and even the fact that in default of a designated religion the tax was destined for secular education did not eliminate the fact that the state intended to "employ Religion as an engine of civil policy."

The preamble of the Assessment Bill stated the purposes of the Bill to be that the general diffusion of religion "hath a natural tendency to correct the morals of men, restrain their vices and preserve the peace of society". Madison made the point that true as this might be, the state was not to employ religion for these or other civil ends.

The preamble to the act under attack in this case is strikingly similar:

> "Whereas, It is in the interest of good moral training, of a life of honorable thought and of good citizen ship, that the public school children should have lessons of morality brought to their attention during their school-days; . . ."[23]

Thus after almost 200 years the legislature of Pennsylvania falls into the precise error that Madison and Jefferson were able to persuade the Virginia legislature to avoid.

But now that the amendment permitting excuse has been added to the statute the similarity between the Assessment Bill generally and the Pennsylvania Bible reading statute becomes ever more marked. The Assessment Bill in its final form, and the form in which it was defeated, provided that those citizens who did not care to have their tax earmarked for a particular religion could designate the tax to be used for secular education purposes. The Bill was therefore what counsel for the School District would insist upon calling a "permissive" assessment.

---

23. Act of May 20, 1913, P. L. 226.

Everyone was going to be taxed and those who objected to the religious use of the tax would be permitted to avoid participation in the support of religion, just as in the amended statute, the Morning Devotions are going to take place, but provision is made for avoidance of participation in them.

This feature should no more serve to save the instant statute than it did the Assessment Bill. Madison went to the heart of the matter when he argued that this was state aid of religion and hence an establishment whether it forced support from a given citizen or not.

Point III.
The Statute Interferes With the Free Exercise of Religion.

Appellees submit that the statute violates the free exercise clause of the First Amendment because it requires that they and their children take public action in order to exercise the freedom of religion or non-religion which the Constitution guarantees to them.

Regardless of the nature of this public action, regardless of whether the consequences are pleasant or unpleasant, the action itself,—the communication to the state authorities is an act of profession of belief or disbelief and it is, per se, a violation of the First Amendment to exact it.

We have adverted to the famous statement of the meaning of the religious clause of the First Amendment as superbly put in *Everson v. Board of Education,* 330 U. S. 1 (1947). The Court said there:

"The 'establishment of religion' clause of the First Amendment means at least this: . . . Neither a State nor the Federal Government . . . can force . . . a person . . . *to profess a belief or disbelief in any religion* . . ." (330 U. S. at 15)

The legislature has now contrived a device which requires the plaintiffs in order to avoid exposure to religious material contrary to the family beliefs of plaintiffs to "profess a belief or disbelief" in a religion.

Plainly the excuse, followed by the excusing, is precisely this. It says to the state authority and to all the world, "I and my children do not believe in the religion promulgated by the Holy Bible".

This is precisely a "profession of disbelief" which the Supreme Court has said the state may not exact.

This statute violates the doctrine of the Everson case totally aside from whether or not other consequences are such as to constitute an inherent penalty for the profession. But there are manifestly such consequences. The action required is such as to mark and set aside from the rest of the students those who desire not to participate in a religious ceremony. The appellee Mr. Schempp testified that he was concerned lest his children be regarded as "odd balls" if they were excused from the morning ceremonies [R. 214]. This is surely a most reasonable apprehension; a view which ignored this fact would be one that ignores reality and the forces of social suasion.

As appellee Schempp testified, few are the children who would distinguish between religious dissent and irreligiousness [R. 214]. It is self-evident, and is a matter of concern to Mr. Schempp, that this is a day when children old enough to be exposed to mass media are told constantly that the epic struggle of all Western civilization is now pitched between the God-fearing West and the atheistic Communists. This side-effect is heightened by the fact that whatever arrangements are made for excusing a child, he would necessarily also be excused from the pledge of allegience to the flag, thus further confusing his classmates as to what it is the child dissents from.

Again, though it may not loom large in the spectrum of the issues here involved, it would appear from the record that unless the excused child remained just outside the threshold of the classroom (as if it were being punished) so as to be ready to enter the room as soon as the Lord's Prayer had ended, the child would also miss the daily announcement [R. 217-218]. No child likes always to be the one in its class that never gets the word.

"That a child is offered an alternative may reduce the constraint; it does not eliminate the operation of influence by the school in matters sacred to conscience and outside the school's domain. The law of imitation operates, and non-conformity is not an outstanding characteristic of children. The result is an obvious pressure upon children to attend": *McCollum v. Board of Education, supra,* 333 U. S. at 227 (Concurring opinion of Mr. Justice Frankfurter).

Appellants argue that no request by these parents to have their children excused has been received, hence there is no compulsion. The argument rests on the assumption that all persons have the courage of their convictions and will act accordingly even though their action may give offense to their neighbors or to a majority of citizens in their community. Again the argument ignores reality and the forces of social suasion. The District Court pointed out its fallacy when appellants first made it: "Indeed the lack of protest may itself attest to the success and the subtlety of the compulsion": *Schempp v. School District of Abington Township,* 177 F. Supp. at 407 [R. 192].

Indeed the requirement that a parent take affirmative action to disassociate himself from the group by requesting an excuse is a greater pressure than in the *McCollum* case where affirmative action was required for association. Moreover, a mandatory requirement of school attendance for every child of school age under criminal penalties imposed on parents or other persons in loco parentis puts both parents and children in the path of the compulsion.

The grounds for rejecting any so-called "voluntary" scheme of Bible reading in public schools for those who choose to attend such reading have been well stated in a number of decisions by state courts of last resort.[24]

---

24. *Herold v. Parish Board of School Directors,* 136 La. 1034, 1050, 68 So. 116, 121 (1915) :

"And excusing such children on religious grounds, although the number excused might be very small, would be a distinct

The separation of the child from his fellows for observance of a religious exercise based on the preference of the parent tends to have a detrimental effect on the child. For the child is torn between an impulse to obey the parents' wishes and the pressure to conform to his group. If the child yields to this pressure, the result is disobedience, a loss of respect for the parent and interference with the parent's right to control in matters of religion. On the other hand, if the child obeys the parent, he suffers a loss of standing in his group.

Hence, this act makes possible a divisive controversy over a religious observance between the parent and the child, between the child and his fellows, between the parent and the school or between the parent who disapproves and

---

preference in favor of the religious beliefs of the majority and would work a discrimination against those who were excused. The exclusion of a pupil under such circumstances puts him in a class by himself; it subjects him to a religious stigma; and all because of his religious belief. Equality in public education would be destroyed by such act, under a Constitution which seeks to establish equality and freedom in religious matters. The Constitution forbids that this shall be done."

State ex rel. Weiss v. District Board, 76 Wis. 177, 199-200, 44 N. W. 967, 975 (1890):

"When . . . a small minority of the pupils in the public school is excluded, for any cause, from a stated school exercise, particularly when such cause is apparent hostility to the Bible which a majority of the pupils have been taught to revere, from that moment the excluded pupil loses caste with his fellows, and is liable to be regarded with aversion and subjected to reproach and insult. But it is a sufficient refutation of the argument that the practice in question tends to destroy the equality of the pupils which the constitution seeks to establish and protect, and puts a portion of them to serious disadvantage in many ways with respect to the others."

People ex rel. Ring v. Board of Education, 245 Ill. 334, 351, 92 N. E. 251, 256 (1910):

"The exclusion of a pupil from this part of the school exercises in which the rest of the school joins, separates him from his fellows, puts him in a class by himself, deprives him of his equality with the other pupils, subjects him to a religious stigma and places him at a disadvantage in the school, which the law never contemplated."

those parents who approve of the law. The result is an injection of religious prejudice tending to subvert the unity basic to an educational system which professes to train good citizens how to live together in a pluralistic society. Discrimination, whether based on religious belief or on race or color, destroys equality in public education.

It is this singling out, this identification, this distinguishing between who believes and who dissents, which is at the root of the prescription that the state may not require a profession of belief or disbelief in any religion.

CONCLUSION.

The American solution of a religiously pluralistic society is unique. It is not the solution of secularism: observers of the American scene from de Tocqueville to the most recent Gallup poll remark upon the high proportion of church membership and attendance. This solution has avoided the anti-clericalism and aggressive secularism which has generally characterized Western European societies. The tradition is not merely the Judeo-Christian tradition insulated and diluted with the secular humanism of rationalist enlightment of the 18th Century. Nor is it quite this rationalism with its secular humanism infused with religion. For inherent in it is the concept of the state of *limited* authority and concerns, a state which is a means, not an end, and which does not assert itself as being the *Whole*.

The wall of separation doctrine implies not antagonism to religion, on the contrary it is the apotheosis of deference by Caesar to God, for it places such matters utterly beyond the ambit of civil power.

"The First Amendment leaves the Government in a position not of hostility to religion but of neutrality . . . The philosophy is that if government interferes in matters spiritual, it will be a divisive force." *Engel v. Vitale,* 370 U. S. at 443, concurring opinion of Mr. Justice Douglas.

The Pennsylvania statute and the practice under it is. unconstitutional.

The judgment and decree of the District Court should be affirmed.

Respectfully submitted,

HENRY W. SAWYER, III,
WAYLAND H. ELSBREE,
Attorneys for Appellees.

Dated: February 1, 1963.

Religion in the Public Schools: A Proposed Constitutional Standard

The place of religion in the public schools is only one aspect of the problem of Church-State separation, but if the emotional response following last year's United States Supreme Court decision in the Regents' Prayer Case is any indication, it is an important one. In this Article, Professor Choper proposes that, for purposes of testing the constitutional validity of religious activity in the public schools, the first amendment's establishment clause is violated whenever the state engages in "solely religious activity that is likely to result in (1) compromising the student's religious or concientious beliefs or (2) influencing the student's freedom of religious or conscientious choice." After analyzing a number of precedents, Professor Choper applies this standard to various situations that involve religious activity in the public schools; he concludes that the price of abolishing certain religious influences in the schools must be paid to protect religious liberty.

Jesse H. Choper*

Thirteen years ago, Father John Courtney Murray stated: "No one who knows a bit about the literature on separation of church and state, that for centuries has poured out in all languages, will be inclined to deny that hardly another problem in the religious or political order has received so much misconceived and deformed statement, with the result that the number of bad philosophies in the matter is, like the scriptural number of fools, infinite."[1] Perhaps Father Murray would similarly evaluate the writing that has

*Associate Professor, University of Minnesota Law School. The author wishes to express his gratitude to Dean William B. Lockhart and to his colleagues, Professors Yale Kamisar, Robert J. Levy, and Terrance Sandalow, for their valuable suggestions in preparing this Article. He also wishes to thank Stephen I. Dokken, of the second year class, for his helpful research assistance.

1. Murray, *Law or Prepossessions?*, 14 LAW & CONTEMP. PROB. 23 (1949).

appeared since 1949. Whether or not one agrees with his judgment on the merits of the literature, no one would deny that the quantity of discussion is indeed overpowering. With the Supreme Court's recent decision in the *Regents' Prayer Case,*[2] it is inevitable that much more will be forthcoming. This term, the Court has already indicated that it will take a more active role in resolving church-state conflicts.[3] Perhaps the wiser course would be to heed the warning implicit in Father Murray's comment. No doubt, many men of wisdom have declined to express themselves on this issue "so likely to generate heat rather than light."[4] But light, in the form of principled standards to determine the constitutionality, under the first and fourteenth amendments, of the multitude of church-state problems inherent in a democracy such as ours, is sorely needed.

The constitutional standard to be developed in this article is not suggested as a solution for every type of church-state conflict. Rather, it is to be confined to a narrow but exceedingly important segment of the question. The two drives that give rise to the greatest current constitutional controversies regarding the church-state separation commanded by the first amendment, according to Mr. Justice Rutledge,[5] involve the use of the public schools to foster religion and the procurement of public funds to support parochial schools. This article will deal only with the first area.

The proposed constitutional standard is that for problems concerning religious intrusion in the public schools, the establishment clause of the first amendment is violated when the state engages in what may be fairly characterized as *solely religious activity* that is likely to result in (1) *compromising* the student's religious or conscientious beliefs or (2) *influencing* the student's freedom of religious or conscientious choice.[6]

---

2. Engel v. Vitale, 370 U.S. 421 (1962).

3. On October 8, 1962, the Court agreed to hear argument in two cases presenting the issue of the validity of daily Bible reading in the public schools. Schempp v. School Dist., 201 F. Supp. 815 (E.D. Pa.), *prob. juris. noted,* 371 U.S. 807 (1962); Murray v. Curlett, 228 Md. 239, 179 A.2d 698, *cert. granted,* 371 U.S. 809 (1962).

4. Kurland, *Of Church and State and the Supreme Court,* 29 U. CHI. L. REV. 1, 2 (1961).

5. Everson v. Board of Educ., 330 U.S. 1, 63 (1947) (dissenting opinion).

6. Use of the phrase "public schools" is meant to encompass all kindergarten, elementary, and high schools maintained under governmental authority and control. The word "state" is used to designate all that is included

I. DEVELOPMENT OF THE STANDARD

A. SOME SETTLED PROPOSITIONS

Certain preliminary issues must be disposed of at the outset. First, the Supreme Court has decisively settled that the first amendment's mandate that "Congress shall make no law respecting an establishment of religion, or prohibiting the free exercise thereof," has been made wholly applicable to the states by the fourteenth amendment.[7] Although the history, logic, and desirability, of this thesis have been articulately questioned,[8] the Court's consistent position renders further discussion unprofitable. Second, the Court has unequivocally rejected the proposition that the purpose of the

---

within the concept of state action under the fourteenth amendment. See Civil Rights Cases, 109 U.S. 3 (1883). This would cover not only the state legislature and executive, see Virginia v. Rives, 100 U.S. 313 (1879), but also all administrative agencies, Home Tel. & Tel. Co. v. City of Los Angeles, 227 U.S. 278 (1913), political subdivisions, Hague v. CIO, 307 U.S. 496 (1939), and individuals (such as school principals and teachers) acting under color of state authority. See Yick Wo v. Hopkins, 118 U.S. 356 (1886).

7. *E.g.*, Cantwell v. Connecticut, 310 U.S. 296, 303 (1940); Murdock v. Pennsylvania, 319 U.S. 105, 108 (1943); Everson v. Board of Educ., 330 U.S. 1, 5 (1947); Illinois *ex rel.* McCollum v. Board of Educ., 333 U.S. 203, 210–11 (1948); Zorach v. Clauson, 343 U.S. 306, 309 (1952); Torcaso v. Watkins, 367 U.S. 488, 492 (1961); Engel v. Vitale, 370 U.S. 421, 423, 430 (1962).

The first part of the first amendment will hereinafter be referred to as the "establishment clause"; the second part, as the "free exercise clause."

8. Howe, *The Constitutional Question*, in RELIGION AND THE FREE SOCIETY 49 (1958). The essence of Professor Howe's position is that the language of the fourteenth amendment that "no State shall . . . deprive any person of life, liberty, or property, without due process of law" indicates that its intention was only to bar the states from infringing on those rights that are "implicit in the concept of ordered liberty." Palko v. Connecticut, 302 U.S. 319, 325 (1937). By virtue of the fourteenth amendment, the states not only are forbidden to deny that liberty that is protected by the free exercise clause, but also are powerless to give any aid to religion that would significantly impair the intellectual or spiritual liberties of individuals. The establishment clause, however, may be read to bar many federal aids to religion that do not appreciably affect individual liberties—for example, the granting of tax exemptions to churches and the public schools' permitting the gift of Bibles to willingly receptive pupils. The fourteenth amendment should not be read to prohibit the states from extending these aids to religion.

In answer, it might be suggested that some of the aids to religion that Professor Howe finds to have little impact on the secured rights of individuals—for example, the distribution of Bibles in the public schools—may well have substantial impact. See text accompanying note 509 *infra*. Furthermore, even those aids to religion that have no *immediate* effect on individual liberty—for example, financial assistance to religion in the form of tax exemption or, for that matter, a direct appropriation to a particular church—historically and logically have tended to cause so much strife among religious sects as to ultimately endanger individual liberty. See Everson v. Board of Educ., 330 U.S. 1, 11, 53–54 (1947).

establishment clause is only to forbid governmental preference of one religion over another.[9] Despite heated (and often intemperate) argument to the contrary,[10] the establishment clause bars certain governmental aids to religion even if impartially afforded to all religious sects.[11] Finally, the Court has firmly determined that the ban of the establishment clause extends beyond the setting up of a state church,[12] a proposition with which there has been relatively little disagreement.

B.   AIMS OF THE PROPOSED STANDARD

Although it has been suggested that "it is not reason but history that must be consulted"[13] to determine what is right and proper in the field of church-state relations, such a dichotomy neither can nor should be drawn. The precise intentions of the framers of the first amendment are surely of great importance, but scholarly investigation has produced antithetic conclusions.[14] The desirable course is to frame a principle for constitutional adjudication that is not only grounded in the history and language of the first amend-

---

9. Illinois *ex rel.* McCollum v. Board of Educ., 333 U.S. 203, 211 (1948).

10. *E.g.,* O'NEILL, RELIGION AND EDUCATION UNDER THE CONSTITUTION (1949); Corwin, *The Supreme Court as National School Board,* 14 LAW & CONTEMP. PROB. 3, 9–16 (1949); Murray, *supra* note 1, at 23. Disagreement with the Court's interpretation of the establishment clause is not limited to nonjudicial commentators. Recently, the Supreme Court of Florida decided that it was

> not impressed with the language quoted [from four Supreme Court decisions] as being definitive of the "establishment" clause. It goes far beyond the purpose and intent of the authors and beyond any reasonable application to the practical facts of every day life in this country. We feel that the broad language quoted must, in the course of time, be further receded from, if weight is to be accorded the true purpose of the First Amendment.

Chamberlin v. Dade County Bd., 143 So. 2d 21, 24–25 (Fla. Sup. Ct. 1962). See also *id.* at 28; Zorach v. Clauson, 303 N.Y. 161, 179–82, 100 N.E.2d 463, 472–73 (1951) (concurring opinion); 9 U.C.L.A.L. REV. 495, 499 (1962).

11. Everson v. Board of Educ., 330 U.S. 1, 15 (1947); Illinois *ex rel.* McCollum v. Board of Educ., 333 U.S. 203, 210–11 (1948); McGowan v. Maryland, 366 U.S. 420, 443 (1961); Torcaso v. Watkins, 367 U.S. 488, 492–93, 495 (1961).

12. Illinois *ex rel.* McCollum v. Board of Educ., 333 U.S. 203, 213 (1948) (concurring opinion); McGowan v. Maryland, 366 U.S. 420, 442 (1961).

13. Herberg, *Religion, Democracy, and Public Education,* in RELIGION IN AMERICA 118, 142 (Cogley ed. 1958).

14. *Compare* the opinions in Everson v. Board v. Educ., 330 U.S. 1 (1947), *with* the authorities cited in note 10 *supra. Compare* Pfeffer, *Church and State: Something Less Than Separation,* 19 U. CHI. L. REV. 1 (1951), *with* PARSONS, THE FIRST FREEDOM (1948). See also Kurland, *The Regents' Prayer Case: "Full of Sound and Fury Signifying . . . ,"* 1962 SUPREME COURT REV. 1, 22–25.

ment,[15] but one that is also capable of consistent application to the relevant problems.[16] When applied, the principle should take into account those values now cherished in our society[17] and should not produce decidedly farfetched or unacceptable results.[18] The last criterion is particularly crucial in the emotionally-charged area of religion in the public schools.

The proposed constitutional standard attempts to meet these requirements. If there are any points of general agreement in the field of church-state relationships, they are that probably the paramount purpose for the enactment of the establishment clause was to safeguard freedom of worship and conscience,[19] and that the protection of religious liberty remains our society's major concern in the church-state sphere.[20] By stressing the security of religious and conscientious scruples of public school children, the proposed standard attempts to fulfill both the predominant histori-

---

15. *Cf.* Henkin, *Shelley v. Kraemer: Notes For a Revised Opinion,* 110 U. PA. L. REV. 473 (1962).

16. See LLEWELLYN, THE BRAMBLE BUSH 43–44 (1951). *But see* 51 GEO. L. J. 185 (1962).

17. *Cf.* Wechsler, *Toward Neutral Principles of Constitutional Law,* 73 HARV. L. REV. 1, 31–32 (1959).

18. *Cf.* Henkin, *supra* note 15, at 477.

19. See, *e.g.,* Engel v. Vitale, 370 U.S. 421, 429–30 (1962) (Black, J.); Zorach v. Clauson, 343 U.S. 306, 313–14 (1952) (Douglas, J.); Everson v. Board of Educ., 330 U.S. 1, 8–11 (Black, J.), 53–54 (1947) (Rutledge, J., dissenting): O'NEILL, *op. cit. supra* note 10 at 96; PFEFFER, CHURCH, STATE, AND FREEDOM 122 (1953); Katz, *Freedom of Religion and State Neutrality,* 20 U. CHI. L. REV. 426, 428 (1953); Kurland, *supra* note 4, at 4; Murray, *supra* note 1, at 32; 31 FORDHAM L. REV. 201, 202 (1962).

20. See, *e.g.,* Butts, *The Relation Between Religion and Education,* 33 PROGRESSIVE EDUCATION 140, 141 (1956): "This movement [from the latter part of the 18th century to the early 20th century] toward separation of church and state in education was undertaken in order to preserve freedom for all." Johnson, *Religion and Education,* 33 PROGRESSIVE EDUCATION 143, 145 (1956): "[P]rotection of religious liberty is the beginning and the end of the separation of church and state." Katz, *supra note* 19, at 436, points out that "fear of the Roman Catholic church as a potential threat to religious freedom" probably explains the strict separationist position of those who oppose government aid to religion, such as financial assistance to parochial schools, that seemingly does not result in an impairment of religious liberty. On the other hand, those who attack the strict separationist position on such issues as financial aid to parochial education and public school released time do so on the ground that complete separation violates the religious liberty of those who attend parochial schools or who wish to participate in released time. See, *e.g.,* Bishops of the United States, *The Place of the Private and Church-Related Schools in American Education,* 33 PROGRESSIVE EDUCATION 152 (1956); Hayes, *The Constitutional Permissibility of the Participation of Church-Related Schools in the Administration's Proposed Program of Massive Federal Aid to Education,* 11 DEPAUL L. REV. 161, 162 (1962); Reed, *Church-State and the Zorach Case,* 27 NOTRE DAME LAW. 529, 540 (1952); Slough & McAnany, *Government Aid to Church-Related Schools: An Analysis,* 11 KAN. L. REV. 35, 72 (1962).

cal and contemporary concerns with religious freedom. It prohibits certain governmental action that is likely to result in (1) a student's doing something that is forbidden by his conscientious beliefs, thus *compromising* his scruples or (2) a student's engaging in religious activities that, although not contrary to his religion's beliefs, he would not otherwise undertake, thus *influencing* his freedom of religious participation or choice. The results the proposed standard produces seem to me to be, for the most part, favorable; those that are not are nonetheless acceptable.

C.   Delimitation of the Area and Definition of Solely Religious Activity

Many writers have considered the problems of religious infiltration in the public schools and financial aid by government to religious schools to be subject to singular treatment.[21] Some have concluded that the result of both is to "aid" religion, and therefore, both must be measured by the same standard.[22] The contention that both "aid" religion is indisputable, but it cannot follow that "aid to religion" is *the* constitutional determinant.[23] If it were, few governmental activities could withstand constitutional attack.[24]

---

21. *E.g.*, Corwin, *Supra* note 10, at 5; Pfeffer, *Religion, Education and the Constitution*, 8 Law. Guild Rev. 387 (1948); Sullivan, *Religious Education in the Schools*, 14 Law & Contemp. Prob. 92, 109, 111 (1949); Pfeffer, *The New York Regents' Prayer Case (Engel v. Vitale): Its Background, Meaning and Implications*, Committee on Law and Social Action Reports 6 (American Jewish Congress June 26, 1962). For a rather intemperate criticism of the Supreme Court's failure to so treat these questions, see Comment, 9 Ohio St. L.J. 336, 340 (1948).

22. *E.g.*, Boyer, *Religious Education of Public School Pupils in Wisconsin*, 1953 Wis. L. Rev. 181, 240; Note, 1 J. Pub. L. 212, 216 (1952).

23. The source of the confusion is undoubtedly the famous dictum of Mr. Justice Black in Everson v. Board of Educ., 330 U.S. 1, 15 (1947): "Neither [a state nor the federal government] can pass laws which aid one religion, aid all religions, or prefer one religion over another." The dictum was repeated by the Court in Illinois *ex rel.* McCollum v. Board of Educ., 333 U.S. 203, 210 (1948); McGowan v. Maryland, 366 U.S. 420, 443 (1961); and Torcaso v. Watkins, 367 U.S. 488, 492–93 (1961). It has been discussed in virtually all of the church-state literature since *Everson.* Curiously, Mr. Justice Black made no reference to this dictum in *Engel v. Vitale.*

24. The public fire and police protection afforded parochial schools undeniably "aid" them. The closing of public schools each Saturday and Sunday, which enables Christian and Jewish children to attend their respective churches and synagogues, clearly "aids" attendance at religious services.

The best evidence that the Court never intended the phrase "aid to religion," as commonly understood, to be *the* constitutional determinant, but rather considers "aid" to be a word of art (perhaps poorly chosen), is that in the first two decisions in which the phrase was used, the Court reached opposite conclusions despite the fact that both situations obviously resulted in "aid" to religion. Everson v. Board of Educ., 330 U.S. 1 (1947)

Nor, when more objective standards are available,[25] is it satisfactory merely to say that the question of what kinds of "aid" are constitutional and what kinds are not "is one of degree."[26]

Various forms of public financial assistance to parochial education are permissible under the first amendment because such assistance, despite its resultant aid to religion, has the accomplishment of a nonreligious public purpose[27] as an independent *primary goal,* as distinguished from a dependent *derivative* goal.[28] Thus, the use of tax-raised funds to pay the bus fares of parochial school pupils was upheld by the Supreme Court as "public welfare legislation" protecting "children going to and from church schools from the very real hazards of traffic."[29] Likewise, the argument, whatever its merit, for the constitutional inclusion of religiously affiliated schools in any federal program providing financial assistance for elementary and secondary school buildings and teachers' salaries is that such government support "confers directly and substantially a benefit to citizen education,"[30] and that such an end is within the legitimate scope of federal concern.[31] Although these governmental programs aid religion, *they may not be fairly characterized as solely religious activities.* However, other practices, such as prayer recitation and Bible reading, *must be fairly characterized as solely religious activities having no independent primary nonreligious purpose.* Their exclusive primary goal is to inculcate the students with religious and spiritual ideals or to assist in such inculcation.

(upholding the use of public funds to transport children to parochial schools); Illinois *ex rel.* McCollum v. Board of Educ., 333 U.S. 203 (1948) (invalidating religious instruction during released time in the public schools).

25. *Cf.* Burton v. Wilmington Parking Authority, 365 U.S. 715, 725 (1961), in which the Court treated the problem of what is sufficient state involvement in private action to constitute state action as a question of degree only "because readily applicable formulae may not be fashioned."

26. Zorach v. Clauson, 343 U.S. 306, 314 (1952) (Douglas, J.).

27. See, *e.g.,* 1 BUFFALO L. REV. 198, 200 (1951); 3 RUTGERS L. REV. 115, 119–21 (1949). The aid obtained by religion is often referred to as being merely "incidental."

28. See text accompanying notes 31–37 *infra.*

29. Everson v. Board of Educ., 330 U.S. 1, 16–17 (1947).

30. National Catholic Welfare Conference, *The Constitutionality of the Inclusion of Church-Related Schools in Federal Aid to Education,* 50 GEO. L.J. 397, 422 (1961).

31. For other instances of the use of this position, see Opinion of the Justices, 99 N.H. 519, 113 A.2d 114 (1955); Schade v. Allegheny County Institution Dist., 386 Pa. 507, 126 A.2d 911 (1956); Slough & McAnany, *supra* note 20, at 62–64. See also Cochran v. Louisiana State Bd., 281 U.S. 370 (1930). Evaluation of this thesis is beyond the scope of this article. Since the governmental action with which it deals may not be fairly characterized as "solely religious," it falls outside the constitutional standard proposed herein and is subject to independent consideration.

Contentions proclaiming a public purpose for these solely religious activities are numerous. It has been argued that their intention is to combat juvenile delinquency among American youth;[32] to teach "tolerance, love of fellow men, kindness, responsibility for the welfare of others";[33] to prevent rape and other crimes;[34] and to develop "deep and intelligent convictions" in our children.[35] It has even been suggested that since failure to engage in these practices causes upset and disturbed community reaction, the prevention of such situations is a secular justification for having the religious exercises.[36]

But these arguments ignore the crucial point. The results that follow from the introduction of religion into the public schools are unimportant. What is relevant is the fact that if such effects are produced, they come about only if the primary goal—the implanting of spiritual and religious beliefs—is achieved; the purported seculars ends are derivative from the exclusively religious end.[37]

Perhaps governmental aid to parochial education may be constitutionally justified on the ground that, despite the fact that aid to religion is a necessary effect, an *equally necessary effect* is the promotion of a secular goal. But to uphold the constitutionality of religious incursions into public education on the basis of their alleged secular benefits, despite the fact that they are merely derived from the *sole necessary effect* of advancing religion not only opens "the doctrinal floodgates for infinitely greater aid to religion,"[38] but literally reads the establishment clause out of the first amendment.[39] Such incursions "employ Religion as an engine of Civil policy."[40] If the instilling of moral, ethical, and spiritual values will sustain these solely religious practices,[41] there

---

32. Brief for the Board of Regents of the University of the State of New York as Amicus Curiae, p. 14, Engel v. Vitale, 370 U.S. 421 (1962). See also Gordon v. Board of Educ., 78 Cal. App. 2d 464, 474, 178 P.2d 488, 494 (Ct. App. 1947).

33. Sullivan, *supra* note 21, at 108.

34. W. S. Fleming, quoted in PFEFFER, *op. cit. supra* note 19, at 300–01.

35. Chairman of New York University Department of Religious Education, quoted in Boyer, *supra* note 22, at 232.

36. See Lieberman, *A General Interpretation of Separation of Church and State and Its Implications for Public Education*, 33 PROGRESSIVE EDUCATION 129, 132 (1956).

37. See McGowan v. Maryland, 366 U.S. 420, 466 (1961) (Frankfurter, J., separate opinion); Note, 3 RUTGERS L. REV. 115, 121 (1949).

38. Note, 57 YALE L.J. 1114, 1120 (1948).

39. See generally Pfeffer, *Court, Constitution and Prayer*, 16 RUTGERS L. REV. 735, 746–47 (1962).

40. Madison, *Memorial and Remonstrance Against Religious Assessments*, para. 5, reprinted in Everson v. Board of Educ., 330 U.S. 1, 67 (1947).

41. The argument that this is the saving "public purpose" has been made

would seem to be no reason why a government could not subsidize the church that it feels best inculcates its members with these qualities.[42]

Nor is it a solution to judge these solely religious activities by balancing the public benefit derived against the quantum of aid extended to religion.[43] This test may have some value in the case of governmental action that results directly in both secular and religious benefit, but when the public benefit is derivative—when it is secured only after the religious inculcation is achieved—the secular benefit will always vary directly with the religious benefit, and any balancing is logically impossible.

The reasons calling for separate treatment of the problem of religious activities in the public schools and the problem of financial aid to parochial education are also applicable in severing the former from that presented by other governmental activity that allegedly violates the establishment clause, but has an independent primary nonreligious purpose.[44] Also, since children of elementary and high school age are far less mature and intellectually developed than the public generally,[45] since they are particularly unable to evaluate conflicting religious beliefs objectively,[46] since they are especially susceptible to being influenced in religious choice,[47] and since they are compelled by law to attend the

by Creel, *Is It Legal for the Public Schools of Alabama to Provide an Elective Course in Non-Sectarian Bible Instruction,* 10 ALA. LAW. 86, 95 (1949); Harpster, *Religion, Education and the Law,* 36 MARQ. L. REV. 24, 47 (1952); Meiklejohn, *Educational Cooperation Between Church and State,* 14 LAW & CONTEMP. PROB. 61, 67 (1949). See also Hart v. School Dist., 2 Lancaster L. Rev. 346, 352 (Pa. C.P. 1885). The writer in 30 FORDHAM L. REV. 509 (1962), asserts: "It would seem quite arbitrary for the Supreme Court to hold that a general day of rest and relaxation served a public purpose but the acknowledgement of a God by people 'whose institutions presuppose a Supreme Being' was not a public purpose."

42. Professor Kauper suggests this result, although somewhat more cautiously: "Moreover, the notion that government can directly aid religion in order to bolster morale suggests implications of a wider use of public moneys in direct aid of religion." Kauper, *Church, State, and Freedom: A Review,* 52 MICH. L. REV. 829, 837 (1954). See also Pfeiffer v. Board of Educ., 118 Mich. 560, 578, 77 N.W. 250, 257 (1898) (dissenting opinion).

43. See Note, 17 GEO. WASH. L. REV. 516, 529 (1949); 57 YALE L.J. 1114, 1120–21 (1948).

44. *E.g.* Sunday closing laws (see McGowan v. Maryland, 366 U.S. 420 (1961)); appropriations to hospital, maintained under religious auspices, for treating indigent patients (see Bradfield v. Roberts, 175 U.S. 291 (1899)).

45. *Cf.* PFEFFER, *op. cit. supra* note 19, at 423; Cosway & Toepfer, *Religion and the Schools,* 17 U. CINC. L. REV. 117, 137 (1948); Comment, 22 U. CHI. L. REV. 888, 893 (1955). Possible distinctions between elementary school children and high school pupils will be discussed *infra.*

46. *Cf.* 16 GEO. WASH. L. REV. 556, 559 (1948).

47. *Cf.* 25 CAL. OPS. ATT'Y GEN. 324 (1955); Cushman, *The Holy*

site of these religious practices,[48] there is a sound basis for giving distinctive treatment to solely religious practices in the public schools instead of treating them together with similar practices existing in our society generally.[49]

D. THE REGENTS' PRAYER CASE

In 1951, the New York State Board of Regents, the governmental agency that supervises the state's public school system, composed and recommended to all local school boards the following prayer: "Almighty God, we acknowledge our dependence upon Thee, and we beg Thy blessings upon us, our parents, our teachers and our country."[50] In 1958, the New Hyde Park Board of Education instructed all teachers that the prayer be recited aloud by each class at the beginning of every school day. An action in the state courts was instituted by parents of attending students, who were Jewish, Ethical Culturists, Unitarians, or non-believers,[51] asserting, *inter alia,* that the practice should cease because it violated the establishment clause.[52] Their claims were rejected at all state levels,[53] although it was made clear that objecting students had the right not to participate.[54] The Supreme Court reversed in *Engel v. Vitale,*[55] holding the practice to be contrary to the establishment clause, a ruling that "aroused more public controversy than any decision since Brown v. Board of Education."[56]

Bible and the Public Schools, 40 CORNELL L.Q. 475, 496 (1955); Kalven, *A Commemorative Case Note,* 27 U. CHI. L. REV. 505, 518 (1960); 74 HARV. L. REV. 611, 614 (1961).

48. *Cf.* Sutherland, *Public Authority and Religious Education: A Brief Survey of Constitutional and Legal Limits,* in THE STUDY OF RELIGION IN THE PUBLIC SCHOOLS: AN APPRAISAL 45 (Brown ed. 1958).

49. Such practices include chaplains in both houses of Congress and in state legislative assemblies and the opening prayer in the United States Supreme Court: "God save the United States and this Honorable Court."

50. Its use was recommended at the commencement of each school day in conjunction with the pledge of allegiance to the flag. Record, p. 28, Engel v. Vitale, 370 U.S. 421 (1962).

51. *Id.* at 12.

52. Other claims presented were that the free exercise clause was violated, that a similar clause of the state constitution, N.Y. CONST. art. I, § 3, was violated, and that the Board of Education had exceeded its statutory power. *Id.* at 16–17.

53. Engel v. Vitale, 18 Misc. 2d 659, 191 N.Y.S.2d 453 (Sup. Ct. 1959), *aff'd,* 11 App. Div. 2d 340, 206 N.Y.S.2d 183 (1960), *aff'd* 10 N.Y.2d 174, 176 N.E.2d 579, 218 N.Y.S.2d 659 (1961) (Dye, J., & Fuld, J. dissenting).

54. 18 Misc. 2d 659, 696, 191 N.Y.S.2d 453, 492–93 (1959).

55. 370 U.S. 421, 424 (1962).

56. 31 U.S.L. WEEK 1038 (1962). The decision was announced on June 25, 1962. Reference to any newspaper or periodical of the time will bear out

At the outset, Mr. Justice Black, writing for the Court,[57] characterized the recitation of the Regents' prayer as "a religious activity."[58] That it was a solely religious activity, having no independent primary nonreligious purpose, is beyond dispute.[59] Examination of the remainder of the opinion, however, leaves somewhat unclear the precise basis and extent of the decision. There is language indicating that the decision holds no more than that the evil in the situation was the fact that a governmental agency had taken it upon itself to *compose* an official prayer for use in the public schools.[60]

---

the Law Week characterization. Many, if not most of the attacks on the case were emotionally oriented and were founded on a basic misunderstanding (unintentional or otherwise) of the decision. Those who found it politically expedient to denounce the "ruling against God" did so, without pausing to learn whether the Court so ruled. Long-time critics of the Court exploited the opportunity to heap further abuse, without regard to the limitations stated in the reasoning and language of the case. For a discussion of this criticism, see Choper, *What Did Court Really Rule on Prayer*, Minneapolis Star, Sept. 15, 1962, p. 6A, col. 5. See generally Kurland, *The Regents' Prayer Case: "Full of Sound and Fury, Signifying . . .,"* in 1962 SUPREME COURT REV. 1; Pfeffer, *supra* note 39.

57. He was joined by Mr. Chief Justice Warren and Justices Clark, Harlan, and Brennan. Mr. Justice Douglas wrote a concurring opinion. Mr. Justice Stewart dissented. For discussion of these last two opinions, see notes 188–89 *infra*. Neither Mr. Justice Frankfurter nor Mr. Justice White participated, the former being ill when the decision was announced and the latter not yet having been appointed when the case was argued.

58. 370 U.S. at 424. The fact that the prayer recitation immediately followed the salute to the flag was not even considered as changing the characterization of the nature of the activity. Record, p. 13, Engel v. Vitale, 370 U.S. at 421. In this connection, see Schempp v. School Dist., 177 F. Supp. 398, 406 (E.D. Pa. 1959). However, the Court's opinion later pointed out that this was an *"unquestioned* religious exercise" (emphasis added) and distinguished this case from "patriotic or ceremonial occasions" such as "singing officially espoused anthems which include the composer's professions of faith in a Supreme Being." 370 U.S. at 435, n.21. Although it appears that this refers only to "The Star-Spangled Banner," the third stanza of which contains references to the Deity, it seems that the Court may be willing to single out those parts of a daily school exercise that are of a religious nature yet unwilling to sever those verses of a song that are solely religious. See text accompanying notes 541–44 *infra*.

59. This was acknowledged in The Regents Statement on Moral and Spiritual Training in the Schools, Record, pp. 28–29, Engel v. Vitale, 370 U.S. 421 (1962).

60.
    The petitioners contend . . . that the . . . prayer must be struck down as a violation of the Establishment Clause because that prayer was composed by government officials as a part of a governmental program to further religious beliefs. . . . We agree with that contention since we think that the [establishment clause] must at least mean that in this country it is no part of the business of government to compose official prayers for any group of the American people to recite as a part of a religious program carried on by government.
370 U.S. at 425.

Even if the Court's holding is this limited, it does not augur well for the closely related public school practices of reading the Bible and reciting other long-established prayers.[61] It can be argued that since the Bible and such prayers as the Lord's Prayer were not *composed* by any governmental agency, they do not fall into the same category as the Regents' prayer,[62] but there seems to be no reason to distinguish between a governmental agency *composing* a religious prayer for use in the schools and that same agency *selecting* a prayer or other religious material composed elsewhere.[63] If anything, the Regents' prayer, which has been described by some as "purely nondenominational,"[64] would be much less objectionable in our religiously pluralistic society than any version of the Bible or the Lord's Prayer, none of which are unobjectionable to all of the major religious faiths.[65] Nor would the circumstances be improved if, instead of the Regents selecting or

---

61. Pfeffer, Committee on Law and Social Action Reports, *supra* note 21, at 5–6, says that it follows from *Engel* that the Lord's Prayer and Bible reading are likewise unconstitutional.

62. See Lewis, *School-Prayer Issue in High Court Again,* N.Y. Times, Oct. 14, 1962, § 4, p. 5, col. 2.

63. It is difficult to believe that the decision in *Engel* would have been different if, instead of the Regents having composed the words of this prayer, they had selected them from a collection of prayers composed by someone else. The opinion laid great emphasis on the bitter controversy in 16th and 17th century England over the governmentally approved Book of Common Prayer. 370 U.S. at 425–27, 429–30. The source of that struggle was the question of what the content of the Book of Common Prayer should be. Surely, it made no difference in that controversy whether the government *composed* prayers that reflected the sentiments of a particular religion or selected prayers already composed of the same kind. See Sutherland, *Establishment According to Engel,* 76 Harv. L. Rev. 25, 38 n.36 (1962).

There is language in the opinion to support the conclusion that this distinction should not be drawn.

[O]ne of the greatest dangers to the freedom of the individual to worship in his own way [lies] in the Government's placing its official stamp of approval upon one particular kind of prayer. . . . [N]either the power nor the prestige of the . . . Government [shall] be used to control, support or influence the kinds of prayer the American people can say. . . .

. . . .

[G]overnment . . . is without power to prescribe by law any particular form of prayer which is to be used as an official prayer in carrying on any program of governmentally sponsored religious activity. . . .

. . . .

[E]ach separate government in this county should stay out of the business of writing or sanctioning official prayers. . . .

370 U.S. at 429, 430, 435. See 31 Fordham L. Rev. 203 n.20 (1962).

64. 9 U.C.L.A.L. Rev. 499 (1962). See also Engel v. Vitale, 370 U.S. 421, 430 (1962). *But see* text accompanying notes 66–74 *infra.*

65. See text accompanying notes 258–81, 230–36 *infra.*

composing the prayer, either the teacher or the students made the choice. Indeed, since these people would be much further removed from the pressures of the political process than the Regents, the product of such selection or composition would much more likely be oriented toward the teachings of a particular religious sect.[66]

Certain other observations may be made from an examination of the Court's opinion. The question of whether the prayer was denominationally neutral[67] was sidestepped by the Court.[68] The answer is manifest. Since it involved a supplication to God, it patently favored the theistic religions over those that are nontheistic, such as Ethical Culture (the religion of one of the complaining parents).[69] The conceded "purpose and effect"[70] of this program was "teaching our children . . . that Almighty God is their Creator, and that by Him they have been endowed with their inalienable rights . . . ."[71] Opposition was expressed even among those religions teaching belief in a Supreme Being; some complained that the prayer was ineffectual, while others found it plainly contrary to their religious beliefs.[72] Furthermore, theistic religions differ on the propriety of offering prayers not specifically decreed by the sect and of seeking divine assistance in certain matters.[73]

---

66. *Cf.* Engel v. Vitale, 18 Misc. 2d 659, 699, 191 N.Y.S.2d 453, 495 (1959).

67. Judge Froessel in the New York Court of Appeals found it to be so. Engel v. Vitale, 10 N.Y.2d 174, 183, 176 N.E.2d 579, 583 (1961) (concurring opinion).

68. 370 U.S. at 430.

69. Other nontheistic religions in this country are Buddhism, Taoism, and Secular Humanism. See authorities cited in Torcaso v. Watkins, 367 U.S. 488, 495 n.11 (1961).

70. McGowan v. Maryland, 366 U.S. 420, 443, 445, 449 (1961). See also *id.* at 453.

71. The Regents Statement on Moral and Spiritual Training in the Schools, Record, p. 28, Engel v. Vitale, 370 U.S. 421 (1962).

72. Although the Catholic Church and most Protestant groups warmly endorsed the prayer,

> *The Christian Century* deemed [it] 'likely to deteriorate quickly into an empty formality with little, if any, spiritual significance.' The leaders of the Lutheran Church of Our Redeemer in Peekskill [N.Y.] charged that Christ's name had 'deliberately been omitted to mollify non-Christian elements,' and that the prayer 'therefore is a denial of Christ and His prescription for a proper prayer. As such it is not a prayer but an abomination and a blasphemy.'

PFEFFER, CHURCH, STATE, AND FREEDOM 396 (1953). Opposition was also expressed by the Schenectady (N.Y.) Methodist Church Board, the Liberal Ministers Club (primarily Unitarians and Universalists), and "every important interested Jewish organization in the state." *Ibid.*

73. See the authorities cited in Brief for American Jewish Committee and Anti-Defamation League of B'nai B'rith as Amici Curiae, p. 20 n.6, Engel v. Vitale, 370 U.S. 421 (1962). See also Brief for Synagogue

Thus, the Court could have easily reached its result by use of the generally noncontroversial proposition that the establishment clause forbids governmental preference of some religions over others.[74] However, since the Court had based a decision just one year before on the thesis that a state cannot "constitutionally pass laws or impose requirements which aid all religions as against nonbelievers,"[75] it would be hypercritical to say that, on this ground, the *Engel* holding is too broad.

The holding may be criticized as too broad on another ground, however. A major defense for the constitutionality of the Regents' prayer was the fact that participation in its recitation was wholly voluntary;[76] objecting students were privileged either to remain silent or to be excused from the room.[77] The Court's opinion found "the fact that its observance on the part of the students is voluntary" to be irrelevant.[78] Although recognizing that "when the power, prestige and financial support of government is placed behind a particular religious belief, the indirect coercive pressure upon religious minorities to conform to the prevailing officially approved religion is plain,"[79] Mr. Justice Black stated that "the Establishment Clause, unlike the Free Exercise Clause, does not depend upon any showing of direct governmental compulsion and is violated by the enactment of *laws which establish an official religion* whether those laws operate directly to coerce nonobserving individuals or not."[80] The essence of this position seems to have emanated from the argument by two amici curiae in the case—one finding an establishment clause violation, irrespective of the privilege of nonparticipation, anytime government is engaged in "undertaking or sponsoring religious programs";[81] the other, whenever there is state "participation in religious affairs."[82] This seemingly

Council of America and National Community Relations Advisory Council as Amici Curiae, p. 10, Engel v. Vitale, 370 U.S. 421 (1962).

74. See text accompanying notes 9–11 *supra*.

75. Torcaso v. Watkins, 367 U.S. 488, 495 (1961). See also authorities cited in note 11 *supra*.

76. Brief for Respondents, pp. 32–34; Brief for Intervenors-Respondents, pp. 11, 42–43; Brief for The Board of Regents of the University of the State of New York as Amicus Curiae, p. 24, Engel v. Vitale, 370 U.S. 421 (1962).

77. 370 U.S. at 430.

78. *Ibid.*

79. *Id.* at 431.

80. *Id.* at 430. (Emphasis added.)

81. Brief for American Jewish Committee and Anti-Defamation League of B'nai B'rith as Amici Curiae, p. 17, Engel v. Vitale, 370 U.S. 421 (1962).

82. Brief for Synagogue Council of America and National Community Relations Advisory Council as Amici Curiae, p. 15 (Mr. Leo Pfeffer, Attorney), Engel v. Vitale, 370 U.S. 421 (1962).

broad interpretation of the establishment clause was not necessary to the decision in *Engel*.[83] The case could have been more discretely decided specifically on the ground that, regardless of the dissenting student's right of nonparticipation, compulsion did exist;[84] that a showing of actual compulsion was unnecessary because of the "indirect coercive pressure" that this program exerted; that the program would result either in the young children[85] of the minority groups involved taking part in a religious exercise that was contrary to their conscientious beliefs or in their being singled out as "oddballs" by their peers; that this is a cruel choice that no state may constitutionally demand if it engages in a solely religious activity.[86]

II. SUPPORT FOR THE STANDARD

A. INDIRECT COERCION

Although the Supreme Court has never explicitly held that indirect coercive pressure constitutes a violation of the establishment clause,[87] there is a plethora of material to support this rationale.

1. *Existence of Indirect Coercion*

It is universally recognized that such pressures in fact exist. Many writers of widely diverse backgrounds[88] have observed that young people of minority religious groups are extremely sensitive about conspicuously absenting themselves from religious exercises conducted by the majority and that there is a powerful, albeit subtle, pressure to conform. The emotional strain is very frequently so great that it results in unwilling participation in preference to some amount of social ostracism. Student commentators

---

83. See text accompanying notes 189–92 *infra*.

84. *But see* Sutherland, *Establishment According to Engel*, 76 HARV. L. REV. 25, 39 (1962).

85. The parents bringing this suit had a total of ten children attending school. The ages of the children ranged from seven to 15. Record, pp. 11–12, Engel v. Vitale, 370 U.S. 421 (1962).

86. *Cf.* Braunfeld v. Brown, 366 U.S. 599, 616 (1961) (Stewart J., dissenting).

87. This is pointed out in 9 U.C.L.A.L. REV. 500 n.25 (1962).

88. These include Cushman, *The Holy Bible and the Public Schools*, 40 CORNELL L.Q. 475, 495 (1955) (professor of government); Levy, *Views from the Wall – Reflections on Church-State Relationships*, 29 HENNEPIN LAW. 51, 55 (1961) (professor of law); Harpster, *Religion, Education and the Law*, 36 MARQ. L. REV. 24, 42 (1952), and Vishny, *The Constitution and Religion in the Public Schools*, Decalogue J., June-July 1960, pp. 4, 5–6; (practicing attorneys); Lewis, *School-Prayer Issue in High Court Again*, N.Y. Times, Oct. 14, 1962, § E, p. 5, col. 1 (newspaper columnist).

have made the same judgment.[89] A recent opinion by the Attorney General of California stated that "children forced by conscience to leave the room during such exercises would be placed in a position inferior to that of students adhering to the State-endorsed religion."[90]

Social psychologists and sociologists have pointed out that children place great importance on how they are esteemed by their classmates.[91] The urge to conform to their classmates' attitudes is peculiarly strong,[92] and "the fear of being accused by the others of wanting to be 'different' " and the "very strong need to remain a member of one's group"[93] are carried so far as to cause these children to do and say things in accordance with the majority that they are convinced are wrong, even with reference to simple perceptual materials.[94] This is particularly prevalent "where the situation is ambiguous and not very clear-cut."[95] The option either to participate in the majority's religious worship or "to suffer the pain of psychic loneliness"[96] has been recently described by Dr. Robert Bierstedt as forcing these immature students "to choose between equally intolerable alternatives."[97] Even religious educators have warned "that so-called voluntary exemption [from religious observances] does not overcome the compulsion exerted by majority behavior."[98]

The insight is not new. As long ago as 1890, state appellate court judges recognized the fact that a nonparticipant in a reli-

---

89. *E.g.*, 11 AM. U.L. REV. 91 (1962); 28 BROOKLYN L. REV. 146 (1961).

90. 25 CAL. OPS. ATT'Y GEN. 316, 319 (1955).

91. BOSSARD, THE SOCIOLOGY OF CHILD DEVELOPMENT 462 (1948).

92. MURPHY & MURPHY, EXPERIMENTAL SOCIAL PSYCHOLOGY 511–16 (1931). See also Cushman, *The Holy Bible and the Public Schools, supra* note 88, at 495: "A number of psychologists, backed by parents . . . point out the tremendous strength of the pressure to conform."

93. BERENDA, THE INFLUENCE OF THE GROUP ON THE JUDGMENTS OF CHILDREN 30 (1950).

94. *Id.* at 16–33.

95. *Id.* at 32.

96. Address by Professor Robert Bierstedt, *The Use of Public Schools for Religious Purposes*, ACLU Biennial Conference, June 22, 1962, p. 10. Dr. Bierstedt is Chairman of the Department of Sociology and Anthropology at the New York University Graduate School of Arts and Sciences.

97. *Ibid.*

98. Committee on Religion and Public Education of the National Council of the Churches of Christ, *Relation of Religion to Public Education—A Study Document*, INTERNATIONAL J. OF RELIGIOUS EDUCATION, April 1960, pp. 21, 29. See also Murray, *Law or Prepossessions?*, 14 LAW & CONTEMP. PROB. 23, 39 (1949): "Thousand of educators of all religious convictions are increasingly agreed that the atmosphere of public schools is *not* free from pressures."

gious exercise "loses caste with his fellows."[99] Lower federal court judges have also made this observation.[100] Four Justices of the Supreme Court subscribed to this theory when they stated: "That a child is offered an alternative may reduce the constraint; it does not eliminate the operation of influence by the school in matters sacred to conscience and outside the school's domain. The law of imitation operates, and nonconformity is not an outstanding characteristic of children."[101]

The fact that these public school religious practices are inherently compulsive may be empirically demonstrated by examining actual situations in some of the litigated cases. Terry McCollum, whose mother, an ardent atheist, successfully challenged a program of released time religious classes on public school premises in Champaign, Illinois,[102] exercised his right of nonparticipation during the first semester of his fourth grade, but the next semester he did attend religious classes. The following year, he changed schools. In the first semester of his fifth grade, he and only one other pupil declined to attend religious classes; during the second semester, the other boy capitulated.[103] In Terry's school, "children of some thirty-one sects, including Catholic, Jewish, and Protestant, as well as many children without any particular religious preference,"[104] *voluntarily* attended a course teaching the tenets of Protestantism. Donna Schempp's father, a member of the Unitarian faith, challenged Bible reading in the Abington Township, Pennsylvania, public schools as contrary to his family's re-

---

99. State *ex rel.* Weiss v. District Bd., 76 Wis. 177, 200, 44 N.W. 967, 975 (1890). In North v. Board of Trustees, 137 Ill. 296, 304, 27 N.E. 54, 56 (1891), the court observed that it was well-known that public schools conduct religious exercises "and that, with rare exceptions, those attending them yield cheerful obedience thereto, regardless of their personal views on the subject of religion." See also Wilkerson v. City of Rome, 152 Ga. 762, 786, 110 S.E. 895, 906 (1922) (dissenting opinion); People *ex rel.* Ring v. Board of Educ., 245 Ill. 334, 351, 92 N.E. 251, 256 (1910); Knowlton v. Baumhover, 182 Iowa 691, 699–700, 166 N.W. 202, 205 (19–18); Herold v. Parish Bd. of School Directors, 136 La. 1034, 1050, 68 So. 116, 121 (1915); Kaplan v. Independent School Dist., 171 Minn. 142, 155–56, 214 N.W. 18, 23 (1927) (dissenting opinion); Engel v. Vitale, 10 N.Y.2d 174, 190, 176 N.E.2d 579, 587 (1961) (dissenting opinion).

100. Schempp v. School Dist., 177 F. Supp. 398, 406 (E.D. Pa. 1959).

101. Opinion of Mr. Justice Frankfurter, in which Justices Jackson, Rutledge, and Burton joined, in Illinois *ex rel.* McCollum v. Board of Educ., 333 U.S. 203, 227 (1948).

102. See Illinois *ex rel.* McCollum v. Board of Educ., 333 U.S. 203 (1948).

103. See People *ex rel.* McCollum v. Board of Educ., 396 Ill. 14, 17, 71 N.E.2d 161, 162 (1947).

104. Record, p. 65, Illinois *ex rel.* McCollum v. Board of Educ., 333 U.S. 203 (1948).

ligious beliefs.[105] Donna had never voiced her objections to school authorities and, on occasion, even volunteered to read the Bible herself.[106] In Southern elementary schools, there are established periods of Christian Bible study; Jewish children have the option of leaving the room, but "some believe that it is better to remain seated than to have forty-three children watch one or two others shuffle out."[107]

2. The Defenses of Indirect Coercion

Although there are a few instances of disagreement with the proposition that subtle coercion inheres in these situations,[108] most writers and state judges,[109] unwilling to find a constitutional violation, argue that "these pressures to conform are part of the normal social pattern and part of the price of being a religious nonconformist is the social stigma which all nonconformists have to bear"[110] and that it "is perhaps not a major hardship and is a sacrifice which a minority might well make to a majority."[111] Some argue that "if the State is going to undertake to protect the child at one point, there seems to be no logical reason for its stopping there—it should protect the child from such mental and

---

105. Schempp v. School Dist., 177 F. Supp. 398 (E.D. Pa. 1959).

106. *Id.* at 400. "Indeed the lack of protest may itself attest to the success and the subtlety of the compulsion." *Id.* at 407.

107. Harry L. Golden, quoted in PFEFFER, CHURCH, STATE, AND FREEDOM 304 (1953). "The Christian children wonder why one or two of their number 'do not want to hear about God,' and the Jewish child is also heartsick as well as bewildered." *Ibid.*

108. People *ex rel.* Vollmar v. Stanley, 81 Colo. 276, 293, 255 Pac. 610, 618 (1927): "The shoe is on the other foot. We have known many boys to be ridiculed for complying with religious regulations, but never one for neglecting them or absenting himself from them." For a singularly acrid and sarcastic (although neither very confident nor persuasive) rejection of the fact, see Chamberlin v. Dade County Bd. of Public Instruction, 143 So. 2d 21, 31–33 (Fla. 1962). The suggestion has been made that non-believing children may simply remain silent when religious invocations are being delivered by all of the others and thereby avoid the appearance of "non-conformity." Lewis v. Allen, 5 Misc. 2d 68, 74, 159 N.Y.S.2d 807, 813 (Sup. Ct. 1957). See also 9 U.C.L.A.L. REV. 499–500 (1962). Such advice is extremely naive; remaining silent conspicuously indicates the nonparticipant's status.

109. See Murray v. Curlett, 228 Md. 239, —, 179 A.2d 698, 704 (1962); Engel v. Vitale, 11 App. Div. 2d 340, 349, 206 N.Y.S.2d 183, 191–92 (1960) (separate opinion); Engel v. Vitale, 18 Misc. 2d 659, 695–96, 191 N.Y.S.2d 453, 491–92 (1959).

110. Cushman, *The Holy Bible and the Public Schools*, 40 CORNELL L.Q. 475, 495 (1955).

111. Sutherland, *Public Authority and Religious Education: A Brief Survey of Constitutional and Legal Limits*, in THE STUDY OF RELIGION IN THE PUBLIC SCHOOLS: AN APPRAISAL 33, 51 (Brown ed. 1958). See also Note, 49 COLUM. L. REV. 836, 843–44 (1949).

emotional abuse in all circumstances. But this is totally impossible."[112] The progenitor of this reasoning is the dictum of Mr. Justice Jackson that "it may be doubted whether the Constitution which, of course, protects the right to dissent, can be construed also to protect one from the embarrassment that always attends nonconformity, whether in religion, politics, behavior or dress."[113]

One need not quarrel with the unfortunate truism that it is probably inherent in our society that aberrant religionists and nonbelievers will be subjected to some scorn and derision. Because of this, societal pressures will be brought to bear on religious nonconformists to forsake their beliefs. As long as these societal pressures are initiated by "private action," the Constitution affords no self-executing relief. But when the state or federal government adopts a solely religious program—whose only immediate effect is the promotion of religion and in which benefit to religion is a condition precedent to any possible public benefit—it has approached the brink of its constitutional power. Some would seem to contend that such governmental activity of itself crosses the first amendment's boundary of church-state separation.[114] However, the proposed standard only requires that when this governmental activity unavoidably results in pressures on the immature to abandon their conscientious scruples, or in the influencing of free religious choice, the establishment clause should be deemed violated. It should not be the function of a governmental program to increase "the price of being a religious nonconformist"[115] when

---

112. Harpster, *Religion, Education and the Law*, 36 MARQ. L. REV. 24, 48 (1952).

113. Illinois *ex rel.* McCollum v. Board of Educ., 333 U.S. 203, 233 (1948) (concurring opinion). Mr. Justice Jackson spoke only for himself. It is difficult to reconcile this statement with Justice Jackson's subscription to Mr. Justice Frankfurter's *McCollum* opinion that takes the opposite stand. See text accompanying note 101 *supra*. See also the statement by Mr. Justice Reed that "one can hardly speak of that embarrassment as a prohibition against the free exercise of religion." 333 U.S. at 241. For discussion of the free exercise issue see note 126 *infra*.

It should be made clear that it is not merely "embarrassment" that results in the situations under discussion. To define the problem with that term "tends to assume that a child of tender years has the necessary courage of his convictions—or perhaps more accurately in this situation, the courage of his parents' convictions—to withstand with emotional impunity some very real pressures to conform to group standards and to avoid being marked by his fellows as an 'outsider.' " 11 AM. U.L. REV. 93 (1962).

114. See text accompanying notes 78–82 *supra*.

115. Cushman, *supra* note 110, at 495. *Cf.* Kamisar, *Betts v. Brady Twenty Years Later: The Right to Counsel and Due Process Values,* 61 MICH. L. REV. 219, 246 (1962), who argues that because an indigent crim-

the only immediate results of the program, if any results are forthcoming at all, are aids to religion. Majority will should not be permitted to impose minority sacrifices when that will is expressed through solely religious governmental action in an area afforded specific protection by the first amendment. Neither unorthodox behavior nor dress fits that category; logical distinctions may be drawn. The contrary position amounts to "no less than the surrender of the constitutional protection of the liberty of small minorities to the popular will."[116]

It is not being suggested that, *in vacuo*, the state is obligated to undertake to protect children of religious minorities, or children of the religious majority who have marginal convictions, from the embarrassment and concomitant pressures that nonconformity brings. The Constitution does not demand that the result of every state activity be free from such effects. Solely religious programs should not be confused, as they have been,[117] with those instances in which the state's program has the accomplishment of a secular purpose as its immediate goal.

The *Flag Salute Case*[118] illustrates this distinction. The Supreme Court held that a state could not compel the pledge of allegiance and salute to the flag by public school children who objected because of religious conviction. The result was that objecting children were excused from participation. Since the daily program of saluting the flag continued, there is no doubt that those who conscientiously objected were faced with precisely the same type dilemma as the children whose beliefs precluded participation

---

inal defendant suffers many handicaps that courts are powerless to eliminate is hardly an excuse for enlarging them or perpetuating others.

116. Minersville School Dist. v. Gobitis, 310 U.S. 586, 606 (1940) (Stone, J., dissenting).

117. See Brief for Intervenors-Respondents, pp. 45–47, 51, Engel v. Vitale, 370 U.S. 421 (1962); Corwin, *The Supreme Court as National School Board*, 14 LAW & CONTEMP. PROB. 3, 8 n.25 (1949). *But cf.* Brief for Synagogue Council of America and National Community Relations Advisory Council as Amici Curiae, pp. 16–19, Engel v. Vitale, *supra*.

118. West Virginia State Bd. of Educ. v. Barnette, 319 U.S. 624 (1943). Complainants in the case were Jehovah's Witnesses. Their religious beliefs included a literal version of *Exodus*, 20: 4–5, which says, "Thou shalt not make unto thee any graven image . . .: Thou shalt not bow down thyself to them, nor serve them." They considered the flag as an "image" within this command.

Although the Court stated that the case did not "turn on one's possession of particular religious views or the sincerity with which they are held," 319 U.S. at 634, and found that the state was generally without power to compel *anyone* to salute the flag, *id.* at 642, the case has been often considered, because of its facts, as presenting a free exercise of religion issue. See, *e.g.*, Braunfeld v. Brown, 366 U.S. 599, 603 (1961); Prince v. Massachusetts, 321 U.S. 158, 165 (1944).

in the recitation of the Regents' prayer. School children whose religious scruples forbid them from taking part in military training[119] or from attending classes in physical education,[120] social dancing,[121] or hygiene,[122] suffer similar difficulties. However, since the requirement of pledging allegiance to the flag is imposed to promote patriotism,[123] and since military training and physical education, dancing, and hygiene classes are placed in the public school curriculum to further national and educational goals, these activities of the state must be fairly characterized as secular. In no way do they promote religion, nor do they rely on religious inculcation for their attainment. Such activities, on their face, are unquestionably within the scope of state power. Some children's religious objections to participating in these secular activities may entitle them to be excused on the ground of protecting the free exercise of their religion,[124] but since the state's program is secular, dissenters cannot require the state to abandon it altogether because its continued operation inherently coerces them to join. *This* is the price the deviator must pay. To hold otherwise would indeed be minority oppression of the majority. It is only when the state engages in a solely religious activity that it should bear the full responsibility for the infringements on freedom of religious choice that such a program brings about.[125] It is un-

---

119. *Cf.* Hamilton v. Regents of the Univ. of Cal., 293 U.S. 245 (1934).

120. *Cf.* Iowa Code § 280.14 (1962).

121. *Cf.* Hardwick v. Board of School Trustees, 54 Cal. App. 696, 205 Pac. 49 (Dist. Ct. App. 1921).

122. *Cf.* Alaska Comp. Laws Ann. § 37-7-12 (Supp. 1958); 1 Fla. Stat. § 231.09 (1) (1959); N.Y. Educ. Law § 3204 (5); Pa. Stat. Ann. tit. 24, § 14-1419 (1962).

123. See 11 Am. U.L. Rev. 91, 93 (1962).

124. The question of whether and when the free exercise clause is violated by the compelling of participation in secular activities irrespective of the fact that such participation is forbidden by one's religion is beyond the scope of this article. The issue is one that the Supreme Court appears not yet to have resolved. See Braunfeld v. Brown, 366 U.S. 599, 605 (1961).

125. Professor Kauper rejects this analysis. He agrees that it would be unconstitutional if actual pressure were exerted on any student to take part in the solely religious activity of released time. See text accompanying notes 467-72 *infra.*

But a proper sense of concern for the non-participant does not require rejection of the program on constitutional grounds. A Jehovah's Witness child may not be required to take part in a public school flag salute exercise. He is permitted to abstain. But the public school is not required in deference to his religious convictions to abandon the flag salute exercise even though it carries religious connotations for persons in this category and may, therefore, in this sense be characterized as a religious exercise. Similarily it should be possible to retain a released time program . . . while doing justice to the non-participants.

necessary to determine whether such infringements result in a violation of the free exercise clause.[126] If the activity is both solely religious and inherently compulsive, it should be found to be a violation of the establishment clause.

B. SUPPORT FROM THE SUPREME COURT

1. The McCollum Case

As already mentioned, there is no Supreme Court decision that articulates this rationale as its basis. However, examination of the *McCollum* case[127] lends strong support. In that case, the board of education permitted teachers employed by private religious groups to hold weekly religious classes in the public school buildings during regular school hours.[128] The classes were attended by those students whose parents signed cards requesting their permission, and nonparticipants were required to continue their public school studies in other classrooms. The parent of a nonparticipant challenged this program under the establishment clause and was sustained by the Supreme Court.

Some writers have interpreted *McCollum* to stand for the proposition that any use of public property for religious purposes is forbidden.[129] The Court's subsequent decision in the *New York*

Kauper, *Church, State, and Freedom: A Review*, 52 MICH. L. REV. 829, 842 (1954). (Footnotes omitted.)

The difficulty with this approach is the characterization of the flag salute as a "religious exercise," thus putting it in the same category as the Regents' prayer. The two activities are intrinsically different. One furthers religion if it does anything; the other in no way advances any religious cause. To say that any governmental activity that offends some religion is a "religious exercise" would mean that a declaration of war could be so characterized. *Cf.* Hamilton v. Regents of the Univ. of Cal., 293 U.S. 245 (1934).

126. It may well be argued that even though these indirect pressures, which accrue when the privilege of nonparticipation is granted, do not result in a breach of the free exercise clause when the state's activity is secular, free exercise is violated when the state action is solely religious. This would certainly be true if the outcome of free exercise problems "depends upon the balancing of the secular needs of the community against the religious rights of the individual . . . ." Brief for Synagogue Council of America and National Community Relations Advisory Council as Amici Curiae, p. 17, Engel v. Vitale, 370 U.S. 421 (1962).

127. Illinois *ex rel.* McCollum v. Board of Educ., 333 U.S. 203 (1948).

128. Originally, classes had been conducted by Protestant teachers, Catholic priests, and a Jewish rabbi. During the final few years, the Jewish classes had been discontinued. The classes were held for 30 minutes in the lower grades and for 45 minutes in the upper grades. *Id.* at 207–09.

129. *E.g.,* Cosway & Toepfer, *Religion and the Schools,* 17 U. CINC. L. REV. 117, 132–33 (1948); Cushman, *Public Support of Religious Education in American Constitutional Law,* 45 ILL. L. REV. 333, 352 (1950); 25 ALBANY L. REV. 318, 319 (1961).

Released Time Case[130] furnishes credence to this analysis. If this reading is accurate, the Court's decision in *Engel* was predetermined by *McCollum* irrespective of the question of inherent compulsion since the Regents' prayer was concededly a religious exercise being conducted on school property. In fact, the Regents' prayer arguably made greater use of public "property" than the released time program since, in the former case, the teachers conducting the religious exercise were publicly employed.[131] But such a reading of *McCollum* must be rejected. In the *Engel* opinion, *McCollum* was not even cited. Although the Court at several points in its *McCollum* opinion did refer to the fact that tax-supported property was being used for the dissemination of religious doctrines,[132] each time it did so it was careful to couple this fact with a reference to the fact that the public school machinery was being used to foster attendance at religious classes.[133] Furthermore, on several occasions the Court has held that the equal protection clause forbids discriminatory treatment in permitting the use of public parks by religious organizations for religious purposes,[134] thus implying that such use of public property is not constitutionally barred.[135] Indeed, at least one commentator has argued that to deny religious organizations the use of public property while permitting its use by other agencies in the community would itself violate the religion clauses of the first amendment.[136]

Even when religious organizations have made the only nonpublic use of public property (which appears to have been the case in *McCollum*), such use has been sustained by state courts when it did not result in any measurable cost to the taxpayers.[137] In

---

130. Zorach v. Clauson, 343 U.S. 306 (1952).

131. Brief for Petitioner, pp. 24–25, Engel v. Vitale, 370 U.S. 421 (1962); Brief for American Jewish Committee and Anti-Defamation League of B'nai B'rith as Amici Curiae, p. 13, Engel v. Vitale, *supra*. *But see* note 146 *infra* for evidence of the more extensive use of the public school building in *McCollum*.

132. 333 U.S. at 209, 212.

133. The author of the *McCollum* opinion, Mr. Justice Black, made clear that it was at least *his* intention that the "decision would have been the same if the religious classes had not been held in the school buildings." Zorach v. Clauson, 343 U.S. 306, 316 (1952) (dissenting opinion).

134. Fowler v. Rhode Island, 345 U.S. 67 (1953); Niemotko v. Maryland, 340 U.S. 268 (1951).

135. See Kauper, *Church, State, and Freedom: A Review*, 52 MICH. L. REV. 829, 836 (1954); Sullivan, *Religious Education in the Schools*, 14 LAW & CONTEMP. PROB. 92, 108–09 (1949); Note, 57 YALE L.J. 1114, 1117–18 (1948).

136. Kurland, *Of Church and State and the Supreme Court*, 29 U. CHI. L. REV. 1, 60 (1961).

137. Southside Estates Baptist Church v. Board of Trustees, 115 So. 2d 697 (Fla. 1959) (temporary use of public school buildings by several

his excellent book, Leo Pfeffer contends that the principle of *de minimis non curat lex*[138] has no application when either the establishment clause or the free exercise clause is concerned; "the right sought to be vindicated is a religious right, not an economic one, and it is therefore inappropriate to measure it in economic terms."[139] The Supreme Court, some time ago, indicated its rejection of the *de minimis* maxim in regard to first amendment freedoms.[140] But when governmental activity, even that fairly characterized as "solely religious," does not infringe on religious liberty, either by violating the free exercise clause or by compromising or influencing the freedom of conscientious choice in a manner that arguably does not violate the free exercise clause,[141] the financial expenditure involved must be subject to measurement by the *de minimis* standard. Otherwise, the appearance of "In God We Trust" on our coins would be unconstitutional. Even Pfeffer has found this to be "insignificant almost to the point of being trivial,"[142] thus impliedly invoking the *de minimis* principle. Examination of his analysis reveals that Pfeffer was concerned solely with those religious programs by government that tend to compromise one's religious beliefs. Likewise, the Supreme Court dictum was concerned with the protection of *liberty*. Other recognized authorities have suggested that there must be a place for the *de minimis* doctrine in this area.[143] State courts have specifically accepted its existence,[144] and the *Engel* case need not be read to

---

churches for Sunday religious meetings); Nichols v. School Directors, 93 Ill. 61, 34 Am. Rep. 160 (1879) (occasional use of school houses by different church organizations for religious services); State *ex rel.* Gilbert v. Dilley, 95 Neb. 527, 145 N.W. 999 (1914) (occasional use of school building for Sunday school and religious meetings). *But see* Hysong v. Gallitzin Borough School Dist., 164 Pa. 629, 30 Atl. 482 (1894) (use of public school rooms immediately after regular school hours for Catholic religious instruction to those students of the school who were Catholic by Catholic sisters who were also public school teachers).

It might be suggested that in this final case, unlike the other three, the facts created an atmosphere that resulted in pressures on both Catholic and non-Catholic children to attend the religious classes. See note 461 *infra*.

138. The law does not concern itself with trifles.

139. PFEFFER, CHURCH, STATE, AND FREEDOM 168 (1953).

140. See Thomas v. Collins, 323 U.S. 516, 543 (1945). More recently, the Court appears to have retreated from this position. See, *e.g.*, Barenblatt v. United States, 360 U.S. 109, 134 (1959); Uphaus v. Wyman, 360 U.S. 72, 77–78 (1959).

141. See text accompanying notes 125–26 *supra*.

142. Pfeffer, *Church and State: Something Less Than Separation,* 19 U. CHI. L. REV. 1, 23 (1951).

143. Kauper, *supra* note 135, at 837; Sutherland, *Due Process and Disestablishment,* 62 HARV. L. REV. 1306, 1343 (1949).

144. Southside Estates Baptist Church v. Board of Trustees, 115 So. 2d 697, 699 (Fla. 1959); People *ex rel.* Lewis v. Graves, 219 App. Div.

have rejected it since it may be explained on grounds of inherent compulsion.[145] Therefore, since the operation of the released time program in *McCollum* involved "no direct appropriation of any kind or direct expenditures of money of any kind,"[146] the use of public property there must be considered *de minimis,* and the Supreme Court's decision cannot be explained on the basis of financial aid to religion.[147]

The *McCollum* decision can only be accounted for on the ground that the operation of the released time program—a program having no independent primary secular goal—resulted in compromising the conscientious beliefs of the complainant's child.[148] This inherent effect of released time must have been the "invaluable aid"[149] that the Court found the state was affording "sectarian groups . . . in that it helps to provide pupils for their religious

---

233, 236, 219 N.Y. Supp. 189, 192 (1927); Nichols v. School Directors, 93 Ill. 61, 63, 34 Am. Rep. 160, 162 (1879). In the first case, the court stated that the state constitution would be violated "if the use of the school buildings [for Sunday religious meetings] were permitted for prolonged periods of time, absent evidence of an immediate intention on the part of the Church to construct its own buildings. . . ." 115 So. 2d at 700.

145. *But see* Pfeffer, *The New York Regents' Prayer Case (Engel v. Vitale): Its Background, Meaning and Implications,* Committee on Law and Social Action Reports 6 (American Jewish Congress, June 26, 1962).

146. People *ex rel.* McCollum v. Board of Educ., 396 Ill. 14, 24, 71 N.E.2d 161, 166 (1947). The court pointed out that

the classes were held in the schoolrooms during the current school period and the rooms were in use during the entire period, and, no doubt, the same cost for lights, heat, janitor service, etc. would exist whether or not the schoolroom was used at the particular time by this particular class. Any additional wear and tear on the floors would seem to be inconsequential. . . . Any additional wear and tear of furniture due to the religious education classes . . . would be negligible.

Ibid. See also Illinois *ex rel.* McCollum v. Board of Educ., 333 U.S. 203, 234 (1948) (Jackson, J., concurring).

147. As this author has suggested elsewhere, the use of the *de minimis* principle in this field may call not only for a measurement of the financial expenditure by government, but also for an examination of the financial benefit to religion. LOCKHART, KAMISAR & CHOPER, SUPPLEMENT TO DODD'S CASES ON CONSTITUTIONAL LAW 358 (1962). Although the former may be negligible, the latter may be quite substantial. See 35 ILL. B.J. 361, 363 (1947). However, this aspect of the problem was not considered at any stage of the *McCollum* litigation. See note 146 *supra.* The Court did find that the released time program afforded unconstitutional aid to religion, but it was not the financial benefit received that turned the decision. See text accompanying notes 148–53 *infra. Cf.* Cushman, *supra* note 129, at 352.

148. See Kurland, *The Regents' Prayer Case: "Full of Sound and Fury, Signifying . . . ,"* 1962 SUPREME COURT REV. 1, 29–30. For a complete discussion of how and why this is the result of the program's operation, see text accompanying notes 376–87 *infra.*

149. 333 U.S. at 212.

classes through the use of the State's compulsory public school machinery."[150] The Court did state that it was unnecessary to consider the contention that the program "was voluntary in name only because *in fact* subtle pressures were brought to bear on the students to force them to participate in it."[151] This declaration may be explained as a response to appellant's argument that the factual evidence in the case belied the trial court's finding that Terry McCollum's teachers and classmates did nothing to subject him to embarrassment because of his religious opinions.[152] The Court's statement should not be read as rejecting the contention that the released time program was in some way inherently coercive and therefore constitutionally defective. Indeed, other writers have found some form of inherent coercion to be the basis upon which the decision was predicated.[153]

Furthermore, it would seem that the only justification for the Court's finding that appellant had standing to maintain the action was the fact that Terry was subject to certain subtle pressures inherent in the released time program.[154] The existing rule is well settled that a "party who invokes the power [of the federal courts to restrain unconstitutional acts] must be able to show not only that the statute is invalid but that he has sustained or is immediate-

---

150. *Ibid.* Further evidence that the Court relied on the inherent pressures of the activity:

The operation of the State's compulsory education system thus assists and is integrated with the program of religious instruction carried on by separate religious sects. Pupils compelled by law to go to school for secular education are released in part from their legal duty upon the condition that they attend the religious classes.

Id. at 209–10.

151. *Id.* at 207 n.1. (Emphasis added.)

152. The trial court's finding may be found in Record, p. 68, Illinois *ex rel.* McCollum v. Board of Educ., 333 U.S. 203 (1948). Brief for Appellant, pp. 26–30, advanced the testimony of a number of witnesses that was contrary to this finding and explained how the testimony relied upon by the trial judge was inadequate. Although counsel for appellant interwove this contention with the "inherent compulsion" argument, the Court's statement was addressed only to those of appellant's arguments that took "issue with the facts found by the Illinois courts . . . ." 333 U.S. at 207.

153. *E.g.,* Sutherland, *Public Authority and Religious Education: A Brief Survey of Constitutional and Legal Limits,* in THE STUDY OF RELIGION IN THE PUBLIC SCHOOLS: AN APPRAISAL 49 (Brown ed. 1958); 16 GEO. WASH. L. REV. 556, 558–59 (1948).

154. The Court perfunctorily rejected the contention that appellant had no standing. 333 U.S. at 206. Mr. Justice Black, the author of the Court's opinion, has indicated on other occasions that his standard on the question of standing in the church-state area is considerably more lenient than is the prevailing rule. See McGowan v. Maryland, 366 U.S. 420, 429 n.6 (1961); Two Guys From Harrison-Allentown, Inc. v. McGinley, 366 U.S. 582, 592 n.10 (1961).

ly in danger of sustaining some direct injury as the result of its enforcement, and not merely that he suffers in some indefinite way in common with people generally."[155] The interest of appellant, Terry's mother, was asserted as that of a resident, taxpayer, and parent of a child then enrolled in a public school having a released time program.[156] The record made clear that appellant was an atheist who desired that her child not be indoctrinated with any religious teachings.[157] Although the Court permitted a local taxpayer to challenge local governmental action as being in violation of the establishment clause in *Everson*,[158] that case involved "a measurable appropriation or disbursement of school-district funds."[159] Since the released time program in *McCollum*, like Bible reading in the public schools,[160] did not involve a substantial disbursement, appellant had no standing as a taxpayer. If appellant had sought standing solely on the basis of the fact that she was a parent of an attending child, she would have failed because there could have been absolutely no showing of any direct injury. It could have been accurately said that there was "no assertion that [he] was injured or even offended thereby or that [he] was compelled to accept, approve, or confess agreement with any dogma or creed or even [attend released time religious classes]."[161] Nor, under existing doctrine,[162] could standing have been conferred on appellant on the ground that those who were injured were unable to assert their rights effectively.[163] Appellant satisfied the existing standing prerequisites by alleging the infringement of a constitutionally protected right—the right of her child to be free from certain inherent pressures to participate in a solely religious governmental activity irrespective of any direct coercion. Only by finding the recognition of such a right in *McCollum* may those who questioned appellant's standing be answered[164] and may the decision be satisfactorily explained.[165]

---

155. Massachusetts v. Mellon, 262 U.S. 447, 488 (1923).

156. 333 U.S. at 205.

157. Record, pp. 1–2, Illinois *ex rel*. McCollum v. Board of Educ., 333 U.S. 203 (1948).

158. Everson v. Board of Educ., 330 U.S. 1 (1947). See text accompanying notes 28–29 *supra*.

159. Doremus v. Board of Educ., 342 U.S. 429, 434 (1952).

160. *Cf. id*. at 429.

161. *Id*. at 432 (dictum).

162. See text accompanying notes 219–27 *infra*.

163. *Cf.* NAACP v. Alabama *ex rel*. Patterson, 357 U.S. 449, 459–60 (1958); Barrows v. Jackson, 346 U.S. 249, 257 (1953).

164. Illinois *ex rel*. McCollum v. Board of Educ., 333 U.S. 203, 232–33 (1948) (Jackson, J.); Corwin, *The Supreme Court as National School Board*, 14 LAW & CONTEMP. PROB. 3, 5–9 (1949); Kauper, *supra* note 135, at 834–35.

165. See generally Sutherland, *Establishment According to Engel*,

2. *Other Doctrines*

There is other support to be found in the decisions of the Supreme Court for the proposed constitutional standard. The Court has unanimously held that, unless justified by some valid overriding interest, a state cannot compel individuals to disclose their membership in an association if such identification, although not directly suppressing the right of free speech protected by the first amendment, nevertheless would have this consequence.[166] It can hardly be said that the state's engaging in a solely religious activity manifests an overriding public interest;[167] in fact, such state activity has been attacked as being in itself invalid.[168] When the state embarks on such a program and then grants the privilege of nonparticipation to conscientious dissenters to avoid problems under the free exercise clause,[169] disclosure of membership in a religious (or nonreligious) group results. Such identification, in turn, tends to compromise religious beliefs[170] that fall within the broad ambit of the first amendment's protection.[171]

This effect is generally unquestioned.[172] The fact that this "re-

---

76 HARV. L. REV. 25, 31–35 (1962). *Cf.* Kurland, *supra* note 148, at 29–30.

166. NAACP v. Alabama *ex rel.* Patterson, 357 U.S. 449 (1958).

167. See text preceding note 114 *supra.*

168. See text accompanying notes 79–82 *supra.*

169. It is undisputed that the free exercise clause, if not also the establishment clause, would be violated if participation in these solely religious activities were governmentally compelled. Engel v. Vitale, 370 U.S. 421, 430–31 (1962); Zorach v. Clauson, 343 U.S. 306, 311–12 (1952); Lewis v. Allen, 5 Misc. 2d 68, 72–73, 159 N.Y.S.2d 807, 811 (Sup. Ct. 1957); Kauper, *Released Time and Religious Liberty: A Further Reply,* 53 MICH. L. REV. 233, 234 (1954); 9 OHIO ST. L.J. 336, 341 (1948).

170. *Cf.* NAACP v. Alabama *ex rel.* Patterson, 357 U.S. 449, 462 (19–58): "Inviolability of privacy in group association may in many circumstances be indispensable to preservation of freedom of association, particularly where a group espouses dissident beliefs."

171. There is persuasive authority for the proposition that it would be unconstitutional for the Government itself to cause a religious nonconformist to be embarrassed, harassed, or humiliated so as to coerce him to compromise his conscientious beliefs. See Bates v. City of Little Rock, 361 U.S. 516, 528 (1960) (concurring opinion); American Communications Ass'n v. Douds, 339 U.S. 382, 402 (1950).

172. See text accompanying notes 87–101 *supra. Cf.* NAACP v. Alabama *ex rel.*Patterson, 357 U.S. 449, 462–63 (1958):

Petitioner has made an uncontroverted showing that on past occasions revelation of the identity of its rank-and-file members has exposed these members to economic reprisal, loss of employment, threat of physical coercion, and other manifestations of public hostility. Under these circumstances, we think it apparent that compelled disclosure of petitioner's Alabama membership is likely to affect adversely the ability of petitioner and its members to pursue their collective effort to foster beliefs which they admittedly have the right to advocate, in that it may

pressive effect . . . follows not from *state* action but from *private* community pressures"[173] is irrelevant;[174] "the crucial factor is the *interplay* of governmental and private action, for it is only after the initial exertion of state power represented by the [introduction of solely religious programs] . . . that private action takes hold."[175]

It is true that all of those Supreme Court decisions in the church-state area that have relied on a compulsion theory to find governmental action to be forbidden by the first amendment have involved instances of compulsion directly imposed by government.[176] However, the Court has shown no inclination to give any weight to differing degrees of governmental compulsion so long as it seems that the state action is likely to compromise conscientious beliefs or influence the freedom of religious choice. Thus, a state requirement that people who wish to become notaries public must declare their belief in God does not as forcefully compel the forsaking or influencing of conscientious beliefs as would be the case if the state prosecuted those who refused to declare their belief;[177] nor does the imposition of a license tax on religious colporteurs compel them as strongly as would a penal provision. But since "the loss of opportunity to obtain private employment . . . may be sufficient to persuade at least some uncommitted persons to adopt a religion,"[178] the Court did not hesitate in *Torcaso v. Watkins*[179] to strike down the required notaries' declaration by a unanimous vote; the license tax was held invalid in *Murdock v. Pennsylvania* because it "tends to suppress" religious practices.[180]

---

induce members to withdraw from the Association and dissuade others from joining it because of fear of exposure of their beliefs shown through their associations and of the consequences of this exposure. 173. *Id.* at 463.

174.

In the domain of these indispensible liberties [under the first amendment], the decisions of this Court recognize that abridgement of such rights, even though unintended, may inevitably follow from varied forms of governmental action. . . . The governmental action challenged may appear to be totally unrelated to protected liberties. *Id.* at 461.

175. *Id.* at 463. (Emphasis added.) This same analysis is implicit in the decision holding an ordinance that forbade the distribution of anonymous handbills unconstitutional on the ground that it tended to restrict freedoms protected by the first amendment. Talley v. California, 362 U.S. 60 (1960). See generally Rosenfield, *Separation of Church and State in the Public Schools*, 22 U. PITT. L. REV. 561, 582–84 (1961).

176. See cases cited notes 177–80 *infra*.

177. *Cf.* West Virginia State Bd. of Educ. v. Barnette, 319 U.S. 624 (1943).

178. 74 HARV. L. REV. 611, 614 (1961).

179. 367 U.S. 488 (1961).

180. 319 U.S. 105, 114 (1943).

It would seem to be only a small step to hold, as state courts have done,[181] that when the state engages in a solely religious activity, its action is constitutionally barred if it inherently produces social compulsion to abandon religious convictions.

Before moving on, it should be noted that the constitutional significance of coercion in the area of church-state problems has not escaped attention. Thus, in evaluating several governmental programs that must be fairly characterized as solely religious, Professor Paul Kauper has relied on the absence of any sort of coercion to sustain their constitutionality.[182] On the other hand, he condemns the appropriation of public funds for church buildings or ministers' salaries since "the maintenance of churches is itself not a governmental function and since it coerces the conscience of nonbelieving taxpayers."[183] Professor Robert Levy has concluded that "any program which operates to compel the young and impressionable to orient to religion should be unconstitutional."[184]

3.   *Application in Engel v. Vitale*

Thus, the way had been well paved for the Supreme Court specifically to restrict its *Regents' Prayer* decision to the compulsive effect on young children inherent in this solely religious activity by the state. Such a definite limitation would have clearly immuniz-

---

181. *E.g.,* Brown v. Orange County Bd. of Pub. Instruction, 128 So. 2d 181 (Fla. Dist. Ct. App. 1960) (distribution of Gideon Bibles in public schools); Tudor v. Board of Educ., 14 N.J. 31, 100 A.2d 857 (1953) (distribution of Gideon Bibles in public schools).

182.   In discussing the chaplains in both houses of Congress, Professor Kauper states that "this is a plain case of spending federal money for religious purposes." Kauper, *supra* note 135, at 837. This seems clearly to indicate that he considers this a solely religious activity. He goes on to state that "it can hardly be considered a substantial use of public funds in aid of religion, and it is not seriously argued that anyone's conscience is coerced by this practice." *Ibid.* The final point is clearly sound although it would not be similarly valid if the chaplains gave daily prayer recitations in the public schools. In raising the question of "substantial use of public funds," Professor Kauper seems to present this as an independent criterion for judging solely religious activities. If it is, as it may well be, one might effectively argue that an annual expenditure of $17,620, see 75 Stat. 320, 324 (1961), is hardly *de minimis,* even when compared to the entire federal budget. See also text accompanying note 147 *supra.*

As to released time programs, Professor Kauper concludes that it has not been demonstrated that they deprive anyone of any liberty. Kauper, *supra* note 135, at 236. An attempted refutation of the conclusion may be found at notes 376–87 *infra.*

183. *Id.* at 846. Here, again, the point made seems to be that this is a solely religious activity.

184. Levy, *Views from the Wall—Reflections on Church-State Separation,* 29 HENNEPIN LAW. 51, 55 (1961). Examination of the context of this statement seems to indicate that Professor Levy was concerned only with those public school "programs" that are solely religious.

ed the Court from the position, taken in the concurring opinion of Mr. Justice Douglas, that government cannot "constitutionally finance a religious exercise . . . whatever form it takes."[185] It would also have effectively distinguished the Regents' prayer situation from most "of the religious traditions of our people, reflected in countless practices of the institutions and officials of our government,"[186] cited by Mr. Justice Stewart in his lone dissent. However, although the language used by the Court appears to be quite comprehensive,[187] it would be rash to conclude that *Engel* passed judgment on (or even hinted at) the long list of governmental activities disapproved by Mr. Justice Douglas[188] or brought forward by Mr. Justice Stewart.[189] The Court's statement that

---

185. Engel v. Vitale, 370 U.S. 421, 437 (1962) (concurring opinion). See note 188 *infra*.

186. Engel v. Vitale, 370 U.S. 421, 446 (1962) (dissenting opinion). See note 189 *infra*.

187. See text accompanying notes 79–80 *supra*.

188. Among the governmental programs and activities that Mr. Justice Douglas would seem to find unconstitutional are congressional and armed service chaplains, use of the Bible for the administration of oaths, "In God We Trust" on coins and currency, and opening prayers in legislative chambers and courts—including the Supreme Court. None of these would seem to produce the inherent pressures that arise from a solely religious activity in the public schools and, thus, are subject to separate consideration. Also included were activities having an independent primary secular goal, such as the availability of funds for parochial schools, G.I. Bill payments to denominational schools, and National School Lunch Act benefits to religious schools. In addition, Mr. Justice Douglas expressed his present disagreement with his vote with the majority in *Everson* (see text accompanying notes 28–29 *supra*), a case raising problems very different from those presented by the Regents' prayer. See text accompanying notes 21–49 *supra*. The evil ingredient that he found to be common to all of these governmental activities was that they "insert a divisive influence into our communities." 370 U.S. at 442, 443. For criticism of this standard, see text accompanying notes 362–65 *infra*.

Mr. Justice Douglas found "no element of compulsion" in the case. 370 U.S. at 438. He stated that there was no more inherent coercion here than there was in the prayers that open sessions of Congress and the Court. *Id.* at 442. This seems to ignore the pertinence of the public school setting and the maturity of the participants. See text accompanying notes 87–107 *supra*.

189. In addition to a number of the matters referred to by Mr. Justice Douglas, Mr. Justice Stewart listed such things as presidential inaugural statements asking the protection and help of God and presidential proclamations of a National Day of Prayer. Neither of these produce effects that are realistically comparable to the social pressures produced in the public school atmosphere. Whether or not constitutional, they must be considered apart from the Regents' prayer.

Mr. Justice Stewart decided that the case was "entirely free of any compulsion . . . including any 'embarrassments and pressures,' " because "the state courts have made clear that those who object to reciting the prayer *must be*" free of these things. 370 U.S. at 445. (Emphasis added.) But no mandate of any court can free this solely religious activity from its concomitant inherent pressures.

"the Establishment Clause . . . does not depend upon any showing of direct governmental compulsion"[190] is entirely consistent with the rationale that the establishment clause is violated by certain laws that produce inherent, albeit *indirect and nongovernmental,* compulsion. So is the Court's pronouncement that the establishment clause "is violated by the enactment of laws which establish an official religion whether those laws operate *directly* to coerce nonobserving individuals or not."[191] Those "laws which establish an official religion" might well be interpreted to mean those laws having no independent primary secular purpose or effect, and the entire pronouncement might not have been intended to deal with those "solely religious laws" that operate *neither directly nor indirectly* to coerce nonobserving persons.[192] In any case, since the governmental program in issue in *Engel did* operate indirectly to compel dissenters, the decision should not, and may not, be read for the proposition that the establishment clause bars all solely religious programs by government.[193]

Close examination of the positions taken by the two amici curiae also indicates that they perhaps meant less than would initially appear. To illustrate the thesis that the establishment clause is violated whenever government undertakes or sponsors a religious program, the argument was made that "the holding of a Mass in a public school during the regular day would violate the Establishment Clause even though all non-Catholic pupils were permitted or required to absent themselves."[194] This would be unconstitutional, but not simply for the reason that the state was "sponsoring [a] religious program"; an establishment clause violation would occur because the minority dissenters would be under the same social pressures from the Catholic majority as the dissenters were in *Engel.*[195] Remove the coercive effect of the public school at-

Mr. Justice Stewart chidingly questioned whether "the Court [was] suggesting that the Constitution permits judges and Congressmen and Presidents to join in prayer, but prohibits school children from doing so?" *Id.* at 450 n.9. The answer would seem to be that (1) the case at bar involved only school children and (2) the pressures inherent in the public school setting may constitutionally distinguish it from the other situations mentioned.

190. 370 U.S. at 430.

191. *Ibid.* (Emphasis added.)

192. This conclusion is supported by the opinion's explicit recognition, immediately following its broad statement, that laws that place the "power . . . and prestige of government . . . behind a particular religious belief" plainly result in indirect coercive pressures. 370 U.S. at 431.

193. *But see* Sutherland, *supra* note 165, at 35–36.

194. Brief of American Jewish Committee and Anti-Defamation League of B'nai B'rith as Amici Curiae, p. 17, Engel v. Vitale, 370 U.S. 421 (1962).

195. See 25 CAL. OPS. ATT'Y GEN. 319 (1955). This assumes that a

mosphere and have the Mass held in the public school on Sunday, and a significantly different question is presented.[196] Further, these amici's thesis was documented by citing *McCollum*,[197] as was the proposition advanced by the other amici that the first amendment's ban on establishment would be violated by state "participation in religious affairs."[198] The sound basis for *McCollum*, however, is the presence of inherent compulsion.[199]

C. DISTINGUISHING THE INDISTINGUISHABLE

Acceptance of the proposed constitutional standard not only effectively circumscribes the *Engel* decision, but also provides a ready means for distinguishing between situations heretofore found by some to be indistinguishable. For example, Mr. Justice Jackson,[200] seconded by several commentators,[201] charged that *McCollum's*

---

program of this sort would only be instituted if there were a Catholic majority. *Cf.* Knowlton v. Baumhover, 182 Iowa 691, 695, 166 N.W. 202, 203 (1918); Williams v. Board of Trustees, 172 Ky. 133, 364 Mo. 121, 129–31, 260 S.W.2d 573, 576–78 (1953). If for some reason this were not the case, the result should be the same because of the program's influence on Roman Catholic students who would not attend Mass otherwise, see text accompanying notes 221, 439–53 *infra*, and because of the influence on free religious choice generated by the public school sponsorship of such an activity. See text accompanying notes 244–46 *infra*.

196. See text accompanying notes 129–47 *supra*.

197. Brief of American Jewish Committee and Anti-Defamation League of B'nai B'rith as Amici Curiae, p. 17, Engel v. Vitale, 370 U.S. 421 (1962).

198. Brief of Synagogue Council of America and National Community Relations Advisory Council as Amici Curiae, p. 15, Engel v. Vitale, 370 U.S. 421 (1962).

199. It must be noted, however, that the Pfeffer brief argued that if the state's "conduct is religious, then it is outside the competence and jurisdiction of the State or its instrumentalities, and even if participation were not compulsory, the conduct would be unconstitutional." *Id.* at 17. The scope of this standard is not clear. From the context, it would not seem to apply only to the state's undertaking solely religious activities in the public schools and granting dissenters the right of nonparticipation; it seems to say that all solely religious activities by the state are barred. This is a matter that was clearly not in issue in Engel, and such a thesis is clearly unworkable and unacceptable. See text accompanying notes 140–44 *supra*. Even if this standard is meant to apply only to those governmental activities that require participation (the context of the statement does lend credence to this), query if these can be found to violate the establishment clause if it can be shown that they are neither inherently compulsive (as only mature adults may be involved) nor involve a substantial use of public funds. See note 182 *supra*. It is difficult to differentiate such a case from "In God We Trust" on coins and currency.

200. See Kunz v. New York, 340 U.S. 290, 311 n.10 (1951) (dissenting opinion); Saia v. New York, 334 U.S. 558, 569 (1948) (dissenting opinion).

201. Corwin, *The Supreme Court as National School Board*, 14 LAW & CONTEMP. PROB. 3, 7–8 (1949); Taylor, *Equal Protection of Religion: Today's Public School Problem*, 38 A.B.A.J. 277–78 (1952).

ban from the public schools of the solely religious activity of released time, *a fortiori,* determined the question of whether the state was permitted to bar the solely religious activities of some people in the public streets and parks. The theory was that since *McCollum* forbade the use of tax-supported school property by any and all sects for the propagation of religion, it was patently anomalous for the Court to hold, as it did,[202] that the state was compelled to permit the nondiscriminate use of tax-supported street and park property for that same purpose.[203] It is not difficult to combat this analysis. The effect of the activity in *McCollum* was to coerce those who were either unwilling to participate or uninterested in doing so. This evil—a significant constitutional ingredient—is not present when the public streets or parks are used for religious purposes. No citizen who declines to participate is in any way compelled to do so, and therefore, no person's religious liberty is impaired.

One writer has stated that he is at a loss to determine "why it is constitutional for a public institution to *purchase* a sectarian book [such as the Gideon Bible], but not to enable its pupils to read such books as *gifts* . . . ."[204] The explanation is the same.[205] While no one has ever argued that dissenters are compelled to desert their religious convictions because public school libraries contain sectarian literature, there has been expert testimony that public school sponsorship of the distribution of Bibles creates coercive pressures to do so.[206]

---

202. See cases cited note 200 *supra.*
203. Professor Corwin put it this way:
[T]he discrepancy between the two holdings is apparent. In one [*McCollum*] it is held that a school board may not constitutionally permit religious groups to use on an equal footing any part of a school building for the purpose of religious instruction to *those who wish to receive it.* By the other [*Saia*] the public authorities are under a *constitutional obligation* to turn over public parks for religious propaganda to be hurled at all and sundry whether they wish to receive it or not. The Court seems to cherish a strange tenderness for *outré* religious manifestations which contrasts sharply with its attitude toward organized religion.
Corwin, *supra* note 201, at 8.
204. Lieberman, *A General Interpretation of Separation of Church and State and Its Implications for Public Education,* 33 PROGRESSIVE EDUCATION 129, 131 (1956).
205. Another reason for distinguishing these situations might be that the state has a secular educational aim in placing Bibles in public school libraries—to make this literature available for academic investigation. See text accompanying notes 333–37 *infra.* No such secular purpose is found in sponsoring Bible distribution. The goal of the Gideons International is to "win men and women for the Lord Jesus Christ." Tudor v. Board of Educ., 14 N.J. 31, 33, 100 A.2d 857, 858 (1953).
206. *Id.* at 50, 100 A.2d at 867. See notes 501–09 *infra* and accompanying text.

In upholding the New York released time plan in *Zorach v. Clauson,* the Supreme Court, per Mr. Justice Douglas, implied that such solely religious activity is equivalent to "prayers in our legislative halls; the appeals to the Almighty in the messages of the Chief Executive; [and] the proclamations making Thanksgiving Day a holiday . . . ."[207] Several state courts have sustained public school Bible reading on similar bases.[208] Because of the presence of inherent coercion, it seems that *Zorach* was incorrectly decided[209] and that daily Bible reading in the public schools is also unconstitutional.[210] Whether or not the other activities referred to are constitutionally valid, it is fairly clear that they are not inherently coercive, and therefore, they should not control the disposition of Bible reading and released time.

Relying on the governmental activities referred to by Mr. Justice Douglas, the House Committee on the Judiciary made the same faulty analogy when it stated that the inclusion of the words "under God" in the pledge of allegiance to the flag did not run afoul of the establishment clause.[211] Immature dissenters from the amended flag pledge will surely be subject to the same coercive pressures in the public school as were the children in *Engel.* Because of this, whether the amended pledge to the flag will withstand attack should turn on whether it may be fairly characterized as a solely religious activity.[212]

In a recent comprehensive article dealing with religion in the public schools, one writer has urged that "the Constitution directs the public school to be a completely secular agency" and that it "proscribes the use of public school funds, facilities, personnel, time, sponsorship, auspices, or authority for religious instruction, practice, or ritual, or for any other religious or religiously-oriented purpose, direct or indirect."[213] Under this standard, not only were prayers, Bible reading, and released time found to be unconstitutional, but so also was the objective or academic study of religion.[214] "On the other hand, where information or ideas about religion are intrinsic to the subjects in the school's normal secular

---

207. 343 U.S. 306, 312–13 (1952).

208. *E.g.,* Murray v. Curlett, 228 Md. 239, —, 179 A.2d 698, 702 (1962); Church v. Bullock, 104 Tex. 1, 7, 109 S.W. 115, 118 (1908).

209. See text accompanying notes 397–403 *infra.*

210. See text accompanying notes 61–66 *supra,* 251–94 *infra.*

211. H.R. REP. No. 1693, 83d Cong., 2d Sess. 3 (1954).

212. For discussion of this question, see text accompanying notes 536–41 *infra.*

213. Rosenfield, *Separation of Church and State in the Public Schools,* 22 U. PITT. L. REV. 561, 570 (1961).

214. *Id.* at 571–78. "Teaching religious doctrine, under any heading, is forbidden." *Id.* at 578.

curriculum, such as history, art, literature, etc., they should be presented factually and objectively."[215] Why a single course in comparative religion makes the school less of a "secular agency" than does the infiltration of religious matter into every other course in the curriculum is unclear. Why the one, and not the other, indirectly instructs in religion is also a mystery. The source of the difficulty seems to be the generality of the standard and the resulting perplexity in its application. Not so, hopefully, with the constitutional standard proposed here.[216]

Finally, it should be noted that use of this suggested standard would even seem to satisfy those, at least for the time being, who contend that since the language of the fourteenth amendment bars only the denial of liberty, "so far as the fourteenth amendment is concerned, states are entirely free to establish religions, provided that they do not deprive anybody of religious liberty."[217]

D. RELIGIOUS PRACTICES CARRIED ON WITHOUT OBJECTION

The seemingly broad standard suggested in *Engel,* as well as the rather sweeping criteria advocated by amici curiae in that case, may be read as stating that any governmental program that is solely religious violates the establishment clause. Under such a reading, there is no question as to the unconstitutionality of such a program, even when no one objects to it. However, since the constitutional principle of the proposed constitutional standard is grounded in the sanctity of the religious and conscientious scruples of public school children, a question does arise as to the extent of its application to a situation in which the public school engages in a solely religious practice and there is no opposition by the attending school children or their parents.

In the two cases in which the Supreme Court has found a practice of this sort to be contrary to the establishment clause, there were conscientious dissenters who instituted the litigation.[218] Thus, if the rationale of these two cases is to be explained on the basis of the proposed constitutional standard, the decisions must be narrowly read to hold no more than that the establishment clause

---

215. *Ibid.*

216. For discussion of the application of the proposed standard to the various religious aspects in the public schools, see text accompanying notes 229–566 *infra.*

217. Corwin, *supra* note 201, at 19. See also note 8 *supra.* It is interesting to theorize whether the establishment of an approved church by a state could be considered an infringement of religious liberty. See text accompanying note 183 *supra.*

218. Engel v. Vitale, 370 U.S. 421 (1962); Illinois *ex rel.* McCollum v. Board of Educ., 333 U.S. 203 (1948).

is violated when a public school engages in a solely religious practice that is objected to by nonconforming students in attendance; if there are no dissenters, the practice may be valid even if, by its nature, it will likely result in compromising of religious beliefs or influencing of the students' freedom of conscientious choice. Furthermore, it may be argued that under prevailing standing requirements, only the parents of a student whose religious beliefs would preclude participation in the school program could be permitted to challenge its constitutionality.[219]

However, the rationale that underlies the proposed constitutional standard calls for rejection of the above conclusions. Despite the fact that the privilege of nonparticipation is extended to religious nonconformists, the societal pressures on children to take part in state-sponsored religious activities often result in their choosing to do so in preference to suffering embarrassment among their peers. This being the fact, if the constitutionality of solely religious activities turns on whether opposition is voiced, these programs most often will be carried on without objection despite the fact that there are nonconformist pupils whose conscientious scruples are being compromised.[220] Even if all the pupils are nominally members of the same religious sect, very likely solely religious programs of that sect conducted in the public schools will result, due to the inherent coercive pressures, in those students with marginal religious convictions being influenced in their freedom of religious choice.[221] Because of these same social pressures, the results of inquiries made by public school officials or parent groups to determine whether all students would be willing to participate in a public school religious activity will probably not reflect the true feelings of those polled.[222] Parents who are

---

219. See text accompanying notes 154–63 *supra*.

220. *Cf.* Kamisar, *The Right to Counsel and the Fourteenth Amendment: A Dialogue on "The Most Pervasive Right" of an Accused*, 30 U. CHI. L. REV. 1, 65–66 (1962), for the view that under the rule of *Betts v. Brady*, 316 U.S. 455 (1942), the uncounselled indigent defendant is caught in a similar vicious circle.

221. Hypothetically, if all of the students of a public school are of the Roman Catholic faith and it is therefore decided to have a daily Mass in the school with attendance being voluntary, the inherent pressures on those non-churchgoing Roman Catholic children to attend this Mass might well be greater than are the pressures on children of minority faiths to take part in majority religious activities.

222. For a decision stating that the unanimous consent of all parents could not save the ceding of public school control to church authorities, see Williams v. Board of Trustees, 173 Ky. 708, 726, 191 S.W. 507, 514 (1917). For a similar case in which the complainant appeared originally to have given his acquiescence, see Knowlton v. Baumhover, 182 Iowa 691, 700, 166 N.W. 202, 205 (1918).

religious dissenters usually refuse to instruct their children to decline to participate because of the fear of their children being subjected to ridicule.[223] Many hesitate to institute litigation because of this and because of "the prospect of disrupted community life, with perhaps devastating consequences to the minority groups themselves, that would result from arbitrary interference with deep-seated community customs."[224] The upshot of all of this would be that those values cherished in our society, which are at the foundation of the standard set forth in this article, would be emasculated by the rule that only those public school religious programs that are in fact objected to by attending students or their parents are unconstitutional. Prophylactic treatment is necessary. The law should be that those solely religious practices in the public schools that are likely to influence free religious choice or to compromise conscientiously held beliefs are per se unconstitutional.

Empirical studies in the church-state field have shown that judicial determinations of unconstitutionality do not substantially deter communities from engaging in patently invalid practices.[225] Thus, the burden of policing falls upon the courts and ultimately upon those willing to risk the time, expense, and hazards, of litigation. If only those parents of attending children who conscientiously oppose public school religious actions were to have standing to attack them, many of these programs would go unchallenged despite the fact that the very values that are afforded the protection of the first amendment are being submerged. The "right" protected in these instances—the "right" to be free from social

223.
[T]he children's father testified that after careful consideration he had decided that he should not have [the children] excused from attendance at these morning ceremonies. Among his reasons were the following. He said that he thought his children would be "labelled as 'odd balls' " before their teachers and classmates every school day; that children . . . . were liable "to lump all particular religious difference[s] or religious objections [together] as 'atheism' " and that today the word "atheism" is often connected with "atheistic communism", and has "very bad" connotations, such as "un-American" or "pro-Red", with overtones of possible immorality.
Schempp v. School Dist., 201 F. Supp. 815, 818 (E.D. Pa.), *prob. juris. noted,* 371 U.S. 807 (1962).

224. Johnson, *Summary of Policies and Recommendations of the American Council on Education Committee on Religion and Education,* in THE STUDY OF RELIGION IN THE PUBLIC SCHOOLS: AN APPRAISAL 9 (1958). See also Harry Golden, quoted in PFEFFER, CHURCH, STATE, AND FREEDOM 304 (1953); Sullivan, *Religious Education in the Schools,* 14 LAW & CONTEMP. PROB. 92 (1949). For an extremely forceful documentation of this point, see PFEFFER, *supra* at 402–04.

225. See Sorauf, *Zorach v. Clauson: The Impact of a Supreme Court Decision,* 53 AM. POL. SCI. REV. 777, 784–86 (1959).

pressures to conform to the majority's religious practices that are governmentally sponsored—depends upon anonymity for its effective vindication. To require that it be claimed by those affected themselves would result in substantial nullification of the "right" at the very moment of its assertion.[226] It would therefore be appropriate here for the Court to fashion an exception to the general requirement of standing because of the weighty countervailing policy of adequately securing these "rights."[227]

III. APPLICATION OF THE STANDARD

As has been observed by another proponent of a constitutional standard for church-state controversies, "the genius of . . . American constitutional law [is] that its growth and principles are measur-

---

226. *Cf.* NAACP v. Alabama *ex rel.* Patterson, 357 U.S. 449, 459 (1958).

227. See United States v. Raines, 362 U.S. 17, 22 (1960). The precise questions of upon whom standing should be conferred and how this may be accomplished doctrinally is beyond the scope of this article. The Supreme Court has permitted litigants to assert the constitutional rights of others, but none of the decided cases appear to be wholly satisfactory in solving the problem at hand. Professor Kenneth Davis has pointed out that this permission has been, and should be, granted much more liberally once the litigant has properly commenced a proceeding to vindicate his own rights. 3 DAVIS, ADMINISTRATIVE LAW TREATISE § 22.07 (1958). This doctrine is not very helpful here. Other cases may be explained on the basis of the fact that the litigant will suffer direct economic injury as a result of the state enactment. See Pierce v. Society of Sisters, 268 U.S. 510 (1925). These, too, are not very useful.

However, in NAACP v. Alabama *ex rel.* Patterson, 357 U.S. 449 (1958), the Court permitted an association to act as the representative of its members in asserting their rights. Similar to the problem at hand, the rights of the NAACP members would have been nullified if the individuals themselves would have been required to assert them. By analogy, perhaps associations composed of religious dissenters may initiate proceedings. Perhaps it may also be said that such an association "is but the medium through which its individual members seek to make more effective the expression of their own views." 357 U.S. at 459. But *NAACP v. Alabama* also stressed the fact, not likely to be present in the case at hand, that there was "reasonable likelihood that the Association itself through diminished financial support and membership may be adversely affected" by the governmental action. *Id.* at 459–60.

Furthermore, the membership of many associations of minority religious groups is well known. In such instances, an action by the association will redound to the members, thus causing the members to discourage association action for the reasons discussed previously. Granting standing to the parent of any attending child, irrespective of religious conviction, on the ground that to force the parent to assert prejudice will expose the child to opprobrium would also probably be inadequate. Parents would realize that whether or not they were in fact religious dissenters, they would be so publicly regarded. It would seem that full protection can be afforded only by a more relaxed standing criterion. *But see* Sutherland, *Establishment According to Engel*, 76 HARV. L. REV. 25, 42 (1962).

ed in terms of concrete factual situations . . . ."[228] Thus, it would be helpful to examine some of the many actual instances of religious intrusion into the public schools, and to determine their constitutional validity when measured by the proposed constitutional standard.

A. PRAYERS

The prayer at issue in *Engel v. Vitale,* neutral and inoffensive as it was,[229] would fail the proposed constitutional test on several counts. Its purpose and effect was admittedly solely religious. The context in which it was delivered was inherently coercive. Due to its theistic basis, it would likely infringe on the conscientious beliefs of some members of the heterogeneous school population.

However, it need not logically follow that every public school prayer would similarly fail. First, if it were possible to devise a prayer against which no one could raise any conscientious objection, it could not be said that its recitation would result in the compromising or influencing of anyone's religious beliefs or choice. Such a prayer would therefore be free from constitutional attack under the proposed standard. Although projects have been undertaken to attempt to satisfy this requirement,[230] the obstacles appear to be insurmountable. Certainly, the Regents' prayer having been rejected, any prayer that invokes the aid or blessing of the Deity runs afoul of this test. Not only would such a prayer

228. Kurland, *Of Church and State and the Supreme Court,* 29 U. CHI. L. REV. 1, 5 (1961).

229. Compare the daily prayer offered by teachers in Hackett v. Brooksville Graded School Dist., 120 Ky. 608, 614–15, 87 S.W. 792, 793 (1905):

Our Father who art in Heaven, we ask Thy aid in our day's work. Be with us in all we do and say. Give us wisdom and strength and patience to teach these children as they should be taught. May teacher and pupil have mutual love and respect. Watch over these children, both in schoolroom and on the playground. Keep them from being hurt in any way, and at last, when we come to die, may none of our number be missing around Thy Throne. These things we ask for Christ's sake. Amen.

This prayer was found not to be "sectarian," and therefore outside the state constitution's prohibition. Whether or not one agrees with the Kentucky court's definition of "sectarian," there is no question that this prayer is a "religious" exercise under the establishment clause. If recited in the same setting as the Regents' prayer, it would be invalid, under *Engel* or the proposed constitutional standard, even if the reference to Christ were omitted.

230. See Abbott, *A Common Bible Reader For Public Schools,* 56 RELIGIOUS EDUCATION 20 (1961); Note, 22 ALBANY L. REV. 156–57 (1958). Efforts to find a commonly acceptable prayer for American citizens are not confined to our time; Benjamin Franklin was among those who previously made the attempt. See Engel v. Vitale, 18 Misc. 2d 659, 660–62, 191 N.Y.S.2d 453, 459–60 (Sup. Ct. 1959).

cause conscientious objections to be raised by atheists, agnostics,[231] and humanists,[232] but it also appears that at least one of the three chief faiths would have religious objections.[233] It has been shown that when many of the attempts to distill a "common core" or nonsectarian religion are scrutinized, the product "comes to mean the common core of orthodox Protestant belief, and . . . what a substantial majority—not of all, but of the believing—agree upon."[234] Furthermore, theologians[235] and educators[236] have pointed out that aside from the fact that the task is extraordinarily difficult, even if it were possible, the result would probably be the reduction of theology to triviality and the creation of a public school sect that would be objectionable to all religious faiths. Moreover, it is likely that some people would conscientiously resist participation in any public supplication, regardless of its content.

Second, if it were possible to find that the prayer recitation had some independent primary secular purpose, it then could not be characterized as a solely religious activity and would thus avoid this requisite for unconstitutionality. Several endeavors of this nature have already been found wanting.[237] The assertion that the prayer's purpose would be "to prepare the children for their work, to quiet them from the outside,"[238] should probably also

---

231. See Vishny, *The Constitution and Religion in the Public Schools,* Decalogue J., June-July 1960, pp. 4, 6.

232. See Nichols, *Religion and Education in a Free Society,* in RELIGION IN AMERICA 148, 157 (1958).

233.
> Jews believe . . . that when a faith in God is taught, it must be achieved in the context of historical associations accompanied by religious rites and symbols that are related to that particular religious group. . . . We do not appreciate the vague and undefined God to which the "American religion" offers lip service. We do not want our children to think of God only in abstract terms, nor in Christian terms. . . . This is a task, therefore, only for the home, synagogue or church.

Gilbert, *A Catalogue of Church-State Problems,* 56 RELIGIOUS EDUCATION 424, 428 (1961). See also note 73 *supra.*

234. PFEFFER, CHURCH, STATE AND FREEDOM 308 (1953). See also Comm. on Religion and Education, Am. Council on Education, *Religion in Public Education,* 42 RELIGIOUS EDUCATION 129, 161 (1947), which stated that permitting instruction in a common core religion "would be, at best, to assume that the support of an overwhelming majority of the people justified overriding the convictions of a minority."

235. Nichols, *supra* note 232, at 157–58.

236. American Council on Education, quoted in PFEFFER, *op. cit. supra* note 234, at 308–09.

237. See text accompanying notes 32–42 *supra.*

238. Billard v. Board of Educ., 69 Kan. 53, 58, 76 Pac. 422, 423 (1904) (Lord's Prayer and Twenty-Third Psalm). See also Doremus v. Board of Educ., 7 N.J. Super. 442, 454, 71 A.2d 732, 740 (Super. Ct. 1950).

fail, either because of disingenousness,[239] or because it would seem that if the prayer did produce placidity, it would be due originally to its religious effect.[240]

Third, if the circumstances under which the prayer were to be recited could be so molded as to remove the likelihood that there would be infringement or influencing of any student's religious or conscientious principles, it would be free from challenge despite its solely religious nature. One suggestion toward this end has been that only one student each day be invited to read the prayer while the others simply remain silent.[241] The difficulty with this is that the same social compulsion that operates on students to participate in group recitation would seem to operate here to force a dissenter to take his turn at reading before the class.[242] Even if only the teacher were to recite the prayer, with the students simply listening in silence, the result should probably be the same. It is likely that the conscientious scruples of some students would forbid even this quantum of "participation" in what is clearly a devotional exercise.[243] Therefore, they would be inherently compelled to compromise their scruples. Furthermore, it is most reasonable to believe that the reading of a prayer, each and every day, "buttressed with the authority of the State and, more importantly to children, backed with the authority of their teachers, can hardly do less than inculcate or promote the inculcation of various religious doctrines in childish minds."[244] Educators have

---

239. The proponent of this justification herself conceded that the prayer recitation "was religious to the children that are religious, and to the others it was not." Billard v. Board of Educ., 69 Kan. 53, 58, 76 Pac. 422, 423 (1904). The court, in sustaining the practice did not do so on the ground that the prayer recitation was not a religious activity. Rather, it found that the exercises "were not a form of religious worship or the teaching of sectarian or religious doctrine" as forbidden by the state constitution. *Ibid.*

240. If the mere recitation of *any* reading would accomplish the teacher's goal, then, as indicated in the text, the practice may not be characterized as a solely religious activity and it is not, for that reason, violative of the establishment clause. However, the establishment clause may be violated for another reason. Although the practice would have the immediate secular end of maintaining order, it would also have the immediate effect of promoting religion. Since, by virtue of the above analysis that saves this practice from being a solely religious activity, the secular end *obviously* could be *just as well* attained by means that do not promote religion (*e.g.*, recitation of one of Shakespeare's sonnets), the selection of a reading that furthers religion should be unconstitutional. *Accord,* McGowan v. Maryland, 366 U.S. 420, 466–67 (1961) (Frankfurter, J., separate opinion).

241. See Engel v. Vitale, 11 App. Div. 2d 340, 348–49, 206 N.Y.S.2d 183, 191 (1960) (Beldock, J., separate opinion).

242. This has occurred. See text accompanying note 106 *supra.*

243. See Schempp v. School Dist., 177 F. Supp. 398, 401 (E.D. Pa. 1959).

244. *Id.* at 404. *Cf. The Effects of Segregation and the Consequences of*

expressed the opinion that even a single instance of school approbation of certain religious principles might have this effect.[245] Surely, the daily repetition of devotional exercises will likely result in instilling religious values, thereby affecting the immature students' freedom of conscientious choice.[246] Many students will be influenced to engage more actively in religious endeavors, and the effect of this practice might be to cause pupils of dissenting religious faiths to compromise their scruples.

Several other suggestions merit consideration. One has been "to have each school day commence with a quiet moment that would still the tumult of the playground and start a day of study."[247] Since each student could utilize this moment of silence for any purpose he saw fit, the activity may not be fairly characterized as solely religious, and since no student would really know the subject of his classmates' reflections, no one could in any way be compelled to alter his thoughts. However, the proposal of recitation of the words of a song that invoke or make other hallowed references to the Deity as a replacement for a traditional prayer[248] falls into a different category. Even if the singing of such a song in the public schools were wholly unobjectionable,[249] the recitation of its words as a devotional exercise transforms its entire complexion. This is clearly no more than the designation of an official prayer, irrespective of by whom it is done, and it is invalid for reasons previously mentioned.[250]

Desegregation: A Social Science Statement, 37 MINN. L. REV. 427, 433 (1953):

> The child who, for example, is compelled to attend a segregated school may be able to cope with ordinary expressions of prejudice by regarding the prejudiced person as evil or misguided; but he cannot readily cope with symbols of authority, the full force of the authority of the State—the school or the school board, in this instance—in the same manner.

See also Levy, *Views from the Wall—Reflections on Church-State Relationships,* 29 HENNEPIN LAW. 51, 55 (1961).

245. See Tudor v. Board of Educ., 14 N.J. 31, 51–52, 100 A.2d 857, 868 (1953). *But see* text accompanying notes 524–25 *infra.*

246. *Cf.* Miller v. Cooper, 56 N.M. 355, 244 P.2d 520 (1952), in which the court permitted occasional public school religious activities, but held invalid the continuous availability of religious pamphlets.

247. Editorial, Washington Post, June 28, 1962, § A, p. 22, col. 2. See also N.Y. Times, Aug. 30, 1962, § 1, p. 18, col. 2.

248. See N.Y. Times, July 29, 1962, § 1, p. 36, col. 4; *id.,* Aug. 10, 1962, § 1, p. 21, col. 1; *id.,* Aug. 30, 1962, § 1, p. 18, col. 3.

249. See text accompanying notes 541–44 *infra.*

250. See text accompanying notes 62–66 *supra.*

B. BIBLE READING

Past and present, one of the most prevalent solely religious practices carried on in the public schools has been Bible reading.[251]
Its legality and constitutionality have evoked a glut of litigation
in the state courts and a surfeit of writing by legal and lay commentators. The Supreme Court has managed to elude the problem in the past,[252] but appears finally to be compelled to adjudicate it on the merits.[253] By any reasonable test, this practice
should be unconstitutional.[254]

The prime reason advanced by many state courts for sustaining
the practice is that since the Bible is a nonsectarian document,
no single religious sect benefits from its use.[255] This factor is
crucial under many state constitutional provisions that prohibit
"sectarian" teaching in the public schools.[256] However, it is irrelevant as far as the first amendment is concerned since, under
the *Everson* dictum, "state action violates the ban . . . if it aids
all religions on a nonpreferential basis."[257] Under the proposed
constitutional standard, the question of whether the Bible is sectarian is likewise inconsequential. This solely religious practice
would be invalid so long as it is likely to cause any student, even
if he belongs to no religious sect, to have his conscientious convictions influenced or compromised.[258]

However, it should be made plain that no version of the Bible
may be fairly characterized as nonsectarian, even in the sense that
none of the *major* religious faiths find it unobjectionable. The
earliest challenges to Bible reading in the American public schools
were leveled by members of the Roman Catholic faith, who con-

---

251. A recent survey estimates that 42% of American public schools
have daily Bible reading. Geographically, the breakdown is: East—68%;
South—77%; Midwest—18%; West—11%. Dierenfield, *The Extent of
Religious Influence in American Public Schools,* 56 RELIGIOUS EDUCATION
173, 176 (1961).

252. See School Dist. v. Schempp, 364 U.S. 298 (1960); Doremus v.
Board of Educ., 342 U.S. 429 (1952).

253. See note 3 *supra.* The Court had little choice but to hear the
Schempp case since it was appealable as a matter of right under § 1253
of the Judicial Code, and the three-judge court below had found that
public school Bible reading was contrary to the establishment clause.

254. See text accompanying notes 60–64 *supra.*

255. See *e.g.,* People *ex rel.* Vollmar v. Stanley, 81 Colo. 276, 255 Pac.
610 (1927); Commonwealth v. Cooke, 7 Am. L. Reg. (o.s.) 417 (Mass.
Police Ct. 1859); Doremus v. Board of Educ., 5 N.J. 435, 75 A.2d 880
(1950); State *ex rel.* Weiss v. District Bd., 76 Wis. 177, 44 N.W. 967
(1890).

256. See cases cited in note 255 *supra;* PFEFFER, CHURCH, STATE AND
FREEDOM 387 (1953).

257. *Id.* at 391.

258. For examples, see text accompanying notes 105–07 *supra.*

scientiously objected to the use of the King James version.[259] Although there has been some indication that this position is in a state of flux,[260] recent litigation has again been undertaken by Catholic parents.[261] Unitarians,[262] members of the Jewish faith,[263] Buddhists,[264] and atheists[265] have all asserted in the courts that public school Bible reading offends their religious and conscientious beliefs. Universalists and some Lutherans and Baptists also oppose the activity.[266]

A number of state courts, although a minority, have recognized the fact that no version of the Bible is acceptable to everyone.[267] Theologians of all faiths encounter no difficulty in arriving at this conclusion.[268] The Roman Catholic religion finds only the Douay version of the Bible acceptable;[269] despite an assertion to the contrary,[270] "a Catholic child commits a grave sin if he knowingly owns or reads from the Protestant version of the Bible."[271] Very recently, Catholic parents protested a New Jersey community's requirement that their children *listen* to readings from a King James Bible.[272] The Roman Catholic position has

---

259. See *e.g.*, Donahoe v. Richards, 38 Me. 379 (1854); Commonwealth v. Cooke, 7 Am. L. Reg. (o.s.) 417 (Mass. Police Ct. 1859); Nessle v. Hum, 1 Ohio N.P. 140 (C.P. 1894); Hart v. School Dist., 2 Lancaster L. Rev. 346 (Pa. C.P. 1885). See also Boyer, *Religious Education of Public School Pupils in Wisconsin,* 1953 WIS. L. REV. 181.

260. See Reed, *Another Tradition at Stake,* Catholic Action, Feb., 1950, p. 4.

261. *E.g.,* Tudor v. Board of Educ., 14 N.J. 31, 100 A.2d 857 (1953).

262. Schempp v. School Dist., 177 F. Supp. 398 (E.D. Pa. 1959).

263. Herold v. Parish Bd. of School Directors, 136 La. 1034, 68 So. 116 (1915); Church v. Bullock, 100 S.W. 1025 (Tex. Civ. App. 1907).

264. Commonwealth v. Renfrew, 332 Mass. 492, 126 N.E.2d 109 (1955).

265. Murray v. Curlett, 228 Md. 239, 179 A.2d 698 (1962).

266. 2 STOKES, CHURCH AND STATE IN THE UNITED STATES 571 (1950).

267. *E.g.,* Evans v. Selma Union High School Dist., 193 Cal. 54, 222 Pac. 801 (1924); Wilkerson v. City of Rome, 152 Ga. 762, 110 S.E. 895 (1922); People *ex rel.* Ring v. Board of Educ., 245 Ill. 334, 92 N.E. 251 (1910); State *ex rel.* Freeman v. Scheve, 65 Neb. 853, 91 N.W. 846 (1900).

268. See Schempp v. School Dist., 177 F. Supp. 398, 401–02 (E.D. Pa. 1959); Tudor v. Board of Educ., 14 N.J. 31, 46–47, 100 A.2d 857, 865 (1953); Harpster, *Religion, Education and the Law,* 36 MARQ. L. REV. 24, 44 (1952).

269. People *ex rel.* Ring v. Board of Educ., 245 Ill. 334, 343–45, 92 N.E. 251, 254 (1910); State *ex rel.* Dearle v. Frazier, 102 Wash. 369, 383, 173 Pac. 35, 39 (1918).

270. See Herold v. Parish Bd. of School Directors, 136 La. 1034, 1040, 68 So. 116, 118 (1915).

271. PFEFFER, *op. cit. supra* note 256, at 384. See also authorities cited in Rosenfield, *Separation of Church and State in the Public Schools,* 22 U. PITT. L. REV. 561, 571 n.49 (1961).

272. Pfeffer & Baum, Public School Sectarianism and the Jewish Child 31 (American Jewish Congress, May, 1957). Roman Catholics "are forbidden . . . to listen to any version of [the Bible] unauthorized by the

been that the King James version is filled with error and false explanations and is used "as an instrument of proselytism."[273] The Protestant stand regarding the Douay translation of the Bible is similar in many respects to the Roman Catholic feeling about the King James version.[274]

The Jewish faith finds the New Testament, whether it be the Douay or King James version, incompatible with Hebrew teachings.[275] Of course, nonbelievers find the dogmatism of every version of the Bible as an imposition on their conscientious scruples.[276] Nonetheless, the argument has been made that the Old Testament is generally immune from objection.[277] Even discounting those minor religious groups that "in this country . . . are numerically small and, in point of impact upon our national life, negligible,"[278] this argument is far from being accurate. Unitarians have testified that much of the Old Testament's content is contrary to their faith.[279] A Jewish theologian has pointed out that there were specific instances in which the King James Old Testament had been

---

Roman Catholic Church." CATHOLIC ENCYCLOPEDIA 524, cited in Tyree, *Should What Is Rendered To God Be Commanded By Caesar?*, 44 PHI DELTA KAPPAN 74, 76 (1962).

273. Encyclicals of the Popes, quoted in Brief for Plaintiffs, p. 24, Schempp v. School Dist., 177 F. Supp. 398 (E.D. Pa. 1959). See PFEFFER, *op. cit. supra* note 256, at 384:

[T]he translators' dedicatory preface [to the King James version] states that the purpose of the translation was to give 'such a blow unto that Man of Sin (the Pope) as will not be healed [and] to make God's holy truth to be yet more and more known to the people whom they ("Papist persons at home or abroad") desire still to be kept in ignorance.'

274. See People *ex rel.* Ring v. Board of Educ., 245 Ill. 334, 344–45, 92 N.E. 251, 254 (1910); Tudor v. Board of Educ., 14 N.J. 31, 47, 100 A.2d 857, 865 (1953).

275. See Kaplan v. Independent School Dist., 171 Minn. 142, 154–55, 214 N.W. 18, 22–23 (1927) (dissenting opinion); Comment, 43 ILL. L. REV. 374, 382 (1948); 27 TEXAS L. REV. 256, 258 (1948).

276. See Comment, 43 ILL. L. REV. 374, 382 (1948).

277. Doremus v. Board of Educ., 5 N.J. 435, 448, 75 A.2d 880, 886 (1950).

278. *Id.* at 449, 75 A.2d at 887.

279.

In content, the father objected to material in the Old Testament regarding blood sacrifices, uncleanness, and leprosy, together with the whole concept of the Old Testament God which was contrary to the concept of deity which he endeavored to instill in his children. He testified that he did not want his children to acquire an image of Jehovah, the God of vengeance. He pointed out that in the very midst of the Ten Commandments was a verse asserting that God would visit the sins of the father upon the fourth generation . . . and the witness went on to assert that this concept of God was in sharp contrast with the God of his own church . . . .

Brief for Plaintiffs, pp. 5–6, Schempp v. School Dist., 177 F. Supp. 398 (E.D. Pa. 1959).

imbued with a Christological significance.[280] Clearly, there is no "English text of the Old Testament accepted fully by the several faiths."[281]

Recognizing this inherent weakness of any complete version of the Bible, it has been suggested that the defect may be remedied by selecting those portions in any version that are in no way religious, but contain only moral principles that are common to *all* men.[282] If this could be done, the practice would be valid under the proposed standard. Not only could it not be fairly characterized as solely religious, but no one's conscientious beliefs could possibly be affected. The difficulty is that those who have advocated this course have concluded, somewhat contradictorily, that there is no one competent to select these portions.[283] Even if it be assumed that such Biblical passages may exist, until there is at least a general consensus as to which ones they are, the establishment clause should forbid any individual or group from choosing some and causing them to be read in the public schools. If this were permitted, for reasons previously advanced,[284] it is very likely that infractions of religious liberty would occur and go unredressed.

Other attempts have been made to justify the constitutionality of public school Bible reading. They also fail on examination. Several state courts have excused the practice on the ground that dissenters are afforded the right of nonparticipation.[285] The inadequacy and fictitiousness of this position have already been belabored.[286] Others have attempted to validate the practice because

---

280. Dr. Solomon Grayzel, cited *id.* at p. 10.

281. Committee on Religion and Public Education of the National Council of the Churches of Christ, *Relation of Religion to Public Education —A Study Document,* International J. of Religious Education, Apr. 1960, pp. 21, 28.

282. See People *ex rel.* Vollmar v. Stanley, 81 Colo. 276, 286–93, 255 Pac. 610, 615–17 (1927); Harpster, *supra* note 268, at 45.

283. *Ibid.* See also Comment, 43 ILL. L. REV. 374, 382 (1948): "However carefully selections for reading may be chosen it is inevitable that some students will be forced to listen to portions which they cannot accept."

284. See text accompanying notes 219–24 *supra.*

285. *E.g.,* People *ex rel.* Vollmar v. Stanley, 81 Colo. 276, 293, 255 Pac. 610, 617 (1927); Chamberlin v. Dade County Bd. of Pub. Instruction, 143 So. 2d 21, 31 (Fla. Sup. Ct. 1962); Pfeiffer v. Board of Educ., 118 Mich. 560, 562–63, 77 N.W. 250, 251 (1898); Kaplan v. Independent School Dist., 171 Minn. 142, 151, 214 N.W. 18, 21 (1927).

286. The consistency of holding, on the one hand, that the Bible is nonsectarian and then holding, on the other hand, that it is saved from religious liberty objection because of the right of nonparticipation has long been questioned. See People *ex rel.* Ring v. Board of Educ., 245 Ill. 334, 351, 92 N.E. 251, 256 (1910); Note, 3 RUTGERS L. REV. 115, 125 (1949). This

it does not transform the public school into a " place of worship."[287] While this contention may satisfy some state constitutional prerequisites, it has no bearing vis-a-vis the establishment clause.

A provision that the reading of the Bible be done without comment has often been submitted as a sustaining feature.[288] This argument ignores the fact that to some sects, "the reading in public of any portion of any version of the Scriptures unaccompanied by authoritative comment or explanation, or the reading of it privately by persons not commissioned by the church to do so, is objectionable, and an offense to their religious feelings . . . ."[289] In addition, since other readings in the curriculum are subjected to critical comment and scrutiny, there is reasonable likelihood that the practice of reading the Bible without discerning comment "will tend to the acceptance by those pupils of the statements in the selections as true."[290] Finally, the daily repetition of this activity, in some schools for a substantial segment of time,[291] under the sponsorship of school and teacher will surely have its effect[292] even if done without comment.[293] These points also

---

dilemma would be solved only if Bible reading could be characterized as a secular activity. See text accompanying notes 117–25 *supra.* It is clear that this may not be done.

287. *E.g.,* Moore v. Monroe, 64 Iowa 367, 20 N.W. 475 (1884); Hackett v. Brooksville Graded School Dist., 120 Ky. 608, 87 S.W. 792 (1905).

288. *E.g.,* Carden v. Bland, 199 Tenn. 665, 288 S.W.2d 718 (1956).

289. State *ex rel.* Freeman v. Scheve, 65 Neb. 853, 871, 91 N.W. 846, 847 (1902). For further documentation of this in regard to the Roman Catholic position, see note 272 *supra;* Brief for Plaintiffs, p. 25, Schempp v. School Dist., 177 F. Supp. 398 (E.D. Pa. 1959).

290. Pfeiffer v. Board of Educ., 118 Mich. 560, 578, 77 N.W. 250, 257 (1898) (dissenting opinion). Of interest also is the following statement in State *ex rel.* Weiss v. District Bd., 76 Wis. 177, 194–95, 44 N.W. 967, 973 (1890):

A most forcible demonstration . . . is found in certain reports of the American Bible Society of its work in Catholic countries . . . in which instances are given of the conversion of several persons from 'Romanism' through the reading of the scriptures alone; that is to say, the reading of the Protestant or King James version of the Bible converted Catholics to Protestants without the aid of comment or exposition.

291. In Chamberlin v. Dade County Bd. of Pub. Instruction, 143 So. 2d 21, 31 (Fla. Sup. Ct. 1962), the court noted that Bible reading consumed from three to five minutes each day.

292. Dean Weigle has written that "the message of the Bible is the central thing . . . . The Bible contains the Word of God to man." Quoted in Brief for Plaintiffs, p. 14, Schempp v. School Dist., 177 F. Supp. 398 (E.D. Pa. 1959).

293. Notice again the inconsistency between finding the Bible to be nonsectarian and, at the same time, finding no infringement of religious liberty only because it is read without comment. See note 286 *supra;* Note, 28 GEO. WASH. L. REV. 579, 611 (1960).

overcome the defenses occasionally asserted that the mere reading of the Bible denotes no implication as to the truth or falsity of the subject matter and that merely listening to it compels no student to *believe* in what he has heard.[294]

1. *Teaching of Moral Values*

The argument is frequently made that Bible reading, religious study, and other devotional exercises in the public schools are indispensable to teaching students moral values and qualities, and that this is a vital function of our public schools in teaching good citizenship and in combating "Godless Communism."[295] If this means that the only available method for inculcating students with these values is first to imbue them with religious ideals, then regardless of how important this may be, the establishment clause should forbid the training.[296]

However, the prospects for the public schools' producing good citizens are not quite so bleak. There is ample evidence that religion in general education is unnecessary to produce better child behavior;[297] moral values may be very effectively taught without the aid of religion.[298] "However we [citizens of the American democracy] may disagree on religious creeds, we can agree on moral and spiritual values."[299] Educators and philosophers have shown[300] that such universally accepted values as justice, property rights, respect for law and authority, and brotherhood[301] may be derived from nonreligious sources[302] and may be enforced

---

294. *E.g.,* Donahoe v. Richards, 38 Me. 379, 399 (1854). See also Spiller v. Inhabitants of Woburn, 12 Allen 127 (Mass. 1866).

295. See, *e.g.,* Taylor, *Equal Protection of Religion: Today's Public School Problem,* 38 A.B.A.J. 277, 339 (1952). See also Hart v. School Dist., 2 Lancaster L. Rev. 346, 352 (C.P. 1885).

296. See text accompanying notes 38–42 *supra.*

297. Seminar No. 4, *The Public School and Religious Education,* 49 RELIGIOUS EDUCATION 143, 144–45 (1954).

298. EDUCATIONAL POLICIES COMM'N, NATIONAL EDUCATION ASS'N, MORAL AND SPIRITUAL VALUES IN THE PUBLIC SCHOOLS 17–30 (1951).

299. *Id.* at 33.

300. *Id.* at 37–45.

301. The public school teaches brotherhood as part of the democratic ideal. The churches teach it as a response to God's commandment to love one's neighbor. The secular humanist practices it as an expression of a purely human value. Comm. on Religion and Public Education of the National Council of the Churches of Christ, *Relation of Religion to Public Education—A Study Document,* International J. of Religious Education, Apr. 1960, pp. 21, 25.

302. "After all, if Aristotle, 350 years before the advent of Christianity, could write a rather comprehensive and enduring work on ethics, I do not see why it should be so difficult for modern American secularists of good will to do likewise." Address by F. E. Flynn, Professor of Philosophy, Col-

by nonreligious sanctions.[303] In fact, there is persuasive authority for the view that moral values are better learned through concrete examples during the school day than through lessons that preach them.[304]

Other generally recognized values, "in the sense that they are common to all segments of our society, irrespective of religious faith or philosophic school,"[305] are "responsibility, honesty, temperance, and self-control."[306] Thus, while the Illinois legislature demands that "every public school teacher shall teach the pupils honesty, kindness, justice and moral courage for the purpose of lessening crime and raising the standard of good citizenship,"[307] it recognizes that this aim may be accomplished on a neutral basis by making clear that the statute "shall not be construed as requiring religious or sectarian teaching."[308] Similarly, New York prescribes courses in "partriotism and citizenship," but implies that this goal may be attained by "instruction in the history, meaning, significance and effect of the provisions of the constitution of the United States, [and of the state of New York], the amendments thereto, [and] the declaration of independence."[309] Surely it may. While teachers should educate their students about the fact that most of our citizens believe that there are various religious sources and sanctions for our moral values,[310] they can successfully instill commonly cherished values without engaging in religious indoctrination.

Although one writer, in his intellectual struggle to validate Bible reading, went so far as to concede that the machinations

---

lege of St. Thomas, to the West St. Paul Federation of Teachers, Sept. 20, 1962.

303. "[T]he [ancient] Greeks are an excellent illustration of a people whose principles of conduct were independent of religious sanction . . . . Buddhism is primarily, if not entirely, a system of ethics; one of conduct, without the inducements of rewards and punishments characteristic of Western religions." THAYER, THE ATTACK UPON THE AMERICAN SECULAR SCHOOL 205–06 (1951). See also THAYER, THE CHALLENGE OF THE PRESENT TO PUBLIC EDUCATION 14–16 (1958).

304. See EDUCATIONAL POLICIES COMM'N, *op. cit. supra* note 298, at 60–70; HARTFORD, MORAL VALUES IN PUBLIC EDUCATION *passim* (1958); THAYER, THE ATTACK UPON THE AMERICAN SECULAR SCHOOL 212–18 (1951).

305. *Id.* at 210.

306. *Ibid.*

307. ILL. REV. STAT. ch. 122, § 27–12 (1961).

308. ILL. REV. STAT. ch. 122, § 27–16 (1961).

309. N.Y. EDUC. LAW § 801.

310. See Nichols, *Religion and Education in a Free Society* in RELIGION IN AMERICA 148, 157 (Cogley ed. 1958). *Cf.* Rosenfield, *Separation of Church and State in the Public Schools*, 22 U. PITT. L. REV. 561, 577–78 (1961).

of his proposal were "contrary to reason,"[311] all others seem to have recognized that there are some religious objections to every version of the Bible.[312] When it is read as part of a devotional exercise, the activity must be fairly characterized as solely religious.[313] While teachers no longer beat dissenting students,[314] the fact is that there is an inherent compulsion to participate, and therefore, conscientious scruples are influenced and compromised. The practice should be held to violate the establishment clause.

2. *Academic Study of Religion*

One last area of discussion concerning the place of the Bible in the public schools must be considered. The suggestion has frequently been made that the Bible (and religion generally) is a vital educational tool. If this means "that the highest duty of those who are charged with the responsibility of training the young people . . . in the public schools is in teaching both by precept and example that in the conflicts of life they should not forget God,"[315] then it must be rejected under any reasonable standard. Aside from the fact that this is educationally unacceptable,[316] the Court has made clear that the establishment clause forbids governmental indoctrination of religious beliefs and public school religious instruction.[317] Under the proposed constitutional standard, this effort to inculcate religious beliefs would unquestionably be a solely religious activity likely to influence and compromise the students' freedom of conscientious choice. However, it is totally inaccurate to conclude, as many have done, that this rejection "sanctions [the public schools'] utilization for the purposes of atheists."[318] This would be correct only if the public schools were

---

311. Harpster, *supra* note 268, at 46.

312. *E.g.*, Kauper, *Church, State, and Freedom: A Review*, 52 MICH. L. REV. 829, 842 (1954); Note, 22 ALBANY L. REV. 156, 172 (1958).

313. See Murray v. Curlett, 228 Md. 239, —, 179 A.2d 698, 708 (1962) (dissenting opinion).

314. See Commonwealth v. Cooke, 7 Am. L. Reg. (o.s.) 417 (Mass. Police Ct. 1859).

315. Carden v. Bland, 199 Tenn. 665, 681, 288 S.W.2d 718, 725 (1956). See also Church v. Bullock, 100 S.W. 1025, 1027 (Tex. Civ. App. 1907): "It may be said that said exercises tended to teach that there was an Almighty God; but this cannot be held objectionable . . . ."

316. American public education "disapproves indoctrination with reference to matters of belief." Comm. on Religion and Education, Am. Council on Education, *Religion in Public Education*, 42 RELIGIOUS EDUCATION 129, 161 (1947).

317. Zorach v. Clauson, 343 U.S. 306, 314 (1952).

318. Schmidt, *Religious Liberty and the Supreme Court of the United States*, 17 FORDHAM L. REV. 173, 185 (1948).

either constitutionally permitted or forced to teach that there is *no* God. Obviously, the first amendment forbids this just as much as it forbids exhortations to the contrary. The result, therefore, is one of true neutrality.

It is also error to deduce that this rejection demands "that the child has a 'legal duty' to put all this time in on secular subjects, none on religious subjects";[319] that it results in "the *compulsory exclusion of any religious element* and the consequent promotion and advancement of atheism";[320] that it "surrender[s] these schools to the sectarianism of atheism or irreligion";[321] that it bans all study of God as connected with our principles of government;[322] or that it compels silence about the Bible, religion, and God, thus impressing school children that these matters are insignificant.[323] It can hardly be denied that "we are a religious people whose institutions presuppose a Supreme Being"[324] since it is a matter of "common notoriety"[325] that the great majority of our citizens are religious in the sense that they do believe in God.[326] Although there is some dispute concerning the percentage of our population that is affiliated with organized religious groups,[327] the most recent government survey showed that less than three percent of all persons over the age of 14 reported that they had no religion whatever;[328] almost 95 percent of the population considered themselves to be either Protestant, Roman Catholic, or Jewish.[329] Nor can it be denied that "acknowledgement of a Supreme Being has . . . been a part of our history."[330]

---

319. Murray, *Law or Prepossessions?*, 14 LAW & CONTEMP. PROB. 23, 36 (1949).

320. Engel v. Vitale, 10 N.Y.2d 174, 184, 176 N.E.2d 579, 583 (1961) (Burke, J., concurring opinion).

321. Luther A. Weigle, formerly Dean of Yale Divinity School, quoted in PFEFFER, CHURCH, STATE, AND FREEDOM 291 (1953).

322. Brief for Intervenors-Respondents, pp. 55–56, Engel v. Vitale, 370 U.S. 421 (1962).

323. Schmidt, *supra* note 318, at 187–88. See also PARSONS, WHICH WAY, DEMOCRACY? 11 (1939).

324. Zorach v. Clauson, 343 U.S. 306, 313 (1952).

325. *Cf.* Black, *The Lawfulness of the Segregation Decisions*, 69 YALE L.J. 421, 426 (1960).

326. PFEFFER, *op. cit. supra* note 321, at 289, has acknowledged that "we are a religious people even though our government is secular."

327. Pfeffer contends that the figure is only about 50%. *Id.* at 303. This must be compared with the fact that the various religious bodies claim church membership in 1960 of 64% of the total population. BUREAU OF CENSUS, U.S. DEP'T OF COMMERCE, STATISTICAL ABSTRACT OF THE UNITED STATES 48 (83d ed. 1962).

328. *Id.* at 46.

329. *Ibid.* Query as to how many of these felt "compelled" to make such a disclosure.

330. VIRGINIA COMMISSION ON CONSTITUTIONAL GOVERNMENT, THE NEW YORK PRAYER CASE 4 (1962).

While there is some dispute as to how religious the founding fathers were,[331] the heritage of this country, both in the past and at present, is replete with examples of theistic and religious influences too multitudinous to enumerate fully.[332]

These being the facts, not only would it be virtually impossible, as a practical matter, to obliterate all references to religion from the public schools, but it would be educationally undesirable.[333] But a public school program that seeks to prevent children from growing up as religious illiterates may not be fairly characterized as a solely religious activity. There is a distinct and weighty public purpose in seeing that all school children comprehend the role that religion has played in this country's evolution[334] and that they have some understanding of the nature of the conscientious beliefs possessed by most of our citizens. Under the proposed constitutional standard there would be no constitutional objection[335] to an academic study in comparative religion[336] or to

---

331. See Pfeffer, *Church and State: Something Less Than Separation,* 19 U. CHI. L. REV. 1, 19–20 (1951).

332. A partial list might include the fact that the Declaration of Independence refers to the Deity four times; that the constitutions of 49 states acknowledge the existence of God and many imply that the rights and liberties of the people issue from God and express gratefulness therefore. See Brief for Respondents, pp. 44–54, Engel v. Vitale, 370 U.S. 421 (1962). "In God We Trust" has been impressed on our coins since 1865. In 1956, Congress adopted these words as our national motto. Lincoln's Gettysburg Address referred to God, as did the Mayflower Compact of 1620 and Madison's famous Memorial and Remonstrance Against Religious Assessments. Such national monuments as the Tomb of the Unknown Soldier, the Washington Monument, and the Lincoln and Jefferson Memorials all contain inscriptions mentioning the Deity. The Northwest Ordinance of 1787 stated that religion was necessary to good government. All of our Presidents have asked for the protection or help of God on assuming office. See Engel v. Vitale, 370 U.S. 421, 446–49 (1962) (Stewart, J., dissenting).

333. See the views expressed at a seminar of educators in Seminar No. 4, *The Public School and Religious Education,* 49 RELIGIOUS EDUCATION 143, 144–45 (1954); Cosway & Toepfer, *Religion and the Schools,* 17 U. CINC. L. REV. 117, 142 (1948). "An educated person cannot be religiously illiterate." Comm. on Religion and Education, Am. Council on Education, *supra* note 316, at 160.

334. "A course in the history of California which did not describe the early Catholic missions is unthinkable." 25 CAL. OPS. ATT'Y GEN. 325 (1955). This same report found prayers and Bible reading in the public schools to be contrary to the first amendment.

335. *But see* text acompanying notes 347–48 *infra.*

336. *Accord, e.g.,* PFEFFER, *op. cit. supra* note 321, at 309. Sutherland, *Public Authority and Religious Education,—A Brief Survey of Constitutional and Legal Limits,* 52 RELIGIOUS EDUCATION 256 (1957); Vishny, *The Constitution and Religion in the Public Schools,* 10 Decalogue J. June-July 1960, pp. 4, 6. *But see* Rosenfield, *Separation of Church and State in the Public Schools,* 22 U. PITT. L. REV. 561, 578 (1961).

the study of the Bible as an artistic work.[337] The salient distinction is that this would be teaching objectively *about* religion and the Bible and would not be religious indoctrination.

The academic study of religion may not take the form of teaching "that religion is sacred"[338] nor present religious dogma as factual material.[339] The only purpose for this approach is to inculcate religious beliefs. Nor may daily devotional Bible reading exercises with the privilege of nonparticipation be validated merely by characterizing them as an "elective course in non-sectarian Bible study."[340] The difference between a devotional exercise and an ordinary literature course that examines the Bible, attempting no indoctrination and therefore not exerting pressure on students, is the difference between a solely religious program that is likely to result in the influencing or compromising of students' conscientious scruples and a secular act by government that is within its power.

It is not easy to deny, at least where younger children are concerned, that even an objectively presented academic examination of the Bible, or of religion generally, will result in some indoctrination.[341] But to concede that there is much truth in the contention that "the young mind cannot grasp the nebulous distinction between the Bible as literature and the Bible as sectarian instruction"[342] is not automatically to invalidate a school board's good faith attempt[343] to educate students with "much useful information about the religious faiths, the important part they have played in establishing the moral and spiritual values of American life,

---

337. See Schempp v. School Dist., 177 F. Supp. 398, 404 (E.D. Pa. 1959); 25 CAL. OPS. ATT'Y GEN. 325 (1955).

338. Such was the announced purpose of a program adopted, in the name of academic study of religion, by the Denver school system for "intergroup education." Herberg, *Religion, Democracy, and Public Education*, in RELIGION IN AMERICA 118, 136 (Cogley ed. 1958).

339. See Emerson & Haber, *The Scopes Case in Modern Dress*, 27 U. CHI. L. REV. 522, 523–24 (1960).

340. This was suggested in Creel, *Is It Legal for the Public Schools of Alabama to Provide an Elective Course in Non-Sectarian Bible Instruction?*, 10 ALA. LAW. 86, 94 (1949).

341. PFEFFER, *op. cit. supra* note 321, at 311; Sutherland, *supra* note 336; Vishny, *supra* note 336.

342. Cosway & Toepfer, *supra* note 333, at 137.

343. The problem of dealing with an unconstitutional legislative "motive" of this kind is a vexing one. See Emerson & Haber, *supra* note 339, at 524. However, it is far from insuperable. See, *e.g.*, Gomillion v. Lightfoot, 364 U.S. 339 (1960); Lane v. Wilson, 307 U.S. 268 (1939); Guinn v. United States, 238 U.S. 347 (1915). See generally Israel, *On Charting A Course Through The Mathematical Quagmire: The Future of Baker v. Carr*, 61 MICH. L. REV.107, 140 n.138 (1962).

and their role in the story of mankind."[344] No doubt, indoctrination often results from academic pursuits. Therefore, although the wisdom of reserving this inquiry to the higher grades may be decided by local authorities,[345] it would not seem to be a proper question for the Supreme Court.[346]

However, despite the fact that the activity is secular and thus immunized from the proposed constitutional standard, it may still be in violation of the establishment clause. The thesis suggested is that when a secular activity by government results not only in attainment of a civil objective, but also promotes religion, the establishment clause is violated if the civil goal may be accomplished *just as well* by means that do not promote religion.[347] Thus, it may be argued that the establishment clause demands that the objective study of religion or the Bible be confined to those higher grades where the influencing or compromising of religious beliefs would not occur because the audience is adult enough to distinguish between indoctrination and academic discussion.[348] The contention would be quite convincing if it could be shown that, by so doing, the state's secular objective of making students religiously literate could be just as effectively achieved.

The Roman Catholic church has voiced strong opposition to allowing its children, at any age, to participate in academic courses in religion.[349] It has also been observed that "the objective teaching of religion is likely to be unacceptable to most churches."[350] In the first analysis, this becomes only one factor to be considered in making the legislative choice. If, however, some religious sect demands that its members do not participate in this instruction as a matter of religious dogma, the question becomes

---

344. EDUCATIONAL POLICIES COMM'N, NATIONAL EDUCATIONAL ASS'N, MORAL AND SPIRITUAL VALUES IN THE PUBLIC SCHOOLS 78 (1951).
345.
The unity of our own country, our understanding of the other nations of the world, and respect for the rich religious traditions of all humanity would be enhanced by instruction about religion in the public schools. Like any other teaching in which deep personal emotions are involved, such instruction should, of course, give due consideration to the varying degrees of maturity of the students.
Id. at 78–79.
346. *Cf.* Braunfeld v. Brown, 366 U.S. 599, 608 (1961). See generally Sutherland, *Public Authority and Religious Education: A Brief Survey of Constitutional and Legal Limits,* in THE STUDY OF RELIGION IN THE PUBLIC SCHOOLS: AN APPRAISAL 67 (Brown ed. 1958).
347. See note 240 *supra.*
348. *Cf.* Kalven, *A Commemorative Case Note, Scopes v. State,* 27 U. CHI. L. REV. 505, 518 (1960). *But cf.* Comment, 32 MARQ. L. REV. 138, 144 (1948).
349. See PFEFFER, *op. cit. supra* note 321, at 310.
350. *Ibid.*

one of whether the free exercise clause is violated by compelling attendance in these courses. Here, as elsewhere,[351] a difficult and delicate free exercise problem is raised when there is a direct conflict between a religious tenet and action compelled by the state—that is, when the state, in pursuit of a secular purpose demands on pain of criminal prosecution that a person compromise his religious scruples.[352] The Supreme Court has not clearly articulated any principle to govern these situations,[353] and the issue is beyond the scope of this article.[354] What should be made plain, however, is that regardless of whether participation in the program may be made mandatory under the free exercise clause, the state is engaging in a secular activity when it introduces the academic study of religion into the public schools. Therefore, with one possible reservation,[355] the establishment clause is not in issue and religious objections to the activity may not result in its abolition.[356]

No doubt there are practical difficulties in administering a program of teaching *about* religion. It may be argued that instructors, who are themselves affiliated with a particular sect, cannot or will not objectively present all points of view;[357] the result, especially

---

351. See text accompanying notes 118–22 *supra*.

352. See Braunfeld v. Brown, 366 U.S. 599, 605 (1961); Prince v. Massachusetts, 321 U.S. 158, 165 (1944).

353. Cases presenting the problem are Prince v. Massachusetts, 321 U.S. 158 (1944); West Virginia State Bd. of Educ. v. Barnette, 319 U.S. 624 (1943); Reynolds v. United States, 98 U.S. 145 (1878).

354. The Court has stated that "legislative power . . . may reach people's actions when they are found to be in violation of important social duties or subversive of good order, even when the actions are demanded by one's religion." Braunfeld v. Brown, 366 U.S. 599, 603–04 (1961) (dictum). If this be the standard, the question of whether the state may demand a religious dissenter to attend classes in the objective study of religion turns on whether the Court feels that any student's failure to attend would be "in violation of important social duties or subversive of good order."
On the other hand, the Court has also noted the importance of whether the religious freedom asserted by the dissenter brings him "into collision with rights asserted by any other individual." West Virginia State Bd. of Educ. v. Barnette, 319 U.S. 624, 630 (1943). It is fairly plain that by absenting themselves from classes engaged in studying about religion, the objectors would not be directly affecting anyone else. Thus, it could be argued that their free exercise claim should be upheld. However, in Reynolds v. United States, 98 U.S. 145 (1878), the Court upheld the conviction of a Mormon polygamist who defended on the ground that the tenets of his church demanded that he practice polygamy. Here it would seem that the defendant's action affected only those persons who volunteered to be affected. For general discussion of this problem, see LOCKHART, KAMISAR & CHOPER, SUPPLEMENT TO DODD'S CASES ON CONSTITUTIONAL LAW 400–01 (1962).

355. See text accompanying notes 347–48 *supra*.

356. See text accompanying notes 117–25 *supra*.

357. See Margolin, Book Review, 72 YALE L.J. 212, 214 (1962).

as far as the younger children are concerned, will be indoctrination at least as powerful as that obtained by a solely religious activity. If the secular purposes of a program of the academic study of religion were inherently subject to abuse, then the only remedy might be to ban the activity.[358] But the alleged defect appears not to be inherent. Educators have stated that "the public school can teach objectively *about* religion without advocating or teaching any religious creed."[359] Theologians "believe that the teachers of the American public school system are, on the whole, qualified to maintain free discussion with genuine respect for religious perspectives."[360] The remedy for teacher abuse is to enjoin it or to get another teacher; it is not to outlaw the program.[361]

Another objection leveled at the academic study of religion in the public schools is that since it is, by its nature, highly controversial, it is likely to engender serious antagonisms among students of the different religious faiths. Instances of this have been recorded.[362] It has been suggested that this matter of "divisiveness" should determine the constitutionality of governmental programs in the religious area.[363] This seems to be neither a desirable nor workable approach to the problem. While this matter is unquestionably relevant to the legislative decision, once a genuinely secular-based program is enacted, it is difficult to see why it should be threatened with preordained abolition under the establishment clause either because some religious group finds it objectionable or because the sensibilities of some students will be offend-

---

358. See Note, 52 COLUM. L. REV. 1033, 1038 (1952); Note, 61 YALE L.J. 412–13 (1952).

359. EDUCATIONAL POLICIES COMM'N, NATIONAL EDUCATIONAL ASS'N, MORAL AND SPIRITUAL VALUES IN THE PUBLIC SCHOOL 77 (1951).
    That religious beliefs are controversial is not an adequate reason for excluding teaching about religion from the public schools. Economic and social questions are taught and studied in the schools on the very sensible theory that students need to know the issues being faced and to get practice in forming sound judgments. Teaching about religion should be approached in the same spirit. General guides on the teaching of all controversial issues may be helpful. If need be, teachers should be provided with special help and information to equip them to teach objectively in this area.
Id. at 78.

360. Nichols, *Religion and Education in a Free Society,* in RELIGION IN AMERICA 148, 159 (Cogley ed. 1958).

361. See Lieberman, *A General Interpretation of Separation of Church and State and Its Implications for Public Education,* 33 PROGRESSIVE EDUCATION 129, 134 (1956); Note, 52 COLUM. L. REV. 1033, 1038 (1952).

362. PFEFFER & BAUM, PUBLIC SCHOOL SECTARIANISM AND THE JEWISH CHILD 34, 37 (1957).

363. See Engel v. Vitale, 370 U.S. 421, 443 (1962) (Douglas, J., concurring opinion). See note 188 *supra*.

ed. If the governmental activity were a solely religious one that would likely result in the influencing or compromising of religious beliefs, the question should be answered differently, as has been maintained throughout this article. But many secular educational programs create dissention and discomfort among students.[364] If the basis of this is due to religious conviction, the free exercise clause may afford individual relief.[365]

Some ardent religionists (and also, undoubtedly some avid non-religionists) have advocated the exclusion of all religious matter from the public school curriculum.[366] This would mean, of course, that the study of European history would ignore the Protestant Reformation and the great religious controversies of the Middle Ages; that American history would be devoid of the struggle for religious freedom in the colonies; that art courses must exclude Da Vinci's "Last Supper" and Michelangelo's "Moses"; and that Beethoven's "Missa Solemnis" and Caruso's rendition of "Adeste Fidelis" could not be played in a music class. This line of reasoning might even prohibit the Bible from the public school library.

Despite the fact that one state court recently could find no difference between studies of this nature and devotional Bible reading,[367] the distinction is quite obvious. The inclusion of that religious material that is an intrinsic part of other disciplines is vitally necessary to a well-rounded education and is, therefore, a secular act.[368] It is thus subject to the same constitutional analysis as the objective study of religion. Unfortunately, from an *educational* standpoint, a recent study of American public education has revealed a "more or less deliberate avoidance of religious subject matter even when it was clearly intrinsic to the discipline concerned."[369] Unfortunately, from a *constitutional* standpoint, the same study "found planned religious activities widely prevalent."[370]

---

364. See note 359 *supra.*
365. See note 354 *supra.*
366. See PFEFFER, *op. cit. supra* note 321, at 287; Johnson, *Religion and Education,* 33 PROGRESSIVE EDUCATION 143, 146 (1956).
367. Chamberlin v. Dade County Bd. of Pub. Instruction, 143 So. 2d 21, 32 (Fla. Sup. Ct. 1962). See also People *ex rel.* Vollmar v. Stanley, 81 Colo. 276, 290, 255 Pac. 610, 616 (1927).
368. See 25 CAL. OPS. ATT'Y GEN. 316, 325 (1955); Johnson, *supra* note 366, at 145.
369. Johnson, *Summary of Policies and Recommendations of the American Council on Education Committee on Religion and Education,* in THE STUDY OF RELIGION IN THE PUBLIC SCHOOLS: AN APPRAISAL 5, 9 (Brown ed. 1958).
370. *Ibid.*

C.   RELEASED TIME

Prior to the Supreme Court's decision on the Regents' prayer, the Court had decided only two other cases on the merits that concerned the question of religious penetration in the public schools. Both of these cases involved released time programs.[371] Such a program may be defined as "a system of religious education in connection with the public school under which those children desiring to participate in religious instruction are excused from their secular studies for a specified period weekly, while those children not participating in religious instruction remain under the jurisdiction and supervision of the public school for the usual period of secular instruction. No distinction is made in the use of the term between religious instruction classes held within or without the public school building; nor between classes held at the first or last period of the school day and those held sometime between these two periods."[372]

Under the proposed constitutional standard, all released time plans should be held in violation of the establishment clause. The only immediate purposes of such a program are to "encourage religious instruction"[373] and to aid in the religious indoctrination of school children. In upholding the constitutionality of these programs, neither the Supreme Court[374] nor the state appellate courts[375] have denied this fact, nor have the many commentators

---

371. Zorach v. Clauson, 343 U.S. 306 (1952); Illinois *ex rel.* McCollum v. Board of Educ., 333 U.S. 203 (1948).

372. PFEFFER, CHURCH, STATE, AND FREEDOM 315 (1953). For a general history of the program, see *id.* at 313–27. Research has revealed one "first-hour-of-the-day" released time program which was said to be voluntary. Nonetheless, "no pupil . . . has refused or failed to attend such morning services for religious instruction." State *ex rel.* Johnson v. Boyd, 217 Ind. 348, 359–60, 28 N.E.2d 256, 261–62 (1940).

373. Zorach v. Clauson, 343 U.S. 306, 314 (1952).

374. *Ibid.*

375. Gordon v. Board of Educ., 78 Cal. App. 2d 464, 178 P.2d 488 (Ct. App. 1947); People *ex rel.* McCollum v. Board of Educ., 396 Ill. 14, 71 N.E.2d 161 (1947); People *ex rel.* Latimer v. Board of Educ., 394 Ill. 228, 68 N.E.2d 305 (1946); Zorach v. Clauson, 278 App. Div. 573, 102 N.Y.S.2d 27 (1951), *aff'd*, 303 N.Y. 161, 100 N.E.2d 463 (1951); People *ex rel.* Lewis v. Graves, 219 App. Div. 233, 219 N.Y. Supp. 189 (1927), *aff'd*, 245 N.Y. 195, 156 N.E. 663 (1927); Perry v. School Dist. No. 81, 54 Wash. 2d 886, 344 P.2d 1036 (1959). Examination of those reported state trial court opinions that have sustained released time programs also bears out this contention. Zorach v. Clauson, 198 Misc. 631, 99 N.Y.S.2d 339 (Sup. Ct. 1950); Lewis v. Spaulding, 193 Misc. 66, 85 N.Y.S.2d 682 (Sup. Ct. 1948); Lewis v. Graves, 127 Misc. 135, 215 N.Y. Supp. 632 (Sup. Ct. 1926). Research reveals only one reported state case striking down a released time program. The grounds for the decision were that (1) since report cards were printed during school hours upon school presses, the state constitutional provision barring state aid to denomination-

who have defended these decisions. That a system of released time is inherently coercive, thereby compromising the students' freedom of religious choice, has already been mentioned and somewhat demonstrated above.[376] Further evidence of its influencing and compromising nature is not lacking. The existence of compulsion has been found in the fact that religious leaders have so strenuously pressed for the establishment of released time systems.[377] While this is not necessarily valid when measured by the strict rules of logic,[378] it is nonetheless quite persuasive. Religious educators who are proponents of the system have noted that released time programs have a "remarkable evangelistic record,"[379] for in those schools where they operate, a substantial percentage of students attend religious classes who would not otherwise do so.[380] Religious leaders who oppose released time view it as "a means of applying public pressures to non-conformists so as to make them 'give in.' "[381] Schools with released time programs have reported "a considerable percentage of pupils in attendance whose parents do not belong to any church."[382] "They want to go to the church with their schoolmates and ask their parents to sign release cards."[383] Where released time systems have been abandoned, attendance at religious classes has declined.[384] Children of minority religious faiths have been known to enroll in the majority's religious classes because they did "not wish to be marked."[385] The

---

al schools was violated and (2) the program violated the state education law's provision requiring public school attendance during the entire time of the school session. Stein v. Brown, 125 Misc. 692, 211 N.Y. Supp. 822 (Sup. Ct. 1925).

376. See text accompanying notes 102–04, 148 *supra.*

377. See PFEFFER, *op. cit. supra* note 372, at 373; Cushman, *The Holy Bible and the Public Schools,* 40 CORNELL L.Q. 475, 497 (1955).

378. Religious leaders may have any one of a multitude of reasons for seeking the establishment of the released time system, and even if their reason is that they believe the system is compulsive, that does not in fact make it true.

379. Dr. Erwin L. Shaver of the International Council of Religious Education, quoted in PFEFFER, *op. cit. supra* note 372, at 328.

380. *Ibid.* Dr. Shaver points out that before a released time system, half of the school population receives no religious training; when the system is instituted, an average of one-third of this neglected half is reached.

381. Glenn Archer, Executive Director of Protestants and Other Americans United, quoted in PFEFFER, *op. cit. supra* note 372, at 332.

382. JACKSON & MALMBERG, RELIGIOUS EDUCATION AND THE STATE 39 (1928).

383. Sullivan, *Religious Education in the Schools,* 14 LAW & CONTEMP. PROB. 92, 94 (1949).

384. See *id.* at 111.

385. PFEFFER & BAUM, PUBLIC SCHOOL SECTARIANISM AND THE JEWISH CHILD 19 (1957). See Record, p. 135, Illinois *ex rel.* McCollum v.

fact that some may not have done so in no way refutes the existence of the inherent pressure.[386] Those who chose not to enroll, or who were forbidden by their parents from doing so, have told of being "ostracized by the other children in after-school activities."[387]

Examination of the reasoning utilized by those few who defend the constitutionality of released time by denying the presence of coercion is revealing. The Illinois Supreme Court, in *McCollum,* "proved" the nonexistence of any coercion by (1) saying that it was no more present there than it was in a prior, similar case, and (2) referring to some testimony by Terry's mother.[388] The first reason, of course, merely avoids the issue, and aside from the fact that the quoted testimony failed to support the court's contention,[389] there was overwhelming evidence to the contrary.[390] Father Murray has taken the position that no threat to any personal rights was visible in *McCollum;*[391] Terry was not pressured into doing anything he did not want to do.[392] However, he then

---

Board of Educ., 333 U.S. 203 (1948), in which Terry McCollum's teacher testified that she spoke to Terry's mother about "the fact that allowing him to take the religious education course might help him to become a member of the group. He was not accepted as a member of our class. I thought if he did the same things that they were doing that might help."

386. The argument that this disproves the existence of coercion was made by Chief Judge Desmond, concurring in Zorach v. Clauson, 303 N.Y. 161, 176, 100 N.E.2d 463, 470 (1951).

387. Affidavit quoted in PFEFFER, *op. cit. supra* note 372, at 357.

When the released time students departed . . . I felt left behind. The released children made remarks about my being Jewish and I was made very much aware of the fact that I did not participate with them in the released time program. I endured a great deal of anguish as a result of this and decided that I would like to go along with the other children to the church center rather than continue to expose myself to such harassment. I asked my mother for permission to participate in the released time program and to accompany my Catholic classmates to their religious center, but she forbade it.

Id. at 356; *accord, id.* at 356–67. *Contra,* Corcoran, Social Relationships of Elementary School Children and the Released-Time Religious Education Program (unpublished doctorial dissertation in Stanford University Library), abstracted in 56 RELIGIOUS EDUCATION 363–64 (1961), concluding that the "degree of participation in the released-time program was not demonstrably related to the sociometric status of elementary school children."

388. People *ex rel.* McCollum v. Board of Educ., 396 Ill. 14, 23, 71 N.E.2d 161, 165 (1947).

389. Mrs. McCollum had testified that, "I do not know it [released time] would bother him [Terry] one way or the other. I *did* not know it *until in court." Ibid.* (Emphasis added.)

390. See, *e.g.,* notes 103, 385 *supra.*

391. Murray, *Law or Prepossessions?,* 14 LAW & CONTEMP. PROB. 23, 24 n.7 (1949).

392. *Id.* at 39.

recognizes that there was "pressure by the school system in the interest of religious sects,"[393] but justifies its existence by stating that the public schools' "sheer omission of religion from the curriculum is itself a pressure against religion,"[394] and that "the system as such has become a formidable ally of secularism."[395] This position may be refuted simply by denying the premises. As has been pointed out, the establishment clause does not demand that the public schools omit religion from their curriculum, nor does it forbid them from objectively educating children as to the important role religion plays and has played in our civilization and in others. And so long as the establishment clause forbids the indoctrination of pupils with the ideas that there is no God or that, if there is, His influence is unimportant,[396] the public schools may not fairly be said to be allied with secularism.

While the Supreme Court did find the *McCollum* released time system in violation of the establishment clause, it sustained the program at issue in *Zorach v. Clauson.*[397] The only significant difference between the cases, so recognized by the Court majority,[398] was that in *McCollum* the public school classrooms were used for religious instruction, whereas in *Zorach* the religious classes were held away from the public school premises. It has already been shown that these cases cannot be meaningfully distinguished on the basis of the use of public property.[399] It may be true that "if the location of the school building makes the trip to a church long or hazardous because of dangerous street crossings, attendance will be improved by securing permission to teach in the school building."[400] But the fact that the system in *McCollum* may have more effectively promoted religious education does not mean that the *Zorach* plan did not promote it at all. It could be argued that the holding of the religious sessions in the same classrooms in which the ordinary daily school activities took place suggested that the religious instruction was an integral part of the public school program and, therefore, created a greater compulsive pressure on dissenters. This may make the result in *McCollum* more understandable, but it does not erase the "ineradicable built-in pressure to 'sign-up' for religious instruction"[401]

---

393. *Ibid.*
394. *Ibid.*
395. *Ibid.*
396. See text accompanying note 318 *supra.*
397. 343 U.S. 306 (1952).
398. *Id.* at 315.
399. See text accompanying notes 129–47 *supra.*
400. Sullivan, *supra* note 383, at 94.
401. Rosenfield, *Separation of Church and State in the Public Schools,* 22 U. PITT. L. REV. 561, 574 (1961).

in *Zorach*. Even those who favor the result in *Zorach*[102] agree with those who do not[403] that the decisions are irreconcilable on the matter of inherent coercion.

Probably the most frequently voiced argument in support of the constitutionality of released time is that its validity is dictated by the Supreme Court's landmark decision in *Pierce v. Society of Sisters*.[404] That case held an Oregon statute requiring public school attendance for children of certain ages unconstitutional on the ground that the fourteenth amendment gives parents the right to direct the education of their children and, therefore, the right to send their children to private or parochial schools that meet state qualifications. One aspect of the argument is that the right recognized in *Pierce* was a right guaranteed by the free exercise clause of the first amendment; to deny the availability of religious instruction in the public schools to those parents who, for financial or other reasons, send their children there, is to confine this right "to parents who can afford to send their children to parochial or other private schools . . . ."[405] The contention that rights protected by the free exercise clause would be suppressed by forbidding released time and other religious programs in the public schools has also been made by a number of others without the aid of the *Pierce* case.[406]

Apart from the question of whether *Pierce* really upheld a free exercise claim,[407] the argument must fail. The shortest answer is that released time programs violate the establishment clause and that ends the matter. Although this point seemingly begs the question, it is strengthened by the fact that the two most articulate proponents of the free exercise argument recognize that the validity of their argument turns on whether the continued operation of re-

---

402. *E.g.*, Kauper, *Church, State, and Freedom: A Review*, 52 MICH. L. REV. 829, 839 (1954).

403. *E.g.*, Zorach v. Clauson, 303 N.Y. 161, 187–88, 100 N.E.2d 463, 477 (1951) (Fuld, J., dissenting); Kurland, *Of Church and State and the Supreme Court*, 29 U. CHI. L. REV. 1, 77 (1961); Comment, 7 ALA. L. REV. 99, 107 (1954); Note, 52 COLUM. L. REV. 1033, 1038–39 (1952); Note, 61 YALE L.J. 405, 413–16 (1952); 74 HARV. L. REV. 611, 614 (1961); 31 TEXAS L. REV. 327, 329–30 (1953).

404. 268 U.S. 510 (1925).

405. Corwin, *The Supreme Court As National School Board*, 14 LAW & CONTEMP. PROB. 3, 20 (1949).

406. *E.g.*, Zorach v. Clauson, 303 N.Y. 161, 178, 100 N.E.2d 463, 471(1951) (Desmond, J., concurring); Zorach v. Clauson, 198 Misc. 631, 636–37, 99 N.Y.S.2d 339, 344 (Sup. Ct. 1950); Harpster, *Religion, Education and the Law*, 36 MARQ. L. REV. 24, 53 (1952); Murray, *supra* note 391, at 33; Reed, *Church-State and the Zorach Case*, 27 NOTRE DAME LAW. 529, 540 (1952).

407. See Kurland, *supra* note 403, at 13–14; Pfeffer, *Released Time and Religious Liberty: A Reply*, 53 MICH. L. REV. 91, 93–94 (1954).

leased time programs infringes on the rights of anyone else.[408] While it has not been contended that the program's imposition on nonconformists violates their rights specifically guaranteed by the free exercise clause,[409] it has been amply shown that the system of released time does infringe on their conscientious scruples.

The more authoritative answer to the argument based on *Pierce* is that the Court has specifically rejected a similar free exercise contention. If the free exercise clause is not violated by a law that "simply regulates a secular activity and, as applied to appellants, operates so as to make the practice of their religious beliefs more expensive,"[410] a decision by the Court to uphold the establishment clause surely must not fail because it has this effect.[411] It may be true that the rights guaranteed by *Pierce* would forbid a state from so regulating its public school system "as to make religious education or exercise impracticable or to limit such education or exercise to Saturday or Sunday"[412] and would preclude a state from "the pre-empting of the whole of the child's time so as to leave no adequate part for religion."[413] Such regulation would effectively bar action "demanded by one's religion."[414] But, since no religion demands that its children be excused early from school to attend religious classes, the abolition of released time "does not make unlawful any religious practices . . . ."[415] At most, the denial of a released time program may be said to impose "only an indirect burden on the exercise of religion . . . ."[416] Clearly, neither the purpose nor the effect of the denial of a released time program "is to impede the observance of

---

408. Zorach v. Clauson, 303 N.Y. 161, 178, 100 N.E.2d 463, 471 (1951) (Desmond, J., concurring); Corwin, note 405 *supra*. See also Johnson, *Summary of Policies and Recommendations of the American Council on Education Committee on Religion and Education*, in THE STUDY OF RELIGION IN THE PUBLIC SCHOOLS: AN APPRAISAL 5, 16–17 (Brown ed. 1958).

409. *But see* Pfeffer, *supra* note 407, at 96–97. See also 1 BAYLOR L. REV. 79, 81 (1948).

410. Braunfeld v. Brown, 366 U.S. 599, 605 (1961).

411. To adopt this free exercise rationale, see text accompanying note 405 *supra*, would be tantamount to saying that the free exercise rights of indigent Roman Catholics would be denied by the state's failure to provide free parochial schools.

412. Fahy, *Religion, Education, and the Supreme Court*, 14 LAW & CONTEMP. PROB. 73, 84–85 (1949).

413. PFEFFER, *op. cit. supra* note 372, at 289.

414. Braunfeld v. Brown, 366 U.S. 599, 604 (1961). Even here, the Court has stated that this is not an absolute test for determining free exercise clause violations. 366 U.S. at 605. See text accompanying notes 351–52 *supra*.

415. 366 U.S. at 605. See also Pfeffer, *supra* note 407, at 96.

416. 366 U.S. at 606. See also Note, 61 YALE L.J. 410–11 (1952).

one or all religions or is to discriminate invidiously between religions . . . ." If it were, the free exercise clause might be violated.[417] Rather, the purpose and effect is to prevent a violation of the establishment clause.[418] Since this "nonreligious" purpose would plainly be thwarted by any program of released time, under the standards set forth by the Supreme Court,[419] there is no credence to the contention that any person's free exercise rights are denied by the exclusion of released time programs.[420]

Another aspect of the argument based on *Pierce* deals with the matter of compulsion. The rationale articulated by the Court in striking down the program in *McCollum* was that "the operation of the State's compulsory education system . . . assists and is integrated with the program of religious instruction carried on by separate religious sects. Pupils compelled by law to go to school for secular education are released in part from their legal duty upon the condition that they attend the religious classes. This is beyond all question a utilization of the tax-established and tax-supported public school system to aid religious groups to spread their faith."[421] The Court concluded that, by the system, "the State . . . affords sectarian groups an invaluable aid in that it helps to provide pupils for their religious classes through use of the State's compulsory public school machinery. This is not separation of Church and State."[422] The argument advanced is that if the *McCollum* plan was defective because it conditioned absence from the public school upon attendance at religious classes, then, *a fortiori,* the parochial school attendance upheld in *Pierce* is also constitutionally defective for precisely the same reason, for it permits children to satisfy the compulsory school attendance law by attending religious classes.[423] Both arrangements produce attend-

---

417. See 366 U.S. at 607.

418. *Cf.* 366 U.S. at 609.

419. If the nonreligious purpose (preventing an establishment clause violation) could be accomplished by means that do not impose an indirect burden on religious observance (exclusion of released time programs may be said to impose such a burden, see text accompanying note 416 *supra*), the Court has indicated that failure to employ the alternative means would violate the free exercise clause. Braunfeld v. Brown, 366 U.S. 599, 607 (1961).

420. *Accord,* Kauper, *supra* note 402, at 848.

421. Illinois *ex rel.* McCollum v. Board of Educ., 333 U.S. 203, 209–10 (1948).

422. 333 U.S. at 212.

423. See Zorach v. Clauson, 303 N.Y. 161, 173–74, 100 N.E.2d 463, 468–69 (1951); Corwin, *supra* note 405, at 20; Meiklejohn, *Educational Cooperation Between Church and State,* 14 LAW & CONTEMP. PROB. 61, 67–68 (1949); Sullivan, *supra* note 383, at 109; 22 SO. CAL. L. REV. 423, 440 (1949).

ance at religious classes by discharging parents from their obligation under the compulsory school provisions. "It is not merely fanciful or frivolous to suggest that [*Pierce*] . . . represents one hundred percent released time."[424]

This line of argument is not wholly unpersuasive. If *McCollum* were based on nothing more than the compulsory education law, it would seem to jeopardize *Pierce*. Or if the main thrust of *Mc-Collum* were that truancy regulations were enforced by reports of attendance at religious classes being made to the public school[425] and that "knowledge that an official record is kept of his attendance necessarily places pressure on the child—accustomed as he is to the discipline of school—to attend these religious classes,"[426] then again the system upheld in *Pierce* might seem to be faulty.

But, even accepting the validity of these bases, the situations are distinguishable. Under the system of released time, the only alternative to remaining in the public school is to attend religious classes. This is not the case in the *Pierce* context. There, children who were excused from public school attendance had a broader range of alternatives; they could attend any accredited private school as well as parochial school.[427] A true analogy between released time and the situation in *Pierce* would exist only if religious classes were but one of several desirable choices available to students.[428] A school board program that would permit students to be released for a certain period of time each week on condition that they attend one of a group of extra-curricular education classes—for example, classes in music, art, religion, drama[429]— might well be valid under the establishment clause.[430] Indeed, the reasoning of one noted commentator suggests that the exclu-

---

424. Kauper, *supra* note 402, at 841.

425. See Illinois *ex rel.* McCollum v. Board of Educ., 333 U.S. 203, 209 n.5 (1948).

426. Zorach v. Clauson, 303 N.Y. 161, 188, 100 N.E.2d 463, 477 (1951) (dissenting opinion).

427. The case itself was prosecuted by both a parochial school and a military training school.

428. Here, again, the question of legislative motive becomes relevant. See note 343 *supra*.

429. "Released time as now practiced had its origin in Gary, Indiana, in 1913 when the Superintendent of Schools directed the dismissal of children an hour earlier one day of each week to enable them to pursue their individual interests such as religion, music or art." Pfeffer, *Religion, Education and the Constitution,* 8 LAW. GUILD REV. 387, 396–97 (1948).

430. The New York courts have upheld released time programs on this basis. People *ex rel.* Lewis v. Graves, 219 App. Div. 233, 239, 219 N.Y. Supp. 189, 195–96, *aff'd,* 245 N.Y. 195, 198, 156 N.E. 663, 664 (1927). See also Cushman, *The Holy Bible and the Public Schools,* 40 CORNELL L.Q. 475, 494 (1955).

sion of religious education as one of the alternatives would violate constitutionally protected religious freedom.[431] Most importantly in regard to the proposed constitutional standard, the difference that might make this program valid is that the provision of attractive alternatives to religious education would remove the inherently coercive element in released time. Students who were religious nonconformists and students with marginal beliefs would not be faced with the choice of either receiving religious instruction, which would compromise or influence their conscientious scruples, or being regarded as "oddballs."[432] They could join with those of their friends of the religious majority who preferred to study art, music, or drama rather than religion.[433] It may be that by instituting such a program, more children would attend religious classes than would be the case otherwise. This is undoubtedly the result of the decision in *Pierce*.[434] But, despite the fact that this represents aid to religion, the absence of coercion calls for a favorable constitutional judgment under the proposed constitutional standard. State action of this nature may be fairly characterized as merely an "accommodation."[435]

However, there is a more compelling distinction between the *Pierce* situation and released time, again based on compulsion. Regardless of the presence of alternative choices, no child of a minority religious faith (or of no faith at all) feels *compelled* to attend a parochial school simply because, under the *Pierce* case, the government must permit him to do so. But, in the released time situation, nonconforming pupils do feel compelled to accept religious instruction, thus compromising their conscientious beliefs.[436] This last argument has been rejected on the ground that

---

431. Kurland, *supra* note 403, at 5.

432. Those children of minority religious faiths who choose to go home to receive religious instruction from their parents, a plan suggested by the counsel for the school board in *Zorach,* would be just as "oddballish" as those who were forced to remain in school because their parents had no religion to impart to them. See PFEFFER, *op. cit. supra* note 372, at 355.

433. In light of the fact that only about half of the public school population would accept religious education without a program of released time, see note 380 *supra,* if attractive alternatives to religious education were available to released students, it is most likely that many religious conformists would accompany the dissenters to the nonreligious classes.

434. It is obvious that if the Court had upheld the statute in *Pierce,* parochial school attendance would be diminished.

435. See text accompanying notes 463–72 *infra.*

436. It might be argued that by the Supreme Court's action in *Pierce,* removing any legal impediment to full time parochial education, the clergy was left free to exert strenuous pressures on their parishioners to send their children to parochial schools and that, in this way, governmental action resulted in private pressures being brought to bear on those

it "is based on the premise that the public school represents a kind of involuntary imprisonment, release from which may be effected by attending religious education classes,"[437] and that it may not "be accepted as an unquestioned proposition of fact that religious instruction is so attractive and public school education so repressive that parents and children will invariably respond by choosing to escape the public school classroom."[438] This is not the premise advanced here. The inherent compulsion does not necessarily arise from the unattractiveness of the public school, but from the urge of the nonconforming students, who would otherwise be left behind, to join the group. Thus, released time is a solely religious activity that is likely to result in compromising and influencing religious beliefs.

Of course, if it could be shown that in those schools that have adopted released time[439] there is majority nonparticipation, it would be difficult to maintain that those students who remain behind will be considered "oddballs" by their colleagues. As a practical matter, it would seem that unless a large proportion of the school were "willing" to participate, the program would be discontinued.[440] For the most part, the available statistics bear out the assumption that most children attend.[441] Those involved in the program have stated that "the enrollment of 90 to 99 percent of the public school constituency in the weekday church school is quite common. To reach less than 80 percent is the excep-

members of the faith with marginal convictions, thus influencing the freedom of religious participation; this then would be no different than that aspect of released time. This argument may be rebutted by pointing out that the *Pierce* decision was dictated by a serious free exercise claim: since the Roman Catholic religion demands that its children attend parochial schools, the Oregon statute was in direct conflict with the religious practice. See text accompanying notes 479–81 *infra*. It has already been pointed out that denial of released time presents no comparable free exercise claim. See generally text accompanying notes 410–20 *supra*. Thus, although released time must be characterized as a solely religious activity, the purpose of the decision in *Pierce* may be fairly characterized as "nonreligious."

437. Kauper, *supra* note 402, at 839.

438. *Ibid.*

439. A recent survey indicates that about 30% of American public schools have released time programs. Dierenfield, *The Extent of Religious Influence in American Public Schools*, 56 RELIGIOUS EDUCATION 173, 177 (1961).

440. In fact, this often happens. See PFEFFER, *op. cit. supra* note 372, at 336–37.

441. There appear to be no published national statistics on the percentage of participation in those schools that do have released time programs. See generally *id.* at 317–21.

tion."[442] Reports from such cities as Spokane, Washington,[443] Champaign, Illinois,[444] Salina, Kansas,[445] and Van Wert, Ohio,[446] confirm this. On the other hand, some schools in Berkeley, California,[447] Mount Vernon, New York,[448] Minneapolis,[449] and Chicago[450] report minority participation. Released time should nonetheless be invalid in most of those schools with minority participation because of the consequences of the unpleasant atmosphere that exists for those pupils, many of them members of the religious majorities, who remain. Educators have complained that one of the major problems involved in the administration of released time programs is what to do with the nonparticipants.[451] The dilemma facing them is that if special programs or normal educational activities are conducted, this in effect penalizes those who attend religious classes; on the other hand, it is unfair to the nonparticipants "to keep them occupied solely with 'busy' work."[452] If the latter course is taken, an unattractive environment is produced for those left behind, thereby influencing attendance at religious classes. Furthermore, if regular school courses are continued, although the religious school may be intrinsically no more attractive than the public school, it is likely that the mere opportunity to change environment and "escape from the classroom and school routine"[453] will act as an incentive to students to go elsewhere. These being the less attractive alternatives available in the public schools, the solely religious program of released time will likely influence the student with marginal re-

---

442. Dr. W. Dyer Blair, Director of the Department of Weekday Religious Education of the International Council of Religious Education, in 1940, quoted in *id.* at 335.

443. "In most instances . . . there are but few children remaining." Perry v. School Dist. No. 81, 54 Wash. 2d 886, 889, 344 P.2d 1036, 1038 (1959).

444. See text accompanying note 103 *supra.*

445. 95%. JACKSON & MALMBERG, *op. cit. supra* note 382, at 50.

446. 81–96%. *Ibid.*

447. Just over 25%. See Nelson, *The Fourth "R" —Religion—In Education,* 51 RELIGIOUS EDUCATION 40, 41 (1956).

448. Over 25%. See Larson, *A Superintendent Looks at the Week-day School of Religion,* 51 RELIGIOUS EDUCATION 43 (1956).

449. Overall, about 50%. But individual schools vary from 12 to 94%. A majority of them are above 50%. Greater Minneapolis Council of Churches, Comparison of Weekday Church School Enrollment with Public School Enrollment, Nov. 13–17, 1961.

450. Less than 10%. See PFEFFER, CHURCH, STATE, AND FREEDOM 348 (1953).

451. See Nelson, *supra* note 447, at 41.

452. PFEFFER, *op. cit. supra* note 450, at 325.

453. Note, 52 COLUM. L. REV. 1033, 1038 (1952). See also Cushman, *supra* note 430, at 496.

ligious beliefs to attend religious classes—something he would not otherwise do.

The same cannot be said for a program of dismissed time, "the system under which, on one or more days, the public school is closed earlier [or opened later][454] than usual, and all children are dismissed, with the expectation—but not the requirement —that some will use the dismissed period for participation in religious instruction."[455] It is no surprise, therefore, that there is general agreement, even among those who find released time unconstitutional, that dismissed time is valid.[456] True, such a program will probably result in greater attendance at religious classes than would otherwise occur.[457] Moreover, it might be demonstrated that the school board's purpose in early closing was solely religious.[458] Nevertheless, the element of state-caused compulsion is absent. Students are not faced with the publicly imposed choice of either going to religious school or remaining behind in an unenticing setting. If they choose to attend religious classes, they will do so in preference to other equally alluring, and, in many cases, more than equally alluring, alternatives.[459] Perhaps dissenters will nonetheless be subject to pressures from their conforming colleagues who choose to attend religious classes,[460] but this would exist even if the schools closed at the regular hour. Unlike the case of released time, the coercion may not be attributed to governmental action.[461] The argument has been made that a

---

454. See City of New Haven v. Town of Torrington, 132 Conn. 194, 197, 43 A.2d 455, 457 (1945).

455. PFEFFER, *op. cit. supra* note 450, at 315.

456. Zorach v. Clauson, 303 N.Y. 161, 190, 100 N.E.2d 463, 478 (1951) (Fuld, J., dissenting); Cushman, *Public Support of Religious Education in American Constitutional Law*, 45 ILL. L. REV. 333, 354, 356 (1950); Sullivan, *Religious Education in the Schools*, 14 LAW & CONTEMP. PROB. 92, 93 (1949); Note, 52 COLUM. L. REV. 1033, 1039 (1952); Comment, 43 ILL. L. REV. 374, 386 (1948); 46 MICH. L. REV. 828, 829–30 (1948); 27 TEXAS L. REV. 256, 259 (1948); Note, 57 YALE L.J. 1114, 1119 (1948).

457. See Katz, *Freedom of Religion and State Neutrality*, 20 U. CHI. L. REV. 426, 439 (1953).

458. A decision to hold the school picnic on Sunday *afternoon*, so as to enable those students who wish to go to church to do so, seems to have a solely religious purpose. But since this action does not inherently compel church attendance, it could not be said to violate the establishment clause under the proposed standard.

459. "[R]eligion can compete more successfully with arithmetic than with recreation." Note, 57 YALE L.J. 1114, 1119 (1948).

460. See generally 31 TEXAS L. REV. 329 (1953).

461. Query if the same could be said if the public school rented its premises for religious classes to commence immediately following the end of the public school day. Would not the coercive pressures here be attributable to the school board's action? See note 137 *supra*.

dismissed time plan "could not be used *if* the effect of the dismissal were to make the total time in school less than that required as compulsory attendance."[462] This would be irrelevant under the proposed consitutional standard because it has no bearing on the matter of compulsion. In any case, it is difficult to determine what merit the argument has since the required time for school attendance could easily be reduced.

There has been much discussion, particularly with reference to released time and other religious infiltration in the public schools, about the state's assuming a role of "neutrality" in this conflict and about the state's making an "accommodation" between the competing interests.[463] While this may have an abstract appeal, it does not adequately substitute for analysis under a principled standard.[464] The New York courts have upheld the constitutionality of the Regents' prayer[465] and released time[466] on this basis. Professor Kauper, a most articulate advocate for the constitutional validity of released time, agrees that it aids religion, but justifies it as a "reasonable accommodation."[467] It is true that "in matters of public education due respect for the democratic process should

---

462. Cosway & Toepfer, *Religion and the Schools,* 17 U. CINC. L. REV. 117, 141 (1948).

463. See, *e.g.,* 9 U.C.L.A.L. REV. 495, 501 & n.30 (1962) and authorities cited therein.

464. Professor Robert F. Cushman calls for "a doctrine of state neutrality." Cushman, *supra* note 430, at 490. He argues that "if all social groups, without regard to purpose, were allowed to come into the schools and conduct meetings which the students could attend, religious groups, since they are social groups, would be included." Perhaps so. But under this same principle, it would be valid for the Community Sandlot Baseball League, the Model Railroad Club (two of Cushman's examples, *id.* at 491), and the Roman Catholic Church (my example) to come into the public schools to prosyletize for members. Professor Philip Kurland's "neutral principle of equality" would appear to call for the same result. Kurland, *Of Church and State and the Supreme Court,* 29 U. CHI. L. REV. 1, 4–5 (1961). Under the principle proposed in this article, the establishment clause would forbid the inclusion of the Church. There is nothing in the Constitution prohibiting the use of the public schools for Little League proselyting; the first amendment stands in the way of any religion doing the same thing. Nor would the prohibition violate the free exercise clause under any Supreme Court interpretation of it. At most, this would be "only an indirect burden on the exercise of religion." Braunfeld v. Brown, 366 U.S. 599, 606 (1961). See generally text accompanying notes 415–20 *supra*.

465. Engel v. Vitale, 18 Misc. 2d 659, 694, 191 N.Y.S.2d 453, 491 (Sup. Ct. 1959).

466. Lewis v. Spaulding, 193 Misc. 66, 73, 85 N.Y.S.2d 682, 690 (Sup. Ct. 1948).

467. Kauper, *Church, State, and Freedom: A Review,* 52 MICH. L. REV. 829, 841 (1954). See also Kauper, *Released Time and Religious Liberty: A Further Reply,* 53 MICH. L. REV. 233, 236 (1954).

permit some discretion to the community in shaping its educational policies,"[468] and that "the interest of parents in the religious education of their children is a legitimate legislative concern."[469] Dismissed time satisfies these appeals. Professor Kauper agrees that "no actual pressure [should be] placed on any student to attend classes in religious education."[470] But he states that "a proper sense of concern for the non-participant does not require rejection of the [released time] program on constitutional grounds,"[471] since "it remains to be demonstrated that the optional released time privilege deprives anyone of [religious liberty]."[472] Hopefully, it has been demonstrated here.

1. *Excusing Children for Religious Holidays*

The argument has often been advanced[473] that excusing children from the public schools for observance of their particular religious holidays is merely an "instance of released time but on a smaller scale,"[474] and, therefore, this practice stands or falls with released time. But there are many distinguishing features. Released time is inherently coercive because it operates to single out the nonconformists *against their will* and compels them to attend religious classes *against their will.* When children are excused from classes on religious holidays, they *ask* to be singled out because they *wish* to attend religious services. Assuming that the public school act of excusing them has a solely religious purpose, the act is requested by the religious nonconformists themselves.

In the case of released time, majority participation works to coerce minority attendance. Minority participation usually results in the practice of excusing children for religious holidays since the public schools ordinarily close on the majority's religious holidays.[475] However, for the same reasons that operated in the re-

---

468. Kauper, *Church, State, and Freedom: A Review, supra* note 467, at 839.

469. Kauper, *Released Time and Religious Liberty: A Further Reply, supra* note 467, at 236.

470. Kauper, *Church, State, and Freedom: A Review, supra* note 467, at 842.

471. *Ibid.*

472. Kauper, *Released Time and Religious Liberty: A Further Reply, supra* note 467, at 236. See also Katz, *supra* note 457, at 439.

473. Zorach v. Clauson, 343 U.S. 306, 313 (1952); Zorach v. Clauson, 303 N.Y. 161, 173, 100 N.E.2d 463, 468 (1951); 20 FORDHAM L. REV. 328, 331 (1951); Brief for Intervenors-Respondents, p. 43, Engel v. Vitale, 370 U.S. 421 (1962).

474. Kauper, *Church, State, and Freedom: A Review, supra* note 467, at 840.

475. Professor Kurland would probably also distinguish these situations, but on other grounds. Since released time makes only religious education

leased time context, it may be that permitting children of religious minorities to be excused from the public school to attend religious services will likely influence students of these religious minorities with marginal beliefs to attend the church or synagogue of their faith.[476] Nonetheless, the situations are distinguishable because, while it has been shown that there is no colorable claim that denial of released time infringes on rights under the free exercise clause,[477] denying children of minority religious faiths their wish to attend holiday religious services does raise a serious free exercise question.[478] Even those who have argued that the two situations are otherwise similar recognize this difference.[479] Attendance at religious services is often an act demanded by one's religion. By the public schools' refusal to permit such attendance, the student faces the choice of either violating his religious principles or receiving whatever penalties the school chooses to impose. The Supreme Court has not held that, in a situation of this nature, the free exercise claim must prevail, but it has recognized that "in such cases, to make accommodation between the religious action and an exercise of state authority is a particularly delicate task."[480] The free exercise claim here does appear to be quite substantial and persuasive because it can hardly be said that a student's action in absenting himself from school for one day is "in violation of important social duties or subversive of good order."[481] For

available, he would likely find it invalid because "it is . . . forbidden the state to confer favors [only] upon religious activity." Kurland, *Of Church and State and the Supreme Court*, 29 U. CHI. L. REV. 1, 5 (1961). Since pupils may be excused from the public schools for many reasons (*e.g.*, funerals, dental appointments), he would likely say that the first amendment *demands* that they also be excused for religious holidays because "inhibitions [may] not be placed by the state on [only] religious activity." *Ibid.* However, it would seem that if the public school forbade absence for *all* extracurricular activities, Professor Kurland's thesis not only would permit the schools to deny excusing children for religious observances, but would actually forbid the schools from granting it. Since there is a substantial and persuasive, albeit not conclusive, free exercise argument for granting children absence from the public schools to observe their religious holidays, see text accompanying notes 478–81 *infra*, one might well disagree with this last point. See LOCKHART, KAMISAR & CHOPER, SUPPLEMENT TO DODD'S CASES ON CONSTITUTIONAL LAW 399 (1962).

476. Of course, if there is majority participation, inherent coercion will exist.

477. See text accompanying notes 414–20 *supra*.

478. See Zorach v. Clauson, 303 N.Y. 161, 191–92, 100 N.E.2d 463, 479 (1951) (Fuld, J., dissenting); Cosway & Toepfer, *Religion and the Schools*, 17 U. CINC. L. REV. 117, 141 (1948).

479. Zorach v. Clauson, 303 N.Y. 161, 173, 100 N.E.2d 463, 468 (1951); Kauper, *Church, State, and Freedom: A Review, supra* note 467, at 840, 848.

480. Braunfeld v. Brown, 366 U.S. 599, 605 (1961).

481. 366 U.S. at 603.

these reasons, the establishment clause may well permit a state to excuse children from school for religious observances despite the influence it may have on them and other pupils. No comparable "nonreligious" justification exists for released time.[482]

2. Shared Time

The newly adopted program of "shared time,"[483] under which parochial school students come to the public schools each day to take certain secular classes, merits brief consideration. As presently constituted, the plan involves a relatively small number of Catholic students[484] joining their public school associates for a few hours each day. There would seem to be no constitutional objection under the proposed constitutional standard in these circumstances, since the activity may not be characterized as being solely religious and it is unlikely that public school students will feel compelled to join their Catholic colleagues when the latter return to the parochial school.[485]

One might suggest that, since the experience over the years with released time has revealed teachers' persistent application of direct pressures on pupils to attend religious classes, despite the fact that teachers have been specifically prohibited from so doing,[486] the program is inherently subject to abuse and, therefore, unconstitutional.[487] However, we need not go this far. Despite the warning that "the critical constitutional issues with respect to released time cannot be solved by any play of language in using the word 'compulsion,' "[488] it is submitted that this solely religious activity should fail, principally for that reason.

D. TEACHERS WEARING RELIGIOUS GARB

Next to Bible reading, the issue involving religious infusion in the public schools probably most often brought before the state courts is whether the schools may employ teachers who wear religious garb.[489] The reason commonly given for the invalidity of

---

482. Cf. note 436 supra.

483. Philadelphia Inquirer, Sept. 5, 1962, p. 25, col. 1.

484. About 10% of those in attendance in the public school. Ibid.

485. The question of whether this program constitutes unconstitutional financial aid to parochial schools is beyond the scope of this article.

486. For extensive documentation, see PFEFFER, CHURCH, STATE, AND FREEDOM 356–67 (1953); Note, 61 YALE L.J. 405, 412–13 (1952).

487. See Note, 52 COLUM. L. REV. 1033, 1038 (1952).

488. Kauper, Released Time and Religious Liberty: A Further Reply, 53 MICH. L. REV. 233, 236 (1954).

489. "A recent survey showed that members of religious orders in

this practice is that "the distinctive garbs, so exclusively peculiar to the Roman Catholic Church, create a religious atmosphere in the schoolroom. They have a subtle influence upon the tender minds being taught and trained by the nuns. In and of themselves they proclaim the Catholic Church and the representative character of the teachers in the schoolroom. They silently promulgate sectarianism."[490]

There is by no means the same general consensus on this point, however, as there is about those practices previously discussed. The pressures on the religiously nonconforming child that are created by his failure to join his colleagues in a particular activity are absent here. Nor can it be said here, as it was in connection with Bible reading, that by engaging teachers who wear religious garb, the state influences the student's freedom of conscientious choice by placing its "stamp of approval" on the Roman Catholic faith. It should be clear to students in the upper grades that when public school teachers are employed, the state approves only of their intellectual qualifications; the state does not endorse their sex, political beliefs, or religious affiliations any more than it sanctions the clothes that they wear or the street on which they live. As to those students in the lower grades, it would seem that any influence of the religious garb would not differ substantially from that produced by the pupils' knowledge of their teacher's religious devotion acquired elsewhere—from statements the teacher has made, from religious insignia the teacher wears, or from general community information.[491] The evidence that this practice is likely to compromise religious beliefs or influence conscientious choice is not very strong.

Even if the evidence were more convincing, the practice of permitting teachers to wear religious garb in the schools would not violate the establishment clause under the proposed constitutional standard unless it could be fairly characterized as solely religious. The practice has been defended on the ground "that to prohibit

---

religious garb were employed as teachers to some extent in the public schools of sixteen states and territories." Fahy, *Religion, Education, and the Supreme Court*, 14 LAW & CONTEMP. PROB. 73, 89 (1949).

490. Rawlings v. Butler, 290 S.W.2d 801, 809 (Ky. 1956) (dissenting opinion). See also Zellers v. Huff, 55 N.M. 501, 523–25, 236 P.2d 947, 963–65 (1951); O'Connor v. Hendrick, 184 N.Y. 421, 428, 77 N.E. 612, 614 (1906); O'Connor v. Hendrick, 109 App. Div. 361, 371–72, 96 N.Y. Supp. 161, 169 (1905); Cosway & Toepfer, *Religion and the Schools*, 17 U. CINC. L. REV. 117, 138 (1948); Comment, 22 U. CHI. L. REV. 888, 893–94 (1955).

491. See Hysong v. Gallitzin Borough School Dist., 164 Pa. 629, 657, 30 Atl. 482, 484 (1894); Harpster, *Religion, Education and the Law*, 36 MARQ. L. REV. 24, 54–55 (1952).

a teaching Sister from wearing the garb would infringe the free exercise of religion."[492] If this premise is valid, it would seem to be a "nonreligious" justification for the practice. However, while it is quite clear that the Constitution prohibits state discrimination against its employees on the basis of religion,[493] it is not clear that the free exercise clause requires the state to permit its teachers to do anything that their religion demands.[494] Aside from the fact that barring teachers who wear religious garb from the public schools would constitute only a rather minor disability,[495] there is some indication that Catholic Sisters may receive dispensation to wear lay clothing while teaching in the public schools.[496] These being the facts, if further research revealed that the wearing of religious garb was likely to act as a compromising or influencing factor, it seems doubtful that the free exercise clause could be read to prohibit a state from barring religious garb from the public schools.[497] If this be true, the wearing of the garb in the schools might fairly be characterized as a solely religious practice.

In any case, if it is found that the practice is influential or coercive, it may be that the establishment clause is violated despite the activity's arguably secular foundation. The secular objective (qualified teachers) may be attained just as well by employing those who do not wear religious garb and, by so doing, the objectionable effects would be eliminated.[498] As of now, the factual premises remain unproven.

The fact that Roman Catholic Sisters contribute their net income from public school teaching to the church should have no bearing whatever on the constitutional validity of the practice.[499] Persons should be able to spend their income for any legal purpose. In fact, the argument may well be made that "to deny the right to make such contribution would in itself constitute a denial of that right of religious liberty which the Constitution guarantees."[500]

---

492. Fahy, *supra* note 489, at 90. *But see* Commonwealth v. Herr, 229 Pa. 132, 78 Atl. 68 (1910); Comment, 22 U. CHI. L. REV. 888, 894 (1955).
493. See Wieman v. Updegraff, 344 U.S. 183, 191–92 (1952); United Pub. Workers v. Mitchell, 330 U.S. 75, 100 (1947).
494. Query if the state could not bar a teacher whose religious faith required that she proselyte while teaching. See Harfst v. Hoegen, 349 Mo. 808, 816, 163 S.W.2d 609, 614 (1942).
495. See text accompanying note 410 *supra*.
496. It has been granted in New York and North Dakota. AMERICAN CIVIL LIBERTIES UNION, 41ST ANNUAL REPORT 28–29 (1961).
497. See generally Braunfeld v. Brown, 366 U.S. 599, 603–07 (1961).
498. See text following note 346 *supra*.
499. Rawlings v. Butler, 290 S.W.2d 801, 806 (Ky. 1956); Zellers v. Huff, 55 N.M. 501, 522, 236 P.2d 949, 961–62 (1951); Hysong v. Gallitzen Borough School Dist., 164 Pa. 629, 656–57, 30 Atl. 482, 483–84 (1894).
500. Gerhardt v. Heid, 66 N.D. 444, 460, 267 N.W. 127, 135 (1936).

The whole discussion of this subject has dealt only with the single practice of teachers wearing religious garb. The result suggested here may be different if the totality of the circumstances in the public school environment, of which the teacher's attire is merely one element, is likely to compromise or influence the conscientious convictions of the students.[501]

E. DISTRIBUTION OF BIBLES

In a recent survey of over 2,000 public school superintendents throughout the country, over 40 percent admitted that the distribution of Gideon Bibles to students was permitted through their schools.[502] This practice is unquestionably solely religious,[503] and the only two cases considering the problem that have reached the appellate level have found it to be in violation of the establishment clause.[504]

There should be no dispute that the King James version of the Bible, which is the version distributed by the Gideons, is objectionable to a large number of religious faiths, and that the scruples of Roman Catholic children will be compromised by receipt of a copy.[505] However, one might agree that this activity is, at best, mildly compulsive on the objectors as compared with some of those programs previously discussed.[506] Consider the situation in *Engel*; it would seem much less likely that a child, during the prayer recitation, would leave the room to stand outside with nothing to do,[507] than that he would decline acceptance of a Bible. This would seem particularly true when the procedures for acquisition of the Bible were carefully drafted so as to avoid the singling

---

501. See Note, 22 U. CHI. L. REV. 888, 890 (1955); text accompanying notes 560–63 *infra*.

502. Dierenfield, *The Extent of Religious Influence in American Public Schools,* 56 RELIGIOUS EDUCATION 173, 175 (1961).

503.
 The Gideons International is a nonprofit corporation . . . whose object is "to win men and women for the Lord Jesus Christ, through . . . (c) placing the Bible—God's Holy Words—or portions thereof in hotels, hospitals, schools, institutions, and also through the distribution of same for personal use."
Tudor v. Board of Educ., 14 N.J. 31, 33, 100 A.2d 857, 858 (1953).

504. Brown v. Orange County Bd. of Pub. Instruction, 128 So. 2d 181 (Fla. Dist. Ct. App. 1960); Tudor v. Board of Educ., 14 N.J. 31, 100 A.2d 857 (1953).

505. See text accompanying note 271 *supra*.

506. See Levy, *Views From the Wall—Reflections on Church-State Relationships,* 29 HENNEPIN LAW. 51, 55–56 (1961).

507. In fact, no child requested such permission although it had been provided for. Brief for Petitioners, p. 31, Engel v. Vitale, 370 U.S. 421 (1962).

out of nonconformists.[508] Nonetheless, there has been expert testimony that the program, as administered, generated pressures to conform.[509] If this factual premise remains unshaken, under the proposed constitutional standard the practice must cease.

F. SCHOOL CREDIT FOR OUTSIDE RELIGIOUS INSTRUCTION

It has been reported that "in a number of communities the public school—generally at the high school level—will give credit toward graduation for religious instruction obtained after public school hours or during week ends under the auspices of the child's church."[510] The purpose and effect of this program—sectarian indoctrination—is solely religious. If those students who do not participate will have to spend extra time in the public school acquiring these credits while the participants are dismissed, this program is no different from released time. Nonparticipants will be conspicuous and, if in the religious minorities, will be subject to pressures to compromise their beliefs. If there is only minority participation, the opportunity to avoid public school routine will likely influence free religious choice. But despite the unquestioned aid that religion would receive, these results would not follow if the public school arranged its schedule so that all students, regardless of whether they participated in outside religious classes, remained in school during the entire school day. Furthermore, if the school were to give credit for a number of extra-curricular educational courses that were of generally equal attractiveness, all pressures and incentives would seem to be removed, and the program should pass the proposed constitutional standard.

The fact that some time of public school administrators and teachers may be taken in insuring that the instruction is being taken by the students and being given by qualified personnel must be excused as *de minimis*.[511] However, if the public schools insist on examining and grading the students on the basis of what they have learned,[512] the program should probably be invalid. In such cases, pupils whose religious beliefs differ from those of the public school teacher will very likely be tempted to learn what they

---

508. In *Tudor*, parents simply had to sign a permission slip. Children whose parents had signed reported to a room "at the close of the session." No other students were present. No reason was to be stated when the announcement calling the students was made. 14 N.J. at 34–35, 100 A.2d at 858–59.

509. 14 N.J. at 50–52, 100 A.2d at 867–68.

510. PFEFFER, CHURCH, STATE, AND FREEDOM 305 (1953).

511. See text accompanying notes 141–47 *supra*.

512. *Cf.* State *ex rel.* Dearle v. Frazier, 102 Wash. 369, 173 Pac. 35 (1918).

believe will be generally acceptable or at least to assert this for examination purposes. Such a compromising element should be barred.

G. BACCALAUREATE AND GRADUATION

Baccalaureate exercises, under public school auspices, are widespread[513] and have divided communities "with bitter conflict and tension."[514] Many of these programs are "occasions to impart spiritual truths"[515] and ordinarily include all the elements of a Protestant church service—processional hymn, invocation prayer, choral hymns, Bible reading, address by a clergyman, benediction prayer, and recessional hymn.[516] These must be fairly characterized as solely religious activities whether the service is held on public school or church property. Certain faiths, particularly the Roman Catholic, forbid participation in exercises of this kind.[517] Although nonparticipation is often permitted,[518] it would likely be ineffective as far as inherent compulsion is concerned for reasons previously discussed.[519] Thus, since participation would directly compromise some students' religious scruples, the establishment clause would be violated under the proposed constitutional standard.[520] Of course, this would neither bar the individual churches from conducting baccalaureate services for members of their own faith nor prevent the public schools from having a nonreligious assembly program that is called a baccalaureate.

---

513. Almost 87% of school superintendents polled stated that the activity was engaged in in their school systems. Dierenfield, *The Extent of Religious Influence in American Public Schools,* 56 RELIGIOUS EDUCATION 173, 175 (1961).

514. Boyer, *Religious Education of Public School Pupils in Wisconsin,* 1953 WIS. L. REV. 181, 196.

515. Sample comment by public school supervisor, quoted in Dierenfield, *supra* note 513, at 179.

516. See PFEFFER, CHURCH, STATE, AND FREEDOM 418 (1953). See also Rosenfield, *Separation of Church and State in the Public Schools,* 22 U. PITT. L. REV. 561, 573 (1961).

517. Boyer, *supra* note 514 at 196, 205.

518. See Chamberlin v. Dade County School Bd., 17 Fla. Supp. 183, 197 (Cir. Ct. 1961). However, in West Virginia and Pennsylvania, recent instances are reported in which nonparticipating Catholic students were denied public awarding of their diplomas. See AMERICAN CIVIL LIBERTIES UNION, 37TH ANNUAL REPORT 64 (1957); PFEFFER, *op. cit. supra* note 516, at 420.

519. However, it may be argued that the pressures on a nonconforming student to attend a single program are virtually nonexistent, especially when compared to the pressures generated to participate in an activity that occurs every day or once each week.

520. An opinion of the Attorney General of the state of Washington, April 20, 1962, agrees. See Jurisdictional Statement, p. 18, Chamberlin v. Dade County Bd. of Pub. Instruction, *appeal docketed,* 31 U.S.L. WEEK 3139 (U.S. Oct. 15, 1962)(No. 520).

There have been several reports of public schools conducting their graduation exercises in church buildings.[521] It this were the only available site for the occasion,[522] it would be difficult to argue that this is a solely religious practice. Moreover, if this be the fact, the alternative argument for establishment clause violation is likewise inadmissible;[523] despite any religious objections to the practice, the secular objective of having a suitable building may not be attained by alternative means.

Graduation invocations delivered by clergymen present a somewhat different problem. This part of the graduation program must be considered as solely religious despite efforts to make it nonsectarian. But there are several reasons why this program may be defended under the proposed constitutional standard. Research has not revealed that listening to the invocation is contrary to anyone's religious or conscientious beliefs. If this is true, the practice could not possibly result in compromising any student's conscientious scruples. And even if there were some objection, the atmosphere is not conducive to inherent compulsion to attend the invocation. The dissenting pupil need not absent himself from the entire program, and he will likely have the comfort of his parents' and relatives' presence and will be in the midst of many people outside his peer group.[524] Finally, the fact that this is but a small segment of a program that a student attends but once makes fairly unpersuasive the "stamp of approval" argument for influencing religious beliefs advanced in connection with daily religious exercises in public school classes.[525]

H. Religious Insignia

A North Dakota staute requires "a placard containing the ten commandments of the Christian religion to be displayed in a conspicuous place in every schoolroom, classroom, or other place where classes convene for instruction."[526] Not long ago, a New York school board passed a resolution that a neutral version of the Ten

---

521. See State *ex rel.* Conway v. District Bd., 162 Wis. 482, 156 N.W. 477 (1916); American Civil Liberties Union, 34th Annual Report 51 (1954).

522. See Miller v. Cooper, 56 N.M. 355, 244 P.2d 520 (1952).

523. See text following note 346 *supra*.

524. The situation has been accurately compared to an opening of Congress or a presidential inauguration. Committee on Religion and Public Education of the National Council of the Churches of Christ, *Relation of Religion to Public Education—A Study Document,* International J. of Religious Education, Apr. 1960, pp. 21, 29.

525. See State *ex rel.* Conway v. District Bd., 162 Wis. 482, 495, 156 N.W. 477, 481 (1916).

526. N.D. Cent. Code § 15–47–10 (1960).

Commandments, amalgamating and modifying the Jewish, Catholic, and Protestant versions, be placed in each classroom.[527] There has been a proposal in Massachusetts to place the words "In God We Trust" in every public schoolroom.[528] All of these practices must be fairly characterized as solely religious,[529] and all of these mottoes undoubtedly would be found violative of someone's conscientious scruples.[530] Aside from the fact that they arguably violate the establishment clause because they involve a measurable and perhaps substantial expenditure of public funds solely in aid of religion,[531] it would seem that they would also fail under the standard proposed herein.

The identification of the public schools with these religiously oriented mottoes,[532] constantly in view of immature students with malleable minds and highest regard for the public school institution, is likely to result in influencing or compromising their religious beliefs.[533] This should be contrasted with the placing of a Christmas creche on the public school lawn that "was not erected or displayed while school was in session"[534] and where "no public funds were expended, nor was the time of any public employee involved in its erection or display."[535] The compromising or influencing potential here seems minimal indeed, as it probably also would if the creche were displayed within the school for a few days while classes were in session.[536]

---

527. See Note, 22 ALBANY L. REV. 156 (1958).

528. See AMERICAN CIVIL LIBERTIES UNION, 37TH ANNUAL REPORT 64 (1957).

529. The announced purpose of the New York program "was to strengthen the moral and spiritual values of the students in the school district." See Note, 22 ALBANY L. REV. 156 (1958).

530. See *ibid.* Note that those theses that propose "neutrality" as the constitutional determinant would seem to permit all of these since there is no constitutional bar to other symbols such as the American or state flag or the sign of the Red Cross or Heart Fund. Indeed, this analysis might well permit the permanent erection of a Crucifix or Star of David or of any extremely sectarian motto. See note 464 *supra.*

531. See note 182 *supra;* 3 N.D. CENT. CODE § 15–47–10 (1960): "The superintendent of public instruction may cause such placards to be printed and may charge an amount therefor that will cover the cost of printing and distribution."

532. *Cf.* Note, 49 COLUM. L. REV. 836, 840 (1949).

533. See text accompanying notes 243–46, 291–94 *supra.*

534. Baer v. Kolmorgen, 14 Misc. 2d 1015, 1019, 181 N.Y.S.2d 230, 236 (Sup. Ct. 1958).

535. *Ibid.*

536. See AMERICAN CIVIL LIBERTIES UNION, 39TH ANNUAL REPORT 39 (1959).

I. FLAG PLEDGE AND PATRIOTIC SONGS

In 1954, Congress amended the pledge of allegiance to the flag to include the words "under God." Whether as a general matter this is unconstitutional is not the question to be considered here. Rather, the issue is whether a school board's requirement that the pledge be stated each day in the public schools violates the establishment clause. This is a difficult question when measured by the proposed constitutional standard. If the only purpose and effect of the inclusion of these words is to have the student recognize the existence of God and to inculcate religious beliefs, then the words should be stricken for reasons previously examined. However, it could be argued that this activity is not solely religious; that, unlike the Regents' prayer that required an invocation of the Deity and a supplication to God,[537] the flag pledge merely requires the recitation of an historical fact—that this nation was believed to have been founded "under God" and that most of our people currently believe this still to be the case. The recitation of the flag pledge would then be no different from the recitation of Lincoln's Gettysburg Address which, while involving the mention of God, does not demand that the student swear allegiance to Him but merely requires the student to learn American history. On this characterization, the activity is secular, and, under the proposed standard, the establishment clause would not demand its exclusion. If some student's conscientious beliefs forbid participation,[538] the free exercise clause demands that he be excused.[539] The fact that he may be inherently compelled to participate is unfortunate but irrelevant.[540]

Even accepting this line of argument, the issue may not be fully resolved. The distinction presented is exceedingly subtle, very likely too fine to be perceived by even an above-average student. There is little doubt that the inclusion of the words "under God" in a daily school exercise will result in compromising of some students' conscientious scruples. Therefore, the argument that the establishment clause is violated because the state may accomplish its secular purpose—teaching students that the founding fathers and

---

537. "The 'Regents prayer' is an acknowledgement of our dependence upon Almighty God and a petition for the bestowal of His blessings." Engel v. Vitale, 10 N.Y.2d 174, 180, 176 N.E.2d 579, 581 (1961).

538. Objections have been raised. See Lewis v. Allen, 5 Misc. 2d 68, 159 N.Y.S.2d 807 (Sup. Ct. 1957), aff'd, 11 App. Div. 2d 447, 207 N.Y.S. 2d 862 (1960).

539. West Virginia State Bd. of Educ. v. Barnette, 319 U.S. 624 (1943).

540. See text accompanying notes 118–26 supra.

most citizens believe that this nation exists under God—just as effectively by less obtrusive means is quite forceful.[541]

An even closer question is presented by the public school activity of singing certain songs as part of the daily opening exercises. Some very popular patriotic compositions, such as "God Bless America" and the final stanza of "America,"[542] undeniably involve supplications to the Deity. This is probably true also of any number of songs. Nevertheless, it seems fair to contend that neither the purpose nor the effect of these is solely religious; the thrust of these songs is to instill love of country and not love of God. This argument becomes even more persuasive when the entire content and spirit of the remaining parts of the opening exercises is nonreligious. Perhaps this argument stretches the principle a bit. But even ardent separationists agree that this activity is secular.[543] Therefore, while the free exercise clause may demand the right of nonparticipation for students whose scruples forbid them from taking part, under the proposed standard, the establishment clause does not forbid the practice. The alternative position for establishment clause violation may also be satisfied by the contention that, since these songs have become something of an American tradition, it is doubtful that the state's secular purpose may be achieved *just as effectively* with their elimination. As to the third stanza of "The Star-Spangled Banner,"[544] the analysis above is even more forceful, especially since the words do not involve an invocation to God but are more like the recitation of historical facts.

J. HOLIDAY OBSERVANCE

The commemoration of certain religious holidays is a very com-

---

541. See text following note 346 *supra*.

542.
Our fathers' God! to Thee
Author of Liberty,
To Thee we sing;
Long may our land be bright
With freedom's holy light;
Protect us by Thy might,
Great God, our King!

543. See Pfeffer, *Court, Constitution and Prayer*, 16 RUTGERS L. REV. 735, 750 (1962); *cf.* McCluskey, quoted in THE STUDY OF RELIGION IN THE PUBLIC SCHOOLS: AN APPRAISAL 25 (Brown ed. 1958). See also Sutherland, *Establishment According to Engel*, 76 HARV. L. REV. 25, 38 (1962).

544.
Blest with victory and peace, may the heav'n rescued land
Praise the Power that hath made and preserved us a nation!
Then conquer we must, when our cause it is just,
And this be our motto—"In God is our Trust."

mon public school practice.[515] Many of the forms that this takes may not be fairly characterized as solely religious. Nor do many of these practices lend themselves to student participation. The presence of these two factors would clearly preclude an establishment clause violation under the proposed principle. Thus, the placing of a Christmas tree or an Easter bunny in the public school has virtually no religious significance and, even if it did, its short lived presence, combined with its scant religious import, would seem to have minimal effect.

The singing of religious songs and the staging of religious pageants are entirely another matter. While the tenor of some holiday songs (for example, "White Christmas" and "Jingle Bells") and of some plays (for example, Dickens' "Christmas Carol") is quite clearly associated with our people's culture rather than with their religious beliefs,[546] this cannot fairly be said of those whose language and purport is Christological, devotional, or otherwise religious. The evidence of the inherent compulsion on members of religious minorities to participate in these songs and pageants is substantial. At a school *in which Jewish children were in the majority,* a sixth grade pupil asked to be excused from the singing of Christmas hymns;[547] after class, she "was belabored by her classmates with such epithets as 'Christ-killer who refuses to sing hymns to Jesus Christ.' "[548] In reaction to or in anticipation of such occurrences, "many Jewish children, with the blend of ingenuousness and ingenuity natural to their age, . . . often engage in one or another subterfuge to produce the appearance of cooperation in the school celebration without at the same time genuinely participating in violation of their religious convictions."[549] The emotional ambivalence

---

545. A recent study showed that Christmas was celebrated in 88% of the public schools polled; Easter, 58%; Hanukkah, 5%; Passover, 2%. Dierenfield, *The Extent of Religious Influence in American Public Schools,* 56 RELIGIOUS EDUCATION 173, 176–77 (1961).

546. THE AMERICAN COLLEGE DICTIONARY 214 (Barnhart ed. 1959) gives, as a definition of Christmas: "Dec. 25 (Christmas Day), now generally observed as an occasion for gifts, greetings, etc." See also PFEFFER, CHURCH, STATE, AND FREEDOM 407 (1953); Rosenfield, *Separation of Church and State in the Public Schools,* 22 U. PITT. L. REV. 561, 573 (1961).

547. *Cf.* PFEFFER, *op. cit. supra* note 546, at 406:
Nor can any non-Jew rightfully assert that such singing ["Come, let us adore Him, Christ the Lord," or "Born is the King of Israel"] will not violate the Jewish child's religious conscience, any more than the school principals in the 19th century could rightfully assert that the Catholic child's religious conscience would not be violated by reading from the King James Bible.
548. *Id.* at 407.

549. PFEFFER & BAUM, PUBLIC SCHOOL SECTARIANISM AND THE JEWISH CHILD 6 (1957). See examples cited *id.* at 7–9; Franck, quoted in

that this produces is quite obvious. No doubt, many less determined children fully sacrifice their religious scruples by joining their colleagues. These solely religious activities that require student participation, whether it be the singing of hymns or the acting in plays, are likely to result in compromising conscientious convictions.[550] Nor is the practice validated under the establishment clause by celebrating the holidays of a greater number of religious faiths. Since religious leaders of all faiths have objected to this,[551] it would only seem to compound the difficulty.

Nothing that has been said would deter examination, in the public school curriculum, of certain aspects of religious holidays as an academic matter. Thus, the singing and learning of religious hymns in a music class, as part of the study of different types of musical compositions, must be fairly characterized as secular activity.[552] Likewise, the occasional showing of motion pictures that depict various religious happenings may be of considerable educational value,[553] and, even if not, the quantum of participation required would be so slight that it is unlikely that the compromising or influencing of conscientious scruples would occur. This last instance is to be contrasted with a public school group activity of making religious cut-outs to be pasted on the schoolroom windows and walls.[554] Here, the element of inherent compulsion seems quite powerful, and under the proposed constitutional standard, *if the children were required to make only religiously significant pictures,* and this practice were contrary to their religious beliefs, the establishment clause would be violated.

K.   PUBLIC SCHOOLS IN PAROCHIAL BUILDINGS

In a small percentage of school districts throughout the country, public school classes are held in church owned buildings.[555]

THE STUDY OF RELIGION IN THE PUBLIC SCHOOLS: AN APPRAISAL 60 (Brown ed. 1958); Gilbert, *A Catalogue of Church-State Problems,* 56 RELIGIOUS EDUCATION 424, 429 (1961).

550. *But see* Levy, *Views From the Wall—Reflections on Church-State Relationships,* 29 HENNEPIN LAW. 51, 56 (1961).

551. See PFEFFER, *op. cit. supra* note 546, at 410–12; AMERICAN CIVIL LIBERTIES UNION, 41ST ANNUAL REPORT 27–28 (1961).

552. See Pfeffer, *Court, Constitution and Prayer,* 16 RUTGERS L. REV. 735, 750 (1962).

553. *But see* Chamberlin v. Dade County School Bd., 17 Fla. Supp. 183, 196 (Cir. Ct. 1961).

554. *Cf.* Sutherland, *Due Process and Disestablishment,* 62 HARV. L. REV. 1306, 1344 (1949).

555. Dierenfield, *The Extent of Religious Influence in American Public Schools,* 56 RELIGIOUS EDUCATION 173, 177 (1961), reports almost 8%.

This practice has spawned a good deal of litigation in the state courts. If the practice involves no more than the school board's renting the only available property,[556] it may hardly be fairly characterized as solely religious. Thus, there would be no violation of the establishment clause, either under the proposed constitutional standard or under the alternative test previously discussed.[557] The fact that the school rooms have religious pictures and decorations[558] would possibly not alter these conclusions, despite the fact that their placement in an ordinary public school would be objectionable; if, irrespective of the religious decor, the church building is still found to be the best available space, the issue is entirely different.[559] It may be reasonably argued that no matter how great the amount of religious infusion in the environment due to quasi-control by the church, the school board's practice of using parochial buildings cannot be said to be solely religious, either in purpose or in effect; in each instance, it is the considered judgment of the public school board that, on balance, these are the best available facilities for public education. Perhaps this would immunize the practice under the proposed standard.

This may not be the case in regard to the alternative criterion for establishment clause violation. It is ultimately the function of the Court to determine whether "on balance, these are the best available facilities" and whether the secular end may not be attained by less objectionable means. It has been suggested that the solution here is: "that which is legally tolerable ends where the religious infusion becomes unreasonably great."[560] But certain guidelines may be established. Public officials should not be permitted to abdicate their responsibility of selecting teachers and textbooks to clerical authorities.[561] The potentiality for unchecked religious indoctrination of public school students in these cir-

---

556. See Rawlings v. Butler, 290 S.W.2d 801, 806–07 (Ky. 1956).
557. See text accompanying note 523 *supra.*
558. See State *ex rel.* Johnson v. Boyd, 217 Ind. 348, 359, 28 N.E.2d 256, 261 (1940).
559. This line of argument assumes, of course, that the pictures and decorations are there without the consent of the public school officials. If they had control over these matters, then the retention of these decorations could be accurately described as a solely religious activity.
560. Sutherland, *Public Authority and Religious Education: A Brief Survey of Constitutional and Legal Limits,* in THE STUDY OF RELIGION IN THE PUBLIC SCHOOLS: AN APPRAISAL 33, 43 (Brown ed. 1958).
561. See Millard v. Board of Educ., 121 Ill. 297, 301, 10 N.E. 669, 671 (1887); State *ex rel.* Johnson v. Boyd, 217 Ind. 348, 358, 28 N.E.2d 256, 261 (1940); Berghorn v. Reorganized School Dist., 364 Mo. 121, 130, 260 S.W.2d 573, 576 (1953). Compare Crain v. Walker, 222 Ky. 828, 839, 2 S.W.2d 654, 659 (1928).

cumstances would seem so great[562] that no justification for it should be held acceptable, perhaps even if the result is tantamount to the temporary suspension of the so-called "public" education. The same, of course, must be said if the result of the use of the parochial buildings is compulsory religious teaching.[563] In such cases, the Court should find that alternative means (for example, construction of an independent public school building or arranging for public education in another school district) must be used to accomplish the secular end of providing a public education. Even if the Constitution permits the use of public funds to aid parochial education, this is no authority for the proposition that the state may demand that children of all faiths who wish a "public education" attend a publicly supported institution that is essentially no different from a parochial school.

On the other hand, if the unalterable consequences of using church property for public education are that the schools, granting the right of nonparticipation, engage in certain solely religious practices such as prayers and worship in daily chapel exercises[564] or programs of religious instruction akin to released time,[565] the Court should place a heavy burden on the state to demonstrate that less objectionable means do not exist. Otherwise, all the protections afforded religious liberty in the public schools that have been discussed may be easily circumvented by turning over some of the control of public education to the clergy of a particular religious faith.[566]

---

562. See, *e.g.*, Knowlton v. Baumhover, 182 Iowa 691, 703, 166 N.W. 202, 206 (1918); Harfst v. Hoegen, 349 Mo. 808, 811, 163 S.W.2d 609, 610 (1942); Zellers v. Huff, 55 N.M. 501, 506, 236 P.2d 949, 952 (1951); Boyer, *Religious Education of Public School Pupils in Wisconsin*, 1953 WIS. L. REV. 181, 217–225.

563. See cases cited note 562 *supra*.

564. See Williams v. Board of Trustees, 172 Ky. 133, 134, 188 S.W. 1058 (1916); Berghorn v. Reorganized School Dist., 364 Mo. 121, 131–32, 260 S.W.2d 573, 577–78 (1953).

565. See Millard v. Board of Educ., 121 Ill. 297, 302, 10 N.E. 669, 671 (1887); State *ex rel.* Johnson v. Boyd, 217 Ind. 348, 359, 28 N.E.2d 256, 261–62 (1940); Zellers v. Huff, 55 N.M. 501, 507–08, 236 P.2d 949, 953 (1951); Boyer, *supra* note 562.

566. *Cf.* Knowlton v. Baumhover, 182 Iowa 691, 725–26, 166 N.W. 202, 213 (1918):

[W]henever the adherents of any particular creed can command a majority of any school board, it may abandon the schoolhouse provided for the common and equal use of all the people, move the school into some church or some parochial or private building established for sectarian use, put in charge of it trained ecclesiastics bound by solemn vows to devote their lives, their services, and all their God-given powers to the advancement of the interest of their church, fill the school with distinctive emblems of their faith, and by a multitude

CONCLUSION

The purpose of this article has not been to reconcile the myriad of state court decisions involving the problems of religion and the public schools. There has been no attempt to demonstrate the existence of an internal consistency even within the very few cases decided by the Supreme Court. Nor has the endeavor been to predict the outcome of future litigation. While the recent decision in *Engel v. Vitale* has been examined, it has not been suggested that the case permits of only one interpretation. Rather, the purpose here has been to submit a rational and desirable standard for constitutional adjudication in this area, and to demonstrate its application in some specific situations. In many of these instances, "nice" distinctions have been drawn. But a "boundary line is none the worse for being narrow."[567] It should be made clear that "the principle offered is meant to provide a starting point for solutions to problems brought before the Court, not a mechanical answer to them."[568] If some of the underlying factual premises advanced here are shown to be incorrect, the results suggested must be changed. But the principle should be adhered to.

Central to the theme of this article has been the fact that it is vital to the preservation of religious liberty to recognize that although "you send your child to the schoolmaster . . . 'tis the schoolboys who educate him."[569] Voluntariness is a concept, not merely a word. "Compulsion which comes from circumstances can be as real as compulsion which comes from a command."[570] If the price for the protection of religious liberty in the public schools is the abolition of certain religious influences,[571] that price must be paid. Although this conclusion may be said to manifest no more than "the traditional American weakness of identifying our own preferences and predilections with the Constitution,"[572] the effort has been made to submerge these preferences and predilections in favor of historical and contemporary national goals.

---

of influences, silent as well as expressed, shape the plastic minds and characters of the young children committed to their care in accordance with their own religious views, and saddle the expense of this sectarian education upon the taxpayers.

567. McLeod v. J. E. Dilworth Co., 322 U.S. 327, 329 (1944).

568. Kurland, *Of Church and State and the Supreme Court*, 29 U. CHI. L. REV. 1, 6 (1961).

569. EMERSON, THE CONDUCT OF LIFE 123 (1860).

570. Public Util. Comm'n v. Pollak, 343 U.S. 451, 468 (1962) (Douglas, J., dissenting).

571. See Kirven, *Freedom of Religion or Freedom from Religion?*, 48 A.B.A.J. 816, 819 (1962).

572. Kauper, *Church, State, and Freedom: A Review*, 52 MICH. L. REV. 829, 848 (1954).

MICHIGAN LAW REVIEW

| Vol. 61 | APRIL 1963 | No. 6 |

PRAYER, PUBLIC SCHOOLS AND THE SUPREME COURT

Paul G. Kauper*

Public reaction to the Supreme Court's decision in *Engel v. Vitale*,[1] decided in June 1962 and holding invalid a nonsectarian prayer prescribed for use in the public schools of the State of New York, made clear that the decision had touched a vital and sensitive spot in the national life.[2] Unfavorable response to the holding ranged from intemperate and abusive denunciation of the Court as Godless to more thoughtful and reflective criticism that was directed to various considerations such as that the Court in interpreting the first amendment had failed to give due weight to the place of religion in American tradition and life, had misinterpreted the original meaning and purpose of this amendment, had conferred a constitutional blessing upon secularism as the official American orthodoxy, and had unduly subordinated the majority will and the community consensus to the sentiments and wishes of a small minority. Some, while not disturbed by the result reached with respect to the problem immediately before the Court, saw large and portentous implications in the decision. Did it mean that the Constitution forbade not only religious practices in the public schools but also any consideration of religion in public school programs? And did it mean that all acknowledgments of Deity on official occasions was forbidden?

Not all of the immediate reaction to *Engel* was critical. Secularists and strict separationists hailed the decision as adding strength to the wall of separation between church and state, while others applauded the decision as a further contribution to religious freedom. Moreover, much of the initial criticism was dissipated when

* Professor of Law, University of Michigan.—Ed.

1 370 U.S. 421 (1962).

2 For some expression of opinion, see 108 Cong. Rec. 11002-08 (daily ed. June 27, 1962); 108 *id.* 10883-86, 10897-98 (daily ed. June 26, 1962); Editorial, *Roundup on Prayer Case*, America, July 28, 1962, p. 541; N.Y. Times, July 1, 1962, § 4, p. 9, cols. 1-6; *id.*, June 28, 1962, p. 1, col. 4, p. 17, cols. 1-3; *id.*, June 27, 1962, p. 1, col. 8, p. 20, col. 3; *id.*, June 26, 1962, p. 1, cols. 6-8, p. 16, col. 7. See also Kurland, *The Regents' Prayer Case: "Full of Sound and Fury, Signifying . . .",* 1962 Supreme Court Rev. 1, 2.

the Court's full opinion was read and understood. A substantial part of the press and a number of religious leaders and groups announced their support of the decision as one which, by restricting the state's power to intervene in the sensitive area of prayer, thereby advanced and protected the liberty of both the believer and the non-believer.[3] Also, some who supported the holding asserted that it did not outlaw all recognition of religion in the public schools and had nothing to say whatever about acknowledgment of Deity in public pronouncements and on official occasions. The decision did not make God an outlaw so far as the national life was concerned. Likewise, any larger implications of the case with respect to the use of public funds or property to aid religious activities were attributable not to the majority opinion but to Mr. Justice Douglas' concurring opinion.

A more complete understanding of the case, while doing much to temper the initial outburst of disapproval, did not by any means dispel all criticism of the decision or allay all the apprehensions aroused by it. Believing that the Supreme Court's opinion was premised on a fundamentally erroneous interpretation of the establishment clause of the first amendment, Bishop James A. Pike headed a movement to amend the Constitution so as to restore what he regarded as the true and intended meaning of its pertinent language.[4] In the meantime, the Supreme Court has agreed to review and has heard argument on cases dealing with the constitutionality of Bible reading and recitation of the Lord's Prayer in public schools.[5] The decisions in these cases may be ex-

---

[3] See, e.g., Editorial, *Prayer is Personal*, N.Y. Times, June 27, 1962, p. 34, col. 1; Editorial, The Christian Century, July 4, 1962, p. 832; Miller, *True Piety and the Regents' Prayer*, The Christian Century, Aug. 1, 1962, p. 934; *Ruling on Prayer Upheld by Rabbis*, N.Y. Times, July 1, 1962, p. 48, col. 3; *Statement of 46 Protestant Clergymen*, Time, Aug. 24, 1962, p. 40.

[4] Bishop Pike proposed before the Senate Judiciary Committee that the first amendment be amended to read as follows: "Congress will make no law respecting the recognition, as an established church, of any denomination, sect or other religious association." For a statement of his views, see Debate by William J. Butler and the Rt. Rev. James A. Pike, *Has the Supreme Court Outlawed Religious Observance in the Schools?*, Reader's Digest, Oct. 1962, pp. 78-85. Bishop Pike declared that the Supreme Court's decision in effect "*deconsecrates* not merely the schools but the *nation*." *Id.* at 79. For discussion and criticism of Bishop Pike's interpretation of the original and intended meaning of the establishment clause, see Smylie, *The First Amendment and Bishop Pike*, The Christian Century, Oct. 31, 1962, pp. 1316-18.

Some fifty-odd proposals to amend the Constitution in order to overcome the result of the *Engel* decision were introduced in the House of Representatives and in the Senate of the United States. For a brief discussion of several of these proposals, see Sutherland, *Establishment According to Engel*, 76 HARV. L. REV. 25, 50-52 (1962).

[5] The cases under review are Murray v. Curlett, 228 Md. 239, 179 A.2d 698, *cert. granted*, 371 U.S. 809 (1962), in which the Maryland Court of Appeals had sustained

pected to result in resumption of the public debate sparked by
Engel.[6]

I. THE NEW YORK TRIAL COURT'S OPINION

The facts of the *Engel* case are simply stated.[7] A local public
school board, acting on the recommendation of the New York
Board of Regents,[8] adopted a resolution directing the daily recitation of the following prayer which the Board had composed for
this purpose:

> "Almighty God, we acknowledge our dependence upon Thee,
> and we beg Thy blessings upon us, our parents, our teachers
> and our country."

The prayer was to be recited at the beginning of the school day,
following the pledge of allegiance to the flag. The school board's
regulation made no allowance for students who objected to participation, but the board did provide in an instruction that was
not incorporated in its resolution or otherwise publicized that
no child was to be required or encouraged to join in the prayer
against his or her wishes. Only one request that a child be excused
from saying the prayer was received in the schools of the district,
which request was respected; and no child had directly asked to
be excused from joining in the prayer, nor had either a parent
or a child sought permission for a child to leave the classroom
during the saying of the prayer. The petitioners, who were taxpayers of the school district and parents of children in the schools
of the district and whose group included Jews, Unitarians, members of the Society of Ethical Culture, and one non-believer, after

the constitutionality of the Maryland school commissioner's rule requiring the daily
reading of one chapter of the Bible and/or daily recital of the Lord's Prayer in
public schools; Schempp v. School Dist., 201 F. Supp. 815 (E.D. Pa.), *prob. juris. noted*,
371 U.S. 807 (1962), a decision of a federal three-judge court holding unconstitutional a
Pennsylvania statute requiring ten verses of the Bible to be read daily in public
schools and also the school district's practice of mass recitation of the Lord's Prayer.
Argument on these cases was heard on February 28 and March 1, 1963.

6 For discussion of the legal aspects of the *Engel* decision, see Ball, *The Forbidden
Prayer*, The Commonwealth, July 27, 1962, p. 419; Kurland, *supra* note 2; Pfeffer, *State-
Sponsored Prayer*, The Commonwealth, July 27, 1962, p. 417; Pfeffer, *Court, Constitution
and Prayer*, 16 RUTGERS L. REV. 735 (1962); Smylie, *supra* note 4; Sutherland, *supra* note
4; 12 DE PAUL L. REV. 128 (1962); 31 FORDHAM L. REV. 201 (1962); 51 GEO. L.J. 179
(1962); 37 TUL. L. REV. 124 (1962); 24 U. PITT. L. REV. 179 (1962).

7 The complete statement appears in the opinion of the trial court in Engel v.
Vitale, 18 Misc. 2d 659, 191 N.Y.S.2d 453 (Sup. Ct. 1959).

8 The recommendation with respect to the prayer was part of a total program set
forth in the Regents' Statement on Moral and Spiritual Training in the Schools, adopted
November 30, 1951. In 1955, this statement was supplemented by the Regents' Recommendations for School Programs on America's Moral and Spiritual Heritage.

an unsuccessful demand upon the school board that the daily prayer practice be terminated, brought a proceeding in a New York court for a mandatory order directing that the prayer practice be discontinued. Asserting that the use of this official prayer in the public schools was contrary to the beliefs, religions, or religious practices of both themselves and their children, they contended that the state's action, both in authorizing the use of this prayer and in ordering its daily recitation by children in public school classrooms, was unconstitutional. Reliance was placed upon the first and fourteenth amendments to the Constitution of the United States and upon the provisions of the New York constitution guaranteeing the free exercise and enjoyment of religious profession and worship, without discrimination or preference, and forbidding public aid to a school in which any denominational tenet or doctrine is taught.

It is unfortunate that all the attention riveted on the final opinion in the case by the United States Supreme Court has served to obscure the opinion by Justice Meyer of the New York trial court.[9] It was an extraordinarily able, thorough and scholarly opinion which did more to illuminate the problems and issues of the case than any other opinions at further stages of the litigation. The gist of the trial court's holding may be briefly stated before we take a closer look at the judge's opinion. He held that the prayer exercise did not violate that clause of the first amendment protecting the free exercise of religion so long as the school board established procedures designed to assure voluntariness of participation in the prayer practice by protecting those who objected to saying the prayer, and found also that it did not constitute an establishment of religion as forbidden by the first amendment. He further found that the prayer practice was not "denominational" within the meaning of the New York constitution and emphasized that this was a prayer *exercise* and not religious instruction in any real sense of the word. While he denied the petitioners the relief they had requested, he did direct the school board to adopt and publicize regulations stating the rules to be observed with respect to the rights of non-participants. He recommended for this purpose the regulation adopted by the New York City Board of Education, which made clear that neither teachers nor any school authority could comment on participation or non-participation in the exercise or suggest or require any par-

---

9 Engel v. Vitale, 18 Misc. 2d 659, 191 N.Y.S.2d 453 (Sup. Ct. 1959).

ticular posture, language, or dress in connection with recitation of the prayer. Non-participation could take the form either of remaining silent during the exercise, or, if the parent or child so desired, of being excused altogether from the exercise. He recommended that the regulations provide that prayer participants could proceed to a common assembly while non-participants attended other rooms, or that non-participants would be permitted to arrive at school a few minutes late or attend separate opening exercises, or authorize any other procedure which assured equal freedom for both participants and non-participants.

The heart of the trial court's extensive and well-documented opinion dealt with the issues raised under the first amendment as made applicable to the states by means of the fourteenth amendment. Stating as a fundamental rule of interpretation that the meaning of a constitutional amendment is to be determined by the "sense of the nation" at the time of its adoption, Justice Meyer, after reviewing historical practices and pointing out that prayer and Bible reading in public schools have been common American practices, concluded that prayer recitation in public schools did not violate the fourteenth amendment as construed by the sense of the nation when this amendment was adopted in 1868. Recognizing, however, that the Supreme Court had held that the first amendment applies to the states by means of the fourteenth amendment, the trial court found no violation of the free exercise clause so long as the right of objectors not to participate in the prayer exercise was adequately protected. So far as the establishment clause was concerned, the court again relied upon historical practice and understanding to demonstrate the sense of the nation that recitation of prayers in public life was not "an establishment of religion" in the sense used in the Constitution or as understood by men such as Jefferson or Madison. Nor did the trial court find that the Supreme Court's opinions interpreting the establishment language required a different result. In the end it placed chief reliance upon the holding and opinion in the *Zorach*[10] case in concluding that some form of prayer would fall within the realm of permissible accommodation of the public school system to the religious needs of the nation.[11]

In weighing the reasons for including this kind of prayer exercise in the public school program, the trial court concluded

10 Zorach v. Clauson, 343 U.S. 306 (1952).
11 Engel v. Vitale, 18 Misc. 2d 659, 693-94, 191 N.Y.S.2d 453, 490-91 (Sup. Ct. 1959).

that it could not be justified on the ground that this was a means of familiarizing students with the religious nature of our heritage since there are other equally effective and constitutionally uninhibited means of achieving that end. Moreover, it could not be justified on the ground that the state could prescribe exercises designed to inculcate in pupils a love of God or to teach "spiritual values," since an exercise directed to such purposes would constitute religious instruction in violation of the establishment clause and in violation of the parents' right to control the education of his child. However, the court concluded that the recognition of prayer as an integral part of our national heritage was demonstrated by practices widely accepted at the time of the adoption of the first and the fourteenth amendments and that, therefore, these constitutional provisions could not have been intended to prohibit prayer in public schools any more than in other aspects of public life.[12]

In summary, the trial court concluded that, since the first and fourteenth amendments should be construed with reference to the "sense of the nation" at the time of their adoption and since recognition of prayer was an integral part of our national heritage, prayer in public schools did not constitute an establishment of religion and did not violate religious freedom so long as the regulations made clear that student participation in the prayer exercise was a voluntary matter and adequate provision was made for those children desiring not to participate.

The trial court's decision was affirmed on appeal by the New York appellate courts.[13] Their opinions rested on substantially the same grounds as those stated more extensively in the trial court's opinion. Judges Dye and Fuld of the New York Court of Appeals dissented on the ground that the prayer exercise violated the establishment clause as interpreted by the Supreme Court in *Everson*[14] and *McCollum*.[15]

II. The Supreme Court's Opinions

The Supreme Court of the United States on review of the case reversed the decision of the New York Court of Appeals and found the prayer practice unconstitutional because it constituted an es-

---

12 *Id.* at 673, 191 N.Y.S.2d at 470.
13 Engel v. Vitale, 11 App. Div. 2d 340, 206 N.Y.S.2d 183 (1960), *aff'd*, 10 N.Y.2d 174, 176 N.E.2d 579, 218 N.Y.S.2d 659 (1961).
14 Everson v. Board of Educ., 330 U.S. 1 (1947).
15 McCollum v. Board of Educ., 333 U.S. 203 (1948).

tablishment of religion in violation of the first and fourteenth amendments.[16] The case was decided by a seven-man court, Justices Frankfurter and White not participating in the decision. The majority opinion written by Mr. Justice Black received the support of Mr. Chief Justice Warren and Justices Brennan, Clark and Harlan. Mr. Justice Douglas concurred in a separate opinion and Mr. Justice Stewart wrote a dissenting opinion.

At the outset, Mr. Justice Black stated the Court's conclusion that New York "by using its school system to encourage recitation of the Regents' prayer . . . has adopted a practice wholly inconsistent with the Establishment Clause."[17] In passages of the opinion that followed he stated that there was no doubt that the New York program of daily classroom invocation of God's blessings was a religious activity, that counsel was correct in asserting that the use of prayer to further religious beliefs breached the constitutional wall of separation between church and state, and that the constitutional prohibition "must at least mean that in this country it is no part of the business of government to compose official prayers for any group of American people to recite as a part of a religious program carried on by government."[18]

In building up his case on the significance of the first amendment's establishment clause in its application to the prayer situation, Mr. Justice Black drew upon the history of practices in England whereby Parliament, in asserting control over the established Church of England and over the Church's Book of Common Prayer, determined what prayers should be included in this book. Objections to this practice led some people to come to this country to find religious freedom, and in England the control by Parliament over prayer led to competition of various groups to secure approval of their particular form of prayer. Mr. Justice Black then stated that many of those who came to this country to find religious freedom in turn established their official religions and were equally intolerant and oppressive. Nevertheless, intensive opposition to the practice of establishing religion by law followed in the wake of the Revolutionary War. This movement crystallized rapidly into an effective opposition that eventually led to the enactment of the famous "Virginia Bill for Religious Liberty," by which all religious groups were placed on an equal footing so far as the state was concerned. By the time, then, that

16 Engel v. Vitale, 370 U.S. 421 (1962).
17 *Id.* at 424.
18 *Id.* at 425.

the Constitution was adopted there was widespread awareness among many Americans of the danger of a union of church and state—the danger to the freedom of the individual to worship in his own way when government places its stamp of approval on one particular kind of prayer, and the bitter strife that comes when zealous religious groups struggle to obtain the government's approval from each ruler that may temporarily come to power. The first amendment to the Constitution was added as a guarantee that neither the power nor the prestige of the federal government would be used to control, support or influence the kinds of prayer the American people can say.

Mr. Justice Black then stated there could be no doubt that the New York school prayer program officially established the religious beliefs embodied in the Regents' prayer and so violated the establishment clause of the first amendment which is operative against the states also "by virtue of the fourteenth amendment."[19] It was immaterial that the prayer was "non-denominational" or that the observance of prayer practice by students was voluntary. Voluntarism might free the prayer from objections under the free exercise clause but not from the establishment clause. The two clauses, even though they overlap, forbid two quite different kinds of "encroachment upon religious freedom."[20] The establishment clause does not depend upon any showing of direct governmental compulsion and is violated by the enactment of laws which establish an official religion, whether these laws operate directly to coerce non-observing individuals or not. But at this point Mr. Justice Black saw fit to inject that this is not

> "to say, of course, that laws officially prescribing a particular form of religious worship do not involve coercion of individuals. When the power, prestige and financial support of government is placed behind a particular religious belief, the indirect coercive pressure upon religious minorities to conform to the prevailing officially approved religion is plain."[21]

But, continued Mr. Justice Black, the purposes underlying the establishment clause go much farther than that. Its first and most immediate purpose is grounded on the belief that a union of government and religion tends to destroy government and to

19 *Id.* at 430.
20 *Ibid.*
21 *Id.* at 430-31.

degrade religion. Another purpose rests upon an awareness of the fact that governmentally established religion and religious persecution go hand in hand.

Denying that this application of the Constitution to prohibit state laws respecting an establishment of religious services in public schools indicated a hostility to religion or toward prayer, Mr. Justice Black, noting that the history of man is inseparable from the history of religion and also that men of faith in the power of prayer led the fight for adoption of the Constitution and the Bill of Rights, concluded:

> "It is neither sacrilegious nor antireligious to say that each separate government in this country should stay out of the business of writing or sanctioning official prayers and leave that purely religious function to the people themselves and to those the people choose to look to for religious guidance."[22]

Referring to the argument that the Regents' prayer did not amount to a total establishment of one particular religion and that governmental endorsement of this prayer was relatively insignificant when compared with the governmental encroachments upon religions which were commonplace two hundred years ago, Mr. Justice Black quoted the following words from James Madison, whom he described as "the author of the first amendment":

> "It is proper to take alarm at the first experiment on our liberties . . . . Who does not see that the same authority which can establish Christianity, in exclusion of all other Religions, may establish with the same ease any particular sect of Christians, in exclusion of all other Sects? That the same authority which can force a citizen to contribute three pence only of his property for the support of any one establishment, may force him to conform to any other establishment in all cases whatsoever?"[23]

Mr. Justice Douglas concurred in a separate opinion in which he premised his whole case on the argument that government cannot constitutionally finance a religious exercise. He made clear that in his opinion there was no element of compulsion or coercion involved in the New York prayer practice. But he condemned New York's action because it financed a religious exercise and went

22 *Id.* at 435.
23 *Id.* at 436.

on to state his opinion that all practices (and in a footnote he referred to numerous ones), whereby a public official on a public payroll performs or conducts a religious exercise in a governmental institution, fall within the same category. While he could not say that to authorize this prayer was to establish religion in "the strictly historic meaning"[24] of those words, yet once government finances a religious exercise it inserts a divisive influence into our communities. The first amendment leaves the government in a position not of hostility to religion but of neutrality. If government interferes in matters spiritual, it will act as a divisive force. "The First Amendment teaches that a government neutral in the field of religion better serves all religious interests."[25]

Mr. Justice Stewart dissented. Emphasizing that it could not be argued that New York had interfered with the free exercise of anybody's religion, he rejected the idea that letting those who wanted to say this prayer say it thereby established "an official religion." On the contrary, he viewed the prayer practice as an opportunity for children to share in the nation's spiritual heritage. Unimpressed by the review in the majority's opinion of the history of an established church in England or in eighteenth century America, he found much more relevant, as an aid to interpretation of the first amendment, "the history of the religious traditions of our people, reflected in countless practices of the institutions and officials of our government."[26] He pointed to the prayers used in opening the Supreme Court's daily session and the daily sessions of both houses of Congress, the prayer found in the third stanza of the National Anthem, the motto "In God We Trust" impressed on our coins, and the inclusion of the phrase "under God" in the pledge of allegiance to the flag. He stated that it was all summed up in the Court's opinion in *Zorach* when it said, "We are a religious people whose institutions presuppose a Supreme Being."[27] What New York had done, as well as the Court, the Congress and the President, had been "to recognize and to follow the deeply entrenched and highly cherished spiritual traditions of our Nation."[28]

24 *Id.* at 442.
25 *Id.* at 443.
26 *Id.* at 446.
27 343 U.S. at 313.
28 Engel v. Vitale, 370 U.S. at 450.

III. THE SCOPE OF THE HOLDING

What then is the significance of the *Engel* case? Viewed with reference to its facts, the case can be limited to a narrow holding, namely, that a state may not prescribe the daily recitation by children under the teacher's supervision of an officially composed prayer in a public school classroom as part of the school's regular program. All of these elements become significant. Not only was the state sanctioning a particular prayer but was using the public school system's machinery to make it an official prayer, and by requiring it as a part of the regular school program conducted by the teacher—the symbol of classroom authority—it was encouraging children to participate. Indeed, in view of all the circumstances, and with due recognition of the psychology of the classroom, objecting children, though free not to participate, were subject to a subtle pressure to conform.

The *Engel* decision reaches only the official prescription of an officially approved prayer for daily recitation in a public school classroom. Of course, it does not outlaw prayer in the public schools. Pupils and teachers are free to engage in silent prayer, and it is consistent with the decision to permit a period for silent prayer. Moreover, it is important to note that the case deals with an officially approved prayer which the teacher is *required* by order of the school board to conduct. The case does not deal with the situation where those in charge of the classroom have a discretionary authority to permit opportunity for children voluntarily to express their individual prayers. Nor does the case deal with the question whether ministers may offer prayers in connection with public school programs. In neither of these situations are public officers or employees charged with a duty of conducting in a public school a religious program centered on a state-approved prayer. It was the degree of the state's involvement in this particular prayer, infusing it with the force and compulsive character of state-sanctioned action, which peculiarly identifies the problem of the *Engel* case and also suggest the limits on the holding.

Even less does the holding in *Engel* suggest that the public schools must display a studied indifference to religion or exclude from their programs a consideration and appreciation of religion in the nation's life or deny opportunity for children, individually or collectively, to engage in exercises that reflect belief in God or acknowledge the nation's dependence upon Him. The following passage taken from a footnote to the majority opinion is of special interest in this connection:

> "There is of course nothing in the decision reached here that is inconsistent with the fact that school children and others are officially encouraged to express love for our country by reciting historical documents such as the Declaration of Independence which contain references to the Deity or by singing officially espoused anthems which include the composer's professions of faith in a Supreme Being, or with the fact that there are many manifestations in our public life of belief in God."[29]

This important statement is a concession by the Court which in a very significant way limits the holding and rationale of the case. Even though the Court goes on to say that "such patriotic or ceremonial occasions bear no true resemblance to the unquestioned religious exercise that the State of New York has sponsored in this instance," the fact remains that whether children sing or recite a prayer and whether the prayer is identified with expressions of patriotic sentiment or not, the school program is being used to encourage an expression of religious faith in accordance with the dominant national and community *ethos*. The distinction is made by the Court that such patriotic exercises are not distinctively religious in character. How solid a basis this is for distinction is questionable. The non-sectarian prayer in its invocation of God's blessing upon "our country" also fosters love of country. Moreover, since the prayer followed the pledge of allegiance to the flag, it could be viewed as part of a total program in which patriotic and religious sentiments were commingled. The Court in the footnote passage referred to did not expressly mention the pledge of allegiance, which now contains the phrase "under God." But if the national anthem, including its third stanza which is distinctively a prayer, can appropriately be sung in the public schools, it should follow also that recitation of the pledge of allegiance is permitted.

Whether a distinction drawn in legal terms between school exercises which are primarily religious in character, even though they include an underlying patriotic sentiment and can be said to be directed to patriotic ends, and those which are primarily patriotic in character and yet are also infused with a religious

29 *Id.* at 435 n.21.

sentiment and consciousness, is a substantial and tenable one is open to question. At most it is a distinction of degree, and under such a test some form of prayer would be permissible. It seems to the writer that the element which adds substance to the distinction drawn by the Court is that the religious beliefs and sentiments expressed in national historical documents and utterances and in the National Anthem have been an established part of the national tradition as compared with a prayer specially composed by state authorities for official use and lacking the sanction established by common and nationwide historical usage. This at once raises the question whether the fact that the non-sectarian prayer was an officially *composed* as well as an officially approved prayer was an important element in the decision. The language in the body of the opinion as well as the distinction made in the footnote discussed above suggest that this was a critical factor. But should it be? On the surface it should be immaterial whether public school authorities themselves compose a prayer prescribed for recitation in public schools or adopt for official use a prayer composed by some other person or persons or regularly used by one or more religious bodies. In either case the government is putting its stamp of approval upon a particular prayer. But if, as suggested above, a distinction can be made between the historic expressions of religious faith that have evolved out of the national life and have become a part of the common national heritage and those not similarly sanctioned by history, the fact that a prayer actually originates with public officials does assume special significance. This question assumes a critical importance in cases which are presently before the Court and which raise the issue whether recitation of the Lord's Prayer in the public schools comes under the ban of the *Engel* decision.[30] Here is a prayer sanctioned by historical usage and one reflecting the common religious heritage of a majority of Americans. It cannot be attributed to the government. On its face the Lord's Prayer is non-sectarian but it is subject to special attack on the ground that it is distinctively the prayer of Christians and that hence the state in presenting or authorizing its use is preferring one religion over another. In this situation it appears likely that the Court, faced with the choice of either approving the recitation of the Lord's Prayer on the ground that it is not officially composed but has its

---

[30] Schempp v. School Dist., 201 F. Supp. 815 (E.D. Pa.), *prob. juris. noted,* 371 U.S. 807 (1962); Murray v. Curlett, 228 Md. 239, 179 A.2d 698, *cert. granted,* 371 U.S. 809 (1962).

own special sanction in history or holding it invalid as sectarian and preferential in character, will follow the latter course. If this proves to be the case, the element of official composition loses its significance, and officially recognized prayers and acknowledgments of Deity may be prescribed for daily ritualistic use in public schools only if incorporated in an exercise of recitation or song which in its totality is characterized as patriotic in character.

The cases[31] before the Court this term also involve state laws which require or authorize the reading without comment of a chapter of the Bible or a certain number of biblical verses at the beginning of the school day. Here the considerations are somewhat different. Students are not asked to recite something as an expression of their own religious belief. The religious and moral ideas of the Bible carry their own spiritual authority, unlike religious ideas stamped as authoritative because they are composed and approved by public officials. In relation to religion, morality and culture, the Bible as a book assumes a prominent place in the world's literature. No one can seriously argue that exposure to or study of the Bible is out of place in the public schools. But the Bible can also be characterized as a sectarian book. For Christians, the Bible is the book of historic revelation on which their faith is founded. The Jewish religious community looks to the Old Testament for its sacred scripture. Any use of the New Testament in the public schools to promote the Christian faith is offensive to persons of the Jewish faith. And in turn Catholics object to the use of biblical translations which they regard as distinctively Protestant in character. Objections may be made by other persons of varying beliefs to any use of the Bible which carries the connotation that it is officially regarded and accepted as revelation of divine truth. Despite these considerations, it should be permissible to read and study the Bible in the public schools both because of its historical and literary features and because it is a source of religious and moral ideas that have influenced our culture and civilization. But to use it in the public schools as a means of religious indoctrination or for the cultivation of religious faith is objectionable. The difficulty with a prescribed daily reading of the Bible without comment is that, rather than a meaningful program of study, it becomes more like a religiously ritualistic exercise, premised on the assumption that the Bible's teachings are inspired and authoritative, and subject to

---

31 Cases cited in note 30 *supra.*

the charge that the state is thereby giving a preference to the religious groups that regard the Bible as their sacred scripture. But to state these considerations is to recognize that Bible reading in the public schools does raise considerations not present in the prayer case. State courts have disagreed on whether Bible reading is a forbidden form of sectarian instruction.[32] In the light of the long history of this practice, its widespread prevalence at present, its sanctioning by a number of state courts, and doubts that the Court may entertain as to whether Bible reading is as distinctively a religious exercise as the recitation of a prayer and whether such reading serves a valid educational purpose, the way is open to the Supreme Court, if it so chooses, to hold that *Engel* does not require the invalidation of Bible-reading practices.

With respect to other aspects of the general problem respecting religion and the public schools, the *Engel* decision makes no directly relevant contribution. The majority opinion does not cite the released-time cases, and the case has no immediate bearing upon the continued validity of the distinction drawn by the Court between released time on the school premises[33] and released time off the school premises.[34] While the *Engel* opinion is premised on the ground that the school program cannot be used to promote religious exercises and religious indoctrination, thereby suggesting that all forms of released time are invalid, a distinction can clearly be observed between the state's promotion of religious faith by means of an officially adopted prayer prescribed for daily recitation under the supervision of a publicly paid teacher, and the state's willingness to excuse children for one hour of the week from the public school's regular program in order to permit opportunity for religious instruction at the hands of teachers furnished by the churches. What the state can do to sanction a state-sponsored religious exercise as part of a public school's daily program and what it can do to accommodate its public school program to a felt need for religious instruction furnished by the churches, thereby acting to implement religious freedom, are two different questions. In both situations it may be claimed that the state is establishing religion, but in the released-time situation

---

[32] The majority of state courts that have dealt with the problem have upheld Bible-reading practices. For a review of the cases, see Engel v. Vitale, 18 Misc. 2d 659, 691-94, 191 N.Y.S.2d 453, 488-90 (Sup. Ct. 1959); Harrison, *The Bible, the Constitution and Public Education*, 29 TENN. L. REV. 360 (1962).

[33] McCollum v. Board of Educ., 333 U.S. 203 (1948).

[34] Zorach v. Clauson, 343 U.S. 306 (1952).

there is a stronger basis for asserting that the establishment limitation should yield to the competing free exercise principle. Even Mr. Justice Douglas, in his far-reaching and, for the most part, gratuitous opinion, in which he stressed that public funds or property cannot be used to finance religious exercises conducted by public officials, gave no indication that he now regards the *Zorach* decision as an incorrect one.[35]

Finally, in appraising the reach of *Engel*, it is clear that it has little if any relevancy in respect to prayers or acknowledgment of Deity in phases of public life apart from the public school situation. Thanksgiving proclamations and declaration of a day of prayer by the President, prayers by ministers on public occasions, the use of chaplains to open sessions of Congress, the inscription of "In God We Trust" on our coins—all involving a recognition of the place of prayer and of the religious consciousness in our national life—are distinguishable. In none of these cases is government prescribing an official form of prayer or an official expression of religious belief for the public's own use. Moreover, the situation is totally unlike that of the problem presented in the classroom, where immature and impressionable children are susceptible to a pressure to conform and to participate in the expression of religious beliefs that carry the sanction and compulsion of the state's authority.

The conclusion that *Engel* does not admit of the wide interpretation given to it, particularly in the immediate response to the decision, is supported by the unusual extra-judicial statement by Mr. Justice Clark who, in the course of a public address and with reference to the criticism directed at the school prayer decision, said that it was a misinterpretation of the decision to say that it barred all religious observances in the public schools or other public places. Nor, according to him, did the Court hold that "there could be no official recognition of a Divine Being . . . or public acknowledgment that we are a religious nation." All the Court did, Mr. Justice Clark continued, was to rule unconstitutional "a state-written prayer circulated to state-employed teachers with instructions to have their pupils recite it in unison at the beginning of each school day."[36]

---

35 *But cf.* McGowan v. Maryland, 366 U.S. 420, 563-64 (1961) (Douglas, J., dissenting).
36 For excerpts of Mr. Justice Clark's address made at the Commonwealth Club in San Francisco, Aug. 3, 1962, see N.Y. Times, Aug. 4, 1962, p. 9, col. 1.

IV. CONSTITUTIONAL THEORY

The attempt has been made up to this point to examine the reach of the *Engel* decision. We turn now to an analysis of the *Engel* holding and opinion in terms of basic constitutional theory respecting the first and fourteenth amendments on which the Court relied.

A. *The Establishment Clause of the First Amendment*

The Court found that the state action involved in the *Engel* situation violated the first amendment as made applicable to the states by the fourteenth amendment. More particularly, the prayer practice prescribed under authority of New York law violated the provision of the first amendment prohibiting laws respecting an establishment of religion. It is important to note that the Court expressly stated that it was not resting its case on the free exercise clause of the first amendment, although it did observe that it was plain that objecting children were placed under implied pressure to conform by participating in the prayer. The Court interpreted the establishment clause as stating an independent limitation which may overlap the free exercise clause in part but which also reaches wider objectives. The officially prescribed New York prayer was held invalid because it established the religious beliefs expressed in the prayer and thereby became a law respecting an establishment of religion.

In commenting on these propositions, it should be pointed out, first of all, that the majority opinion did not cite a single case in support of the conclusions reached by it. Indeed, the decision is unique in its failure to cite, much less discuss, earlier opinions dealing with the interpretation of the establishment limitation. This is all the more remarkable since the Court in the celebrated *Everson* opinion[37] had laid down broad statements on the meaning of this limitation, and in its *McCollum* decision[38] had invalidated a program of released time on public school premises on the ground that this constituted a use of the publicly owned and operated school system to enlist students for religious instruction in violation of the ideas first advanced in *Everson*. In the well-known dicta of his *Everson* opinion, Mr. Justice Black had stated that the effect of the first amendment's twin phrasing was to establish a principle of separation of church and state, and

---

37 Everson v. Board of Educ., 330 U.S. 1 (1947).
38 McCollum v. Board of Educ., 333 U.S. 203 (1948).

he had referred to Jefferson's letter in which he characterized the Constitution as establishing a wall of separation between church and state. He had further stated that the effect of the first amendment's establishment clause was not only to forbid an established church or to forbid giving a preference to one or more religions, but that it went farther and forbade aid to all religions, whether preferential or not, and that tax monies could not be spent to support any religious activities or institutions. Thus, the *Everson* opinion had read into the first amendment a theory of strict separation of church and state going far beyond the notion of an established church in the historic sense of the word.

The simplest explanation of the Court's failure to cite any precedent is that the earlier cases, dealing with use of public funds to provide for the transportation of children to parochial schools, with programs of released time for religious instruction furnished by the churches—whether on or off the school premises —and with Sunday closing laws, were not directly in point. The closest analogy was furnished by the *McCollum* decision, where the Court had invalidated a program of released time for religious instruction conducted on the school's premises by teachers who were furnished by the churches. This case supported the broad proposition that no part of the public school program could be used in the furtherance of religious instruction or exercises on the school premises. But *McCollum* involved a close working relation between the schools and the churches and a substantial use of public school property for religious instruction. Neither factor was present in *Engel*. Apart, however, from reliance on the precedent furnished by the *McCollum* decision, Mr. Justice Black could have found much in the language he used in his prior opinions for the Court in *Everson* and *McCollum* to support the ideas relied upon in *Engel*. He had stated in *Everson* that government cannot pass laws "which aid one religion, aid all religions, or prefer one religion over another."[39] In the *McCollum* opinion he had cited this language with approval. The prescribed non-sectarian prayer could easily be characterized either as an aid to all religions or as a preference for the particular religious beliefs embodied in this prayer. Why Mr. Justice Black chose to disregard his opinions in *Everson* and *McCollum* is a matter for speculation. In view of the statement by Mr. Justice Douglas in his concurring opinion, that he now regards the actual decision in *Everson* as

39 330 U.S. at 15.

incorrect,[40] it may be that Mr. Justice Black's failure to cite *Everson* assumes substantial significance. His failure to cite *McCollum* is perhaps more readily explained, since any reference to *McCollum* would have been incomplete without citing *Zorach* as well. Not only did *Zorach* limit *McCollum* by holding that a program of released time for religious instruction was valid if conducted off the school premises, but Mr. Justice Douglas' opinion had indicated a substantial retreat in the interpretation of the establishment clause from that enunciated in the *Everson* opinion. He had stated there that the first amendment did not establish an over-all principle of separation of church and state, that the state could take account of the religious interests of its people and that it could accommodate its public school program to these interests. The *Zorach* opinion thus undermined the absolutism expressed in *Everson* and *McCollum* and appeared to recognize that the establishment limitation must at times be balanced against the free exercise principle and that the legislature may in appropriate instances, in the interest of neutrality, choose to advance the free exercise of religion at some expense to the establishment prohibition. It is for these reasons that *Zorach* was generally regarded as substantially limiting, if not undermining, much of what was said in *Everson* and *McCollum*[41]—a view that seemed to be shared by the four Justices, including Mr. Justice Black, who dissented so vigorously in *Zorach*. It is understandable, therefore, that Mr. Justice Black in writing the opinion in *Engel* wished to avoid any discussion of precedents that might involve his approval of *Zorach* and the views stated there. Finally, it is open to speculation also that differences within the Court in interpreting and reconciling the prior cases and the supporting opinions made it prudent for Mr. Justice Black, in writing an opinion that would command the support of at least four other Justices, to avoid all discussion of prior cases. But Mr. Justice Black's opinion, although it does not rely on prior cases, does appear to restore the broad and absolutist interpretation of the establishment clause first stated in the *Everson* opinion.[42]

40 370 U.S. at 443.

41 See Engel v. Vitale, 18 Misc. 2d 659, 686-89, 191 N.Y.S.2d 453, 483-86 (Sup. Ct. 1959); Kauper, Civil Liberties and the Constitution 17-19 (1962) [also located in Kauper, *Church and State: Cooperative Separatism*, 60 Mich. L. Rev. 1, 10-13 (1961)].

42 Mr. Justice Douglas' views may have a vital impact on the course of the Court's future decisions in this area. Opinions expressed by him in dissent in the Sunday closing law cases [See, e.g., McGowan v. Maryland, 366 U.S. 420, 563-64 (1961).], together with his emphasis in his separate opinion in *Engel* on the idea that no public funds or properties can be used to finance religious exercises and his express questioning

Whether the *Everson* opinion, postulating a broad no-aid-to-religion idea, correctly stated the meaning of this clause is open to serious question.[43] As Mr. Justice Douglas frankly recognized in his concurring opinion in *Engel*, the prescription of a school prayer for voluntary participation by students is not an establishment of religion within the historic meaning of this language. In *Everson*, Mr. Justice Black relied in large part on the views of James Madison and Thomas Jefferson in giving the establishment language its broad construction.[44] Madison and Jefferson viewed this language as furnishing protection for freedom of conscience and protection against ecclesiastical domination of political affairs by imposing a barrier to any kind of governmental sanction or support of religious activities. In their view the establishment language served as a counterweight to the free exercise clause. But there is no evidence that the committee that approved the text of the first amendment and the Congress that submitted the amendment and the state legislatures that approved it supposed that the establishment language carried the wide connotations attributed to it by Madison.[45] There is, however, some evidence to support the conclusion that those responsible for the final wording used in the first amendment—and this included persons besides Madison[46]—did have in mind something more than an officially established church and something more than giving a

of the result reached in *Everson*, raise the question whether Mr. Justice Douglas still adheres to the ideas he expressed in *Zorach*. On the other hand, his failure in his separate opinion in *Engel* to repudiate the result in *Zorach*, all the more conspicuous because of doubts he expressed as to the holding in *Everson*, may indicate that he continues to draw the line between use of public funds, property and personnel in aid of religious instruction and exercises and "accommodation" of the public school program to religious instruction given under church auspices off the school premises.

For discussion of the *Engel* opinion with reference to *McCollum* and *Zorach*, see Kurland, *supra* note 2, at 25-29; Sutherland, *supra* note 4, at 30-35.

[43] For varying interpretations of the intended meaning of the establishment language, see Parsons, The First Freedom (1948); 1 Stokes, Church and State in the United States 538-61 (1950); Katz, *Freedom of Religion and State Neutrality*, 20 U. Chi. L. Rev. 426 (1953); Pfeffer, *Church and State: Something Less Than Separation*, 19 U. Chi. L. Rev. (1951).

[44] For Madison's view and for a discussion of his part in the drafting of the text of the first amendment, see Brant, James Madison: Father of the Constitution, 1787-1800, at 264-75 (1950). See also Brant, *Madison and the Prayer Case*, The New Republic, July 30, 1962, p. 18.

[45] For a detailed examination of the proceedings of the congressional committee that drafted the religion clauses of the first amendment, see 1 Stokes, *op. cit. supra* note 43. See also Smylie, *supra* note 4.

[46] 1 Stokes, *op. cit. supra* note 43, at 543-48, attributes chief credit to Samuel Livermore for the wording and questions the widely held idea that Madison composed the final draft. He states also that Madison's great emphasis was on securing a "legal equality" among sects. *Id.* at 548.

preference to one or more religions. Fragmentary evidence supports the idea that this language was intended to keep Congress "from establishing articles of faith or a mode of worship."[47] It does not appear to be a distortion of words to say that prescription of an official prayer for recitation in public schools is the establishment of an official mode of worship and is, therefore, forbidden. But, as a practical matter, even this interpretation in its application to prayer in schools is open to question when consideration is given to the practical construction afforded by the whole course of American history. Here the opinion of the New York trial court is particularly illuminating in showing that public recognition of prayer and of Deity reflected the "sense of the nation" at the time of the adoption of the first and fourteenth amendments and should be taken into account in the process of constitutional interpretation. It is indeed remarkable that Mr. Justice Black in his opinion in *Engel* completely disregarded the long history with respect to prayers in public life and in schools.

Mr. Justice Black did refer to history—the control of the Book of Common Prayer by Parliament and the evils resulting from it and the concern that eventually developed in this country that there should be no union of church and state, since such a union tended to degrade religion and to subject the state to risk of ecclesiastical domination. But, as Mr. Justice Stewart pointed out in his dissenting opinion, it is a far cry from control of prayer in an officially established church to a public school program that gives opportunity for voluntary participation in common prayer.[48] Insofar as the Court relied on history in *Engel*, it followed a highly selective process in determining what history was relevant. The Court's selection of history in determining what it will read into the establishment clause is in itself a highly subjective process. But in this respect *Engel* again demonstrates that the Constitution is what the judges say it is.

It seems clear that, if the no-aid-to-religion principle is a valid interpretation of the establishment language, the Court reached a correct result in the *Engel* case. In *Everson*[49] the Court upheld the expenditure of public funds to reimburse parents for the cost of transporting children to parochial schools. The Court recog-

---

47 1 STOKES, *op. cit. supra* note 43, at 546; Katz, *supra* note 43, at 434. See also Smylie, *supra* note 4.
48 For a brief discussion of the historical arguments and their relevancy, see Kurland, *supra* note 2, at 22-25.
49 Everson v. Board of Educ., 330 U.S. 1 (1947).

nized that this resulted in aid to parochial school education but said that this result was incidental to the valid secular purpose of promoting the safe transportation of children to school. In the Sunday closing law cases[50] the Court held that the validity of Sunday laws as proper exercises of the police power to promote the general welfare was not impaired by the fact that they had the incidental effect of favoring the Christian day of worship. Thus, the Court, in the cases where it has purported to follow an absolutist interpretation of the establishment language, has, nevertheless, permitted aid to religion as an incident to a lawful secular purpose. But in the *Engel* case the prayer practice was seen to be directed to wholly religious ends and the aid to religion was primary and not incidental. The opposing argument that the prayer exercise was intended to serve a patriotic purpose by creating an awareness and appreciation of prayer as part of the American heritage proved too much and if accepted would have undermined the whole no-aid idea. Nevertheless, the Court itself came perilously close to this idea and created difficulties for itself when it recognized that school children may properly be encouraged to recite patriotic passages containing references to Deity and to sing the National Anthem which in its third verse incorporates a prayer that expresses some of the same sentiments found in the New York Regents' prayer. As pointed out earlier, this is justified on the ground that such activities are not distinctively religious exercises. To put the matter in another way, schools may engage in religious exercises if they are incident to patriotic purposes. All of this suggests that the no-aid principle is not so absolute as it sounds and is not a very viable principle for solving problems with respect to the interrelationship of government and religion. Moreover, the whole course of American governmental practices, not only in giving recognition to the nation's religious heritage and consciousness but also in sanctioning various forms of direct and indirect assistance for religious activities, is a repudiation of the extreme Madisonian view and lends no support to the kind of absolutism that appears on the surface in the *Engel* opinion.[51]

Reference may be made at this point to alternative theories

---

[50] McGowan v. Maryland, 366 U.S. 420 (1961); Two Guys from Harrison-Allentown, Inc. v. McGinley, 366 U.S. 582 (1961); Braunfeld v. Brown, 366 U.S. 599 (1961); Gallagher v. Crown Kosher Super Mkt., 366 U.S. 617 (1961).

[51] See examples cited in Engel v. Vitale, 370 U.S. 421, 437 n.1 (1962) (Douglas, J., concurring); FELLMAN, THE LIMITS OF FREEDOM 40-41 (1959); KAUPER, CIVIL LIBERTIES AND THE CONSTITUTION 35-39 (1962) [also located in Kauper, *Church and State: Cooperative Separatism*, 60 MICH. L. REV. 1, 26-29 (1961)].

on the construction of the free exercise and establishment clauses of the first amendment. Mr. Justice Douglas in speaking for the majority in *Zorach*[52] stated that government must be neutral between sects, and in his concurring opinion in *Engel*[53] stated that government must be neutral in the field of religion. Professor Katz has advanced the idea that the primary thrust of the first amendment's religious clauses is to protect religious liberty, that this objective is best attained when government remains neutral in respect to religious matters, but that government must abandon neutrality in some situations where adherence to the establishment limitation would result in an interference with the free exercise of religion.[54] Professor Kurland proposes the thesis that the first amendment requires the government to be neutral in the sense that it can do nothing to hinder or promote religion as such, that is, religion or religious activities cannot be the basis for classification.[55] The difference between the Douglas and Katz view, on the one hand, and the Kurland view, on the other, is that the former is addressed to the problem of neutrality within the framework of a first amendment view that recognizes the free exercise and establishment principles as independent, sometimes overlapping, and sometimes competing principles, whereas the Kurland thesis accepts these principles as mutually exclusive of each other. It is fair to say that the Supreme Court's opinions on the whole reflect the view that the two religion clauses of the first amendment state independent limitations, and that the problem of neutrality may be approached on this basis.

It is clear that government must be neutral as between competing religious claims. It may not prefer one religion over another. But to say that government must be neutral as between religion and non-religion raises more questions. If this means that government can do nothing which in fact aids religion, this may in some situations mean that government must discriminate against religion and thereby violate the free exercise clause. The Constitution does not require this. On the contrary, any meaningful concept of neutrality must permit government some dis-

52 343 U.S. at 314.
53 370 U.S. at 443.
54 Katz, *supra* note 43, at 428.
55 KURLAND, RELIGION AND THE LAW 17-18, 111-12 (1962). The *Engel* decision is clearly in accord with Professor Kurland's thesis since, by prescribing a religious exercise, the state was acting on the basis of a classification that promoted religious activity as such. For his analysis and comments on *Engel*, see Kurland, *The Regents' Prayer Case: "Full of Sound and Fury. Signifying . . .",* 1962 SUPREME COURT REV. 1.

cretion in striking a balance between the establishment and the free exercise principles since they may conflict. If neutrality means that government must be indifferent to religion, and must base its policies, actions and programs on the theory that religion is irrelevant to life, it means that government is committed to a philosophy of secularism, and then the question must be raised whether secularism as an officially established orthodoxy is any more consistent with the first amendment than a religious orthodoxy.[56] But such a conception of neutrality is inconsistent with the unbroken tradition of American life in giving expression to the religious habits and consciousness of the American people, a tradition supporting the Court's assertion in *Zorach* that "we are a religious people whose institutions presuppose a Supreme Being."[57] Indeed, if the public schools disregard the religious factors in the educational process, they are not neutral. Neutrality is a two-edged sword and its application in a given situation invites study of a variety of considerations.

The decision in *Engel* may be measured by the standard of neutrality. Clearly the state's action in sanctioning a particular prayer was an expression of governmental preference for the religious beliefs embodied in that prayer, and to this extent it discriminated against persons who did not accept these principles or who preferred to pray in another way. The state, then, was not being neutral in the narrower sense of the term. But did the Court in denying the state the power to prescribe an official prayer for recitation in public schools thereby compel the state to discriminate on the basis of religion or to interfere with religious freedom? Although the argument was made before the Court that the prayer exercise implemented the religious freedom of children who wanted to participate, the proposition that the right to recite prayers in public schools is *essential* to religious freedom is hardly convincing. The general right of prayer is not affected by the decision and, as previously noted, some form of prayer in the classroom is consistent with the *Engel* decision. Nor can it be said that a prohibition of officially sanctioned prayer in public school classrooms violates neutrality by forcing the state

---

[56] See Torcaso v. Watkins, 367 U.S. 488, 495 n.11 (1961), to the effect that non-theistic religions such as Ethical Culture and Secular Humanism come within the scope of the free exercise clause. See also the statement in West Virginia State Bd. of Educ. v. Barnette, 319 U.S. 624 (1943), that government may not prescribe what shall be orthodox in politics, nationalism, religion or other matters of opinion. *Id.* at 642. See also Ball, *supra* note 6.

[57] 343 U.S. at 313.

to use its schools to promote secularism as the officially established orthodoxy. Consistent with the decision the schools and government may still follow practices and educational programs that reflect a sympathetic awareness of religion and its relevancy to the life of the individual and the community. The state, then, was supporting a practice which sanctioned and gave a preferred position to the expression of religious ideas even though it was not constitutionally required to do so in the interests of either religious freedom or strict neutrality. This leaves the basic question of whether the Constitution does require a strict or absolute neutrality in regard to religious matters, or whether, in at least a limited way, government may in its institutional life and programs express a preference for the expression of religious ideas that are in accord with the national tradition and reflect the beliefs shared by a preponderant element of the community.

Numerous governmental practices at all levels make clear that government has never been absolutely neutral in religious matters. Moreover, the Court's opinion in *Engel* in sanctioning public school exercises which are viewed as primarily patriotic in character but also have religious significance seems to make clear that the public schools are not required in the interest of a strict neutrality to abandon exercises that invite student participation in expressions of religious faith.[58] What seems to be really important is not that government be strictly or abstractly neutral but that government in its policies and programs does not trespass in any significant way upon the rights of minorities. To criticize *Engel* on the ground that it permits a minority to exercise a commanding influence in determining public school policy is in itself a pointless argument since a major purpose of a constitutional system is to place a check on the will of the majority in the interest of protecting minority rights. There can be no quarrel with the Court's overruling the majority will in *Engel* if it may be assumed that minority rights were involved.

---

[58] For examples of governmental practices that reflect the nation's religious tradition and for criticism of the distinction made in the majority opinion between "patriotic or ceremonial occasions" and "an unquestioned religious exercise," see Mr. Justice Stewart's dissenting opinion in *Engel*, 370 U.S. at 446-50. See also the discussion in the text *supra* at 1040, 1042, 1046.

Reference may be also made at this point to the decision in *Zorach* sustaining the validity of a released-time program for religious instruction conducted off the school premises as supporting the proposition that the state may accommodate its official program to the recognition and furtherance of the religious interests of its citizens even though it is not constitutionally required to do so. Mr. Justice Douglas, who wrote the opinion in *Zorach*, had no difficulty in reconciling the released-time program with his concept of neutrality.

B. *Personal Rights and the Standing Question*

This leads to a consideration of a major difficulty raised by *Engel*. The Court did not rest its decision on the ground that the prayer practice subjected objecting children to an implied pressure to participate and thereby offended freedom of religion or a personal freedom of conscience. Instead, the Court made it clear that it was resting its case on the establishment clause, and that this clause, while designed in part to protect individual freedom, was also designed to prevent a union of government and religion. But insofar as the establishment clause is invocable by individuals, must it not be shown that a practice alleged to constitute an establishment of religion infringes on constitutionally recognized freedoms or interests? At this point it is useful to inquire whether the prohibition of laws respecting an establishment of religion can be translated into a protection of some kind of fundamental freedom. For Madison and Jefferson it assumed significance as a protection for freedom of belief and conscience which transcends the more limited concept of freedom of religion. This view finds support in the following statement taken from Mr. Justice Roberts' opinion for the Court in *Cantwell v. Connecticut:*

> "The constitutional inhibition of legislation on the subject of religion has a double aspect. On the one hand, it forestalls compulsion by law of the acceptance of any creed or the practice of any form of worship. Freedom of conscience and freedom to adhere to such religious organization or form of worship as the individual may choose cannot be restricted by law. On the other hand, it safeguards the free exercise of the chosen form of religion. Thus the Amendment embraces two concepts—freedom to believe and freedom to act."[59]

Mr. Justice Roberts went to the heart of the matter when he interpreted the establishment clause to protect freedom of belief by forestalling *compulsion by law* of the acceptance of any creed or the practice of any form of worship.[60] This freedom is violated when

---

[59] 310 U.S. 296, 303 (1940). See also Madison's statement, when the first amendment was pending in Congress in substantially its final form, that "he apprehended the meaning of the words to be, that Congress should not establish a religion, and enforce the legal observation of it by law, nor compel men to worship God in any manner contrary to their conscience." 1 ANNALS OF CONG. 730 (1834) [1789-1791]. This statement is quoted by Mr. Justice Reed in his dissenting opinion in McCollum v. Board of Educ., 333 U.S. 203, 244 (1948).

[60] See, however, Professor Howe's criticism of Mr. Justice Roberts' interpretation on the ground that the establishment language, as stating a federal principle, namely, that Congress has no authority to deal with matters relating to religious establishment,

a person is forced to profess a belief whether or not contrary to conviction, is denied a right or privilege because of refusal to profess an officially sanctioned belief, or is forced to pay taxes in support of a church or religious practices. Unless the New York prayer practice, though voluntary in form, had the effect of indirectly coercing objectors who did not care to participate, it is difficult to see what rights were violated. It can hardly be claimed that taxpayers were subjected to any additional burden because of the use of school facilities or personnel in connection with the prayer exercise.[61]

Moreover, apart from the question of whether an individual in order to claim the protection of the establishment clause must show that his freedom of conscience is violated, the requirement of proper standing as a party in interest to raise constitutional questions must still be considered. What standing did the petitioners have in this case? They brought this suit as parents and the theory of the trial court, relying on the *Zorach* decision, was that the petitioners were asserting their right to control the education of their children and the right to be free from a religious practice in the public schools which was contrary to their own beliefs or unbeliefs and those of their children.[62] The Supreme Court did not even discuss the question of standing. It seems proper to infer then that the standing requisite to maintain the suit in the state court carried forward as a basis for standing before the Supreme Court. Since the Supreme Court has not disavowed the party in interest requirement, since it accepted a standing premised originally on a claim of violation of the petitioners' rights, and since it stated that it had agreed to review the case because it involved "rights protected by the First and Fourteenth Amendments,"[63] it appears to be implicit in the decision that some substantial legal interests of the petitioners were at stake in the case. Admittedly, however, the Court's express statement that it was not basing its holding on the ground that the prayer exercise

goes beyond the purpose of protecting individual rights. Howe, *The Constitutional Question*, in RELIGION AND THE FREE SOCIETY 49, 52-53 (The Fund for the Republic pamphlet, 1958). See also notes 64 and 75 *infra*.

61 Mr. Justice Douglas' concurring opinion was squarely based on the theory that tax funds and property were used to support a religious exercise, but this emphasis does not appear in the majority opinion. See Doremus v. Board of Educ., 342 U.S. 429 (1952), holding that taxpayers did not have standing to challenge the constitutionality of Bible reading in a public school, absent a showing that this practice resulted in added out-of-pocket costs to the operation of the school system.

62 Engel v. Vitale, 18 Misc. 2d 659, 666-67, 191 N.Y.S.2d 453, 464-65 (Sup. Ct. 1959).

63 370 U.S. at 424.

was a violation of religious freedom and its failure to discuss the standing question emerge as puzzling aspects of the decision.[64]

Whatever questions are raised respecting the rights and the standing of the petitioners under the first amendment become even more acute when the restrictions of this amendment are translated into fourteenth amendment limitations. There is a danger of forgetting that the first amendment was not directly involved in the *Engel* case, since by its terms it is a limitation only on Congress. It becomes involved only on the theory that the fourteenth amendment operates in some way to make the first amendment applicable as a limitation on the states. On this question Mr. Justice Black's opinion is extraordinarily interesting. All that he found it necessary to say is that the first amendment's provisions "are operative against the States by virtue of the Fourteenth Amendment."[65] What language of the fourteenth amendment has this effect? On this point, Mr. Justice Black's opinion is eloquently and discreetly silent. But the fourteenth amendment is not an abstraction or some mysterious event in history achieving constitutional change without resort to words. Is it not pertinent to ask what language of the fourteenth amendment has the effect of making the first amendment applicable?

Any thorough exploration of the questions with respect to the interrelationship of the first and fourteenth amendments would unduly extend the scope of this article. But some basic theories of interpretation should be stated. Three lines of thought may be identified:

(1) The main line of interpretation of the fourteenth amendment, as a basis for protecting substantive and procedural rights against state impairment, has turned on the clause of its first section which states, "nor shall any State deprive any person of life, liberty or property, without due process of law." The classic theory expressed in the judicial gloss on this language is that the

---

[64] Although the opinion in *Engel* does not expressly deal with the question of whether the establishment clause protects a broad freedom of conscience, as distinguished from a narrower freedom of religion protected by the free exercise clause, it does on its face accord with Professor Howe's view [note 60 *supra*] that the establishment clause as a limitation on Congress goes beyond the purpose of protecting individual rights. In turn, the Court's failure to discuss the standing question may then be interpreted as suggesting a substantial modification, if not virtual abandonment, of the traditional party-in-interest concept so far as standing to raise the establishment question is concerned. For analysis and discussion of *Engel* with respect to the standing problem, see Sutherland, *Establishment According to Engel*, 76 HARV. L. REV. 25 (1962). See also Kurland, *supra* note 55.

[65] 370 U.S. at 430.

"liberty" clause serves to protect those freedoms which are ranked as fundamental and that there is no necessary relationship between these and the Bill of Rights.[66] In the application of this theory the *freedoms* of the first amendment came to be recognized as fundamental. Thus, in the *Cantwell* decision Mr. Justice Roberts stated that "the fundamental concept of liberty embodied in [the fourteenth amendment] embraces the liberties guaranteed by the First Amendment."[67] Whether the language used is that first amendment freedoms are ranked as fundamental or that they are absorbed or selectively incorporated into the due process clause, the result is the same, namely, the first amendment freedoms are a part of the liberty protected under the due process clause.

(2) A variant of the fundamental rights theory is that when liberties specified in the Bill of Rights are recognized as fundamental they have the same dimensions and quality, when incorporated into the due process clause, as they have in their original setting in the Bill of Rights and are subject only to the limitations there recognized. This may be characterized for purpose of convenience as the Brennan theory, since Mr. Justice Brennan has most clearly articulated this idea in recent cases.[68] This theory of interpretation becomes a means of enlarging the fundamental freedoms as limitations on state action since it by-passes the usual due process consideration that the fundamental liberties may be restricted so long as the state is acting reasonably to achieve legitimate governmental purposes. But this theory is still centered on the protection of fundamental freedoms.

(3) A third view, the one advanced by Mr. Justice Black and supported by Mr. Justice Douglas, which may be referred to as the Black theory, is that the effect of the fourteenth amendment was to make the entire Bill of Rights apply to the states.[69] Mr. Justice Black persists in this theory which he bases on an interpretation of historical intent despite its being discredited by legal historians.[70] The significance of this view is that it subjects the states to the Bill of Rights, without reference to the fundamental

66 See Adamson v. California, 332 U.S. 46 (1947); Palko v. Connecticut, 302 U.S. 319 (1937).

67 310 U.S. at 303.

68 See, *e.g.*, Ohio *ex rel.* Eaton v. Price, 364 U.S. 263, *rehearing denied*, 364 U.S. 855 (1960).

69 See Adamson v. California, 332 U.S. 46, 68 (1947) (Black, J., dissenting).

70 See Bartkus v. Illinois, 359 U.S. 121, 124 (1959); Fairman, *Does the Fourteenth Amendment Incorporate the Bill of Rights? The Original Understanding*, 2 STAN. L. REV. 5 (1949); Freund, *The Supreme Court and Civil Liberties*, 4 VAND. L. REV. 533, 547 (1951).

freedoms concept and without regard to usual due process considerations.[71]

The relevancy of these three approaches to the first amendment question is apparent. Under all three views, the first amendment is recognized to have a special significance with respect to the states. But the "fundamental rights" interpretation and the Brennan theory place emphasis upon the freedoms of the first amendment, as part of the liberty protected under the due process clause, whereas under the Black view all of the first amendment is applicable to the states and hence it is not necessary to inquire whether a question of fundamental freedoms is involved. The practical effect of his theory is that by judicial act the first amendment is amended to read, "Neither Congress *nor the States* shall make any law respecting an establishment of religion . . . ." Thus, he could rest his opinion in *Engel* on the establishment clause without finding that the petitioners' freedoms were violated. Moreover, since the first amendment's language is absolute, there is no place in Mr. Justice Black's thinking for an inquiry into whether the state had acted in an arbitrary or unreasonable way in impinging upon the petitioners' interests.[72]

The interpretation of the first amendment's establishment clause as a limitation on the states without regard to the usual due process considerations was already foreshadowed in the *Everson* and *McCollum* decisions. But *Everson* turned on the right of a taxpayer not to have out-of-pocket expenditures of tax funds made in support of religious activities,[73] and *McCollum* could be interpreted to turn on the right of a person who was both taxpayer and parent not to have school property used in a substantial way for religious instruction and not to have her child's freedom impaired by a public school attendance requirement imposed only on those who did not attend the religious education classes.[74] The *Engel* opinion, however, is unique in that it finds a state practice

71 In Adamson v. California, 332 U.S. 46 (1947), Mr. Justice Black in his dissenting opinion indicated that the Bill of Rights is made applicable to the states by means of the privileges and immunities clause of § 1 of the fourteenth amendment. *Id.* at 71-72.

72 See Konigsberg v. State Bar, 366 U.S. 36, 56 (1961) (Black, J., dissenting).

73 The preamble to the "Virginia Bill of Religious Liberty," quoted in the Court's opinion, 330 U.S. at 12-13, contains the following passage: "[T]o compel a man to furnish contributions of money for the propagation of opinions which he disbelieves, is sinful and tyrannical."

74 There was, however, no showing in *McCollum* that students were *in fact* coerced to attend the religious education classes. For a discussion of the *McCollum* and *Zorach* cases with respect to the standing problem posed by *Engel*, see Kurland, *supra* note 55; Sutherland, *supra* note 64.

invalid as an establishment of religion without regard to whether it offended any rights or interests of the petitioners.

It is not surprising that Mr. Justice Black in his *Engel* opinion saw the problem as wholly a first amendment establishment question, unrelated to the due process clause and the deprivation of liberty, since he has committed himself to this view. What is surprising is that some other members of the Court who supported the majority opinion appeared *sub silentio* to endorse a view of the first and fourteenth amendment interrelationship which rests on a spurious interpretation of history, disregards the main line of fourteenth amendment interpretation, and marks a bold high in the long history of judicial free-wheeling in the construction of this amendment.[75]

Whatever significance may attach to the surface of the opinion in *Engel*, some aspects of the case do suggest that the decision finds its ultimate justification on the ground that the prayer practice carried a compulsive force notwithstanding its apparent voluntary character, and that it therefore resulted in violation of freedom of conscience. Why should the Court otherwise have emphasized all the elements of the exercise that gave it such an official nature? Indeed, Mr. Justice Black stated that the "indirect coercive pressure upon religious minorities to conform to the prevailing officially approved religion is plain."[76]

Regardless of its underlying theory, the *Engel* decision does suggest substantial problems with respect to protection of minority rights. How far may the dominant sentiment of the community be given expression in the public schools, or for that matter in public life generally, where the expression of this sentiment is offensive to minority groups? The answers to these questions, inherent in our pluralistic society, are not easy. Must all practices offensive to minority groups be barred, or is it enough that they be free not to participate? We may put alongside the problem of *Engel* the question presented in *West Virginia State Bd. of Educ. v. Barnette*,[77] where the Court held that a Jehovah's Witness could not be denied the privilege of attending a public

---

75 On the question whether the establishment limitation of the first amendment, as stating a federal principle in placing a jurisdictional limit on congressional power, should have any carry-over to the fourteenth amendment except in terms of protection of fundamental rights, thereby permitting states to take such action "in aid of religion as does not appreciably affect the religious or other constitutional rights of [others]," see Howe, *supra* note 60, at 53-57; Freund, *supra* note 70, at 533-34. See also note 64 *supra*.

76 370 U.S. at 431.

77 319 U.S. 624 (1943).

school because of his refusal to stand up and salute the flag at a school exercise held at the beginning of the day. For the Jehovah's Witnesses a salute to the flag is an obeisance which is idolatrous and, therefore, offensive to their religious beliefs. Mr. Justice Jackson, delivering the opinion of the Court, did not rest the case on the ground of religious freedom but significantly on the broader ground of freedom of thought. In the well-known passage from his opinion, he said:

> "If there is any fixed star in our constitutional constellation, it is that no official, high or petty, can prescribe what shall be orthodox in politics, nationalism, religion, or other matters of opinion or force citizens to confess by word or act their faith therein."[78]

But there was no indication that the school board was under a duty to eliminate the flag-salute exercise in order to protect the Jehovah's Witnesses against the embarrassment and pressures arising from their non-participation. It was enough that the Jehovah's Witness could not be compelled to take part. What distinguishes this case from *Engel* where the Court finds that the prayer exercise must be discontinued? Superficially, the distinction suggests itself that in the flag-salute case the state is promoting a proper secular purpose—cultivation of patriotic sentiments. Even if this distinction is tenable, it does indicate that the extent to which public schools may engage in practices that are offensive to conscience is a question of degree. But actually the distinction is not as convincing as it seems. Mr. Justice Jackson's opinion in *Barnette* rested on the ground that the state may not prescribe any orthodoxy or force citizens to confess their faith therein. In other words, quite apart from the specific prohibition on the establishment of religion, the state may not officially establish any faith—political or religious. At this point it should also be noted that Mr. Justice Black said in *Torcaso v. Watkins*[79] that religious freedom under the Constitution extends to such non-theistic religions as Ethical Culture and Secular Humanism. Putting *Barnette* and *Torcaso* together, it may be said, then, that the Constitution forbids the establishment of either theistic or non-theistic orthodoxies. If this is so, then it may be questioned whether in the interest of protecting the non-conformist a distinction should

---

[78] *Id.* at 642. It should be noted, however, that Justices Black, Douglas, and Murphy in their concurring opinions laid stress on the religious freedom argument.
[79] 367 U.S. 488, 495 n.11 (1961).

be observed between the state's promoting a non-theistic political orthodoxy which offends a minority religious group and its action in promoting a theistic orthodoxy which offends a minority of believers and non-believers. If the protection afforded in the name of religious freedom against a state-prescribed non-theistic orthodoxy is that a person cannot be compelled to participate, whereas the protection afforded in the name of the establishment clause is that a person may demand that any exercise promoting theistic belief be completely eliminated, the result is that the freedom protected by the establishment clause is regarded as having a higher value than the freedom protected by the free exercise clause. Perhaps the simplest explanation of this situation is that the Jehovah's Witnesses have not demanded that the flag salute exercise be completely eliminated in order to avoid an implied coercion on their children to participate, but to point up this problem is to indicate that the degree of protection accorded nonconformists who object to public practices they find offensive is a matter requiring further careful probing.[80]

To state the problem in this way is to recognize that the first amendment's explicit clause respecting an establishment of religion, as well as its implied prohibition of the establishment of any kind of orthodoxy, as recognized in *Barnette*, cannot be given an absolute construction but must be balanced against a variety of competing factors, including considerations of community interest that are legitimated by American life and experience. In construing the freedoms expressly safeguarded by the first amendment—freedom of religion, freedom of speech and freedom of press—the Court has recognized that these freedoms, whether as first amendment freedoms, or as absorbed into the liberty protected by the fourteenth amendment, are not absolute, but may be restricted by legislation directed to the protection of appropriate public interests as defined by the legislature.[81] Why

80 The New York trial court recognized that, even with restrictions on the prayer practice designed to secure freedom of non-participation, some subtle pressures might operate on persons not desiring to participate. But on this point Justice Meyer stated that the disadvantages of non-conformity are inherent in the American situation, and that objections to pressure placed on private persons by persons other than the state cannot be elevated to the level of a constitutional freedom. Engel v. Vitale, 18 Misc. 2d 659, 695, 191 N.Y.S.2d 453, 491-92 (Sup. Ct. 1959).

81 See, e.g., *Freedom of Religion*: Prince v. Massachusetts, 321 U.S. 158 (1944); Reynolds v. United States, 98 U.S. 145 (1878); *Freedom of Speech*: Scales v. United States, 367 U.S. 203 (1961); Dennis v. United States, 341 U.S. 494 (1951); *Freedom of the Press*: Roth v. United States, 354 U.S. 476 (1957); Beauharnais v. Illinois, 343 U.S. 250, rehearing denied, 343 U.S. 988 (1952). See also the majority opinion in Konigsberg v. State Bar, 366 U.S. 36 (1961).

the establishment limitation and the liberties implicit in it should be elevated to a higher place than these freedoms has not been made clear. James Madison's "three pence" argument,[82] if valid to support an absolutist interpretation of the establishment principle, should be equally valid to support the absolutist interpretation which the Court has rejected in its interpretation of the first amendment freedoms generally.[83]

Is it the effect of the *Engel* decision to bar the recitation of prayers by public school children in the situation where no parents voice an objection? Conceivably there are communities in the United States where all parents are ready and willing to have their children participate in such a practice. If the *Engel* case rests on an abstract and absolute non-establishment limitation, unrelated to infringement upon personal liberty, all school boards are in principle bound thereby, even though in the absence of objecting parents a serious standing problem would be presented as regards the bringing of a lawsuit to compel the school board to comply with the law as established by the *Engel* decision.[84] If, as has been suggested, the *Engel* case finds its real justification in the consideration that the officially prescribed prayer subjected all children to a compulsion to participate and thereby impaired the liberty of children and their parents, then *Engel* has no relevancy where all parents are willing to have their children participate. In a country as large as the United States, with great variations in the communities so far as religious elements are concerned, there is no compelling reason why the Constitution should be interpreted to require a uniform rule prohibiting all prayer exercises, without regard to the elements of coercion, impairment of rights of objectors and the effect of the exercises in promoting community divisiveness.

[82] See text *supra* at 1039 for the passage from Madison quoted in the *Engel* opinion.

[83] In an address delivered at the University of Utah, Feb. 27, 1963, in which he criticized the "absolutist" approach of the majority opinion in the *Engel* decision, Dean Erwin N. Griswold of the Harvard Law School said: "If one thinks of the Constitution as a God-given text stating fixed law for all time, and then focuses on a single passage, or indeed on two words—'no law'—without recognizing all the other words in the whole document, and its relation to the society outside the document, one can find the answers very simply. . . . The absolutist approach involves, I submit, a failure to exercise the responsibilities—and indeed the pains—of judgment. By ignoring factors relevant to sound decisions, it inevitably leads to wrong results." Excerpts from Dean Griswold's address appeared in the public press. See, *e.g.*, Ann Arbor News, Feb. 28, 1963, p. 13.

[84] In Doremus v. Board of Educ., 342 U.S. 429 (1952), the Court held that a taxpayer did not have standing before the Court to contest the validity of a Bible-reading practice, in the absence of a showing that the practice resulted in added out-of-pocket costs to the operation of the school system. See Sutherland, *supra* note 64, at 32-35, 39-42.

V. CONCLUSIONS

Viewed with respect to the precise problem before the Court, the decision in *Engel* is not a disturbing one, when evaluated in terms of underlying policy considerations. Prayer, religious faith, and the freedom of religion are not damaged by the Court's holding. On the contrary, the decision maintains the dignity and religious significance of prayer by keeping it free from state compulsion and interference, and, by the same token, it preserves the freedom of both the believer and the non-believer in respect to prayer. Nor should it be of consequence that the prayer was "non-sectarian." Even such a prayer can be productive of religious divisiveness, not only because it is objectionable to non-believers or non-theistic religionists, but also because theistic believers may find it an offense to conscience to engage in prayer except in accordance with the tenets of their own religion. Moreover, religionists can have little enthusiasm for an officially sanctioned non-sectarian expression of religious belief which at most reflects a vague and generalized religiosity. Any usefulness of a prayer practice in public schools as symbolic of the religious tradition in our national life, of the values of religion to our society, and of religious ideas shared in common, must be weighed against the peril that the official promotion of common-denominator religious practices, conspicuous by their vagueness and syncretistic character, will contribute to the furtherance and establishment of an official folk or culture religion which many competent observers regard as a serious threat to the vitality and distinctive witness of the historic faiths.[85]

The decision makes sense in terms of constitutional considerations if the case is confined to the fact emphasized by the Court and if the constitutional rights of objecting parents and children are viewed as vital to the result. It is, however, the Court's broad and absolutist interpretation of the first amendment, its disregard of the sanctions furnished by history for religious practices in the public schools, its indifference to the problem of standing, its failure to relate the establishment limitation to meaningful considerations of personal liberty—a failure all the more conspicuous when the relevancy of the fourteenth amendment is taken into account—and its failure to come to grips with the delicate problem of the rights of non-conformists in a com-

---

85 See HERBERG, PROTESTANT, CATHOLIC, JEW 254-72 (Doubleday paperback ed. 1960); MARTY, THE NEW SHAPE OF AMERICAN RELIGION 31-89 (1959).

munity that recognizes a common religious heritage that present the constitutional problems and difficulties. A decision resting on the narrower ground of freedom of religion or of conscience, explaining why the considerations advanced in support of the prayer practice were outweighed by the rights of the objectors, and why under the circumstances the feature of voluntary participation did not sufficiently protect the interests of objectors, would have been much more satisfactory. The Court's reliance instead on a broad and abstract ground of establishment warrants Reinhold Niebuhr's criticism that the Court used a meat-axe when it should have used a scalpel.[86]

The issue raised in *Engel* is symptomatic of the problem we face in a religiously pluralistic society. Protestantism can no longer claim a dominating position in shaping the American *ethos*. It is understandable that practices such as prayers and Bible reading in public schools, which had their origin in days of Protestant domination, should come under fresh scrutiny as the Court exercises its role of accommodating constitutional interpretation to the changing social scene, although it would be refreshing to have the Court acknowledge its creative and policy-making function in this respect instead of making it appear that the result is required either on the basis of a literal textual exegesis or by reference to the intent of the Founding Fathers. The larger question, however, is whether and to what extent the government and its institutions may reflect a dominant religious consciousness of the community that has its roots in the nation's history and tradition. Due regard for our religious pluralism as well as for the larger pluralism that takes account of non-theistic ideologies and nonbelief requires that government, in any recognition it gives to the dominant religious consciousness, carefully abstain from practices that in any significant way coerce conscience or otherwise impair minority rights. On the other hand, it is equally clear that the Constitution, in establishing a secular state that cannot prescribe any official belief or creed for its citizens, whether theistic or non-theistic and whether religious or political, does not require and, indeed, does not permit government to establish secularism or secular humanism as the nation's orthodoxy.

Religionists have ground for complaint if the public schools by studied indifference teach that belief in God is irrelevant to

[86] Niebuhr, *The Court and the Prayer: A Dissenting Opinion*, The New Leader, July 9, 1962, p. 3.

life. The *Engel* decision does not require such indifference. Consistent with it the schools may follow practices and teaching programs that help to create awareness, appreciation and understanding of the religious factor in the life of the nation and its citizens. They may create respect for the moral values which reflect the community consensus and which illuminate the purposes and processes of our democratic society. But it is not their responsibility or function to cultivate an official faith or ideology, whether religious or humanistic in character, or to indoctrinate students in any system of beliefs and values that rests on a claim of insight into ultimate truth with respect to the meaning and purpose of life. Parents who desire religious instruction for their children as part of a school program have the option of sending them to parochial schools. One effect of the school prayer decision is to highlight the importance of private schools and of the parents' freedom of choice in our free and pluralistic society that does not recognize governmental monopoly of the educational process. But the majority of Americans who are concerned with the relevancy of religious teaching to the total educational program do not see the parochial school as the answer to the problem. Their interest may lie in the further development of dismissed- or released-time programs in connection with the operation of the public school systems.[87] Moreover, in view of the present impasse with respect to the parochial school situation, it may well be that the shared-time plan offers the greatest promise for reconciling the felt needs for religious instruction with the secular limitations placed on the public school systems.[88] All proposals of this kind deserve careful study. Needless to say, any constructive solution to the problem will require a generous measure of sympathetic understanding, good will and tolerance on the part of all concerned elements of the community.

Whatever the merits of plans for accommodating the educational system to programs of formal religious instruction, they should not serve to obscure the fundamental consideration that

[87] On the question whether in the light of the *Engel* case the Supreme Court will continue to adhere to its decision in the *Zorach* case, sustaining the validity of a released-time program when conducted off the public school premises, see the discussion in the text *supra* at 1045.

[88] For a discussion of shared-time proposals whereby children will receive a part of their instruction in parochial schools and a part in the public schools, see STAFF OF HOUSE COMMITTEE ON EDUCATION AND LABOR, 87TH CONG., 2D SESS., PIONEER IDEALS IN EDUCATION 55-59 (Comm. Print 1962); Cassels, *A Way Out of Our Parochial-Public School Conflict*, Look, Aug. 28, 1962, p. 54; *Symposium: Shared Time*, 57 RELIGIOUS EDUCATION 5 (1962).

the cultivation of religious faith is the responsibility of home and church. If secularism triumphs as the dominant American ideology, it will not be because of the Constitution or the Supreme Court or because the public schools have failed in their limited tasks, but because meaningful and vital religious faith has lost its place in the hearts and lives of the people. The *Engel* decision is a forceful reminder to parents and the churches that theirs is the task and responsibility of making prayer, worship and religious instruction rich and meaningful in the lives of their children.

PRAYER AND POLITICS: THE IMPACT OF *ENGEL* AND *SCHEMPP* ON THE POLITICAL PROCESS*

William M. Beaney†

Edward N. Beiser††

To MANY AMERICANS THE OUTRIGHT REFUSAL of some state and local authorities to accept the constitutional rules set forth in the 1954 *School Segregation Case*[1] was shocking and unprecedented. Students of American public law, however, have long recognized that the pronouncements of any court, high or low, may prove in practice to have far less significance because of the conscious resistance of officials whose duties include the administration of the newly announced law. A quite different explanation of non-enforcement occasionally arises from the ignorance of officeholders as to the actual law applicable to a situation confronting them, but non-enforcement resulting from official ignorance has far less negative impact on social values than do inaction and opposition originating in avowed resistance to court declared norms of behavior. While the openness and pervasiveness of resistance after 1954 seemed novel, Americans of every generation since the founding of the Republic have chosen at times to disregard unpopular laws, or to temper their application so that they remain formally alive, but become meaningless in practice.

Students of constitutional law have, on the whole, been disinclined to examine the impact of Supreme Court decisions.[2] They have preferred to trace the development of doctrine in successive Court decisions with the tacit assumption that the law is obeyed except in those relatively rare instances where state or lower federal courts have refused to follow the

---

* The authors wish to acknowledge their indebtedness to the following individuals whose personal assistance, and where indicated, that of their staff, provided valuable data and helpful insights: Hon. Frank J. Becker (R. N.Y.) and his staff; Hon. Emmanuel Celler (D. N.Y.), and from his staff Mrs. Bess E. Dick, Staff Director, and Mr. Stuart H. Johnson, Jr., Counsel; Rev. Dean M. Kelley, Executive Director, Department of Religious Liberty, National Council of Churches; Dr. Leo Pfeffer, General Counsel, American Jewish Congress and members of his staff; Mr. Sol Rabkin, Chief of the Law Department of the Anti-Defamation League of B'nai B'rith, and members of his staff, especially Mr. Robert Frankel; and Mr. John Bechler, Washington correspondent of the Associated Press, who covered the Becker Amendment hearings.

† Professor of Politics and Cromwell Professor of Law, Princeton University; co-author with MASON, AMERICAN CONSTITUTIONAL LAW (3d ed. 1964).

†† Kent Fellow, Assistant in Instruction, Princeton University; currently engaged in a study of the treatment of the reapportionment issue by the lower state and federal courts.

1 Brown v. Board of Educ., 347 U.S. 483 (1954).

2 Some exceptions include Patric, *The Impact of a Court Decision: Aftermath of the McCollum Case*, 6 J. PUB. L. 455 (1957); Patric & Sorauf, *Zorach v. Clauson: The Impact of a Supreme Court Decision*, 53 AM. POL. SCI. REV. 777 (1959). A notable study of the impact of Supreme Court decisions on Congress is MURPHY, CONGRESS AND THE COURT (1962). There are numerous studies examining various aspects of efforts to implement the desegregation rulings. See, for example, PELTASON, FIFTY-EIGHT LONELY MEN (1961).

mandate of the highest court. Just as lower courts presumably accept the highest court's decisions, all officials presumably feel bound to obey the law. The reasons for this attitude are not hard to find. Despite a long history of resistance to certain laws, our political system, which has been remarkably viable, is based on the principle of the rule of law and all that is implied by that principle. The fair and even application of law is part of the official doctrine. The status of the Constitution as fundamental law raises Supreme Court decisions interpreting that document to the highest position in the hierarchy of law.

If our official doctrine tends to prevent recognition of reality, the practical difficulty of tracing a pattern of non- or partial observance is an equally substantial reason for eschewing such studies. In such a vast nation it is impossible to take more than a sampling of the many thousands of communities which refuse to accept, or fail to comply with, a Supreme Court decision. An explicit act or statement signifying outright opposition to, or announced refusal to adhere to, a decision by responsible officials permits obvious conclusions to be drawn, but how is one to discern the more subtle forms of resistance—the averting of official eyes from local practices, the whispered suggestion that officials or citizens are free to do as they have been accustomed to doing, or the *subrosa* encouragement to do what has not previously been done? Even if these and other patterns of circumvention are discovered, documentation may be all but impossible.

Yet, it seems obvious that students of our legal system should not be satisfied with an acceptance of the official theory that court decisions, and particularly Supreme Court decisions that affect important public policy issues, are universally accepted as the law. It is grossly misleading and dangerous to treat law as a significant form of social control by concentrating on the rules handed down by courts. The realist persuasion in legal philosophy, if it has done nothing else, has warned us against ignoring the ways in which law affects or may leave untouched the daily lives of those to whom it ostensibly applies.

When a court decision impinges on an activity of only a few persons, the tracing of impact is a simple and obvious process. A *Steel Seizure* case,[3] for example, poses a single question with respect to consequences: Did the United States relinquish control of the seized mills to their private corporate owners? But seldom will the question and the answer be so simple. Some decisions, such as those affecting the right of free speech of a curbstone orator, may have few consequences beyond resolving the specific dispute because of the varying contexts in which official action curtailing speech takes place. The impact of decisions affecting behavior of law enforcement officials are difficult to trace because of the difficulty of observing post-decision conduct. If any conclusions are to be reached

---

[3] Youngstown Sheet & Tube Co. v. Sawyer, 343 U.S. 579 (1952).

they must inevitably be based on the judgment of a few well-placed observers, or on the frequency of future cases where a breach of the rule of the earlier decision can be documented.

These preliminary remarks are intended to serve as qualifications of the present brief study of some of the principal political and governmental responses to *Engel v. Vitale*[4] in June 1962, outlawing the use of a Regent's prescribed prayer in New York public schools, and the decision of *School Dist. v. Schempp*[5]—*Murray v. Curlett*[6] in June 1963, prohibiting the reading of Bible passages or saying of prayers as religious exercises in public schools throughout the nation, a decision which is analyzed at length in another part of this symposium. A careful state-by-state study of what has occurred since these Court pronouncements has not been undertaken because of limitations of time and resources. What follows is based on data available in newspaper and other printed accounts, supplemented by interviews with those possessing first-hand knowledge of various facets of this subject.

THE NEW YORK PRAYER CASE

The reaction to the Court's decision declaring unconstitutional the use in public schools of a prayer prepared by the New York Regents was not long in forthcoming. And, at least in Congress, it was as one-sided as it was violent. Senator Talmadge (D. Ga.) denounced the decision as "unconscionable . . . an outrageous edict. . . ."[7] Congressman Williams (D. Miss.) insisted that the decision constituted "a deliberately and carefully planned conspiracy to substitute materialism for spiritual values and thus to communize America."[8] Congressman Sikes' (D. Fla.) description of the Court's action as infamous was probably closer to the mood of Congress than Senator Sparkman's (D. Ala.) milder comment: "a tragic mistake."[9] And Congressman Becker (R. N.Y.), who was to become the leader of the opposition to the Court on this issue, informed his colleagues that *Engel* was "the most tragic decision in the history of the United States."[10]

The immediate congressional reaction stressed what was to become one of the major themes of opponents of the Court's decisions: any opposition to religious activities in the public schools was an attack upon religion and upon God Himself. For Senator Robertson (D. Va.) this was the most extreme ruling the Supreme Court had ever made in favor of atheists and agnostics.[11] And Congressman Abernathy (D. Miss.) insisted that it would be "most pleasing to a few atheists and world Com-

---

4 370 U.S. 421 (1962).
5 374 U.S. 203 (1963).
6 *Ibid.*
7 108 CONG. REC. 11675 (1962).
8 *Id.* at 11734.
9 *Id.* at 11775, 11844.
10 *Id.* at 11719.
11 *Id.* at 11708.

munism."[12] Representative Rivers (D. S.C.) denounced the Court for having "now officially stated its disbelief in God Almighty," while Senator Ervin (D. N.C.), widely regarded as an authority on constitutional law, insisted that "the Supreme Court has made God unconstitutional."[13] Nor was this reaction limited to Southerners. Senator McCarthy (D. Minn.) denounced the decision as leading to "not only a secularized government but a secularized society."[14]

Congressman Andrews of Alabama managed to criticize the Court on two counts in one pithy utterance, "They put the Negroes into the schools and now they have driven God out of them."[15] The extent and one-sidedness of Congressional reaction is indicated by the fact that the Court's usual friends by and large did not attempt to defend the *Engel* decision, but restricted their activities to attempts at minimizing the scope of the decision. Senator Javits (R. N.Y.), for example, insisted that *Engel* did not prohibit prayer per se, but only governmentally prescribed prayer.[16] Except for Congressman Celler's (D. N.Y.) statement that he would oppose attempts to overturn *Engel* by amending the Constitution, the lone voice heard in support of the decision in the face of this onslaught was that of Congressman Lindsay (R.) of New York.[17]

Congressional reaction was expressed in several other forms as well. Congressman Haley (D. Fla.) offered an amendment to a judiciary appropriations bill to earmark out of the Supreme Court's appropriations funds to purchase "for the personal use of each justice a copy of the Holy Bible," but his resolution was rejected 47-66.[18] And on September 27, the House voted unanimously to place the motto "In God We Trust" behind the Speaker's desk. Lest the motivation behind this sudden religious impulse escape anyone, Congressman Randall (D. Mo.) pointed out that "we have given perhaps not directly but yet in a not so subtle way" our answer to the Supreme Court's decision.[19]

The type of Congressional action which posed the most serious threat to the Court's holding, and with which this article will be primarily concerned, was the introduction of proposed amendments to the Constitution to allow public schools to conduct religious exercises. Congressman Frank Becker (R. N.Y.) introduced his amendment the day after *Engel* was decided. His language is typical of this type of proposal: "Prayers may

---

[12] *Id.* at 11718.

[13] Dr. Leo Pfeffer, *Information Bulletin No. 6*, Commission on Law and Social Action of the American Jewish Congress, p. 2, August 15, 1962 [hereinafter cited as *CLSA Bull.* 1].

[14] 108 CONG. REC. 11844 (1962).

[15] Quoted by Kurland, *The Regents' Prayer Case: "Full of Sound and Fury, Signifying . . .,"* SUPREME COURT REV. 3 (Kurland ed. 1962).

[16] For Sen. Javits' comments, and similar remarks by Sen. Wiley and Congressmen Van Zant and James W. Davis, see *Congressional Record* of June 29, 1962, *passim.*

[17] As of June 27, 1962. *Congressional Record Digest*, Anti-Defamation League of B'nai Brith.

[18] 108 CONG. REC. 14360 (1962).

[19] *Id.* at 21102.

be offered in the course of any program in any public school or other public place in the United States."[20]

Twenty-two senators and fifty-three representatives introduced amendments in response to *Engel,* as indicated in the following table:[21]

TABLE I

Members of Congress Introducing Anti-*Engel* Amendments. 87th Congress, 2d Session.

	House	Senate
PARTY AFFILIATION		
Republicans	26	12
Southern Democrats	19	8
Non-Southern Democrats	8	2
	—	—
Total	53	22

Congressional hostility toward the Court's decision was further demonstrated at hearings conducted by Senator Eastland's Judiciary Committee, just one month after *Engel* was decided. Testimony by various senators shows that they were acutely aware that the Court was soon to consider the constitutionality of Bible reading and the recitation of the Lord's Prayer in public schools, and that it was fully expected that both practices would be prohibited. Thus one of the joint resolutions before the committee anticipated the Court's action in *Schempp,* by proposing to amend the Constitution to allow prayer and Bible reading in public schools. It is interesting to note that in their general frame of reference as well as in their specific resolutions, the senators were significantly affected not only by what the Court had done—but by what it might be expected to do in the future.

One who reads the hearings cannot help but be impressed by the tremendous impact of Mr. Justice Douglas' concurring opinion in *Engel.*[22] Again and again witnesses pointed to it as an example of what the Court would do in the future. Critics of the Court's action, especially California's Episcopal Bishop James A. Pike and Senator Stennis (D. Miss.), relied heavily on statements in his opinion. The fact that Mr. Justice Douglas had already taken an extreme position which the critics charged that the Court as a whole might assume in the future greatly strengthened their position, since Douglas' opinion made concrete what might otherwise have been dismissed as idle speculation.

---

[20] Quoted in *Hearings on Prayer in Public Schools and Other Matters Before the Senate Committee on the Judiciary,* 87th Cong., 2d Sess. 71 (1962) [hereinafter cited as *1962 Senate Hearings*].

[21] "Southern Democrats" includes representatives of the eleven states of the old Confederate States of America. This is the usage of V. O. Key in SOUTHERN POLITICS (1949).

[22] 370 U.S. at 437.

The short Senate Judiciary Committee hearings, with Senator Eastland, the chairman, absent, provided a field day for opponents of the Court. While the critical statements of such organizations as the American Legion and Young Americans For Freedom were countered by statements submitted by such groups as the American Civil Liberties Union, Anti-Defamation League, The Baptist Joint Committee on Public Affairs, and others, the oral testimony of the witnesses was unanimous in opposing the Court's action. The principal theme of the several witnesses—as had been the case in the initial congressional reaction—was that the decision represented a concerted attack on God and on religion in American life. Bishop Pike, for example, insisted that the result of the decision was "secularism, whether by intent or by default. I am not implying for a moment that the proponents or supporters of the decision of the Supreme Court intentionally wish an atheistic result. Nevertheless, when it is by default we simply *cut off the whole spiritual dimension of life,* and without even a reference to it. What we have left is actually a secularist view of life."[23]

The Eastland Committee hearings also provided a platform for those who had other bones to pick with the Court. There were repeated references in the testimony to persistent abuses by the Supreme Court of its judicial function. It is hardly coincidental that the overwhelming majority of congressmen and senators who participated in these hearings were Southerners. Table I indicated that more than half of the amendments to the Constitution introduced to reverse *Engel* were introduced by representatives of the 11 states of the former Confederacy. And Bishop Pike—the one non-congressional witness at the hearings—began his testimony with a strong states' rights argument.[24] Apart from allowing opponents of the Court and of the *Regents' Prayer* decision to vent their spleen, the hearings accomplished nothing. No final report was issued, nor was any legislation proposed.

The reaction of the late President Kennedy differed significantly. In response to a question at his regular news conference, he said:

> The Supreme Court has made its judgment. Some will disagree and others will agree. In the efforts we're making to maintain our Constitutional principles, we will have to abide by what the Supreme Court says. We have a very easy remedy here, and that is to pray ourselves. We can pray a good deal more at home and attend our churches with fidelity and emphasize the true meaning of prayer in the lives of our children. I hope, as a result of that decision, all Americans will give prayer a greater emphasis.[25]

---

[23] *1962 Senate Hearings* 56. (Emphasis added.)
[24] *Id.* at 51. Bishop Pike misstated the text of the 10th amendment in his comment that the amendment "makes clear that those things not *specifically* given to the federal government by authority, are reserved to the States and the people." (Emphasis added.)
[25] *CLSA Bull.* 3.

The late President Hoover, however, voiced a strong dissent:

> The interpretation of the Constitution is a disintegration of one of the most sacred of American heritages. The Congress should at once submit an amendment to the Constitution which establishes the right to religious devotion in all government agencies —national, state, or local.[26]

If the two former Presidents divided evenly, the governors did not. At a meeting at Hershey, Pennsylvania, on July 3, the Governors' Conference resolved that:

> Whereas the recent majority opinion of the United States Supreme Court in the New York *School Prayer* case has created far reaching misunderstanding as to the nation's faith and dependence in God; and
>
> Whereas the Governors assembled . . . acknowledge their dependence upon God and the power of prayer to Him; . . .
>
> Resolved, that the Governors' Conference urge upon the Congress of the United States to propose an amendment to the Constitution of the United States that will make clear and beyond challenge the acknowledgment by our nation and people of their faith in God and permit the free and voluntary participation in prayer in our public schools.[27]

The resolution passed unanimously, with only Governor Rockefeller of New York abstaining.[28]

The reaction of the nation's press was mixed. As might have been expected, the Court was defended by such newspapers as the *New York Times, New York Herald Tribune, New York Post, St. Louis Post-Dispatch, Washington Post, Milwaukee Journal,* and *Chicago Sun-Times,* among others. Critics of the Court included the Hearst newspapers, the *New York News, Baltimore Sun, Boston Globe, Chicago Tribune,* and *Los Angeles Times.*[29] The moderate *New York Herald Tribune* was amazed at "the sight of so many otherwise responsible newspapers getting completely swept off their feet by the tide of emotionalism."[30] Twenty-seven of the sixty-three newspapers examined by one writer were found to have published editorials opposed to the *School Prayer* decision; sixteen favored the decision in editorials; and eleven were more or less neutral. "The strongest opposition came from papers in the northern Midwest. Contrary to common newspaper reports, more southern papers were neutral or favorable to the opinion than opposed. . . . Twenty papers published critical cartoons; twelve published favorable cartoons."[31]

---

[26] *Ibid.*
[27] *1962 Senate Hearings* 210.
[28] *CLSA Bull.* 3.
[29] SUPREME COURT REV., *op. cit. supra* note 15, at 2 n.7.
[30] *Ibid.*
[31] Newland, *Press Coverage of the U.S. Supreme Court,* 17 WESTERN POLITICAL Q. 15, 30 (1964).

Of particular interest and no little surprise, was the reaction of the Negro community. Dr. Martin Luther King, actively engaged in the Albany, Georgia kneel-in controversy, called the Court's action "a sound and good decision reaffirming something that is basic in our Constitution, namely, separation of church and state."[32] Such leading Negro newspapers as the *Amsterdam News, Chicago Defender,* and *Pittsburgh Courier* expressed their support of the decision.[33] And the NAACP, which rarely takes public positions on issues that do not directly affect Negroes, and which had never done so in the area of church-state relations, unanimously passed a resolution supporting the *Engel* decision at its national convention in Atlanta on July 2-8. In addition, it submitted a strong pro-decision statement to the Eastland Committee.[34]

This reaction seemed to indicate a realization on the part of the Negro community that the attack on the Court which followed the *Engel* decision was in fact directed at the Court for its civil rights' decisions as well as its stand on the Regents' prayer, and that if the Court were slapped down in this area, it might be more cautious in cases which directly affect the Negro community.

The leadership of the religious community tended to divide on denominational lines. Roman Catholic spokesmen were extremely critical of the Court. Cardinal Spellman, for example, was "shocked and frightened that the Supreme Court had declared unconstitutional a simple and voluntary declaration of belief in God by public school children. The decision strikes at the very heart of the Godly tradition in which America's children have for so long been raised."[35] Cardinal Spellman's representative at the Senate hearings supported an amendment to the Constitution to reverse *Engel,* denouncing the decision as "a grave error in judicial judgment, a decision out of line with the conscience and religious heritage of the American people and one which foreshadows an ominous tendency to undermine cherished traditions of this Nation."[36] "Preposterous" was the term used by the *Brooklyn Tablet* to describe the decision, while the Jesuit weekly *America* used the adjectives "asinine," "stupid," "doctrinaire," and "unrealistic."[37]

Jewish religious and organizational leaders, on the other hand, were almost unanimous in their support of the Court's action. The New York Board of Rabbis, the Rabbinical Assembly of America, and the Commission of Social Action of Reform Judaism were among the many organizations expressing their support.[38]

---

[32] *CLSA Bull.* 1. We rely heavily on Dr. Pfeffer's analysis at this point.
[33] *Ibid.*
[34] *1962 Senate Hearings* 149. The statement refers to the NAACP Convention's action.
[35] Kurland *op. cit. supra* note 15, at 2 n.5.
[36] *1962 Senate Hearings* 140.
[37] SUPREME COURT REV., *op. cit. supra* note 15, at 2 n.5.
[38] *Ibid.* See also *CLSA Bull.* 4.

Protestant leadership was divided. Episcopal Bishop James A. Pike announced that "the Supreme Court has just deconsecrated the nation." The Reverend Dr. Billy Graham and Dr. Reinhold Niebuhr reacted critically, Graham in the following words: "God pity our country when we can no longer appeal to God for help."[39] And, as noted above, Bishop Pike appeared in person before the Eastland Committee to urge strongly the modification of the first amendment to prohibit not the "establishment of religion," but rather "the recognition as an established church of any denomination, sect, or organized religious association."[40] Dr. Leo Pfeffer notes with some amusement that if this amendment were achieved, "use of tax-raised funds for parochial schools would become constitutional— a development which Bishop Pike along with practically all other Protestant leaders strongly opposes."[41]

Equally strong statements supporting the Court's decision were issued by other elements within the Protestant camp. The Joint Baptist Committee on Public Affairs, with a constituency of more than 17 million members, reacted very favorably to *Engel.*[42] *Christian Century,* widely regarded as the leading Protestant publication in America, endorsed the decision, as did a group of Protestant theologians, including the Dean of the Harvard Divinity School.[43]

THE RESPONSE TO THE LORD'S PRAYER AND BIBLE READING DECISIONS[44]

When the decision in *Schempp* was handed down on June 17, 1963, the immediate reaction was less violent than those who had experienced the stormy reaction to *Engel* had anticipated. A careful observer concluded that "the reaction in the total American community to the ruling was markedly more positive than it had been to the Court's decision in the *Regent's Prayer* case one year earlier."[45] *Time* magazine called the reaction "relatively mild" and "nothing compared to that of 1962."[46] The Attorney General's office reported that it had received many fewer letters reacting against *Schempp* than it had in response to *Engel,* and a Court aide reported that the volume of critical mail was well below that of the previous decision.[47] A study of 185 editorials in newspapers published in 35 states and the District of Columbia found that 61 percent approved the Court's decision, a marked shift from earlier editorial stands, especially in the Northeast and Midwest.[48] It appears that there was also a decrease

---

39 SUPREME COURT REV., *op. cit. supra* note 15, at 2 n.5.
40 *1962 Senate Hearings* 55.
41 *CLSA Bull.* 4.
42 *Ibid.*
43 *Ibid.*
44 School Dist. v. Schempp, 374 U.S. 203 (1963).
45 Arnold Forster (Director of civil liberties division, ADL), *Memorandum to All ADL Regional Offices,* July 11, 1963, p. 1 [hereinafter cited as Forster].
46 Time, June 28, 1963, p. 13.
47 Chicago American, June 30, 1963.
48 Forster *supra* note 45, at 1. The survey included 169 papers in 115 cities.

in the number of hostile "Letters to the Editor" in these same papers, although a majority opposed the decision. The reactions expressed in readers' letters to periodicals also were milder in tone when contrasted with the bitter outpouring which had followed the earlier decision.[49]

But there is little doubt that an overwhelming majority of the public disapproved of the Court's position. The Gallup Poll posed the following question: "The U.S. Supreme Court has ruled that no state or local government may require the reading of the Lord's Prayer or Bible verses in public schools. What are your views on this?" Results released on August 30, 1963, showed that 70 percent of those polled opposed the decisions, only 24 percent approved, while 6 percent had no opinion.

The greater restraint shown by editors and readers was matched by a more moderate tone in the responsive statements of religious leaders. The most significant shifts occurred in the ranks of Protestant and Catholic spokesmen, with the dominant note a plea for respect for the Court's decision coupled with assertions that the banning of Bible reading and required prayers in public schools did not represent a new judicial attitude of hostility toward religion. In many instances spokesmen seemed intent on calming public fears arising from the attention paid by the press and other news media to Mr. Justice Douglas' concurring opinion in *Engel*, which was widely accepted as a threat by the Court to sweep away every recognition of religion in American public life. Some of the positive points enunciated by Protestant spokesmen were: the church and home had responsibility for developing proper religious attitudes in the young; perfunctory religious observances, which was the proper characterization of many school ceremonies, were a waste of time at least and perhaps bred improper views of religious doctrine; the church now had a duty to improve its own program of religious instruction; and finally, the decisions did not prevent public schools from initiating programs of effective teaching about the past and present roles of religion in society.[50]

Whereas expressions of opinion by Catholic leaders after *Engel* had been almost uniformly critical, several Catholic Bishops and Archbishops now issued statements calling for restraint.[51] The distinguished Catholic legal scholar, Father Robert F. Drinan, S.J., Dean of the School of Law at Boston College, said "formal religion rightfully belongs in the home, in churches, and synagogues, and in their respective schools. . . ." Cardinal Ritter joined the St. Louis Church Federation and the Rabbinical Association in a statement pledging cooperation and respect for the decision "as the law of the land" regardless of the merits or lack thereof, of the de-

---

[49] *Id.* at 2.
[50] *Id.* at 4.
[51] *Id.* at 3. A survey of Roman Catholic diocesan papers by the weekly *Ave Maria* revealed that 35 had gone on record opposing any congressional action to overturn the court decision, while only eight favored it. After *Engel*, a large majority of the same papers had attacked the Court's decision. Time, June 19, 1964, p. 62.

cision itself.[52] Part of the Catholic press, including *America,* opposed the ruling, a position probably shared by their readers. And, it seems clear that the majority of people of both the Catholic and Protestant faiths opposed the banning of prayers and Bible reading from the public schools, despite the statements of church leaders supporting the Court or counseling acceptance of its mandate.

As had been the case a year earlier, the reaction of Jewish groups was almost uniformly favorable. Among the organizations which issued statements supporting the Court's action were The American Jewish Committee, the American Jewish Congress, the Anti-Defamation League, The Rabbinical Council of America, and the Synagogue Council of America.[53] Since the Gallup poll cited above did not classify respondents according to religion, it is impossible to know the extent to which the unanimous position of the Jewish organizations reflected the attitudes of the Jewish community.

The failure of the 1963 decision to touch off public and press outcries comparable to those engendered by the *Regents Prayer* case, while at first glance surprising, seems readily explainable. The shock value of the first decision was great—both the public and press seem to have been caught unawares—so that much of the bitter first commentary was uninformed, and frequently was based on sentences ripped out of the context of the Court's opinion, or to be found only in the concurring opinion of Mr. Justice Douglas. The 1963 decision, on the other hand, was anticipated, although some defenders of the Court had given the misleading impression that the *Regents'* case represented the judicial response to an officially prescribed prayer and had no wider application. It had also become evident that many of the severest critics of the Court's 1962 decision were staunch opponents of the Court's desegregation stand, a fact which gave pause to religious spokesmen who were unwilling to help weaken the Court's moral authority in the crucial area of race relations. It appears also that some of the more perceptive Catholic leaders believed other church-state issues to be of greater importance, particularly the question of federal financial assistance to education and thus did not choose to become involved in the present controversy. In any event, the generally milder initial reaction to the 1963 decision was to prove illusory to those who thought that this portended widespread acceptance of the Court's ruling. Both in the affected states and in Congress, unmistakable evidence of resistance and opposition in various forms soon appeared and battle was joined.

---

[52] Forster, *supra* note 45, at 3.
[53] *Id.* at 5.

THE STATE RESPONSE TO SCHEMPP

The *Regents' Prayer* case affected only an estimated ten percent of the public school districts in a single state—New York. But the *Schempp* decision was directly applicable to a very substantial portion of the nation's school systems. In mid-1963 when these cases were decided, thirty-seven states and the District of Columbia permitted religious exercises in the public schools.[54] Thirteen of these *required* Bible reading by law,[55] and twelve others specifically permitted Bible reading by law or judicial decision.[56] It was reported that the *Bible* was read in 76 percent of the Southern schools, 67 percent of Eastern schools, 18 percent of Midwestern schools, and 11 percent of the Western schools. Overall, the Court's 1963 decisions affected almost 42 percent of the nation's public schools.

As one might expect, state reaction to the *Schempp* decision ranged from forthright declarations that a state or a specific school's system would not be bound, to equally strong statements advocating and insisting upon full compliance. In between these clearly defined attitudes were various official stances in which spokesmen suggested either that the Court's decisions were not applicable, or that each local system was to be permitted to decide its own policy, or, as was common, said nothing to acknowledge that a new rule was in effect, which left to local school officials the decision to continue or terminate religious ceremonies.

Most of the instances of outright defiance occurred in the South where, since 1954, opposition by public officials to any of the Court's controversial rulings can be anticipated almost as a reflex action. The Alabama State Board of Education denounced the Court for issuing a decision that was "a calculated effort to take God out of the public affairs of the nation."[58] Governor Wallace was even more explicit: "I would like for the people of Alabama to be in defiance of such a ruling. . . . I want the Supreme Court to know we are not going to conform to any such decision. I want the State Board of Education to tell the whole world we are not going to abide by it."[59]

And several days later, perhaps copying a tactic from the civil rights movement he has so bitterly opposed, the Governor told newsmen that he was prepared to stage a pray-in. The Governor stated that if the Court rules "that we cannot read the Bible in some school, I'm going to that school and read it myself."[60] Having stood in the doorway of a schoolhouse to

---

54 N. Y. Times, June 18, 1963, p. 27, col. 5, quoting a study by R. H. Diernfield, for the Public Affairs Press.

55 *Ibid.* The states were Alabama, Arkansas, Delaware, Florida, Georgia, Idaho, Kentucky, Maine, Massachusetts, New Jersey, Pennsylvania, Tennessee, and the District of Columbia.

56 *Ibid.* The states were Colorado, Iowa, Indiana, Kansas, Michigan, Minnesota, Mississippi, Nebraska, North Dakota, Ohio, Oklahoma, and Texas.

57 *Ibid.*

58 Religious News Service (Domestic). Aug. 6, 1963 [hereinafter cited as RNS].

59 *Ibid.*

60 N. Y. Times, Aug. 6, 1963, p. 17, col. 3.

thwart the federal courts, Wallace was apparently prepared to pray in a classroom to accomplish much the same end. Showing an appreciation of legal niceties, the Alabama State Board of Education ordered daily Bible reading as a part of a "prescribed course of study," which on its face placed the state practice within a category permitted by the decisions.[61] Wallace's Mississippi colleague, Ross Barnett, announced that he was "going to tell every teacher in Mississippi to conduct prayers and Bible reading despite what the Supreme Court says."[62] And Mississippi's chief law enforcement officer, Attorney General Joe Patterson, advised "all principals to continue to recognize the supremacy and many blessings of a great and just God as we have always done in our public schools."[63] South Carolina's State Superintendent of Education, Jesse Anderson, obviously felt that the decision did not apply in his state, for he announced that "South Carolina will continue to feel free to do in each school or classroom the normal thing which the teacher feels should be done."[64]

Outright defiance was not confined to the deep South. The Kentucky State Superintendent of Public Instruction, Wendell Butler, instructed local school districts to "continue to read and pray until somebody stops you. I don't want to make anybody stop."[65] The Kentucky State Board of Education opened its June 26th meeting with the customary Bible reading, sermon, and prayer, one Board member saying, "If the procedure is illegal, I move to violate the Constitution."[66] And Rhode Island State Commissioner of Education Robinson declared that he did "not now or in the future intend to prostitute the office of Commissioner of Education of Rhode Island to further the cause of the irreligious, the atheistic, the unreligious, or the agnostic."[67]

Many who did not openly defy the Court sought to evade the impact of the decisions by employing one or more of the following devices: attempting to distinguish the case; limiting the scope of the case by interpretation (usually by misinterpretation); reading a patriotic song such as "America" or the fourth stanza of the Star Spangled Banner ("In God is our trust"); using hymns, prayers, etc., as part of "music appreciation"; using the Bible as "literature" with no intention of conducting literary study, or, as noted above in the case of Alabama, making Bible reading part of a "course of study." The first of these tactics was employed by the Attorney General of Delaware, David Buckson, who insisted that his state's statute had not been considered by the Court:

---

[61] American Jewish Committee, Jewish Information Service, *Bible Reading After the Schempp-Murray Decision,* December, 1963, at 43 (Prepared by Mrs. S. Dawidowicz) [hereinafter cited as Dawidowicz].
[62] New Orleans Times Picayune, June 20, 1963, p. 6.
[63] Jackson Clarion Ledger, June 18, 1963, p. 1.
[64] RNS, June 18, 1963.
[65] Louisville Courier Journal, June 27, 1963. (The following September, the Kentucky Attorney General reversed this decision. RNS, Sept. 11, 1963.)
[66] *Ibid.*
[67] Providence Evening Bulletin, Oct. 8, 1963.

Despite the expressed opinion that this particular [Bible reading] law may be unconstitutional and may be unenforceable if challenged, the fact remains that the Delaware statute is still the law of Delaware and will remain so until repealed or modified by the General Assembly or declared by a court of competent jurisdiction to be violative of the State or Federal Constitution.[68]

Similar arguments were used by the defiant residents of Hawthorne, New Jersey when they refused to comply with the State Commissioner of Education's orders to terminate religious practices on the ground that the New Jersey statutes had not been tested in court.[69]

The most prevalent misinterpretation of *Schempp* was the insistence that prayers and Bible readings were permissible as long as state compulsion did not enter the picture. Governor Sanford of North Carolina announced that:

> We will go on having Bible reading and prayer in the schools of this state just as we always have. . . . We do not require the Bible reading and prayer, but we do these things because we want to. . . . As I read the decision, this kind of thing is not forbidden by the Court, and indeed, it should not be.[70]

Much the same views were expressed by U.S. District Judge Johnson J. Hayes, at the First Baptist Church of Statesville, N. C., when he said that the ruling prohibited the government from requiring religious observances, but did not preclude a teacher from leading students in the Lord's Prayer on a voluntary basis.[71] Arkansas Attorney General Bennett told state school officials that the Arkansas Bible reading law was *not* struck down because children were not compelled to participate.[72] Perhaps the most interesting "interpretation" of the decisions was that of the Superintendent of Schools of Little Rock, Arkansas: "We understand the Supreme Court ruling was not mandatory. . . ."[73]

The device most widely used to permit the continuation of religious practices in the schools, however, was to avoid establishing any official policy. Oklahoma State Superintendent of Public Instruction Hodge felt that since the state had no law requiring Bible reading, the decision as to whether religious practices could continue was a matter for the individual teacher to decide. Ohio State Superintendent Holt insisted that the State Board of Education take no position, and leave all interpretations to local school systems.[74] The Manchester *Union Leader* quoted New

---

[68] Wilmington Morning News, Aug. 16, 1963, p. 24.
[69] For further details, see the N. Y. Herald Tribune, Sept. 5, 1963, p. 3, col. 2.
[70] RNS, Sept. 16, 1963.
[71] Dawidowicz, *supra* note 61, at 43-44.
[72] *Id.* at 43.
[73] RNS, Sept. 9, 1963.
[74] ADL, *Report on Reactions in Public School Systems Throughout the Country to the Supreme Court's Decisions on Bible Reading and Prayer*, Fall, 1963, p. 9 (unpublished).

Hampshire State Board of Education chairman John C. Driscoll as saying that "it is up to each local school board to determine for itself, consistent with the Constitution as interpreted by the Supreme Court . . . , what it is going to permit for practices within the format of regular school exercises."

And, lest any of its readers fail to realize the significance of this "local option" policy, the *Union Leader's* editorial continued by adding that "there is nothing to prevent school teachers or the students themselves from conducting their own non-compulsory prayer exercises within the classroom. . . ."[75] In Iowa, Superintendent Johnston felt that since this was a local matter, "custom in their own community ought to determine what they should do."[76] There is little doubt that in each of the states in which the authorities chose to rely on "local custom" rather than on the Court's decisions, they had an accurate idea of what "local custom" would dictate.[77]

The picture was not completely one sided, however. There are states in which the Court's decisions are apparently being enforced. Silent meditation is allowed in some. In Maryland, for example, State Superintendent of Schools Thomas C. Pullen, Jr. informed all school superintendents that "any attempt to circumvent the decision of the Supreme Court by indirection or chicanery would be improper and not in the spirit of the administration of the public schools in Maryland."[78] In New Jersey, the Hughes administration insisted on strict compliance. State Commissioner of Education Raubinger informed local school boards that "there can be no option or discretionary choice in the matter."[79] The State Board of Education threatened to cut off state aid, and in one case obtained a state supreme court injunction, in order to force compliance by a defiant school district.[80] In Massachusetts, Attorney General Edward W. Brooke issued a twenty-two page directive urging compliance without resort to sophistry of any sort. "No official of government of whatever station can, in good conscience, disobey the mandate of the Supreme Court. . . ."[81] As in New Jersey, some Massachusetts towns resisted the state's attempt to bring about compliance; Brooke was forced to go into court to compel the town of North Brookfield to comply.[82] Similarly, in Pennsylvania, the

---

[75] Manchester Union Leader, October 30, 1963, Editorial.
[76] Des Moines Sunday Register, Aug. 25, 1963.
[77] Other "local option" states were Florida, Georgia, and Virginia.
[78] Dawidowicz, *supra* n.61, at 44.
[79] Newark Star Ledger, Sept. 5, 1963, p. 1.
[80] 5 N.J. 435 (1950). The major battle took place in Hawthorne, New Jersey, site of Doremus v. Board of Education, 342 U.S. 429 (1952), in which the state courts had sustained Bible reading in the public schools. The issue was avoided by the Supreme Court on jurisdictional grounds. See the Newark Evening News, Sept. 12, 1963, for details surrounding the issuing of the injunction.
[81] Directive from Attorney General's office, Aug. 20, 1963, at 21.
[82] See the Boston Herald, Oct. 14, 1963, p. 1.

state authorities were faced with open defiance at one time of as many as twenty-two school districts.[83]

It should be noted that in some sections of the country the Court's decision would have little impact, for Bible reading and prayer were not widely practiced. Eleven states—mostly Western— specifically barred such activities.[84]

Of course, the official reactions of state and local officials do not give us anything like a complete picture of what is actually going on in classrooms throughout the country; and the available data are at best fragmentary. A careful survey, which probably tends to understate the situation, reported that at the time school opened in 1963, prayer or Bible reading took place in the public schools of 10 states, and that in three— Arkansas, Alabama, and Delaware—Bible reading or the Lord's Prayer were *required* by law.[85] In addition, it was estimated that in some seven other states the official "hands off" policy allows religious practices to continue on a local basis. Spot checks indicate that the Court's decisions are being violated in many other areas. The *Religious News Service* reported, for example, that as of September 27, 1963, less than 20 of Connecticut's 169 towns had acted to implement in some way the Court's decision.[86] The *Des Moines Sunday Register* observed that "as Iowa's public schools prepare to begin another year the impact of the U.S. Supreme Court's latest ruling against school prayers is *almost unnoticeable. . . .* Most schools will make no change from past policy."[87] The *Atlanta Journal* reported that most Georgia school boards are unofficially encouraging continuation of religious exercises, including chapel.[88] A major study of policy and practice in Indiana, published in April, 1964, showed that the reading of the Bible at the opening of the school day was permitted or practiced in approximately one-third of the responding school corporations and that nearly one-half permitted or practiced the reciting of the Lord's Prayer, while 60 percent allowed a pupil or teacher to lead the saying of a prayer, commonly in conjunction with the noon meal. Less than 6 percent of the respondents reported a change in school board policy as a result of the 1963 Court decision.[89] These figures, it should be noted, are based on replies of school board superintendents, who might be expected to *minimize* the extent to which illegal practices are going on in their schools.

How are we to understand this apparently widespread defiance of a

---

[83] RNS, Sept. 26, 1963.
[84] Diernfield study, *supra* note 54.
[85] ADL report, *supra* note 74.
[86] RNS, Sept. 27, 1963.
[87] Des Moines Sunday Register, Aug. 25, 1963. (Emphasis added.)
[88] Quoted in a memo in the ADL files from its Atlanta office, dated Oct. 1963.
[89] John C. Hill, *Religion and the Public Schools: Policy and Practice in Indiana,* Research Bulletin No. 14, School of Education, Indiana University, April, 1964. Summary and conclusions. (No pagination.)

Supreme Court ruling? A comment in the *Indianapolis Star* probably answers this question. "No Supreme Court decision handed down to us because of a disgruntled [*sic*] atheist mother who doesn't want her child to know there is a God should influence our School Board."[90]

Reports from many other states that could not be accused of having an anti-Court bias tend to support the conclusion that forthright compliance with the Court's mandate has been the exception rather than the rule in many parts of the nation, and that a tremendous number of suits will be necessary to convert many state and local officials to a policy that conforms to the rulings of the supposed "final arbiter" of constitutional question.[91] Whether or not President Jackson ever said "John Marshall has made his decision, now let him enforce it," his sentiment aptly describes the response of many of the nation's school districts to the Court's decisions in *Schempp* and *Murray*.[92]

THE BECKER AMENDMENT

In light of popular support for the continuation of Bible reading and prayers in the public schools, and the obvious reluctance of many states to abandon practices which have been in effect for several decades, it was hardly to be expected that Congress would stay out of the controversy engendered by the 1963 decision. The initial congressional reaction, though largely reflecting opposition, was more restrained than that of a year earlier when the *Regents' Prayer* decision was handed down. There was some of the damning language which followed the earlier decision. Congressman

---

[90] Indianapolis Star, Nov. 25, 1963.

[91] Delaware provides an example of the difficulties which may be involved in bringing such suits. Mrs. Mary DeYoung of Middletown, Delaware, brought suit in August 1963 to enjoin the practice of prayer in the public schools. Mrs. DeYoung was both a parent and a teacher in the Middletown Public School. The court found in favor of the plaintiffs. However, before the decision was handed down, Mrs. DeYoung was informed that her contract as a teacher in the Middletown school would not be renewed. She did not have tenure, and was thus not entitled to receive specific reasons for her "discharge." Mrs. DeYoung, it should be noted, had an excellent teaching record, and had received an "A" rating for her work during the school year 1962/63. The Board of Education claimed that her participation in the Bible case had caused administrative problems, especially because parents requested that their children be taken out of her class, a contention disputed by her attorney. If the Court's decisions are to be implemented in the absence of vigorous enforcement by state officials, local citizens must be prepared to bring suit, and to subject themselves to the kinds of pressures illustrated by Mrs. DeYoung's experience. We are grateful to Mr. Irvin Morris, Esq. for details of the DeYoung case. Letter to the authors, July 17, 1964.

[92] On May 20, 1964, Mr. Hugh L. Elsbree, Director of the Legislative Reference Service of the Library of Congress, sent a telegram to the Attorneys-General of the fifty states, asking them to report any actions taken in response to the 1963 decisions, and to indicate the policies and practices then in existence. While many of the replies were not fully responsive, it is clear that at least the following states were *admittedly* not in compliance with the Court's pronouncements: Alabama, Arkansas, Florida, Idaho, Mississippi, North Carolina, North Dakota, and Oklahoma. The tone of numerous other state responses indicated a "hands off" policy by state officials.

We noted above the action taken by New Jersey state officials to insure compliance with the Court's action. Yet despite these sincere and vigorous efforts, the authors are aware of at least one case in which the Lord's Prayer was used in a New Jersey public school as recently as the Spring of 1964, and suspect that this was not an isolated incident.

O'Konski (R. Wis.), for example, suggested mental tests for the Justices, and Senator Ellender (D. La.), continuing a long standing quarrel with the Court, referred to the "eight silly old men."[93] Senator Thurmond (D. S.C.) called it "another major triumph of secularism and atheism which are bent on throwing God completely out of our national life," while his colleague Senator Robertson (D. Va.) insisted that "we will become as Godless a nation as is the Soviet Union."[94] Striking a more positive note, Senator Johnston (D. S.C.) urged teachers to defy the decisions, and Congressman Ashmore (D. S.C.) moved that "In God We Trust" be placed in the Supreme Court building in much the same spirit that had led the House to place that motto behind the Speaker's desk a year earlier.[95] By and large, however, the violent outburst which had followed *Engel* was missing.

But whatever personal views members of Congress may have held, those of their constituents were made increasingly clear by a barrage of letters and petitions heavily weighted against the prayer and Bible reading decisions. And this unusually heavy flood of mail was soon followed by Congressional action in the form of numerous bills proposing amendments to the Constitution intended to reverse the *Schempp* decision. A comparison of Tables I and II indicates that almost twice as many members of Congress felt impelled to introduce such amendments as had been the

TABLE II

Party Affiliation of Authors of Constitutional Amendments to Reverse *Schempp*.
88th Congress, 2d Session.

	House	Senate
PARTY AFFILIATION		
Republicans	64	15
Southern Democrats	30	8
Non-Southern Democrats	19	4
Total	113	27

case after *Engel*. In all, 146 amendments were introduced as of March 24, 1964. We are thus faced with an interesting paradox: popular reaction to *Engel* was much greater than the outcry after *Schempp;* yet at the

---

[93] Forster, *supra* note 45, at 6.
[94] *Ibid.*
[95] *Ibid.*
[96] "Southern Democrats" represent the 11 states of the former Confederacy. The table is based on the *Congressional Record*, 88th Congress, both sessions. One might have expected many Southerners would have introduced such resolutions. It is important to realize that the pattern of behavior among Southern Congressmen was far from uniform. As indicated below, there were Southern states in which resentment against the Court would be expected to be high, in which the Congressmen did not feel called upon to introduce such amendments.

same time positive political action was much more significant after *Schempp* than it had been a year earlier. Several factors may help us to understand this situation. First, as indicated above, the 1963 decisions directly affected a much wider segment of the American public than had the *Regents' Prayer* case. Thus while the immediate outcry from public figures may have been greater after *Engel*, the *Schempp* decision was much more likely to stir up a widespread wave of opposition. Second, while it was not likely that Congressional action in response to *Engel* could have been taken in time to affect the 1962 Congressional elections, the elections of 1964 were constantly in the minds of Congressmen as Congress convened after the summer 1963 recess. And finally, we must interject into the 1963/64 situation the effects of the untiring efforts of Congressman Frank Becker (R. N.Y.).

Although the Senate had chosen to act following *Engel*, through its Judiciary Committee, the House was to be the center of the fight between supporters and opponents of amendments following *Schempp*. And the battle focused increasingly on the efforts of Representative Becker to push through such an amendment, and those of Representative Emmanuel Celler (D. N.Y.), powerful chairman of the House Judiciary Committee, to forestall any attack on the Court's ruling. Becker had proposed an amendment after *Engel*, and on the day after the 1963 decision was handed down, he introduced another. Firmly convinced that the Court had struck a serious blow against the religious training of the nation's youth, Becker devoted all his personal efforts to a crusade to convince the public and his colleagues that the great majority of Americans favored and were entitled to the continuation of religious ceremonies in the public schools. A devout Catholic, Congressman Becker had been educated in

TABLE III
Number of Congressmen Introducing Amendments to Reverse *Schempp*.
88th Congress, 1st & 2d Sessions.

STATE	DEMOCRATS	REPUBLICANS
Alabama	3 out of 8	———
Arkansas	0 out of 4	———
Florida	5 out of 10	1 out of 2
Georgia	3 out of 10	———
Louisiana	1 out of 8	———
Mississippi	5 out of 5	———
North Carolina	7 out of 7	2 out of 2
South Carolina	4 out of 6	———
Tennessee	0 out of 3	3 out of 3
Texas	2 out of 19	0 out of 2
Virginia	0 out of 6	2 out of 2
Total	30 out of 86	8 out of 11

Note that almost all Southern Republicans introduced "anti-Court" amendments. But compare the behavior of Congressmen from Mississippi and North Carolina with that of Democrats from Virginia and Arkansas. The authors attempted to correlate the above indicated pattern with such factors as V. O. Key's "Black Belt" thesis; income distribution; presence of an opposition party; and religious affiliation of both Congressmen and population, without success. Whatever caused this interesting pattern, it warns us to avoid the danger of viewing the South monolithically in this matter.

public schools, as had his children, and he regarded as wholly salutary the modest practices by which the public schools recognized the roles of God and of religion. Becker's zeal was reinforced by his conception of the opponents he was combatting: "I certainly believe that the atheists intend to bury religion. . . ."[97] Since he did not intend to seek re-election in 1964, Becker was prepared to devote virtually his entire energies to the task at hand. He made numerous public addresses, carried on a heavy correspondence, and made himself available as a leader in the fight to get an amendment through both Houses of Congress. Recognizing that the Chairman of the Judiciary Committee was unalterably opposed to any such amendment and would not let such a bill out of his committee unless compelled to do so, Becker sought to unite those who agreed with him on one form of amendment, and, by introducing a discharge petition, either to force the holding of hearings, or to get his amendment out of Celler's committee and to the floor, where he anticipated favorable action by the required two-thirds of the House. With the unprecedented number of almost 115 fellow amendment seekers, he thought his chances of success were high, since only 218 signatures were necessary to discharge the bill from the committee. Becker faced two major difficulties from the start: one was the ingrained reluctance of many members to sign a discharge petition on any subject, particularly where the powerful Judiciary Committee was involved, the other was the coincidence of this issue and the Civil Rights Bill, eventually enacted in 1964, which tended to divide supporters of a prayer amendment.[98]

The bill which was to become identified in the public's mind as the "Becker Amendment" was not the bill introduced originally by the Representative, but was the product of a drafting effort by six members of Congress designated to perform this task following a meeting of amendment supporters in late August, 1963.[99] The amendment proposed in House Joint Resolution 693, introduced on September 10, 1963, provided that:

> Sec. 1. Nothing in this Constitution shall be deemed to prohibit the offering, reading from, or listening to prayers or Biblical scriptures, if participation therein is on a voluntary basis, in any governmental or public school, institution or place.

> Sec. 2. Nothing in this Constitution shall be deemed to prohibit making reference to, belief in, reliance upon, or invoking the aid of God or a Supreme Being in any governmental or

---

[97] *Hearings on School Prayers Before the House Committee on the Judiciary*, 88th Cong., 2d Sess. 2008 (1964) [hereinafter cited as *1964 House Hearings*].

[98] Note that the battle over Becker's discharge petition probably hurt the attempt to discharge the Civil Rights Bill from the House Rules Committee at about the same time. Many Congressmen who were afraid to "fight God" but who opposed Becker refused to sign his petition on the grounds that as a matter of principle they never signed discharge petitions. This prevented some from signing the civil rights discharge petition.

[99] RNS, Aug. 26, 1963. The six were Becker, W. Baring (D. Nev.), W. Cramer (R. Fla.), D. Fuqua (D. Fla.), H. R. Kornegay (D. N.C.), and D. Latta (R. Ohio).

public document, proceeding, activity, ceremony, school, institution, or place, or upon any coinage, currency, or obligation of the United States.

Sec. 3. Nothing in this article shall constitute an establishment of religion.

Ratification by three-fourths of the state legislatures within seven years was required by the last section of the proposed amendment.

During this period petitions and letters continued to pile up in congressional offices, and especially in those of members of the House Judiciary Committee. The campaign on behalf of an amendment to overcome the Court's decisions now had a clearer focus. From now on the battle was to be waged exclusively in terms of the Becker Amendment.

Although the volume of mail favoring the Becker Amendment continued to mount and members of the House continued to sign Becker's discharge petition, supporters of the decision did not view the matter seriously. The natural congressional opposition to discharge petitions under any circumstances and the feeling that the Judiciary Committee and especially its chairman could not be stampeded, along with the relative mildness of the initial reactions to the 1963 decision, led usually well-informed observers to believe that the Becker Amendment would peacefully die in committee. But support for the amendment from constituents of all types continued to mount, largely as a result of the activities of Congressman Becker and of organizations supporting his position. The *New York Times* reported that "largely through his efforts, it is conceded widely in Congress that Congressional mail on this issue has grown to flood proportions, exceeding the mail of the civil rights controversy."[100] Congressman Lionel Van Deerlin (D. Cal.) wrote that his colleagues "are being inundated with constituent mail, the great bulk of which favors such an amendment."[101] A form letter used by Congressman R. G. Stephens (D. Ga.) to reply to constituents apologized for the fact that a printed reply was being used, but said that it was necessitated by the fact that he had had over one thousand letters on the subject. On February 18, the House Republican Policy Committee voted to support the Becker Amendment.[102] Congressman Alec G. Olson (D. Minn.) informed a constituent that he believed "this is a result of the large volume of mail running in favor of this amendment. In my case, I have received correspondence which is at least 200 to 1 in favor of such an amendment. . . ."[103] Gradually the number of signatures on the discharge petition rose so that eventually it contained almost 170 names.[104] And, the *Wall*

---

100 N. Y. Times, April 23, 1964, p. 14, col. 5.
101 Personal letter to Mr. Dore Schary, in the ADL files.
102 N. Y. Times, Feb. 19, 1964, p. 21, col. 3.
103 Letter to Mr. Merrill Keller, St. Paul, Minn., March 13, 1964, in ADL files.
104 It is impossible to know exactly how many signatures appear on a discharge petition at a given moment, as this figure is never officially released, and members can

Street Journal reported, "it is no secret that many more members including some hostile to the proposal and others adverse to the irregular procedure, have warned Mr. Celler that pressure from home would force them to sign unless he made some move."[105]

How is it that the members of Congress—who were surely well aware that much of the mail they were receiving was "inspired"—were sensitive to public sentiment to the extent that the *Wall Street Journal* pointed out that "for the most part, even lawmakers adamant in their opposition have kept silent in public"?[106] The answer is probably to be found in the way the issue was phrased by Becker and his supporters. In an election year, no Congressman wanted to be placed in a position of appearing to vote against God, which was exactly the role into which supporters of the Court were being forced. One powerful Southern committee chairman who had recently tied the house up in knots by the exercise of his individual power, wrote to a clergyman in his district that, despite his personal opposition to the Becker Amendment, "I have been somewhat silent on the subject matter, waiting for the hysteria to subside."[107] Congressman Neil Staebler (D. Mich.) felt constrained to begin a form letter: "Thank you for your recent letter concerning the question of religious practices in the schools. *As you know, we use prayers regularly in Congress.*" And Congressman Holifield's (D. Cal.) form letter opposing Becker began by stressing the fact that it was as "a believer in true freedom of religious choice . . . as a believer in a Supreme Being . . . [and] as a believer in the efficacy of. sincere prayer" that he could not support Becker's proposal.[108] The bind in which Congressman Charles Wilson (D. Cal.) found himself is illustrated by a letter in which he urged opponents of the bill to obtain support for their position from the ministers of religion. "Any help you can give in this regard will be much appreciated."[109] Congressman Becker put additional pressure on his colleagues by threatening to come into the district of every congressman who failed to support his amendment and actively campaign against him in the forthcoming election.

Early in 1964 it became apparent that Congressman Celler would have to schedule hearings, in order to avoid having the bill taken out of his committee. And indeed, by the middle of February he reacted to the Republican Policy Committee's demand for hearings by dryly remarking that a staff study was in progress, and that hearings would be scheduled when it was completed.[110] Opponents of the Becker amendment who had

---

withdraw their names at any time. The *Wall Street Journal* reported that 166 signatures were said to have been obtained. This appears to square with other published reports, and with Becker's claims. Wall Street Journal, April 22, 1964, p. 1, col. 4.

105 *Id.* at 1.
106 *Ibid.*
107 Letter on file at the ADL.
108 These form letters are on file at the ADL. (Emphasis added.)
109 Letter to Mr. Dore Schary on file at the ADL.
110 N. Y. Times, Feb. 19, 1964, p. 21, col. 5.

previously been relatively inactive suddenly realized that if they did not stop Becker's juggernaut at the Committee hearings, their worst fears would be fulfilled. Meeting in New York on St. Patrick's Day, 1964, an *ad hoc* committee consisting of representatives of numerous Protestant, Jewish, and civil liberties groups opposed to the amendment decided that at that time the Becker amendment had an excellent chance of receiving the approval of a majority of the Judiciary Committee, that if reported out favorably it was likely to pass easily in the House, and that while the Senate might delay passage of the bill, it would eventually pass there as well, an estimate concurred in by close students of the situation not present at the meeting.

Faced with this prospect, the members of the *ad hoc* group decided to coordinate their organizational efforts. It was agreed that probably the most important function the group could play would be to mobilize leaders of the religious community to oppose the Becker Amendment, in order to make it "respectable" and "safe" for Congressmen to oppose the Becker proposal. Similar attempts would be made to get law school deans and teachers to voice their opposition. And a drive to "inspire" a countervailing flood of mail would be undertaken. In order to maximize the support which they could hope to mobilize, it was decided to pitch the anti-Becker campaign in terms of protecting the sanctity of the first amendment. It was hoped that this tactic might be particularly useful in obtaining the support of liberal Catholic elements.

Two days after the *ad hoc* committee met, Chairman Celler announced that hearings would begin on April 22. He indicated that he was in no hurry to report out an amendment, and that the nature and importance of the subject matter required mature and deliberate consideration of the best thinking on both sides of the question.[111] Congressman Becker was "amazed" that Celler had scheduled the hearings for the end of April, having expected them to begin on April 1. He denounced him for employing delaying tactics, and threatened to continue to push his discharge petition, which, he claimed, contained over 160 signatures.[112] Accusing Celler of "total and unalterable opposition" to his proposal, he insisted that it was only after "insurmountable pressure"—largely from the discharge petition—that the chairman had acted. He further accused Celler of having deliberately scheduled the hearings to begin on the first day of the New York World's Fair, so as to minimize the amount of public attention they would receive. The chairman replied: "I never dreamed of the World's Fair."[113]

As the hearings commenced, the *ad hoc* committee of organizations opposing the Becker Amendment, and their coordinator—Rev. Dean M.

---

111 N. Y. Times, March 20, 1964, p. 17, col. 1.
112 CONG. REC. 5696 (1964).
113 N. Y. World Telegram and Sun, March 24, 1964.

Kelley of the National Council of Churches[114]—believed that a majority of the Judiciary Committee members were in favor of the amendment. Their immediate goal, therefore, was to attempt through personal visits with the uncommitted and, hopefully, changeable members of the Committee to reverse this balance. In addition, they made plans to present an imposing group of witnesses against the amendment, paying particular attention to religious leaders and legal scholars.

The anti-Becker campaign received some assistance from the Judiciary Committee's staff study, published on March 24, 1964, which pointed out in considerable detail the various difficulties presented by proposed amendments, including that of Congressman Becker. Though, in true staff style, it avoided taking an overt position on the merits, it raised so many questions and doubts concerning the form and substance of the several proposals that several members of the Committee strongly objected to its release.

The *ad hoc* committee representatives quickly discovered that one of the major factors weakening the opponents of the Becker Amendment was their lack of communication on this matter. Congressmen contacted by Rev. Kelley were amazed to find out that certain of their colleagues shared their views.[115] As indicated above, the antireligion charge raised by Becker's side had silenced many opponents. And in their silence they assumed that they were alone.

We have here an interesting insight into the legislative process, particularly with respect to the role of political parties in that process. One of the benefits a busy Congressman derives from his party affiliation is information. He can quickly determine how most of his colleagues stand on a given issue. But the Becker Amendment fight had not become a partisan issue, and thus the party whips were not performing their usual function of consolidating support for, or opposition to, this piece of legislation. Congressman Becker's monumental efforts on behalf of his cause had taken the place of the party machinery for supporters of the bill, but opponents of the amendment were left in virtual legislative isolation. Kelley and the interest groups he represented quickly moved into this gap, making every effort to bring members opposed to the amendment together and providing them with "ammunition" for use during the hearings.

As the result of the efforts of the *ad hoc* committee, a substantial volume of anti-amendment mail began to arrive in Congressional offices and that of the Committee as the hearings began on April 22, a flow that continued until their termination. While it never equaled the volume of

---

[114] It is likely that one of the reasons that Rev. Kelley was chosen to represent the *ad hoc* group—in addition to his experience in such matters—was the desire of the Jewish groups involved to minimize their role in the fight against the Becker Amendment. They were very sensitive to the charge that the Court's decision had been brought about by a minority of "Jews, atheists, and Communists."

[115] Interview with Rev. Dean Kelley, July 20, 1964.

proamendment mail, it was sufficient to justify some Congressmen in concluding that public sentiment was hardly as one-sided as they had suspected.

The hearings themselves were originally planned to last two weeks, or so Becker thought.[116] But once Chairman Celler decided to hold the hearings with the entire committee present, previous plans had to be abandoned. The hearings ran from April 22 through June 3, 1964, giving both sides an ample opportunity to parade their forces. The three volumes and 2774 pages of testimony by 197 witnesses, with numerous prepared statements, letters, and other data, are evidence that the opportunity was seized by both sides, but particularly by Becker's opponents. It may well be that, realizing that the Becker forces were in a position of advantage as the hearings opened, the Chairman felt that delay would give opponents a chance to catch up. It is extremely likely that Representative Celler was aware that by June Congress would be rushing toward adjournment in time for the Republican Presidential Convention in San Francisco. In any event, efforts made from time to time by pro-Becker Committee members to limit the prolonged questioning of witnesses came to naught.[117] In addition, the Chairman, who is generally regarded as a very effective presiding officer, used his position to blunt the effectiveness of proamendment witnesses, helped the critics over rough spots, and clearly sought to shape arguments that might appeal to the uncommitted members. It is a gross understatement to say that had Celler favored the proposed amendment, the anti-Becker forces would have had a much more difficult time.

Although any effort to summarize briefly or evaluate the testimony of the contending forces is inevitably highly subjective, a few observations reflecting the authors' impressions may be of some value. The arguments of the Becker supporters followed the pattern previously established: the people favor such practices; the Court's decisions are an attack on God and on religion; this country was founded on a belief in God, and cannot exist without it; majorities have rights, and they need not always bow to the will of an "atheistic" minority.

Without question, the most significant testimony in opposition to the proposal was that of the religious leaders organized by Rev. Kelley and his associates. The unanimous opposition of such distinguished theologians as Dr. Eugene Carson Blake, chief officer of the United Presbyterian Church, and former president of the National Council of Churches, Methodist Bishop John Wesley Lord of Washington, D.C.; Dr. Edwin Tuller, General Secretary of the American Baptist Convention; Dr. Fredrik Schiotz, President of the American Lutheran Church; Presiding Protestant Episcopal Bishop Arthur Lichtenberger; and many others, made it

---

[116] See his letter to Chairman Celler, published in the Committee Report, *1964 House Hearings*, 1058.
[117] See, *e.g., 1964 House Hearings*, 690-91.

difficult for Becker supporters to insist that only the Godless opposed them, and made it considerably "safer" for election-conscious Congressmen to oppose the Becker Amendment.[118] While it is quite probable that the virtual unanimity of these spokesmen did not correspond fully to the actual views of all their religious constituents—and indeed, the Becker forces strove valiantly to establish this point—they placed the prestige of organized religion against the attempt to tamper with the first amendment. Important, too, was the union in opposition of leading Protestant, Jewish, and Catholic spokesmen (especially those from Catholic law schools) so that an appearance of transdenominational solidarity was maintained. It is likely that the impact which the testimony of the religious leaders had on the members of the Committee, the membership of Congress as a whole, and on the general public was the major factor which tipped the balance against the Becker forces.

Equally impressive, and perhaps almost as significant, was the testimony of legal scholars who attacked the amendment. Such distinguished professors as Paul A. Freund of Harvard, Philip B. Kurland of Chicago, and Paul E. Kauper of Michigan bolstered the position of the opponents.[119] Particularly striking was a statement of opposition signed by 223 of the nation's best known law school deans and teachers, drawn up by Professors Freund; Wilbur G. Katz of Wisconsin; Robert P. Drinan, S.J., Dean of Boston College Law School; and Leo Pfeffer, General Counsel of The American Jewish Congress, as the hearings came to their close.[120]

The testimony of the opponents of the amendment was intended to sway the opinion of wavering congressmen. Which version of the *Bible* would be used? Would the *Koran* qualify under the amendment? Who would decide which prayers to say? Could the "Ave Maria" be employed? And again and again they returned to the basic theme: "thou shalt not touch the Bill of Rights."

The Becker Amendment movement, while endorsed widely, was essentially a one-man crusade. Although various organizations lent their support, and vigorous statements were made by several witnesses, the strategy used and the calibre of the witnesses did not match the efforts of the anti-amendment forces.[121] To one who tries to read the pro-Becker

---

[118] Among the many religious leaders who opposed the Becker Amendment at the hearings were: Father George Bacopoulos, Chancellor, Greek Orthodox Archdiocese North and South America; Rabbi Irwin Blank, Synagogue Council of America; Dr. E. Carlson, Baptist Joint Committee on Public Affairs; Rt. Rev. Wm. Creighton, Protestant Episcopal Bishop of Washington; Rabbi M. Eisendrath, Union of American Hebrew Congregation; Mr. Moses Feuerstein, Union of Orthodox Jewish Congregations; and Rabbi Harry Halpern, United Synagogues of America.

[119] Other law school professors who testified against the Becker Amendment were: C. J. Antieau (Georgetown); Dean J. B. Fordham (U. of Penn.); W. G. Katz (Wisconsin); W. G. Keneally, S.J. (Boston College); and J. C. Kirby (Vanderbilt).

[120] *1964 House Hearings* 2483-85.

[121] Among the organizations which supported Becker were: Committee for the Preservation of Prayer and Bible Reading in Public Schools; Constitutional Prayer Foundation; Massachusetts Citizens for Public Prayer; Project Prayer; Foundation for Religious Action

testimony objectively, it seems that in the minds of many witnesses popular support for continuance of school prayers and Bible reading was regarded as the decisive factor. With notable exceptions, such as Charles Wesley Lowry,[122] many pro-Becker witnesses seemed to have adopted the simple equation—The people want prayers in schools; the Court took them away; we, on behalf of the people, must restore them. When the Chairman or other Committee members attempted to draw them out as to the effects of the various provisions of the amendment, they were often unable to follow the subtleties of the questioner. They frequently seemed annoyed by the complexities of issues framed by opponents.

Press coverage of the hearings was relatively full, and though the public was unable to gain a very coherent notion of the trend of the debates, it appears that the testimony of the anti-Becker church leaders and that of the legal authorities opposing the measure dominated the reports, especially in the later sessions. This may help to explain the increase in the anti-Becker mail, and a number of editorials throughout the nation urging that the amendment not pass.[123]

---

in the Social Order (FRASCO); International Council of Christian Churches; International Christian Youth in the U.S.A.; and the American Legion.

In addition, the legislatures of the following states petitioned Congress to approve a Becker-type amendment: Kentucky, Massachusetts, Michigan, New Jersey, Pennsylvania (Senate), and South Carolina.

It is interesting to speculate about the extent and significance of right wing support for the Becker Amendment. Rowland Evans and Robert Novak, writing in the New York Herald Tribune of May 12, 1964, p. 12, col. 1, stated that "although members of the House Judiciary Committee do not know it, the 'Citizens Congressional Committee' now flooding Capitol Hill with mail backing the prayer amendment is operated, financed, and directed by Gerald L. K. Smith, notorious promoter of extreme Right Wing causes. Smith's backstage maneuvering is the best evidence to date that neo-Fascist hate groups have infiltrated the high pressure campaign to change the Bill of Rights. . . ." They pointed to the May, 1964, issue of Smith's The Cross and the Flag, which said: "The bill has been held up by the Jew, Emmanuel Celler, who is Chairman of the Judiciary Committee."

Of all the groups supporting Becker, perhaps the most active was Dr. Carl McIntire's International Christian Youth, and its "Project America." They presented petitions alleged to contain 1,000,000 signatures to the Committee. McIntire threw the full weight of his many organizations—and his radio broadcasts on over 500 stations—behind Becker. In its November 21, 1963 article headed "Fighting the Bible," McIntire's Christian Beacon spoke of Congressman Celler—"A Jew" who was blocking hearings on this Amendment. Id. at 8. And, it went on: "It is going to be up to the great rank and file of the Christian people of the United States to stand against this coalition of modernists, Jews, infidels, Unitarians and atheists in their determination to keep the Bible out of the schools."

It is often unfair to blame the leaders of a movement for the kind of extremist support they may inadvertently attract. But in the case at hand this does not appear to have been unwelcomed support. McIntire's Christian Beacon of March 26, 1964, quoted Becker in a front page story as encouraged by International Christian Youth's "Project America" petition drive. And the Rev. Billy James Hargis' magazine Christian Crusade, of August 1964, printed abstracts of a letter it received from Congressman Becker thanking it "sincerely for the work the Christian Crusade has been doing in behalf of the 'Prayer Amendment' to the Constitution. Your great ability to reach the people throughout the United States has helped immeasurably in rallying their support for this truly vital Cause. . . ." Id. at 13. Note that the capital "C" appeared in the original! It is interesting to note further that several pro-Becker witnesses who appeared before the Celler Committee —including representatives of the American Legion's Americanism Committee and Victor Jory's "Project Prayer"—felt compelled to disclaim any connection with the extreme Right's attacks on the Court.

122 1964 House Hearings, 1125.

123 See, e.g., N. Y. Herald Tribune, May 10, 1964, p. 22, col. 1, editorial entitled "It's not a vote against God."

The real test of the effectiveness of the opposition lay in the impact on members of the Judiciary Committee. Although any judgment must be made with considerable reservation, it would seem that the direction of change of views of committee members was almost exclusively in one direction—against the amendment. At the beginning of the hearings, as noted above, the *ad hoc* committee had estimated that the Becker amendment would easily win a majority in the committee; by the end of May, they expected that the Becker Amendment would probably be opposed by as many as 20 of the 35 members. By that time it was doubtful that any amendment then in prospect could attract a majority of the committee. It was apparent that the drive for a discharge petition had passed its crest; not only could it not gain the necessary 218 signatures, but members who had signed the petition were prepared to remove their names should the total approach 210. And even if a bill were discharged, it was doubtful that it could obtain a majority in the House, much less the required two-thirds majority. The *Wall Street Journal* doubted that as many as 8 members of the Committee still supported an amendment.[124]

The use of public hearings as a means of shaping the thinking of committee members has been increasingly discounted by political analysts in recent years. They have tended to view them as a show with little relevance to the actual struggle over important public issues. The Becker Amendment hearings would appear to cast serious doubt as to the validity of these conclusions, for, as we have seen, the hearings had a significant impact *both* on Congressional opinion and on public opinion. The Becker hearings point to many aspects of the legislative process which students of future contests would do well to keep in mind. A combination of factors: expert, if belated, planning by opponents; their ability to gain the support of heavier "guns" at the hearings; and the natural advantage that our political system provides those opposing legislative action, was all too much for the Becker cause, regardless of its popular support. Also, the skillful operation of an experienced committee chairman and ally was of inestimable value to the anti-amendment forces.

One might be tempted to conclude as Congressman Becker did that the final outcome—the failure of the Committee to report the Becker bill and of the drive to gain enough signatures to discharge the Committee—represented a defeat for the democratic process. But it is probably correct to say that this is precisely a situation envisaged by and acceptable to the framers of the Constitution. The great danger, according to Madison in *Federalist No. 10,* lay in factions representing a majority. To prevent these majorities from riding roughly over minorities our elaborate system of separated powers and checks and balances was established. The nature of the committee system of the Congress is clearly consistent with the spirit of the legislative "filter" of which Madison spoke.

---

124 Wall Street Journal, June 16, 1964, p. 3, col. 2.

Although Congressman Becker has continued his efforts to win accept-ance for the constitutional recognition of prayers and Bible reading, and promises to continue the work after his retirement from Congress, the momentum of the proamendment forces is gone. "Unleashing Frank Becker at this point is about like unleashing Chiang Kai-Shek," comment-ed one member of the Judiciary Committee in the middle of June.[125] It had been widely assumed that the committee would report out a resolution expressing the "sense of Congress" that the Court reverse or restrict its decisions as a face-saving device to get many Congressmen "off the hook." However, this suggestion dropped out of sight, and Congress adjourned without considering such a proposal.

Congressman Becker took his battle to the Republican National Conven-tion, where the Chairman of the Platform Committee commented on the large amount of mail he had received on the subject.[126] The Convention approved a plank in the platform pledging support for a constitutional amendment:

> permitting those individuals and groups who choose to do so to exercise their religion freely in public places, provided religious exercises are not prepared or *prescribed* by the state or political subdivision thereof and no person's participation therein is coerced, thus preserving the traditional separation of church and state.[127]

But little was made of the prayer issue in the Presidential campaign save as a small part of a broadside attack on the Supreme Court. In American politics a succession of major issues emerge and disappear too swiftly to provide many second chances for any one. It is unlikely that the Becker Amendment will prove an exception to that rule.

---

[125] *Ibid.*
[126] N. Y. Times, July 5, 1964, p. 32, col. 3.
[127] N. Y. Times, July 13, 1964. p. 16, col. 1.

ROBERT H. BIRKBY
Vanderbilt University

The Supreme Court and the Bible Belt:
Tennessee Reaction to the "Schempp" Decision *

IT HAS BECOME commonplace to observe that the Supreme Court is a political body. It is belaboring the obvious to assert that judicial decisions, particularly in the constitutional area, have effects beyond those on the parties to the litigation. Yet both lawyers and political scientists have, by and large, tended to move on to greener pastures once the inner logic, doctrinal contribution, and possible legal implications of a particular decision have been explored and the votes by the judges tabulated for analysis with many other cases. All too frequently, despite the outpouring of words and printers' ink, no attention has been paid to the implementation and effect of the Court's decisions.[1] And this even though it is a part of the profession's "conventional wisdom" that judicial decisions are not self-executing. To speculate why so few have studied the aftermath of the Court's decisions would be profitless. We can simply note that there are few such studies.[2]

---

* Research for this article was supported by a grant from the University Research Committee, Vanderbilt University.

[1] The major exception is in the area of race relations and there the pressure of events and not professional interest has been responsible for the examination.

[2] Arthur S. Miller has recently issued a call for more impact studies. Miller, "On the Need for 'Impact Analysis' of Supreme Court Decisions," 53 *Georgetown Law Journal* 365 (1965). The existing impact studies can be quickly listed: Gordon Patric, "The Impact of a Court Decision: Aftermath of the McCollum Case," 6 *Journal of Public Law* 455 (1957); Frank J. Sorauf, "*Zorach v. Clauson*: The Impact of a Supreme Court Decision," 53 *American Political Science Review* 777 (1959); Jack W. Peltason, *Fifty-Eight Lonely Men* (New York: Harcourt Brace & World, 1961); Walter F. Murphy, *Congress and Court* (Chicago: University of Chicago Press, 1962); David R. Manwaring, "The Impact of *Mapp v. Ohio*," paper delivered at the 1964 Annual Meeting of the American Political Science Association, Chicago, Sept. 9-12, 1964; Stephen L. Wasby, "The Supreme Court, Obscenity, and Oregon Policy," paper delivered at the 1964 Annual Meeting of the American Political Science Association, Chicago, Sept. 9-12, 1964; Richard M. Johnson, "Separation of Church and State: The Dynamics of Supreme Court Decision-Making" (unpublished Ph. D. Dissertation, Department of Political Science, University of Illinois, 1965); W. M. Beaney and Edward Beiser, "Prayer and Politics: The Impact of Engel and Schempp on the Political Process," 13 *Journal of Public Law* 475 (1964).

304

This paper is a presentation of research findings and the posing of a research problem growing out of examination of the impact of one decision in one state.

I

Since 1915, the policy of the State of Tennessee has been that "it shall be the duty of the teacher . . . to read, or cause to be read, at the opening of the school every day, a selection from the Bible and the same selection shall not be read more than twice a month."[3] In addition to the statutory requirement, it has been common practice for students and teacher to recite the Lord's Prayer. In 1956, this statute survived a challenge in the state courts.[4] A taxpayer and parent had contended that Bible reading in the public schools violated both the First Amendment to the United States Constitution and Article I, Section 3 of the Tennessee Constitution.[5] Relying primarily on *Everson* v. *Board of Education*[6] and several state cases, the Tennessee Supreme Court unanimously upheld the statute. The Court said:

Counsel, it seems to us, confuses an hour, or a short period of reverence, or a simple act of spiritual devotion as being a form of worship that is being sponsored and approved by an agency of the State to the prejudice of other religious groups. We find it more or less difficult to conceive that these simple ceremonies amount to "establishment of a religion," or any attempt to do so; nor is it an infringement with any student's secular belief contrary to law.[7]

Declaring the King James version of the Bible to be non-sectarian, the Court justified the devotional exercises on the ground that

the highest duty of those charged with the responsibility of training the young people of this state in the public schools is in the teaching both by precept and example that in the conflicts of life they should not forget God. And this in substance is about all that our statute requires. For this Court to hold that the statute herein assailed contemplates the establishment of religion, and that it is

---

[3] Sec. 49-1307 (A), Tennessee Code Annotated. Note that this requirement unlike those in some other states does not specify the version of the Bible to be used nor does it restrict the choice of selections to the Old Testament.

[4] *Carden* v. *Bland*, 199 Tenn. 665, 288 S. W. 2d 718 (1956).

[5] Tenn. Const., Art. I, Sec. 3: "*Right of Worship Free*—That all men have a natural and indefeasible right to worship Almighty God according to the dictates of their own conscience; that no man can of right be compelled to attend, erect, or support any place of worship, or to maintain any minister against his consent; that no human authority can, in any case whatever, control or interfere with the rights of conscience; and that no preference shall ever be given, by law to any religious establishment or mode of worship."

[6] 330 U. S. 1 (1947).

[7] 288 S. W. 2d 718, 722.

a subtle method of breaking down Mr. Jefferson's " wall of separation " between church and State, would be a spectacular exhibition of judicial sophistry.[8]

No appeal or petition for certiorari apparently was filed with the United States Supreme Court and so the matter rested until 1963.

Engel v. *Vitale*[9] had foreshadowed the Supreme Court's decision in the 1963 case of *Abington School District* v. *Schempp*.[10] In *Engel* the Court declared the New York Regents' prayer invalid as an establishment of religion. The narrow holding was " that the constitutional prohibition against laws respecting an establishment of religion must at least mean that in this country it is no part of the business of government to compose official prayers for any group of the American people to recite as a part of a religious program carried on by government." [11] The broader implications of the decision brought an immediate reaction from all parts of the country. Religious groups split over the wisdom of the decision, newspapers praised or damned the Court, and private individuals quickly took sides.[12]

After the initial reaction, church groups began to assess the probable future of all types of devotional exercises in the public schools. Despite differing opinions concerning the desirability of such exercises most conceded that, if challenged, required exercises such as Bible reading and recitation of the Lord's Prayer were doomed. Some churches tried to prepare their members for this eventuality. The relative lack of outcry when the *Schempp* decision confirmed the predictions may be looked upon as an index to the success of the churches' "educational" program.[13]

In its simplest form *Schempp* declared that the required reading of the Bible without comment and the use of the Lord's Prayer as a regular religious exercise in the public schools was constitutionally impermissible as an establishment of religion. The Court was careful to note that "nothing we have said here indicates that . . . study of the Bible or of religion, when presented objectively as part of a secular

[8] *Ibid.,* p. 725.

[9] 370 U. S. 421 (1962).

[10] 374 U. S. 203 (1963).

[11] 370 U. S. 421, 425.

[12] For the reaction to Engel see Phillip Kurland, " The School Prayer Cases," in Dallin H. Oaks, ed., *The Wall Between Church and State* (Chicago: University of Chicago Press, 1963), pp. 142-46; and Donald F. Boles, *The Bible, Religion and the Public Schools*, 3rd ed. (Ames: Iowa State University Press, 1965), chs. 6-8.

[13] There was, of course, a reaction in 1963. It was mild only when compared to the outburst of a year before.

program of education, may not be effected consistently with the First Amendment." [14] As a result of this decision there was no doubt about the invalidity of the practices in Pennsylvania and Baltimore where the cases originated. In theory there should be no doubt about the status of similar programs in other states including Tennessee. Yet a cursory reading of the newspaper documents a definite lack of compliance in several states.[15] One school superintendent in Tennessee explained why his schools had not changed their practice: "In that the state law has not been voided, I as Superintendent instructed the teachers to proceed as before."

II

If the *Schempp* decision had any effect in Tennessee it should be noticeable in the policies adopted and enforced at the school district level. The State Commissioner of Education was reported as saying that it was permissible to read the Bible in public schools despite *Schempp* but he left the final decision to local school officials.[16] The school boards were left free to continue the practice required by state law or to comply with the Court's ruling. This study was undertaken to determine what the school boards did and, if possible, why. Even though it was expected that, in Gordon Patric's words, the "decision was put into effect in diverse ways and 'obeyed' to varying degrees," [17] board action in response to *Schempp* was classified as changing or not changing policy. All districts reporting a departure from the pre-*Schempp* provisions of state law were considered changing districts. It was believed that one of several factors could be used to explain the differences between changing and non-changing districts. These were degree of urbanization, extent of religious pluralism, articulate opposition within the district to devotional exercises, or differences in the socio-economic composition of the school boards.[18]

To test these suppositions three questionnaires were prepared and

[14] 374 U. S. 203, 225.

[15] "Good Book Going Back to School Too," *Nashville Tennessean*, August 25, 1963, p. 1; "Kentucky Schools Keep Prayer Policy," *New York Times*, August 30, 1964, p. 36; "Prayer Decision Skirted in Jersey," *New York Times*, October 4, 1964, p. 122.

[16] *Nashville Tennessean*, August 23, 1963, p. 1. In an interview October 16, 1964, the Commissioner confirmed that he had left the decision to local officials. He said at that time that he had taken no official position on the issue.

[17] Patric, *op. cit.*, p. 455.

[18] Boles, *op. cit.*, p. 340, suggests the urbanization and religious pluralism explanations.

sent out in late 1964 and early 1965. One was mailed to each of the 152 superintendents of schools in the state. The second was mailed to the chairman and two other randomly selected members of each school board. The third was sent to the remaining school board members in those districts from which responses were obtained to either or both of the first two questionnaires. The superintendents were asked what the policy on Bible reading and devotional exercises had been in their district before June, 1963, and what it currently was. They were asked to identify any factors inducing change and to describe, in each time period, the policy-making role of the board, superintendent, principals, teachers, parents, religious groups, and any other participants. The first group of board members was asked about current (post 1963) policy, how it differed from that of the past, what groups or persons made policy suggestions to the board, and what groups or persons were consulted by the board. The second group of board members was simply asked to supply information on age, occupation, education, income, religious affiliation, length of service on the board, and length of residence in the school district of its members. Response to the first and third questionnaires was good. Ninety-two (60.5%) of the superintendents responded; ninety-seven (21.2%) of the first group of board members representing eighty-four of 152 districts replied; and 237 (56.1%) of the second group of board members from 109 out of a possible 121 districts returned the questionnaire. By combining the reports of the superintendents and the first group of board members (cross-checking where possible) the policy currently in effect in 121 of the state's 152 school districts was determined.

Of the 121 districts, 70 were reported to be still following the requirements of state law. The other 51 districts were reported to have made some changes in their policy but only one of these completely eliminated all Bible reading and devotional exercises. The other fifty merely made student participation voluntary and left the decision whether to have devotional exercises to the discretion of the classroom teacher. Thus 42 percent of the reporting school districts no longer adhere strictly to the provisions of state law even though all but one could have some form of classroom devotional exercise.

The most reasonable explanation for these differences in response to *Schempp* seemed to lie in the extent of urbanization. Table 1 shows the distribution of changing and non-changing districts according to this factor.

TABLE 1.

Relationship of Urbanization and School Religious Exercise Policy Change

% of District	Number of Districts	
Population Urbanized *	Changing	Not Changing
90–100	17	19
80–89	1	0
70–79	0	0
60–69	0	0
50–59	1	0
40–49	3	1
30–39	2	0
20–29	5	9
10–19	3	4
0–9	19	37
Totals	51	70

Using the point bi-serial correlation [19] the relationship between urbanization and tendency toward partial compliance with *Schempp* was found to be practically non-existent ($r_{pb} = -0.08$).[20] Thus, on the basis of questionnaire responses, school boards and superintendents in urban areas showed no greater tendency to change Bible reading and devotional exercise policy than the respondents from rural areas.

The possibility that increasing religious pluralism may account for objections to religion in the schools must remain largely in the realm of speculation since accurate figures on denominational membership by school district or even county do not exist. The National Council of Churches has issued a rough compilation by counties [21]

* On the basis of 1960 census data.

[19] Allen L. Edwards, *Statistical Methods for the Behavioral Sciences* (New York: Rinehart & Company, 1954), pp. 182-85.

[20] As a cross check on this finding the districts were grouped by per cent rural non-farm and per cent rural farm. These were equally inconclusive. Rural non-farm $r_{pb} = 0.20$. Rural farm $r_{pb} = -0.12$.

[21] *Churches and Church Membership in the United States* (New York: National Council of Churches of Christ in the U. S. A., 1956). These figures are no more than approximations since 137 denominations furnished no data and the membership of the Jewish and Roman Catholic faiths are estimated. Of particular importance in Tennessee, the Church of Christ is one of the denominations for which no figures were available. For this study the number of this group's congregations per county was determined and an average membership per congregation was used to estimate county figures.

and in lieu of anything else these figures were used to test this possibility. Only those counties with a single area-wide school district (no city districts) and those counties in which the county district and the city district took the same position could be used. This distorts the results somewhat but was made necessary by the impossibility of breaking county religious affiliation figures down into smaller units. On this rough test there is only slight correlation between religious pluralism and tendency to change ($r_{pb} = 0.02$). The pattern of change classified by total population of the district was also checked on the theory that heavily populated districts would be more likely to be religiously heterogeneous; again only a slight correlation was found ($r_{pb} = 0.24$).[22]

The other two possibilities advanced above are equally ineffective in explaining the pattern of change. From only one of the eighty-four districts represented by responses from the first group of board members was there a report that the board had been approached by an individual who objected to a continuation of the Bible reading and devotional exercises. In this instance the protester's efforts were in vain since that district still complies with state law. Either there was no significant opposition to devotional exercise or else no board member wanted to admit that there had been any.

Using the chi square test and rejecting the null hypothesis at the 0.01 level of significance, tabulation of the responses of the second group of board members produced no significant differences in socio-economic characteristics between changing and non-changing boards. Tables 2 and 3 show the distribution and significance level of occupation and religious affiliation.[23]

In each instance the null hypothesis must be accepted.

Thus far this paper has presented only negative results. Partial compliance with *Schempp* is not explained by degree of urbanization. There are no significant differences in the socio-economic characteristics of changing and non-changing board members. In the changing districts the board members did not report any overt pressure for compliance. And, by a rough test, the extent of religious pluralism in

[22] This was expected since heavily populated districts are also the more urban areas. There is some indirect confirmation that religious pluralism was unimportant. Two large urban city districts still comply with state law while the two rural county districts which surround them have changed their policy.

[23] The other characteristics collected and their level of significance are: Age, 0.20; Education, 0.20; Income, 0.30; Length of Service on the Board, 0.50; Years Resident in the District, 0.80.

the district had no effect. These findings are significant and justify reporting. It may well be that the population of the State of Tennessee is too homogeneous—socially, religiously, and economically—for any of

TABLE 2

OCCUPATION OF SCHOOL BOARD MEMBERS

Occupation	Non-changing Districts	Changing Districts
Attorney	7	12
Professional and Banker	19	33
Self-employed	46	34
Managerial	15	12
White Collar	16	12
Skilled and Semi-skilled	18	4
Farmer	38	32
Retired	4	9
Other	15	11
Totals	178	159

$X^2 = 18.76$; $p > 0.05$

TABLE 3

RELIGIOUS AFFILIATION OF SCHOOL BOARD MEMBERS

Denomination	Non-changing Districts	Changing Districts
Baptist	55	39
Methodist	49	42
Church of Christ	20	17
Presbyterian, Congregational, and Episcopalian	14	28
Christian and Lutheran	22	12
Unspecified Protestant	12	10
Jewish	0	2
Totals	172	150

$X^2 = 11.84$; $p > 0.10$

these tests to be significant.[24] In some other state with greater diversity, urbanization and religious pluralism might be more important. Even so, Tennessee reaction would remain unexplained.

[24] A semi-humorous comment of one of my senior colleagues is relevant: " In Tennessee the cities are made up of rural people who just happen to live close together."

III

The reported response by Tennessee school districts to *Schempp* might be explained by one other hypothesis. There is in the questionnaires some support for it but not enough to make it possible to assert that it is correct. What follows then is largely speculative. The line of reasoning starts with a distinction between procedural and substantive change in policy. Policy change in any situation may take the form of (1) altering procedure without altering the policy goal, (2) changing procedure to reach a new policy goal without, however, making the new goal explicit, or (3) changing the policy goal with or without a change in procedure. Although we cannot be sure, it seems fairly safe to say that in the fifty school districts which overtly changed their policy on Bible reading and delegated the decision to the teachers there has been little change in fact. That is, it is suspected that the classroom teachers are "voluntarily" conducting Bible reading and devotional exercises just as they did before *Schempp*.[25] One might go a step further and assert, without being able to prove it, that the school boards were aware that this would probably happen. I am suggesting that the board members acted consciously either to save the substance of the program or to avoid upsetting the community status quo by making slight procedural changes. In the language of Sayre and Kaufman, the contestants who had the prizes of the game were able to keep them by responding to a rules change with a rules change of their own.[26] A comment by a lawyer on the board of a changing district indicates the compromise nature of the policy adopted:

> My personal conviction is that the Supreme Court decisions are correct, and I so told the Board and Superintendent; but I saw no reason to create controversy. If the Board had made public a decision abolishing devotional exercises, there would have been public outcry. I believe all staff members understand that the continuance of devotional exercises in their schools and in their rooms is entirely voluntary and subject to discontinuance upon objection of any individual or minority group.

There are other reasons that a board might adopt this strategy of procedural change. It could be used to reduce disagreement within

[25] This suspicion is based on unsystematic conversations with classroom teachers from two or three districts which made this formal change and on the questionnaire responses of a few superintendents who indicated doubt that any actual change had occurred.

[26] Wallace S. Sayre and Herbert Kaufman, *Governing New York City* (New York: Russell Sage Foundation, 1960).

the board itself. It could be suggested by an individual as a means of reducing his own tensions between a desire to comply with the Court's decision and a desire to retain perceived advantages of devotional exercises. Finally, change in procedure without change in substance might be made to forestall demands for even greater change. There is nothing in the questionnaire responses to indicate which of these alternatives is correct and it is possible that all were present to some extent. If any or all of these suppositions are correct, a desire to retain the program rather than religious pluralism and urbanization would be responsible for the formal change. To this point the hypothesis does not provide an answer to the question of why the form was changed in some districts and not in others. It does emphasize that the answer must be sought in psychological rather than in demographic or socio-economic factors.

The question being asked in any impact study is why the Court's decision is not self-executing. In a different context Richard Neustadt has concluded that a self-executing order must have five characteristics: (1) the issuer of the order must be unambiguously involved in making the decision, (2) the order must be unambiguously worded, (3) the order must receive wide publicity, (4) those receiving the order must have control of the means of implementation, and (5) there must be no doubt of the individual's authority to issue the order.[27] Neustadt was speaking of orders issued by the President but there is no reason that the same analysis cannot be applied to Court decisions. In this instance, there was no doubt that the Court did in fact make the decision though one school board member suggested that the Court was "controlled by small pressure groups." When applied to the Tennessee statute the wording of the order, although negative in content, was clear enough.[28] There was wide publicity. The members of the boards of education had control of the means of implementation. However, the fifth factor was not so obviously present.

There was some confusion about the Court's decision. It was clear enough that required devotional exercises were forbidden but the Court did not commit itself on the status of voluntary programs such as those adopted by the fifty changing districts in Tennessee. This

[27] Richard E. Neustadt, *Presidential Power* (New York: John Wiley and Sons, 1960), p. 19.

[28] In some instances this criterion will not be met by a decision. The best examples are the confusion resulting from the "with all deliberate speed" formula in school desegregation and general ambiguity in the majority opinion in *Zorach v. Clauson*, 343 U. S. 306 (1952). See Peltason, *op. cit.*, and Sorauf, *op. cit.*

ambiguity caused one superintendent to assert confidently "we believe our policy [voluntary participation] is in accordance with the ruling of the Supreme Court and in accord with the desires of the people in this community."

More important is the question of the Court's authority to issue the order. The policy maker's reaction to a judicial decision will be conditioned by his perception of the Court's role in general, his beliefs concerning the importance of the challenged activity or program, his perception of the attitudes of his reference groups and constituents on the issue, and his perception of his role. The differences in policy position may be the result of a general attitude toward the Court and its role in the American system of government.[29] The following comments are typical in content and intensity.

Changing Districts

A Surgeon: We must conform with Federal law. If we are to teach our children to obey laws we must set an example.

A Farmer: We did not want to violate any federal law.

A Superintendent: I think the Supreme Court is correct. Very few people understand the religious issue, less seem to understand what is meant by religious freedom, and relatively few seem to understand the Supreme Court's role in our government.

A Farmer: We are commanded by the Bible to be subject to civil powers as long as their laws do not conflict with laws of God.

Non-Changing Districts

A Superintendent: Impeach Earl Warren.

A Housewife: The decision of the Supreme Court seemed senseless and I could see no advantage in making changes.

A College Professor: The Supreme Court decision didn't mean a damn.

A Banker: The general public in this county do not have the respect for the U. S. Supreme Court as they once did. They think it is packed, so to speak, and

[29] Speaking to the American Philosophical Society in 1952, Justice Felix Frankfurter observed that "broadly speaking, the chief reliance of law in a democracy is the habit of popular respect for law. Especially true is it that law as promulgated by the Supreme Court ultimately depends upon confidence of the people in the Supreme Court as an institution." Frankfurter, *Of Law and Men*, Elman, ed. (New York: Harcourt, Brace & Co., 1956), p. 31. Brehm and Cohen report an experiment demonstrating that the more credible the source of a communication the greater the change in the recipient's attitude even when there was wide discrepancy between the recipient's initial attitude and the content of the communication. Jack W. Brehm and Arthur R. Cohen, *Explorations in Cognitive Dissonance* (New York: John Wiley and Sons, 1962), pp. 247-48.

doubt very much if all are qualified and unbiased and listen to the whims of the President that gave them the appointment. The standards are on a lower level than back several years ago.

A Superintendent: I am at a loss to understand the necessity for this survey. I am of the opinion that 99% of the people in the United States feel as I do about the Supreme Court's decision—that it was an outrage and that Congress should have it amended. The remaining 1% do not belong in this free world.

A Lawyer: We felt that in the absence of some good specific objection, there was no compelling reason to change previous policy.

If one had these comments without information on the policy adopted, it would not be too difficult to predict the position taken by each of these school boards.

The Court-attitude is only one of the variables affecting the impact of a judicial decision. The other major variable is the policy maker's assessment of and commitment to the challenged program or activity.[30] Comments on the benefits and value of Bible reading and devotional exercises came only from the school board members and superintendents from the non-changing districts. These are typical:

A Farmer: I believe that if the Bible is removed from our schools and is not read that would be the first step toward removing the Holy Bible from our free society. Then we would eventually drift into heathenism.

A Merchant: This nation was founded and has grown under the firm belief in God. For those who do not believe it, there are places where they do not believe. Let them go there if they choose.

A Locomotive Engineer: I thought the Bible should be read and prayer held on account this was the only time some of our students ever had any spiritual guidance.

A Surgeon: This is a free country. If Bible reading is offensive to a very small minority then this minority may do homework or look out the window. However, we shall not discard Bible reading in order to coddle them.

A Bookkeeper: While this is a federal law, we do not intend to stick strictly to same. We permit Bible reading and devotional exercises in our school. If it was not being done, I would insist that it be done, bearing in mind that perhaps this is the only place some children are exposed to same. I cannot bear to think of communist atmosphere being exercised through our schools and children.

A Superintendent: Political leaders should read Bible and quit playing politics.

In some of these instances the belief in the importance of the program was sufficiently intense to override any desire to comply with

[30] See Thomas Schelling, *The Strategy of Conflict* (New York: Oxford University Press, 1963), pp. 24-28 for a discussion of the effect of making a public commitment on an issue or course of action. Brehm and Cohen, *op. cit.*, pp. 7-10, discuss the effect of commitment on the process of reaching a decision.

the decision. In other instances, respondents combined attacks on the Court with a defense of the program. It seems reasonable to assume that the relative intensities of the Court-attitude and the program-attitude determined in large part the policy position taken by the school board.[31] In changing districts the board must have felt a greater obligation to follow the Court ruling than to continue to enforce their beliefs in the value of devotional exercises. In the non-changing districts *Schempp* was repudiated either because of a pre-existing negative attitude toward the Court or because of a strong belief in the value of the program, or both.

Perceptions of the attitudes of constituents or clientele are important but seem to be secondary. They play the role of reinforcing or modifying the Court-attitude and/or the program-attitude. A dentist on the board of a changing district observed that "we thought public opinion would want us to comply with Federal Law," while a chairman of a non-changing board (who did not indicate his occupation) said that the most important factor influencing him was that "we would have had complaints if we did not have Bible reading." Both of these board members were reacting to their perception of constituent attitude. The officials' constituents or clientele are not the only reference group they have. Other official bodies, such as the State Board of Education and the Commissioner of Education, may

---

[31] The Court-attitude and the program-attitude may be either complementary or divergent. If complementary, one attitude would be positive and the other negative; they would reinforce each other and make reaching a decision relatively easy. If the two attitudes were divergent they would carry the same sign and the policy position would be unpredictable if no more were known. The possibilities and results can be diagrammed:

Court-attitude Direction	Program-attitude Direction	Policy-Position Expected
+	—	compliance
—	+	non-compliance
+	+	variable
—	—	variable

In the last two instances shown the intensity of the basic attitudes and the effect of secondary perceptions will determine the final policy position adopted.

Of those responding to this survey from changing districts only one indicated a negative Court-attitude as compared to twenty-six who expressed a favorable attitude. In non-changing districts the ratio was two favorable to thirteen negative expressions. No respondent expressed a negative program-attitude but only two from changing districts as contrasted to twenty-one from non-changing districts made positive statements. Both groups indicated a belief that their course of action had the approval of their constituents.

constitute another while non-official groups and opinion leaders could make up a third. The Commissioner's statement that Bible reading was permissible was not mentioned by any respondent but undoubtedly played a part in the making of decisions. The state has also continued to print the statutory requirement in the handbook of regulations for teachers. This prompted one superintendent to remark that "most teachers consider Bible reading a state law since it is still in their register." And a merchant in a non-changing district said that he was influenced by the necessity of "complying with the laws of the State." Another superintendent indicated his valuation of the Court's decision by reporting that he "suggested teachers continue practices of past until forbidden by law." While official reference groups, constituents, and perceptions of the ranking of state law and Court decisions played an admitted role in the policy making process, no board member indicated that he had been influenced by any non-official reference group. However, the possibility cannot be ruled out. One superintendent justified the lack of change in his district by pointing out that the county education association had adopted a resolution favoring continued compliance with state law.

On the basis of the information available, it is impossible to weigh the value of the perceptions that went into the making of the policies. But one might hazard a guess that in the changing districts a perception of the Court as an authoritative body exercising legitimate power was strong enough to override any commitment to devotional exercises. The reverse, of course, would hold true in non-changing districts. The weight given to reference group attitudes and the direction of those attitudes probably, though not necessarily, varied in the same direction as the final policy decision and served to reinforce attitudes toward the Court or beliefs in the value of devotionals. That is, public opinion in changing districts probably was perceived by the board as favoring or at least not opposing compliance with *Schempp* and strengthened the board's desire to comply.[32]

One warning is in order. It is not asserted that procedural change to save substance and intensity of attitude explains what took place in Tennessee. All that is claimed here is that with the failure of the initial hypotheses in this study this additional explanation is possible and is supported to some extent by the response to the questionnaires.

[32] One board chairman reported that he and the superintendent made the decision to leave devotional exercises to the teacher's discretion "since no one else seemed to be interested."

IV

In the light of the findings of this study, future research on the impact of Court decisions should obtain information on the policy maker's attitudes toward the Court, knowledge of the content and meaning of the specific decision and group of decisions into which it fits,[33] and attitudes on the particular issue under consideration. It should be possible to obtain responses to declarative statements on an "agree very strongly" to a "disagree very strongly" scale to get some indication of the intensity of feelings and perceptions.[34] It is believed that the collection of this attitudinal data would enable the researcher to predict whether the policy makers would or would not comply with the Court's decision. It would also lead to the conclusion that the same variables condition response to judicial decisions as affect reaction to other political stimuli.[35]

One must conclude with Robert A. Dahl that "by itself, the Court is almost powerless to affect the course of national policy."[36] It may delay or accelerate adoption of policy but cannot impose or reverse policy. Court decisions, therefore, will increase in effectiveness as those who have to implement them are either in accord with the Court's position or are sufficiently convinced of the legitimacy of the Court's exercise of power that this conviction overrides any prior commitment to an alternative policy. A limit is thus placed on the ability of the Court to make policy and this impales the justices on the horns of a strategic dilemma. Their decisions have the greatest effectiveness when the policy laid down is non-controversial and the Court's prestige is high. But in a period of massive social (and therefore legal) change the justices' policy choices will be controversial and as a result the Court's prestige will be lower than in quieter periods.[37] The

---

[33] Compare Sorauf, *op. cit.* The fact that a policy maker is mistaken or uninformed about the meaning of a decision is important but his reaction will have to be evaluated in light of his understanding of the Court's order.

[34] See Johnson, *op. cit.*, Appendix B, for a questionnaire which could easily be adapted for use in any impact study.

[35] If this conclusion is correct the findings of the various voting behavior surveys, e.g. Angus Campbell, *et al.*, *The American Voter* (John Wiley and Sons, 1960), will become highly relevant to impact studies.

[36] R. A. Dahl, "Decision-Making in a Democracy: The Supreme Court as a National Policy-Maker," 6 *Journal of Public Law* 279, 293 (1958).

[37] It may be that the making of more controversial decisions and weakened prestige plus abandonment of the mechanical explanation of the judicial decision-making process explain the differences in public and professional reaction to President Roosevelt's "court-packing plan" of 1937 and the Jenner-Butler Bill

options available are to deal with one problem area at a time in an attempt to maximize effectiveness by minimizing controversy or to take the problems as they come since any decision will have some, even if not total, effect. Unless we are to counsel judicial abdication the only way to resolve this dilemma is for the Court to utilize every legitimate means at its disposal to convince other policy-makers and the general public that its policy choice is the best of the possible alternatives.[38]

in 1957. See Joseph Alsop and Turner Catledge, *The 168 Days* (New York: Doubleday, 1938) and Walter F. Murphy, *Congress and the Court* (Chicago: University of Chicago Press, 1962).

[38] On this point see: Martin Shapiro, *Law and Politics in the Supreme Court* (New York: Free Press, 1964), pp. 17-32.

SURVEY RESEARCH ON JUDICIAL DECISIONS: THE PRAYER AND BIBLE READING CASES

H. Frank Way, Jr.

University of California, Riverside

W
ITHIN the past decade research in public law has undergone considerable change. The focus has shifted from traditional content analysis of
Supreme Court decisions to a focus on the Court as a political-policy
making agency. The battle within the discipline has largely centered on the via-
bility of unidimensional versus multidimensional methods of analysis. For all of
the limitations of the new research in this area, the net impact has been a positive
advancement of our understanding of the Court as one of the actors in the policy
process. Nonetheless, one of the greatest limitations of the new methods for systems
analysis has been to assume that the output was politically significant. Unfortunately little attention has been devoted to measuring the impact of policy output. In
no area of the discipline is this statement truer than the output of the judiciary.
We need empirical data (for example in order to determine whether the anti-trust
decision of the Supreme Court in *United States* v. *Du Pont*[1] has had an impact in
controlling vertical monopoly practices); and similarly we need data to measure
the impact of the *Miranda* and *Escobedo* decisions on state and local police practices or indeed, even on state and local judicial decisions.

This study is one attempt to gather national data on the impact of a new
Supreme Court policy. It involves the 1962 and 1963 decisions of the Court
banning prayers and Bible readings in public school.[2] We know that the Court is
not always successful when it attempts to alter deeply rooted practices, as for example the limited judicial impact of the desegregation decision. Religious practices
in public school were deeply rooted in 1962 and were probably more geographically widespread than governmentally imposed racial segregation was in the public
school system in 1953. Indeed, many commentators otherwise friendly to the
Court feared that the Court had pronounced in an area where it was likely to be
openly and widely disregarded.[3]

By using standard methods in survey research it was determined that indeed
the proscribed practices had been widespread and further, that with the exception
of the South, the practices had largely disappeared in public elementary schools
by the academic year 1964–65. The remainder of this article reports the results
of the survey.

The Survey

The survey was conducted during 1964–65 and was a national random sample
of 2,320 public elementary school teachers. It was arbitrarily decided that 5

Note: The author wishes to acknowledge the support of the Center for the Study of Law
and Society, University of California, Berkeley, and the Faculty Committee on Research,
University of California, Riverside.
[1] 353 U.S. 586 (1957).
[2] *Engle* v. *Vitale*, 370 U.S. 421 and *Abington* v. *Schempp*, 374 U.S. 203.
[3] See Erwin Griswold's "Absolute Is in the Dark," *Utah Law Review*, Summer 1963.

189

teachers per school would be sampled. This meant 464 schools would be in the sample. Since no enrollment figures are available on a state-by-state basis which separate public elementary and secondary enrollments, the national figure of 38,644,000 was used. This represents public school enrollments for the academic year 1962–63 for kindergarten through twelfth grade. This total enrollment was divided by 464, giving a quotient of 83,284. The quotient was then used as the basis for selecting school districts. Starting with Alabama and working through Wyoming, school district enrollments were progressively tabulated and at every point where the tabulation added up to 83,284 the district was included in the sample.[4] Then the districts selected were located by state in each state educational directory. Using a table of random numbers 464 elementary schools were selected, as were 464 alternates. A request was then sent to each school for the current academic roster of teachers. When the replies were received a table of random numbers was used to select five teachers from each school. The questionnaire was then mailed to the 2,320 randomly selected teachers. The return rate was 74 per cent or 1,712 replies.[5]

Assumptions

Two basic assumptions were made in undertaking this study. The first derives from the view that Court decisions generate an expectancy that persons not party to a suit but who are legally similarly situated will adhere to the Court's decision. Thus the prayer and Bible reading decisions of 1962–63 generated an expectancy that prayers and Bible readings in all public schools would cease. The second assumption was that adherence to the decisions would in no small measure depend on the classroom teachers. The assumption here was that a classroom teacher exercises considerable independence in determining whether her classroom will engage in religious exercises. This is not to deny that other factors would play an important part in the decision to adhere or not to adhere to the new precedents. School boards, superintendents, principals, PTA's, ministerial associations, state

---

[4] The U.S. Office of Education's *Education Directory, 1962–1963, Part 2*, was used for this tabulation.

[5] There is a possibility that the sample response contains a rural bias. While the over-all response rate was 74%, the response rate from the smallest school districts, presumably rural, was 82% whereas the response rate from the largest district was only 50%. The percentage distribution of the sample and the final response by school district population was:

School Population	Distribution of Original Sample	Distribution of Response	Rate of Response
0 – 2000	20.2	22.5	82
2001 – 4000	12.9	14.4	82
4001 – 8000	16.1	16.7	76
8001 – 16000	14.8	15.5	77
16001 – 32000	10.5	9.4	66
32001 – 64000	7.9	6.7	62
64001 – 128000	9.6	8.7	66
128001 – 512000	2.5	2.4	70
512001+	4.9	3.3	50
	99.4	99.6	
	N = 2320	N = 1712	

officials and state laws all have been influential in this area and would likely continue to be so.

Religion in the School

The average teacher in the survey did feel the impact of the Supreme Court's decisions. As the following figures indicate there has been a noticeable shift in actual classroom practices in regard to prayers and Bible readings. Prayers were said in over 60 per cent of the classrooms of teachers responding to the questionnaire and who were teaching at the time the Court decisions were announced. Within this group the practice was overwhelmingly a daily one. By the academic year 1964–65 the situation had changed from the pre-1962 figure of 60 per cent of the classrooms saying prayers at sometime to only 28 per cent.[6]

MORNING PRAYERS BEFORE 1962

	Daily	Weekly	Less Than Weekly	Not at all
Before 1962	720	33	19	498
1964–65	321	24	29	946

While classroom prayers were common before 1962, classroom Bible readings were somewhat less common. Forty-eight per cent of the respondents teaching before 1962 indicated that Bible selections were read in their classrooms on a daily to less than weekly basis. Again, this situation changed radically after the Court decisions. By the academic year 1964–65 only 22 per cent of the respondents indicated Bible selections were being read in their classes.

BIBLE READINGS

	Daily	Weekly	Less Than Weekly	Not at all
Before 1962	512	72	106	745
1964–65	208	43	103	1261

Other Religious Practices

In addition to prayers and Bible readings there are numerous other classroom and school practices which have religious overtones. Undoubtedly many of these are consistent with the First Amendment. Eighty per cent of the respondents indicated they use religious percepts, such as the Golden Rule, in their classrooms and 35 per cent said they made use of religious hymns such as "The Old Rugged Cross."

Previously one of the most controversial programs was the released time program.[7] This survey found that the program is not extensively used. Twenty-three per cent of the respondents said their schools had such a program. However, 47 per cent of the respondents who indicated their schools have a released time pro-

---

[6] It should be noted, however, that there was an increase in 1964–65 in the practice of "silent meditation" in the classroom. This rose from 178 before 1962 to 294 during 1964–65.

[7] *McCollum v. Board of Education*, 333 U.S. 203 (1948), and *Zorach v. Clauson*, 343 U.S. 306 (1952).

gram were from two states — California and New York. Of those schools who participated in released time programs slightly over 15 per cent allow the program to be conducted on the school premises. This, of course, is in violation of the Court's decision in *McCollum* v. *Board of Education*.[8] While the released time programs are not extensively used in the United States, they are not confined to any particular size of city. They are as likely to be found in small towns as in large urban areas.

DISTRIBUTION BY POPULATION OF RELEASED TIME PROGRAMS

0–10,000	10,001–75,000	75,001–250,000	250,001+
128 (32.90)	128 (32.90)	43 (11.00)	90 (23.20)

It is not uncommon for a school district to oppose regular religious exercises but to sanction occasional breaks in this policy. Christmas, Easter, and Thanksgiving are the occasions which are most frequently observed by religious exercises. Graduation services, particularly baccalaureate exercises, traditionally include some form of religious observance. When asked whether prayers were currently offered in their schools on special occasions such as assemblies, the respondents replied as follows: Yes, 517; No, 1,100; Don't know, 70.

A further indication of accommodation is the frequency or infrequency students are allowed excused absences in order to attend religious services or to practice for a religious exercise. Out of a total response of 1,424, 595 respondents indicated students in their schools were given excused absences for such things as practice for first communion, holy days of obligation and high holy days.

While the positive response rate here was 41 per cent nationally, such practices are episodic in all states except New York, Pennsylvania, and New Jersey. These three states accounted for just over one third of the 595 positive responses.

UNREPORTED VARIABLES

A number of variables were found to have little or no significance in affecting teacher practices or opinions. Race, marital status, grade level taught, and the number of school age children of respondents failed to develop any statistically significant trend.

Since the sample was drawn on the basis of school district population, it might be expected that district size would be a significant variable. However, cross-tabulations of districts by size revealed only that districts of over 128,000 were significantly different in their responses. This probably reflects an urban influence rather than other factors associated with the size of school districts. Due to consolidation of school districts, size no longer reflects an urban-rural influence, except for the strongly urban influence in the largest districts.

SCHOOL POLICY

Respondents were asked about their school's policy regarding classroom prayers and Bible readings. The results confirmed the assumption that teachers exercise

[8] *Zorach* v. *Clauson*, however, gave judicial approval to a released time program conducted during school hours but off the school premises.

considerable individual discretion in this area. The following are the responses on school classroom prayer policy:

A Favors some or all prayers 155
B Opposes all types of prayers 492
C Not aware of policy, has no policy, or
   leaves it to teacher discretion 1,011

Of those respondents who indicated their current classroom practice, 43 per cent of the teachers in schools favoring prayers actually said prayers, 4 per cent of those in schools opposing prayers said them, and 40 per cent of those in schools with no policy, or where the policy was to give the teacher discretionary power, or where the teacher was unaware of any policy said prayers.

The results were similar for Bible readings:

A Favors Bible readings 121
B Opposes Bible readings 570
C No policy, teacher discretion, or
   unaware of any policy 1,084

Of those who indicated their current practice, 91 per cent of the teachers in schools favoring Bible reading had Bible readings, 3 per cent of the teachers in schools opposing Bible readings had them, and 25 per cent of the teachers in category C had Bible readings.

There is only a small difference in categories A, B, and C in school prayer policy as opposed to school Bible reading policy. The distinctive feature of both sets of data is the size of category C.

CHURCH ATTENDANCE

In a survey concerned with a religious issue one would expect that the frequency of a teacher's attendance at religious services might well influence her attitudes and practices in the public classroom.[9] The results were as expected. The more frequently a teacher attended church the more likely she was to have prayers and Bible readings in her classroom before the Court decisions and to continue them after the decisions were announced. This same trend is noted in the results on opinions about religion in the public classroom. The three sets of percentages which merit the closest attention are those reporting current practices on morning prayers, Bible readings, and grace. Here infrequency of church attendance appears to have had its most pronounced influence. The average difference of responses to all questions on classroom practices between those who rarely or never attend religious services and those who attend more than weekly was 29 per cent. An even greater variation occurs between these same groups on opinion questions relating to religion in the classroom. Here the average disagreement between those who

---

[9] The following is a breakdown of number of respondents in each attendance level:

Never-rarely 271
Monthly 360
Weekly 761
More than weekly 308

             1,700

TABLE 1*

RELATIONSHIP BETWEEN TEACHER-CHURCH ATTENDANCE
AND CLASSROOM PRACTICES AND ATTITUDES

(in percentages)

	CHURCH ATTENDANCE				SIGNIFICANCE LEVEL
	Never-Rarely Attend	Attend Monthly	Attend Weekly	Attend More Than Weekly	
Opinions About Religion in Public Schools					
Prayer and Bible readings decisions interfere with teacher freedom	36	61	65	74	p < 1%
Devotional services have no place in the public school	69	41	31	20	p < 1%
Released time programs interfere with class schedules	68	58	46	36	p < 1%
Don't stop prayers and Bible readings because of a few	51	77	83	92	p < 1%
Bible readings and prayers are beneficial to students	68	83	90	95	p < 1%
Public school not proper place to develop religious values	78	58	48	55	p < 1%
Classroom Religious Practices					
Bible readings, pre-1962	32	44	49	63	p < 1%
Bible readings, 1964–65	7	16	25	38	p < 1%
Morning prayers, pre-1962	42	60	59	67	p < 1%
Morning prayers, 1964–65	12	23	30	42	p < 1%
Religious precepts, 1964–65	71	79	81	86	p < 1%
Grace, pre-1962	30	57	59	67	p < 1%
Grace, 1964–65	17	31	35	47	p < 1%

* The chi-square test of the significance of difference of two independent samples was used in Tables 1 through 8.

never or rarely attend religious services and those who attend more than weekly was 35 per cent. It should also be noted that not only is there a wide disagreement between those who rarely or never attend and those who attend more than weekly, but also there is frequently a consensus among all those teachers who attend monthly or more than monthly, a consensus which the "never-rarely" group does not share.

RELIGIOUS AFFILIATION

Denominational affiliation was coded raw, and on the basis of similarity of responses denominations were grouped.[10] Minor sects and those respondents who checked no affiliation, and who noted they were agnostic or atheist, were discarded in this matrix. This was done because the groups were so small that it was felt no

[10] In some respects certain religious groups probably do not fit the categories they have been placed in here. It is certainly questionable whether the Latter-day Saints are liberal in either the religious or political sense of this word. The only justification for this grouping is that on the matter surveyed here teachers who professed membership in the Church of Jesus Christ of Latter-day Saints were more similar to, for example, Methodists, than they were to denominations within the conservative category.

statistical significance could be attached to the responses. The two Protestant groups and the number of respondents in each are as follows:

Liberal Protestants — 904
Methodist
Presbyterian
Episcopalian
Congregational, including
United Church of Christ
Lutheran
United Brethern
Christian Science
Latter-day Saints

Conservative Protestants — 354
Church of Christ
Assembly of God
Christian
Church of God
Baptist
Disciples of Christ
Free Methodist
Nazarene
Holiness
Pentecostal

There were 60 respondents in the Jewish group and 266 in the Roman Catholic group.

The most surprising result in this matrix is the position of the Roman Catholic teacher. Contrary to the general assumptions of a conservative outlook among many Roman Catholics, there is a significant liberal trend among Roman Catholic teachers. On religious issues they responded more like liberal Protestants than like conservative Protestants. Indeed on current classroom religious practices, prayers, Bible readings and grace, the Roman Catholic teacher responded more like the Jewish teacher than like either group of Protestant teachers. This suggests that once the Court decisions were announced the Roman Catholic and Jewish teachers were more willing to accept a ban on classroom religious practices than were Protestant teachers.

TABLE 2

RELATIONSHIP BETWEEN TEACHER RELIGIOUS AFFILIATION
AND CLASSROOM PRACTICES AND ATTITUDES

(in percentages)

	RELIGIOUS AFFILIATION				SIGNIFICANCE LEVEL
	Jew	Roman Catholic	Liberal Protestant	Conservative Protestant	
Opinions About Religion in Public Schools					
Prayer and Bible readings decisions interfere with teacher freedom	12	66	64	68	p < 1%
Devotional services have no place in the public school	93	39	37	18	p < 1%
Released time programs interfere with class schedules	64	39	54	46	p < 1%
Don't stop prayers and Bible readings because of a few	19	78	79	90	p < 1%
Bible readings and prayers are beneficial to students	47	87	87	92	p < 1%
Public school not proper place to develop religious values	95	55	54	40	p < 1%
Classroom Religious Practices					
Bible readings, pre-1962	44	38	44	72	p < 1%
Bible readings, 1964–65	0	7	21	47	p < 1%
Morning prayers, pre-1962	56	55	57	71	p < 5%
Morning prayers, 1964–65	5	11	27	51	p < 1%
Religious precepts, 1964–65	61	76	80	89	p < 1%
Grace, pre-1962	30	45	56	75	p < 1%
Grace, 1964–65	5	13	35	55	p < 1%

A number of factors could affect the religious affiliation variable and help to explain some of the results. The conservative Protestant results could have been influenced by the Southern Baptists in this category. Southern teachers were distinctly more conservative in all of their responses. Furthermore there is probably an urban-rural influence at work here.[11] Forty-seven per cent of the liberal Protestant teachers were from towns of similar size. At the urban level 20 per cent of the conservative Protestant teachers were from cities of over 75,000 whereas 27 per cent of the liberal Protestant teachers were from the larger urban areas. When conservative Protestant teacher responses were cross-tabulated against city population, there was a marked tendency for the responses to become more liberal as the city population increased.

As suggested above, Roman Catholic teachers' responses were more liberal than one might have expected. When their responses were cross-tabulated against city population the expected pattern of increased liberalism in the largest cities did not emerge. On the contrary, in cities of over 250,000 there was a distinct decline in liberal responses. Although the data itself does not suggest an explanation for this, one could speculate that since the very large urban areas are also the headquarters of Roman Catholic hierarchy, Roman Catholic teachers in these areas may be subject to greater influence by their bishops and cardinals than Roman Catholics in smaller and more removed areas. Furthermore, these large urban areas are also the centers of what is left of Irish Catholic immigrant groups, who follow a distinctly conservative religious tradition.

In summary, the denominational affiliation of an elementary public school teacher has a sharp cutting edge in predicting practices and attitudes about religion in the public school.

City Population

A normal hypothesis of a study of religion in public schools would be that large cities are more likely to oppose religion in the public schools than are small towns. It is not mere chance that the Supreme Court prayer and Bible reading cases originated in either large cities or suburban areas. The metropolitan areas have been the centers of liberal Protestant, Jewish, and agnostic thought. The large cities also provide a degree of anonymity to an individual to challenge traditions which is not afforded by the smaller towns and rural areas. Furthermore income and education levels are higher in metropolitan areas.

Table 3 confirms the expected hypothesis except for cities of 75,000 to 250,000. Here there is a regression in the expected liberal response. The explanation for this is a bias in the sample response. According to 1960 census figures 9 per cent of the American population lived in cities of this category. The regional distribution of cities of this size showed that the South also had 9 per cent of its population in this category. However, the sample response for these Southern cities was 14 per cent. Southern responses were considerably more conservative than responses from other regions. The unexpected regression can be explained by this difference.

----

[11] Although no sample bias is present.

TABLE 3

RELATIONSHIP BETWEEN CITY POPULATION AND TEACHER
ATTITUDES AND PRACTICES

(in percentages)

	CITY POPULATION				SIGNIFICANCE LEVEL
	0–10,000	10,001–75,000	75,001–250,000	250,001+	
Opinions About Religion in Public Schools					
Prayer and Bible readings decisions interfere with teacher freedom	65	57	60	52	p < 1%
Devotional services have no place in the public school	32	41	32	45	p < 1%
Released time programs interfere with class schedules	48	55	51	49	p > 5%
Don't stop prayers and Bible readings because of a few	83	73	82	70	p < 1%
Bible readings and prayers are beneficial to students	90	83	88	77	p < 1%
Public school not proper place to develop religious values	52	54	50	63	p < 5%
Classroom Religious Practices					
Bible readings, pre-1962	52	44	49	45	p > 5%
Bible readings, 1964–65	26	21	24	16	p < 5%
Morning prayers, pre-1962	65	56	53	52	p < 1%
Morning prayers, 1964–65	32	26	28	21	p < 5%
Religious precepts, 1964–65	82	78	84	77	p > 5%
Grace, pre-1962	65	49	58	46	p < 1%
Grace 1964–65	40	29	37	26	p < 1%

Indeed when a random elimination was made to reduce the percentage from 14 to 9 the bias was corrected.

AGE

Age presents one of the more interesting of the significant variables. There is a predictable trend from a liberal to a conservative position as the teacher moves up the age scale. However, there is interesting deviation from this trend in the youngest age group, the 20–29 teachers. The youngest group of teachers were frequently more conservative or traditionalist than the age group 30–39. This could suggest that the younger and probably more inexperienced teacher is less sure of her position and perhaps somewhat fearful of showing greater independence from her more experienced colleagues. However when the 20–29 group is divided into those who have taught less than and those who have taught more than five years one discovers that there is little difference in their practices or opinions. This in turn suggests that in the 20–29 group it is not as much a question of the length or lack of length of experience which is significant, but rather that experiences outside of teaching are sufficiently common and strong so as to influence their attitudes and practices. The 26-year-old teacher of 1964 was born in 1940 and was a high school student during the McCarthy era, whereas the 36-year-old teacher of 1964 was born in the depression and was a high school student during World War II.

TABLE 4

RELATIONSHIP BETWEEN AGE AND TEACHER
ATTITUDES AND PRACTICES

(in percentages)

	Age					Significance Level
	20–29	30–39	40–49	50–59	60–69	
Opinions About Religion in Public Schools						
Prayer and Bible readings decisions interfere with teacher freedom	56	55	57	65	69	p < 1%
Devotional services have no place in the public school	39	46	37	35	27	p < 1%
Released time programs interfere with class schedules	47	52	53	54	52	p < 1%
Don't stop prayers and Bible readings because of a few	73	71	79	81	87	p < 1%
Bible readings and prayers are beneficial to students	87	78	85	88	87	p < 1%
Public school not proper place to develop religious values	50	58	57	53	57	p < 1%
Classroom Religious Practices						
Bible readings, pre-1962	45	40	48	53	51	p < 1%
Bible readings, 1964–65	18	18	25	26	29	p < 1%
Morning prayers, pre-1962	55	51	56	65	62	p < 1%
Morning prayers, 1964–65	21	21	28	34	38	p < 1%
Religious precepts, 1964–65	79	76	83	81	80	p < 1%
Grace, pre-1962	33	32	33	37	42	p < 1%
Grace, 1964–65	25	28	36	41	42	p < 1%

REGIONS

Since the sample was a national one all areas should be represented in approximate proportion to the distribution of population by regions. For purposes of this study New England consists of those six states from Maine through Connecticut. The Middle Atlantic states include New York, New Jersey, Pennsylvania, and Maryland.[12] The South is made up of the eleven states of the Confederacy plus Oklahoma, West Virginia, and Kentucky. The Middle West is used to designate the eleven states west of Pennsylvania to the Rocky Mountains.[13] The designation Rocky Mountain-Far West was used for the twelve states beginning with Colorado and west to the Pacific Coast.[14]

The sample responses by regions were closely parallel to 1960 census statistics:

	1960 Census	Responses
New England	5%	5%
Middle Atlantic	21%	18%
South	29%	29%
Middle West	29%	29%
Rocky Mountain-Far West	16%	19%

[12] Delaware and District of Columbia did not appear in the sample.

[13] Excluding South Dakota which did not appear in the sample.

[14] Hawaii was not included in the sample because it did not have a published roster of school districts by population in 1964.

TABLE 5

RELATIONSHIPS BETWEEN REGIONS AND TEACHER
ATTITUDES AND PRACTICES

(in percentages)

	REGIONS					SIGNIFICANCE LEVEL
	South	New England	Middle West	Middle Atlantic	Rocky Mt-Far West	
Opinions About Religion in Public Schools						
Prayer and Bible readings decisions interfere with teacher freedom	69	73	54	58	53	p < 1%
Devotional services have no place in the public school	11	25	48	41	60	p < 1%
Released time programs interfere with class schedules	43	59	57	48	47	p < 1%
Don't stop prayers and Bible readings because of a few	94	89	71	70	65	p < 1%
Bible readings and prayers are beneficial to students	94	91	86	75	80	p < 1%
Public school not proper place to develop religious values	34	43	62	58	72	p < 1%
Classroom Religious Practices						
Bible readings, pre-1962	80	64	28	62	14	p < 1%
Bible readings, 1964–65	57	20	12	5	6	p < 1%
Morning prayers, pre-1962	87	95	38	80	14	p < 1%
Morning prayers, 1964–65	64	27	21	7	5	p < 1%
Religious precepts, 1964–65	89	69	81	72	77	p < 1%
Grace, pre-1962	87	73	43	56	23	p < 1%
Grace, 1964–65	68	28	33	11	8	p < 1%

The central tendency which emerges from a study of region as a variable is that we are a nation, but with a unique regional variant, the South. In the responses to five out of six opinion questions about religion in the public school the South was the most conservative area. The average variation between the most liberal and the most conservative responses to these six questions was 27 per cent. The South's regional uniqueness is further demonstrated when we turn to classroom religious practices. Both before and after the Supreme Court decisions prayers and Bible reading were more likely to occur in Southern classrooms than elsewhere in the nation. Here the average variation in regional responses was 56 per cent. This high percentage is largely accounted for by the discrepancy in current practices between the South and the rest of the nation. Prayers, Bible readings, and grace were reported practiced by a majority of all Southern teachers and only by a minority of teachers in all other regions.

The only region which slightly approximates the South is New England. The pattern of opinion which emerges, at least on religious questions, is one suggested by William Warren Sweet's *Religion in Colonial America.*[15] The South and New England reflect more religious homogeneity of opinion. They are also the colonial areas where established churches had their greatest influence. The Middle Atlantic states, particularly New York, Pennsylvania and New Jersey were in colonial times

---

[15] New York: Scribner's, 1953.

more religiously heterogeneous. In the colonial South and New England, with a more homogeneous religious population, it was commonly accepted that the state and the church would actively cooperate. When religious dissenters in these areas moved west they left behind this established tradition of church-state rapport. Thus we note that the responses from the Rocky Mountain-Far West states are today the more liberal in all questions relating to religion than those from all other regions. An ironic aspect of such a proposition is that minority groups in the colonial South and New England, Baptists and Roman Catholics, who resented the established church position, have become today the upholders of church-state cooperation in these areas.

College Education

The presumption of the college education variable is that a higher level of college attainment will free a teacher from traditional practices and opinions. If college education is intended as a liberating force then a teacher with a graduate degree would be more likely to challenge the position of religious exercises in public schools. There is little evidence in this table to support such a position. The average percentage variation among the three levels of college-educated respondents is minimal.

TABLE 6

RELATIONSHIP BETWEEN COLLEGE EDUCATION
AND TEACHER ATTITUDES AND PRACTICES

(in percentages)

	College Education			Significance Level
	Less than Baccalaureate	Baccalaureate	Graduate Degree	
Opinions About Religion in Public Schools				
Prayer and Bible readings decisions interfere with teacher freedom	67	60	55	$p < 1\%$
Devotional services have no place in the public school	37	38	38	$p > 5\%$
Released time programs interfere with class schedules	55	50	56	$p < 1\%$
Don't stop prayers and Bible readings because of a few	84	77	72	$p < 5\%$
Bible readings and prayers are beneficial to students	88	85	83	$p > 5\%$
Public school not proper place to develop religious values	58	53	56	$p > 5\%$
Classroom Religious Practices				
Bible readings, pre-1962	50	48	46	$p < 5\%$
Bible readings, 1964–65	26	23	19	$p < 5\%$
Morning prayers, pre-1962	59	58	57	$p > 5\%$
Morning prayers, 1964–65	30	28	25	$p > 5\%$
Religious precepts, 1964–65	77	80	80	$p > 5\%$
Grace, pre-1962	58	56	52	$p > 5\%$
Grace, 1964–65	36	33	31	$p > 5\%$

YEARS TAUGHT

As in the case of age, the presumption of the variable years taught is that the longer she teaches the more conservative a teacher becomes. This assumption was supported by the sample results, particularly as applied to classroom practices. The more years taught the more likely a teacher was to continue classroom religious practices. The same assumption did not hold true in all opinion questions but the over-all results in opinion questions indicated the assumption has some validity.

TABLE 7
RELATIONSHIP BETWEEN YEARS TAUGHT AND TEACHER ATTITUDES AND PRACTICES
(in percentages)

	YEARS TAUGHT				SIGNIFICANCE LEVEL
	0–10	*11–20*	*21–30*	*31–45*	
Opinions About Religion in Public Schools					
Prayer and Bible readings decisions interfere with teacher freedom	54	60	66	73	p < 1%
Devotional services have no place in the public school	42	40	31	24	p < 1%
Released time programs interfere with class schedules	51	52	52	48	p > 5%
Don't stop prayers and Bible readings because of a few	73	77	83	86	p < 1%
Bible readings and prayers are beneficial to students	84	84	86	93	p > 5%
Public school not proper place to develop religious values	55	54	56	50	p > 5%
Classroom Religious Practices					
Bible readings, pre-1962	44	48	52	60	p < 1%
Bible readings, 1964–65	19	23	28	29	p < 1%
Morning prayers, pre-1962	54	58	65	70	p < 1%
Morning prayers, 1964–65	22	28	37	35	p < 1%
Religious precepts, 1964–65	79	81	82	81	p < 1%
Grace, pre-1962	48	59	65	66	p < 1%
Grace, 1964–65	28	37	42	40	p < 1%

SEX

The male position in American society has been freer than that of the female. In the area of religion the female has had stronger membership and attendance ties with churches. Thus an assumption is made that the male, with his weaker religious ties, would be less opposed to the abolition of religious exercises in public schools. The data supports this assumption as it relates to actual classroom religious practices. Here the average variation in the responses to the seven questions was 13 per cent. However, the responses to the opinion questions on religion in the public schools were not significantly different. The average variation was only 5 per cent and the chi-square test indicates the responses to two of the six questions were of doubtful statistical significance.

TABLE 8

RELATIONSHIP BETWEEN SEX AND TEACHER ATTITUDES AND PRACTICES

(in percentages)

	Sex		Significance Level
	Male	Female	
Opinions About Religion in Public Schools			
Prayer and Bible readings decisions interfere with teacher freedom	58	60	p < 5%
Devotional services have no place in the public school	45	37	p < 5%
Released time programs interfere with class schedules	52	51	p > 5%
Don't stop prayers and Bible readings because of a few	74	77	p > 5%
Bible readings and prayers are beneficial to students	78	86	p < 5%
Public school not proper place to develop religious values	62	54	p < 1%
Classroom Religious Practices			
Bible readings, pre-1962	35	49	p < 1%
Bible readings, 1964–65	19	23	p > 5%
Morning prayers, pre-1962	43	60	p < 1%
Morning prayers, 1964–65	19	29	p < 1%
Religious precepts, 1964–65	76	81	p < 1%
Grace, pre-1962	35	58	p < 1%
Grace, 1964–65	18	35	p < 1%

COEFFICIENT AND MULTIPLE REGRESSION

None of the previous tables give any indication of the relative importance of each independent variable in influencing the dependent variables. By using a multiple correlation program it is possible to arrive at a more definite idea of their importance.

The first step was to eliminate all respondents who failed to answer any of the variables to be considered in the multiple correlation. Out of 1,712 respondents 785 were eliminated for non-responses. When the two groups were compared (i.e., the 785 non-response group and the 927 full response group), it was evident that there were no significant differences in the independent variables — age, sex, years taught, city population, region, and religious attendance. This determination was made separately for each independent variable by means of the K S chi-square test,

$$X^2 = 4D^2 \frac{N_1 N_2}{N_1 + N_2}.$$

One difficulty encountered in using a multiple correlation program is that it assumes a normal distribution in each variable. Thus it is questionable whether sex and region can be utilized. While sex probably contributes little to the dependent variables under consideration, region unquestionably does. At some sacrifice to statistical theory both variables have been included in the multiple correlation. Regions were collapsed to two — South and Non-South.

ANALYSIS OF R^2 AND MULTIPLE R

The results of the multiple correlation are not startling but they do contain some interesting nuances. In Bible readings and prayers, pre-1962 and 1964–65, neither sex nor size of city population contribute much to the variance in teacher practice. The raw data had previously indicated that the Bible readings were most widely practiced in the South, both before and after the Supreme Court decision. The multiple R confirms that it was regional custom and by this we mean a Southern custom which is associated with the greatest percentage of variance in this dependent variable.

TABLE 9

MULTIPLE CORRELATION

Morning Prayers Percentage of Variance (R^2)			
Pre-1962		**1964–65**	
R^2 age deleted	= 18.17	R^2 years taught deleted	= 36.57
R^2 sex deleted	= 18.06	R^2 sex deleted	= 36.57
R^2 population deleted	= 17.81	R^2 population deleted	= 36.55
R^2 religious attendance deleted	= 17.44	Multiple R, region, age, and religious attendance	= 36.00
Multiple R years taught and region	= 16.59	Percentage of Variance Associated with:	
Percentage of Variance Associated with:		Age	= 02.52
Years Taught	= 01.49	Religious Attendance	= 01.97
Region	= 14.33	Region	= 30.53

Bible Readings Percentage of Variance (R^2)			
Pre-1962		**1964–65**	
R^2 age deleted	= 18.78	R^2 years taught deleted	= 35.14
R^2 population deleted	= 18.76	R^2 sex deleted	= 35.14
R^2 sex deleted	= 18.69	R^2 population deleted	= 35.14
R^2 religious attendance deleted	= 18.32	Multiple R, age, region and years taught	= 34.92
Multiple R, years taught and region	= 17.74	Percentage of Variance Associated with:	
Percentage of Variance Associated with:		Age	= 01.25
Years taught	= 01.54	Religious Attendance	= 01.24
Region	= 15.42	Region	= 30.96

Also it is interesting to observe the contrast of the multiple R for 1962 and 1964–65. Here we see deletion of religious attendance in 1962 and its inclusion in 1964–65. Thus when prayers and Bible readings were continued after the Court decisions the teacher was influenced by her degree of formal religious attachment, as measured by attendance at religious services.

The most significant result of the multiple regression analysis is the confirmation it gives to the influence of region, or more particularly to distinctiveness of the South.

"Southness"

The South, as previously defined, constituted 28.75 per cent of the total sample response. On the other hand it disproportionately accounts for item responses which could be taken as an indication of a traditionalist-conservative attitude. For example, Southern respondents indicated they attend religious services more frequently than non-Southern respondents; 23.78 per cent attend more than once a week in contrast to only 15.67 for non-Southern respondents. Similarly 39.23 per cent of the Southern respondents taught a Sunday school class sometime during 1963–64, in contrast to 21.14 for the non-Southern respondents. As one might expect, a high percentage of Southern respondents indicated their schools operate under a policy which favors Bible readings and prayers: 22.56 per cent of the Southern teachers reported their school policy favors Bible readings, in contrast to less than 1 per cent for non-Southern teachers. Only 11 per cent of the Southern teachers reported a school policy which opposes Bible readings, whereas 42.32 per cent of the non-Southern teachers reported a similar policy. Similar responses were received from both groups regarding school prayer policy.

Another possible explanation of the distinctiveness of Southern behavior could be the legal framework. At the time of the Schempp decision eighteen states had statutory or constitutional provisions either allowing or requiring daily Bible readings. Nine of these states were located in the South or border areas.[16] The remaining nine were scattered in other regions. Thus the South had the strongest legal framework supporting religious exercises in public classrooms.

Yet the legal fabric cannot itself explain the strength of this tradition in the South. The New England and Middle Atlantic states also had long legal traditions quite similar to the South's. Pennsylvania, New Jersey, Maine, and Massachusetts all had statutorily required daily Bible readings. Prior to 1962 classroom Bible readings were practiced by 96 per cent of all respondents from the above-mentioned four states. After the Court decisions 97 per cent of the respondents from these same states indicated that they did not have classroom Bible readings.[17] Thus in a situation where the legal framework was quite similar to the South's, the Court decisions resulted in an almost complete reversal of traditional policy. Why?

We are now at the point in our analysis where the technique of survey research is at its greatest disadvantage. As political scientists we are interested in the "whats" of behavior but we are equally interested in the more puzzling "whys" of such empirically reported data. Why does a tradition die so quickly in some situations and not in others?

Another possible independent variable one might suspect as contributing to the causal direction is mobility. The assumption here is that a highly mobile group is more likely to be exposed to the clash of cultures and thus less insular and more tolerant. The respondents were asked in what state did they reside between the ages of 1 and 17. Of the non-Southern respondents, 68.79 per cent indicated they were reared in the state in which they were currently teaching. This was true of

---

[16] See Hugh C. Keenan, "Provisions of State Constitutions and Statutes Relating to God . . . ," contained in Part III of House of Representatives, Committee on the Judiciary, *Hearings, School Prayers* (Washington, D.C.: GPO, 1964), pp. 2599–2752.

[17] N = 182.

75.96 per cent of the Southern respondents. Yet even this difference of approximately 7 per cent loses any significance one might want to attach to it when it is recognized that the higher degree of mobility in non-Southern teachers can be accounted for by the influence of the Pacific Coast and Rocky Mountain states where only 45.67 per cent were locally reared. Indeed, the least mobile group came from New England where 86.25 per cent were raised in that area.

Thus we are left with what America's historians and novelists have been describing for several generations, an envelope Southern culture. The empirical data from this survey reinforces the proposition. It does not, however, offer data to explain the roots of this culture. The traditional independent variables apparently hold little promise in explaining the riddle of the South.

This study suggests that the more difficult task of analysis of dependent variables cannot be tied to mainstream techniques of survey research. In explaining the particular dependent variables involved in this research, it would possibly have been more fruitful for the research design to have been tied to a wider variety of cultural variables, for example the influence and degree of mass communication on respondents or the structure of educational, political, and religious leadership. The implications of this for further research may well mean the forgoing of the search for national empirical data until such time as local case studies can provide us with greater insights into the types of independent variables that can be tested nationally and quantitative methods more suitable than we presently have for the analysis of variables. This poses a dilemma for political science in that it restricts our knowledge of political-reality by the demands imposed by a search for a rigorous theory.

≡ACKNOWLEDGMENTS≡

"Engel et al. v. Vitale et al." *United States Reports* 370 (1962): 421–50. Courtesy of the Yale University Law Library.

"School District of Abington Township, Pennsylvania, et al. v. Schempp et al." *United States Reports* 374 (1963): 203–30. Courtesy of the Yale University Law Library.

"Robert E. Lee, Individually and as Principal of Nathan Bishop Middle School, et al., Petitioners v. Daniel Weisman etc." *United States Law Week* 60 (1992): 4723–41. Reprinted with the permission from *United States Law Week*. Published by the Bureau of National Affairs, Inc. (800-372-1033). Courtesy of Yale University Law Library.

"Brief for Petitioners, Engel v. Vitale." 370 U.S. 421 (No. 468) (1961). Courtesy of the Yale University Law Library.

"Brief of Respondents, Engel v. Vitale." 370 U.S. 421 (No. 468) (1961). Courtesy of the Yale University Law Library.

"Brief for Appellants, Abington v. Schempp." 374 U.S. 203 (No. 142) (1962). Courtesy of the Yale University Law Library.

"Brief for Appellees, Abington v. Schempp." 374 U.S. 203 (No. 142) (1962). Courtesy of the Yale University Law Library.

Choper, Jesse H. "Religion in the Public Schools: A Proposed Constitutional Standard." *Minnesota Law Review* 47 (1963): 329–416. Reprinted with the permission of the *University of Minnesota Law Review* and the author, who retains copyright as indicated in original publication of article. Courtesy of the Yale University Law Library.

Kauper, Paul G. "Prayer, Public Schools and the Supreme Court." *Michigan Law Review* 61 (1963): 1031–68. Reprinted with the permission of the Michigan Law Review Association. Courtesy of the Michigan Law Review Association.

Beaney, William M. and Edward N. Beiser. "Prayer and Politics: The Impact of *Engel* and *Schempp* on the Political Process."

Journal of Public Law 13 (1964): 475–503. Courtesy of the Yale University Law Library.

Birkby, Robert H. "The Supreme Court and the Bible Belt: Tennessee Reaction to the 'Schempp' Decision." *Midwest Journal of Political Science* 10 (1966): 304–19. Reprinted with the permission of the University of Texas Press. Courtesy of the Yale University Law Library.

Way, Jr., H. Frank. "Survey Research on Judicial Decisions: The Prayer and Bible Reading Cases." *Western Political Quarterly* 21 (1968): 189–205. Reprinted by permission of the University of Utah, copyright holder. Courtesy of the *Western Political Quarterly*.